TRUE STORIES OF FALSE CONFESSIONS

TRUE STORIES OF
FALSE CONFESSIONS

Edited by **ROB WARDEN**
and **STEVEN A. DRIZIN**

NORTHWESTERN UNIVERSITY PRESS | EVANSTON, ILLINOIS

Northwestern University Press
www.nupress.northwestern.edu

Printed in the United States of America

10 9 8 7 6 5 4 3 2 1

Library of Congress Cataloging-in-Publication Data

True stories of false confessions / edited by Rob Warden and Steven A. Drizin.
    p. cm.
    Includes bibliographical references and index.
    ISBN 978-0-8101-2603-9 (trade paper : alk. paper)
    1. Confession (Law)—United States. 2. Confession (Law)—Psychological aspects.
    3. Self-incrimination—United States. 4. Police questioning—United States.
    I. Warden, Rob. II. Drizin, Steven A.
    KF9664.T77 2009
    364.1092273—dc22

                            2009005931

CONTENTS

Of all the factors that lead to wrongful convictions, the most difficult to comprehend is the false confession—the ultimate abrogation of one's self-interest. Yet false confessions are amazingly common. And, of course, they are extremely powerful evidence in the courts—often perceived as proof positive of guilt—even when they aren't corroborated or don't fit the facts of the alleged crimes, and regardless of the circumstances under which they were made and the mental state of the person who confessed.

The principal purpose of this anthology—which includes thirty-eight articles adapted from newspapers, magazines, and books—is to show why and how there are so many false confessions and to provide insight into what might be done to reduce their frequency. But there is a secondary purpose as well. With the future of the newspaper business uncertain, there is a concern that investigative reporting may go the way of the linotype machine. Thus, we want to underscore the critical importance of investigative reporting in exposing and helping us understand the counterintuitive phenomenon of false confessions.

We have divided the articles into eleven categories.

Brainwashing—cases in which interrogators deceitfully persuaded suspects that they simply must have committed the crimes. The technique typically involves lying to the suspects about the evidence, suggesting that there is no doubt they committed the crimes, and offering possible explanations of why they cannot remember committing them.

Desperation—cases in which exhausted suspects confessed for no reason other than to bring their grueling interrogations to an end, figuring that, because they are innocent, they will be able to straighten out the facts after getting some rest.

Inquisition—cases in which interrogators led suspects to believe that confessing is the only way they will be able to avoid death sentences or other draconian consequences.

Child Abuse—cases in which interrogators elicited false confessions from children by exploiting their susceptibility to suggestion and manipulation.

Mental Fragility—cases in which interrogators elicited false confessions from adults with the minds of children or who suffer from mental illness.

Inference—cases in which the authorities misconstrued the suspects' statements as admissions to the crimes. In these cases, the statements were real—only the inferences drawn from them were wrong.

Fabrication—cases in which, try as they might, the authorities could not get confessions, so they fabricated them.

Opportunism—cases in which suspects or prospective informants, in a naive belief that they could dupe the authorities out of a reward or favor, falsely claimed to have information about crimes with which they wound up being convicted.

Pretense—cases in which mentally disturbed persons who are not suspects simply come forward and confess to crimes they did not commit. The motives for these confessions are elusive and no doubt varied—a delusional belief, perhaps, that they actually committed the crimes, or a perverse desire for notoriety.

Police Force—cases in which interrogators coerced confessions with physical violence. These cases are not difficult to understand—Navy Lieutenant Commander John McCain, under torture in North Vietnam, confessed to war crimes—yet it may be hard to fathom that torture could be a systemic problem in modern American criminal investigations.

Unrequited Innocence—cases in which defendants were convicted of crimes based on confessions or incriminating statements that in all probability were false but who have been denied relief.

The articles in this anthology were selected on the basis of the quality—the thoroughness and insightfulness—of the reporting and writing. The facts of the cases themselves were not necessarily more compelling than the facts of scores of other cases that simply did not attract the attention of a talented and committed journalist.

Some articles in the collection could have fit into more than one category. For instance, the very first article—the story of Michael Crowe, in the "Brainwashing" section—could just as easily have gone into the "Child Abuse" section. But each article was placed where it seemed to fit best.

It should be noted that the articles are adaptations, not verbatim reprints. No substantive changes have been made, but ancillary information that did not pertain to how the confessions came about has been deleted. Many of the originals, for instance, included discourses on the overall problem of false confessions—information that would have been redundant in this collection.

Although many publications have policies of allowing only verbatim reprints, gracious exceptions were made for this book. The articles were fact-checked against published appellate decisions and other sources, and the adaptations were reviewed and approved by the authors, except, of course, when they were deceased.

We have added an epilogue after each article to update the case.

Many talented and knowledgeable persons, in addition to the authors of the articles themselves, made invaluable contributions to this anthology.

Two members of the Center on Wrongful Convictions Advisory Board— Donald S. Connery and Thomas P. Sullivan—read much of the manuscript and made many excellent suggestions, as did five members of the center's staff—Dolores Angeles, Dolores Kennedy, Jennifer Linzer, Heather Lyster, and Karen Ranos. And the project would not have come to fruition, at least not in as timely a fashion, without the able assistance of ten center interns—Saiba Arain, Kate Fontaine, Danielle Golaman, Patrick Kuehnle, John Lee, Amy Malinowski, Nicole Ostrowski, Chris Rapisarda, Dana Snyder, and Susan Sperling.

TRUE STORIES OF FALSE CONFESSIONS

BRAINWASHING

You did the crime—and forgot it.

Happens all the time, particularly to good, decent people like you, people who'd never consciously do anything so horrendous.

But you did it. No doubt about that. We've got witnesses. And overwhelming physical evidence.

Why can't you remember it?

Probably because it was so out of character. You're a good person.

Maybe you just blacked out—that's common in these situations.

What you need is help. That's what we're here for—to help you.

Or so your interrogators tell you.

But it's a ploy.

Not a word of truth to it—except of course that you are a good person and would never consciously, or unconsciously, for that matter, do anything so awful.

You wouldn't stab your sister to death. Or shoot your paramour. Or set apartments afire. Or kill your mother. You wouldn't rape and murder your neighbor.

You wouldn't—yet there's all this evidence.

The police wouldn't lie about that—they want to help you.

So, after hours of grilling, you allow that, yes, it's possible you did it.

Only possible. You don't remember. Very vexing.

Maybe you don't consider what you just said to be a confession—but the police do.

And you are in serious trouble, as exemplified by the following articles.

MICHAEL CROWE

He considered it a blessing that he didn't remember killing his sister

MARK SAUER AND JOHN WILKENS
ESCONDIDO, CALIFORNIA

The nightmare began on January 21, 1998. At 6:30 A.M., time for Stephanie Crowe to rise for another day of seventh grade at Hidden Valley Middle School, her alarm carried to the bedroom of her grandmother, Judith Kennedy, who was on an extended visit from her home in Florida. Wondering why Stephanie hadn't turned it off, Kennedy flipped on a hallway light and went to Stephanie's room. There she found her granddaughter sprawled on the floor from the foot of her bed into the doorway.

Kennedy rushed screaming to the master bedroom, where the door was ajar.

"Come quick! It's Stephanie," she yelled. "She's covered in mud!"

Steve Crowe got to her first. He bent down and realized that it was blood, not mud. He lifted his twelve-year-old daughter's head. Her brown eyes were open, but lifeless. Her body was rigid. Her long brown hair was pulled back in a ponytail. She was dressed in the purple T-shirt and blue jeans she had on the night before.

As Cheryl Crowe rushed to the room, she heard Steve's cries, "No! No! My God, no!"

Cheryl threw herself on her daughter's body.

"Oh, Mom," Cheryl said to Kennedy, "she's so cold. My baby! My baby, my baby!"

A call was placed to 911.

At 6:37 A.M., when paramedics arrived, they had to pry the thirty-three-year-old mother from Stephanie's body.

The case was assigned to Detective Ralph Claytor, a twenty-three-year veteran of law enforcement. He had been a full-time homicide investigator,

From "The Night She Was Killed" and "The Arrest," *San Diego Union-Tribune*, May 11–12, 1999. Copyright © San Diego Union-Tribune. Adapted with permission.

one of three in the Escondido Police Department, for about two years after several years working juvenile cases. It was about 7:30 A.M. when he joined other officers at the Crowe family's single-story, yellow stucco ranch house off Valley Center Road, up a paved driveway bordered by avocado trees.

Walking the perimeter of the home, officers found no broken doors or windows or other evidence of a forced entry. Stephanie's bedroom window was unlocked and the screen was bent—it had been pulled out at the bottom, so that the line for her new phone could be run into her room—but dust and cobwebs indicated that no one had come through the window. A sliding glass door from the parents' bedroom to the backyard also was unlocked. To enter through it, however, an intruder would have had to open a sliding screen door, which was locked, and get past a plastic vertical blind, which was closed, without alerting Steve and Cheryl, who said they were sleeping in the room.

Claytor immediately suspected that the killing was an inside job—not a surprising theory, because most domestic murders are committed by someone known to the victim. The initial suspects, thus, were Stephanie's grandmother, parents, and her siblings, Michael, fourteen, and Shannon, ten.

The Crowes were working-class people. Steve and Cheryl had been sweethearts at Orange Glen High, the same school Stephanie and Michael attended. They had been married in August 1982, three years after Steve graduated from Orange Glen and a year before Michael was born. They had never owned a home. They bought their cars used. But there was enough to cover the monthly bills and provide a comfortable home for the kids, as long as they didn't splurge.

The family members were ushered into their living room and told not to talk to each other—standard police procedure to guard against witnesses' sharing information and contaminating the investigation.

Shortly after Claytor arrived, the family was taken to police headquarters in downtown Escondido, where each of the five was placed in a room and told to undress, one piece of clothing at a time, until they were naked. They were photographed at each stage—also standard procedure. Detectives were looking for scratches, cuts, marks of any kind that could have been caused by either a knife or a struggling victim. They found none. The police took blood, hair, and fingernail samples and took the family's clothing for further testing.

Back at the Crowe house that morning, on the public side of yellow crime-scene tape, a handful of neighbors gathered.

Some of them told officers about the strange-looking man with dirty blond hair and beard who was roaming the rural neighborhood the night before. The description rang a bell instantly with police—Richard Raymond Tuite, a drifter with a long history of arrests and severe mental illness, was no stranger to street cops and narcotics detectives. He had been questioned by police the previous day after he followed two kids into an apartment complex. He had served time recently for methamphetamine possession and vandalism and had been diagnosed while in custody as paranoid schizophrenic.

Around eight o'clock the night Stephanie was stabbed, Tuite had peered through the windows of Sheldon Homa's house, across Valley Center Road from the Crowe home. When Homa confronted him, Tuite said he was looking for someone named Tracy. Homa called 911. Thirty minutes later, Homa's son and his son's girlfriend saw Tuite walking along the road toward the Crowe house and were sufficiently alarmed to stop at a nearby church and warn leaders of a youth group.

Next, Tuite knocked on the door of Dannette Mogelinski, who told him to come in. He asked for Tracy. Mogelinski said no one by that name lived there. Tuite left but moments later walked in again, unannounced, and the conversation was repeated.

About 9:20 P.M., Tuite crossed to the Crowes' side of the road and knocked on the door of Patrick and Misty Green's trailer home. Again, Tuite asked for "Tracy" and was told no one by that name lived there. Tuite then went to the main house on the property, where the Reverend Gary West, the Crowes' immediate neighbor to the south, lived. West told Tuite to go away and not come back. Like Sheldon Homa before him, West called 911.

An officer arrived in the neighborhood at 9:37 P.M. He did not see Tuite, but reported noticing the laundry-room door by the Crowes' garage closing. Two other neighbors reported that they had seen Tuite standing in the Crowes' driveway looking up at their house at 12:30 A.M., six hours before Stephanie's body was discovered.

The FBI trains homicide investigators that when a child is killed at home, the parents are the first suspects. If the parents are ruled out, under the FBI protocol, the next suspects should be siblings, then others living in the house, then persons with frequent access to the child, a babysitter, for example, then friends and business associates of the parents, and, last, strangers.

Detectives accordingly focused first on Steve Crowe, wondering whether he might have been molesting his daughter and killed her to keep her quiet. But they also were suspicious of Stephanie's fourteen-year-old brother Michael, whom some officers had found curiously unemotional that morning.

Around noon, Claytor obtained a search warrant, and detectives and evidence technicians converged on the Crowes' eighteen-hundred-square-foot house, taking dozens of photographs and hours of videotape. They measured distances and drew diagrams and compiled detailed lists of what was where. They found almost ninety fingerprints, including bloody ones on Stephanie's bed frame, on her door, and on the hallway door frame of her parents' bedroom. Stephanie's bedding was stained with blood, and her comforter had been slashed numerous times.

Stephanie's body yielded clues. When police arrived, she was lying on her right side, with her head just outside the doorway, which is in an alcove about two feet from the hallway. In that spot, her door could not be closed. Her right foot was resting on a book, a mystery novel titled *The Twisted Window*. Pools of blood were on the bed, at the foot of the bed, and near the door. There were several hairs in her hands, including one woven between the ring and middle fingers of her right hand.

Brian Blackbourne, San Diego County's chief medical examiner, did a preliminary examination of Stephanie before her body was removed from the home and performed an autopsy the next day. He determined that Stephanie had been stabbed nine times—twice on the top of the right shoulder and once each on the left cheek, the left ear, the right ear, the left side of the neck, the back of the neck, the back of the right shoulder, and the left side of the chest. The wounds to the back of the right shoulder and the left side of the chest were lethal—each penetrated more than five inches and cut major arteries. She had not been molested. From her stomach contents, Blackbourne concluded that the death occurred between 9:00 P.M. and 12:30 A.M.

At 1:35 P.M. on January 21, Detective Barry Sweeney began a videotaped interview with Steve Crowe, who detailed the family's activities of the night and morning. He described Stephanie as very outgoing and well-liked. He said she recently had received an award for volunteering at the Escondido Public Library. He talked about how guilty he felt about not being able to prevent her death, and said he didn't know anyone who would want to hurt her. He was not asked whether he had heard anything in the night, whether anything was missing, whether anything unusual had happened the day before.

Steve mentioned that Michael loved video games. Indeed, the police had found numerous Nintendo and Sony PlayStation games in Michael's room—games with names like *Underground*, *Final Fantasy VII*, *Gauntlet*, and *Double Dragon*. Also in the room, police found books and drawings and Lego sets decorated with medieval imagery and a handmade book-let mentioning the role-playing game *Dungeons and Dragons* and stating, "Many have entered, none have left alive."

At about 5:30 P.M., Michael was allowed to make a phone call. He called his best friend, Joshua Treadway, tearfully relating that Stephanie was dead, that somebody might have broken into the house and killed her, and that he had seen her body on her bedroom floor. About an hour and a half later, Detective Mark Wrisley told Steve and Cheryl that Michael and their surviving daughter, ten-year-old Shannon, would be taken to a facility for abused and neglected children known as the Polinsky Children's Center in Kearny Mesa. Steve exploded, bellowing that nobody was taking his kids away and demanding that they be brought to him. Several officers rushed in from adjoining offices to quiet him. "We were going to let you say goodbye to them," Steve would recall being told, "but you have lost that privilege."

Cheryl was allowed to meet briefly with the sobbing children. They begged her not to let the officers take them away, but she told them to be strong, to trust the police because "they are here to help us."

After the children left, the police checked Steve and Cheryl into a motel, where they collapsed together on the bed and cried all night.

Meanwhile, Richard Tuite had been spotted at a laundry and picked up by police for questioning. Like Steve Crowe, he was interviewed by Detective Sweeney. Unlike Steve's interview, Tuite's was not recorded, but Sweeney wrote a report. The report said he told Tuite that "possibly a homicide had occurred out on the east end of Escondido" and asked whether he had had contact with anyone there.

Tuite replied that he had talked to several people but, according to Sweeney's report, "absolutely did not go inside any houses."

Officers photographed Tuite, who had a cut one and a half inches long on his right palm and scrapes on his body. Tuite was released after police took fingernail scrapings and clippings and confiscated his clothing, giving him sweat clothes to replace his black jeans, white T-shirt, and a red turtle-neck sweat shirt. The police had forgotten to fingerprint him.

When a patrol officer found him the next day, he didn't mind going back to the station.

"I want to help you guys out," said Tuite.

After fingerprinting, he again was released.

Whatever inappropriate grieving the police might have observed in Michael was absent by the time social worker Sharon Gordon saw him at the Polin-

sky Center. Both he and Shannon were quite upset and crying, according
to Gordon.

The children were not allowed to see their parents for the next two
days, but the children had other visitors—detectives came and talked to
them separately, without their parents' knowledge. Twice the police took
Michael away for extended interviews at the police station. When Shannon
asked where he was, she was told he was on a field trip.

Detective Claytor sat down with Michael in an interview room at the station. The room was about fourteen by fourteen feet, carpeted, with white
walls and no outside windows. It was furnished with a desk, bookcases, and
a hidden video camera.

Three factors heightened the police suspicions of Michael. First, to
some officers, he had seemed oddly unaffected by his sister's death. Second, there was his infatuation with games like *Dungeons and Dragons*.
Third, when initially interviewed the previous day, Michael said that he
had awakened with a headache at 4:30 A.M., gone into the kitchen, and
taken Tylenol with milk, yet somehow, when he passed Stephanie's room,
he had not seen her body in the doorway, although the autopsy indicated
the crime had occurred several hours earlier.

"Do you have any idea who may have wanted to harm your sister?" Claytor began.

"No," Michael said.

"If you had anything to do with it, would you tell me?"

"Yes."

At Claytor's request, Michael retold his story—going to the kitchen for
Tylenol and milk. He said he thought Stephanie's door was closed, but
added that he "was still half asleep at the time" and that the lighting was
"dim but I could still see pretty well."

After the first of several pauses in which Michael was left alone in the
interview room, Claytor returned and told him, "We're really trying to
believe what you say. Would you have any problems with taking a truth-
verification exam?"

Michael said he wouldn't mind, but Claytor thought he detected trepidation and asked, "What's the problem, Mike?"

"I've spent all day away from my family," Michael replied. "I couldn't
see them. I feel like I'm being treated like I killed my sister, but I didn't. It
feels horrible. I'm being blamed for it."

"Mike, you need to trust me on this," Claytor said. "This is going to work
out. What we're after and what's important is that we get to the truth of the
matter."

With that, Claytor brought in Detective Chris McDonough of the Oceanside Police Department. McDonough had been in law enforcement seventeen years, the last ten as a violent-crimes investigator. He was called in because he operated a Computer Voice Stress Analyzer (CVSA).

The CVSA was described by its manufacturer, the Florida-based National Institute for Truth Verification, as an almost foolproof lie detector, but no independent research supported this claim; numerous independent tests had shown it to be no more reliable than a coin flip. Nonetheless, the CVSA had been used by hundreds of law enforcement agencies nationwide since its introduction eleven years earlier.

The theory behind the device is that the voice emits inaudible vibrations called microtremors. Under stress, such as when a person lies, the vocal muscles tighten and the vibrations decrease. When the vibrations are recorded on a grid, the pattern of a supposedly truthful response looks like a Christmas tree, while a supposedly deceitful response is more squared-off.

McDonough twice asked Michael a series of questions, including "Did you take Stephanie's life?" and "Do you know who took Stephanie's life?"

Both times Michael answered no to both questions.

After reviewing the results, McDonough told Michael that he was showing deception on the question "Do you know who took Stephanie's life?"

"I don't know why it would say I was lying right there because I was being truthful," Michael said.

McDonough told him that police were combing the crime scene for evidence. "They're going to find all kinds of stuff and you know that," McDonough said. "I'm looking at you right now, OK, and inside you're about ready to burst."

Michael said he had been "afraid from the beginning" that "this was going to happen, where they're going to blame something on me." He began to cry.

McDonough pushed on. "The only thing you can give back in totality is the truth, everything," he said. "You're going to have to put all the cards on the table. Science is in our favor. Technology is on our side."

"I'm being told that I'm lying and I'm not lying," Michael protested. "I don't know who did this. I swear. I don't know."

Referring to the hair that had been found in Stephanie's hand, McDonough pressed, "What if that's your hair?"

"It couldn't be," said Michael.

McDonough pointed again to the CVSA results.

"I don't know why it says that," Michael responded. "I told the truth on every question . . . I mean, I've truly lost everything if I can't even believe myself."

At this point, Michael had been interrogated for almost two and a half hours. McDonough left and Claytor returned.

"It's very difficult for the person who did it not to get blood on them and not to transfer that blood to other parts of the house," Claytor said.

Then he dropped a bombshell—"We found blood in your room already."

"God, where did you find it?" asked Michael—apparently not suspecting that Claytor might be lying.

"I'm sure you know," Claytor responded, although in truth no blood had been found in Michael's room. "It's easy to make mistakes in the dark. We know who did it. What we need to do now is get over the fact that it's been done, and get down to why it was done, and get on with our lives here. Nothing we can do is ever going to change the fact that Stephanie is not with us anymore."

Michael began crying again.

"What I'd like you to do right off the bat, rather than put our team through any more, can you tell me what you did with the knife?" Clayton continued.

"Why? God. No. I don't know. I didn't do it. I'll swear to that."

Claytor then confronted Michael with "inconsistencies" in his story about waking up at 4:30 to take Tylenol. "I know that there's no way that the door could have been closed at four thirty in the morning," Claytor said. "Our evidence has already shown that. What you need to do, Mike, is you need to help us determine how we're going to help you get through it."

"I didn't do this. I didn't. God," Michael insisted.

"You need to help us understand what's going on here," said Claytor. "You need to help us understand how to help you. Just because a person makes a mistake—just because a person does something bad . . . A, it doesn't mean that the world comes to an end, and B, it doesn't mean that you're a bad person."

"Why are you doing this to me?" Michael pleaded. "I didn't do this to her. I couldn't. God. Why? I can't even believe myself anymore. I don't know if I did it or not. I didn't, though."

Claytor continued, "Well, I think you're on the right track. Let's go ahead and think through this now."

"I don't think—if I did this, I don't remember it," said Michael. "I don't remember a thing."

"You know what, that's possible," Claytor told him.

"What's going to happen to me now?" Michael asked. "Even though I don't even know that I did it. What's going to happen?"

"I'm going to try everything . . . that the system can muster to help you through this," Claytor assured him. "And you know what, it can be done."

"My whole life is just down the drain now and I don't even remember," Michael said.

The interview ended about three and a half hours after it began, and Michael was taken back to the Polinsky Center. He was emotionally drained and so tired he could barely walk, but detectives weren't through with him.

At about 4:00 P.M. the next day, January 23, Michael was taken from the Polinsky Center to the police station for another videotaped interview. It was conducted by Ralph Claytor and Mark Wrisley and lasted approximately six hours.

Wrisley, who has been in law enforcement for about ten years, wondered aloud whether there might be two Michaels—one who is "very compassionate towards his sister" and another who lives in the violent fantasy world of video games. Claytor echoed the theme, asking Michael "to help the bad part in Michael be understood by the rest of us."

Michael replied, "If that's true, then the other Michael has taken over because I don't know what's going on because I don't remember." A few minutes later, he asked what would happen to him if the "bad Michael" had taken over and killed Stephanie.

"You're a child," Claytor said. "You're fourteen years old. Nobody's going to hold you to the same standards that they would some criminal on the street. You're going to need some help through this." But, Claytor added, "It's a two-way street. We put out that effort, we need that effort."

Claytor told Michael to write a letter to Stephanie "and ask for that forgiveness" and Michael complied, writing:

> Dear Stephanie,
>   I'm so sorry that I can't even remember what I did to you. I feel that it is almost like I am being convinced of this than really knowing it. I will always love you and can still remember you in life.
>   You have always given so much that you truly must be an angel. I tried to be as loving as possible to you. I'm still crying for you and I pray to God that you forgive me for what they say I did.
>   Sometimes I think it would be better if I could remember but I don't really want to try. The fact that I can't remember is a

blessing from God. I only want to remember the way you were when you were with us.

I hope that you love me forever and that I never forget what you were, a truly loving person.

They are putting me through hell and I think that is what I deserve. I will always hold you dear to my heart. If I did do this then I am insane. I hope both you and God will forgive me for this.

We all miss you and I feel that I am being ripped from everything I know. I never ment [*sic*] to hurt you and the only way I know I did is because they told me I did. I hope you understand that I don't know what I was thinking when I did this. I hope I never remember because I don't think I could ever forgive myself if I knew what I did.

I want you to know that I was not myself when I did this. They want me to help them but I can't. I feel because of that that I am letting you down. I should help you but I simply can't. If you don't forgive me then I can understand.

You showed me what God could do for you and now I have excepted [*sic*] him myself. I shall one day see you in heaven and I hope that I shall have an eternity to serve you for this.

Never forget that I always loved you.

Wrisley pressed Michael for details about the killing, about the location of the stab wounds. "God," Michael said, sobbing. "It's a blessing that I can't remember. Please don't make me."

"We can prove that nobody came in the house," Wrisley said. "So we know that the person that did this was inside that house." Michael started sobbing again, as Wrisley asked him, "If we can prove to you without a doubt through all the science and everything else that we have at our disposal that it was you, would you believe it then?"

"I'd believe it, yes." Michael replied. "I don't know if I'd remember it, though." He added, "I don't want it to be anyone else in my family. I don't want to believe that. I don't want it to be me, but you say the evidence points toward me. I don't know what to do anymore. I can't remember. You keep asking me questions I can't answer."

A few minutes later, he said, "I'm afraid you're going to put me some-where with a lot of bad people."

Now about four hours into the interrogation, Claytor told Michael there were two paths he could take. He could say nothing and make the police prove their case, which would lead to jail. Or he could confess and provide details about the killing, which would lead to getting "help."

Claytor added, "We're going to let the evidence lead you down one path or we're going to let you, a repentant you, lead us down another path. That's the only two roads we're traveling, OK? It's as simple as that."

"I want to go down that path, but I can't," said Michael.

"Cut it out, Mike. Cut it out," Claytor said, and then added, "The reason I'm sounding impatient, Mike, is the eleventh hour is rapidly approaching. All this evidence is going to be in. We put a rush on some things that, quite frankly, is going to bury you, my friend. And you need to head that off at the pass. Let's hear it, Mike."

"You know, I'll lie," Michael said. "I'll have to make it up."

"Tell us the story, Michael," Wrisley pressed.

"OK. I'm telling you right now, it's a complete lie."

"Tell us the story."

"OK. This is true. I am extremely jealous of my sister."

"OK."

"She's always had a lot of friends. Good friends and stuff like that. She was friends with people my age, I mean with all the popular girls and stuff like that. That's true, OK?"

"You let me know when you get to the lie part."

"OK. Here's the part where I'll start lying. That night I got pissed off at her. I couldn't take it anymore. So I got a knife, went into her room, and I stabbed her. After I was done, I pulled her off the bed . . ."

"How many times did you stab her?"

"This is going to be a lie—three times."

"When you went in to do that, Mike, was she on her back or on her stomach or on her side when she was in bed?"

"On her side. That's a lie. I don't know. I told you it was going to be a lie."

"Well, tell me what the truth is."

"The only reason I'm trying to lie here is because you presented me with two paths, one I'm definitely afraid of. I'd rather die than go to jail."

After a pause, Claytor took over, saying, "Now, quite frankly, I'm offended that you'd want to play this game with me because you're a lot smarter than that. If you want to test my intelligence, then do so, OK. If you want to play the game, then do so."

Michael asked to be returned to the Polinsky Center, then said, "I know I did it, but I don't know how. I don't know when I'm going to be able to tell you anything."

"How about beginning at the beginning? Where did you get the knife?"

"I don't know."

"What did you do with the knife afterwards?"

"I don't know what I did with the knife."

"Give me some of these details, not your hollow lying."

"Take me back to Polinsky. I can't tell you. I'm sorry."

Claytor and Wrisley escorted Michael to another part of the police station and left him alone for thirteen minutes as a video camera recorded the empty room.

When Michael was brought back into the interview room, he was noticeably changed, seemingly more under control and animated. His answers were longer, more involved, almost a monologue.

During the thirteen-minute gap, Claytor and Wrisley told him he was under arrest for killing his sister.

Michael's reaction, Claytor would testify, was, "I thought so. I really didn't like her anyway." But Michael would have a different recollection—that Wrisley told him his parents believed he was the killer and never wanted to see him again.

"They said, 'This is your last chance, buddy,'" Michael would say. "'You need to tell us your story now or you'll never get another chance.' I took it."

For the next hour, on videotape, Michael talked openly about animosity toward his sister, saying such things as: "Every time I was going to be in the spotlight, she grabbed it right away from me." "She made me feel ugly." "She made me feel worthless." "The oldest [child] is supposed to be the one who has everyone in their shadow, but I was in hers."

Michael said his parents once took an important award he won off the wall so they could paint, then never put the honor back up. Stephanie's awards, meanwhile, got prominent display. He said he hated his family so much that he hid in his room, escaped to a world of video games and books.

"I've made up my own fantasy world," he said. "It's like I'm three people." One of those people, he said, was evil—he called this person Odin. "I just split myself apart," he said. "I think Odin came out to play," he said, and he was "positive" he had killed Stephanie. "I'm not sure how I did it. All I know is I did it."

When asked about the killing, he said, "I can't get into details because I don't remember details . . . just pure rage."

The detectives again asked him about the knife, about the clothes he wore, and about what he did to clean up after the attack. Michael said he couldn't remember. "Like I said, the only way I even know I did this is that she's dead and that the evidence says I did it. You could find that someone else did it, and I pray to God someone else did. I think it's too late for that. I think I did it."

Claytor asked him, "Having killed once, do you think it would be easier to kill again?"

"No, definitely not because I just feel, you know," Michael replied, "I thought it would solve everything. It solved nothing. It made everything worse."

Michael was taken to Juvenile Hall.

Just after midnight, Detective Sweeney called Steve Crowe, who had taken a sleeping pill and was asleep.

"We have arrested someone for your daughter's murder," Sweeney told him.

"What?" Steve Crowe replied, groggy, uncomprehending.

"We arrested your daughter's murderer."

"Oh? You did? Who is it?"

"Your son, Michael."

Epilogue

Michael Crowe, who had nothing to do with his sister's murder, was not the only Escondido teenager to falsely confess to the crime. His friend, Joshua Treadway, also confessed over two lengthy interrogation sessions. Based on information fed to him by the interrogators and his knowledge of *Dungeons and Dragons*, Joshua created a quite plausible confession implicating a third youth named Aaron Houser. The three were indicted for Stephanie's murder in May 1998, but the charges were dismissed on the eve of trial the following February after DNA testing established that tiny spots of Stephanie's blood were on a sweatshirt worn by Richard Raymond Tuite, the transient who should have been the prime suspect from the beginning. Subsequent testing revealed drops of Stephanie's blood on the hem of the undershirt Tuite wore the night of the murder.

It was not until May 2002 that Tuite was finally charged with the crime, and the trial did not begin until twenty-one months after that. On the first day of jury selection, February 2, 2004, Tuite slipped out of handcuffs during the lunch break, fled the courthouse in downtown San Diego, hopped a bus, and made it more than ten miles to Claremont, where he was arrested late that afternoon. Jury selection resumed and the trial proceeded. The defense contended that Michael, Joshua, and Aaron had committed the

crime and that the blood on Tuite's two shirts was the result of police contamination. Although there was no question that detectives had botched
the investigation miserably, prosecution experts discounted the possibility that the blood spots could have been the result of contamination. On
May 26, the jury found Tuite, who had been diagnosed as suffering from
chronic schizophrenia, guilty of voluntary manslaughter. Tuite sat expres-
sionless as the verdict was read, as he had throughout the three-month trial.
On August 25, San Diego County Superior Court Judge Frederic Link
sentenced him to thirteen years in prison. Three months later, Tuite was
sentenced to an additional four years and four months for escape, to be
served consecutively with the manslaughter sentence. It was never determined precisely how he'd entered the Crowe home.

The Crowe, Treadway, and Houser families filed federal civil rights suits
against the police for depriving the boys of their civil rights, but in 2004
and 2005 the federal courts dismissed most of the claims, holding that the
plaintiffs had failed to prove that the police had acted in bad faith. A separate action brought on behalf of Michael against the National Institute
for Truth Verification, maker of the Voice Stress Analyzer, was settled for
an undisclosed amount. On December 14, 2006, the Court of Appeal of
California unanimously affirmed Tuite's conviction and sentence for manslaughter; Tuite did not appeal the escape conviction.

BEVERLY MONROE

She concluded she'd been there—and erased it from her memory

JOHN TAYLOR

RICHMOND, VIRGINIA

Early on the evening of February 29, 1992, Roger Zygmunt de la Burde was alone in his bedroom at Windsor Farm, dressing for a ball. The property was on Huguenot Trail, bordering the James River west of Richmond. It dated back to the seventeenth century. Charles Carter Lee, the oldest full brother of Robert E. Lee, had acquired it in 1853 and it earned a footnote in Civil War history when, after surrendering at Appomattox, Lee and his officers returned to Richmond along the Huguenot Trail, spending the last night before they disbanded in the farm fields.

Roger had lived at Windsor for twenty-five years, first with his wife, Brigitte, and their two daughters. Then, after the girls left for college and he and Brigitte divorced, he lived there by himself. Windsor was a functioning horse farm with 220 acres of pasture and woodland. The dozen or so horses grazing on his fields belonged to other people, who stabled them at Windsor. Roger had little interest in animals, crops, or gardening. He was by profession a chemist and had, until retiring four years earlier, worked in the research department of Philip Morris, where he had been the coauthor of some seventeen patents. But most of Roger's money had come from real estate speculation.

Roger took his tuxedo out of the closet. The ensemble had a wing-collared shirt and a rakish green-and-black-plaid jacket with black silk lapels. The jacket, when he tried it on, felt tight. Roger led an active life. He was an accomplished skier and an aggressive tennis player. But he had a weakness for fatty food—meat and cheese and desserts—and in the last couple of years he had gained twenty-five pounds. Most of it had gone to his gut. He felt himself aging.

Roger was sixty. He had an olive complexion, an infectious smile, and penetrating dark eyes. Women considered him handsome, and this encouraged his vanity. The sagging skin beneath his jaw dismayed him, as did his receding hairline; he'd had a hair transplant that had not come out as well as he'd have liked. In fact, it looked terrible. And he worried about his health. He suffered from insomnia, heart pains, and high blood pressure. Recently, he had discovered blood in his semen—and that, he could tell you, was a sight to tighten the sphincter.

Roger was originally from Kraków, Poland, where he grew up during the Nazi occupation and came of age under postwar Communist rule, which he found even more oppressive. His father, a lawyer, had managed a small factory, and his family, considered part of the reactionary bourgeoisie, was forced to surrender its house to a workers' collective.

After receiving a Ph.D. in chemistry from Kraków University, Roger fled his Soviet-bloc country. During a trip to East Berlin he slipped into West Germany, then made his way to the United States, living in Buffalo and Chicago before settling in Richmond when Philip Morris offered him a job in the 1960s.

Roger claimed he was a count. He was descended, he told people, from a French aristocrat who had settled in Kraków after the Napoleonic Wars. His neighbors and colleagues never knew how seriously to take these claims. They considered the man himself an extraordinary oddity. He could be witty and engaging, an enjoyable raconteur of wickedly funny stories told in thickly accented English, but he also had what to people in the Virginia Piedmont seemed to be strange eccentricities. He bowed. He wore ascots and smoking jackets. He collected abstract and African art. He routinely propositioned women he scarcely knew.

They also considered him unscrupulous. After the local fire department put out a fire in a cottage at Windsor that contained part of his art collection, the blaze started again the following night, and that time Roger tried to fight it alone with a garden hose. His insurer, Lloyd's of London, refused to honor the policy, citing the suspicious circumstances; Roger sued and the case was settled out of court. He also had been tried and acquitted of extortion (for threatening a business partner's girlfriend) and tried and convicted of malicious destruction of property (for cutting down a neighbor's trees).

But to his friends, Roger's roguishness was part of his charm. He was devoted to high culture and given to sudden enthusiasms—in the last few years he had taught himself to speak French and to play the piano. His taste in music ran from Telemann to Bill Evans; in books, from Goethe to Lawrence Durrell. But his foremost enthusiasm was for African art. He had, as an art critic for the *Richmond Times-Dispatch* noted, "one of the best collections of African sculpture in the country." Roger had begun assembling it on an extended trip to Nigeria in 1968, and owned more than four hundred objects.

Despite its size and the unquestioned value of some of the pieces, a taint had become attached to the collection because Roger lied about its provenance. To avoid acknowledging that he had violated Nigeria's antiquities law by exporting valuable artifacts, he claimed that his father had collected the pieces during trips to West Africa in 1912 and 1916. Confronted by an associate curator of African art at the Metropolitan Museum of Art, he sheepishly admitted that he may have embellished the facts. But that was fifteen years ago, and Roger had worked since then to restore the collection's reputation. For two years, he had been putting together a book about it, complete with photographs of the important pieces and essays by five academics.

Aside from the book, which was still unfinished, Roger's life lately was full of vexations. After leaving Philip Morris, he had sued the company for a share of the profits from one of his patents and, instead of settling, as he had hoped it would, the company had countersued. Roger also had money problems. Most of his wealth was tied up in illiquid real estate, and in the past year he had grown so short of cash that he had concocted a scheme to sell forged art created by a local stonemason, who changed his mind and backed out before the project got off the ground.

That was just as well, Roger later decided, after he learned that a man named Wojtek Drewnowska had reported him to the FBI for trafficking in fraudulent art. Drewnowska had good reason to feel hostile—Roger had been having an affair with his wife, Krystyna, who now presented Roger's most pressing worry. Two months ago, after leaving her husband and their two teenage children, she had become pregnant by Roger. Recently, she had drafted an agreement for her and the child and was pressing him to sign it. She also wanted to move in with him at Windsor to see if they were suited for marriage. Before that could happen, he would have to leave his primary companion for the past twelve years—Beverly Monroe.

Beverly knew about his affair with Krystyna, but did not know Krystyna was pregnant. If Beverly found out, the long relationship Roger had enjoyed with her would quite possibly be destroyed. Upheaval now seemed not just inevitable but imminent.

Roger's entanglement with the two women had become terribly complicated. This evening he would be leaving the pregnant Krystyna alone on

her birthday in order to accompany Beverly and her family to the ball at
the Virginia Museum of Fine Arts. Roger probably did not feel particularly
guilty about this. He was used to doing what he pleased, without much
regard for the feelings of others.

From his bedroom window Roger had a view of the James River, high
with early runoff from the Blue Ridge Mountains. The view was through a
gap in the trees of the neighboring property. When the owners had refused
permission to create the gap by cutting down the trees, he had hired someone to do the job anyway. The man leveled a couple of acres of trees—
mostly sycamores, some two hundred years old and so big you couldn't get
your arms around them—and left them toppled in the river in violation of
water-conservation board restrictions. Roger had paid fines and settled a
suit the owners brought against him, and now he had the view he wanted.

It was dark by the time Roger finished putting on his tuxedo. He switched
on the outdoor floodlights, set the alarm, locked the front door, and crossed
the gravel driveway to his sienna-brown Jaguar sedan. Overhead, stars glim-
mered in a clear but moonless night sky.

Roger and Beverly, and Beverly's daughter, Katie, and son, Gavin, and their
dates arrived at the Virginia Museum just as the ball was getting under
way. It was a masked ball, celebrating Mardi Gras, and some people wore
full costumes. Beverly had bought everyone in her group a handheld mask.
Laughing, made slightly giddy by the infectious silliness of the party, they
raised their masks to their faces and made their way past Picassos and
Braques into a huge chamber crowded with revelers, its walls and floor and
columns paneled in glistening pink marble.

A few months earlier the curators of the museum, whom Roger had
been trying to persuade to sponsor an exhibit of his African art to coincide
with the publication of his book, had turned him down; the collection
was still too controversial. Since then, a woman named Katharine Lee had
been named director of the museum, and Roger hoped to charm her into
reversing the decision. As the ball reached its climax and the raucous swing
band launched into a Count Basie tune, he asked Katharine to dance.

Roger was a good dancer. He liked to throw in little moves he'd picked
up in Africa, shimmies and shakes that Beverly found hilarious. As he and
Katharine began to jitterbug, a photographer for the *Richmond News Leader*
sensed the night's shot. His exploding flash caught Roger, in his wing-
collared shirt and plaid dinner jacket, swinging the museum director across
the floor by the hand. His face had a look of rapturous concentration.

It was the last photograph taken of him while he was alive.

On Sunday, after the ball, Beverly was at Windsor helping Roger with his book when she found a copy of the support agreement Krystyna Drewnowska had drafted. Roger broke down. In the long conversation that followed, he acknowledged that Krystyna was pregnant. He had been talking for years about finding a surrogate mother to bear him a male heir, but Beverly was unsure if Krystyna was merely a casual mistress who had agreed to serve as a surrogate mother, as Roger insisted, or a true lover.

Beverly left in the early evening to avoid encountering Roger's attorney, who was coming in from out of town to discuss Roger's lawsuit against Philip Morris. Beverly herself worked at Philip Morris as a coordinator in the patent department. Some people at the company regarded her with suspicion for continuing to see a man who had filed a lawsuit against it, so she made a point of drawing a very distinct boundary between her job and her relationship with Roger.

The next morning, before going to work, Beverly drove back out to Windsor to give Roger some photographs of the two of them that he'd mentioned the day before. His attorney's car was still in the driveway, so she left the pictures on the front steps. Roger called later and asked her to take the afternoon off and spend it at Windsor. She agreed. It was a brisk, sunny day. They sat on redwood chairs on the front lawn and tried to talk calmly about the big question that hung over them.

That evening Roger dropped by Beverly's house, thirteen miles from Windsor, on Old Gun Road in Chesterfield County. He brought a bouquet. The following night, Tuesday, Roger again appeared without warning at Beverly's house. She was playing the piano when he arrived. She rose and offered him some food or wine. "No," he said, "just play." Hoping to break Roger's unsettling quiet mood, she put on a tape of Saint-Saëns' adagio, *The Swan*. When it ended, he asked her to play it again, then a third time. At 9:30 he said he was tired and left.

The next day, Roger called Beverly several times at her office, asking her to come out to Windsor as soon as possible. She agreed, but wasn't able to leave the office until after 5:00 P.M. Then she got caught in traffic, stopped by home, and arrived at Windsor after the sun had fallen behind the tree line to the west.

Shortly after 8:00 A.M. on Thursday, March 5, Joe Hairfield left his home on Huguenot Trail to make the two-mile drive to Windsor. Roger had hired Joe's teenage son to help around the farm the previous summer, but the job turned out to be a little more than a fifteen-year-old could handle, and Roger hired the father as well. Joe soon became Roger's farm manager.

As Joe was turning into Windsor's driveway, he saw Beverly's blue Mercury about to pull out onto Huguenot Trail. Joe knew Beverly fairly well. She was at Windsor most weekends. Although demure and proper, she liked working outdoors—doing actual labor, not just gardening. Joe and Beverly rolled down their windows and talked car to car over their idling engines. Beverly said she had been with Roger the night before. But Roger's usual practice was to call after she left to make sure she had gotten home safely. When the call didn't come, she called him several times but got a busy signal. When she called this morning, the line was still busy. She was afraid something had happened to him. He could have had a heart attack. She had just been at the house, but the door was locked and no one answered the bell.

Beverly returned to the house to try again, while Joe went to the barn and called on the phone, but there was no response. Joe told her to keep ringing the bell while he circled the house to look in the windows. The first few rooms he looked into were empty, but then he worked himself between two old boxwoods in front of the library windows. Craning to peer over the air conditioner, he saw Roger lying on one of the couches. It looked like he was asleep.

Joe went around the corner of the house and jimmied open the lock on a sliding glass patio door and pushed open heavy gold curtains. The library was a strange room and utterly silent now. Roger was lying on his side on the couch nearest the sliding door, facing into the backrest. Joe circled the couch. Roger had on dark sweatpants and a navy sweatshirt. He had taken his shoes off, and the soles of his white socks were slightly dirty. His bifocals rested on a coffee table, next to a copy of *Time* opened to an article about Toulouse-Lautrec.

As Joe approached Roger, he saw a bullet hole in his forehead. He could tell right away that Roger was dead. The upholstery in front of Roger's head was splattered with dried blood. Blood had streaked across Roger's face and pooled below his right eye, which was swollen shut. Rigor mortis had set in. Joe recognized Roger's revolver, a .38 Special with a double-action hammer, on the couch beside him. There was no note, but it seemed clear to Joe that Roger had killed himself. Joe started back out the sliding glass door just as Beverly appeared on the patio.

"Don't go in," Joe said. "Roger committed suicide."

Beverly rushed past him. Sobbing, she knelt by the couch and leaned her head on Roger's shoulder. Joe went into the foyer. He saw that the phone had been taken off the hook. He hung it up and called the Powhatan County Sheriff's Office.

Powhatan County Deputy Sheriff Greg Neal was at home when the dispatcher called and told him Roger de la Burde had committed suicide. It was Neal's day off, but he was one of two investigators in the department. The other, Captain Vernon Poe, was scheduled to appear in court that day, so the task of investigating Roger's death, and writing a report, fell to Neal. When Neal reached Windsor, after stopping at the office to pick up cameras and other equipment, two uniformed patrolmen were already there. One of them explained the situation—apparent suicide—and showed Neal into the library.

Neal had been with the office nearly eleven years. Originally from West Virginia, he had lived in Powhatan County since he was thirteen, attended Powhatan High School, and worked as a mechanic before making a switch to law enforcement. After graduating from the police academy, he worked the road for seven years as a patrol deputy. When he started doing investigations they mostly involved uncomplicated rural crimes that tended either to be spontaneously conceived, badly planned, or stupidly executed—and therefore pretty easy to solve.

As he surveyed the scene, Neal had no reason to doubt that Roger had killed himself, but he was puzzled by black marks on the fourth and fifth fingers of Roger's right hand. The marks were more extensive than any Neal had seen before, and he thought they were powder. Perhaps, he thought, Roger had wrapped his hand around the cylinder of the gun when he pulled the trigger. Neal took several photographs and slipped paper bags over Roger's hands, to prevent contamination until the medical examiner could swab them. The swabs would be sent to the state forensic laboratory to be tested for gunshot residue to determine if Roger actually had been holding the gun.

The sheriff's department had no hard-and-fast rules about how a suicide, as opposed to a homicide, should be investigated. That was left to the investigator's judgment. And so, operating on the assumption that Roger's death was a suicide, Neal did not do many things he would later come to regret not doing. He did not have officers secure the house, or even the library, with yellow crime-scene tape. He took the gun into evidence, but not the couch, and he did not look for signs of forced entry.

Roger's body lay on the couch until Lester Brown, the local medical examiner, arrived at 11:30. He too treated the death as a suicide, staying only thirty minutes and neglecting to record the temperature of the corpse. Shortly after Brown left, a hearse from a funeral home took the body to the chief state medical examiner's office in Richmond, where it was placed in cold storage to await an autopsy.

Shortly before 2:00, Neal asked Beverly to follow him into Roger's bedroom, down the hall from the library, and give her version of what happened the night before. He sat on the bed and took out a notepad. He didn't ask many questions. He didn't have to—Beverly was one of those people who, once they got started talking, didn't stop.

She said she had arrived at Windsor sometime after 6:00. She and Roger had intended to talk over "difficulties" but decided to delay the discussion until the coming Friday and instead played the piano together. Roger suggested that she read the Toulouse-Lautrec article while he fixed a dinner of shrimp and rice. It was a peaceful, pleasant evening. She said Roger kept telling her how nice it was to have her there, and kept repeating that word— *nice.* After dinner, Roger decided to work on his book. Beverly brought out the research and he began leafing through it, but soon stopped. Roger's earlier cheerful mood dissipated. He began to act as if something was wrong.

A number of things had been worrying Roger the last couple of years, she said. The upkeep of the farm was one. The lawsuit with Philip Morris was getting him down. And he had health problems—he complained about his chest and heart and was afraid he had prostate cancer. Furthermore, she said, he had been unfaithful to her. While she had come to accept his infidelities, knowing that she was aware of them distressed him.

For the last year, he had been obsessed with the idea of having another child. He talked about finding a surrogate mother. Although Beverly was fifty-four, they had discussed the possibility of her bearing the child. She had gone so far as to ask her daughter Katie if she would supply an egg. The idea hadn't panned out, and Roger began having an affair with Krystyna Drewnowska, who had left her husband and had been trying to get Roger to marry her. When he refused, she drew up a child-support agreement and demanded that he sign it. Once the child he had thought he wanted was actually on the way, Beverly said, Roger felt trapped. He saw no way out of the situation. Krystyna was determined to bear the child against his wishes and to hold him financially responsible.

When Neal put his notepad away, he thanked Beverly. She seemed truthful and genuinely grieving, but as he drove back to the sheriff's office he began to wonder about the nature of Roger's death. Those stains on his fingers were puzzling.

The pathologist who conducted the autopsy saw nothing that contradicted the story that the deceased had killed himself. A determination of that, however, was beyond the scope of his responsibilities. In his report, under the heading for cause of death, he stated, "Gunshot wound to the head and brain."

On Friday morning, March 6, an article appeared in the *Richmond Times-Dispatch* with the headline "Art Collector Found Dead in Powhatan." The article reported that the authorities were investigating whether Roger's death was a suicide, and quoted Captain Vernon Poe as saying, "It's really too early to tell." The *Richmond News Leader* gave greater prominence to the official uncertainty, declaring in the lead sentence, "Police have not determined whether the shooting death of Roger de la Burde, a Powhatan art collector, is a homicide or a suicide."

Poe's desk was next to Greg Neal's, and Neal had shown him Polaroids of the body he'd taken at the scene. It seemed to Poe that the bullet's entry hole, just above the deceased's right eyebrow, was in an unusual spot. Most suicides who use guns, he told Neal, shoot themselves in the mouth or temple. As Neal was pondering that, he received a call from Krystyna Drewnowska. He had talked to her briefly before at Windsor, and she didn't think Roger would have committed suicide. Now she had heard Beverly's story, and thought it didn't make sense. If Beverly had called Roger and gotten busy signals three times between 10:00 P.M. and midnight, she would have been back on his doorstep by 1:00 A.M., said Krystyna.

A little later, Neal received a call from Don Beville, who identified himself as Roger's publisher and said Roger had called him around ten the night before his body was found. The conversation had been short, but what Roger had said seemed so strange that Beville had written down the words. It was "a new day," Roger had declared, adding that he was going to "make some changes" in his life, and that the "weight of the world" was off his shoulders. Roger didn't seem depressed. In fact, they had agreed to have lunch the following day. Roger had said he would bring a friend.

On Monday, March 10, Neal drove to First Division State Police Headquarters in Henrico County, north of Richmond, where Dave Riley worked in a small, low-ceilinged office with two other investigators. Neal knew the others but had never heard of Riley and at first didn't like him. Riley seemed to think Neal was a rube who didn't know what he was doing and had muffed the death-scene investigation. Riley didn't say this—it was just Neal's impression.

As he studied the Polaroids of the dark smudges on Roger's right hand, Riley could not understand how they occurred as a result of a suicide. Roger was right-handed. Assuming the stains were from gunpowder, he couldn't have used his right hand to pull the trigger. His right hand would have had to have been close to the source of the discharge—the muzzle or the cylinder—which meant he would have used his left hand to pull the trigger.

The position of the body, lying sideways on a couch, also seemed strange. Typically, Riley thought, a suicide's goal was to kill himself instantly, avoiding at all costs botching the job and winding up maimed but alive. That Roger would lie on his side and pull the trigger with his left hand didn't make a lot of sense.

Riley thus had a gut feeling that Roger's death was a homicide. He theorized that Roger might have been asleep and awakened just before the shot was fired and thrown up his right hand in an effort to ward off the shot. It was only a hunch. But, as hunches went, it was powerful.

If Roger had been found dead in a car in downtown Richmond, there would be a whole range of suspects. But under the actual circumstances the universe of potential suspects was small. Although Beverly seemed the prime suspect, there were, of course, Krystyna Drewnowska and Roger's daughter, Corinna de la Burde, and his part-time secretary, Barbara Samuels.

Corinna had seemed stunned by her father's death, although they hadn't had a very loving relationship and at the funeral she didn't appear to shed a tear. Afterward, she called Greg Neal. She said he'd probably hear from people who knew her father and who thought it impossible that he would have killed himself. But her father was, in her opinion, a very intense man. He experienced radical mood swings. He jumped from project to project. He constantly changed his mind. Anyone who knew him well would suspect he had a chemical imbalance. He had been unhappy recently. And there was a history of suicide in the family; his mother had tried to kill herself.

That there was no suicide note was the only thing that gave her pause. Roger had been obsessed with what would happen to his art collection and, in addition to his will, which he constantly revised, he'd written detailed instructions about what his children, mistresses, relatives, and friends should do if he died. She would have expected him to leave an extensive suicide note.

But because Riley had to start somewhere, he questioned Barbara Samuels first, thinking the secretary was more likely to be neutral than anyone else. Barbara was a stout woman who looked to be in her early forties. In a brief interview at Windsor after the funeral, she said Roger hadn't seemed suicidal, that he was looking forward to finishing his book, and was planning a ski trip with Beverly in only a week and a half. She recalled that, when a Powhatan teenager had committed suicide a short while back, Roger had described it as a tragedy and commented, "There's no reason ever to give up. There's always hope." At the end of the interview, Barbara said she would share more details of Roger's life, but not while Corinna was in the house.

Two days later, Riley again interviewed Barbara at Windsor. He told her he felt he had to put it on the table right away—whether she and Roger were having an affair. No, she said, matter-of-factly. Roger tried, she refused, and he gave up. She hadn't held it against him because that was just the way he was—he tried with every woman. There had been some sexual activity between Roger and a woman who kept his books and perhaps other help, but the two main women in his life were Beverly and Krystyna. He had felt torn between the two, but had toyed with leaving Beverly for Krystyna.

Riley wondered if Barbara was in some way biased against Beverly, but didn't feel that she was. Barbara clearly liked Roger, and didn't seem to have any love for Krystyna. If Roger had been contemplating leaving Beverly for Krystyna, that could have been a motive for Beverly to kill him.

Krystyna also had a motive, and had hired an estate attorney and left the country shortly after Roger's death and did not return until after police had charged Beverly. But if she had killed Roger, it seemed unlikely to Riley that she would have called Greg Neal and urged him to investigate the case as a homicide. It would have been in her interest to pass it off as a suicide. Krystyna's husband, Wojtek, also clearly had a motive—Roger more or less had stolen his wife—but he wouldn't have had the sort of easy access to the house that the killer apparently enjoyed.

Riley had no intention of letting Beverly know he considered Roger's death a homicide, much less that he considered her the likely murderer. Summoning her in for an official interrogation and advising her of her Miranda rights would instantly create an adversarial relationship. She would clam up and insist on a lawyer. But if he could lull her into a false sense of security, if he could allow her to think she had gulled the police into thinking Roger had killed himself, she might say or do something that would betray her guilt.

In preparation for an interview, Riley talked with Larry McCann, the state police psychological profiler, about how best to approach her. And he made notes on what he might ask or say: "Did you ever handle the gun?" "Beverly, after several calls & no answer, weren't you concerned that he still wasn't answering til after midnight, yet you went to bed without reaching him or going back over to check on him, especially since you said he was having chest pains." "Tell her I *know* she had already found the body, but was afraid, due to the circumstances, to be the one to find him. Or that she was actually in the house *when* he killed himself but was afraid to say so."

To get as much information as possible to help him establish rapport with Beverly, Riley called Barbara Samuels. She filled him in on Beverly's background. Beverly was cultured. She was interested in art, classical music, and history. Riley had once been interested in art himself. He'd have that going for him. Plus, he was interested in history, another point of common ground. He listened to classical music, to help him understand who Beverly was.

Riley called Beverly, introduced himself, and said he had been brought in to make an official determination about the cause of death. She agreed to meet him at Windsor, the morning of March 26. He wanted the meeting there to see how she would react to the scene of the crime. But she walked in, Riley thought, like she owned the place, so he didn't get anything out of that. He told her he was investigating the death from a psychological perspective and that he needed to determine Roger's state of mind in the final days of his life.

Beverly struck Riley as intelligent, articulate, attractive, and sophisticated. She had a master's degree in chemistry from the University of Florida, where she had met her husband, a Ph.D. candidate in the same field. They had three children, the oldest of whom was Katie, now an attorney. In 1982, after the marriage ended, Beverly built the house on Old Gun Road. It had cedar siding stained gray, a massive fireplace of rugged Maryland fieldstone, and big windows and glass doors that ensured the interior was filled with sunlight. Roger, with whom she began an affair before he left Philip Morris, had helped her acquire the property.

Riley brought a suicide-assessment form, but found he didn't need it. Beverly was extremely cooperative, surprisingly so, Riley thought. She required no prompting. All he had to do was nod and take it all down. She talked for nearly two hours. From time to time, she broke down in tears, but for the most part she retained her composure. In the last year, she said, Roger had become depressed, confused, and so forgetful that she had taken to writing down what he said to prove to him later that he'd actually said it. But in retrospect, she said, it had always seemed that he had psychological problems. He tried to dominate every aspect of the lives of those around him. He could be cruel to loved ones. "Would it be accurate," Riley asked, "to say that Roger had a Jekyll-and-Hyde personality?" Beverly agreed that it would.

Roger had asked her to marry him several times, she said, once getting down on bended knee, but she refused because she didn't think he'd be faithful. After she found the child-support agreement Krystyna had drafted, she said, he again had asked her to marry him and help raise the child

Krystyna was carrying. She said she'd think it over. She then described how three days later she and Roger had spent his last evening. He became melancholy when the subject of Krystyna came up. He said he'd spoken to her and she had rejected the idea of giving the child over to him and Beverly. He became disconsolate and finally rolled over into a fetal position on the couch.

Listening to Beverly, Riley tried to maintain an air of neutrality. From what he had come to understand, Roger wasn't about to marry Beverly, or anyone else, but Riley didn't want to give the slightest sign of disbelief, which might cause her to rethink her willingness to cooperate.

Because she was the last person to see Roger alive and was present when the body was discovered, Riley told her, keeping his voice friendly, the next natural step in the investigation would be for her to take a polygraph examination. He made it sound like a mere formality, a minor nuisance that could be taken care of quickly and, in fact, the sooner the better. "It would be convenient," he said, "if we could finish this up today."

Beverly worried that her nerves might adversely affect the outcome, but Riley shrugged off her concern, and she agreed to take the test. Riley gave her directions to First Division headquarters in Henrico County and asked her to come at 1:00 P.M.—the less time that elapsed, he thought, the less opportunity she would have to reconsider.

Beverly arrived at the First Division, a brick-and-cement building with brown-tainted windows, right on time. Riley met her in the lobby, thanked her for coming, and escorted her to an elevator. Upstairs, there were corridors with offices, all very quiet—nothing like the bustling atmosphere you might expect from watching television, with ringing phones and men wearing shoulder holsters.

Riley led her into a small interrogation room and introduced her to the polygraph examiner, Wyatt Omohundro, a huge, balding man, with a ponderous, looming presence. In a slow, rumbling voice with a heavy Southern accent, he began the session, which was tape-recorded, by explaining the process. "Basically," he told her, "when I get through, I grade the charts, I reach a determination, I will look you right in the eye, and tell you the determination."

As required by law, Omohundro read her the standards-of-practice form, advising her that the test could not be administered without her written permission and that she had a right to end the examination at any time. "Is it standard for someone to do this without a lawyer?" Beverly asked. "My daughter's a lawyer. She's concerned with everything I do." Omohundro replied, "Sure, I can understand." If she insisted on calling a lawyer, he would abandon the polygraph. He handed her the form and told her, "Just sign your name right there." She signed, but she still wanted Omohundro's advice on legal representation. "If a person does this, would it be wrong to have a lawyer?" she asked. "Should I get a lawyer?" In a casual voice, he said, "Well, some do and some don't."

Beverly asked how reliable polygraphs actually were. "In situations where there is a clear, specific issue," he said, "the polygraph is extremely accurate." He told her that polygraphs have a bad name only because private examiners, without proper training, sat on pasteboard boxes in the back rooms of convenience stores running dozens of job applications at a time and charging one hundred dollars a person.

Omohundro then handed her a Miranda waiver form. "It all sounds so serious," Beverly said, to which he replied, "Well, this is a very serious matter." "My one question," she said, "is whether I should have my daughter here." Omohundro ignored the question. "OK," he said. "Do you understand your rights as I've explained them to you?" When she said she did, he asked, "With your rights in mind, do you waive your rights?" "Yes," she said. She signed the form, Omohundro signed as a witness, and for the next hour they talked about her relationship with Roger, about the child Krystyna was expecting, and about the evening of March 4.

"Now, listen," Omohundro said, "I've got some very heavy questions I've got to ask you. This boils down to the very reason as to why you're here so we can put this thing away forever and ever and ever."

Then, in a pre-interview without the polygraph hooked up, he asked her questions he had formulated.

"Do you know who shot Roger?"

"I think he killed himself."

"You think it was Roger that killed himself. OK. Did you yourself shoot Roger?"

"Oh, no."

"You did not."

"Oh, no."

"Listen to what I'm saying. At the very moment Roger was shot, were you there?"

"No."

"You did not see this happen. Before Roger was shot, did you know he was going to be shot?"

"No. Let me tell you something—"

"I'm trying to help you by not letting you go into too much detail. At the same time, I don't want to cut you off."

After a few more pre-interview questions, he told her, "The bad part is over now. I'm going to go in and make a few notes and write a few questions down, and when I come back we can get this over with."

When he returned, he hooked up the attachments, and told her to sit very still and remain silent. He told her he would turn on the instrument and balance its readings on her present conditions. Once he had done this, he took out a pack of notes and began reading questions.

"Were you present when Roger died?"

"No."

Did you yourself fire the shot that caused the death of Roger?"

"No."

Omohundro conducted two separate tests, and ran both of them twice. After each run, he pulled rolls of paper out of the machine and left the room, joining Riley, who had been watching the test through a one-way mirror. They studied the charts, and Omohundro concluded her responses were deceptive. To Riley, his initial hunch about the case—that Beverly had murdered Roger—seemed verified.

Riley told Omohundro he didn't think Beverly would put up with much in the way of confrontation at this point, that if their talk veered into an interrogation, she might stop cooperating. They agreed not to lean on her.

When Omohundro returned to the interrogation room, Beverly was pale and red-eyed. It was almost 3:00, and she had been in the room for close to two hours without a break. Looking her straight in the eye, as he had promised he would, he told her that her answers indicated deception on relevant issues.

"You're kidding," Beverly said.

"No, I am not kidding," Omohundro told her. "You are not telling the truth."

Then he asked, "Isn't it true that you killed Roger?"

"No."

"Well, Agent Riley would like to talk to you."

For days, Riley had been thinking about what to do if Beverly failed the test.

John Reid, who worked at the Chicago Police crime lab in the 1940s and helped develop the polygraph machine, had developed a technique that involved presenting a subject with scenarios—he called them "themes"—

that would appear either to explain a suspect's suspicious behavior or lessen his or her culpability.

One theme that occurred to Riley was to suggest to Beverly that Roger had committed suicide in her presence, and then to offer two possible explanations for why she had failed the polygraph—either she had lied because she didn't want people to know she was present and unable to stop Roger from killing himself, or she didn't remember it because she blocked it out. The beauty of the theme was that it placed her at the scene while seeming to get her off the hook.

But if forensic evidence showed that Roger's death was homicide, acknowledging that she was present would be the equivalent of a murder confession. It would in fact be tantamount to an admission not only that she killed him but also that she staged a suicide. That would constitute first-degree murder.

Before leaving the interrogation room, Omohundro switched off the tape recorder, which had been running without Beverly's knowledge. Later Omohundro would recall encountering Riley outside and telling him how to turn the recorder back on with a hidden switch. But Riley didn't turn it on. Thus, there was no verbatim record of the ensuing session, which lasted about an hour and a half, and was observed through the one-way mirror by witnesses in the observation room.

Riley told her he didn't believe she was telling him everything, and claimed that there were inconsistencies in her story. In a prior interview, for instance, she had said that she and Roger had watched a PBS program about Charles de Gaulle after he fixed dinner the evening of March 4. Riley told Beverly that the show had not been on that night—that it had aired earlier—although in fact it had aired on March 4, precisely as Beverly had recalled. Also, Riley said, it had come to his attention that she had called the medical examiner's office and asked the time of Roger's death. Beverly responded that she didn't remember calling the medical examiner's office, but clearly remembered the de Gaulle program. Actually, although Roger's ex-wife had called the medical examiner's office, Beverly had not. Beverly told Riley that the inconsistencies were baffling, as was her failure of the polygraph test.

When Riley proposed the first of his alternative explanations—that she had been present when Roger killed himself but didn't want anyone to know—she resisted the idea. Riley kept pushing, saying people often wouldn't admit to such things for any number of reasons. Maybe they found it too painful. Maybe they felt responsible. Maybe they feared they would be blamed for what happened. Beverly shook her head.

Roger moved on to the other alternative—maybe she was so traumatized by Roger's suicide that she blacked it out. Sometimes, he went on, when people are involved in traumatic incidents, the shock is so bad that they can't recall the actual event. That's a natural fact, he said, it's documented. To drive it home, Riley told her that when he was a boy his father committed suicide in front of him and he blocked it from his memory; he only knew what people told him about it. This was a lie. Riley's father did commit suicide, but Riley wasn't present and was much too young to remember it at all. But Riley had no compunction about lying to Beverly. It was part of his job. John Reid had encouraged the practice, referring to such fabrications as "transitional themes," which offered a suspect a "crutch" that made it easier to admit guilt.

Beverly seemed to go for the idea that if he'd blocked out the memory of a loved one's suicide, she might have done the same. With Riley leading the way, prodding, suggesting details, insisting again that this was the only possible explanation for the failed polygraph, and with Beverly at first reluctantly consenting to his proposals and then, in a tentative, halting voice, offering possibilities of her own, they together constructed a series of events that Riley convinced her she had blocked from memory. At this point, he turned the recorder back on—he would later insist that he had only then realized he had forgotten to do so at the start of the interview—and tried to get her to recite the scenario they had just worked out.

After she said she'd seen Roger's gun and had "this vision" of him lying on the couch, Riley said, "You remember seeing him there, and all night long, all you wanted to do was go to him and be with him and see that he was found, and it just ate at you all night long." She murmured in a confused manner, and he told her, "It's eating at you right now. Beverly, you're going to sleep better. You'll sleep better if you remember this."

"I'll try," she said.

As the session continued, Beverly seemed to be struggling to visualize the events Riley was encouraging her to recall. Prompting her to focus on his scenario, he told her, "You called him. And you knew he wouldn't answer the phone, but you kept hoping that he would. And then all night long you didn't sleep, because you knew where he was. And you couldn't stand the thought. You thought, what a horrible person I am, because I have left him without somebody to take care of him. And it ate at you all night long. That's the worst thing that's bothering you, isn't it? Tell me the truth."

"I think so." Her voice had become almost inaudible.

Moments later, she said, "But I have to tell you this. If you hadn't said I was with him, I would have never—"

Riley interrupted, "But you do remember now, don't you. Tell me yes. Tell me you remember."

"I remember some of it."

Riley repeated the scenario again, and then again, finally telling her, "You might not want to accept it consciously, but you know from talking to me what happened, don't you? Give me that much."

"OK."

"You do know that, don't you? Tell me yes."

"Yes, I guess so." She paused. "I wish I could see it somehow."

When Riley felt he had gotten as much as he was going to get, he asked, "You want to go home now?"

"Yeah, I really must," she said. The questioning had gone on eight hours.

"I'll walk you outside," Riley said. "Let's use the stairs."

Beverly had been with police all day, with nothing to eat and nothing to drink except coffee. She was exhausted and confused and beginning to question her memory of her last night with Roger; she would describe the feeling as like being hypnotized.

The next day, March 27, Beverly called Riley, who was surprised to hear from his suspect. "I was supposed to take care of him, Dave. I always promised him I would take care of him and I couldn't," she sobbed.

"Beverly, quit beating yourself over the head," Riley said. "He was a man that enjoyed controlling things. That's what it all boiled down to, the money and the art and the friends and the prestige, all was part of being in control. . . . And he could not stand the thought of not being able to have you and control the situation with Krystyna."

It was a curious state of affairs—Riley, who considered suicide nothing more than a concoction to hide a murder, talking about why Roger had killed himself. But he was only doing it because he thought Beverly was trying to make herself seem more credible by pretending to be confused about it.

When Beverly said, "I feel like I have to clear this up somehow," Riley told her that the only person to whom she had a responsibility to explain her behavior in the aftermath of Roger's death was Corinna. But Beverly said she couldn't tell Corinna what happened because "I don't remember exactly."

To put a stop to Beverly's ambivalence, Riley said they'd figured out the previous day "that the reason your behavior was so strange and inappropriate—even though you didn't realize it at the time—had to do with the fact that you were present."

Riley continued, "Nobody's blaming you for leaving him that night. . . . There wasn't a damn thing in the world that you could have done for him that night. He was dead the instant the gun went off."

"I wish I had that coherence in my mind," she said. "I really feel like I need to talk to someone."

"Well, if you feel that need, why don't you find a psychologist?"

What she couldn't understand, she said, was the contradiction between her memory and the facts as Riley presented them.

"I feel like my integrity has been questioned," she said.

"I haven't questioned your integrity."

"I know you haven't, but I just feel like—"

Riley interrupted, repeating forcefully, "I have *not* questioned your integrity. . . . All of my questions have been answered, as far as I'm concerned."

She asked about the other investigators, and he told her, "I think we're pretty much on the same wavelength."

Beverly had never been to a psychologist. Going through the yellow pages, she saw an advertisement for a mental health clinic at St. Luke's Hospital in Richmond. She once had taken her younger daughter, Shannon, there after she broke her arm. If nothing else, St. Luke's was a familiar name, so she arranged for an evaluation.

Marsha Alon, a nurse clinician, took her background information. Beverly tried to explain what had happened, how she must have gone into shock after Roger's death, and then suppressed any memory of it.

"Is it possible, that someone can block something like this out?" Beverly asked.

"Yes, it happens all the time," the nurse told her. "It's very common."

On Monday, March 30, Corinna called Riley because she'd heard nothing about the status of the investigation. The call, Riley felt, was fortuitous. He thought he'd persuaded Beverly to tell Corinna that she'd been present when her father killed himself. But Riley didn't want Corinna to be blindsided—she might blow up at Beverly and accuse her outright of murder. That would interrupt the smooth flow of the investigation, which depended on Beverly's cooperation. Thus, Riley decided to bring Corinna into the investigative circle, asking her to come to First Division headquarters.

When she heard Riley's theory of the case, she was stunned. To her, the notion that Beverly could be a murderer was unthinkable. But when Riley told her there simply was no other way to account for the facts, she found herself forced to accept the idea, and she agreed to cooperate with the investigation. When she spoke to Beverly, Riley told her, she would need to appear neutral, friendly, and sympathetic. "If you react adversely, it will shut her down," Riley said. "We want to play this out as long as possible."

The following day, Corinna and Beverly met for lunch at a downtown Richmond hotel. Beverly said she had decided to complete Roger's book as a tribute to his memory, and they talked about the questions of fraud surrounding his collection. Then, suddenly, Beverly said, "Corinna, I would like to talk to you about what happened that last night with your father." She started crying and held out her hand to take Corinna's hand. Then she said she had been there when Roger committed suicide.

"Beverly, are you sure?" Corinna asked. Despite being prepared by Riley, she was absolutely horrified by the words coming out of Beverly's mouth. "You've been under so much stress," Corinna said. "It's been a very difficult time for all of us. You're sure you're not imagining this?

She wasn't imagining it, she said, but it was all unclear. She had been in a daze and was unsure exactly what happened. She was still struggling with herself to find the answers. She remembered a loud noise and remembered trying to get the gun out of Roger's hand, but she thought she might be mixing up her memories of what happened that night with what happened the following morning after Joe Hairfield discovered the body. And now she was plagued by an overwhelming sense of guilt—a feeling that she could have said or done something to stop Roger.

"Beverly," Corinna told her, "you really need to get some help to deal with your guilt issues. Then, as if she had known nothing in advance, Corinna told her, "And you really need to tell the police." Beverly said she already had.

Corinna was now convinced that Riley was right—Beverly had killed her father. Wanting to get away from Beverly as quickly as possible, Corinna said she had to go.

"I couldn't believe she said it," Corinna said, recounting the conversation to Riley. He felt satisfied that the commonwealth now had a witness outside the police force—a sympathetic, reliable witness—who could testify that Beverly had confessed to being with Roger at the time of his death.

It wasn't until May 21 that Ann Jones, the firearms expert at the state forensic lab, sat down to study the evidence in the case. She had Roger's gun, the four cartridges that had remained in its cylinder, the bullet fragments that had been removed from his brain, a box of the same ammunition taken from Windsor, and the pillows that had been on the couch alongside the body.

Jones test-fired several rounds from the cartridge box to see what sort of residue traces the ammunition would leave. It was extremely dirty ammunition, some of the dirtiest she had seen in eight years on the job. She held the gun into a target from one inch. The shot produced a four-to-five-inch spread. From two inches away, the soot spread seven to eight inches. From photographs Greg Neal had taken, Jones reasoned the gun barrel had been close to the skin.

To replicate Roger's head, Jones formed cotton padding into an ovoid shape. To replicate his right hand, she filled a white glove with clay. Then she arranged the ovoid head and the pillows in a configuration resembling that depicted in Neal's photos, and covered the pillows with a white sheet. She angled the gun so it would create a pattern of gunshot residue contained on the pillows underneath and slipped the muzzle between the fourth and fifth fingers of the clay hand.

When she fired, the clay hand toppled forward. On it were soot marks that were similar to, although not exactly like, those on Roger's fingers. Jones then filled a second glove with clay and placed it in the position Riley had suggested it would have been in if Roger had awakened and used his right hand to ward off the shot. When she fired the gun again, the blast tore through the glove, down to the clay. If Roger's hand had been in that position, it would have been injured, but the photos showed no injury.

Nonetheless, Jones called Riley and told him that her test results were consistent with his theory that Roger had been asleep with his right hand cupping his forehead when the murderer had slipped the muzzle between the fourth and fifth fingers of his hand and pulled the trigger.

Riley called Powhatan County Commonwealth's Attorney Jack Lewis and said he thought the forensic results, together with Beverly's confession that she had been with Roger when he died, was enough evidence to seek an indictment for murder. But Lewis wished, if possible, to avoid a trial. He had been the prosecutor for sixteen years. It was only a part-time job; he also had a private practice, doing mostly real estate closings and title examinations and handling loans for deeds of trust. A murder trial would be time-consuming and expensive. It also was risky in a case where the evidence was circumstantial.

Lewis suggested trying to work out some sort of plea bargain with Beverly. Riley was a natural person to make this overture, but he didn't think Beverly would ever agree to a plea. That would destroy her reputation and forfeit her job. That would be the end of her life as she knew it. But on June 3, Lewis called Riley and they agreed on a strategy: Riley would tell Beverly he was contacting her on his own and tell her he was bringing her the inside scoop—which was that everyone except him on the commonwealth team believed she had committed first-degree murder and were inclined to indict her. Riley would appear as a friend and confidant, someone who was there to help by offering her a way out—the possibility of a lesser sentence if she admitted killing Roger. "It isn't going to work," Riley told Lewis, "but I'll try."

As soon as he hung up, Riley called Beverly at Philip Morris. "Beverly, I need to talk to you," he said. "What does your schedule look like today?" She hadn't heard from Riley in almost a month. He had left her with the impression that the investigation had ended and that the final report, with its conclusion of suicide, would be issued any day. "Well," she said, "I'm busy, but I'm always available. What's the problem?" Riley said he wanted to talk in person "someplace where there isn't anybody else around."

"That sounds ominous," Beverly said, but Riley told her, "Don't read too much into it. It's just to talk." He proposed meeting at Fort Darling, a national park a few miles south of the Philip Morris plant, and she agreed to be there at 11:00 A.M. When she pulled into the parking lot, he was waiting. He climbed into her car, saying he was there as a friend, adding, "I've got bad news."

He told her a laboratory analysis of the powder-burn patterns indicated that Roger could not possibly have shot himself. The finding, together with her admission that she had been present when he died, indicated that she was the one who shot him. Riley said both he and the commonwealth attorney were convinced she had killed Roger. But he didn't blame her, considering Roger's abominable behavior and his affairs with Krystyna Drewnowska and other women. What surprised him, Riley said, was that she had tolerated the heartless monster for so long. "You should get a medal," Riley said. His objective was to appear to commiserate with Beverly—on the theory that sympathizing with a suspect and blaming the crime on the victim's evil nature increases the chance for a confession.

As Riley expected, she vehemently denied killing Roger. Also, as he'd expected, she said she was now convinced she had only dreamed about being at Windsor when Roger died. Furthermore, she said, she thought she had proof that she had left Windsor by the time Roger spoke to his publisher that night. She said her son, Gavin, had reminded her that after coming home that night she had gone to a nearby Safeway store and bought groceries. She said she always kept her receipts and could find the one from Safeway showing the time and date.

"Anybody can get receipts," Riley said. You could pick up receipts in a supermarket parking lot and it was extraordinary, if she had such a receipt, that she hadn't mentioned it before. The evidence, he told her, was over-whelming and included signs of premeditation.

Beverly had grown very quiet, almost paralyzed. Finally, she said she couldn't conceive of killing Roger. She loved him too much. But that evening had become such a blank that she no longer could recall what had happened.

The commonwealth attorney hadn't authorized him to provide the details he had just revealed, Riley said. No one knew he was here. He had come only because he sympathized with her and felt that Roger's behavior had been despicable. In yet another deception, Riley said the forensics indicated someone had wiped the gun clean. If the two of them could craft an explanation for that, he said, he would present it to Jack Lewis, and it might prevent Lewis from proceeding with an indictment for first-degree murder. Maybe, Riley said, it would convince Lewis not even to prosecute at all. In fact, an admission by Beverly that she had wiped the gun would strengthen the case against her.

Riley was improvising. Maybe, he told Beverly, she had been asleep and panicked when she heard the gun go off, had picked up the gun in a state of confusion, wiped it, and placed it in Roger's hand. That would account for the presence of Roger's fingerprints and the absence of hers—which was what the forensics really showed. Riley told her he wasn't saying she had done this, just that it was hypothetically possible. Beverly replied that it was possible, although she couldn't remember what happened.

Amazingly, Beverly once again was accepting the she-was-there scenario, only minutes after repudiating it. Riley had brought her full circle. On a notepad, he started drafting a statement, checking each sentence with Beverly before committing it to paper. It said she and Roger had fallen asleep on separate sofas in the room. A noise made her jump, and she suddenly found herself standing over Roger and seeing the gun. "The above I remember clearly but I don't remember exactly what happened next." But her natural reaction, not knowing that Roger was dead, would have been to take the gun away from him. And then it "would have been natural for anyone realizing they shouldn't have touched the gun" to wipe it off.

When Riley finished writing the statement, Beverly signed it. "I'll give this to Jack Lewis," Riley said. "He's the one making the decisions. Maybe this will explain enough to sway him a little bit."

Then they took a short walk. In a ploy he hoped would lead to an admission that she had shot Roger, Riley told her, "If you did this, Beverly, it's understandable considering the way Roger treated you in the relationship and throwing you aside."

"I'm not a criminal or murderer," she said.

"No, you're not," Riley said. "This is something you would never do again. This was something that was forced on you. It was irresistible, an irresistible impulse." He told her that an irresistible impulse could be the basis for a defense of temporary insanity. That would require overcoming a reservoir of jury skepticism, but it occasionally succeeded. But she might want to consider a plea bargain.

"I know the commonwealth attorney would be more than willing to be very, very lenient in any sentencing against you," he said, "you know, the bare minimum. Maybe he would even go for a manslaughter charge, which would be a very short prison term. Maybe, if you're trying to save face, you know, you could not actually have to admit guilt but acknowledge that there was enough evidence to convict you." Despite anguish, Beverly seemed to be listening to everything he said.

"I'm not a killer," she said.

"Beverly, I know you're not a killer," he said. To show how much he trusted her, he held out his gun, telling her, "Here's my gun. I hand you my gun. I know you're not that kind of person. This was a onetime thing." She was taken aback. "Oh, no," she said.

As their conversation was ending, Beverly asked, "Do you know a good lawyer, somebody that can help me?"

"Beverly," he said, "I'm not the person that you should be talking to about this. You have a daughter that is a lawyer. You should be talking to her."

That afternoon, Beverly finally called Katie, her lawyer-daughter who was clerking for an appellate judge in Charlottesville. "Buggy," said Beverly, using Katie's childhood nickname. "Something terrible's happened. They think I did something terrible to Roger."

Katie told her to come to Charlottesville immediately. When Beverly arrived, she told the story in reverse. Katie couldn't believe her mother could have been so dumb. But for all her outward sophistication, Beverly had been raised in rural South Carolina—brought up to believe that you could trust the police, that you could always turn to the police, that the police were your friends.

Katie called her boyfriend, Alan Block, a lawyer in Washington, D.C., and asked him to help find a lawyer. After talking to other lawyers, Alan recommended Peter Greenspun, in Fairfax, Virginia, a suburb of Washington.

They made an appointment with Greenspun for the following morning and drove to Fairfax to meet him. Like Katie, Greenspun was appalled that Beverly had taken a polygraph and signed a statement without talking to a lawyer. His intuition told him that even if Beverly were willing to do so, the prosecutor would not let her plead down to manslaughter. A trial appeared inevitable, he said, and Beverly would have to prove her innocence because the presumption of innocence—the requirement that the prosecution prove guilt beyond a reasonable doubt—was fairly dead in Virginia.

In Greenspun, Katie thought, her mother had someone who appreciated the true peril of her circumstances. Beverly wrote him a check for $10,000. But back in Richmond, Beverly talked to others about her situation and became concerned that Powhatan County jurors might be ill-disposed toward a lawyer from Washington. Thus, she decided to speak with Murray Janus, the most prominent criminal defense lawyer in Richmond. He told Beverly he would take her case for $150,000, and would need $50,000 up front. Katie asked several judges to rate Greenspun and Janus. No one had anything critical to say about either lawyer. But one judge told Katie, "I have to say, if it was my mother, I'd want her in the hands of Murray Janus." Beverly was already leaning toward Janus, called Greenspun, who was gracious and professional and said he would promptly return her retainer. Beverly then wrote a $50,000 check to Janus.

On June 9, Jack Lewis obtained a grand jury indictment charging Beverly with first-degree murder and the use of a firearm in the commission of a crime. The next morning, Beverly surrendered at the Powhatan County Sheriff's Office, where she was fingerprinted and promptly freed on a $25,000 bond, under an arrangement Murray Janus had worked out in advance.

The trial opened on Monday, October 26, before Powhatan County Circuit Court Judge Thomas V. Warren and a jury. The prosecution was led by Jack Lewis, who had been joined by Warren Von Schuch, a capable, experienced prosecutor from Chesterfield County. Their case relied primarily on the words that had come out of Beverly's mouth, but also on the testimony of Ann Jones that her test firings of Roger's gun produced a residue pattern consistent with murder, the testimony of various witnesses who said Roger seemed cheerful and looking to the future, and the testimony of a woman named Zelma Smith, a convict with an extensive criminal record who claimed Beverly had tried to buy an untraceable gun from her before Roger's death and denied that the prosecution had promised anything in exchange for her testimony.

Janus countered with a seemingly seamless alibi. Beverly's son Gavin testified that on March 4 his mother came home around 10:00 P.M., went out to buy groceries, and returned about 11:00 P.M. Janus produced a timed receipt placing Beverly at the Safeway at 10:40 P.M., and the alibi was corroborated by a disinterested witness who told the jury he had been in the Safeway checkout line behind Beverly and had spoken with her. Thus, Janus contended, Beverly hardly could have been with Roger after he spoke to his publisher around 10:00 P.M.

Janus also called Herbert MacDonell, a renowned firearms expert who had testified in many high-profile cases, including those following the assassinations of Robert F. Kennedy and Martin Luther King. From tests of a gun similar to Roger's, MacDonell concluded that Roger had held the gun upside down, with the fingers of his right hand clenching the barrel and the cylinder frame, and then pulled the trigger with his left thumb. "This is not at all uncommon in suicides," MacDonell told the jury, "because of a wish to steady the revolver in some fashion." Finally, Beverly took the stand, firmly denying that she had killed Roger.

On Monday, November 2, a week after the trial began, the jury returned a verdict. A clerk passed it to Judge Warren, who read it and said, "On the murder indictment, you find the defendant guilty of first-degree murder as charged in the indictment. . . ."

"Witch trial!" Shannon Monroe, Beverly's younger daughter, cried out.

Warren looked up sternly, then continued, "and you fix her punishment at twenty years in prison. Signed by your foreman. On the use of a firearm in the commission of a murder, you find the defendant guilty and fix her punishment at two years. Signed by your foreman."

Judge Warren set a hearing for December 22, at which time the defense could argue for a reduced sentence. Janus requested that Beverly be allowed to remain out on bail pending the official sentencing. "It is rather unusual on a murder charge for it to be granted," Jack Lewis told the judge, "but if the court is so inclined, the commonwealth wouldn't oppose it." Warren granted the motion, but reminded Beverly that her status had been irrevocably altered. "You have now been convicted," he said. "You are no longer presumed innocent."

The next day, the attorney general of Virginia advised Judge Warren that under state law persons convicted of first-degree murder were not entitled to bail. That statement was incorrect, but based on it Warren ordered Beverly to surrender within twenty-four hours. After Janus pleaded for more time, Warren relented, allowing Beverly until the following Monday to get her affairs in order.

On November 9, a week after Beverly was convicted, the Monroe children drove her to the Powhatan County Sheriff's Office, where Greg Neal awaited her. He turned her over to a uniformed deputy. Beverly, carrying a small cardboard box containing a few belongings, followed the deputy and a female secretary to an unmarked car. A rack on the dashboard held a shotgun. With the children following, the deputy headed for the Virginia Correctional Facility for Women just outside the small town of Goochland on the north bank of the James River. Throughout the trip, the secretary kept up a stream of polite conversation about the accomplishments of their respective children, as if they were at a church social.

The prison was a cluster of old brick buildings with slate roofs and white casement windows set among magnolia and pecan trees. It was surprisingly pastoral. Black Angus cattle grazed in a pasture across the road. At a guard station, the guard halted the children, while the sheriff's car proceeded to an administration building. Beverly looked back at her children. They waved. She waved back and followed the deputy inside.

Epilogue

On November 7, 1992, just six days after Beverly's conviction, Common-wealth's Attorney Jack Williams filed a motion seeking a sentence reduction for Zelma Smith, the convict who had denied at the trial that she had been offered anything in exchange for testifying that Beverly had tried to buy a gun from her. In February 1993, Chesterfield County Circuit Court Judge Herbert Gill held an in-camera hearing on the motion, which he granted, cutting the sentence Smith was serving for check fraud from seven to four years.

In May 1994 Beverly was released on appeal bond, but she returned to prison in December 1995 after the Virginia Court of Appeals affirmed her conviction and the Virginia Supreme Court declined to hear the case. She remained in prison until May 2002, when Senior U.S. District Court Judge Richard L. Williams granted her petition for a federal writ of habeas corpus on the grounds that prosecutors withheld important evidence supporting Beverly's innocence. Among the withheld evidence were forensic reports, including one concluding that Roger committed suicide. Williams called her case a "monument to prosecutorial indiscretions and mishandling." Williams also described the police interviews of Beverly as "deceitful and manipulative." The U.S. Court of Appeals for the Fourth Circuit affirmed Williams's decision in March 2003. Three months later the prosecution dropped the charges.

PETER REILLY

After grilling, he thought maybe he'd killed his mother—
and blocked it out of his mind

DONALD S. CONNERY

FALLS VILLAGE, CONNECTICUT

Barbara Gibbons was still alive at nine thirty Friday night, September 28, 1973. She was alone, probably, in the small, unkempt cottage in Falls Village that she shared with her son, Peter Reilly, an eighteen-year-old high school senior.

She was drunk. That was not unusual. Often Peter would telephone home to let her know that he was all right and receive no answer. Because she was partly deaf, he would explain to his friends that "my mom must be sleeping on her good ear and can't hear the phone." Maybe so, they would think, but it was just as likely that she had passed out on the lower bunk of their bedroom.

That night, however, Barbara was still functioning and she was worried. She had been operated on for cancer of the uterus three years earlier, and she had recently been tested to see if there had been a recurrence. She thought she was dying of cancer.

Anxious to know the results of the tests, she called her surgeon, Dr. Frank Lovallo, at his home in nearby Sharon. He was not home, but she finally reached him at a dinner party "between 9:20 and 9:40," as the doctor would tell the police. He advised her to call him on Monday when he might know the test results. "Her manner of speaking was aggressive, and she sounded upset." His patient would never learn that she was not dying of cancer.

At about the time Barbara was speaking with Lovallo, Peter was about five miles away by car, saying good night to friends outside the Canaan Methodist Church on West Main Street in North Canaan, a town north of Falls Village. He and two dozen other people had been meeting in the

From *Guilty Until Proven Innocent* (New York: G.P. Putnam's Sons, 1977). Copyright © Donald S. Connery. Adapted with permission.

church basement since 8:00 P.M., discussing the future of the Canaan Youth Center.

Many of the participants were older than Peter, but he was comfortable in their company. Better spoken and better mannered than most of his contemporaries, he was a slight, almost frail youth who looked younger than his eighteen years. He was easygoing, more lethargic than energetic, but he was bright and well-informed despite his average grades.

His deportment was exemplary; everyone from his school principal on down had a good word for him. As far as the police were concerned, he was, in the words of one officer, "clean as a whistle." They thought this surprising because his mother, despite her intellectual interests and her background as an insurance company employee in Manhattan, was "a screwball."

In recent years, she was mainly known for her drinking and belligerence. She liked to play practical jokes, sometimes even placing prank phone calls to the police. Neighbors were accustomed to seeing her reading books outdoors: under a light at night, under an umbrella in the pouring rain, or wrapped in a raccoon coat during a snowstorm, her book protected by a transparent plastic sheet.

Some townspeople thought Barbara was a lesbian; others spoke of the men she entertained. Some suspected she was bisexual. Yet Peter seemed to have a way of floating above it all. Here was a young man who had never known his father and didn't know why his last name was Reilly. His mother said she had made it up. Yet he seemed more proud than ashamed of Barbara's eccentric ways, believing her to be more sophisticated and more liberated than their neighbors.

After the meeting at the church, Peter agreed to give a ride to sixteen-year-old John Sochocki. Peter drove a royal blue Corvette with a white convertible top. His wealthy godmother in New York, Barbara's longtime friend, had bought the car for him the year before. He was a fortunate young man, people thought, to be able to drive such a car while he and his mother lived on welfare. Still, no one seemed to resent him for it; he was too nice a boy for anyone to dislike.

After leaving Sochocki at his house, Peter drove home and parked the Corvette. As he passed through the front door, he noticed a book on the living room card table face-down in a way that might hurt the binding. He found this surprising because his mother "was a library sort of person, with a respect for books."

He called out, "Hey, Mom, I'm home," but there was no answer. He noticed that the reading lamp was on in the bedroom to his right. When he looked in, he saw his near-naked mother sprawled on a rug that was crimson with blood.

People react in different ways to horrifying sights. Peter might have rushed into the bedroom to touch or shake or embrace his mutilated parent. He might have tried to determine whether she was dead or alive. He might have rushed out of the house screaming for help. What he did do, with self-possession that would count against him in the minds of the authorities, was most sensible—he went straight to the telephone.

Peter called the Madow family. They were close friends and volunteers for the VFW ambulance squad. They had told him what to do in case of a medical emergency: don't touch anything unless you're qualified; summon help.

Marion Madow answered Peter's call. It was 9:50 P.M. He told her something was wrong with his mother; there was "blood all over the place." He thought she was unconscious. She told him to call his family physician. Then she and her husband, Mickey, headed for the ambulance garage.

Peter called the home of the family physician, Dr. Carl Bornemann, who was on vacation. The call was forwarded to the doctor's daughter-in-law, who advised Peter to call Sharon Hospital, where he spoke to Barbara Fenn, the evening supervisor. Fenn notified the state police.

Within minutes, the Madows' seventeen-year-old son, Geoffrey, arrived at the Gibbons cottage. He too had been at the meeting in the Methodist Church. Shortly after Geoff's arrival, his parents drove up in the ambulance.

The first officer at the scene was State Trooper Bruce McCafferty, who had been cruising in East Canaan when he received orders to go to the Gibbons cottage. He was quickly followed by Lieutenant James Shay, commander of the Canaan state police troop, and Sergeant Percy Salley, the shift supervisor.

The first thing Shay did was berate Mickey Madow for covering the body with a blanket. Mickey said he had done that "because her son was standing there and she was nude. I only did it out of decency."

"Well, don't ever do it again," Shay said.

Barbara's legs were spread and her arms outstretched. Her body had been slashed, smashed, and stomped upon. She was naked except for a white T-shirt and an unbuttoned shirt that had been pulled above her breasts. The shirt covered a great gaping neck wound and severed vocal cords. She had almost been beheaded.

Peter realized he was under suspicion when Sergeant Salley peered at his fingernails and asked him to remove his shirt, looking for signs of blood or bruises. There were none. Geoff Madow also was briefly a suspect, due to his presence at the scene when police arrived. The teenagers were placed in separate police cruisers, about twenty-five feet apart, on the other side of the road from the Gibbons cottage, where they sat while the investigation proceeded.

Shortly before 11:00 P.M., Trooper McCafferty asked Peter to read and sign a form describing his constitutional rights. Peter, of course, had a right to remain silent, but he willingly described his activities leading up to the discovery of his mother lying motionless on the floor. He spoke slowly, and the officer wrote down what he said. This took more than half an hour.

For the next three and a half hours, Peter sat in the police cruiser, alone with his thoughts, as the homicide investigation continued.

At about 2:00 A.M., he was taken to the state police barracks in Canaan, a grim, two-story, red-brick building with a green neon "State Police" sign out front. There Sergeant Percy Salley read Peter his rights again after telling him that he was not being charged with anything.

Further questioning did not begin, however, until Lieutenant Shay returned to the barracks at about 6:30 A.M. Shay began the session, which he secretly tape-recorded, by again advising Peter of his rights.

As the audiotape rolls, Peter tells Shay that when he saw his mother on the floor he either said or thought, "Oh, my God," and started making calls. "I didn't touch her. If you touch someone you can get into trouble."

"How long were you on the phone?" Shay asks.

"Four or five minutes, maybe less. I looked and saw blood all over the place. I never went into the room. I never went through the bedroom door."

"Was your mother alive?"

"She was breathing but having trouble. She was unconscious. She didn't answer when I called to her."

"Were her eyes open?"

"No, I think they were closed. I'm almost sure, but I can't definitely say."

"How long did you observe her breathing?"

"Just a couple of seconds. Then she stopped."

"How was she dressed?"

"She had on a T-shirt and nothing else, maybe a coat. I'm not sure."

"Did you see any blood?"

"Yes, the T-shirt was pulled up and there was blood on the chest. And on the floor. Possibly on her face and throat. I'm not sure. . . . I was really shaken. We were very close. She did as much as she could. She did a very good job. She always tried to do things. If I wanted something, if there were any problems, we'd always work them out."

"Could someone think otherwise?"

"I haven't been at home that much in the evenings for the last several months. We swore at each other when we got mad."

"Which was quite often?"

"Not really. She changed a little after the hysterectomy. I wouldn't want to discuss things with her. She'd fly right off the handle."

"Did she have a drinking problem?"

"She drank wine quite consistently."

"Did you ever see your mother having sex?"

"No, but I heard it once. I heard heavy breathing and the bedsprings."

"Did it bother you?"

"No. I argued that if I can do it she can."

"Do you have any brothers or sisters?"

"No, an only child."

"What names did you call your mother?"

"Fuck you, dumb bitch. She called me the same, you sonofabitch and things like that. Otherwise we got along fairly well."

"Why didn't you touch her?"

"I knew I didn't know what I was doing. The first thing I'd do was to get someone who knew what they were doing. First person I could think of was Mrs. Madow. I wanted to get someone there. You don't expect to see your mom in a pool of blood. It's been drilled into me not to touch her. I'd be more than willing to take a lie detector test."

"We'll arrange it."

Though the full dialogue lasted an hour and a half, most of the rest of the tape was garbled beyond transcription. Later, Peter would recall being asked about his godmother and relatives and about his mother's sex life and whether he had ever had sexual relations with her. When Shay stepped out of the room, Sergeant Salley upset Peter by coming in and asking some of the same questions.

At 8:30, Shay took Peter down the hall to a bedroom. Having been awake for twenty-five hours, he lay down on the bed fully clothed, except for his sneakers, which were taken, presumably for testing. Left alone for four hours, he tried to sleep. The door was kept open so that an auxiliary trooper, sitting on a chair in the hallway, could watch him.

On the first floor of the police building there was great commotion, as if the place were under siege. While some troopers handled routine police business, other officers, working full-time on the Gibbons murder, rushed in and out. People were being questioned about their movements the night before and what they knew about Barbara Gibbons and Peter Reilly.

Solving the case quickly would be a great feather in the cap of the commanding officer, but to let the killer slip away by mischance would be a personal disaster. By midday Saturday, however, Lieutenant Shay had no physical evidence pointing to Peter's guilt and no other suspects. The boy's claim of innocence rested on an extraordinary coincidence: that he had appeared on the scene just minutes or seconds after a murderer finished the job and vanished.

At noon, Peter awoke to Trooper James Mulhern's voice. He knew Mulhern and his wife Joanne. In fact, Joanne had attended the church meeting and was now scrutinizing Peter through a one-way glass. She said the clothes he had on were the same ones he had worn at the youth center discussion.

Trooper Mulhern then drove the suspect to state police headquarters in Hartford for the polygraph examination Peter had offered to take. Lieutenant Shay arrived soon afterward. He briefed Sergeant Timothy Kelly, the head of the polygraph unit, and his associate, Sergeant Jack Schneider, on the Gibbons crime-scene details and his thoughts about Peter Reilly as his best suspect.

Through a one-way mirror, Shay would spend the next few hours watching Kelly use the so-called lie detector test as a means of leading Peter into a full-blown interrogation and a possible confession.

What happened has never been in dispute because a reel-to-reel audiotape recorder captured every word of the eight-hour confrontation between the teenager and a tag team of police officers. Thanks to the tape, the dialogue lives on.

Sergeant Schneider begins by asking Peter for some basic data about himself, saying, "This is confidential information. It stays here. Everything that we do today or any forms we make out remain here."

His approach is friendly and relaxing, as if Peter has nothing to worry about and would soon be free to go.

Asked if he has consumed liquor or drugs during the past twenty-four hours, Peter says he has not. He does, however, admit to having smoked marijuana in the past. Schneider says cheerfully, "Who don't smoke grass at eighteen years of age, right?"

He takes Peter to a room where the polygraph machine is fitted into a regular desk. Peter is asked to sit next to the desk in a straight chair with adjustable arms. Schneider calls it "the seat of honor."

Placing a cardio cuff on Peter's left arm, the officer explains, "We're measuring your blood pressure, your heartbeat, your pulse, you see, because that's very important because that's the only muscle in your body you can't control."

A rubber device is fastened to Peter's chest to measure his respiration. Electrodes are attached to two fingers of his left hand to measure his body electricity.

Schneider has a final word for Peter before handing him over to Sergeant Kelly: "There are three things we can say here today. You told us the truth, you didn't tell us the truth, or there's some mental or physical problem, we can't test you. For some reason we can't test you, we'll test you again some other day. OK? As long as you want to."

Peter sits silently until the door squeaks open and Kelly enters. "Peter, how are ya?" says Kelly. His deep voice is warm and friendly. He says, "You can leave here any time you want. You just say, hey, Tim, I want to go home, let me take the equipment off, and you can go home. Fair enough?"

When Peter agrees, Kelly assures him, "I'm not here trying to trick you or anything like that."

Tricks, however, are the stock-in-trade of police interrogators. The leading textbook, *Criminal Interrogation and Confessions* by Fred E. Inbau and John E. Reid, states flatly, "We do approve of such psychological tactics and techniques as trickery and deceit that are not only helpful but frequently necessary in order to secure incriminating information from the guilty."

Before beginning the test, Kelly, revealing that an autopsy has found that Barbara's legs were broken, tells Peter that he will soon know whether he has been truthful in his earlier statements. The polygraph "reads your brain for me."

"Does it actually read my brain?" Peter asks.

"Oh, definitely, definitely. And if you've told me the truth, this is what your brain is going to tell me."

"Will this stand up and protect me?"

"Right, right."

"Good. That's the reason I came up to take it, you know."

When Kelly asks Peter whether he has ever done anything that he is really ashamed of in his life, Peter asks for assurance that his words will not leave the room. When Kelly promises that the answer will stay "right here," Peter says a homosexual once made an advance but "nothing really happened." And he lied to his mother about smoking marijuana. That seems to be the extent of his shameful memories.

He agrees with Kelly that murdering his mother would be "a damned shameful thing." If he weren't innocent, "it would be ridiculous for me to come down and volunteer for this test."

Kelly observes, "I've had people actually come in here and take this test because they knew they were guilty but they didn't know how to tell somebody. . . . Maybe you're looking for somebody to help you, I don't know."

After the test questions are discussed, Kelly leaves the room "to write these up on a form so I can read them intelligently." He tells Peter that "the truth will be on [the polygraph chart] very shortly."

When he returns, Kelly tightens the arm cuff. "Your arm may get slightly red, but I guarantee it won't fall off."

The test begins. There are twelve questions, a mixture of relevant, irrelevant, and "control" questions, standard practice in the polygraph field.

"Were you born in the United States?" ("Yes.")

"Do you live in Connecticut?" ("Yes.")

"Last night do you know for sure how your mother got hurt?" ("No.")

"Are you wearing a brown shirt?" ("Yes.")

"Last night did you hurt your mother?" ("No.")

"Did you ever deliberately hurt someone in your life?" ("No.")

"Is your first name Peter?" ("Yes.")

"Do you know how your mother's legs were broken?" ("No.")

"Last night did you talk to your mother when you came home?" ("No.")

"Do you know how your mother's clothes got wet?" ("No.")

"Besides what we've talked about, have you done anything else you're ashamed of?" ("No.")

"Is the statement you made to the police the truth?" ("Yes.")

When it is over, Peter asks "How'd I do?"

"You're very cooperative, let me put it that way."

"What do you mean?"

Kelly explains that the first test was just a warm-up. To give the results wouldn't be fair because "you're nervous . . . definitely nervous this first time. We run it once to show you there's no electric shock or tricks. I'm not going to lie to you one iota. . . . I don't make it a habit to lie to people."

Kelly asks whether any of the questions bother Peter.

"Well, one thing I noticed is that, like, the question whether I harmed my mother or not."

"Why?"

"Well, that question—like they told me up at the barracks yesterday that— how some people don't realize—all of a sudden fly off the handle for a split second and it leaves a blank spot in their memory. Well, I thought about that last night, and I thought and I thought and I thought, and I said no, I couldn't have done it. . . . And now, when you ask me the question, that's what I think of."

"If you did it, this is probably how it could have happened."

"What do you mean?"

"Bango, just like this. . . . If you did it, it was a split-second thing that you did. You lost your head."

Kelly suggests that Peter might have been high on narcotics when he did the killing or maybe there was an argument or maybe his mother attacked him. "If anything like that happened, I'll know it over here on these charts."

Kelly tells Peter that in the next exercise he will be asked to deliberately lie to make sure they are getting proper recordings from him.

Sergeant Schneider returns to the room to run a test with a deck of playing cards. "This is the person's opportunity to beat the polygraph," he tells Peter, because if the instrument cannot detect a person lying about the number of the card in his hand then it will be of no use on the serious questions.

When the test ends, Schneider compliments Peter on being a "textbook reactor." "When you tell a lie you go right to the top of the chart," he said. "This is great for us because we'll have no trouble here today. . . . You're no pathological liar."

As Kelly replaces Schneider, Peter boasts, "I'm a textbook reactor."

They run through the twelve questions again. Same answers. Then one more time, except now the questions are asked in a different order. Instead of, "Are you wearing a brown shirt?" as the final question, Kelly asks, "Do you have a clear recollection of what happened last night?"

"Yes."

"Is there any doubt in your mind, Pete?"

"Can you stop the test?"

"OK."

"I didn't understand that last question. I didn't understand . . ."

"I think we've got a little problem here, Peter."

". . . that last question."

"I was trying to probe your subconscious there a little bit, OK?"

"But, the thing was, I wasn't sure whether you meant what happened to her or whether I knew who did it to her and everything?"

"Well, I think we got a little problem here, Pete."

"What do you mean?"

"About hurting your mother last night."

"I didn't do it."

"You're giving me a reaction, that's why I put in these questions towards the end there. I'm just wondering, do you have any doubt in your mind?"

"About hurting my mother. Because the thing is, like, when we went over, and over, and over it. . . . When he told me I could have flown off the handle, I gave it a lot of consideration."

"All right."

"But, I don't think I did."

"But, you're not sure, are you?"

"That's right. Well, I could have."

"OK. Now I think you possibly did from what I'm seeing here, OK?"

Peter says, "I'm sure what I did" but not sure what happened in the house.

Kelly suggests he might have hit his mother with the car outside the house and then "set it up to look like something really violent happened in the house."

"It wouldn't have been like me . . . honestly. If I had hit my mom, the first thing I would have done was call the ambulance."

"I think you got doubts as to what happened there last night. Don't you?"

"I've got doubts because I don't understand what happened and—"

"What do you mean you don't understand?"

"Well, I mean, I'm afraid to—"

"Are you afraid that you did this thing?"

"Well, yeah, of course I am. That's natural."

A little later, Peter says that not being sure "scares me a little bit."

Kelly offers comfort. "I don't think you're *crazy* or anything like this, but I think you need a little help."

"With a psychiatrist?"

"Yes."

Peter is led to believe he has a mental problem that explains why he cannot remember murdering his mother. He thinks his bad reaction on the polygraph must be due to his nervousness—"I mean my mother did die"—and asks for another test.

Kelly puts him off, saying that "what I'm interested in here, Pete, is that you said you're not sure if you hurt your mother or not last night."

"What I say I did, I'm absolutely sure of. But if I had a lapse of memory, that's what I'm not sure of."

Kelly asks whether he thinks he has a lapse of memory and Peter says flatly, "No." He is just as firm in denying that he is covering up for somebody else.

No longer able to rely on the lie detector to get him out of this fix, Peter turns to another hope: "If I did it and I didn't realize it, there's got to be some clue there in the house anyway that's gonna connect with it . . . there *has* to be something in that house, someplace. If I did it. Or whoever did it. There's got to be something, somehow, somewhere."

Peter is asked whether he has any doubt about hurting his mother. He says, "This test is giving me doubt right now." He recalls being told in the Canaan barracks that he might have killed his mother. "The fact that I could have forgotten . . . that really shook me because I never heard of anything like that before."

Kelly, after briefly leaving the room, relates the news that Peter's mother had talked on the telephone to Dr. Lovallo shortly before she was murdered. Kelly says this "puts you home almost at the exact same time."

Peter believes this was the time he left the church. Saying he is speaking of the approximate time, Kelly drops the bomb: "Pete, I think you got a problem. I really do. . . . And Jack feels the same way when he looked at these charts. . . . These charts say you hurt your mother last night."

In fact, this is not true, but police interrogators routinely use "lie tests," whatever the results, as a means of sowing confusion in the minds of suspects.

When Peter says he cannot remember hurting her, Kelly suggests that "what happened here was a mercy thing." Perhaps his mother had a fatal disease and he was doing her a favor by ending her life. On the other hand, he might have hit her with his car and then panicked. If so, "this is only an accident."

But Peter insists that he did not even hit her with the car.

"Then if you didn't, then you killed your mother deliberately."

"I didn't though. I don't remember it."

"Then why does the lie chart say you did?"

"I don't know. I can't give you a definite answer."

"You see? But you don't know for sure if you did this thing, do you?"

"No, I don't."

"Why?"

"I just don't. I mean, like your chart and everything says I did."

"OK."

"But I still say I didn't."

The interrogation is a contest of wills: Peter versus the polygraph as interpreted by Kelly. Peter is still attached to the machine, two hours after the session began. Kelly removes the last of the connections, but the dialogue continues.

Kelly speculates that "something happened between you and your mother last night and one thing led to another and some way you accidentally hurt her seriously."

"But how? It's not like me. I wouldn't mind so much if they could *prove* I did it. . . . I'm positive to myself that I didn't. Consciously. But subconsciously, you know, who knows?"

His confidence is gone. "Now I'm afraid," he says, "because I was so sure, you know, that I didn't do something. . . . And I still want to stay in school. I don't have any place to go. . . . I don't want to go into—like Newtown or something."

By "Newtown" Peter means Fairfield Hills Hospital in Newtown, Connecticut, a mental-health institution. Peter seems persuaded that he has a mental problem. Kelly encourages this belief, saying, "This isn't the end of the world. I've talked to a lot of people who have been involved in a lot of serious things and they're normal individuals today. Once they got it straightened out upstairs."

When Kelly insists that Peter "did it" despite his inability to remember doing it, Peter asks if there is any way "they can kind of pound it out of me, if I did it?"

Kelly exclaims, "Peter!"

Soon Peter admits, "There's doubt in my mind. Maybe I did do it." He says, "We got to keep drilling at it."

He again tells the familiar story of arriving home but now he says that when he entered the house he looked up at the top bunk in the bedroom and "I thought I saw her" lying there.

"See?" Kelly says. "I think this is probably where you flipped over a little bit. You probably *did* see your mother standing there."

Peter insists, "No, laying in bed." He explains that she had a habit of lying in bed reading with her clothes on when it was too cold to read outdoors.

"The thing that's messing me up," he says, is not whether or not he killed his mother but "the fact that *if* I did do it, why don't I remember it?"

Kelly says that Peter is so ashamed that he is afraid to admit it. He suggests that Peter is deliberately lying to him. Denying that he is being untruthful, Peter again asks about clues: "Are my footprints going into the bedroom there?"

Saying that such things take time to check out, Kelly assures him, "Once we get this out in the open and we get you the proper help it will be over with. . . . No one's going to lock you up and throw the keys away."

"I *want* to tell you I did it, now, but I'm still not sure I did do it."

Kelly suggests that the only penalty will be a short spell of psychiatric treatment. "As I said, Peter, three months out of your life—that's not a very long time."

Peter agrees that he has a problem. "I think I've been sliding for a long time, to something. . . . I've *always* had a question in my mind if I was mentally right" because of his family's history of mental problems and alcoholism.

The dialogue becomes increasingly unreal. As Kelly speaks of the crime victim as "hurt" instead of murdered, with the punishment limited to psychiatric counseling, Peter talks about band practices.

He tells the officer that "if I had to give up the band, I'd have no outlook on life any more." He wouldn't want to go away for mental treatment because "it would stop the band." He says, "I got to go to the dance this week. We got contracts and can't break contracts." Kelly says he can continue in the band only if he faces up to what he has done.

Together they speculate about why Peter "went off the handle." Or what he did when his mother "flew off the handle and went at you or something and you had to protect yourself." Peter is being offered an opportunity to claim that he acted only in self-defense. He does not accept it because "self-defense goes just so far."

After they both agree that Peter is not a cold-blooded killer but just "a guy sitting here with a problem," Kelly asks again what happened. Peter says, "I'm still in a fog. I don't know."

They seem to be getting nowhere. There are long pauses as Peter thinks and thinks, but he cannot come up with any reason for having a battle with his mother. "I'm so damned exhausted," he says. "I'm just going to fall asleep. I know I am." Kelly says, "I bet you won't fall asleep," and leaves the room. Peter lets out a long sigh.

Like police interrogators elsewhere in the country, the detectives in Hartford had been taught that an isolated room without distracting noises is vital to good questioning. Within such a room, the deprivation of cigarettes, food, and sleep will keep emotional tension high. They can be offered as rewards for cooperation. The interrogator should be friendly but persistent. He should seem to be on the side of the suspect by sympathizing with him and condemning the victim of his crime.

In *Criminal Interrogation and Confessions,* Inbau and Reid urge interrogators to maintain a "trusting" atmosphere and "display an air of confidence in the subject's guilt." They should "call attention to the subject's
physiological and psychological 'symptoms' of guilt," and minimize the
seriousness of the crime by suggesting that "anyone else would have done
the same, under the circumstances."

If the subject clings to his story and refuses to confess, then an alternate
method of interrogation is to try to unnerve the suspect with a "bad cop"
and offer him relief with a "good cop." Finally, a written confession should
be obtained as soon as possible after an oral confession so that the subject
will not have time to think things over and change his mind.

The U.S. Supreme Court, in *Rogers vs. Richmond* in 1961, said that "ours
is an accusatorial and not an inquisitorial system—a system in which the State
must establish guilt by evidence independently and freely secured and may
not by coercion prove its charge against an accused out of his own mouth."

Policemen understandably see intense questioning of the likeliest suspect as the shortest and fastest route to the solution of a crime. The abuse
of police interrogations and the risk of false confessions have been so great,
however, that the police are obliged to work under tight restraints.

Although the U.S. Supreme Court's 1966 *Miranda* decision on the
admissibility of confessions has obliged police officers to be meticulous
about reading the defendant his constitutional rights to remain silent and
ask for an attorney, it is debatable whether this is enough of a safeguard.

"For most, if not all of us," says Henry H. Foster Jr., professor of law at
New York University, "the policeman and prosecutor are authority figures,
and the situation of being subjected to their questioning triggers off emo-
tions varying from apprehension to panic. The physical setup of a station
house in itself is intimidating. In the absence of counsel or some friend or
relative to lend a supportive role, most suspects will talk, although the experienced or professional criminal may preserve his silence. If the interrogation is protracted, done in relays, and fatigue sets in, suspects may confess
to almost anything."

When Sergeant Kelly returns to the polygraph room, he tells Peter that he
has been on the telephone with the investigators in Canaan. "I think I have
a reason why it happened." The police have learned from Peter's friends
that "your mother was always on your back. Constantly." She was always
telephoning around for him. "She'd been bugging you so fucking long that
last night you came in the house and she started bugging you again and you
snapped. Am I right?"

"I would say you're right," Peter replies, "but I don't remember doing the things that happened. That's just it. I believe I did it now."

These words mark the beginning of the confession. Peter has snapped at the bait. He is hooked. Now it is just a matter of reeling him in and getting his signature on a formal confession. But the process will take many more hours of "drilling, drilling, drilling," as he told his attorney later. "They started brainwashing, making me think I really had a mental problem. So you know, I started really believing that maybe I'm a little nutty. So I started dreaming things up."

Kelly tells Peter that he "lost self-control" and was "like a prisoner being tortured." His mother had treated him so badly that naturally he finally blew up.

"Am I right, Pete?"

"You're right."

Straining to be helpful, Peter adds, "Somewhere in my head a straight razor sticks in." He remembers that there is a straight razor in the house.

All the while, he yawns repeatedly. He asks if he can have something to drink, maybe even something to eat. "I haven't had anything to eat in about twenty-four hours except a candy bar—part of one."

Kelly sends Schneider for soft drinks while telling Peter that "you're not going to be able to eat because this is going to be preying on your mind." First talk, then eat.

"Once you get this out," Kelly says, "you're going to eat like you've never eaten before." When Peter mentions how tired he is, Kelly adds, "Well, once you get this out, Pete, you'll be able to sleep for a week."

"When I get this out, I'd possibly be totally cured too?"

"Could be," Kelly answers.

For a moment, Peter seems almost exultant about a situation that seems to be purging him of his troubles. He speaks of feeling so free now, "like all the things that have had a hold of me all around are letting go."

Yet he suddenly remembers what his mother was like, at her best, and how, just a few hours ago, he had awakened and thought of going to his mother for help "because, if I ever got in trouble—like something like this—she'd be right there."

Peter vacillates. He says, "I believe I did it," but then, after further questioning, he doubts that he did it because he doesn't think he had any right to take his mother's life. He still cannot remember any details about the murder, so he takes incidents from earlier days—his mother complaining about cigarettes or the old Ford that he tried to repair in the backyard—and wonders whether they could have cropped up on the murder night.

Kelly, like Shay, asks if he ever had relations with his mother. Peter says no, but he recalls an affair his mother had. "Once she started to have relations with this other guy it all started going downhill."

He is encouraged to feel sorry for himself. He speaks of the nice homes of his friends in contrast to his own and how annoying sharing an automobile with his mother was. "I hated being home."

On the other hand, when he was away from home, "I'd miss my mom." But once home again he would want to get away because of her nagging. Kelly wants to know specifically what she was nagging him about that caused him to "go off the deep end."

Peter says he doesn't know, but as he rummages through his mind he finds that "violence is coming into it now. With the straight razor, slashing and stuff. But, not much. I—one thing toward her throat, I think. I may be imagining it. And shaking her up a lot."

"How about her legs?" Kelly asks. "What kind of vision do we get there?"

"I don't want to remember that because I think I'm going to get sick if I do."

"Why?"

"Because something like that makes me sick anyway—and to think I did it."

"Peter, you're not going to get sick. Did you step on her legs or something? When she was on the floor, and jumped up and down or something, and break them like that or what?"

"I could have."

"Or did you hit her?"

"That sounds possible."

"Or did you hit her with something?"

"No, 'cause if I hit her with something it probably would have been my guitar and no matter what I did, I'd have never used my guitar."

"I don't blame you."

Kelly asks, "Can you remember stomping her legs?"

"I think. But I'm not sure because you say it then I imagine I'm doing it."

"No, no, no. You're not imagining anything. I think the truth is starting to come from you now. Because you want it out. You want that second chance."

Peter speaks of his worry that people will look at him and say, "Hey, he murdered his mother." Kelly says it was not murder because "I don't think you planned it. I don't think it was premeditated. I think something happened between you and her there last night and you just went off the fucking deep end and you just kept slashing and kicking and hitting, and it was too late. You had lost all your composure because of all the buildup over the past year or two years and all this came out at one time. And it came out violently."

When he is asked about the straight razor, Peter thinks he "probably" found it on the kitchen table and then, after using it, "maybe I gave it a heave or something."

Kelly wants to know where Peter disposed of the razor because this might be the murder weapon. (Back in Canaan, an investigator has already come upon the straight razor, closed and without bloodstains, on a living room shelf.) Peter speculates that he might have thrown the razor behind the gas station or over the barn.

When Kelly asks where he cut his mother with this razor, Peter says "the throat is the only thing I can think of."

As for cleaning up his mother with water afterward, Peter asks, "Wouldn't I have been out of breath if I'd carried her in and back and done all that? . . . If I'd taken her into the bathroom and cleaned her up or something?"

He asks Kelly, "Do you think we could quit now—where we are—so I could get some sleep? I'm so tired, nothing's happening."

"I think it's happening now, Pete. I think it's coming out now. I think it's coming right out now."

"I think I'm saying things that I don't mean to say though."

When Kelly insists that Peter is now finally telling the truth and that "you know it was you," Peter asks, "What would you do if something came up where it turned out that it absolutely wasn't me? If it happened?"

"I'd apologize to you," Kelly replies, "but this isn't going to happen, Peter."

The speculation continues. Peter wonders whether he could have put himself into a state of hypnosis the night before. "Wish I weren't so tired because things come into my head and they go right out again."

He supposes that either his mother or he picked up the razor. He is not sure, but "I remember slashing like that. . . . I remember doing the damage." And he thinks he "could have jumped up and down on her. . . . Maybe I could have kicked her." He thinks so because, even though he has never been in a real fight, he thinks you have to fight dirty to win.

The interrogation has been under way for four hours. Kelly seems to feel that he has done all he can do for the moment. He wants Lieutenant Shay to take over for a while. He suggests to Peter that they go across the hall to another room where they can be more comfortable. He leads him to the interrogation room of the polygraph unit, complete with a leather lounge chair and a leather couch. Peter sits on the couch by himself while Kelly confers outside with Shay. A window is open and children can be heard playing on the street.

When the two men enter the room together, Peter tells Shay, "The polygraph thing didn't come out right. It looked like I've done it."

Kelly asks, "Well, what's it look like now?"

"It really looks like I did it."

"You did it?"

"Yes."

Peter thinks he used the straight razor. Shay suggests that he used a knife as well. "Maybe, I think," Peter says. "I'm not absolutely sure of it, though."

Kelly leaves and Shay carries on. He explains to Peter that "we on the State Police are not your enemies." They want to help him. Peter says that before he goes any further, "I've got to have someone to talk to." Shay tells him that "you got us to turn to in this case."

Peter seems to feel more alone and vulnerable than before. He speaks of needing "one particular person who's going to be on my side and help me. I don't mean a lawyer or something like that. I mean someone like an adult, a father, a mother, or something." He is afraid of being taken out of school. He feels "so guilty" about what has happened. He wouldn't mind seeing a psychiatrist once or twice a week, "but I *cannot* be taken away from the band. That's my life." He wants to find the answer to the puzzle. "I've got to get this out in the open so I can see what happened. And say, it's done, I've done it, I've got to live with it."

He is now so convinced of his guilt that he apologizes for causing the interrogators so much trouble: "I didn't realize I was lying on that lie detector. . . . You're really busting your ass trying to help me right now and I really appreciate it."

Shay asks Peter to trust him and to begin trusting people, and then lies to him. "We have, right now, without any word out of your mouth, proof positive that you did it."

"So OK," Peter responds, "then I may as well say I did it."

Soon, however, as Peter worries about what is going to happen to him—his name in the papers, having a record, missing school—he becomes a little less convinced of his guilt. When Kelly returns to the room, Peter asks, "Should I really come out and say something that I'm not sure?"

"Peter, I think you're sure," Kelly says.

"Pete, you're sure," Shay adds.

"No, I'm not. I mean, I'm sure of what *you've* shown me that I did it, but what I'm not sure of is how I did it. It's still not all coming to me."

He tries to describe the murder to them, but nothing is clear except his coming home and seeing his mother on the floor. He can't seem to fill in the space between looking at the top bunk and the sight of the body on the floor. Shay becomes exasperated and accuses Peter of "not being honest." He says Peter is trying to trick him.

Peter offers to go back on the polygraph, but Shay says "You've been playing head games with us. . . . You know it and I know it."

Peter protests: "I don't know it! . . . I'm trying hard as I can. I mean it's bad enough realizing and finding that my mom's dead, but to find that I did it and not realizing that I did it makes it even worse."

He had earlier protested when Shay spoke of his need for decent parents by saying, "I don't think my mom was that indecent." Now he agrees that he's been treated like an animal. "I've been given my food and I've been given my place where I slept, but I've never been shown affection."

Now that his mother is off his back, he says, he has to find someone to help him. "If you trust me," Shay says, "I'll see that you get the help you need."

"You personally?"

"Yes."

Peter speaks of his dream of finding someone like Shay to help him. He begins to cry. He explains that "I haven't cried 'til I found someone to turn to." He asks where Shay lives and whether there is any chance that he would take him in.

"Sure there's a chance."

"God, I'll do anything. Work around the house, chores, anything. I'd love to do it."

Peter says he now knows that "I definitely did do what happened to my mother last night. But the thing that I don't realize is the exact steps that I took doing it."

Shay allows him to ramble on about life and death and God and the wonder of good, close families. He speaks of "getting more and more trusting" and asks for a chance to get at the truth gradually. Shay decides that a little food might help the situation. He leaves the room. Peter sits alone.

Jim Mulhern appears with a ham-and-cheese sandwich, two chocolate cupcakes, and a Coca-Cola. Peter tells him, "It turned out I did it."

"Did what?"

"What happened to my mother."

"You killed your mother? How did you do that?"

Peter says he does not really know. He can't figure out why there is no blood on him. "There's nothing on me. I'm still wearing the same clothes. I can't understand that."

It is now past 8:00. Lieutenant Shay returns to the room and orders Mulhern to reduce Peter's admissions to writing. This is a difficult assignment because Peter is saying he can "imagine" himself cutting his mother's throat "and the chances are that I did do it . . . but I'm not positive."

Shay accuses him of playing "head games" and leaves the room.

Peter appeals to Mulhern: "I don't know what to do, Jim. I'm still not positive any of that happened . . . It seems like I'm being pushed into saying things. . . . Why should I say something that I'm not sure of if it can be used against me?"

Mulhern does not respond. He is conscious, as Peter is not, that every word being said can be overheard by his superiors and is being recorded. The time has passed, anyway, to give advice to his young friend. He says he will write down whatever Peter tells him.

Peter asks him three times to be sure to put in the statement that he is not really sure of what he is saying. Mulhern agrees but, ultimately, that qualification is left out of the confession.

Shay returns in time to hear Peter tell Mulhern that it is "almost like I'm making it up." Now angry as well as frustrated, Shay accuses Peter of "playing head games with us now for too long a period. . . . We have definitely established that you were in that house when your mother was killed. OK, now look. There are many things that we can do to make this thing a very difficult process for you."

He launches into a five-minute tirade, telling Peter that "I've been fooling around here now for a lot of hours with you and I'm getting tired. I don't want you to treat me like some kind of jerk." He is bellowing as he says, "I tried to treat you like a human being. I tried to be understanding but. . . . you reject every offer that we've made to be kind to you. . . . Now you're trying to treat us like muck. . . . If you want to play this way we'll take you and we'll lock you up and treat you like an animal."

In a long, rambling statement, Shay tells Peter, "You are here because you are responsible for the death of your mother. . . . Let's stop the nonsense and let's get going here. . . . You've got to trust us. . . . Somebody is dead. You are responsible. . . . We can prove it with extrinsic evidence. Now, we're telling you that we are offering you our hand. Take it."

The lieutenant has calmed down and is no longer yelling, but when Peter asks, "You say you can prove it?" Shay erupts again and says, "I'm not going to play head games." He tells Peter that "your mother called the doctor at nine thirty. You called the hospital at ten minutes of ten."

"I called there at ten of ten?" Peter asks.

"That's correct," Shay says. "We can place your mother's death in that fifteen-minute period. . . . Now, if you think you can beat that, you're crazy. And if you're going to act like a hardened criminal, John Dillinger, try to beat the police, you're nuts."

Peter says softly, "I'm not." Shay tells him to "sit there like a man" and understand that he is going to go to a mental hospital, not the gas chamber or prison. "You are in no condition to think or to make judgment as to what your problem is."

The questioning goes on, but Peter insists that all he can remember is cutting his mother's throat and jumping on her stomach. The only blood he can remember seeing is "when I was back in reality again" after having "flown off the handle."

Peter, at this moment, is not exactly in "reality." When Shay steps out of the room, Peter asks Mulhern, "After having this on my record, is there any chance I can still get on the State Police?"

The trooper says it depends on what happens. There are long pauses as Mulhern laboriously writes out the confession for Peter to sign. Peter asks if "you could put little quotes in between the part where I was slashing my mother's throat to where I jumped on her legs? You know, so you can tell that section is the stuff I—that I'm digging up."

Peter looks over the confession and signs it.

Mulhern leaves with the document and Shay returns to the room. Peter has a question for the man who only minutes before threatened to treat him like an animal.

"I was wondering if some way . . . I could possibly live with your family if you had the room? . . . I wouldn't want to impose and I know my godmother would pay my way."

"It would be a rather unusual turn of events."

"I've taken a liking to you—you know, kind of father image and I trust you. . . . I would like to live with a family, like a complete family, for a while anyway."

Peter rambles on about the pleasures of real families, apparently thinking his ordeal is over. But Sergeant Kelly reappears to say that "Something's still wrong here, Pete." Shay and Kelly have learned the details of Dr. Izumi's autopsy and they know that Barbara Gibbons was sexually mutilated. A large object was thrust into her vagina with sufficient force to cause internal wounds.

"What's really burning inside of you that you don't want to tell us about," Kelly asks, "that you did to your mother?"

"I think I raped her. It seems like I did. That's what everything looks like I did."

But the answer is not the right one. Yet all Peter can think of is rape. He explains that rape sticks in his mind because of Geoff Madow's comment at the crime scene that he thought someone had raped his mother.

Again, the officers switch places. Mulhern comes in to ask for more details about the throat slashing. Peter thinks he used his right hand and is "pretty sure" he saw the razor cut through, but "it's almost like in a dream."

As Mulhern adds these details to the confession, Peter asks, "Do you feel bad about knowing me now that you know what I've done?" Mulhern replies that what Peter did is not all that bad: "Five years from now I may do the same thing."

Mulhern, having combined Peter's statements into a single confession, asks for his signature again. As Peter signs, he wonders whether he will need a lawyer. "You can have an attorney at any time that you want," Mulhern replies. Peter, still clinging to the idea that a lawyer is needed only if you lie to the police, says, "Everything I said I mean. I mean, it *is* the truth."

At nearly eleven o'clock at night, twenty-six hours after the death of Barbara Gibbons, the tape recorder is turned off. Five boxes of audiotapes, each numbered and marked "MURDER, FALLS VILLAGE, 9/29/73," are placed on top of a filing cabinet. A confession, said to be "the queen of evidence," is in hand. The police are satisfied that the crime has been solved.

> I, Peter A. Reilly, age 18, DOB 3/2/55 of Rte. 63, Falls Village, Conn., make the following voluntary statement without fear, threat or promise, knowing it may be used in Court against me.
>
> On the evening of Friday, September 28th, 1973, I attended a meeting of the Canaan Youth Center at the Methodist Church in North Canaan, Conn. I left the church at about 9:30–9:35 p.m. and took John Sochocki of West Main Street, North Canaan, home. After leaving him at his house I proceeded to my home arriving at about 9:50–9:55 p.m. I parked directly in front of the house, got out of the car and pushed down the front left headlight unit, and turned off the car. I entered the front door of the house and yelled, "Hey Ma, I'm home."
>
> There was no answer so I looked to the right into the bedroom. At first, I thought I saw my mother, Barbara Gibbons, in the top

bunk and then I saw her on the floor. I remember "slashing once at my mother's throat with a straight razor I used for model airplanes. This was on the living room table. I also remember jumping on my mother's legs." I am not sure about washing her off. Next I saw blood on her face and throat, and, I think, I'm pretty sure on her T-shirt which was rolled up to the bottom of her breasts.

Then I went to the telephone and called the Madows to get an ambulance. Next I called information for the family doctor's number, Dr. Borneman [sic]. I spoke with Dr. Borneman's wife, I assume or a woman answered, and she gave me two other doctor's names who were covering for Dr. Borneman who was on vacation. I again called information for the Sharon Hospital's telephone number as Mrs. Borneman instructed me. I was connected with the hospital emergency room and was asked if I knew artificial respiration to which I replied, "No." I was told they would notify the State Police and dispatch an ambulance. I told the woman I already called the ambulance.

I hung up the phone and went outside and unlocked the car and moved it to the side of the house, the north side, facing the road and left on the flashers. I also threw a hibachi grill out of the way as it was near the front steps on the cement. I stood in the driveway until Geoffrey Madow arrived and we both went inside to look at my mother. Geoffrey stated she looked as though she had been raped. We both went back outside and waited for the police cruiser to arrive.

I would like to clarify one point in this statement. When I slashed at my mother's throat with the straight razor I cut her throat. This is all I wanted to clarify. I have read the above statement and it is the truth.

[signed] PETER REILLY

Epilogue

After six months in the Litchfield jail, and just before his nineteenth birthday, Peter Reilly was brought to trial for his mother's murder. Though no forensic evidence linked him to the killing, the jury believed his confession and accepted the word of the state's experts who said that only he could have committed the crime. He was sentenced to an indeterminate term of six to sixteen years in prison for manslaughter.

All the while, however, certainty about the boy's innocence was voiced by his small-town neighbors. The absence of time for Peter to do the crime, quite apart from his always-obvious good nature, made it impossible to imagine his carrying out the most vicious killing in Litchfield County history.

After the neighbors raised sixty thousand dollars for a bond to free him during the appeal process, Peter, the "convicted killer" of the headlines, returned to school for his senior year. Playwright Arthur Miller, a resident of nearby Roxbury, used his influence to recruit a new attorney, a private investigator, and top experts, all working pro bono. Investigative reports in the *New York Times* and on *60 Minutes* drew national attention to Peter's plight.

At the end of a long hearing for a new trial in the spring of 1976, the original trial judge, John A. Speziale, whose integrity soon made him the state's chief justice, erased Peter's conviction, calling it "a grave injustice." Critical to his decision was evidence pointing to suspects ignored by the police and the compelling testimony of psychiatrist Herbert Spiegel, an authority on mind-control dynamics, explaining how psychological pressures can compel a naive teenager to confess falsely.

A fresh trial proved to be unnecessary. The state's attorney's heart-attack death led to the revelation that he and the police had all along concealed vital exculpatory information placing Peter five miles away at the time of the murder. The boy was fully exonerated after a grand jury inquiry condemned the misconduct. Knowing how critical the tapes were to the exposure of their tactics, the state police gave up recording suspect questioning for the next three decades even though the practice is a widely recommended means of avoiding miscarriages of justice.

Peter Reilly's experience entered the legal annals as perhaps the classic instance of a suspect under interrogation becoming convinced that he committed a crime he did not do.

Despite an independent investigation ordered by Governor Ella Grasso in 1977, the Barbara Gibbons case remains unsolved—the coldest of all of Connecticut's cold cases.

MICHAEL ALTENBURGER

The fire was dreadful, and his interrogators' deceptions
convinced him he must have set it

JOHN KENDALL AND WILLIAM FARR
LOS ANGELES, CALIFORNIA

It had been quick work. Within hours of the fire that claimed twenty-five lives at the Stratford Apartments late on the night of November 15, 1973, police picked up Michael Altenburger, an eighteen-year-old transient from Tucson with a record of setting fires. Sixteen hours later, Altenburger was booked for murder and arson. Many of the dead still had not been identified when a *Los Angeles Times* headline proclaimed, "Transient Admits Setting Apartment Fire, Officials Say."

In addition to his alleged confession to the most dreadful fire in Los Angeles history, the case against Altenburger was supported by three supposedly positive, although belated, eyewitness identifications.

Eighty-five days after his arrest—without physical corroboration of the evidence against him, Altenburger was ordered to stand trial on twenty-five counts of murder and one count of arson.

Only two days after that, however, he was exonerated and released.

In the end, it took just six hours for authorities to verify facts establishing Altenburger's innocence—facts that could have been checked, but weren't, before the charges were brought.

"This is *1984*, ten years before," said Deputy Public Defender Stanley Mathiesen, Altenburger's lawyer.

With money donated personally by Mathiesen and Los Angeles District Attorney Joseph P. Busch, Altenburger left town. He declined to speak with reporters, but Mathiesen quoted him as saying, "I'm getting out of here."

Altenburger was lucky—he could have spent the rest of his life behind bars for a crime he didn't commit.

As it was, he spent eighty-seven days.

71

Altenburger, a skinny six-footer in a green corduroy coat, tan corduroy pants, and green T-shirt, got off a Greyhound bus from Tucson in downtown Los Angeles shortly after 8:30 A.M. on November 15, a week after his eighteenth birthday.

Like others who suddenly leave a place, the brown-haired, 125-pound teenager left Tucson to escape unpleasantness. He had been in trouble for setting fires and he had argued with his mother—again. So he left it all behind. He thought.

A day later, he would be in custody, under suspicion of setting the most dreadful fire in Los Angeles history, struggling to describe a twenty-one-hour odyssey in a strange city.

Shortly after daybreak on November 16, roughly seven hours after the fire began, two Los Angeles traffic officers spotted Altenburger on a bus bench near the San Diego Freeway and Sunset Boulevard, about three miles west of the campus of the University of California, Los Angeles, and some fourteen miles from the burned-out hulk of the old, mustard-color, three-story Stratford.

"Why are you out here at this time of morning?" Officer Terry Schauer would recall asking the youth.

Altenburger answered something to the effect, "I'm trying to get to Venice, to the beach."

At first, Schauer and his partner, Robert Kehoe, thought the youth might be a runaway. He had no identification, less than a dollar, and, to them, he looked about sixteen. There was something about him that aroused the officers' suspicion—at first he was very calm, but then, for no apparent reason, he became extremely nervous, wiping his sweaty hands on his pants.

After arriving at the bus depot on Sixth Street, Altenburger said, he walked toward the ocean. Walking had been uncomfortable—his slip-on shoes were not meant for hiking on concrete. He accepted a ride from a man, who asked him if he was gay and let him out when he said he wasn't. He resumed walking and made it to Hollywood by noon. He went to two department stores, climbed a hill to see the ocean, and then went to the La Brea Tar Pits, arriving at about 7:30 P.M. A little later, he took a bus on Wilshire Boulevard toward UCLA. He went to an all-night restaurant, where he ate a bowl of chili, which cost one dollar, and then he rested at a nearby McDonald's restaurant. After leaving the McDonald's, he went into the alcove of a building a couple of blocks away. He hoped to sleep there, but left when a man and woman taunted him.

It was obvious to Schauer and Kehoe that walking west on Sixth Street from the bus depot, Altenburger would have passed the Stratford. Or, what if, instead of taking the bus toward UCLA from the Tar Pits, he had taken the bus downtown? He would have passed within a block of the Stratford right around the time that the fire began. The officers' suspicion was further aroused, to say the least, when, in response to questions, Altenburger revealed not only that he had been in trouble in Tucson—but that it had been for, among other things, setting fires.

Schauer and Kehoe took Altenburger into the West Los Angeles Police Station for questioning and were completing paperwork when copies of the *Los Angeles Times* arrived. Pointing to a photograph of the burning Stratford, Schauer asked, "Is this the apartment house you were at last night?"

Altenburger "looked at the picture briefly," Schauer said later, "and his eyes went down to the headline, which said words to the effect, 'Twenty-five Dead, Forty Injured in Apartment Blaze.' And his eyes looked at the words and he looked away from the paper and started muttering to himself hurriedly, 'dead, death, dead,' a number of times extremely fast."

When asked if he knew anything about the fire, Altenburger answered, "No, no, I don't know anything about it."

Schauer and Kehoe took the youth in handcuffs to the Rampart Station, a mile and a half from the Stratford. On the way, Schauer noticed, or so he would say later, that when Kehoe lit a cigarette Altenburger turned toward the flame and stared "as if hypnotized."

It was 7:30 A.M. when they arrived at Rampart, where Altenburger waived his right to counsel and was interviewed by Investigator Michael O. Lambert and Sergeant L. M. Orozco.

Altenburger told Lambert and Orozco that in September 1972, when he was sixteen, Tucson authorities had arrested him for setting several fires, including five in a trash bin and one in a shed.

After a year in the Arizona State Industrial School at Fort Grant, he had been assigned to the Columbus Halfway House in Tucson. He had been released just a week earlier, on November 8, his eighteenth birthday.

He had argued with his mother, Maria C. Henry. She left, and he thought she was going to call police, so he took the 11:20 P.M. bus to Los Angeles.

Later, others would learn that Altenburger was an only child, born in Germany; that he had thought of killing his mother; that she had been divorced, then wed an American soldier, and then divorced again. He had gone to school through the ninth grade and liked mathematics. He would be described as intelligent, introverted, maladjusted, lacking self-confidence, inarticulate, and so extremely self-conscious that he thought people were always looking at him.

At Rampart that morning, however, Lambert and Orozco began a tape-recorded interview by asking Altenburger about the building where he tried to sleep.

Altenburger offered to sketch it, and Lambert gave him a pencil and paper. "OK, there's this complex right underneath here," Altenburger said, "and there were a number of other buildings along with this, apartments, and there was this area right here, there were two doors out here, and I remained here because it was well-lighted and it was fairly warm, see."

He added the building was white and modern, about ten stories tall, not far from Wilshire Boulevard, and in the same area as a McDonald's where he had eaten the one-dollar bowl of chili and lingered because he was tired.

"OK," Lambert said. "We'd like to give you a polygraph examination and we can do that right now. And if you show that you've been truthful with us and you're truthful about not being involved in this we're going to release you. Would you like to do that so you can be on your way?"

"Yes," Altenburger agreed.

"OK," Lambert continued, "because we do have some people that saw somebody that fits your description around that area."

In fact, no one had provided any such description at this point. Claiming otherwise was Lambert's first deception. A second deception came a bit later when Lambert showed Altenburger items that had been in his pockets when he was picked up—two Tucson bus tokens, a used bus ticket, and a book, *Star Trek Night*, and less than a dollar in change.

Lambert had added an item that actually had not been in Altenburger's pocket—a book of matches.

"Are these yours?" Lambert asked.

"No," Altenburger replied. "You see, I don't carry matches or anything of this type. I do not carry lighters or anything."

Altenburger was taken to the Parker Center, LAPD administrative headquarters, where the polygraph examination he had agreed to take was administered by Ray Inglin, a nineteen-year veteran of the police force.

Before attaching electrodes to Altenburger's body, the white-smocked examiner told his subject that "the $35,000 piece of equipment" would measure his heart rate, galvanic skin response, and respiration, and record his involuntary responses on graph paper. If he didn't set the fire, Inglin said, the polygraph would establish his innocence—but if he didn't tell the truth, well, then, the consequences went without saying.

The examination began at 9:30 A.M. and lasted about two hours, as Lambert watched through a one-way window.

Like Altenburger's previous interrogators, Inglin began by taking him through his wanderings after his arrival in Los Angeles. Then, showing Altenburger a photograph of the Stratford, Inglin asked, "Does that look like the alcove you went into?"

"No," Altenburger answered. "It was a building which was much taller."

"Can you be certain of that?" Inglin asked.

"I'm positive," Altenburger said.

After eliciting denials that Altenburger had set any fires in Los Angeles, Inglin turned to the matches that Lambert had shown Altenburger—falsely stating, as Lambert had, that the matches had been found in his pocket.

"You had some matches on you when they picked you up," Inglin said. "Where'd you get those matches?"

Altenburger responded not with a denial, but rather with, "I don't know."

"Well, where did they come from?" Inglin asked. "Did you pick them up in a restaurant?"

"I just don't think—anywhere," Altenburger replied.

"What are you going to tell me?" Inglin persisted. "You're telling me those aren't your matches? Just tell the truth. You don't believe they are your matches."

"They are not my matches."

Several times Inglin asked whether Altenburger had set any fires in Los Angeles. The answers were always "No"—but sometimes Altenburger seemed equivocal.

"You're positive?" Inglin asked at one point. "Or, are you saying you had some lapses of memory. Do you think you had a lapse of memory last night?"

"The thing is—the matches," Altenburger said. "If there were matches on my person, then I think I would have doubts and believe maybe I did and did not know it."

"Well, it's what you know," Inglin said. "What do you know for sure in your heart?"

"I think I did not set the fire."

Inglin concluded that many of the answers had been deceptive—and Lambert informed Altenburger that he was under arrest for murder.

Before returning to Rampart, Altenburger asked Lambert and Orozco to let him show them where he had been the day before, but they refused.

Back at Rampart, Lambert took Altenburger into an interview room and emerged ten minutes later to report that Altenburger had confessed. He said he had set the fire, Lambert said, because he wanted to kill his mother.

The statement was not recorded, and Lambert's supervisor sent him back to the interview room to get the admission on tape.

"Hi, Mike," Lambert resumed. "Kind of tired, huh?"

Altenburger had not slept in a bed for more than thirty-eight hours.

The ensuing interview was rambling, but Altenburger seemed to be having trouble remembering what he allegedly had said minutes earlier.

"OK," Lambert said, "but you remember that that's why you set the fire because you wanted to kill your mother, right?"

"Yes, sir," Altenburger said.

Lambert then told Altenburger he was going to take him back to the Parker Center, where he could get some sleep. As Altenburger put on his jacket, Lambert harked back to his first deception—now asserting flatly not that witnesses had merely seen someone fitting his description but rather had seen *him*.

"OK," Lambert said, "that's the jacket you were wearing last night?"

"Yes."

"That's the one the lady recognized. She said it stood out like a—like a sore thumb. Like I say, you were seen, you know, by quite a few people there."

Three days later, Inglin administered a second polygraph test to Altenburger at the Parker Center.

Inglin began by asking whether Altenburger had told any lies during any of the previous questioning.

Altenburger said he hadn't—and then added, "Except, one time they asked me if I was in that room. . . . I said, yeah, but I was not."

"What room?" asked Inglin.

"The Stratford Apartments," Altenburger replied.

Inglin then introduced yet another deception, asking, "How come your clothes smelled like smoke when they picked you up? That's the first thing they told me. They said your clothes smelled like smoke. How come?"

"Un uuh," Altenburger responded.

"Well, there had to be a reason. You had to be around smoke since you came to Los Angeles."

"Maybe they were lying."

"Were you in that lobby?"

"No, I was not."

Inglin concluded that Altenburger was not telling the truth.

A little more than two months later, when Altenburger's preliminary hearing began before Los Angeles Municipal Judge Antonio E. Chavez, the case might have seemed ironclad—to an outsider.

An arson expert would testify the Stratford was set on fire. A detective would recite a confession and, by this time, the three purported eyewitnesses had come forward, claiming to have seen Altenburger run out of the Stratford.

What more could a prosecutor want?

Actually, Deputy District Attorney Stephen Kay, at thirty-one, a relatively youthful prosecutor with experience in several big cases—including the Charles Manson murder trial—had serious doubt about Altenburger's guilt. And so of course did Stanley Mathiesen, a fifty-three-year-old veteran of the Special Trials Division of the Public Defender's Office.

Kay had poked through the Stratford and listened to hours of the tape-recorded questioning. The recordings gave Kay pause.

"It was like he was fighting a battle," Kay said in a recent interview. "Like, 'I know this isn't so, but yet I can't explain the matches and the smoke.' I'll tell you, I lost more sleep on this case than any other I've ever been involved in and that's because of great doubts I had."

Because he wanted a public record, Kay rejected suggestions from other prosecutors that he avoid a preliminary hearing by taking the case before a grand jury, where the proceedings would be secret. In returning an indictment, the grand jury would determine that there was probable cause to believe that Altenburger had committed the crime. By rejecting that course, Kay left the determination of probable cause to the preliminary hearing judge in a public proceeding where Mathiesen could cross-examine the prosecution witnesses.

The purported eyewitnesses, all residents of the Stratford before the fire, claimed to have seen Altenburger in the lobby of the building before the fire, but on cross-examination their accounts proved to be conflicting on key points.

Arson Investigator Donald E. Brian offered the opinion that the fire had been set in a mattress next to a desk in the lobby "with open flame held in human hands," but Mathiesen got him to admit that it was "possible" that the fire had been of electrical origin—perhaps not arson at all. Even if set by human hands, however, Brian's testimony shed no light on whose hands those might have been.

The main prosecution witness was Lambert, who recounted Altenburger's confession. On cross-examination, Mathiesen focused on the deceptions that Lambert had employed during interrogation.

"Now you told Mr. Altenburger, did you not, or asked him, whether or not some matches on the desk were his when he emptied his pockets. Isn't that correct?" Mathiesen asked.

When Lambert acknowledged that he had, Mathiesen continued, "You knew those weren't Altenburger's, did you not?"

"Yes, that is correct."

"Did you tell Mr. Altenburger that a lady had seen him running away from the scene of the fire?"

"Yes, I did."

"You knew that wasn't the truth, did you not?"

"That is correct."

Mathiesen dealt with the other police deception by establishing that neither of the officers who picked up Altenburger had smelled smoke on his clothing and that neither had told anyone otherwise. Next, Mathiesen called Inglin as a defense witness, principally to establish that he had used two of the police deceptions during the polygraph testing—first the matchbook fabrication, then the false assertion that officers had smelled smoke on Altenburger's clothes.

Inglin was the final witness, and immediately after he left the stand, Kay gave a summation acknowledging weaknesses in the prosecution case, including the facts that Altenburger had confessed to setting the fire in a chair although, according to the Fire Department, it had started in a mattress, and the eyewitness identifications were dubious—two of the witnesses had seen a newspaper photograph of Altenburger before identifying him and the third had claimed to have seen Altenburger only briefly, from his apartment window, while not wearing his glasses.

Kay said the use of deceptions was sometimes a good interrogation technique, but added, "On the other hand, if you get somebody in a situation where they start believing something that didn't happen, well, then that is the problem."

In a recent interview, Kay said, "I think everybody in the courtroom, certainly the officers around me, knew what I was talking about. One of them said afterwards, 'Well, you sound like a public defender.' . . . Well, I'm just not going to get up and argue something I don't believe—I never will."

Mathiesen sounded like the deputy public defender he was, accusing the officers involved of "thumb-and-screw" tactics that stripped Altenburger of "every semblance of human decency."

Judge Chavez held that there was probable cause to bind Altenburger over for trial, but added, "Were I the trier of fact, on what has been presented here, [there] would be great reasonable doubt in my mind. But I am not the trier of fact, and that is a standard I as a magistrate cannot hold."

When Kay arrived at his office the next morning, he was surprised to find Sergeant Joe Goodman, the supervisor of the LAPD investigation of the Stratford fire, waiting for him.

The conversation, as Kay recalls it, went something like this.

"Gee, Joe, what are you doing here? I didn't think we had a meeting this morning?"

"Well, we don't, but I don't buy the case we have against the defendant and I'd like to prove him innocent, if he is."

Kay called DA Investigator Alex Acosta, and the three of them decided to ask Mathiesen, Altenburger's public defender, if he would agree to let them take his client out of jail to verify his story, promising that nothing Altenburger said could be used against him.

Mathiesen agreed, but asked to go along, which was acceptable to Kay.

After checking Altenburger out of jail at 9:00 A.M. on February 8, Acosta told him, "You direct us and we'll go anywhere."

As they drove, Kay thumbed through transcripts of Altenburger's various statements to compare what he said now with what he had said before.

They headed for the La Brea Tar Pits, passing May Company, which Altenburger identified as the store he had entered the evening of the Stratford fire.

He recalled that at closing time he had been asked to leave by a clerk, whom he described as a black man in his mid-twenties with a slim but sturdy build.

"We went up and checked out the records to see who was on duty that night and sure enough it was the guy he said," Kay recalled afterward. "He described the clerk just perfectly."

Altenburger related that after May Company closed—closing time was 9:30 P.M.—he walked around a bit, then took a bus on Wilshire Boulevard, got off, and went into the all-night restaurant where he ordered chili.

At first, Altenburger didn't recognize Tiny Naylor's in Westwood as the restaurant, but when they went inside, he said, "This is it."

The price of chili was one dollar, as he had previously said.

After leaving Tiny Naylor's, the group found the McDonald's that Altenburger had initially described. It was on Westwood Boulevard, and closing time, as Altenburger had initially said, was midnight.

Finally, they located the alcove into which Altenburger had said he had gone in the hope of sleeping. It was in a combination office-apartment building known as Monty's, not far from McDonald's, and it matched the description of the building Altenburger had given as he sketched the building during his initial interrogation.

It was clear to Kay, Goodman, and Acosta that Altenburger could not have set the Stratford fire between 11:10 and 11:15 P.M., made it to Tiny Naylor's and eaten chili, and arrived at the McDonald's before midnight.

On the way back downtown, Kay told Mathiesen he would request that charges against Altenburger be dropped and would seek his immediate release.

But it was Friday—too late to fulfill the promise before the weekend.

On Monday, February 11, at Kay's request, Superior Court Judge Ross Bigelow dismissed the indictment against Altenburger—"because he did not and could not have committed those crimes."

Within hours, Altenburger left town on a Greyhound bus.

Epilogue

No other charges were ever brought in connection with the Stratford Apartments fire. It remained possible, as Stanley Mathiesen had argued at Altenburger's preliminary hearing, that the fire had been accidental—not arson.

GERALD MARTIN ANDERSON

After hours of tag-team interrogation, his belief in
his innocence cracked at its foundation

JAMES R. PHELAN
MOUNTAIN HOME, IDAHO

On the night of April 9, 1962, someone stabbed and slashed to death Nancy
Johnson, the pretty young wife of Airman Alec Johnson, and their two-
year-old son Danny. The bodies were found in the kitchen of the modest
Johnson home by Alec Johnson early in the morning of April 10, when he
returned home from Mountain Home Air Force Base, ten miles from the
town.

What heightened the fear and outrage of Mountain Home was that the
double murder seemed wanton and pointless. Nancy had been stabbed
viciously more than a dozen times, once with such force that one of her
ribs was broken, and her small son's throat had been cut. Police examination of the little home showed that it had been ransacked of some odds and
ends of almost no value—a saw, a hatchet, a hammer, the base of an old
lamp, and two of Nancy's purses containing less than two dollars. Police
immediately surmised that the burglary had been a hasty afterthought of
the killer and not his motive for the crime. Nancy Johnson's reputation
deepened the mystery. She was a pleasant girl without any known enemies,
a good wife to Alec Johnson, and highly unlikely to strike up any clandes-
tine affair that might erupt into a crime of passion.

There were few clues at the murder scene. What proved to be the most
important single piece of evidence was not a clue but the absence of one.
There was no murder weapon. Whatever instrument the killer had used,
he apparently had taken it with him when he fled.

Mountain Home is a raw little "bedroom city" for the huge Strategic Air
Command base. Growth of the air base in recent years has spawned acres
of trailer homes in the town, pushing its population from 1,887 in 1950

From "Innocent's Grim Ordeal," *Saturday Evening Post*, February 2, 1963. Copyright ©
Saturday Evening Post Society. Adapted with permission.

to more than 11,000. Most of these new thousands are lonely wives and children of men at the air base. News of the murders sent terror coursing through the trailer camps of Mountain Home and stirred anxiety among the men at the base. The tension also put pressure on the law authorities to solve the two hideous killings.

In less than forty-eight hours the civil authorities came up with a suspect. When his identity was made public a week later, the rank and file at the air base were stunned. He was a fellow airman and a friend of the Johnsons—a slight, gaunt-faced, twenty-five-year-old Californian, Airman First Class Gerald Martin Anderson. Anderson and his attractive young wife Jane had three children, and the Andersons and Johnsons frequently babysat for each other and picnicked and fished together. The rented home of the Andersons was scarcely a hundred yards from the Johnson residence, where Nancy and little Danny had been killed.

Airman Anderson came under suspicion through some tenuous evidence, if it can be called evidence at all. In fairness to the law officers, Anderson was certainly a proper subject for questioning. He was the last person to have seen Nancy and Danny Johnson alive, and his details of this event were essential to a proper investigation of the crime.

The time of the murders was estimated roughly between 8:00 P.M. and 11:00 P.M. At approximately 8:00 P.M. Airman Anderson had left his home to drive to a nearby dairy for two gallons of milk, one for his family and one for the Johnsons. By his account, he had walked over to the Johnson home first and picked up an empty milk jar from Nancy. He had found her alone with Danny getting the child ready for bed; Airman Johnson was at the air base, celebrating the news of his impending transfer to Spain. Anderson said he was in the Johnson home only a couple of minutes, that he had bummed a cigarette from Nancy, and that he was still smoking it when he got the jars filled at the dairy, approximately two blocks away. He said that he had then delivered the milk to Nancy and talked briefly to her. She had given him two cans of condensed milk that she owed his wife, and he had then gone home. He fixed his return to his own home firmly at 8:25 P.M. because he recalled in detail the windup of the television program, *The M-Squad*, which finished at 8:30. Then, without leaving the house again, he and Jane had watched the two-hour Academy Awards show and had gone to bed at about 10:45.

At 1:00 A.M. the Andersons were awakened by Airman Johnson pounding frantically on their window. They let him in and he cried, "Nancy's over there all cut up and dead, and I can't find Danny. Get the police." Later it turned out that in his anguish he had overlooked the body of his son, lying alongside that of his wife, half concealed by their washing machine.

Anderson threw on some clothes and drove to the police station, where the woman dispatcher summoned a squad car. Anderson rode with the police to the Johnson home. Then occurred the first of a series of events that soon were to weave a monstrous web around Airman Anderson. He knew that there was only one usable entrance to the Johnson house—the rear door to the kitchen. Anderson insists that he said something to the effect, "Around in back." The officers, reconstructing the conversation later, reported that he said, "The bodies are around in back."

The next day Anderson foolishly wove a few more strands of the web of suspicion around himself. He stayed home from the base, and shortly before noon he went downtown and got drunk. Anderson is strictly a beer drinker, with a limited capacity, and after a few beers he began to talk almost compulsively about the murders. "The murders were big news," he said later. "Since I was the guy who called the police and all, I figured I'd be the center of attention."

Anderson became the center of attention—but in a way he had not expected. He talked at length at the Cozy Bar to a married couple. They told the police that they had driven Anderson home from the bar and that a peculiar conversation had occurred between Anderson and his wife Jane upon his arrival. They said that Anderson had broken down and sobbed, "I didn't want to do it, but I had to," and that Jane had comforted him and replied, "Shhhh, don't say another word."

"Heck, I was just talking about going into town and getting beered up," Anderson says now. "Jane doesn't like for me to drink, and I went under false pretenses, telling her I was going to get some Pepsi. And I bawled because when we drove up I looked over at the Johnson home and I got thinking about those terrible murders. I felt sorry for Nancy and Danny, and I thought how it might have easily been Jane and my kids."

But when this ambiguous statement—"I didn't want to do it, but I had to"—was relayed to Mountain Home officials, they decided Airman Anderson had better be questioned. They asked air base officials to question him, because he was a military man. It was apparent from what ensued that no one at this time considered Airman Anderson a serious suspect. The Air Police merely called into town and left word for him to drop around the next day when he reported for duty at the base. Anderson dutifully showed up at the Air Police office the following day, April 11. In an ironic touch straight out of Kafka, he said later, he walked into the murder interrogation expecting, with considerable apprehension, to get "chewed out" over having allowed the insurance on his car to lapse.

Instead, the Air Police began questioning him about his movements the night of the Johnson murders. The questioning went on through the day and into the evening; as it ground on and on, Anderson's apprehension began to mount. Then at 9:00 P.M. the Air Police summoned two plainclothes agents of the Office of Special Investigations. They took him outside while they carried out a thorough search of his car, even carefully sweeping up the dirt from the floor into envelopes and turning an ultraviolet light on the upholstery.

"There's a spot of blood on the upholstery," one of the agents said to Anderson. "How did it get there?"

With that question, Airman Anderson panicked. Long before, he had been out with his wife and in an argument had slapped her, starting a nosebleed. He was ashamed of what he had done and saw no reason why he had to disclose a private family quarrel to the OSI agents. "It's an old spot," he told the agent truthfully. "How did it get there?" the agent persisted.

"It was there when I got the car," Anderson said. This was a lie with a simple motive that could have been easily explained and easily understood, but it was to swell to nightmarish proportions in the days to come.

"Come with us," the agents said. They took him across the base to the OSI headquarters and into their crude, bare-looking interrogation room. It was a deceptive little room, because it actually was well equipped for its purpose. Hidden in the wall was a microphone, leading to a tape recorder in an adjoining room. On the wall was what appeared to be a mirror. It was actually a one-way window, through which a hidden agent in the tape-recording room could look out unseen upon what was said and done in the interrogation room.

Thus began the ordeal of Airman Gerald Martin Anderson.

In the next five days he was grilled for more than forty hours by relays of OSI agents until finally, exhausted, confused, and his will broken, he signed a statement that he had killed Nancy Johnson. The statement left the murder of Danny Johnson unexplained, and it embodied incriminating statements that Anderson consistently denied up to the moment of signature, and that he promptly repudiated when he got out of the hands of the OSI. It was bare of many vital details of the crime and was almost totally lacking in corroboration by physical evidence. And finally, it failed to convince one of the interrogating OSI agents that Anderson had committed the crime.

The grilling was done by four agents working in shifts. Three of them were from the regular OSI force at the base and the fourth, Joe Townsend, was a lie-detector operator flown in from Lowry Air Force Base in Denver, regional headquarters of the OSI. The first inquisitor was William Welsch, head of the Mountain Home OSI detachment. He began the questioning in a friendly, relaxed manner. He read Anderson Article 31 of the Military Code—the counterpart of the Fifth Amendment. "This is the routine we go through" he told the airman. "Generally what it means is that you don't have to make any statement, and any statement made by you can be used in evidence against you."

"Anything I would say wouldn't hurt me?" Anderson asked. Welsch avoided answering the question and moved easily into the questioning. With the hidden tape machine recording every word, he told Anderson, "You understand that everything we say here is between you and me. In other words, the only thing, I just want to shoot the bull and get a little background from you. . . ."

They talked about Anderson's early life, his parents, his schooling, his religion, how he joined the service, his marriage. In this easygoing little chat, the OSI picked up four pieces of information. First, Anderson revealed the truth about the blood on his car—that it was from Jane's nosebleed when he slapped her. Second, he related that he had been in trouble as a juvenile and had been sent to a reform school. Third, he said he had once gotten into a fight with his wife's stepfather, who had moved in on them without paying his own way. Fourth, he volunteered that when he was a boy he had fallen at a skating rink, struck his head, and had blacked out from the blow.

When Anderson mentioned the juvenile trouble that had sent him to the reform school, he told Welsch that he would rather not talk about it because "it's all past and done with, and I'd just as soon not bring it up." Welsch, all geniality, replied, "Surely," and passed over the incident. But he promptly relayed it to the next interrogator for his own use against Anderson. Welsch led Anderson around to the day of the murders. By now the airman, who had already related his account to the Air Police, was groggy with fatigue, but he ran through his story again in detail. When he finished, he let out a big sigh. "Whew!" he said to the agent. "When are we going to call it quits . . . ? Boy, I tell you, I'm getting sleepy."

This exchanged revealed much about Anderson. Legally he was not in custody and could have got up and walked out of the interrogation room without asking the agent's permission. But he had a passive personality and an awesome respect for authority. The transcript showed, too, that at this point he was eager to assist the OSI; he repeatedly stated that he wanted "to help you fellows." Welsch ignored Anderson's complaint of fatigue and led him again over the events after he had left the Johnson home after delivering the milk to Nancy. Then without warning Welsch threw a frightening question at the young airman.

"Why did you get rid of those two people?" the agent demanded.

"I beg your pardon?" Anderson said.

"I said," repeated Welsch, "why did you get rid of those two people?"

"Get rid of what two people?" Anderson asked.

"Nancy and Danny."

"You're out of your mind!" said Airman Anderson.

Welsch withdrew from the questioning and was replaced by another agent, Robert Jent. He started where Welsch left off, with the unexplained and unsupported assumption that Anderson was guilty of the two killings. One of the basic techniques of procuring confessions is to give the suspect a way to admit guilt and still save face, and Jent began opening a path for Anderson to confess the hideous killings and still save some remnant of self-respect.

The agent told Anderson that "due to environment, due to illnesses, due to many reasons, people don't follow the straight and narrow path. . . . Sometimes we can't help what we do. Sometimes we do things in a moment of passion, a moment of anger and maybe because things just aren't clicking off right up here in our head. Normal human beings want to get things straightened out, where we know we have done wrong. Whether there are circumstances that drove you to do this, I don't know."

When Anderson clung to his insistence that he had done nothing to the Johnsons, the agent turned the questioning to the juvenile incident that Welsch had graciously passed over. He demanded to know what kind of "trouble" Anderson had been in. Anderson resisted him, insisting that it had nothing to do with the investigation. When the agent continued to press him relentlessly, Anderson's composure cracked slightly for the first time.

"Can't I have someone in here with me?" he asked the agent.

The legally correct answer to this was "Yes." Under Article 31 of the Military Code, Anderson was entitled to the advice of a lawyer, whether a civilian attorney, if he wanted to pay for one, or free counsel from the air base legal office, which was right next door to the interrogation room.

"You've got to stand on your own two feet," the agent told him. "You're a man. Everything is going to come out. Something like this there is no stopping. This investigation can go on for years and years. . . . We're going to check out everything, every stinking thing that happened to you. . . . We're going to stop nowhere until this matter is solved."

Reluctantly, Anderson told him that he had been involved in a minor sex offense. It had stemmed from an adolescent curiosity; the girl had not been harmed; the offense had never been repeated, and Anderson said he had felt an enduring sense of guilt and shame about it ever since.

The agent told Anderson that some of the people at the base had been saying for a year that he was "mentally off" on certain things, psychologically speaking.

Anderson bristled at this accusation. "Like what?" he challenged the agent.

"Well, I'm not going to sit here and . . . tell you exactly, because I don't know exactly. I just know that . . . it's all putting you in a bad light."

He worked over Anderson on the incident when he had returned home from the Cozy Bar the day after the murders and had broken down when he met his wife. Then he went back to Anderson's "lie" about the blood on his car and began upbraiding him.

"I think you're a psychopathic liar," the OSI man told Jerry Anderson. "That's what I think you are. I think you're sick. You're sick whether you admit it to yourself or not. You're sick in the head. When are you going to admit you need help? . . . The only way you are going to get help is by coming clean and asking for forgiveness for what you've done, and you're never going to do it by sitting there telling me little piddly . . . lies . . . You have told lies when the truth would have served the same purpose. Why? What are you trying to hide?"

"I've told you the truth."

"You have lied to me, and now you're sitting there telling me another lie by telling me you told the truth. . . . You're a sick man. . . . You are a man of violence. You know you are. Will you say it to yourself? Will you admit to yourself that you aren't quite right? Huh?"

"There isn't anything wrong," Anderson insisted.

"There you go again," snapped the agent. "You're a sick man that took the life of that young mother and little boy. It could happen again. It could happen to your own family. . . . Where is it going to lead? Where is the next bit of violence going to be?"

"Sir," said Airman Anderson, "I didn't do it."

"You don't know you didn't do it because you don't know what the truth is. . . . Is your conscience something that left you many years ago, huh?"

"Please leave me alone," Anderson pleaded. "I didn't do it, I tell you."

"I'm not going to let you alone until I get the truth out of you. . . . Now we will stay here until tomorrow night at this time . . . until I get the truth. . . . You're a sick man. You're sick. You're a twisted up, violent, sick man. That's what you are. Look at yourself. Inspect your heart, inspect your mind, look at your brain. . . . Are you proud of what you are, huh?"

Throughout this sustained assault on his personality, Anderson responded with unbroken denials. Early in the morning the agent gave up. Between the Air Police and the OSI, Anderson had been under interrogation for more than fifteen hours. Now the OSI moved in a fresh agent, a smooth-cheeked, boyish fellow, David Mangold, with a soft voice and a sympathetic manner. Mangold was only twenty-three and looked five years younger. He was a "veteran" of eighteen months with the OSI, and his total training in criminal investigation consisted of a ten-week course at the OSI school in Washington. He had never investigated a homicide.

One of the established techniques is the "good guy and bad guy" ploy. This consists of alternating harsh, aggressive, hostile agents with a gentle and sympathetic one. The psychology is to build up bitter resentment of the "bad guy" agent and then give the suspect an understanding audience in the form of a "good guy" agent. Suspects on the verge of confessing often pour out their admissions to the "good guys" just to show up the inadequacies of the "bad guys" as interrogators.

"Now I don't know what your trouble has been with Mr. Welsch or Mr. Jent, and I don't care," Mangold said. "All I'm interested in is what you're going to tell me, and I'd like to hear it, hear your story of what happened. Would you like to tell me, Jerry?"

"No more," mumbled the exhausted Anderson. "No more."

"Just one more, huh?" Mangold wheedled.

In a remarkable display of endurance, Anderson outlasted the fresh young agent. Near dawn Anderson was stubbornly maintaining his innocence, and the exasperated Mangold suddenly broke and abandoned his assigned role of the sympathetic "good guy."

"If you're afraid of getting in any deeper, you needn't have any worries," he told Anderson, "because you're at the bottom of the well, man, and they're getting ready to put the plug in over you. . . . I want you to get it off your chest, and don't give me any of this . . . because I've had it. You know the answers. . . . If a man had nothing to hide, he'd come out with these answers. . . . You are the type of man who hits his own wife. I don't hold with any man who hits a woman at all. Frankly, I think he's the lowest son of a bitch on the face of the earth."

Agents led Anderson over to the detention facility and let him go to bed. Although he was under no detaining order and had been charged with no crime, he did not question their right to lock him up. He turned in just as everyone else was getting up for the new day. "They were banging around, going in and out, cleaning the place, with the radio going," Anderson re-called. "I didn't get much sleep."

The next day they brought in Joe Townsend and his lie detector. The OSI built up Townsend and his "lie box" in advance to Anderson, condi-tioning him to the belief that the machine was infallible. "This man's a specialist," Welsch said. "I have never known him to be wrong, and if a man is lying he can tell it." Before strapping Anderson to the machine, Townsend explained how it worked and told him, "If a person tells me the truth, I know it. If he doesn't tell me the truth, I know it."

"Well, I'm pretty sure I'll pass it," Anderson said.

"No, there is no pretty sure about it," Townsend told him. "You know right now whether you will or not . . . because you know right now whether you did commit this act. If you didn't there's no way in the world that I'm going to show that you did."

This is a gross misstatement of the polygraph machine. The lie detector is a useful tool, but it is not an omniscient judge. The readings obtained from it are not admissible in court as evidence of guilt. Capable operators readily concede that reactions require human interpretation, that there are guilty suspects who can "beat the box," and that there are circumstances where innocent people will yield readings that indicate guilt.

Townsend ran two long series of tests on Anderson. By his own account, he got a completely contradictory set of readings. The first tests produced reactions that Townsend interpreted as guilty knowledge of the murders and of the murder weapon. He then tested Anderson specifically on the nature of the weapon and what he had done with it, because at this time the weapon—a major piece of evidence—was still missing. Townsend got a complete negative from Airman Anderson, both on the weapon and its whereabouts. Baffled, the lie-detector operator ran five tests on the airman. All showed no knowledge of what was used to kill the Johnsons or what had been done with the weapon. In the face of these contradictory readings and despite clear indication that Anderson showed negative on key aspects of the crime, Townsend informed the airman that he had failed the lie test.

Abandoning his role as polygraph technician, Townsend took over as interrogator, and in the next three days grilled Anderson for twenty-seven hours. The transcript of the grilling shows the lie detector test had a pro-found effect on the young airman. To his continued protests of innocence, Townsend simply insisted, "We've already crossed that bridge, and there's no going back. . . . We both know it happened, and you and I are the only two that know for certain it happened." Townsend now began pressing Ander-son for the motive. He suggested repeatedly that perhaps Anderson was insane, or that he had blacked out and killed the Johnsons without knowing it. "You can say that you were completely off your rocker," Townsend told him. "Neither myself nor anybody could prove that you weren't momentarily insane for a period of ten minutes."

"I swear to God I didn't do it," Anderson replied, but by now his protestations were becoming more and more uncertain. He began to discuss with the agent, on a "just suppose" basis, that maybe he had blacked out. Under the hammering of accusation his memory of the night of April 9 began to fade. On the fourth day of interrogation, for the first time, he told inquisitors that now he could not clearly recall his actions after delivering the milk to Nancy Johnson. "I can't remember leaving her house," he said. The agents seized on this and began pushing the idea that he had killed the mother and son without his conscious mind admitting that he had done so. Anderson began to entertain this frightful possibility.

"The first couple of days there was no doubt in my mind," he told the agents. "And I started talking to you people . . . and I began to question myself, because nothing is impossible. I could have blacked out, and I can't remember doing it. . . ."

On April 16, in the middle of the night after five days of interrogation, Anderson's will finally broke. What broke it, by his account, was a statement by OSI agent Joe Townsend, who told him that his wife Jane had been interrogated and had incriminated him in the crime. Jane Anderson bitterly denies having made this statement. In an interview with the *Los Angeles Times* she stated, "There couldn't be anything of the sort. I don't know what Townsend was talking about."

Anderson frantically pleaded with the OSI men to let him talk to his wife. Shaken by his lie detector tests and the constant suggestions that he had killed in a "blackout," his belief in his innocence began to crack at its foundation with the claim that his wife thought him guilty. The final shove over the brink came when Townsend threatened to name his wife as an accessory, Anderson recalled. Townsend told him, "And when I do that, I put those three young kids in a reformatory or an orphanage."

The alleged confession of Airman Anderson surely must be one of the most peculiar documents in modern criminology. At no point in the marathon interrogation did he state that he had killed either Nancy or Danny Johnson. When his will to resist shattered, he asked the OSI agent to tell him what his motive could have been, if he had killed them. Townsend unhesitatingly reconstructed the crime for him, and it is Townsend's version of the murders that is set forth in Anderson's confession. After explaining to Anderson how he might have killed Nancy, and why, Townsend summoned Mangold and began dictating a confession as if it were being made by Anderson.

"Townsend did all the talking, Mangold did all the writing, and I did all the listening," Anderson recalled. The tape recorder clearly showed that Townsend spoke to Anderson only sporadically throughout the dictation, to check a few minor details. On the key passages related to the murder, Anderson sat silently while Townsend and Mangold composed his supposed confession.

The statement sets forth that when Anderson brought the milk jar back from the dairy, he made a verbal pass at Nancy, and she rebuffed him with a slighting reference to his manhood. "This remark of Nancy's enraged me," Townsend dictated. "I immediately became violent. . . . We scuffled shortly, and I possibly knocked her down; however, I am not certain. I recall seeing some blood on the floor and know that I did stab her, but I do not know what knife or instrument I used to stab her, and I have no idea where the instrument is now. During this short period it seemed to me that I blacked out, and I do not recall seeing or doing any harm to Johnson's son Danny."

Near the end, there was a revealing dialogue:

> TOWNSEND: "My wife and I remained awake [early in the morning after the murders] and discussed the—what—incident—or?"
> ANDERSON: "Whatever you want to call it."
> TOWNSEND: "The murder or stabbing?"
> MANGOLD: "Call it the murder or stabbing."
> TOWNSEND: "Happenings at Johnson's home. We'll just let them draw their own cotton-picking conclusions."

In dictating the supposed confession, Townsend changed the time that the airman said he had returned to his own home. The statement puts the time at 8:35 P.M. Throughout the interrogation, Anderson had clung stubbornly to one fact—that he had arrived home before 8:30, in time to watch the conclusion of M-Squad, which he recalled vividly and in detail. One can only speculate at the reason for this alteration in time, but Townsend's reconstruction of the crime gives a clue. Independent testimony had placed Anderson at the dairy after 8:00 P.M. The murder scene was violently splashed with blood. With Anderson leaving the dairy after 8:00 P.M., it would have been virtually impossible for him to have driven to the Johnson home, delivered the milk, talked to Nancy, become enraged, killed her and the boy, washed up the blood on himself, looted the house, and disposed of the murder weapon in time to get home and sit down to a television program by 8:25. The statement presented to Anderson for signature conveniently gave him an extra ten minutes to get this all done.

When Mangold finished his writing, the agents swore in Anderson and presented him with the document they had prepared. In a final burst of resistance, he threw down the pen and refused to sign it. "I want to know one thing, Joe," he appealed to Townsend. "Did my wife really say it? . . . I'm so mixed up I don't know what I want to do. . . . My wife really said I did it, huh?"

Townsend assured him that this was the truth, they swore him in again, and this time he affixed his name to the OSI's version of the death of Nancy Johnson. They had him initial each page and each of Mangold's corrections in the manuscript. When the tape recording of the event is timed, from the moment he began initialing the six pages until he signed the last one, only forty-five seconds elapsed. "Well, that's it," said Townsend. "I thank you for your cooperation."

As Airman Anderson was led away, he asked what proved to be a prescient question: "What happens to a guy when he confesses to something he didn't do—and then they find out someone else did it?"

Even then the ordeal of interrogation was not over. The civil authorities in Mountain Home examined his confession and pointed out a glaring inadequacy. The autopsy of Nancy Johnson had shown that she had been sexually violated. The statement dictated by Townsend had not touched upon this aspect of the murder. The OSI agents hauled Anderson back in and tried to plug this gap in another long inquisition, but by now Anderson was through cooperating. He fought off every suggestion that, in addition to killing his friend and neighbor, he also had raped her. During this last interrogation, OSI agent Jent, sickened with the affair, asked to be relieved of questioning Anderson further. "I felt in my mind," he said later, "that he wasn't the man."

The Air Force turned Anderson over to the civilian authorities early on the morning of April 18, just nine days after the murders in Mountain Home. Later in the same day, searchers found the weapon that had killed Nancy and Danny Johnson. It was discovered on the roadside more than a mile from the murder scene—a fact that ripped a hole through Townsend's tight time schedule for the murders. But by now the OSI had finished its job, and there were other investigations to pursue. No one bothered trying to fit the task of disposing of the knife, with a two-mile round trip, into Anderson's confession.

Seven months later, with Anderson sitting in the Elmore County Jail, charged with the murders, the case blew wide open. In the middle of November a twenty-one-year-old civilian named Theodore Dickie confessed to the killings. Unlike Anderson, Dickie confessed under his own volition, with no interrogation reconstruction or suggestions from anyone. Unlike Anderson, he supplied details of the murder that not even the OSI or Idaho law officials knew. When he admitted the murders, Dickie was being held in Boise for the slaying of a ten-year-old girl, to which he had already confessed. The civilian officials, aware of the danger that Dickie, facing one murder charge, might falsely confess another crime, put Dickie's account to the severest test.

They found an impressive array of corroboration in the accumulated evidence in the Johnson murders. The most damning point of verification, virtually riveting Dickie to the crime, concerned the murder weapon. Dickie stated that he had killed the Johnsons with an old hunting knife and that the blade had broken when he stabbed Nancy Johnson. During the autopsy, a moon-shaped piece of a knife blade was found inside her chest. When the murder weapon was found at the roadside—the weapon Townsend's "lie box" showed Airman Anderson had no knowledge of— the blade had a moon-shaped gap in it. FBI tests proved that the piece in Nancy's body came from Dickie's knife. Dickie not only told officers where he had discarded the knife, he also told them something they didn't know—where the knife had come from. He said he had stolen it shortly before the murder from a trading post in Mountain Home.

Queried by officers after Dickie's confession, the owner of the knife confirmed that it had been stolen from him, described it accurately and, when shown the weapon, identified it as stolen from his store in April. Dickie named the articles he had stolen from the Johnson home, accurately described the two purses and their contents, and told where he had thrown them. He described the interior of the Johnson home in detail, down to the location of a shotgun shell on the top of the television set and the position of a baseball bat on the rear porch. He described how Nancy was dressed and stated that he had had sexual relations with her. He stated that shortly before going to the Johnson house, his car stalled in Mountain Home and he got a push from a resident. The man and his wife both verified this. He supplied a motive for the crime; he said he had got into a violent argument with Nancy, and she had rushed into the kitchen and got a knife, and that he had knocked her down and stabbed her, and then killed Danny when he came in and began crying.

When the last lead in Dickie's story had been checked and verified, the Idaho civilian authorities moved swiftly to rectify Airman Anderson's plight. The prosecuting attorney of Elmore County moved to dismiss the murder charge against Anderson, declaring that "evidence has now been discovered which completely exonerates the defendant" and informing the court that "an investigation of the facts has revealed physical evidence in full corroboration of the confession . . . of Theodore Thomas Dickie."

In a highly unusual action, the district judge entered an order that Anderson was "adjudged and decreed . . . not guilty" of the Johnson murder and that the prosecution be dropped and Anderson released.

With a known slayer confessing to the Johnson crime and a court finding that Anderson was guiltless, Anderson assumed that his long agony had come to an end. After seven months of sitting in a cell for a murder another had now confessed, Anderson was released and reunited with his wife. He told newsmen that "it's wonderful, just wonderful. I knew I didn't commit this crime, and I just waited, hoped, and prayed for some break."

What seemed a storybook ending to a tragedy of errors was shattered within twenty-four hours. While Anderson celebrated the end of his ordeal, the Air Force was suffering through an ordeal of its own. To drop the charge against Anderson would be a public admission that the OSI had obtained a fraudulent confession.

To resolve this dilemma, the Air Force flew in a legal expert from March Air Force Base in California and announced that Anderson would be held in custody for twenty-four hours, while the expert reviewed the entire case and recommended a course of action. On the basis of his one-day examination of the long, involved case—the transcript of the OSI interrogation alone runs three hundred pages—the Air Force on November 27 charged Anderson with the murder of both Nancy and Danny Johnson. Back went Airman Anderson behind military bars.

The announcement set a storm of controversy swirling around Mountain Home Air Force Base. Idaho newspapers raised a cry that the military was flouting the civilian courts. The Idaho Statesman charged that the Air Force was operating under a law of its own. Senator Thomas Kuchel of Anderson's home state of California requested an inquiry by Congress. Investigations of the case were begun by the Department of Justice, the Inspector General's office, the Defense Department, and the Senate Subcommittee on Constitutional Rights.

Amid the uproar, a select team of OSI agents came swarming into Mountain Home and Boise. Early in December the Air Force convened an "Article 32" hearing—the military equivalent of a grand jury—to determine whether Airman Anderson should be sent to court-martial or cleared of the killings. A week-long hearing, conducted by Major James Goddard of the Judge Advocate's Office at Biggs Air Force Base in Texas, produced new sensations in the case.

Under bitter cross-examination by Anderson's civilian attorney, Robert McLaughlin, and by his military attorney, Major Peter McKinney, testimony was produced that:

- OSI agents, on learning that Dickie had confessed to the crime their men had pinned on Anderson, had subjected Dickie to a lengthy interrogation. Although he told them from the outset that he had killed the Johnsons, OSI agents continued to interrogate until he gave them an oral repudiation of his confession. (As soon as the OSI agents left town again, Dickie called in newsmen and said, "I just gave the OSI a big old spiel. I knew what they wanted—to tie Anderson into that crime, and I told them what they wanted to hear.")
- The OSI agents who obtained Anderson's "confession" ignored his requests for legal counsel and neglected to enter these requests in their records, in violation of OSI regulations.
- Townsend, the agent who threatened to name Anderson's wife as an accessory and put his children in an orphanage, swore that he did not consider this coercion.
- Townsend also stated his belief that accusing a suspect of murder, suggesting to him that he was mentally unsound and might have killed in a blackout, and then running a lie detector test on him would not affect the polygraph readings.
- Laboratory tests of the material "shaken down" from Anderson's car had shown no connection with the crime.
- Male skin and hair samples scraped from Nancy Johnson's fingernails and body had already proved, under analysis, not to be Anderson's.

At the conclusion of the hearings, Major Goddard announced that he would study the entire record and then recommend to the commander of the Fifteenth Air Force either the release or the court-martialing of Airman Anderson.

On January 9 Theodore Dickie shattered the remnants of the OSI's case against Anderson when he gave a detailed confession—his sixth—to OSI agents and then took, and passed, their lie detector test.

At this writing, the Air Force does not expect to make a final decision until February 7. And so Anderson still sits in his cell at Mountain Home Air Force Base, waiting for the red tape to unwind. While his ordeal is not over, it has toughened and matured him and restored his faith in ultimate justice.

After nine months behind bars he still can say, "The Air Force is a good outfit to be in. It's got some good people and I won't run it down." Then he turned his memory back to the long nights he spent in the bare little interrogation room. "Just one thing," said Airman Anderson. "What I say about the Air Force doesn't go for the OSI."

Epilogue

On January 29, 1963, three days before the cover date of the *Saturday Evening Post* carrying the foregoing article, the military charges against Gerald Martin Anderson were dismissed and he was released. Two days later, he had what the *Los Angeles Times* described as a "reserved but friendly" reunion with his wife Jane. She had been flown to Los Angeles from Ogden, Utah, where she had been living since her husband's arrest. "I lost my husband and my home, and I never want to see Mountain Home, Idaho, again," she said. The couple never reconciled.

The following April, Major Peter J. McKinney, Anderson's military lawyer, was passed over for promotion and forced into retirement in what he alleged was a reprisal for his vigorous defense of his client. Robert F. McLaughlin, Anderson's civilian lawyer, told reporters, "Major McKinney is a very competent, capable attorney. It strikes me as highly unusual that a man of his capability would be passed over and lost to the service."

Theodore Thomas Dickie pled guilty to the slayings and on September 28, 1963, was sentenced to two consecutive life terms in prison, to be served consecutively with a life sentence he already had received for the murder of the ten-year-old girl in Boise. Passing sentence, Judge Clay V. Speer said, "It is the recommendation of this court to the Idaho Board of Probation and Parole that the defendant be perpetually ineligible for probation, parole, or pardon, for this court is of the opinion that society in general should be protected from any further crimes by the defendant through incarceration for the entire remainder of his natural life."

Joe R. Townsend retired from the Air Force in May 1963 and took a job as a polygraph operator with the Florida Sheriff's Bureau. There he coerced a false statement from a nineteen-year-old woman implicating two innocent African-Americans, Freddie L. Pitts and Wilbert Lee, in the murder of two white filling station attendants. Pitts and Lee were sentenced to death but exonerated and released in 1975 after the actual killer, a white man named Curtis Adams, confessed that he had killed the two men.

Anderson filed a federal lawsuit seeking $250,000 damages from Air Force Secretary Eugene Zuckert and nine officers, but the suit was dismissed in 1967.

DESPERATION

You've been advised that you have a right to remain silent, but somehow you simply can't.

It's unfathomable to you that your interrogators can't see the truth, but they don't.

The interrogation is relentless and, seemingly, endless.

You're at wits' end, but now they offer you a way out—just say it was an accident, or self-defense, or your buddy did it, or something, and the questioning will stop.

You'll be able to go home.

You haven't taken complete leave of your senses, but you're so desperate to end the relentless grilling that you tell them what they want to hear.

You think you'll set the record straight later.

You are, after all, innocent—surely, the truth will out.

After resting, you come to your senses. You try to take back what you told them.

But it's too late.

You're presumed guilty, in practice if not in theory.

It's no consolation, but—as the following articles show—you're not the only person who, desperate and exhausted, has fallen into such a trap.

DONNELL VAUGHN

Anguish brought on by a sick trick sapped his will to resist

BRENDAN SMITH
WASHINGTON, D.C.

While shackled to the wall during a four-hour interrogation in 2005, twenty-four-year-old Donnell Vaughn learned that the grandmother who had raised him—the woman he described as "my heart"—was dead.

District of Columbia Metropolitan Police Department Detective Anthony Greene told Vaughn his grandmother was frightened by officers and suffered a heart attack during a search of her home for evidence linking Vaughn to a gun battle in Southeast D.C. that injured two women.

"You've got your grandma laying in the motherfucking hospital with tubes in her because she had a fucking heart attack over some shit you did," Greene told Vaughn during the videotaped interrogation. "You basically telling me you don't give a fuck about your grandma."

Vaughn later sobbed and banged his head against a table after an officer told him his grandmother died at the hospital. Fearing his family would never speak to him again and appearing exhausted, Vaughn eventually confessed to being one of the shooters.

Vaughn's grandmother, however, was alive and well, and the lies MPD investigators told were part of a tangled web of deception that ultimately undermined their case. On July 21, 2006, District of Columbia Superior Court Judge Herbert Dixon Jr. ruled Vaughn's confession was inadmissible because Greene and Sergeant Joseph Thomas had "exceeded the bounds of permissible police conduct and techniques" and engaged in a "sufficient course of misconduct that had resulted in involuntary and inadmissible statements." Dixon said the ongoing deceit about Vaughn's grandmother "crossed the line" and was "the seminal lie in this case."

According to Vaughn and his defense attorney, Bernard S. Grimm, Vaughn's confession was also false, a product of police coercion and psychological manipulation that left Vaughn overwhelmed and that cost him thirteen months of his life while he was held without bond in the D.C. jail awaiting trial.

Four days after Vaughn's confession was suppressed, the U.S. Attorney's Office dropped all fourteen charges against him, including assault with intent to kill, aggravated assault, fleeing a police officer, and several firearms offenses. The case hinged on Vaughn's confession because no physical evidence or witness accounts linked him to the shooting or to a machine gun recovered in the street.

Now twenty-five years old, Vaughn is living again with his grandmother while searching for work to support himself and his three young daughters. Before his arrest, Vaughn's only encounter with the MPD had been for a public-drinking violation, and he has no prior adult record at D.C. Superior Court.

"You're locked up for something you didn't even do," Vaughn told *Legal Times*. "The government now don't even care. All they want is a conviction. They don't care if they take somebody's life or not."

The videotape of Vaughn's interrogation shows the corner of a dingy interview room at the MPD's Seventh District station, where chunks of plaster have fallen from the wall and crumbled into a fine, chalky dust on the black floor. A police officer handcuffs Vaughn's right hand to a bolt protruding from the pockmarked wall before leaving him with Greene, the lead detective on the case.

Wearing a white T-shirt, baggy jean shorts, and high-top tennis shoes, Vaughn hunches his six-foot, 150-pound body over a chair, occasionally scratching his handcuffed wrist or resting his head on the bare white table.

Vaughn tells Greene he simply was in the "wrong place at the wrong time" during the early morning hours of June 25, 2005, when he was riding in the back seat of a stolen red 1998 Acura 3.0 CL with two friends he would describe only as "T.J." and "Rock." An eleventh-grade dropout who grew up in Southeast D.C., Vaughn may not have been in serious trouble with the police before, but he knew one cardinal rule of the street: you don't snitch on your friends. During his entire interrogation, Vaughn refused to name the two friends who escaped arrest or describe their role in the shooting, prompting Greene to shift his focus to implicating Vaughn even though Vaughn repeatedly said he was sitting in the back seat during the shooting.

According to police reports, the driver of the Acura and a man on the passenger's side opened fire with a 9mm handgun and a .223-caliber Ruger Mini 14 machine gun. The barrage of bullets tore through a Dodge Neon, occupied by two women, at the intersection of Ninth and Yuma streets Southeast. The women were victims of an apparent case of mistaken identity, but someone other than the women returned fire on the Acura, shattering its rear window.

"I'm in the back seat, you know what I'm saying? The window bust. Glass flew in my back and all in my shoes," Vaughn told Greene. "I'm like, man, go, go, go!"

One woman suffered a gunshot wound to her stomach and left side, while the other woman was hit in her left leg. Both victims were treated at Greater Southeast Community Hospital and survived their injuries.

Two officers in a police cruiser heard the gunshots and tried to stop the red Acura, speeding northbound on Ninth Street Southeast, police reports stated. The driver refused to stop, resulting in a high-speed chase through the streets of Southeast D.C., with the Acura running three stoplights and a stop sign and reaching an estimated speed of one hundred miles per hour in a thirty-miles-per-hour zone. An ambulance driver saw an occupant of the Acura toss the machine gun, which officers later recovered on Thirteenth Street Southeast. Two men bailed out of the car when it finally stopped on Raynolds Place Southeast, where Vaughn lived.

Vaughn, the second man to exit the two-door car on the driver's side, was the only one who was caught. He was arrested and initially was charged only with unauthorized use of a motor vehicle. He was transported to the Seventh District station, where he was questioned by Greene.

At the beginning of the interrogation, Greene tells Vaughn the written waiver of his Miranda rights is "procedural stuff," and Vaughn agrees to sign the form after reading it. Approximately thirty minutes into the interrogation, Greene lies about Vaughn's grandmother suffering a heart attack and says, "It don't look too good for her." If Vaughn will confess, Greene says, he can try to get Vaughn released under police custody to see his grandmother at the hospital or at her funeral. Frustrated by Vaughn's unresponsiveness, Greene even suggests that Vaughn should kill himself.

"You need to come clean, Mr. Vaughn, to give your family some closure for this shit because this is going to eat your ass alive. The stress is going to get so overwhelming you're going to fucking have a heart attack your motherfucking self or want to hang yourself, because what else is there to live for?" Greene says. "You might as well because you ain't helping yourself here. All you want to do is rot in motherfucking jail for something you ain't do?"

Investigators also tell Vaughn what Judge Dixon would later call "the normal assortment of lies to a defendant," or lies about the evidence that routinely have been allowed by the Supreme Court. Greene lies about Vaughn's fingerprints being on the recovered machine gun and witnesses seeing him toss the gun, while Sergeant Thomas lies about a second suspect being arrested who will snitch on Vaughn.

But Dixon ruled the lies about Vaughn's grandmother "went beyond a lie about the evidence" and was "a psychological ploy to create an urgency in Mr. Vaughn to gain his release to pay his last respects to his grandmother."

During the interrogation, Greene repeatedly refuses to allow Vaughn to call his family and ignores his pleas that he is tired and just wants to rest. Thomas also falsely claims that Vaughn could receive a D.C. Youth Act expungement and be released on his own recognizance.

Near the end of the four-hour interrogation, Vaughn finally gives a motive for the shooting and implicates himself as one of the shooters. He says a man who murdered a friend more than a year earlier at a U Street nightclub was supposed to be in the Neon occupied by the two women. After persistent questioning about which gun he used, Vaughn mumbles he used the "big gun."

Vaughn told *Legal Times* he reached his breaking point during the interrogation. "I was tired, and I was trying to check on my family," he says. "I just said anything. I would say anything they wanted me to say. [Greene] was leading me through that whole thing. He was leading me what to say."

Greene did not return phone calls seeking comment. In an interview with *Legal Times*, the MPD's Thomas denied making any promises of leniency, even though he told Vaughn during the interrogation he could "almost guarantee" Vaughn would be released on his own recognizance if he cooperated. (Promises of leniency or threats of harm during a confession are, the Supreme Court held in 1961, "a denial of the state and federal constitutional guarantees of due process of law.")

Thomas, who is one of Greene's supervisors, calls Greene a "very intelligent detective," but he differed with Greene on his decision to lie about Vaughn's grandmother. Nevertheless, Thomas, who entered the interrogation midway and talked about religion and God as an interrogation tactic, played along with the lies and even asked Vaughn what he would say to his dead grandmother if she appeared in the room.

"Me, per se, I may not go the route [Greene] went. That's not my forte. I use a different technique," Thomas says. "They have all kinds of techniques that detectives use, and it's almost whatever works."

Grimm, Vaughn's defense attorney, who has practiced in the District for twenty-two years, filed the motion to suppress Vaughn's confession, stating the interrogation violated Vaughn's Fourth, Fifth, and Fourteenth Amendment constitutional protections. Grimm questioned Greene during a July 15 preliminary hearing, in which the detective admitted lying about the death of Vaughn's grandmother. Greene testified there was no evidence linking Vaughn to the shooting other than his confession.

"It's not the worst confession I've ever heard about, but it's the worst one I've heard that I was able to prove in court," Grimm says. "[Vaughn] was willing to say he was involved in the Kennedy assassination if it would get him home to his grandmother's funeral."

Grimm says Vaughn "ended up confessing to a crime he didn't do, based even on the government's own theory of what happened." Since the arresting officers stated Vaughn was the second person to exit the two-door Acura on the driver's side, Grimm says it supports Vaughn's statements that he was in the back seat during the shooting. Grimm says that Vaughn will speak with another attorney this week about a possible lawsuit against the MPD over his case and his incarceration.

Last year the D.C. Council passed an act requiring that the MPD record custodial interrogations of violent-crime suspects when the interrogations take place in an interview room equipped with electronic recording equipment.

MPD commander Michael Anzallo, superintendent of the detective division, says detectives receive regular in-service training and training from a retired FBI agent on interrogation techniques. But he adds, "The only way to really practice the concepts and techniques that are taught is by doing it."

The MPD doesn't tell detectives whether to lie to suspects during inter-rogations, but "we do what is allowable within the confines of the law," Anzallo says.

The U.S. Attorney's Office held a six-hour training class last year with approximately 350 MPD detectives, with ninety minutes focused on Fifth and Sixth Amendment issues, including involuntary confessions, says Dan-iel Friedman, the office's director of training. Both Anzallo and Friedman say they will review Dixon's ruling in Vaughn's case to see if MPD detec-tives need additional training. For Vaughn, any improvements to the D.C. criminal justice system will come too late. He already had lost the thirteen months of his life spent in jail before his case was dismissed last month.

"Whatever hell is, it's got to be something similar to that," he says about being locked up.

Vaughn says that Greene and Thomas just wanted to make a case and they "went through the extreme to get it done."

"That was my first time going in for something like that," Vaughn says. "I'm glad it's over, but I hate the police."

Epilogue

Vaughn brought no civil rights case, and no disciplinary action was taken against the officers who coerced his confession.

KEVIN FOX

They promised to stop the grilling—if he'd just say
it had been an accident

BRYAN SMITH

WILMINGTON, ILLINOIS

Dressed in a tuxedo—dapper but slightly self-conscious—Kevin Fox took his place at the wedding altar inside Holy Name Cathedral in Chicago, awestruck by the majesty that surrounded him: the light slanting through the stained glass windows, the arches soaring up to gilt ceilings, the bas-relief of Abraham offering to sacrifice his child. A self-described small-town boy from Wilmington, he was there to act as best man for his older brother, Chad. But if he felt out of place as the ceremony began, his discomfort melted at the sight of his two children now making their way down the aisle.

Tyler, the six-year-old spitting image of his dad, bore the ring; beside him toddled Tyler's three-year-old sister, Riley. Her hair a tiara of chestnut curls, she wore a snow-white "princess" dress, a gossamer confection of satin and lace over white satin slippers. Reaching into a tiny white basket, she doled red rose petals along the aisle like a pixie spreading fairy dust.

The ceremony's original choreography called for Riley to turn right at the front of the aisle and join her mother's pew. Instead, she marched up the marble stairs and past the groom. With a huge smile on her face, she headed straight to her daddy, who scooped her up into his arms. As Kevin and countless others in the sanctuary laughed with delight, he returned her to her mother, who shook her head with resignation and took the girl to the pew.

A few hours later, at a reception at the Park Hyatt, Kevin drew on the moment as he stood to toast his brother, Chad, and Chad's new wife, Stacy. "Throughout my life, I've always followed in your footsteps," Kevin said. "I tagged around when we were in high school. I made you drive me around when you got your license. I pledged the same fraternity. But now that I have a wonderful wife, and the two most beautiful children in the world, you get to finally follow me and make a family. It's your turn to follow in my footsteps."

Chad hugged Kevin as the room burst into applause. The band broke into song. The extended Fox family danced the night away, though before too long Riley and Tyler had curled up under a table and fallen sound asleep. A picture of the children would make its way into Chad's wedding album, a cherished memento of a perfect day.

The image was almost as precious, in fact, as the photo a few pages later of Chad, Stacy, Kevin, Melissa, Tyler, and Riley smiling back at the camera in their wedding formalwear. At the time, it seemed like a happy though standard family portrait. In fact, it would be the last photo of all of them together, taken as it was just two weeks before the little girl would be found floating face-down in a creek.

Five months later, in October 2004, a gallery of stunned observers packed the hearing at the Will County Courthouse in Joliet. The collection of friends, family, reporters, and onlookers watched as Kevin Fox, red-eyed and shell-shocked, shuffled into the courtroom. He wore a red jumpsuit and was shackled at the legs and hands. Already, the shocking news had been splashed across the front of every local newspaper—Fox was being charged with an unspeakable crime, murdering his three-year-old daughter.

The state's attorney, a heavyset man named Jeffery Tomczak, swept into the room, shaking hands and nodding toward a line of police officers who stood stone-faced and imposing near a cadre of assistant prosecutors arrayed around the prosecution table. After the bailiff called the court to order, Tomczak laid out what he called cold, hard evidence of the father's guilt, including a confession. "He admitted duct-taping the child's mouth. He admitted placing her on the bank of the river, under the water. He admitted placing his finger in the vagina of the child. . . . He then went home and slept," the prosecutor said.

Tomczak added other details: the girl had been placed in the water while she was still "alive and moving and kicking." As if the image wasn't terrible enough, he said, she had been "able to remove the duct tape from her wrists prior to succumbing to drowning in the water."

At one point an assistant interrupted the presentation by bursting into the courtroom and thrusting a document into Tomczak's hand. "I've just been handed our certificate of intent to seek the death penalty in this case," the prosecutor declared. "I'm asking leave to file same." Tomczak wrapped up the hearing by asking for a $25 million bond, a request that drew gasps from the gallery.

To the people who knew Kevin Fox, the hearing seemed unreal. The Kevin Fox they knew was a wonderful father, devoted to his wife and son and daughter. His little girl had seemed to hold a special place in his heart. If you saw Kevin, you most likely saw Riley, on his shoulders or carrying their fishing poles down to the lake together. To his family, the event seemed staged, a dog-and-pony show orchestrated by Tomczak. To those who didn't know Kevin Fox, the hearing seemed to offer a shocking solution to a terrible crime . . . the cops, the judge, the seeming confidence of the state's attorney, and, most of all, the confession. Who would admit to such horrible things if he hadn't really done them?

Yet, despite the overwhelming implication of guilt produced by the hearing, a number of troubling questions lurked within the prosecutor's case. How solid was the evidence? What about DNA testing? And what were the circumstances of the "confession"? The timing of the charges also seemed curious, coming just six days before a tight election for state's attorney between Tomczak, the incumbent, and a bitter rival, James Glasgow. What's more, Tomczak's father, Donald, second-in-command at the City of Chicago's water department, had just been named in a federal indictment for corruption.

As if in anticipation of unavoidable criticism, Tomczak had earlier stopped at the defense table where Kevin Fox's attorney, Kathleen Zellner, was seated.

"This isn't political," he said.

"We'll see," the defense attorney shot back.

The murder of Riley Fox has since turned into a mystery extraordinary for reasons beyond the heartbreaking death of a little girl. The case has set in motion a series of events that bitterly divided what had been a neighborly town; cast a shadow of suspicion over a tight-knit, well-respected family; and raised questions about whether justice was forsaken for personal and political ambitions.

Kevin Fox was eventually released, and the case against him was dismissed. The murder of his daughter remains unsolved. The aftershocks of his arrest, however, reverberate in the form of a lawsuit he and his wife have brought against Will County authorities. The complaint accuses them of conducting a sloppy investigation that, from the start, focused almost exclusively on Kevin Fox and ignored any evidence that might have cast doubt on his guilt. The interrogation and arrest of Fox, the suit alleges, were part of a last-ditch effort by Tomczak to win reelection.

Tomczak did not return calls requesting an interview, but in court pleadings he has denied any wrongdoing, including any suggestion that Kevin Fox's arrest was related to his reelection campaign. "Any charges of politics are baseless," Tomczak said in a statement the day after Fox's arrest. The Will County Sheriff's Office defends its detectives' handling of the case, including the fourteen-and-a-half-hour interrogation that led to Fox's confession.

"We were not happy about [Fox's release]," says Pat Barry, spokesman for the Will County Sheriff's Office. "I'm not saying he shouldn't have been . . . but we firmly believe, and the sheriff firmly believes, that [the detectives] did a good job . . . and we stand behind them."

Virtually none of the principals involved in the case has gone untouched. The original detectives on the murder have been reassigned, the former state's attorney is now in private practice, and the little town where it occurred has suffered a loss of innocence, as well as wounds to its pride that may take years to heal.

Until now, the Foxes have remained silent about their ordeal. They agreed to tell their story to *Chicago Magazine*, they say, in hopes of calling attention to the injustices they believe they have suffered and to breathe new life into an investigation that, even authorities admit, has not yielded any promising leads for months. Meanwhile, the members of Kevin's family hold firm to their unwavering belief in the man who they say became, like his murdered daughter, a victim.

Wilmington, Illinois, just south of Joliet, stands amid the vast cornfields and high-grass prairies of the Kankakee River valley, a little more than fifty miles southwest of Chicago. Its 4.2 square miles occupy a rural stretch of old Route 66 (now Route 53) and offer the picture-perfect icons of Midwestern America. A faded water tower bearing the words "Wilmington Wildcats" overlooks Main Street, and a collection of modest ranch homes, ornamented with basketball courts and large American flags, lies sprinkled along the tree-lined streets. There's a bowling alley and a post office and a small movie house. As often as not, the town's dozen full-time police officers are looked on less as faceless authorities than as neighbors and friends and former high-school classmates.

The Fox family had called Wilmington home for generations. Like their father before them, Kevin and his older brother, Chad, were born here, rode their bikes here, fished here, and graduated from the town's only high school. While Chad talked about leaving for the big city, Kevin couldn't imagine living anywhere else. It was here, after all, that the lanky, blond, gentle-natured teenager had met a pretty, impetuous girl named Melissa Rossi, who eventually became his wife. The Rossi family had moved to Wilmington when Melissa was in the third grade. Her father, an avid fisherman, had learned he had cancer, and he wanted to spend what time he had left in a peaceful place along a river, she says. Melissa first saw Kevin at a high-school volleyball game. Sensing his shyness, she took matters into her own hands. "That night she asked me to her homecoming," Kevin recalls with a laugh. "I guess we were going out on a limb, but it turned out she was the one."

The relationship evolved quickly and, just after Kevin started college at Illinois State University, Melissa, then eighteen, became pregnant with Tyler. Kevin, twenty, was overwhelmed by the sudden turn of events, and the two broke up for a short period. "We were still young, so it was scary," Kevin says. But Kevin knew he was meant to be with Melissa. And he realized he needed to take responsibility for his child. He quit school and the two moved in together. Three years later, in 2000, with Kevin having found work as a union painter and Melissa as a waitress, the two were married.

For all his initial trepidation, Kevin took to fatherhood in a way that surprised even his closest family. "He is an amazing dad, I tell you what," says his mother, Dawn. "He changed more diapers and fed and bathed the kids way more than the average father."

A year after their marriage, they added a daughter to the family—an apple-cheeked princess with a pile of light brown hair. She quickly became known around town as the precocious little girl who loved Dora the Explorer, the kind of child who insisted on picking out her own flower girl dress—only after pliés and curtsies in front of a mirror. She adored her father. "They did everything together," recalls Curt Fox, Kevin's dad. Kevin even attached a cart to his bicycle, and Riley quickly adopted it as her favorite mode of travel. "If you saw one, generally the other was right behind," Curt Fox says.

The parents' doting nature meant that Riley and Tyler rarely strayed far from their sight. Only once, in fact, had the little girl wandered away from the small ranch house—that time, to play with a friend. Which made what happened even more mysterious and frightening.

The weekend of June 5 and 6, 2004, Melissa Fox left Wilmington to participate in a breast cancer walk in Chicago. That Saturday night, she stayed at a campsite with friends in Skokie. It was one of the first times she had spent the night away from the kids, but for her, it was a worthy venture—a way to honor her late father.

That night, Kevin drove to Chicago, too, to attend a concert with a friend and one of Melissa's brothers. He left Tyler and Riley with Melissa's mother, Sandy Rossi. According to a statement he later gave police, he picked the kids up and drove them home at around 1:00 A.M. Then, too tired to make up their beds, he laid them down in the living room—Riley on the couch and Tyler on a chair with a footstool. He locked the front door and retired to his room. Unable to sleep at first, he watched some TV, snacked, then went to bed around 2:30, turning on a fan against the hot night in the un-air-conditioned house. He planned to drive the kids to Chicago in the morning to catch Melissa at the finish line.

A little before eight in the morning, however, Tyler came into Kevin's room. "Riley's gone," the boy said. Trying not to panic, Kevin searched the house. He immediately noticed that the front door and screen were ajar. He then ran next door, where Riley's best friend lived. No sign of her. He called Wilmington police, but not wanting to raise an alarm prematurely, he would later explain, he decided to call the nonemergency line—a choice that was later questioned. He says the police told him he was right not to panic, that "in a lot of cases a child wanders off, and they can't find them at first." Even so, as time passed and word spread that Riley Fox was missing, a search was mounted. In less than an hour, it seemed the whole town had turned out. Kevin told police that Riley was wearing a white T-shirt with a pink flamingo on it and pink capri pants.

Melissa got the word when she called Kevin to arrange to meet the family at the finish line. "He was crying," she recalls. "He said, 'I can't find Riley.' I said, 'What are you talking about?'" Within minutes, Melissa and a friend were barreling down Interstate 55. As she neared Wilmington, Melissa felt a chill. "For some reason," she says, "I had this terrible feeling that I was never going to see her again."

By now, hundreds of townsfolk were clawing through brush and woods. "They'd come back with their legs scratched up and bleeding," recalls Kevin. As the day wore on, local merchants pitched in with food and pop. Television satellite trucks roared into town, deploying their parabolic dishes and disgorging reporters. By the afternoon, more than five hundred people were scouring the area, some on horseback, others on bicycles or all-terrain vehicles. At one point, Chad received a call from a friend watching the Cubs game. An Amber alert for Riley Fox had flashed on the scoreboard. "Isn't that your niece?" the friend asked.

Suddenly, at about three o'clock that afternoon, police jumped in their cars and sped off. Bewildered and frightened, Kevin and Melissa prayed that the sudden departure was less ominous than it looked.

About a mile away as the crow flies, a Wilmington mother and daughter had decided to search Forsythe Woods, a sprawling forest preserve with dense growth cut by a tributary of the Kankakee River called Forked Creek. The elder woman had just made her way to the edge of the creek when she noticed something that looked to her like a plastic bag. She screamed when she realized what she had found.

A Wilmington crime scene investigator arrived within minutes. In the cold, shallow, murky water of Forked Creek, Riley's body floated, face-down. She wore a flamingo-decorated T-shirt, dirtied now by mud and silt. Gone were any underwear and capri pants. An autopsy would later reveal that the girl had been sexually abused and probably died from drowning. Her mouth had been covered with duct tape, and adhesive residue on her arms led authorities to surmise she had been bound. The medical examiner also noted light bruising on Riley's head. "Rape kits"—samples of DNA collected from Riley's body—were sent to the Illinois State Police crime lab for analysis. A preliminary report indicated no signs of foreign DNA—with one possible exception: a test for saliva in her vagina came back "inconclusive."

Three miles away, a Wilmington police cruiser returned to Kevin and Melissa's house. "We need you to come to the police station," an officer told them.

"What's happened?" Melissa recalls asking, still holding out hope that their daughter was alive. Police would reveal nothing.

At the small brick-and-concrete station, just off Main Street, police put Kevin in one room and Melissa in another. "They made me sit in a room for forty-five minutes," Melissa says, still furious at the memory. "I kept saying, 'What's going on? Why can't I see my husband!'" Finally they were brought out into a waiting room, where Curt, Dawn, Chad, and Stacy had already gathered.

Melissa knew by their faces that the news was grim. But when she looked for confirmation from two detectives who stood in the room—including Todd Lyons, a burly, bald Wilmington investigator to whom Kevin had delivered papers when he was a boy—they "just stared at us," she says.

"Where is she?" Melissa asked.

"They found her at Forsythe Woods," Curt answered in a broken voice. "She didn't make it."

Kevin began to pound the walls. He turned to Lyons, incredulous that the detective hadn't told him earlier. "Todd, what the hell! Are you kidding me?" The detective shook his head. Kevin's knees buckled. Melissa begged her husband, "Please hold me, hold me."

Today, Chad fumes that his brother was not told earlier. "What kind of Cracker-Jack-box cops don't have the decency to tell the parents of a murdered little girl that their daughter is dead?" he asks.

In hindsight, the couple believes that either the police "were just completely overwhelmed by the fact that there was a murder in Wilmington and they had no idea what to do," Melissa says, "or they were watching to see how we would react."

In fact, the case was already out of their hands. Will County Sheriff's detectives had taken charge, assuming jurisdiction because the crime scene was in a forest preserve.

To accommodate the expected crowds, Riley's viewing, five days after the murder, was held at the town's largest church, St. Rose Catholic. The girl's body lay in a small polished white casket with stainless steel handles. She was wearing the same "princess dress" she had picked out and worn as a flower girl in Chad and Stacy's wedding. For hours, Kevin and Melissa shook hands and gave hugs, receiving mourners until they could barely stand.

More than six thousand people attended the wake—nearly one thousand more than the entire population of Wilmington. Hundreds more turned out the next day for the funeral, many wearing pink ribbons and ties and butterfly pins. A steady drizzle fell, while inside, mourners wept at a slide-show collage set to the songs "My Girl" and Sarah McLachlan's "Angel." "Let the little children come to me," said the Reverend Mark M. Strothmann, pastor of the First Presbyterian Church of Wilmington, quoting Mark 10:14. "For it is to such as these the kingdom of God belongs."

Among those in attendance, unobtrusive but noticeable, were two men holding video cameras. Their lenses, the family later learned, were trained not on the ceremony, or the casket, but on the mourners, including Kevin Fox. The men, the family learned, were Will County detectives.

In the weeks that followed, Melissa and Kevin found the investigators to be supportive, even friendly. One detective, Scott Swearengen, played toss with Tyler and often dropped by for coffee at Curt and Dawn's house, where Kevin and Melissa had moved after Riley's murder. He would eventually become such a fixture that the family would refer to him simply as "Scott."

From his Joliet offices, Will County State's Attorney Tomczak kept close tabs on the investigation's progress. If charges were to be filed, he would be the one to bring them. Tomczak, forty-four at the time, had earned his law degree in Chicago, but settled in Will County with his wife, who today is a judge there. A father of two, he made a failed run for Congress in 1994, but in the 2000 race for Will County state's attorney, the Republican Tomczak beat the incumbent Democrat, James Glasgow.

Bad blood had existed between the men for years. The two had clashed on nearly everything, from elections to court cases to ethical conduct. Everything about the men, even their appearance, seemed at odds. Tomczak was bulky with thinning hair. Glasgow was trim with a blow-dried pompadour of silver. In that summer of Riley's disappearance, the men were again locked in a tight race against each other in a campaign that, the *Chicago Tribune* said, "was bound to get ugly" given the men's history.

Kevin Fox and his family paid little attention to the politics of the race. But as the summer wore on, they came to believe that the investigation was dragging. "We felt we could never get an answer on the progress of the case," Kevin says. "We'd ask, but they'd always say something like 'We can't really discuss it.'" More often than not, the detectives would instead question Kevin and Melissa.

On one level, the couple could understand that the authorities might hold them—or at least Kevin—under suspicion. With the death of a child under these circumstances, the police look first to the family. Kevin, after all, had been the last person known to have seen Riley alive. But the parents believed they had cooperated in every way possible, including providing DNA samples, consenting to searches, and answering questions.

Other family members were less comfortable. They urged Kevin to hire an attorney. But after briefly talking to one lawyer, Kevin dismissed the idea. "I felt like I had nothing to hide," he says, and he worried that hiring an attorney might make him look guilty. Most important, Kevin says, he trusted the detectives' motives. "I was raised with the idea that authorities were good people and that they should be respected."

In late June, Kevin and Melissa consented to let the authorities question Tyler. After all, the boy could be crucial in helping the parents find their daughter's killer. A videotape captured the session, conducted by a forensic interviewer named Mary Jane Pluth, who works for the Will County Children's Advocacy Center. On the tape, her manner suggests a strict schoolteacher. Pluth starts off with basic questions about where Tyler lives and what kind of sports he likes.

The boy, who is extremely shy with strangers, answers reluctantly, with head shakes and nods. The questions quickly shift to what Kevin did or didn't do that night. "I don't know," Tyler says. "Did he leave the house?" Tyler shakes his head "no" several times. Once, he nods. Pluth pursues. "What did he do when he left? Did he take Riley somewhere?" she asks. The boy shakes his head. Pluth asks again. "No." "Where did he take Riley? You can tell me," she says. The boy weeps. His little chest heaves and his thin shoulders shake. He claws his sweatshirt hood over his head. At one point, he asks for his "mommy and daddy." Still, Pluth pursues her questioning.

After an hour, the boy draws into a fetal position. His blotchy face shines with tears. He looks away. He struggles to catch his breath between sobs. Finally, after more than an hour of interrogation, Pluth reaches for a box of tissues and thrusts it at Tyler. He shakes his head one final time. No.

By the end he has answered "no" approximately 178 times. He has also, on matters unrelated to the case, been in error in at least thirteen instances, according to the Fox suit. The entire time, Detective Edward Hayes, who would become the lead detective on the case, watches from the other side of a one-way mirror. His image hovers ghostlike in the frame.

Later that same afternoon, detective Michael Guilfoyle took Tyler to the Fox family's home. This time there were no cameras or tape recorders. Instead, Guilfoyle later wrote a summary of the interview. According to that report, Tyler became much more specific and descriptive. He recalled that his father "took Riley somewhere" during the night. When pressed, however, the boy seemed less sure. Guilfoyle reported that Tyler claimed he stood in the kitchen and saw his father using the clothes dryer after he returned. (A water usage report from that night suggests that the washing machine did not run.) By Guilfoyle's account, the boy also said things that seem to contradict known facts—that Kevin had dressed Riley in pajamas, for instance.

Until the night of Kevin's long interrogation several months later, authorities never told him and Melissa what Tyler allegedly had said. Guilfoyle's report did not surface until May, seven months after Kevin had been arrested. Kevin's lawyer, Kathleen Zellner, says that when she asked to see the handwritten notes from which the summary was drawn, Will County authorities told her that they were gone.

Also unknown to Kevin and Melissa, the police were pursuing another lead that might point toward Kevin. The Foxes owned a dark blue Ford Escape. A tip came in claiming that video surveillance cameras at the town's Mobil station might have captured a car like that at four in the morning of Riley's disappearance. If the car turned out to be the Fox vehicle, Kevin's alibi that he was asleep all night would be seriously undermined. What's more, investigators would be able to place the car along the route that led to Forsythe Woods, where Riley's body had been found. Will County detectives spent considerable time and effort establishing that other local owners of dark Ford Escapes were not in sight of the video camera that morning. But Zellner, who has viewed a copy of the videotape, says it's too fuzzy to make out a license plate or even to positively identify any vehicle. The authorities did not mention the videotape in court, though they did bring it up during the interrogation before Kevin confessed.

Around Wilmington, rumors began to swirl that the Foxes were using money donated to a "Riley fund" for extravagant vacations and luxury purchases. Melissa was seen getting a fancy haircut at the mall. She had traded in the Ford Escape for a new car. The couple had gone gambling in Las Vegas. They were vacationing in the Ozarks. Some questioned why a reward had never been offered. On October 11, a report by Amy Jacobson, a tall blond reporter from Chicago's NBC 5, gave voice to the whispers. A "source," his face hidden behind a black blob, his voice disguised, repeated the rumors in Jacobson's "exclusive" interview.

The next day, an article and editorial in the local paper, the *Free Press Advocate*, excoriated Jacobson and NBC 5 and told the family's account: Melissa had traded in the car because she couldn't bear how it reminded her of trips around town with Riley. The Las Vegas trip was to attend a friend's wedding and had been planned and paid for months before Riley's death. The trip to the Ozarks had been for another friend's wedding. And the Fox family had indeed suggested a reward be offered, only to be told by police it was unnecessary.

Nonetheless, the family members were deeply hurt by the TV report, as well as by the realization that people in town were gossiping about them. Chad Fox looked on the rumors as confirmation that Kevin—still not represented by a lawyer—was a suspect, perhaps the only suspect. In early October, Chad, a stockbroker, approached Zellner, who coincidentally worked across the hall from Chad in Naperville. She had been following the case in the media, and she urged Chad to get his brother to talk to her. Kevin again refused. "He kept saying, 'The DNA will clear me,'" Chad says. "I felt helpless and frustrated."

Indeed, by late October 2004, Kevin was the prime suspect. "Everything that [detectives] had was still pointing to this guy," says Will County Sheriff's spokesman Pat Barry. "There was nothing to eliminate him." Zellner insists that there was exculpatory evidence—in the so-called rape kits with material taken from Riley. But after the initial testing by the state crime lab, with its inconclusive finding on saliva, the DNA had been sent to the FBI lab in Quantico, Virginia, which had a nine-month backlog.

Meanwhile, Tomczak and Glasgow were said to be running neck and neck in the state's attorney's race. A break in the case could well tip the scales. For Tomczak it could also provide a diversion from a new headache that had suddenly surfaced. On October 21, his father, Donald Tomczak, was arrested on a federal indictment in the Hired Truck scandal in Chicago. Among the allegations was that the father had made illegal contributions to his son's campaign. Glasgow seized on the charges, suggesting his opponent would be soft on crime. The *Chicago Tribune* quickly threw its editorial support to Glasgow, saying on October 22 that he didn't "carry the burden of doubts about the ethical conduct of his campaign."

On October 25, a little more than a week before the election, the four detectives working on the Riley Fox murder—Scott Swearengen, John Ruettiger, Michael Guilfoyle, and Edward Hayes—convened at the Will County Sheriff's Office in Joliet to discuss bringing Kevin in for an interrogation.

Pat Barry insists that Tomczak knew nothing of the meeting, and that, no matter how questionable the timing appears, politics had nothing to do with it. Zellner is skeptical. "For a state's attorney not to know of such a meeting of his detectives in such a high-profile case would be unheard of," she claims. Fox's lawsuit alleges that the meeting was conducted with Tomczak's support and consent.

In preparation for the possible interrogation, the detectives contacted several polygraph experts, including Fred Hunter, a Hinsdale-based examiner with more than thirty thousand tests under his belt. None was available. Ultimately the detectives went with a far less experienced examiner— Richard C. Williams, a Cook County detective who, according to the Fox lawsuit, had conducted only about ninety tests.

On October 26, Swearengen called Kevin Fox to say, by Kevin's account, that there was news about the case and that the Foxes should come to the police station that night. The timing was less than ideal for the couple. Kevin had been up since four thirty that morning and had spent much of his day working at a painting job. He'd barely had time to grab a bite to eat all day. Still, he says, "we had waited so long. Months. This was our daughter, our little girl. We wanted to know if they had found out what had happened."

Kevin alerted his parents and Chad, who was immediately wary. "Something didn't feel right," Chad recalls. "I told my mom that they should not answer any questions. And if it became clear that there was no new information they should leave immediately."

The couple held hands as they made their way across the parking lot to the Will County Sheriff's Office in Joliet at about seven thirty that night.

"We felt like we were finally going to find out what had happened," Kevin says. "We put all our faith in them. We thought, this is the night."

They were greeted at the door by Swearengen. He was cordial, they recall, but he also insisted that the two be separated. "I thought it was a little strange," Melissa says. "But Scott said not to worry, that they just needed to ask us a few questions before they told us whatever they wanted to tell us."

They took Kevin into another part of the building. Melissa, meanwhile, was led into a conference room where, Swearengen told her, Detective Guilfoyle would be along shortly to ask a few questions. What more can they possibly want to know? she thought. And why did the door lock when he left the room?

Elsewhere in the building, in a small, cramped room with a low ceiling and a one-way mirror about the size of a cereal box, Kevin sat in a corner, facing a group of detectives, including an intense man with strawberry-blond hair and a flushed complexion: Ed Hayes. The questions started out easy, but quickly became pointed. Why did Kevin call the nonemergency line instead of 911 the morning of Riley's disappearance? Why would Tyler say Kevin had walked out during the night with Riley? Did he know his car had been spotted passing the Mobil station at four in the morning?

Kevin says he told the detectives that he didn't call 911 because he didn't want to panic prematurely. As for Tyler, Kevin had no idea his son had made such a statement—it was the first he'd heard of it. Maybe the boy thought Kevin had left when he stepped outside for a quick smoke. And he had no idea how his car wound up on a security tape. Again, this was the first he'd heard of it. When pressed about the car, Kevin recalls, he became exasperated and suggested sarcastically that someone must have snuck into his house, stolen his keys, taken the car, and returned it later. But if Kevin was joking, the police apparently didn't get it. They later portrayed his statement as an attempt to provide a possible alibi.

Kevin says Swearengen's tone changed abruptly. "We think you know more than you're telling us," Kevin says the detective told him. "We think you were involved." Kevin says he was incredulous. "Are you kidding me?" he recalls saying. "You guys are nuts!"

After three hours alone, Melissa grew furious. "I finally kicked the door really hard," she says. Within moments, Swearengen appeared and led her into an adjoining room. "There are some red flags that are making us look at Kevin," Melissa recalls the detective saying.

Melissa says that Swearengen told her about the videotape of the car and about Tyler's statement and then laid out an "accident" scenario for the death of Riley. By her account, Swearengen said that he suspected that Kevin had bumped Riley's head, perhaps while opening the bathroom door, and had panicked when it appeared she was dead. The detective surmised that Kevin had applied the duct tape and committed the sexual assault to make it look as if the little girl had been kidnapped.

Melissa reeled. The story seemed preposterous. Even if Kevin had accidentally hurt Riley, he would have tried to resuscitate her—he was certified in CPR. As for sexual abuse, "I'm not a stupid person," Melissa says. "If someone was abusing my child, I would have known about it. There would have been some sign. I knew it wasn't true."

And yet, "I'm sitting there thinking there's videotape of the car," she says. "And wondering, why would they lie to me?" For the briefest of moments, "they were making me question myself. I hated that, but I had no idea what to believe."

By now, Melissa's brother had arrived at the jail, as had Kevin's father. Chad was on the phone to his father, desperately urging Kevin and Melissa to leave. According to the sheriff's summary of the interrogation, when Curt Fox told the detectives that he wanted them to stop questioning his son, Swearengen replied, "Kevin is twenty-seven years old and he came to the investigation office voluntarily." Kevin claims he asked for an attorney and his father several times, but was given the same response: "[The detectives] said, 'You're twenty-seven years old. You don't need your father.'"

By midnight that night, Kevin says, the detectives had dropped all pretense of friendliness. "We know you killed your daughter," they said, according to the lawsuit. The only way to dissuade them, he says they told him, would be to take a polygraph test.

At 12:20 A.M. on October 27, according to the detectives' summary of events, Detective Richard Williams arrived to administer the exam. According to the lawsuit, Williams told Kevin that if he passed he would be cleared in his daughter's death; if he failed, he would be charged with murder.

The exam began at just before one in the morning and took a little over an hour. When it was over, Williams told Kevin that he had failed. As for the murder of Riley, "You did it," the lawsuit quotes Williams as saying. "It's all right to say you did it." Melissa, who was also told that Kevin had failed, demanded to see the results. She was led into Kevin's room where, she claims, Williams showed her a computer screen. "See all that red?" she quotes him as saying. "That's 'failed.'"

At this point, Melissa says, she knew something wasn't right. She put her hand on Kevin's leg. "Everything's going to be OK," she told him. "I didn't do it, Melissa," he answered back, looking her in the eye. "I swear to God I didn't do it." Suddenly, she says, Ed Hayes "got right in my face. He yelled, 'Your fucking husband killed your fucking daughter and he doesn't love you or her.'"

"I started shaking and crying," she says. "I had never even met him before and he was just screaming in my face. I had never been treated like that before. I told him, 'Don't you talk like that about my husband and family.'" From that moment, Melissa says, she never doubted Kevin. "They thought they had me convinced," she says. "When I reached out to Kevin and said, 'I believe you,' I think they got pissed."

The detectives then took Kevin back to the interrogation room and resumed the questioning, according to the lawsuit. Hayes made Kevin watch as he filled out an arrest sheet for first-degree murder. Guilfoyle, meanwhile, began banging handcuffs on the table in front of Kevin. "You don't have much time," Hayes warned. "If I finish the sheet, you are being charged with first-degree murder with thirty years to life."

At one point, according to the lawsuit, Hayes leaned close and told Kevin that he "knew people" at the jail, "and would 'make sure' that Kevin was 'fucked' every day unless he told them what they wanted to hear." Ruettiger straddled Kevin's legs, pressing his testicles into Kevin's knees. He grabbed the back of Kevin's shirt and pulled his face close. "Your family doesn't love you," he shouted. "So just say you did it." Finally, Kevin claims in the suit, he was shown pictures of his dead daughter, her mouth still covered with duct tape, nude from the waist down, taken moments after she had been pulled from the creek. "Riley is in the room with you right now," the lawsuit quotes Guilfoyle as saying. "She is in pain and needs closure."

Today, in recalling this part of the interrogation, Kevin weeps. "I didn't know what had happened to her," he says. "When I saw the pictures . . . I don't even know how to describe it. When you see your daughter dead, with dirt and mud on her face. . . ." His voice trails off. "But the awful truth is," he says, "I wanted to see more. I wanted to see if I could find anything in those pictures that would help me figure out for myself what had happened, who had done this to my baby."

Kevin's account of the interrogation continues: Swearengen burst into the room, out of breath and saying he had just talked to Tomczak. "Hurry back. I can help this kid if he acts now," the detective quoted the state's attorney as saying. "I can make a deal for him."

Kevin says that Swearengen suggested the same "accident" scenario that he had proposed to Melissa nearly nine hours earlier. "It's now or never," the lawsuit claims the detective said. "Say it was an accident. Get your help from the state's attorney so you can go home to your family. If you pass it up, you will spend your life in prison. If you say it was an accident, it's involuntary manslaughter with a three to five year sentence. You'll serve half. Go home now on bond."

Promising a suspect leniency to confess is forbidden under Illinois law, and the detectives have denied in court pleadings that they did so. Since the prelude to Kevin's confession was not videotaped—a law requiring interrogations be videotaped would not go into effect for several more months—the purported promise pits detectives' word against Kevin's.

It was now after 6:00 A.M. Kevin had been up for more than twenty-four hours and he'd had little to eat. He had been undergoing questioning for nearly twelve hours. The terms of the "offer" echoed in his head. He knew he was innocent, he says. But if he could get out on bond, he could straighten this mess out.

At 8:32 A.M., detectives turned on the video camera and began to tape Kevin's statement. According to the sheriff's summary, this is what he said: He came home at about 1:30 A.M., ate a snack, and then watched television, including an adult video. Around 2:15, he went to the bathroom and swung the door open quickly, striking Riley and knocking her down. The girl appeared "lifeless," and Kevin thought she was dead. Panicking, he scooped her up and carried her to his car, retrieving some duct tape from the back. According to the summary, Kevin thought of driving to his mother-in-law's house, or perhaps taking Riley to the hospital. Instead, he decided to make her death look like an abduction. He duct-taped his daughter's mouth and bound her wrists together with tape. He drove to a bridge over Forsythe Creek and then carried the girl down a muddy bank, slipping on the way down. Before putting the girl in the water, he inserted his finger inside her to make it look like she had been sexually assaulted. He then went home, cried for a while, and went to sleep.

A copy of the tape has not been released to the public, but Zellner has viewed it and she claims Kevin's manner is vague and halting. "They were putting words in his mouth," she claims. Rather than providing a running narrative, she says, Kevin often simply answered "yes" or "no" to the detectives' questions. Beyond that, she says, the details left several obvious questions unanswered. Why would a father with CPR training make no attempt to revive his daughter? Why was no duct tape found? If he slipped in the mud, why were his clothes not muddy? How could a lightweight bathroom door knock a little girl out so completely that she appeared dead? Why was no blood or other physical evidence found in the Ford Escape? And, most telling, how could detectives ignore that Kevin had not provided a single piece of information that only the killer would have known, such as the whereabouts of Riley's capri pants?

All told, Kevin was interrogated that night for more than fourteen hours; only twenty minutes were taped. Just before he was booked and taken to jail, Kevin says, the last thing he heard was the sound of the detectives in the hallway, laughing and congratulating themselves.

After being photographed and fingerprinted, Kevin arrived at the Will County Adult Detention Center less than a mile from the sheriff's office, spent and sick with anxiety. The enormity of what had just happened, what he had just done, had not yet sunk in. But the sense of betrayal he felt at the hands of the detectives, especially when he learned that he would not, indeed, be "bonded out" to go home and straighten things out, was crushing. Not only was he not being charged with involuntary manslaughter, as he believed he'd been promised, but he was now facing first-degree murder, a charge that carried the possibility of the death penalty.

It had all happened so quickly—had seemed to make so much sense in the moment. Experts on interrogation and false confessions say that's not uncommon. They describe a series of emotional and intellectual manipulations designed to break down even the strongest of personalities. Northwestern University School of Law's Center on Wrongful Convictions reports that 60 percent of the forty-two wrongful murder convictions since 1970 in Illinois have rested in whole or in part on false confessions. Kevin knew virtually nothing about such statistics or the theories of interrogation techniques. But it slowly dawned on him that the whole thing—the supposed sympathy of the detectives, the "friendship" of "Scott," the seemingly cordial questioning—had been a ruse. Now, just a handful of minutes after giving his statement, he sat behind a Plexiglas window with a phone in his hand, shaking his head and crying as his older brother, Chad, and Kathleen Zellner watched helplessly and offered what comfort they could.

Tall and striking, with dark brown shoulder-length hair, Zellner has made a name for herself by winning wrongful conviction cases. In one resolved in December 2001, she helped free three men who had falsely confessed to the 1986 murder and rape of a Rush University medical student named Lori Roscetti.

That morning in the Will County jail, Zellner watched the interaction between the two brothers closely. Chad recalls the moment vividly: "Kevin looked at me and said, 'I didn't do this. They tricked me.' Immediately, we both started crying. I looked at him square in the eyes the whole time, and I knew my brother was not lying to me."

Today, Zellner says that what impressed her was Kevin's immediate denial of the crime. "It wasn't like there was any time to cook up a story," she says. "Within minutes he was sitting there saying he felt like they'd tricked him, they'd lied to him." Zellner says she also was struck by the unwavering belief in Kevin's innocence by the family, particularly Melissa. "I've had other families come in a situation like this and they've had some hesitancy—'Well, he's always been kind of troubled but I don't think he'd do anything violent.' But this family's response—and I have to say when I met Kevin I understood—was that it isn't conceivable that someone like Kevin Fox could hurt anybody."

Shortly after the bond hearing, Tomczak, Will County Sheriff Paul Kaupas, and other authorities held a press conference outside the Wilmington police station. Kaupas acknowledged that the detectives had had no substantial new evidence when they called in Kevin. Instead, going on a "gut feeling," he said, they "rolled bones" in the hope they could elicit a confession. Among the questions the two men fielded were queries about whether politics influenced the timing of the interrogation. Absolutely not, Kaupas said. "We really tried to stay the course," he told reporters. "We didn't want to turn it into another JonBenét Ramsey case."

The people of Wilmington seemed to divide into two camps. Most of those who knew Kevin and the rest of the Fox family believed in his innocence. Many of them questioned the confession. Many other people assumed he was guilty. Some expressed bitter feelings of betrayal to reporters. "He watched everybody search for his child the whole day," one woman, a ten-year resident of Wilmington, told the Chicago Sun-Times. "I feel sad for the whole community that we were betrayed." Another resident told the paper, "It's what a lot of people suspected."

The Fox family expressed staunch support of Kevin. Melissa, describing her husband as a wonderful father, made it clear immediately that she believed he had been railroaded. A statement by Kevin himself saying he had been tricked into confessing was posted on a Web site three days after the interrogation.

With bond set at $25 million, the family decided, on Zellner's advice, not to try to get Kevin out, but to put their money toward clearing his name. "I hated leaving him there," Chad says. "But she was right."

Meanwhile, several statements by Tomczak, which later proved unfounded, cast another shadow over Kevin. The state's attorney was quoted in the Chicago Tribune on October 29 as saying "the evidence shows us that [Riley] was sexually abused during life." The claim triggered an investigation from a representative of the Illinois Department of Children and

Family Services. More than six months later, DCFS reported finding no evidence to support the allegation. Riley's pediatrician has said there was never a hint of prior sexual abuse.

Also, Tomczak alleged during Kevin's initial hearing that "the autopsy report indicated [Riley] was alive and struggling when placed in the water." This gruesome detail helped form the basis for the death penalty charge. Later, Scott Denton, the forensic pathologist who performed the autopsy on Riley, signed an affidavit swearing that he had never talked to Tomczak and did not share his opinion about Riley's being alive when she was placed in the water.

On November 2, six days after Kevin's arrest, Glasgow defeated Tomczak 121,000 votes to 112,000 to win the state's attorney's race. Chad and Zellner viewed the change in office with a wary eye. Glasgow seemed like a fair man, but he had given no indication that he planned to drop charges against Kevin. Indeed, he had promised to press ahead with the death penalty.

With the possibility of a trial, Zellner began to reinvestigate the case. She initially hired Ernie Rizzo, the big, blustery, and controversial private eye. With his help, an investigative team began to reenact each element of Kevin's statement to test it for plausibility. They first tested where Kevin said he had left the body—according to his confession, he had placed it in the water at the base of the Kahler Bridge, slipping once as he made his way down the muddy embankment. But when one of Zellner's assistants tried to do so with a forty-pound bag—the approximate weight of Riley at the time of the murder—the bag was blocked by debris. When the bag was thrown from the bridge, however, it twice floated to the spot where the body had been found.

Zellner also reexamined the bathroom door that had supposedly hit Riley. "That door was paper thin," Zellner says. "And you'd have to have hit her on the head with a hammer to get the effect" Kevin described in the interrogation. (Tomczak later accused Kevin of lying during his confession—concocting the story of the bathroom door to hide his guilt in molesting Riley.) Zellner also began looking into an element that seemed to have been forgotten: the DNA evidence taken from Riley.

Meanwhile, the family launched a public-relations counteroffensive against the barrage of media coverage suggesting Kevin's guilt. As they had wanted to do all along, the family began to offer a reward, for twenty thousand dollars. Chad Fox took the lead, assuming the role of family spokesman and coordinating other family interviews, including an unequivocal expression of support by Melissa. For Chad, the fight to clear his kid brother's name became a crusade. "I knew he was innocent, and I knew my family was in for the fight of its life," he says.

Christmas passed with Kevin still in jail, then New Year's, and Kevin's twenty-eighth birthday on January 4. He had been moved to protective custody, but that didn't protect him from threats on his life and threats of being raped. "People would walk by my cell and sit in front and look at me," he says. "I felt like a zoo animal."

On the outside, the stress of trying to free Kevin weighed heavily on the Fox family, especially Chad. He began having nightmares in which he would see Kevin strapped to a gurney, about to receive a lethal injection. "I felt as if I had aged five years since Kevin's arrest," he says.

At a hearing on January 28, 2005, Will County prosecutors turned over several police reports to Zellner and her defense team. As for the long-awaited DNA evidence originally taken from Riley, the news was not good for Kevin. As far as Glasgow knew, the little girl's rape kits had not contained sufficient genetic material to yield a usable profile. The FBI would be returning the DNA evidence within a week, he said.

What neither Zellner nor Glasgow apparently realized was that the FBI had not tested Riley's DNA. In fact, a day after the election, an order had come from the Will County Sheriff's Office halting any testing of DNA evidence in the Riley Fox murder. The order, it would later be revealed, had come from Detective Ed Hayes.

Zellner returned to her office facing the daunting prospect of going to trial with a client who had confessed. "The only way to guarantee that Kevin Fox would not be executed was to find DNA that excluded him with 100-percent certainty," she says. And that she did not have.

But several days later, while reviewing the state crime lab's report, Zellner puzzled over the "inconclusive" finding for the presence of male saliva. She phoned a forensic scientist, who explained what that meant: the state crime lab simply didn't have the sophisticated capabilities that would be needed to test properly for the substance.

Buoyed over the finding, Zellner secured a court order to have the material tested by a private lab—Bode Technology Group in Virginia. The judge ordered that the genetic material be sent right away. After three weeks, however, the lab still had not received Riley's DNA. On April 5, Zellner says, she learned why. The DNA had been sent to the state crime lab, not Virginia, and then returned to Joliet. The person behind the mix-up, the lawsuit alleges, was Ed Hayes.

The delay enraged the family. Worse, when Bode finally got the DNA, the family was told testing would take two months, and that the chances of finding male saliva in Riley's DNA were slim because there was so little genetic material to test.

The weeks dragged by. Then, on June 7, came the answer. The lab had found a man's saliva—just enough to extract a full DNA profile. The next day, Kevin Fox's DNA was compared with the sample. He was not a match, Bode reported. Not even close. When Zellner told Chad, the older brother laid his head down on a table and wept.

The Fox family wanted Kevin's immediate release. But Bode, insisting on following protocol, said they'd have to wait for the final report. At last, eight days later, Zellner stood near a fax machine in Glasgow's office. The lab had said the results would arrive around 6:00 P.M. The machine clicked on at a couple of minutes before the hour. Glasgow would later say he was "shocked" at the results. But he agreed with Zellner. Kevin would have to be freed.

Nine days later, Chad and Stacy packed more than one hundred T-shirts bearing the words "Test Before Arrest" and "376 Days of a Killer on the Loose" in bold black lettering into a van that Zellner had rented for the occasion. Then they drove to the Will County courthouse, where Kevin had first been charged with murdering his daughter. On this day, however, the mood was festive. Outside the courtroom, more than a hundred friends and family greeted them. Once the hearing was under way, Glasgow came right to the point: the DNA resulted in an "absolute exclusion of Kevin Fox as a donor," the prosecutor told the judge. "The people lack the probable cause to continue to hold him on these charges and would be unable to meet our burden of proof beyond a reasonable doubt." (The DNA was subsequently retested at a different laboratory, and the results again excluded Kevin.)

As Glasgow spoke, Kevin began to weep. By the time the state's attorney had finished, Kevin's shoulders were shaking. During his stay in jail he had lost more than twenty pounds. He had suffered threats and the ridicule of guards, according to his lawsuit. Now he was free. When Judge Dan Rozak dismissed the case, the courtroom exploded into applause and cheering. After a brief reunion with Melissa and Tyler, Kevin emerged from the jail with his arms raised in triumph and stood before a mob scene of cameras and well-wishers. What did he want to do on his first night out, he was asked. "Spend it with my wife and son," he said, something he had dreamed about "every day, every single day" since the ordeal had begun.

At a press conference, Glasgow stopped short of directly criticizing Tom-czak, but the implication was clear: he thought the case had been mis-handled, particularly when it came to the long delay in DNA testing. "So when you send something to the lab, you monitor it," the *Tribune* quoted Glasgow as saying. "The state's attorney's office at that point needs to get involved and say, 'Wait a minute. We've got to get this to the laboratory so that we can process it quickly.'"

After pizza and champagne at Zellner's office, Kevin, Melissa, and Tyler spent the evening at Chad and Stacy's apartment in Chicago, safely away from the media. That night, before turning in, Chad peeked into the guest bedroom, where Kevin, Melissa, and Tyler had already crashed. There he saw three pairs of feet poking out of the bottom of the bedcovers. "I don't think I've ever seen a more beautiful sight," he says.

Later, however, he would reflect on the bittersweet nature of the day. "My niece was kidnapped and murdered from her own home," he said; "no answers from the cops for months, a deliberate railroading of my brother, my family nearly falls apart because of the sadness and stress, the terrible perception by the public of us defending Kevin. . . . Life will never be the same for any of us."

The town of Wilmington, struggling to heal, tends a small garden that hon-ors Riley's memory. Set just off a playground around the corner from the house where she disappeared, the garden includes a statue of a young girl with butterflies alighting on her raised hands. Kevin and Melissa have vis-ited it many times, as they have Riley's grave in Wilmington's Oakwood Cemetery. "It's hard," Kevin says. "You look at a stone with your daughter's picture, knowing that her body is in the dirt rather than in your arms. . . . But we feel closer to her when we go there."

The couple, however, moved out of Wilmington. They live in Naper-ville now, a place they feel has given them a fresh start. "I used to love it," Kevin says of his hometown. "But I lost so much there. The only reason I go back now is to visit Riley's stone."

Despite the elimination of all charges against Kevin, some still wonder how a child could be abducted from under a father's nose. One study sug-gests that, though rare, it happens. From 1997 to 1999, more than fifty thou-sand children in the United States were abducted by persons other than family members, according to a 2002 study funded by the U.S. Department of Justice. Eighteen of those children were stolen from the home.

Meanwhile, the mystery of what happened to Riley Fox remains. The few clues that might have pointed to other suspects were either discounted or ignored. Police have tested the DNA found in Riley against every male in the Fox family, as well as numerous people in the neighborhood, including several previously convicted sex offenders, with no luck.

In the sorrow-filled twilight of their little girl's death, in the aftermath of an ordeal that could have sent Kevin Fox to death row, Kevin and Melissa have searched for meaning in their anguish. On a recent April evening, however, their attentions are devoted to gentler undertakings: their new baby girl, Teagan, who was born on March 8. Though the girl has Riley's apple cheeks and sweet disposition, neither parent would ever look on the child as a replacement for their lost daughter. Still, both wept when they learned Melissa was carrying a girl. "In a way, though, it's hard," Kevin admits. "Because I think to myself what Riley would be doing right now. She'd be a great big sister."

For a long time, the family could not bear to look at photos of Chad's wedding, of Kevin in his tuxedo with the single red rose, of Riley and Tyler sleeping under the table. Harder still was the family portrait with Riley in her princess dress and white satin slippers. On this night, however, leafing through a picture book, with Kevin holding Teagan, and Tyler peering over Melissa's shoulder, they can smile when they reach the photograph of the happy family they once were, when the biggest worries were a best man's toast and a little girl wanting to stand beside her daddy. And they turn the page.

Epilogue

On December 20, 2007, a U.S. district court jury awarded Kevin and Melissa Fox $15.5 million for violations of their civil rights. The killer had not been found when this volume went to press.

DENNIS DEONTE GREEN

Exhausted, he confessed to a crime in which he'd
actually been a victim

APRIL WITT

LANHAM, MARYLAND

Shivering in his summer shirtsleeves in the cold, cramped room across a tiny table from a homicide detective, seventeen-year-old Dennis Deonte Green figured he'd be home as soon as he set the record straight.

Thus, according to police records, at about 2:20 P.M. on August 24, 2000, the Bowie High School student signed a Miranda waiver and proceeded to tell a Prince George's County detective that late the night before he had been standing outside his Lanham home, talking with several buddies, when a band of strangers approached, pointed guns at them, and forced them to the ground.

The attackers were looking for revenge. Someone in the neighborhood had squirted a teenage girl in the face with a water pistol a few hours before. The girl's older brother and a few of their friends confronted Green and his friends as payback for the prank.

A scuffle and a chase ended with a volley of gunshots fired blindly in the dark. One of the avengers who didn't have a gun, Reginald Woodard Jr., a clerk at a mall music store, fell dying. Two others were wounded.

Green said that he and his friends had been surprised by the attack, hadn't been armed, and didn't fire the shots. He said he hadn't seen who did the shooting. It was too dark. But for the homicide detectives interrogating Green the day after the shooting, his story didn't add up. Two groups of youths collided in the night and three members of one group were shot. It seemed clear to them that the shots must have come from the group that emerged unscathed.

The detectives pressed Green and some of his friends—who were in adjoining interrogation rooms—to confess, Green said.

"The cop said, 'We heard that you had a .22,'" Green recalled.

Green was stunned, he said. If the cops were so confused that they thought he was the shooter instead of a victim, then he needed a lawyer after all, he decided.

"I had been asking to get a lawyer when it appeared they thought I did it for real, and they weren't going to give up until they got what they wanted," Green said. "They said, 'You are not getting a phone call until I hear what I want to hear.'"

Green was relieved when a man wearing a jacket emblazoned "forensics" entered the interrogation room, swabbed the teenager's hand and said he was performing a scientific test to determine if Green had fired a gun recently. Finally, they'd believe that he didn't shoot anyone, Green recalled thinking.

"When they come back and the test is negative, I'll forgive you and then I can just go home," Green remembered telling a detective.

The "test" apparently was a bit of interrogation-room theatrics designed to persuade Green to confess. Green said a detective told him that the test showed he'd not only fired a gun, he'd used a .22—a degree of specificity that a gunshot residue test doesn't provide.

Convinced that police were trying to set him up, Green said he wanted a lie detector test. According to Green, the detective then told him, "All right, but if this lie detector comes back wrong, I'm going to kick your ass."

The same detective backed him into a corner, screamed that it was his fault Woodard lay dead in the morgue, and poked him hard several times, Green recalled.

After that, Green said, he was too intimidated to take the test or ask again for a lawyer or phone call.

"I know my limit," Green said. "I wasn't saying nothing. That's like asking for it, to get beat up."

In other interrogation rooms nearby, Green's friends also were under pressure to implicate themselves and each other in the shooting, according to records and interviews.

One steadfastly maintained that none of the youths who had been standing outside Green's house had guns when the avengers attacked, said Green's attorney, Michael Worthy. One caved in and told police that Green had been armed and met the attack with gunfire, Green said.

Disheartened, Green figured that if people were going to lie about him to save themselves, he'd toss the blame back at them. Green wrote a second statement in which he suggested vaguely that a couple of his friends might have had guns, after all, because when the attack began he saw them reach for their waistbands.

By the time Green gave the second statement, he was tired, he said. He was cold. He had to go to the bathroom. He had no idea what would happen to him next. He was scared.

The last detective to enter the interrogation room brought Green a soda, gave him a blanket, and escorted him down the hall to use the bathroom.

"I figured he was decent, maybe I can get through to him," Green said.

So Green tried once more to say that he hadn't shot anybody.

This detective seemed very sympathetic, but then he provided Green with a bit of unsolicited legal advice, Green said: sticking with his story wouldn't play well in a courtroom, but he'd have a good claim of self-defense if he confessed.

"He came in and was like, 'They know you did it. What's it going to look like when you go to court and you are still saying you didn't do it? We can get you a good self-defense claim' or something like that," Green recalled. "He was like, 'You might not even see any time.' He was like, 'Them guys came around there, and they were trying to get you. They probably were trying to kill you. So you pulled out your gun and said, "I'm not going to let them get me first." So you shot them.'"

Green said he had no will left to resist.

"I had been cracked by then," Green said.

"I'd been sitting in that room for hours. When I seen that he still believed whatever was circulating with the rest of the cops, I don't know, I just gave up. I didn't feel like going through no more. I started answering questions the way they wanted. Because they wouldn't let me make no phone call.

"I kept thinking, in my mind, once I get out and make a phone call and I get a lawyer, he's going to prove the truth anyway. When I get out, I'm going to change my story and say: 'Look, they lied, they made me write this.'"

Green wrote a third statement. In this one, he said that he had a gun—a .22-caliber revolver—and that he fired at his attackers without aiming, dropped the gun, and ran. By the time he was answering the detective's follow-up questions, he was too tired to sit up. "I was so tired that at one point, I was laying down on the floor," he said.

At 6:25 A.M. on August 25—some sixteen hours after Prince George's homicide detectives took him into custody—Green appeared before a court commissioner who informed him that he'd been charged with one count of first-degree murder and two counts of first-degree assault. Police also charged one of Green's friends, Chris Evans, with Woodard's murder.

Six weeks later, the charges against Green and Evans were dropped.

Prince George's County Assistant State's Attorney Mary Crawford did her own investigation, walking the crime scene with a witness, diagramming the complicated chain of events, and repeatedly reviewing the case with her colleagues.

"I had additional evidence that was uncovered after the arrest warrants were obtained," Crawford said. "Based on additional information, we dismissed the charges against Mr. Green and Mr. Evans. We always try to prosecute the people who we believe are responsible for the crime."

Ballistics showed that the gun that killed Woodard was a .22-caliber semiautomatic, not the revolver that Green had described in his confession, according to Worthy, Green's lawyer. Statements from witnesses and analysis of the angle from which Woodard and the two wounded were shot made it clear that Green could not have been the shooter.

Why did Green confess to a crime he had not committed?

He said no one could understand without having been in the interrogation room.

"What's so bad about the room is you don't know what's coming next," Green said. "You don't get to go to the other side of the door and see who is out there, what they're preparing next. You've just got to sit in the room and wait, and talk to yourself.

"The time goes so slow that it's almost like solitary confinement. You haven't got anybody but yourself in there. So you pray for somebody to come in the room, even if it is a cop that's coming in there to holler at you. You don't know what's going on other than what they say. I couldn't contact nobody so I had no help. Being in the room, you are like, 'Man, I've got to get out.'"

After Green's release, members of the avenging group have pleaded guilty to charges of carrying handguns and assaulting Green and his friends— exactly what Green tried to tell his interrogators had happened.

Green's name is still listed in a criminal file, but with a new designation: "victim."

Epilogue

A third man charged in the case after Green's release was acquitted following a jury trial.

INQUISITION

More than six centuries ago, in an ecclesiastical manuscript known as the *Directorium Inquisitorum*, the inquisitor general of Aragon, Nicolas Eymeric, prescribed a protocol for extracting confessions from suspected enemies of the faith: First, the alleged heretics were threatened with torture. Second, they were taken to the torture chamber. Third, they were shown the instruments of torture. Only after scrupulous adherence to those steps was torture of the physical kind allowed.

The threat of physical pain usually achieved the desired result, rendering the final step unnecessary—a point memorably made in Bertolt Brecht's *Life of Galileo*: "He is not to be tortured. . . . At the very most, he may be shown the torture instruments," the Pope tells the Inquisitor, who replies, "That will be adequate, Your Holiness. Mr. Galileo understands machinery."

The rack, thumbscrews, and other medieval instruments of torture are not found in modern American interrogation chambers. They have been replaced with an armory of psychological pressures, often involving polygraph machines and voice-stress analyzers as props to break suspects' will to resist. Among proven effective instruments are threats of execution and, in terrorist investigations, extraordinary rendition—transferring suspects to countries likely to employ physical torture.

Thus, while the torture devices may have changed, the protocol prescribed by the *Directorium Inquisitorum* hasn't. The fundamental idea is simply to persuade suspects that it's better to confess than to persist in futile denials—and face a draconian consequence.

Some confessions extracted with modern inquisitorial techniques are true. Others aren't, as the following articles demonstrate. But, absent substantial corroboration, they're all unreliable.

The story of Joseph Jesse Dick Jr., Derek Tice, Danial Williams, and Eric Wilson in the "Unrequited Innocence" section of this anthology (page 415) is a further example of an inquisitorial confession.

ABDALLAH HIGAZY

Facing rendition to Egypt, he promptly chose to confess

JIM DWYER
NEW YORK, NEW YORK

This month, Abdallah Higazy managed to crawl from the landslide of forgotten history on a slow-motion journey toward the truth.

Higazy, now thirty-six, was briefly and wrongly known as a mysterious figure who fled a hotel room directly across Church Street from the World Trade Center on the morning of September 11, 2001, leaving behind a Koran, an Egyptian passport, and an aviation radio that might have allowed him to communicate with the hijacked airliners that flew into the towers. A security guard reported the discovery of these items.

After first adamantly denying any knowledge of the aviation radio, and then sitting in solitary confinement for ten days, Higazy finally conceded. It was his radio, he confessed. He was charged with making false statements.

One month after Higazy was locked up, the story took a sharp turn.

An airline pilot walked into the hotel asking for the very same radio, saying that he had left it behind in his room on the morning of September 11. The pilot, a United States citizen from the Midwest, knew nothing about Higazy. On further inquiry, the hotel security guard then admitted that he had lied about where he had found the radio. He later pleaded guilty to making false statements to the FBI.

And so it was discovered that Higazy, an engineering student at Brooklyn Polytech who was being put up at the hotel by the federal agency that was sponsoring him, had confessed to something he had not done, and to a crime that had not taken place.

Why?

Only now are some answers emerging from a civil rights lawsuit brought by Higazy that has been grinding through the federal courts. In a decision released two weeks ago that allows Higazy's lawsuit to proceed, an appeals court said that if his claims are all true, then a jury could conclude that his confession was obtained by the force of threats.

So far, all parties agree on one thing: a fear of brutal handling and outright torture by Egyptian security forces loomed over the interrogation when Higazy made his false confession.

Higazy says that when he was questioned on December 27, 2001, an FBI agent raised the specter of Egyptian security forces' tormenting his family to get him to drop his denials about the radio.

The government says that no such threat was made. While Egyptian security was discussed during the interrogation, Justice Department lawyers said, that was only because Higazy had raised the subject. Moreover, the government said, he could have stopped the questioning at any time to speak with his lawyer.

The decision released on October 19 quoted from sealed testimony by Michael Templeton, the FBI agent who questioned Higazy. Templeton said he did not threaten Higazy. But, the ruling noted, Agent Templeton was aware of the fierce reputation of the Egyptian security forces.

"Templeton later admitted that he knew how the Egyptian security forces operated: 'that they had a security service, that their laws are different than ours, that they are probably allowed to do things in that country where they don't advise people of their rights . . .'" Judge Rosemary Pooler wrote.

Higazy said he felt utterly cornered during his questioning, according to the decision. The agent told him that if he did not cooperate, the authorities would "make sure that Egyptian security gives my family hell," Higazy said. "I knew that I couldn't prove my innocence, and I knew that my family was in danger."

The agent, however, has given a different account, according to an internal Justice Department report. He was trying to administer a polygraph test that had been requested by Higazy and his lawyer. Agent Templeton "stated that he asked Higazy about the Egyptian security services in order to alleviate any concerns that might be a barrier to Higazy's successful completion of the examination. The polygrapher stated that this was the only time during the examination that the Egyptian security services was mentioned."

The FBI does not tape its interviews and interrogations, so there is no known recording of the encounter between Agent Templeton and Higazy. The appeals court ruling may mean that a jury will ultimately decide who is telling the truth about the events of almost six years ago.

"We're now going to get disclosure and a trial on whether or not his constitutional rights were violated," said Jonathan Abady, a lawyer for Higazy.

As for Higazy, he went on to complete the engineering program at Brooklyn Polytech. He is now teaching computer engineering in Cairo, Abady said, and he had a simple reaction to the news that his case will go ahead: "relief."

Epilogue

A federal civil case brought on Abdallah Higazy's behalf against Michael Templeton and the Millennium Hotel was pending as this volume went to press.

CHRISTOPHER OCHOA

To avoid a death sentence, he implicated himself
and a friend, with tragic results

ALAN BERLOW

AUSTIN, TEXAS

At 9:55 P.M. on February 27, 1991, an inmate named Richard Danzinger at a Texas prison near Amarillo was brutally assaulted by another inmate, who threw him to the ground and kicked him in the head repeatedly with his steel-tipped boots. Danzinger was taken to a nearby hospital where emergency surgery was performed and part of his brain was removed. The other guy, Armando Gutierrez, was serving an eighteen-year sentence for assaulting a police officer, and had an additional twenty-five years put on his sentence for nearly killing Danzinger. And as it turns out, Gutierrez had thought Danzinger was someone else entirely. He'd jumped the wrong man.

So too, it now appears, did the state of Texas. Two of them, in fact.

At the time Danzinger was attacked, he and another man, his onetime roommate and friend, Christopher Ochoa, were serving life sentences for the brutal 1988 murder of twenty-year-old Nancy DePriest, the mother of a fifteen-month-old baby girl. According to the sordid testimony in Danzinger's trial, the two men repeatedly raped DePriest at an Austin Pizza Hut where she was working, including twice after she'd been shot in the back of the head.

Now a third man, Achim Josef Marino, insists that he—not Ochoa, and not Danzinger—raped and murdered DePriest. And one DNA test showed that DNA evidence discovered on DePriest did not match Ochoa's or Danzinger's. It did, however, match Marino, who is serving a life sentence for aggravated robbery with a deadly weapon and a handful of other felonies. Sources close to the investigation confirm that there is no evidence that Danzinger or Ochoa ever met Marino.

Marino says he has been trying to come clean for more than four years. As reported by *Salon,* Marino sent a letter to Texas Governor George W.

Bush two years ago confessing to the crime, and insisting Bush was "morally obligated" to notify attorneys for Danzinger and Ochoa. Bush's office filed the letter away but apparently notified no one, not the lawyers for Danzinger or Ochoa or the police or the district attorney.

Bush's office might not have been the only one to ignore Marino's plea. Marino says he wrote to Bush because earlier confessions sent to the police, the American Civil Liberties Union, and the *Austin American-Statesman* had failed to elicit any response. Ochoa's attorneys provided *Salon* with a copy of a six-page letter, dated February 5, 1996, that Marino says he sent to the *Statesman*. In it he confesses to the rape and murder of DePriest.

He also, in digressions, writes of how he'd been "possessed by a spirit" that appeared to him as "a serpent dragon type of animal" when he was a child. He discusses his hatred of his mother while growing up—trying to kill her on one occasion—and how he emerged in 1988, after five years in prison, hating "people in general, and women in particular." Eventually, Marino circles back to his main point, insisting that he was writing the *American-Statesman* for "Danzinger and Ochoa sake [sic]" and, as he did in his subsequent letter to Bush, he appealed to the paper to contact their lawyers.

The police, it turns out, did look into Marino's letter in March or April 1996, according to sources familiar with the investigation, and appear close—four years later—to completing an investigation that might free both Ochoa and Danzinger. Sources also say that assertions Marino makes in his letters—that keys from the Pizza Hut and two bank moneybags from the restaurant could be picked up from his parents' home—have also proven true.

This comes amid a major review by the police and Austin district attorney of four hundred cases prior to 1996—when DNA testing began being regularly used in trials—to see how many may have resulted in wrongful convictions. It also coincides with a presidential campaign starring a Texas governor who has repeatedly defended the quality of the Texas criminal justice system, insisting that its use of the death penalty under his watch has been error-free.

Bush's only comment on this particular matter, to ABC News: "Marino's case was fully looked at by the Austin Police Department." Perhaps. But the issue is not "Marino's case" but the cases of two ostensibly innocent men Marino pleaded with the governor—unsuccessfully—to address. The reexamination of those cases, by all accounts, is expected to lead to a completely different conclusion than that reached by police nearly twelve years ago.

Looking back on the Danzinger-Ochoa trial, Robert A. Perkins, the presiding judge, insists that "any jury hearing that testimony would have found those two guys guilty." Now it looks like Danzinger and Ochoa may turn out to prove that even a case that seems error-free can wind up dead wrong.

Ochoa and Danzinger had met at the Austin Pizza Hut where they both worked, not far from the one where Nancy DePriest was employed. They were picked up a day after toasting DePriest's memory at the Pizza Hut, according to Danzinger's trial record. Employees at the restaurant, finding their behavior odd, called and reported it to the police. Three days later, Christopher Ochoa, twenty-two, confessed to the crime, and he became the state's star witness against his friend and coworker, Danzinger. Judge Perkins describes the testimony by Ochoa as "very compelling." Not only was it emotional, but it contained details police said only a witness to the crime could have known.

Now, Ochoa and his lawyers insist that his confession and his testimony were a fabrication coerced by police who had given him a Hobson's choice. "He was made to feel that he was doomed one way or the other," says Keith Findley, a lawyer with the Wisconsin Innocence Project who is working on the case. "His doom could either be death or it could be [life in] prison."

But with a life sentence came another ugly reality. The police were convinced that Ochoa and Danzinger had committed the crime together, and in exchange for avoiding a death sentence, Ochoa had to take Danzinger down with him. "That was part of the plea bargain. He had to testify against Danzinger," Findley said.

Danzinger always refused to plead. He maintained his innocence throughout his 1990 trial, insisting he had no idea why Ochoa implicated him. The homicide detectives who testified against him were lying, he said. Ochoa maintained his innocence in conversations with family members; his attorneys say he would not assert the claim publicly for fear the state would try to execute him.

"He said, 'They made me confess and how am I going to prove my innocence now? It's my word against theirs,'" says Ronald Navejos, Ochoa's uncle and closest friend.

But if Ochoa's confession and his testimony at Danzinger's trial were all lies, where did he get the facts—and the story line—that allowed him to appear completely credible to the judge and jury? Ochoa didn't just say he and Danzinger raped and murdered the victim but described Danzinger's elaborate plan for the robbery, such as how they planned to meet at a McDonald's near the Pizza Hut at seven o'clock the morning of the murder; how they entered the crime scene by a side door using a key Danzinger had obtained; their conversation with the victim, who was cutting pizza dough when they entered; and how the two men bound her, gagged her, and raped and sodomized her eight different times.

Ochoa's lawyers say he got his story line and the key crime scene facts from the police. "There isn't any way [Ochoa] would have known the facts about the case unless they told him the facts about the case," says Bill Allison, an Austin attorney representing Ochoa.

Allison doesn't believe the police necessarily fabricated their case against Ochoa, but that they "violated every rule of taking down a statement that you can violate." Ochoa asked for a lawyer the first day he was interrogated but was denied one on the ground that he hadn't been charged with anything. "The invocation of asking for a lawyer should have stopped the interrogation at that point," says Allison, who claims the police were "feeding him [Ochoa] facts about the case" as they questioned him. Allison also alleges that a critical tape recording of Ochoa's interrogation, occurring just prior to the confession, has mysteriously disappeared.

Allison also likes to point out that the police sergeant primarily responsible for the interrogation, a man named Hector Polanco, "can be very intimidating." Polanco is a controversial figure who has been accused of coercing confessions from suspects in several other cases. In 1992, four years after Ochoa and Danzinger were convicted, the Austin Police Department fired Polanco after an internal investigation determined he had presented perjured testimony in a murder trial.

Polanco was reinstated nine months later by an arbitrator who attributed an alleged false statement in a murder trial to a memory lapse, and he later won a $350,000 jury judgment in a subsequent lawsuit against the department over his firing.

Ochoa told his mother, Dora Ochoa, and others in his family that Polanco threw chairs around the room during his interrogation. Ronald Navejos says Ochoa told him, "If he didn't confess they'd crush his head." His current attorneys also maintain that there were threats of physical violence. Meanwhile, Donna Angstadt, Danzinger's former girlfriend, describes her questioning by Polanco and Sergeant Bruce Boardman as "the most horrific, the most horrible experience I've ever been through in my life. I had nightmares about this forever."

Angstadt was the manager of the Pizza Hut where Danzinger and Ochoa worked. She says Polanco and Boardman tried to link her to the crime and threatened to have her children, then nine and four, removed from her custody. "They threatened that if Richard gets out, he's going to hunt me down and kill me like he did Nancy DePriest. . . . They told me Richard had told Chris [Ochoa] that I'm the one who supplied the gun. Another time, Hector Polanco said, 'Your boyfriend's holding her head and you're the one who pulled the trigger for your little love interest.'"

Polanco, who is on medical leave, could not be reached. Boardman refused to comment. A source close to the investigation into Marino's claims said that neither man is a subject of the current inquiry, in part because the statute of limitations would have expired on any crime they might have committed in extracting a false confession from Ochoa in 1988.

Still, if the police did coerce Ochoa into confessing a crime that Marino committed, as Ochoa's lawyers now assert, that means Ochoa is guilty of fingering another perfectly innocent man—his friend, Danzinger—to save himself. It's a prospect, says Danzinger's sister, Barbara Oakley, that haunts her and her family. "To be very honest with you, we're very, very angry," she says. "We'd like to meet [Ochoa] and know why he did this. He and Richard were supposed to be friends. I can understand, as far as he's concerned, his making a false confession. But why did he implicate my brother? Why? Why? Why not John Doe? And why hasn't he tried to contact us or his family members and tried to say something? He knows my brother's been hurt. Why not come forward after all these years?"

Today Oakley describes her brother as extremely nervous and fearful of having anyone stand or even walk behind him. "He's very intimidated. He doesn't want anyone messing with him," she says. "He's like that the entire time you talk to him." She says the last time she visited her brother, he continually mistook Oakley's daughter for Oakley. Danzinger has been confined to the Skyview psychiatric prison in Rusk, Texas, since March 1997.

If the Austin police were prepared to intimidate someone into coercing another suspect, Bill Allison says they picked the perfect subject in Ochoa. "I tell you, I think in the first fifteen seconds of seeing Chris Ochoa, they knew they could get him to talk. It's his demeanor. He's not a real strong person. He's small. He wasn't experienced."

Friends and family members describe Ochoa in similar terms. His mother, Dora Ochoa, says, "He was a timid little boy" who dreamed of being a baseball player or a priest. His uncle, Ronald Navejos, described him as "a smart kid, but a real loner. I tried to pull him out of that by taking him out and doing things with him. But he was real quiet."

Ochoa's background provides nothing that comports with the profile of a cold-blooded murderer. He grew up in a tightly knit, third-generation, churchgoing Mexican-American family and graduated in 1984 with honors from Riverside High School in El Paso.

He was manager of the Riverside football team, but a fellow team member, Andres Martinez, says Ochoa didn't fit the macho, football player stereotype. "He wasn't hanging out with the rest of us off the field," says Martinez, now a truck driver who lives in Chaparral, New Mexico. "We were the rowdy bunch and Chris was very quiet. He kept to himself."

Ochoa's temperament seemed better suited to Riverside High's literary magazine, where he was one of the editors. To this day, he writes songs and poems to friends and family members. A handful of these, provided by his mother, suggest an understandably bleak, suffocating outlook on life. In one song, "Walkin' in the Dark," he writes that "hopes and dreams are no longer with me/There's nothing left for me to say/Gone is my imagination and inspiration." In another song, he writes: "I look for my future somewhere/It's so dark out there I can't see/Don't see it as hard as I stare."

Ochoa has now spent about a third of his life in two medium-security Texas prisons, first at Coffield Prison near Tennessee Colony, and for the last two years at the state prison in Huntsville. According to his uncle, Navejos, Ochoa was "shocked" and "really didn't know how to handle" his incarceration at first. Navejos says there was a time when he believed Ochoa was depressed and had given up hope. "He thought he was going to die there. I kept telling him to keep his faith up, to try to keep positive thoughts in mind."

He says Ochoa has been on good terms with the warden and has had his "good conduct" rewarded with decent jobs, most recently in the prison's shipping and receiving unit. Ochoa's mother claims her son has received two college diplomas while in prison, one in business administration and another in computer science.

Navejos says he "never doubted he was innocent because I know Chris, and I know what he is capable of. He was too timid to do something like this." He also, Navejos and Dora Ochoa say, has never mentioned Danzinger to them.

Before the prison assault that left Richard Danzinger severely brain damaged, Barbara Oakley says her brother was "a very happy, very loving individual who always found something to laugh about."

Although his childhood was hardly predictive of a future life of crime, Oakley says it was also no picnic, in part because his parents, who were in the military, were always moving around, and in part because they went through a "nasty divorce." As a teenager, Danzinger was sent to Brown Schools in San Marcos, Texas, which specializes in services for troubled youth and juvenile offenders, where he reportedly received psychological treatment. (At his trial Danzinger told jurors he didn't want them to conclude from this experience that he was "some psycho or some lunatic," an assurance that likely had just the opposite effect.) When he was arrested in 1989, Danzinger was on parole for forging one of his mother's checks. Oakley says she didn't think her brother had many friends at the time other than Donna Angstadt and Ochoa.

Oakley says her top priority now is getting Danzinger released and getting the state of Texas to pay for his care for the rest of his life. She says she would like to have her brother released soon so he can see his mother, who is dying of lymphoma.

Although the Austin police seemed to give little credence to Marino's confession until recently, it is safe to say that without it, Danzinger and Ochoa would have practically no hope of ever being released. Why it has taken so long to get to the bottom of Marino's claims is not at all clear. Police approached Ochoa sometime in 1998, says attorney Allison, but Ochoa didn't understand why. He assumed the police were trying to get him to confess to some unsolved crimes, the ostensible carrot being that his cooperation might lead to parole.

"You don't get parole by claiming you're innocent," Allison says.

Danzinger was not even provided an attorney until two weeks ago, more than four years after police had Marino's first confession. And it was not until February of this year, under prodding from the Wisconsin Innocence Project, which had taken up Ochoa's cause, that the police and the Austin district attorney conducted DNA tests that had been unavailable at the time of Danzinger's trial.

Attorneys who have been critical of the Texas death penalty and, more broadly, of its criminal justice system, think what happened to Ochoa and Danzinger is significant for several reasons. One is that it suggests how the death penalty can be misused to intimidate an innocent person into making a false confession.

Secondly, perhaps obviously, a false confession perverts the entire judicial process. Prosecutors and jurors relying on perjured testimony are likely to produce a tainted verdict. "If in fact the two men are not guilty," says Travis County District Attorney Ronnie Earle, "it is a tragedy for everybody concerned. It is a tragedy for the two men involved and it is a tragedy for the community because of the general sense of justice that people in this community have."

One way of preventing abuses that lead to wrongful convictions is to provide sufficient money to pay competent defense lawyers from the time of arrest. But the state of Texas has been loath to finance full-time public defenders—and Bush vetoed legislation that would have required the state to provide a lawyer within twenty days of an arrest. Most states provide attorneys within no more than three days.

While the Austin district attorney's current investigation of wrongful convictions has been roundly applauded by defense attorneys and may yet find some innocent people in Texas prisons, it is designed to look primarily at cases in which DNA is available. (Earle says other cases "might also be included.") No one in Texas is talking about reinvestigating cases in which defendants were assigned incompetent lawyers or no lawyers, or about convictions that resulted from potential police coercion or testimony by unreliable jailhouse witnesses. Innocent people convicted in those circumstances will probably just have to serve out their time.

But no matter what happens, nothing will give Richard Danzinger back his health—or restore the last twelve years of his and Ochoa's lives.

Epilogue

Christopher Ochoa and Richard Danzinger were released from prison on January 16, 2001. Shortly thereafter Achim Josef Marino was charged with the murder of Nancy DePriest. On December 13, 2001, DePriest's mother, Jeanette Popp, met with Marino in the Travis County Jail, where he was awaiting trial. After the meeting, Popp told reporters that she hoped he would be spared a death sentence. "If they kill this man they will be victimizing me yet again," said Popp, who had long opposed capital punishment for religious reasons. "I will not dishonor my daughter with the taking of another life in her name."

In November 2002, a Travis County jury convicted Marino of Nancy DePriest's murder. In keeping with Jeanette Popp's wish, he was sentenced to life in prison—in addition to the life sentence he already was serving. Within days of Marino's conviction Ochoa and Danzinger filed federal civil rights suits alleging that Austin homicide investigators Hector Polanco, Bruce Boardman, and Edward Balagia had violated their civil rights by threatening them with violence, fabricating Ochoa's confession, and destroying and hiding exculpatory evidence in the case. The City of Austin settled the suits in 2003 with payments of $5.3 million to Ochoa and $9 million to Danzinger.

Meanwhile, Jeanette Popp had befriended Ochoa and the two began appearing together at legislative hearings and public forums at which they championed criminal justice reform and, especially, ending capital punishment. Their efforts were instrumental in persuading the Texas legislature to guarantee the right to post-conviction DNA testing.

Polanco, Boardman, and Balagia were never personally held to account for the misconduct that cost Ochoa and Danzinger a dozen years of their lives and Austin taxpayers $14.3 million. Balagia was deceased by the time of the settlement. Polanco, who had been fired in 1992 for committing perjury in another case but had won reinstatement in 1994, was reassigned to the department's Patrol Division. Boardman was reassigned—as incredible as it might seem—to the department's Office of Professional Standards, which investigates complaints of police misconduct.

Ochoa was admitted to the University of Wisconsin Law School, from which he graduated on May 12, 2006. He entered private practice in Madison.

LAVALE BURT

He was told the consequences of denying the crime
were worse than the consequences of confessing

ROB WARDEN

CHICAGO, ILLINOIS

*They say, "You're a smart ass. You ain't gonna tell us what happened." I kept
tellin' them, "I dunno what happened." They slap me around, in the face, a
lot of body shots, but that is not what made me give the confession. I gave
it because I got scared. I thought I was gonna get convicted of something I
didn't do.*

*The detective was sayin', "You're stupid. Nobody believe you meant to do
it. You know, everybody know you're not a baby killer. You got a good background and you'll get off with involuntary manslaughter and probation."*

*They told me the two young ladies say they saw me do it. That's when I got
scared and started to make the phony confession. They took me to the scene
and made me look for the gun an' everything. They asked me, "Where do you
think you might have thrown it?" I picked out an area where someone was
growing a garden and I told them, "I threw it over there."*

*I kept asking if I could call home, but they kept sayin', "You tell us what
happened, and then you can make a call." I didn't ask for a lawyer. They
didn't mention nuthin' about rights until I was going to make a statement. At
the time they called in the court reporter was the first time they said anything
about rights.*

Those are the words of LaVale Burt, a twenty-year-old Chicagoan, explaining why he falsely confessed to firing a bullet that killed a child in the city's
Bridgeport neighborhood.

Two days after he confessed, Burt told his lawyer that he was not involved
in the murder but had believed the police when they told him he would
get probation if he confessed. He said he decided that confessing to a crime

From "LaVale Burt—Victim of a Modern Form of Torture," *Chicago Lawyer,* January 1987.
Copyright © Chicago Lawyer. Adapted with permission.

he did not commit was better than risking a jail sentence or even the death penalty.

When Associate Judge Ronald A. Himel was faced with the choice of believing the confession or the recantation, he chose the confession. After a bench trial last October, Himel found Burt guilty of murder. He later told *Chicago Lawyer* that his verdict was based solely on the confession.

While Burt was awaiting sentencing, however, Himel received new evidence that indicated that the child's mother fired the fatal bullet and that Burt had nothing to do with it. Himel reopened the case and acquitted Burt.

The shooting with which Burt was charged, convicted, and then acquitted occurred the morning of September 19, 1985. The victim, Charles Gregory, was shot once in the head with a .22-caliber weapon outside his home near Comiskey Park.

After the shooting, police discovered gunpowder residue on the child's mother, Carolyn Collins, indicating that she fired a gun. Collins gave conflicting accounts of what happened in different interviews with police and in telling the story to the child's paternal grandmother.

Despite the powder residue and her inconsistent statements, the police chose to focus their investigation not on Collins but rather on one of the various stories she told about what happened—that she had seen Burt, a school acquaintance from many years earlier, come across a vacant lot adjacent to her home and fire at two girls, missing them and accidentally hitting the infant.

Collins told this story belatedly. In her initial accounts, she claimed she did not see what happened. In one version, she said she at first thought the child had been bitten by a dog. In another, she said she heard a shot but saw no one who might have fired it. Only after Collins learned that tests showed that there was gunpowder residue on her—making her the prime suspect—did she implicate Burt.

Collins identified the two girls at whom Burt supposedly fired as sisters, Linda (Fay) Leatherberry and Gloria Leatherberry Walls. Both initially denied having been shot at, but after interrogation Linda stated that she had in fact been shot at by Burt. However, she soon recanted this statement, claiming that the police coerced her to make it by refusing to let her go home until she told them what they wanted to hear.

After taking Linda's statement, police developed a complex theory of Burt's motive for shooting at the girls. Their brother, Robert Leatherberry, had been shot in the leg a day or two earlier by an acquaintance of Burt's. The police suspected that the shooting was gang-related and, therefore, that Burt might have shot at the sisters to discourage any thought their brother may have had of testifying against the shooter.

This theory seems to have had little basis in fact. The Leatherberry shooting apparently was accidental. Burt was one of several youths questioned, and after questioning he located the weapon involved and took it to the police. There is no evidence that he was a gang member.

Apparently because they knew Burt from the Leatherberry incident—he had never been in trouble for anything else except underage drinking—the police decided to see if he knew anything about the shooting of Charles Gregory. Detective Donald Barton went to Burt's home about noon the day of the shooting. Burt was not home, but his grandmother took Barton's card and promised to have Burt call when he came home. Burt evidently was not a suspect at that time. He called twice before police came to talk to him. When they finally did come and took him to the Brighton Park district station, he was not handcuffed.

As he was led into the station Burt said he saw Carolyn Collins. She had not, she would testify later, identified Burt prior to seeing him at the police station.

After hours of interrogation, Burt said Barton and other detectives told him that both Carolyn Collins and Linda Leatherberry had told them he fired the shot that killed Charles Gregory. Because the detective repeatedly suggested that he would be better off confessing than facing the consequences that might flow from not confessing, he said, he decided to confess.

Burt said that during interrogation the officers gave him the details that he reiterated in his confession, which he gave to Assistant State's Attorney Peter J. Troy and a court reporter the next day.

After Burt was charged with the child's murder, his first cousin, Thomas Brewer, an assistant Massachusetts attorney general, arranged for him to be represented by Chicago criminal defense lawyer Francis X. Speh Jr. Brewer and Speh had worked together several years earlier as assistant Cook County state's attorneys.

When Speh first interviewed Burt in the county jail, Burt recanted and explained why he had confessed in the first place. Because of the gunpowder residue on Collins, the lack of any on Burt, the failure to find the gun, and the conflicting statements made by Collins, Speh came to believe Burt.

Speh said he did not move to suppress the confession because there appeared to be no basis for such a motion. While Burt had asked permission to call home, he had not asked for an attorney, and he was advised of his right to counsel before he made his formal statement.

The case was scheduled for trial before Judge Thomas J. Maloney, and Speh demanded a jury. When the trial date came around, however, Maloney was on vacation. Because Brewer had come to Chicago to serve as co-counsel, Speh objected to a delay until Maloney returned, and Himel agreed to try the case. Because Himel is a former defense attorney with a reputation for fairness, Speh said, he and Brewer then elected to have a bench trial.

"They made the cardinal mistake of saying bench instead of jury," Himel told *Chicago Lawyer*. "They were asking a judge to throw out a statement made to an excellent state's attorney. If this man, Peter Troy, was part of any conspiracy to feed the defendant information and force him to make a statement, my ideals would be shattered. They were asking a judge to disbelieve Peter Troy."

Himel said when he heard Collins's testimony the day before he heard Troy, he thought he would have to throw out the case. "After her testimony, I immediately thought she was involved because they had impeached her on a lot of material points," Himel said. "In the car ride home with my wife [attorney Lorna Propes] that night, I said, 'If this is it, I'm going to have to throw this out.' Then they came in the next day with the defendant's statement, and the statement corroborated everything she said. We didn't hear from the Leatherberry sisters, and I just attributed that to fear."

The day after Himel found Burt guilty, Charles Gregory's maternal grandmother, Josephine Collins, arranged for a friend to contact Himel. The friend told Himel that Josephine, who lived with Carolyn Collins and who had attended the Burt trial, had important information about the case.

Himel agreed to speak with her. "She wanted to clear her conscience," Himel said later. "She, in her own mind, wanted to make certain that the wrong person wasn't punished." She told him that, after learning during the trial of the gunpowder residue on her daughter, she checked a .22-caliber pistol in the family home and found a bullet missing. Himel sent police to pick up the pistol, and a ballistics examination indicated it in all probability was the weapon that killed Charles Gregory.

Because the bullet recovered from the child's body was damaged, a police ballistics expert said it was impossible to absolutely link it with the gun from the Collins apartment. Nonetheless, Himel told *Chicago Lawyer*, "The ballistics guy convinced me that the gun was the murder weapon. There is no question in my mind. There was no question in his mind."

Himel reopened the case. Despite all the facts favorable to Burt and unfavorable to Collins, the lead prosecutor in the case, John T. Groark, continued to profess that Burt did it. "There was no reason for him to give the statement unless he was there and he did do it," Groark told reporters.

Himel concluded otherwise. After a brief hearing on December 10, he acquitted Burt. "All these things came together and created such a massive doubt that I had no alternative," Himel told *Chicago Lawyer.*

Himel added that he still does not understand why Burt confessed to the crime if he did not commit it.

John H. Langbein, a University of Chicago law professor, offers a possible explanation.

"This is charge bargaining, isn't it?" asked Langbein when told about the Burt case.

That is what it was, assuming that Burt's explanation for his confession is analogous to an explanation given by a public official condemned to death in seventeenth-century Germany after confessing under torture to witchcraft: "It's all a falsehood and invention, so help me God. . . . They never cease to torture until one says something."

The interrogation method to which Burt was subjected in the back room of a Chicago police station in 1985 was vastly more polite than that employed in medieval dungeons, but the effect was the same, according to Langbein: a coerced confession.

Because of the inherent danger in charge bargaining, safeguards have been established in modern law to ensure that promises have not been made to a confessing defendant and that there is independent evidence pointing to guilt, Langbein said, but the safeguards presuppose that the bargaining will be done by prosecutors—not by police.

"Our safeguards are directed at the prosecutorial management of charge and sentence bargaining," he said, "but what you're discovering is a situation of police management—and, indeed, fraudulent management—of the situation. What really happened here was charge bargaining, but by people who could not deliver on it. The safeguards are not directed at this situation."

When police have the power to charge bargain, there is a danger, according to Langbein, that they will use it as a substitute for investigation.

Langbein quoted a response elicited by James Fitzjames Stephen when he commented on the proclivity of the native Indian police to torture suspects in 1883: "It is far pleasanter to sit comfortably in the shade rubbing red pepper into a poor devil's eyes than to go about in the sun hunting up evidence."

Epilogue

Carolyn Collins was never charged in connection with her son's death.

JOHN A. JOHNSON

He denied guilt—until he considered the alternative

EDWIN M. BORCHARD
MADISON, WISCONSIN

On Wednesday, September 6, 1911, residents of Madison were startled as news spread that a seven-year-old girl named Annie Lemberger had disappeared during the night from her home on South Francis Street, where she lived with her parents, Martin and Magdeline Lemberger, and two brothers, nine-year-old Alois and six-year-old Martin Jr.

Magdeline Lemberger told the police that, at about ten o'clock the night before, she had tucked Annie into bed, checked all doors and windows to make sure they were locked, and awoke early the next morning to find Annie's bed empty.

The Lemberger boys, who slept in another bed in the same room, had not been disturbed. And Martin and Magdeline said they heard nothing, although the door between their room and the children's had been ajar.

Police found that a small triangular piece of glass had been broken out of the window next to Annie's bed and there were footprints outside. As word of the apparent abduction spread, alarmed neighbors joined authorities in a thorough search. They searched vacant lots, culverts, manholes, and nearby marshes, but to no avail.

Tips and rumors flowed in to police, all leading nowhere. Magdeline theorized that gypsies had kidnapped Annie, and a spiritualist opined that the child had been kidnapped and carted off in a covered wagon. And, because the hole in the windowpane was thought to be too small for an adult hand to get through, there was speculation that a boy or boys might have been involved.

All such notions proved baseless on Saturday, September 10, when Annie's body was found in Lake Monona. An autopsy determined that she had not drowned, but had suffered a small wound behind her left ear, caus-

Adapted from *Convicting the Innocent* (New Haven: Yale University Press, 1932). Copyright © Yale University Press.

ing a clot on her brain—the probable cause of death. There was no evidence of sexual assault or other likely motive for the murder.

Nothing like this crime had ever occurred in Madison, and public indignation naturally ran high. A reward fund was established for information leading to the arrest and conviction of the killer or killers. The *Wisconsin State Journal*—editorializing that "the fiend must be found"—launched a public subscription campaign and used the proceeds to retain the W. J. Burns Detective Agency, which assigned Detective Edward L. Boyer to the investigation.

When Boyer arrived in Madison, the police already had questioned John A. Johnson, a loafer and barroom hanger-on known as "Dogskin." Johnson had been among the first to join the excited crowds in search of Annie. After her body was found, he had nosed around the undertaking parlors, attracting the authorities' suspicion.

Through an all-night grilling, Johnson asserted his innocence and was released, but was rearrested when the police learned that he had a record— he had served time for nonsupport of his wife and two daughters, and had twice been committed to insane asylums for taking liberties with girls.

Under rapid-fire questioning by Boyer and others, Johnson continued to stoutly maintain his innocence, saying that he had gone to bed at about 9:00 P.M. on September 5—an hour before Magdeline said she'd tucked Annie into bed—and that he had not left home until about 6:00 A.M. the next day. Johnson's wife, who actually supported the family, backed him up, telling the authorities that he couldn't have left without her knowledge because she'd been sitting up all night with a sick daughter. Both of the Johnsons' daughters corroborated the alibi.

Nonetheless—with neither physical nor circumstantial evidence linking Johnson to the crime and no confession—Dane County District Attorney Gaylord A. Nelson charged Johnson with the murder of Annie Lemberger. On September 13, Johnson was taken before Dane County Municipal Court Judge Anthony Donovan. After the charge was read, Johnson entered a plea of not guilty and Donovan set bail at ten thousand dollars. Since Johnson was indigent, Donovan assigned a prominent Madison lawyer, Emerson Ela, to defend him. The trial was set for September 26.

Johnson was returned to jail, where a short time later—inexplicably in view of his prior statements—he confessed to the crime:

> I had been drinking hard the last two months and on this night
> I went to bed drunk. Sometime after one o'clock I awoke and
> wanted another drink of whisky. I got out of bed and dressed

quietly and crept downstairs and got my shoes from behind the stove. When I got outside I put them on with the intention of going to some saloon close by and begging for a drink.

I walked up Francis Street as far as the Lemberger house which is four doors away from my home. When I reached there I remembered I had often looked into the window of the little cottage and seen the Lemberger children going to bed. Some devilish impulse caused me to step over to the window and reach my hand through the broken pane and raise it. I lifted Annie out without making any noise and the cold air awakened her and she saw me and yelled, "Johnson!"

I hit her with my fist and began to run. She kept making a noise and I kept hitting her until she was limp in my arms. By that time I had reached the middle of the vacant lot and I laid her down in the weeds to catch my breath and get my bearings. In a few seconds I began to realize what I had done and I thought I had better throw the body into the lake. I walked to the bay, five blocks away, and by keeping in the shadows of the barns and fences I got there without anyone seeing me. I threw the body as far as possible out into the water and then ran home. I took off my shoes and put them back and got upstairs without waking any of the family. I want to plead guilty and make this confession so I will be taken to prison today.

Johnson insisted that he be taken back before Judge Donovan. The various officials involved were quickly called together. Emerson Ela explained the seriousness of changing the plea to Johnson, but Johnson persisted. Thereupon, Donovan sentenced Johnson to life at hard labor. The authorities acceded to Johnson's desire that he be taken to prison immediately, slipping him out of a little-used side door of the courthouse, secreting him beneath a blanket in a car, and rushing him out of Madison before word spread about the rapid turn of affairs.

Upon arrival at the Waupun Penitentiary about sixty miles northeast of Madison, Johnson began writing letters contending that he was innocent, and that he had confessed and pled guilty solely to save himself from death at the hands of what he apparently had been led to believe was an angry mob amassing outside the jail.

In view of Johnson's record and a widely held belief that he was not of sound mind, his letters were ignored for years by their recipients. But in 1920, a Madison lawyer named Ole A. Stolen was moved by a pleading letter to visit Johnson at Waupun. And, after studying the record, Stolen became convinced that Johnson was innocent.

Stolen filed a pardon application for Johnson, and on September 14, 1921, Governor John J. Blaine appointed a commissioner, Rufus B. Smith, to conduct a hearing, which opened two weeks later. Stolen represented Johnson and Dale County District Attorney Theodore G. Lewis represented the state. It was rumored that Stolen would prove who the actual murderer was. That did not happen, but Stolen did prove that the hole in the windowpane over Annie's bed was far too small to admit the hand of a man.

After Johnson's wife and two daughters testified that he had retired at ten o'clock the night Annie disappeared and had not left the house until six o'clock the next morning, Johnson took the stand. On direct examination, he said that Detective Boyer had told him a mob was waiting outside the jail. In fact, there had been no mob, but Johnson testified that the ruse had made him livid with fear. Johnson said he once had seen a black man lynched—strung up with a rope, riddled by bullets, cut down, and stabbed. The fright of something like that happening to him, Johnson said, prompted him to seize what seemed the only alternative—signing the confession, which Boyer had helped prepare.

Stolen elicited that Johnson had adamantly maintained his innocence throughout grueling interrogation, but District Attorney Lewis countered by calling several witnesses who testified that Johnson had displayed no signs of fear or duress when he pled guilty. Among those witnesses was Gaylord Nelson, the district attorney who had charged Johnson with the crime in 1911. Nelson testified that he had urged Johnson not to change his plea, but that Johnson had persisted in doing so—from which Nelson drew a strong inference of guilt.

Following Nelson's testimony, Johnson's chances of winning a pardon seemed slim. But then Stolen received an anonymous letter followed by a telephone call from a woman who claimed to know who had killed Annie and who offered to testify in exchange for protection from the killer. When Stolen assured the woman that she could be protected, she identified herself as Mae Sorenson, saying she was a close friend of Magdeline Lemberger. She proceeded to relate that Magdeline had called her on September 6, 1911, and told her of Annie's disappearance. Mae immediately went to the Lemberger home to console Magdeline, whom she found in the kitchen burning what appeared to be a bloodstained nightgown. Magdeline was weeping bitterly and finally fainted. Then, regaining consciousness, Magdeline cried, "Martin, Martin, why did you do it?"

On the day of Annie's funeral, Sorenson continued, Alois Lemberger told her that on the evening of September 5 his father, in company with other men, had been drinking heavily. Annie had risen to get a drink, and on passing through the kitchen, was asked by her father to hand him the poker. She couldn't find it. In a drunken fury, he struck her behind the ear with a beer bottle and she fell against the stove unconscious. Martin Lemberger then carried her to her cot, and she died. The Lembergers denied Mae's allegations, but Martin was arrested and charged with the murder of his daughter.

On December 13, 1921, Commissioner Smith rendered a report to Governor Blaine recommending a pardon for Johnson with these words: "An attentive consideration of all the testimony taken before me and of all the facts and circumstances attending the disappearance of Annie Lemberger, has produced the profound conviction in my mind that Mr. Johnson was not guilty of the crime. . . . It is of course clear that ordinary people do not ordinarily accuse themselves falsely of the commission of crime. If Mr. Johnson were a man of ordinary strength of character, and of ordinary prudence and sagacity, I should find it difficult to disbelieve him when he stated that he committed this offense. But I find that he was and is far below the ordinary individual in mentality. The testimony establishes in fact, to my satisfaction at least, that he was a man conspicuously weak, weak almost to the degree of irresponsibility."

Two weeks later, Martin Lemberger was taken before Judge A. C. Hoppmann for a preliminary hearing, the purpose of which was to determine if there was probable cause to hold him for trial. After five days of testimony, Ralph Jackman, who had been named special prosecutor in the case, announced in court that, although Annie, in his view, had met her death at her father's hands, "I am equally satisfied that her death was not the result of any premeditated design." Thus, Jackman said, the appropriate charge was not murder but manslaughter—a crime for which the statute of limitations was ten years. On that ground, Martin was discharged from custody on January 5, 1922.

In a report to Governor Blaine the following month, Jackman stated, "It is my judgment that Martin Lemberger accidentally hit Annie Lemberger, that she went against the stove, hitting her temple, and became unconscious, that Martin Lemberger started to take her to the hospital, and that she died and was thrown into the lake. The death was entirely accidental with no premeditation of any kind. It is my judgment that Johnson had nothing whatever to do with her death."

Based on the conclusions of both Commissioner Smith and Special Prosecutor Jackman, the governor commuted Johnson's sentence to expire at 8:00 A.M. on February 7, 1922. "I am convinced that the whole truth has not been told in connection with the murder," Governor Blaine said. "There is only one fact that stands out clearly, and that is that Johnson did not murder Annie Lemberger."

Stolen filed a claim for Johnson under a 1913 Wisconsin statute authorizing compensation to innocent persons erroneously imprisoned. On December 5, 1922, however, the state board administering the statute denied the claim on the ground that Johnson had contributed to his wrongful conviction and therefore was excluded from the benefits of the statute.

Epilogue

In 1935 the Wisconsin legislature approved and Governor Philip La Follette signed a bill to compensate James A. Johnson at a rate of about forty-five dollars a month up to five thousand dollars. Three years later—on April 25, 1938—Johnson died, having collected roughly two thousand dollars. In 1993, seventy-two years after the murder, Prairie Oak Press of Madison published a book by Mark Lemberger, a grandson of Martin and Magdeline Lemberger, contending that Johnson had been guilty after all. The book, entitled *Crime of Magnitude: The Murder of Little Annie*, claimed that the author's grandparents had been the victims of a "Kafkaesque nightmare."

JESSE AND STEPHEN BOORN

Hoping to avoid the gallows, they confessed—but that didn't help

GERALD MCFARLAND

MANCHESTER, VERMONT

In April 1819, Amos Boorn had a dream. So urgent was its message that the dream was repeated three times. In it, the ghost of Russell Colvin, who had disappeared seven years earlier, came and stood beside the slumbering Amos. The ghost said he had been murdered and wanted to show Amos where his mortal remains had been laid. Amos followed the ghost to the location, an old cellar hole in the field that, at the time of Russell's disappearance, had belonged to Amos's brother, Barney Boorn.

Barney had sold the field in 1815 to a neighbor named Thomas Johnson. Shortly after the transaction, three things happened that, in light of Amos's dream, would play into a widespread assumption in Manchester that Russell had been murdered. First, a sheep barn on the property mysteriously burned down. Second, Johnson's children found a "very moldy and rotten" hat in the field—a hat that resembled one Russell had worn. Third, and most curiously, according to Johnson, a volunteer apple tree that had grown out of the cellar hole mysteriously disappeared—and the ground "appeared to have been moved."

Until Amos reported his dream, the townsfolk had regarded the happenings as mere curiosities. Russell's disappearance had portended nothing nefarious because, during eleven years of marriage to Barney Boorn's daughter Sally, he had wandered off several times without telling anyone he was leaving. Once he had disappeared for nine months. But Amos Boorn was regarded as a solid citizen. He was, in the words of the local Congregational minister, "a gentleman of respectability, whose character is unimpeachable." Thus, his ghost story gained immediate plausibility among a sizeable segment of the populace. And although the ghost seems not to have explicitly identified his murderers, local opinion immediately sup-

From *The "Counterfeit" Man* (New York: Pantheon Books, 1990). Copyright © Gerald McFarland. Adapted with permission.

plied their names—Stephen and Jesse Boorn, Barney's sons and Russell Colvin's brothers-in-law.

Suddenly other residents of the area began reporting visions and ghost sightings. Although Manchester's leading citizens—its lawyers, clergy, and merchants—saw the stories as products of ignorance and superstition, the visions and sightings, together with Amos's dream, prompted town officers to act. They arrested Jesse Boorn and convened a court of inquiry—a panel of town officials and prominent citizens—to investigate whether a crime had occurred. Stephen Boorn was not arrested because he had moved and was living two hundred miles away in Denmark, New York.

The court of inquiry opened on Tuesday, April 27, 1819, led by Joel Pratt, the town clerk who also was a justice of the peace, and Truman Hill, the town's grand juror, an elective office. Jesse was housed in a log jail that had been constructed during the American Revolution as a prison for Tories and since had undergone few physical improvements. Ordinarily, prisoners were brought from the jail directly across the street to the court-house, a two-story clapboard structure with courtrooms above a tavern on the first floor. In this case, however, the courthouse was too small to accom-modate the crowd clamoring to attend, so the proceedings were moved to the Congregational meeting house, which was larger.

On its first day, the court of inquiry interrogated Jesse Boorn, an exer-cise that produced little beyond denials of wrongdoing. The next day, April 28, the court of inquiry began fieldwork in search of evidence. Guided by Amos Boorn, the court and a substantial following went to examine the old cellar hole in Thomas Johnson's field. One member was designated to dig, and before long the excavation turned up a few pieces of crockery, a coat button, and two knives, one "an old fashioned long jack-knife," the other a penknife.

Two members of the court, Pratt and Richard Skinner, a wealthy young lawyer, were designated to take the artifacts to Sally Colvin for possible identification. Before showing the presumed widow the items, Pratt and Skinner asked her to describe the design of the buttons on the coat Russell had before he disappeared. Then, in Skinner's words, "we in her presence rubbed the button and discovered the color and flower in the centre"—pre-cisely the color and design Sally described.

On Friday, April 30, the key witness was Lewis Colvin, the seventeen-year-old son of Russell and Sally. The last time Lewis saw his father was the day he disappeared, which other testimony had established as May 10, 1812. Lewis testified that they—just the two of them—had been picking up stones in the field when his father began to behave in a deranged way, "throwing fence-rails about," at which point Lewis ran to his grandparents' house. The testimony was not at all damaging to Jesse, who again testified and scarcely blinked when shown the battered hat Thomas Johnson's children had found in 1815 and the old jackknife that had been unearthed earlier in the week.

At this point, the court of inquiry seemed to have run out of leads. The items recovered from the cellar hole, assuming they were in fact Colvin's, were insufficient to establish that he had been murdered. The testimony had yielded nothing incriminating, and interrogation of Jesse had produced no useful information. There were the stories of the visions and ghost sightings, of course, but the members of the court of inquiry were unanimously insistent upon keeping spectral evidence out of the record, lest they and the entire legal process be discredited.

But Truman Hill, the elected grand juror, was not quite ready to give up. On Saturday morning, May 1, Hill obtained the keys to the jail and took Thomas Johnson to speak with the prisoner. What Johnson said was not revealed, but whatever it was, it produced a result. Contrary to his earlier denial, Jesse said he had recognized the jackknife. It was Russell's. When Johnson came out, Hill entered the cell and found Jesse "much agitated." Hill, according to his written account, asked, "What was the matter?" to which Jesse replied, "There was matter enough." Urged to continue, Jesse proceeded to say that Stephen—during a recent visit to Manchester, his first since moving to New York—had revealed that he had given "Russel [sic] a blow, and laid him aside, where no one would find him" Only then, Jesse insisted, had he realized that Stephen had killed Russell. Not having had a chance to mull things over, Jesse "thought he knew within a few rods where Colvin was buried."

News of the breakthrough set off a wild rush to find Russell's bones the next day. Although it was the Sabbath, "nearly all the people for miles around" joined the search, or so one old-timer recalled, adding that "stumps were overturned, cellar holes examined, and the side of the mountain back of the premises carefully searched"—all to no avail.

Meanwhile, a smaller party of searchers pursued a different lead, which had been provided by an East Manchester boy only the day before. The boy reported that he had been walking his pet spaniel along the road that ran from the Battenkill River past Barney Boorn's house to the field that now belonged to Thomas Johnson. Near the east bank of the river, the dog ran over to a birch stump, dashing about, whining, and pawing at the ground. Peering into the opening, the boy discovered a cache of bones. When the searchers overturned the stump and began picking through the bones, some of which had been charred by fire, they found what appeared to be parts of human thumbnails or toenails.

The discovery spawned an elaborate theory to which a sizable segment of the citizenry promptly subscribed. The theory was that Russell's first resting place had been the old cellar hole where his coat button and jackknife had been found, but his remains had been moved—accounting for the disappearance of the apple tree and Thomas Johnson's discovery that the ground had been disturbed. According to this theory, Russell's remains then were placed beneath the floor of the sheep barn. When the barn burned down, the bones were charred and exposed, and the murderer or murderers moved them again, depositing them in the hollow stump down the road.

Four physicians were summoned to examine the charred bones. What followed resembled at times an opéra bouffe in which the limited anatomical knowledge of the time would become all too painfully evident. At first, doctors agreed that among the bones were remnants of a human foot. But one of them, who came from the neighboring town of Arlington, owned a skeleton. When he got home, he concluded from an examination of his skeleton that the bones found in Manchester were not human. The next day the physician returned to Manchester, but was unable to budge his colleagues from their conviction that the bones were human. After much debate, the group decided to settle the issue in an empirical way.

A man who lived four or five miles from Manchester had recently had a leg amputation. A delegation was sent to exhume the leg, which the physicians then compared with the foot-like bone found in Manchester. All four doctors then agreed that the Manchester bones were not of human origin. Of course there was still the thumbnail or toenail, or whatever it was, but that fell far short of establishing that Russell Colvin had been murdered.

Although the gentlemen conducting the court of inquiry would have preferred to have physical evidence, it was not necessary to have the victim's remains in order to prosecute a murder case, but rather only proof that the murder had in fact occurred. And the court of inquiry now had such proof, or so it seemed—Jesse's statement that Stephen had admitted murdering Russell Colvin. Also, subsequent to Jesse's revelations, two members of the court had grilled Lewis Colvin, who now, contrary to his previous statement, claimed to have witnessed a fight between Stephen and his father the day his father disappeared. Based on the statements of Jesse and Lewis, the court issued a warrant for the arrest of Stephen Boorn.

A three-man posse, including Thurman Hill, was immediately dispatched to Denmark, New York, to take Stephen into custody. It took the men three days to get there, which meant that they pushed themselves and their mounts hard, covering an average of sixty-six miles a day. Fearful that their quarry might escape, the posse enlisted the aid of several local residents, including an innkeeper, who guided them to Stephen's house. One of the Denmark men went into the house and kept Stephen occupied with small talk, while the posse and new volunteers surrounded the house. When they moved in for the arrest, they encountered no resistance. Stephen was stoic. According to Hill, Stephen "peremptorily asserted innocence, and declared he knew nothing about the murder of his brother-in-law." The next morning, with Stephen manacled, the posse started back for Manchester, where they arrived on Saturday, May 15.

Once back in Manchester, Stephen at first was put into a cell separate from that of his brother Jesse. Calvin Sheldon, the state prosecuting attorney, joined a chorus of voices urging Stephen to come clean, but he continued to profess innocence. Finally, hoping that bringing the brothers together would loosen their tongues, court officers had the two men placed in the same cell. The result, however, was that Jesse, after a tongue-lashing from Stephen, retracted his earlier statement accusing Stephen of Russell's murder.

With the tide of public opinion going strongly against the brothers, their father, Barney, also came under scrutiny. He had tried to provide an alibi for Jesse and Stephen, falsely claiming that neither had been working at home and thus could not have been in the field when the alleged crime occurred. As a result of the lie, Barney was arrested as a possible accessory in the murder. He was fortunate, however, that the examining magistrate, John S. Pettibone, had the independence of mind to resist popular prejudices. After giving Barney "a severe examination," Pettibone discharged him, much to the indignation of the public.

The main targets of the indignation, of course, were Stephen and Jesse Boorn, who remained in the town jail as days and weeks passed. There was little to break the monotony except frequent interrogations by town officials who were intent on getting Stephen to confess and Jesse to reaffirm the statement he had recanted. But by early June it was obvious to the inquisitors that they were making no headway and, thus, they turned to subterfuge—enlisting another prisoner to act as a stool pigeon.

Stephen and Jesse, who had been sharing a cell, were separated. Stephen was moved to a dark, windowless room and placed in triple chains—he had shackles on his hands and feet and was also chained to the floor. Jesse was put into another cell with the enlisted stool pigeon, a man named Silas Merrill, who was being held on charges of perjury. Although neither Merrill nor town officials would ever admit it, there was strong circumstantial evidence indicating that Merrill had been promised lenient treatment if he could provide significant information about Colvin's murder.

Before June was over, Merrill claimed to be the recipient of stunning revelations from his cellmate. One Sunday, after having received a visit from Barney Boorn, Jesse seemed upset and nervous, Merrill said. And that night, after Merrill fell asleep, Jesse awakened him and, according to Merrill, said "he was frightened about something that had come into the window, and was on the bed behind him." If Merrill was to be believed, the incident—the only example of spectral activity that made it into official records of the Boorn-Colvin case—loosened Jesse's tongue in a big way.

Jesse supposedly then began sharing confidences with Merrill, beginning with what happened in the field on May 10, 1812. According to Merrill, Jesse confided that he, Lewis, Stephen, and Russell were picking up stones when a fight broke out between the latter two. Stephen clubbed Russell to the ground, and Lewis ran off. Then Stephen struck Russell again and "broke his skull" so that "blood gushed out."

After a while, Barney Boorn arrived and asked whether Russell was dead. Stephen and Jesse said he was not. Barney went away, returning twice more, only to receive the same answer each time. On his third visit to the field, according to Jesse, "the old man said damn him," and directed Jesse to grab Russell's legs and Stephen his shoulders. Together the three men carried Russell to the cellar hole, where Barney used Stephen's penknife to cut Russell's throat. By the time they buried Russell in the old foundation it was nearly dark.

Later, according to Merrill's account of Jesse's revelations, the Boorn brothers dug up Russell's remains—this would have been in 1814 or 1815—and hid them under the floor of the nearby sheep barn. When the barn burned down in 1815, Jesse and Stephen went back and retrieved Russell's bones, pounded them into small bits, and dumped them into the Battenkill River. The skull was so badly burned that it crumbled into small pieces. Finally, a few leftover bone fragments were gathered up by Barney Boorn and stuffed into "a hollow birch stump near the road."

At his earliest opportunity, Merrill passed along the news of Jesse's middle-of-the-night confession—which of course tracked the theory that some of the citizens of Manchester had confabulated following the discovery of the bones in the stump two months earlier—to Joel Pratt and his colleagues. When confronted with Merrill's allegations, Jesse denied that he had told Merrill any such thing and Stephen declared that there was no truth to the account.

But as June became July, the inquisitors continued to press for full confessions, no doubt with sincerity. They were pillars of Manchester society— Calvin Sheldon, Truman Hill, and Joel Pratt, among others—conscientious men, possibly overzealous in their methods at times, but nevertheless striving to do their best to solve a difficult case, in the face of intense pressure. "All, all was consternation!" wrote Samuel Putnam Waldo, a lawyer from Hartford, Connecticut, who studied the case in 1820. "Every mouth was ready to exclaim, murder! murder!" And, as Richard Skinner, the young lawyer who had joined Pratt to interview Sally Colvin, would be quoted as saying, "It would have been as easy to resist the cataract of Niagara as to arrest [the] torrent of passion and prejudice."

The trouble was that the case against the Boorn brothers was weak, cobbled together from less-than-dispositive and highly circumstantial scraps of physical evidence, Jesse's equivocated accusation against Stephen, Lewis Colvin's contradictory statements, and the claims of Silas Merrill, who was hardly an unimpeachable witness.

Two members of the court of inquiry—Samuel Raymond and Josiah Burton, wealthy partners in mercantile endeavors—took a very hard line in the ongoing interrogation of the brothers, particularly Stephen. Raymond told Stephen that he had "no doubt of his guilt," and Burton chimed in that Stephen was "a gone goose." His only hope for escaping the noose, the businessmen unabashedly acknowledged telling Stephen, was to confess to having killed Colvin. The businessmen, in turn, would support a move to get him a light sentence.

Stephen resisted until late August, when his mood abruptly changed. Precisely what precipitated the change would never be known—perhaps he was simply worn down by more than three months in jail and being told over and over that confessing was his only hope. In any event, on August 27, 1819, Stephen asked Burton to bring Pratt, Hill, and Sheldon to the jail. When they arrived, they led him across the street to the courthouse where he asked Pratt "about some small points." Writing materials then were brought to Stephen, who proceeded to write a detailed confession that Pratt and Hill signed as witnesses.

The confession was in two sections, the first of which was the core statement in which he admitted killing Russell: On the morning of May 10, 1812, Stephen had visited the field where Russell and Lewis were working. He and Russell fell into an argument. When Russell boasted of "how many dollars benefit" he had been to Barney Boorn, Stephen ridiculed his claims. Russell flew into a rage, picked up a beech limb, and struck

Stephen a glancing blow. Stephen then grabbed the club away from Russell and delivered two blows, the second of which landed on the back of Russell's neck at the base of his skull and knocked him to the ground. Russell died shortly thereafter.

The second section was a lengthy description of how he had disposed of and later twice moved Russell's remains: The night of the fight, Stephen dug a grave, buried Russell, and, in his own words, "went home crying . . ." A year or two later, he went back, dug up Colvin's bones, and carried them to the sheep barn, where he hid them in a hole he dug under the floor. In March 1815, after learning that the barn had burned down, he visited the site and recovered the bones that had survived the fire. The largest of these he carried down to the Battenkill and threw into a deep part of the stream. Shortly thereafter, he returned to the barn site again and scraped up a few smaller bits and pieces, which he stuffed into a hole in a stump beside the road near the river.

At first glance, the vividness of the confession made it seem ingenuous and authentic, but it was not without its artful aspects. Leaving Jesse out of the story eliminated any need on Jesse's part to defend himself by providing further evidence against Stephen. And by claiming that he had simply returned Russell's blow—that is, acted in an unpremeditated way and without murderous intent—he gave Raymond and Burton solid grounds to fulfill their promise to seek leniency on his behalf. On the other hand, Stephen did not contend that he had to kill Russell to save his own life—a necessary element of self-defense, a ground on which he would have had a shot at an acquittal.

Somewhat ironically, in view of all of the efforts that went into getting the confession, State's Attorney Calvin Sheldon, as far as can be determined, chose not to use it when he took the case to a grand jury in Manchester on September 26, 1819. Most likely that was because the confession made no mention of Jesse, whom Sheldon sought to indict along with Stephen. The key grand jury witness was Silas Merrill, who related the story he claimed to have heard from Jesse three months earlier.

Based primarily on that tale, the grand jury returned indictments charging that Stephen "feloniously, willfully, and of his malice aforethought" struck and killed Russell Colvin, and that Jesse "then and there, feloniously, willfully, and of his malice aforethought, was present aiding, helping, abetting, comforting, assisting and maintaining the said Stephen Boorn [in] the felony and murder aforesaid."

Epilogue

On October 31, 1819, after a four-day trial, a jury returned guilty verdicts. The convictions carried automatic death sentences. The law provided no judicial review of criminal convictions, but did provide a clemency process through the Vermont General Assembly, a unicameral body in adjournment until January 1820. Once back in session, legislators promptly commuted Jesse's sentence to life at hard labor but denied relief for Stephen, whose hanging was scheduled for January 28.

Meanwhile, however, something most serendipitous and fortuitous had happened. In November 1819, an anonymous letter appeared in the *Albany Gazette and Daily Advertiser* marveling that "a most striking example of divine agency" had brought Jesse and Stephen Boorn to justice for the murder of Russell Colvin.

The letter was reprinted several days later in the *New York Evening Post* and read aloud in the public room of a New York City hotel. Among those who happened to be present were Tabor Chadwick, a Methodist minister from Shrewsbury, New Jersey, and James Whelpley, a New York tavern keeper and native of Manchester.

Upon hearing the name Russell Colvin, Chadwick proclaimed that he knew a man who called himself that—and who, for the last several years, had been working as a farmhand in Dover, New Jersey. Whelpley, who had known Colvin slightly years before, promptly set off for Dover. There he found the man who had been presumed dead to be quite alive. Colvin returned to Manchester, effecting the exoneration and release of his brothers-in-law.

CHILD ABUSE

Kids, Art Linkletter famously observed, say the darndest things.

The kinds of things to which he was referring, of course, were harmless and (at least mildly) humorous.

Not so the things children are liable to say under police interrogation when they are suspected of having committed serious crimes.

In interrogation, whatever they say is neither harmless nor in any sense humorous.

It can, and will, be used against them.

The younger crime suspects are, the greater their tendency to be submissive, compliant, and naively trustful of authority figures.

And the less sense they have of the gravity and severity of the consequences of anything they say.

They may not have the capacity to understand a Miranda warning, and certainly not the judgment to invoke their rights to silence or counsel.

If mature, intelligent, sober adults are unable to withstand police interrogation, then inflicting it upon those of tender age is cruel, if not unusual, and nothing short of child abuse—as the following stories disquietingly illustrate.

ROMARR GIPSON AND ELIJAH HENDERSON

After the prepubescent boys confessed, semen was found
on the victim's panties

ALEX KOTLOWITZ
CHICAGO, ILLINOIS

On the morning of Monday, August 10, 1998, the Chicago Police Department held a press conference in the auditorium of a station on the South
Side. Five detectives, in jackets and ties, stood shoulder to shoulder, their
hands folded, looking very much like preoccupied prep-school kids. Seated
in front of them was their boss, Sergeant Stan Zaborac. The night before,
two boys, seven and eight, had been arrested and charged with first-degree
murder. Zaborac solemnly told the throng of reporters that the two boys
had confessed to killing an eleven-year-old girl named Ryan Harris. Zaborac's tone was measured, but he was clearly proud of his men's work. The
statements of the boys, he told the assembled crowd, contained details that
could be known only by the individuals who committed the crime and
the detectives who investigated it. "Their statements indicate that they are
perpetrators," he said, "and we have some physical evidence that is corroborated by their statements."

The reporters pressed him for details. By fits and starts, Zaborac described
what the police believed had occurred. The boys, he said, wanted Harris's
blue Road Warrior bicycle, so the seven-year-old threw a rock at her, and it
knocked her off the bike. Then they molested her and stuffed an article of
clothing in her mouth. The boys lived near Harris and knew her.

"Did they, Sergeant, indicate an understanding of what they'd done?"
one reporter inquired.

"You would have to use conjecture or logical thoughts," he said. "We're
being set off on two various tangents by one of the children involved. You
would have to suspect that they knew what they had done and that they

were coming up with various accounts to point the blame toward someone else." Zaborac ended by saying that his detectives had performed "magnificently."

Five hours after Zaborac's press conference, the children, Elijah Henderson and Romarr Gipson,* were taken from Hartgrove Hospital, the locked psychiatric facility where they had been held overnight, to the Cook County Juvenile Justice Center. They were brought in through the loading dock to attend a hearing on whether they could return to their families. There were so many reporters that the hearing had to be moved to the building's largest courtroom.

"The press was waiting to see the demons," Maurice Possley, who covered the case for the *Chicago Tribune*, says. "We're waiting to see John Wayne Gacy or some serial rapist, we've been told the story by the police. I think we were expecting to see burly oversized kids with glinty eyes. We were not expecting to see what we got."

Elijah, the eight-year-old, was stick skinny, with gangly limbs that moved out of sync with the rest of his body, like those of a marionette. He was four feet two and weighed fifty-six pounds. Romarr, the seven-year-old, who was missing many of his front teeth, was two inches shorter but more stockily built, and he weighed sixty-two pounds. Before the boys entered the courtroom, they had both been "wailing," one attorney told me, and first they seemed dazed and lost. Their families—parents, grandparents, even a great-grandmother—sat in the front row. Only one parent was absent—Romarr's father, Jeremy. That morning, unable to face the thought that his son had been arrested for murder, Jeremy got into his 1988 Ford Taurus and drove ninety miles north to Milwaukee and then back, listening to his and his son's favorite song, Al Green's "Love and Happiness."

When the boys entered the courtroom, there was brief silence, followed by an audible gasp. Possley recalls that, as an adult led the boys to their seats, their small hands were swallowed up in his long fingers. A television sketch artist says that she had to lean over a raised bench to see more than just the tops of their heads. A public defender who represented Romarr kept the doodles he made on her yellow legal pad that day: on one sheet he drew a house with heart-shaped balloons overhead; on another he simply wrote his name and his father's all over the page. Another attorney took one look at the boys and began to cry.

---

* Because the boys were minors, Kotlowitz used pseudonyms to identify them in the *New Yorker* article. Their real names—Romarr Gipson and Elijah Henderson—became public in subsequent litigation and have been substituted here for the pseudonyms.

Probable-cause hearings are usually brief, and one of the few people to testify at this one was Detective Allen Nathaniel, who had interrogated the boys with his partner, James Cassidy. Nathaniel, who is black, spoke in clipped sentences and referred to Romarr and Elijah as "young men." He told the court that Romarr had admitted knocking Harris off her bike, and then confessed that he and Elijah had dragged her and the bike into the high weeds of a vacant lot. Nathaniel provided some details of the crime which had not been mentioned at the press conference, including the fact that Harris had a laceration in her vagina. Nathaniel also said that Romarr had told him that after the attack he went home to play with his puppies. The judge ordered the two boys held a few days longer at Hartgrove, so that psychiatrists could determine whether they posed any danger.

The press, the public, and even children's advocates reacted to the boys' arrest with horrified dismay. In the ten months preceding Harris's murder there had been four highly publicized incidents around the country in which boys between the ages of eleven and sixteen had opened fire on their schoolmates. But no children as young as Romarr and Elijah had ever been charged with murder—at least, not in recent memory. An editorial in the *Los Angeles Times* said that their case marked "The End of Innocence," and the *Chicago Sun-Times* warned that "more and more, we are seeing child play replaced with predatory behavior." Because I had written a book about children in a Chicago public-housing complex, I was invited to join in the laments. On *CBS This Morning*, I earnestly declared that we must figure out how "to prevent other Ryan Harrises." Only the residents of Romarr and Elijah's neighborhood steadfastly maintained that the boys could not be killers.

Chicago had already been the scene of two brutal crimes by children, just months apart, that shocked and frightened the nation. In the summer of 1994, eleven-year-old Robert (Yummy) Sandifer shot and killed a fourteen-year-old girl and was gunned down a few days later by two teenage fellow gang members. That October, two boys, ten and eleven, dangled five-year-old Eric Mores from a fourteenth-floor window, and then let him fall because he refused to steal candy for them. These incidents came at the end of a seven-year period in which arrests for juvenile homicides had more than doubled nationwide, and the stories that accompanied the statistics—of teenagers killed for leather jackets, or caught in drive-by shootings—evoked a latter-day "Lord of the Flies."

But Chicago is also the birthplace of the juvenile court, which was founded a hundred years ago by Jane Addams and her colleagues at Hull House on the premise that children require special treatment. Until 1899, children who broke the law were prosecuted and jailed like adults. Addams believed that the legal system should be designed to rehabilitate young people who got in trouble, not punish them. She persuaded state lawmakers to create a separate court for juveniles, without lawyers or rigid rules, in which the judge was free to act as a jurist, social worker, and "kind and just parent" in order to do what was in the best interests of the child.

As Chicago's juvenile-justice system celebrates its centennial this year, that notion has begun to look like an outmoded relic from another era, when children stole hubcaps and fought with fists. By the early 1980s, it was clear that the more lenient juvenile laws were being exploited by urban gangs, who dispatched "shorties" to commit felonies, and Illinois was among the first states to begin dismantling that system. The chief state's attorney at Cook County Juvenile Court at the time was a nun named Cathy Ryan. As a member of the School Sisters of St. Francis, an order dedicated to helping the poor, she was very much in the helping tradition of Jane Addams. But Ryan was alarmed by the viciousness of some juvenile criminals, and she helped write one of the nation's first automatic-transfer laws—state legislation that required fifteen- and sixteen-year-olds accused of murder, rape, and certain other violent offenses to be tried in adult court, where they would receive stiffer sentences. By last year, every state in the country had made it easier to try violent juvenile offenders as adults. In some jurisdictions, children of any age can be moved to regular court, and in many states children are transferred for nonviolent offenses such as drug dealing and fish-and-game violations.

Illinois transfer law does not apply to children as young as Romarr and Elijah. But they were arrested and prosecuted as if they were adult suspects, and their case shows just how deeply the special protections for children have eroded.

Chicago's Englewood neighborhood, which is on the city's South Side, across the expressway from the infamous Robert Taylor Homes, has one of the highest homicide rates in the city. In 1977 this community, of roughly fifty thousand, recorded fifty-five murders. It also has the largest number of registered sex offenders in the city—159, which is the equivalent of one every five blocks.

Englewood is an impoverished, dispirited community. Many of its single- and two-family frame houses, which lean like drunkards in the wind, sit on vast expanses of empty ground, because so many lots are vacant. On summer evenings, men used to gather after work at a place called the Hump, a raised vacant lot across from two taverns. But those taverns are gone, and fewer people have work. What civic life remains is centered on small bodegas and currency exchanges and, on Sundays, a multitude of storefront churches with names like United in Love Missionary Baptist Church, Get God in the Mind Ministries, and Blooming Rose Deliverance Church.

Ryan Harris, who lived in a Chicago suburb, was spending the summer in Englewood with her godmother, babysitting and attending a swimming program at Robeson High School. On a Monday afternoon, she left on her bike for the corner store and disappeared. The next day, neighbors organized a search, distributing 250 copies of Harris's school portrait. A teenage boy found her body behind a two-story red brick house, in a thicket of high weeds and shrubs near a short, steep embankment leading to a set of railroad tracks.

Harris was sprawled on her back, her bare legs wide apart, and one arm bent above her head, as if she were striking a pose. Her face and head were badly beaten, and her flowered underpants had been ripped off her body and stuffed in her mouth. It was later determined that she had skull fractures on both sides of her head, and that her underpants had been pushed so deep down her throat that she swallowed her tongue. A leaf, neatly folded, had been inserted in each nostril. Her striped short-sleeved shirt had been pulled up, partly exposing her breasts, and her lime-green shorts lay in a curled mess around her right ankle. She was still wearing a pair of white Nike sneakers, the only articles of clothing that were undisturbed.

Four neighbors dialed 911. When the first squad car arrived, fourteen minutes after the first call, the officers asked for backup to control the crowd that had already gathered. In that time, neighbors estimated, more than fifty people, mostly children, had tramped through the weeds to look at Harris's body—including, according to one woman at the scene, Elijah and Romarr. Elijah later told a psychologist he'd been playing basketball when a friend came running over to tell him he wanted to show him Harris's body. And Romarr at one point told the police that he and Elijah had seen the body the day it was discovered. After one young man fainted at the sight of the corpse, someone had the presence of mind to cover it with a green shirt.

Elijah lives with his parents and grandparents one block from where Harris's body was found. He is a year older than Romarr, and more easygoing and socially mature. When he smiles, it's as if someone had plugged him in—his two wide front teeth protrude slightly over his bottom lip, and his cheeks press upward toward his eyes. When I visited his family recently, Elijah, in white shirt, blue pants, and stocking feet, instructed me to wipe my shoes before coming in. He then ran off to the kitchen to finish his math homework.

Elijah likes school. Last year, in second grade, he received mostly As and Bs. In first grade, he won the Most Improved Speller Award. Often, after school, Elijah swept the floor at the corner Laundromat for a dollar. Elijah's mother and father, Rachel and Elijah, are not married, but they have lived together for twelve years. Rachel doesn't work; the elder Elijah is a self-employed car mechanic. The younger Elijah visited with us briefly in the living room and told me, in a quiet voice, about some newborn kittens in the basement which he had helped nurse.

Romarr and Elijah became friends during regular visits Romarr made to his grandmother, who lives across the alley. Romarr's parents, Sylvia and Jeremy, were high-school sweethearts, and both worked at Kentucky Fried Chicken. Sylvia is a supervisor; Jeremy works in maintenance. Each wears a tattoo with the other's name. Romarr, who seems restrained and cautious, idolizes his father and imitates him, wearing flannel shirts and braids tightly bound along his scalp.

Romarr had perfect attendance last year in first grade, and no major discipline problems. But he struggles with his studies and brought home mostly Cs and Ds. Remarkably, none of the school reports submitted to the court mentioned what is most striking about Romarr—his speech is muddy and atonal, like that of someone who is deaf, and he speaks in sentence fragments, often stopping in mid-thought. When I visited Romarr, his parents had to translate his one- and two-word answers.

"What's his name?" I asked, pointing to a figure he'd sketched while sitting on the kitchen floor.

"Bambam," he replied.

"Bambam?" I asked. "Like in *The Flintstones?*"

"Bambam," he insisted. "Bambam."

"Batman," his mother explained.

Louis Kraus, a psychiatrist who examined Romarr recently, concluded that he had "significant" cognitive disabilities. "You asked him a question and his answer wouldn't always be what you asked him," Dr. Kraus told me. "What he would say was not what he necessarily meant." When Romarr looked out the fifth-floor window of the hospital where Kraus met with him, instead of saying "We're high" he said "We're tall."

"I noticed that if I would suggest something to him, such as a place or period of time, that he would then incorporate it in his story," Kraus wrote in a report submitted to the court. "Within two or three more versions, it appeared that he was unclear what he had incorporated into his story and what potentially had occurred."

I haven't spoken to either of the boys about Harris's murder, but even if their lawyers had permitted me to, it would have been difficult to discern what actually occurred and what they believe occurred, given all that has happened since—the neighborhood rumors, the boys' interrogation by the police, the courtroom sessions, their lawyers' advice, their parents' counseling. What follows has been pieced together from the police report, from neighbors, from the boys' families, and from their attorneys. Department policies do not permit police or prosecutors to discuss their cases.

In the two weeks between Harris's death and the boys' arrest, the crime received scant notice in the Chicago press. But it was not taken lightly by the police, who immediately began a door-to-door canvass. They spoke with children and adults, and heard all kinds of stories. They were told that a group of kids had been riding their bikes with Harris behind Robeson High School. These children, Elijah among them, claimed that Harris had got into a red car with two men, and that the men had put her bike in the trunk—an account that the police came to doubt. One boy, who later admitted he'd lied, claimed that he'd seen a man carrying Harris down the street, and that she had a sock stuffed in her mouth. The police initially suspected a middle-aged man who lived in the building behind which Harris's body was found, but he had a solid alibi.

One account especially bothered the detectives. Harris's godmother, according to notes taken by the police, said that two days before the girl's disappearance a group of boys had thrown rocks at her and her friends as they rode their bikes to the store. Harris had taken her godmother to the house where one of the boys lived; it was Elijah's home. Harris's sister said that one of the boys wore his hair in braids. The police also received an anonymous tip that Harris's death had resulted from a "rock-throwing incident" in which some boys tried to take her bike. They began to focus their attention on Elijah and Romarr, dropping by their homes to talk informally with them and their parents.

On Sunday, August 9, detectives visited both boys' houses and asked Elijah's mother and Romarr's grandmother to bring the boys down to the police station. The detectives wanted to talk with them about what they might have seen or heard. They did not say that the children were suspects.

Sometime in the mid-afternoon, the boys arrived at Area One Police Headquarters, which handles violent crimes for much of the South Side. The detectives' bureau is on the second floor, at the end of a long, bare hallway. The two lead detectives in the case, Cassidy and Nathaniel, have been on the force for twenty-five and twelve years, respectively. Cassidy, who is white, has a boyish look, his hair parted on the side and brushed neatly across his forehead. Nathaniel is stocky and somewhat brash, and often cocks his head when he speaks. The detectives received permission from Elijah's mother to interview the boy alone, then took him into the lineup room. Elijah told the police, according to their report, that Romarr had led him to Harris's body right after it was discovered and that Harris had been naked with something in her mouth. He told this story twice.

The two detectives then told Romarr's grandmother that they wanted to interview him alone, and took him into their lieutenant's office, a ten-by-fifteen-foot room with three chairs, a desk, and several filing cabinets. Cassidy and Nathaniel asked the boy general questions about his favorite sport, and whether he was looking forward to going back to school—presumably to make him feel comfortable. They told Romarr that good boys only told the truth. They asked him if he was a good boy. Each detective took one of Romarr's hands, and they told him they were his friends and asked if he'd taken his friend to Harris's body.

At that point, according to the report:

> Romarr said in essence without further questioning . . . that he and Elijah were playing throwing rocks when they saw Ryan Harris riding her bicycle. Romarr said he threw a rock, hitting the girl in the head and knocking her off her bike. After she fell off the bicycle, she wasn't moving, so he and Elijah each took one of the girl's arms and moved her into the weeds, where they began "to play with her soft." He said they took her panties off and put them in the girl's mouth and rubbed leaves on her. Romarr said they put leaves in the girl's nose and also a stem. They took her bicycle and moved it into the weeds by the railroad tracks. He said "someone must have come and taken the bike, because he never saw it again."

Though Romarr and Elijah both had family members waiting in nearby rooms, Cassidy and Nathaniel then asked for two youth investigators to join them. Under Illinois law, a youth investigator or a parent must be present when a child is interrogated and is read the Miranda warnings. A youth investigator ordinarily handles crimes committed against children by parents but is sometimes used in a case like this as the designated adult in order to, as the detectives wrote in this report, "watch out for the best interests of the child." But the report does not indicate that these investigators did anything but observe silently.

Nathaniel told Romarr that he didn't have to speak with them, that he could have his grandmother in the room if he wished, and that he could have a lawyer present—"a person [who] is on his side looking out for him." Romarr told his story again to the officers, and as he ate a Happy Meal, brought by another detective, added a few new details. This time, he said he—not Elijah—had stuffed Harris's panties in her mouth and put the leaves in her nose.

Romarr's grandmother recalls that after three and a half hours the detectives emerged and told her about Romarr's statement. She remembers that one of the detectives said, "It was an accident. You can take him home. It'll be all over." She told me, "I got hysterical. I said, 'That boy didn't do nothing like that. He ain't no murderer.'" She refused to let her grandson speak any further to the detectives, who asked that she and Romarr remain at the station.

The detective then approached Elijah and his mother and told them that they considered him a witness, not a suspect. The detective told Rachel that they only wanted her son to identify some photographs, and that she did not need to accompany them. In an office nearby, Cassidy informed Elijah that Romarr's story had differed from his. Tell me again what you saw, Cassidy said, showing him Harris's school picture. According to the report, Elijah then changed his story and confirmed Romarr's account but he would not repeat this new version of events in his mother's presence. She says the police told her, too, that they considered the death an accident and that everything would be all right. "We were cooperating with them," she explained to me. "We thought we were helping out."

Cassidy called the medical examiner and asked whether a thrown rock would be consistent with Harris's injuries. No, he was told, the injuries were so severe that someone had to have delivered blows to her head as she lay on the ground. Cassidy concluded that the boys were lying and that they must have acted in concert, one of them holding Harris down while the other beat her head with a rock. At roughly eleven thirty that night, Elijah and Romarr were charged with killing Ryan Harris.

Romarr's mother, Sylvia, had arrived at the station sometime earlier, and she remembers seeing her son nodding, half asleep, a toy car from the Happy Meal still clutched in one hand. She carried him to the squad car and held him tight against her chest as they rode to Hartgrove. "I asked them to let him sleep till after I left," she said. "He'd never been away from home."

Elijah was still awake, and his father, who had also come to the station, tried to comfort the boy. "I didn't know how to explain to my child that he was being charged with murder," Elijah senior said. "I tried to keep a clear face. I told him they were just going to take some tests, that he'd be home soon, that there wasn't really anything to worry about."

Since no recording was made of the boys' statements, there is no way to know exactly what information Romarr and Elijah volunteered and what they parroted back to the detectives. Still, it is well known that interrogating children, especially under stressful conditions, can produce unreliable results.

Thomas Grisso, a clinical psychologist who heads the Department of Forensic Training and Research at the University of Massachusetts Medical School, is helping conduct one of the few national studies of the competency of accused children. In the early 1970s, Grisso's research demonstrated that most children under fourteen are unable to understand their Miranda warnings, and many states have passed laws requiring police to make their best efforts to have parents present for interrogations. I showed Grisso a copy of the police report on the questioning of Romarr and Elijah. He said, "The holding of hands. We're friends. Only bad boys lie. Even if all you're looking for is the least distorted, most accurate report from these kids, this is not the way to do it, because it heightens their feeling that they need to comply with what it is the authority figure wants to hear or what they think he wants to hear. They themselves told more than one version. By definition, either all of those versions are wrong or one is right. By that measure, there seems to be some degree of distortion."

I asked Grisso about the detectives' conclusion that the children had been truthful about part of their story—that they threw a rock at Harris—but had been misleading about other parts, such as not confessing to holding Harris down and pummeling her to death.

"Can kids lie? Can kids mislead? Yes. Kids can be afraid and say things they didn't do," he said. "But if they had bludgeoned her later, it would be more likely for them to lie and say they hadn't thrown a stone at her. To say they had done something that might have been injurious if they were trying to hide the fact that they had indeed bludgeoned her with a brick would be odd. Kids at that age just don't think things through at that nuanced level. We attribute intentions to kids that are adult-like."

Moreover, adults often fail to take account of all the factors that can influence their conversations with children. An article in the March issue of the *Journal of Experimental Psychology: Applied* reports on an experiment in which mothers were asked to interview their preschool-age children about a series of play activities. The study found that the mothers often later confused what the children had told them and what they had, in fact, asked the children. "The mothers are guided by hypotheses, as the police are," Stephen Ceci, a coauthor of the article, told me. All the time the police "are asking questions and not getting answers—firing blanks—they're not writing it down," he went on. "They don't write down what I consider is significant. It's not just important what the kid ultimately tells you. It's equally important how many times he was asked it and denied it before he finally assented, and what the emotional atmospherics were."

There is a psychological term for what may have happened during Romarr's and Elijah's interrogations—cryptomnesia. It means that someone unwittingly claims to have generated an idea that was generated by someone else—a phenomenon more common in children than adults. It is possible that Romarr unconsciously created a narrative of events in his mind based on the detectives' questions to him, then later repeated it as a confession. Dr. Kraus, the psychologist who evaluated Romarr, said that, given Romarr's speech deficits, it's doubtful that he could have spun out an intelligible yarn, from beginning to end, without prompting. Moreover, some of what the children told the detectives, by the detectives' own admission, was patently false. Some of it was clearly the result of confusion. Romarr told the detective that after Harris was killed he went home to play with his puppies. According to his parents, he didn't have any puppies at the time. He got a puppy the day before he was interviewed by the police—nearly two weeks after Harris's murder.

R. Eugene Pincham is still fit and trim at the age of seventy-three, a tall, broad-shouldered African American with a shaved head offset by a graying mustache. Pincham is a legendary figure in Chicago. When he was practicing law full-time, other attorneys would break away from their cases in the Criminal Courts Building to hear his spellbinding closing arguments. After twenty-five years as a lawyer, Pincham spent fourteen years as a judge, first on the circuit court, then on the appellate court. His long legal career, however, has been somewhat overshadowed by a quixotic foray into politics. During the 1987 reelection bid of Harold Washington, the city's first African American mayor, Pincham declared that anyone on Chicago's South Side who didn't vote for Washington should be hanged—a statement that earned him the sobriquet Lynch'em Pincham. When Washington subsequently died in office, Pincham left the bench to first run for mayor and then for state's attorney, but was soundly defeated in both races. Though he no longer practices full-time, Pincham provides guidance to several of the young black attorneys in town, including Andre Grant, who was hired by Elijah's parents. Just five years out of law school, Grant felt overwhelmed by the press attention, and begged Pincham to join the case. "You keep doing

what you're doing," Pincham advised him at first. "You've got them vexed."
But Grant kept calling, and Pincham finally relented.

When I visited Pincham, in his office at home on the South Side, he
said, "We have a saying in our culture, in our church, 'You ain't lived on
my street,' and if you ain't lived on my street you don't see what I see, you
don't hear what I hear. The accusations against these children spread like
wildfire in part because of racism. Racism was involved in that they"—
the media—"were saying, 'You see, inner-city black children are literally
uncivilized. They'll kill each other for a bicycle. And then they'll rape the
person.'" He continued, "If you're gonna steal a bicycle, you're gonna steal
a bicycle from some kid you don't know anything about. You ain't gonna
ride around with a girl all day on a bicycle. That doesn't make sense. Both
Romarr and Elijah had a bicycle. What they gonna steal her bicycle for?"
Pincham was also convinced that the boys were too physically slight to
inflict such a mauling and too immature to commit a sex crime.

At a court hearing four days after the boys' arrest to consider whether
they could go home, Pincham appeared in his signature black cowboy boots
and black Stetson, his face, as always, set in a self-assured grin that borders
on mischievous. It is unusual for a lawyer of Pincham's stature to appear
in juvenile court, which is almost exclusively the domain of poor clients
represented by public defenders. Two experienced defenders, Catherine
Ferguson and Beth Tarzia, represented Romarr. They understood the idio-
syncrasies of juvenile court better than Pincham did, yet their hard work
was eclipsed by his theatrics. The minute Pincham arrived at the courthouse and demanded seats for the crowd of reporters, his presence promised to transform the hearing into a full-blown courtroom drama. "Things
crackled," one reporter recalls.

Pincham lugged a medical scale into the courtroom, placed it before
the judge, and weighed his client, Elijah, who was fourteen pounds lighter
and five inches shorter than the police estimates. To demonstrate Elijah's
featheriness, Pincham placed a hand under the boy's armpit and lifted him
a foot off the carpeted floor. He lectured the bench on the Constitution
and quoted the Bible instructing the judge to "do unto others as you would
have them do unto you." He sparred with the state's attorneys in the courtroom and, in the judge's chambers, chided them for their inexperience.

The rancorous session went on for five hours. Romarr spent much of the
afternoon leaning on an attorney's shoulder, whispering in her ear, "Wanna
g'home." The boys drew in coloring books, and at one point Ferguson made
paper airplanes for them under the table. They clearly had little understanding of the proceedings. A few days earlier, when Grant first met Elijah and

told him he was his lawyer, Elijah asked, "Like a policeman?" To explain his role in terms that Elijah would understand, Grant, who has a five-year-old son, asked Elijah which Power Ranger was his favorite. "The blue one," the boy said, and from then on Elijah referred to Grant as the Blue Power Ranger and to Pincham as the Black Power Ranger.

Dr. Kraus, who had interviewed Romarr, and a second therapist, who had interviewed Elijah, testified that neither boy posed a danger. Both also said that they were struck by the stability of the boys' families. Kraus reported that Romarr's parents had brought to their interview with him a paper bag full of paraphernalia, including two trophies for perfect attendance, a science-fair award for flipping spoons into a cup, a basketball trophy, and a "good helper" award. The other therapist reported that Elijah's parents had arrived with an aunt, three grandparents, and a great-grandmother.

But the prosecutors fought hard to keep the boys in state custody. They argued that the two therapists had not spent enough time with the boys to make a complete evaluation, then aggressively challenged the credentials of one therapist. In a closing statement, Patti Sudendorf, a prosecutor who had recently transferred from adult court, countered Pincham's Bible verses with one of her own. She stood in front of the lawyers' table and turned to point an index finger at Romarr and Elijah. Drawing out each word slowly and clearly, she declared, "Thou shalt not kill." Romarr started to cry; he bowed his head and mumbled, "I din't do nothing."

Judge Gerald Winiecki, who was handling the initial proceedings before the case went to trial, struck a compromise—the boys would be confined to their homes and fitted with ankle monitors. Court officials had to punch extra notches in the anklets. The boys received automated calls at all hours asking them to repeat a password, which they often didn't remember. Within days, the officials had stopped the calls. Three weeks later, the presiding judge decided that it was inappropriate to detain young children, even at home, and ordered the monitors removed.

The confrontational tone and the legalistic antics at the boys' pretrial hearing showed just how far the juvenile-justice system had strayed from the model of an informal conference focused on the best interests of the child. Things had begun to change in 1967, after an Arizona judge sentenced a fifteen-year-old boy, named Gerald Gault, to up to six years for making an obscene phone call. Gault, who had not been represented by a lawyer, appealed the ruling. The case eventually went to the Supreme Court, which held that children charged with a crime were entitled to the same legal rights as adults, including the right to counsel and protection against self-incrimination.

As a result, juvenile proceedings began to look more like those of an adult court, at a time when the crimes committed by young people were beginning to look more like adult crimes. Between 1965 and 1985—when the drug trade exploded and handguns and automatic weapons became readily available—the number of minors arrested for violent felonies doubled. (By the early 1990s, the number had tripled.) The public began to lose confidence in the juvenile-justice system. By 1994, according to a Gallup poll, 68 percent of those surveyed believed that children charged with violent crimes should be prosecuted as adults.

That certainly was Cathy Ryan's opinion during her first tour as chief prosecutor at Cook County Juvenile Court, in the early 1980s; in her first year, the number of youths sent to prison in the county jumped 113 percent. "She was pretty typical of your state's attorneys," recalls a colleague from that period. "Cathy was very much a law-and-order person."

But by the time Ryan returned to the juvenile court post, in January 1997, she had a radically different view. She had spent thirteen years in private practice and had seen the system from the other side as the lawyer for parents of neglected or delinquent children. She became convinced that the juvenile courts had become too intent on punishment.

Today Ryan sounds a bit like Jane Addams. The justice system, she says, should take a less adversarial approach to children and begin "reaching their hearts and minds." Shortly after returning to the prosecutor's job, she told me, "This is a historical moment at juvenile court." The system, she believed, had "lost its way." She went on, "In the whole climate that we're in, what you hear about is, 'We're going to get tougher, we're going to punish, we're going to send these kids away.' Now, there's always a group that requires more creativity and direction of resources."

Ryan, fifty-two, is a reserved, unimposing woman who is five feet two and who wears buttoned-to-the-collar suits, the newest of which she bought four years ago. She lives in an apartment with three other nuns and gives her $153,000 salary to the order. In her quiet way, she has set out to reverse the trend toward prosecuting children without any special consideration of their immaturity and vulnerability. "The juvenile court at its best is really a commitment on our society's part that we care about youth and that we are going to work to provide at least an opportunity for a productive future," she explained, though she was quick to admit that this "was perhaps not the traditional view of what a prosecutor is." Since 1997, Ryan has reduced the number of requests for transfer to adult court and has experimented with neighborhood tribunals to oversee nonviolent juvenile cases.

When Romarr and Elijah were arrested, Ryan was on vacation, driving along the Mississippi with her mother and her sister. Another senior prosecutor was put in charge of the case, but Ryan rushed back to Chicago, and the next day I ran into her in the juvenile court building. "What do you think?" I asked. She told me that neither family had a record with the Department of Children and Family Services. Ryan has been at this long enough to know that when young children commit sex crimes there is almost always some history of abuse. The sexual aspects of Harris's murder clearly raised questions for Ryan, though she believed that Romarr and Elijah might have been involved in the death in some way. And although she would not comment publicly on the case, she implied that, had it been her call, she would not have prosecuted them. She described two other homicides she had recently handled. In one case, a ten-year-old boy left at home to babysit for five younger children had repeatedly hit a fifteen-month-old to stop him from crying. In the other, a nine-year-old boy, trying to make a three-month-old baby stop crying, tossed her into the air several times and fractured her skull. Ryan did not file charges against either boy. (In the first incident, she charged the mother with neglect.) Instead, both children will receive therapeutic treatment.

Working behind the scenes in the Harris case, Ryan and another high-ranking prosecutor convinced their colleagues that they should ask the court to order competency exams for Romarr and Elijah. Did the boys understand the proceedings? Had they understood what took place in the police station? Such requests are made routinely by the prosecution. Yet, short of dropping the charges, such evaluations seemed the only way to avert a messy trial in which the boys' lawyers would no doubt point out that the police had rushed to charge Romarr and Elijah before they had any physical evidence linking the boys to the crime. The police had not searched the boys' homes for bloody clothes, or for Harris's bike—which was never found.

Meanwhile, Pincham had received the police report, which mentioned that three youngsters had separately told detectives they'd seen an unidentified man walking with Harris near where her body was found. The police had taken these sightings seriously enough to have a police artist draw a composite sketch of the man. Convinced that an adult pedophile had murdered Harris—and that police had evidence to that effect—Pincham defied standard legal practice and handed out portions of the report to the press. As he had hoped, this led to a number of articles recounting how the detectives had coaxed statements from the boys; Maurice Possley's coverage in the *Chicago Tribune* was particularly aggressive. As a result, the editorial pages, which only weeks earlier had been deploring the savagery of today's children, began to decry the lax police procedures for interrogating young suspects and to call for the videotaping of confessions.

Andrew Berman, the judge scheduled to preside over Romarr and Elijah's trial, later told me that he read the news stories and asked himself if he would be forced to throw out the confessions. Most states, including Illinois, require a judge to consider what is called "the totality of circumstances"—the child's age, his criminal history, his IQ—in deciding whether to admit a statement made when parents were not present. Romarr and Elijah were so young, and the charges against them so serious, that it seemed obvious that the parents should have been there.

On September 4, four weeks after the boys' arrest, Berman called the lawyers to a preliminary hearing at 11:00. (The judge had excused Romarr and Elijah from pretrial proceedings.) The state's attorneys asked for a ten-minute postponement, then an hour later, Berman convened the session, and Sudendorf asked to speak for the prosecution. She stood and, without much inflection, read a three-paragraph prepared statement. "Yesterday afternoon," she read, "we received a telephone call from the crime lab advising us that semen was present on the panties of the victim Ryan Harris. After we received that information, we were informed by medical experts that the possibility of semen coming from seven- and eight-year-olds is highly remote." Sudendorf then announced that the prosecutor's office was dropping all charges against the boys. As at the first hearing on the case, there was a prolonged hush, but then, Berman recalls, "pandemonium." Pincham threw his arms around Grant, who burst into tears. One of the public defenders embraced a reporter. The other whispered into the air, "Thank God."

Three weeks later, a state police crime lab technician found that the DNA in the semen closely matched that of Eddie Durr, a convicted sex offender, who had been in jail at the time of Harris's murder. The technician began to look at relatives, and got a precise match with Durr's brother, Floyd, a twenty-nine-year-old Englewood resident. Floyd was in the county jail awaiting trial for allegedly raping three girls, two of them under thirteen, but he had not been incarcerated at the time of Harris's death.

It rankles many in the African American community that the police have not charged Floyd Durr with Harris's murder. According to a high-placed source, Floyd had told the police that as he happened to be walking past the vacant lot he heard a commotion; when he walked into the thicket of high weeds, he saw two boys—he couldn't identify—and Harris's body.

He also told police that he then masturbated over the girl. One teenager identified Floyd in a lineup as having been with Harris shortly before her disappearance, but the police have questions about his credibility.

Police and prosecutors refuse to comment on the Harris murder investigation, other than to say that it is ongoing. Floyd Durr, who could be sentenced to as many as 125 years if convicted on the three pending rape charges, is off the streets—being held without bail in the county jail. The authorities still believe that Elijah and Romarr were present at Harris's death because they knew details about the condition of her body. While neither the police nor the state's attorney will say so, the boys remain suspects, and investigators are not yet ready to admit that their confessions are flawed. (However, a directive has been issued to ensure that a parent or guardian is present whenever a child twelve or under is interviewed, and a commission—which includes Cathy Ryan—has been convened to explore the competency of children under eleven to understand their Miranda warnings and to stand trial.)

Pincham is preparing to file a civil suit against the police, charging that Romarr and Elijah were framed. He will argue that Detective James Cassidy was involved in a similarly troubling case in 1994, in which an eleven-year-old African American boy told Cassidy that he had killed his neighbor, an eighty-three-year-old white woman. There was no physical evidence linking the boy to the crime, and his parents were not present at the interview. Cassidy testified that the boy, who had originally been brought in as a witness, confessed spontaneously, and that when Cassidy then tried to reach the mother she was away from home. The boy was convicted, and made a ward of the Department of Children and Family Services. The Northwestern Law School legal clinic, along with lawyers working pro bono at Jenner & Block, a corporate law firm, have taken steps to overturn the verdict on procedural grounds. They have also identified apparent lapses in the investigation, including the failure of the police to check whether a palm print and a partial shoe print at the crime scene matched the boy's.

Still, there is little to suggest that Cassidy is a rogue cop. There are not complaints of brutality or verbal abuse in his file, and one former prosecutor described him as "a gas pumper"—a detective who goes about his work without an agenda. Moreover, as one detective said to me, "What reward does a detective get for railroading a kid?"

But the possibility that Cassidy and Nathaniel were just workaday cops, going by the book, makes the treatment of Romarr and Elijah—as if they were just like any other suspects, despite their obvious immaturity—even more disquieting. "That comes from a drumbeat that echoes across the country," Robert Schwartz, the head of the Philadelphia-based Juvenile Law Center, says. "Phrases like 'adult time for adult crimes,' the use of labels like 'superpredators,' the political bandwagon to see who can get tougher on younger and younger kids—all this creates a climate in which law enforcement can react with a knee-jerk response, as it did with Romarr and Elijah, that gets everything wrong about where these kids are developmentally." Franklin Zimring, the author of the recent book *American Youth Violence*, says that the prosecution of the two boys "is a cautionary tale," and he adds, "We just don't know what its persuasive power will be until the next time the TV cameras line up to tell us how bad our children are."

Elijah and Romarr have tried to return to their normal activities, but they have been taunted in school about Harris's murder, and they both have nightmares. When I visited Elijah at home recently with Pincham, he still seemed disoriented by the events of the summer. Pincham marched up to him, clapped a hand on his shoulder, and asked, "Do you know who I am?" Elijah got flustered and replied, "The principal?"

During the court proceedings, Romarr's parents managed to insulate him from the press. But in November he saw a television report that showed a sketch artist's drawings of his tightly braided hair. That night, Romarr took a pair of scissors and began cutting off his braids. His father finished the job for him, and carries one of the braids in his wallet. "That's a good-luck piece," he told me, holding up the six-inch braid. "It could have been worse."

Epilogue

Floyd Durr eventually was charged with the crime. Because he had an IQ below sixty-five, making him ineligible for the death penalty, prosecutors agreed to a sentence of life plus thirty years in exchange for a guilty plea. The sentence had little practical significance because Durr already was serving 125 years for his previous assaults on young girls.

Civil rights claims were brought on behalf of both boys against the City of Chicago. The case of the younger child, Elijah Gipson, was settled in October 2004 for an amount that would come to be seen as paltry—$2 million. The older child, Romarr Henderson, held out for another eleven months, until September 2005, when the city offered and he accepted a $6.2 million settlement.

On April 3, 2008, R. Eugene Pincham died at age eighty-two of complications from lung and brain cancer.

ANTRON McCRAY, KEVIN RICHARDSON, YUSEF SALAAM, RAYMOND SANTANA, AND KHAREY WISE

The confession was unanimous—they beat and raped the Central Park jogger

SYDNEY H. SCHANBERG

NEW YORK, NEW YORK

Every now and again, we get a look, usually no more than a glimpse, at how the justice system really works. What we see—before the sanitizing curtain is drawn abruptly down—is a process full of human fallibility and error, sometimes noble, more often unfair, rarely evil but frequently unequal, and through it all inevitably influenced by issues of race and class and economic status. In short, it's a lot like other big, unwieldy institutions. Such a moment of clear sight emerges from the mess we know as the case of the Central Park jogger.

She was horribly beaten and raped and left near death on an April night thirteen years ago. Five Harlem teenagers who were part of a "wilding" spree by more than thirty youths in Central Park that night were accused of the rape. Other charges included sexual abuse, assault, riot, and robbery. Under intense questioning, they at first confessed, in written statements and on videotape, but shortly thereafter retracted everything—contending that they had been intimidated, lied to, and coerced into making the statements.

There was no physical evidence linking them to the crime—no blood match, no semen match, nothing. The victim could not provide an identification of any assailant because the battering left her with no memory whatever of the episode or even of starting out on her jog. But in two court trials a year later, the juries were persuaded by the vivid confessions that each of the five had at least some role in the attack on the young woman. Four—because they were under sixteen—were sentenced under juvenile

From "A Journey Through the Tangled Case of the Central Park Jogger," *Village Voice*, November 26, 2002. Copyright © Village Voice Media. Adapted with permission.

guidelines and served jail terms of five to ten years. The fifth, Kharey Wise, who was sixteen and thus classed as an adult, got a sentence of five to fifteen years. He came out of prison just last August.

Sometime last winter a serial rapist and murderer named Matias Reyes, who is serving a sentence of thirty-three and one-third years to life in state prison, sought out the authorities, told them religion had entered his life, and confessed that he and he alone had brutalized and raped the jogger. His DNA, it was soon learned, matched that of the semen found in the jogger's cervix and on one of her running socks.

The public wasn't told any of this for several months as the shocked "justice system" wrestled with the gargantuan problem.

Manhattan District Attorney Robert Morgenthau, whose office prosecuted the case, began an investigation. It was not as hurried as the first one, nor were as many detectives assigned to it. Despite the new evidence, the police department, whose leadership is reported to still believe that the five teenagers had at least some connection to the rape, recently started its own investigation. Morgenthau has a court date of December 5 to deliver his recommendations on whether the convictions should be vacated. Unseen backstage, the two assistant district attorneys in charge of Morgenthau's reinvestigation, Nancy Ryan and Peter Casolaro, are said to be under heavy lobbying from the players who produced those convictions. It's now a tug-of-war between a fair decision and one that would try to protect some carefully crafted reputations.

State law would seem to favor the five convicted youths. New York's Criminal Procedure Law—section 440.10(1)(g)—states that if "new evidence" is produced that probably would have affected the original verdicts, then a court may "vacate" the convictions. There is no requirement for the court to rule that the confessions were coerced.

Back in 1989, the atmosphere surrounding this crime was, modestly put, emotional. The city was crackling with racial aggravation. And the mayoral campaign had begun—David Dinkins, who is black, would be opposing Rudolph Giuliani, who was already showing his disdain for many in the black leadership.

And then, on the night of April 19, in the city's premier greensward, a white, twenty-eight-year-old honors graduate from Wellesley and Yale, a rising star at Salomon Brothers investment bank, was allegedly raped by a group of black and Latino youths who, the authorities said, had thrown her to the ground, stripped her of her clothes, and, as she struggled desperately, bashed her all over her body with a rock and other objects to stop her flailing. Her left eye socket was crushed and her skull broken through to the brain. She lost 80 percent of her blood. The doctors at Metropolitan Hospital, who initially told police her chances to live were almost nil, saved her.

Press coverage was wall-to-wall. The rape wasn't the only crime committed in the same area that night. During the roving band's hour or two in the park, a number of cyclists and pedestrians and joggers had also been assaulted. Two of them, both men, were beaten into the dirt and, like the jogger, left in pools of blood. In such crimes, given the media attention and the potential for community anxiety and even unrest, pressure on police and prosecutors is immense. The unwritten edict from on high is: solve this case instantly and put the perpetrators behind bars. In less than forty-eight hours, the police had rounded up a dozen or so suspects and reported that a few had already confessed.

A week later, with five youths of color charged, Donald Trump, a loud real estate developer and casino operator whose kinship with either truth or justice has never been obvious, took out a full-page ad in each of the city's four daily papers urging New Yorkers to ignore those like Mayor Koch and Cardinal O'Connor who had counseled against "hate and rancor." Of the accused, Trump wrote: "I want to hate these muggers and murderers. They should be forced to suffer and, when they kill, they should be executed. . . . I am looking to punish them. . . . I want them to be afraid." Ugliness was in the air.

Linda Fairstein, who controlled the case as head of the Manhattan district attorney's Sex Crimes Prosecution Unit, says now: "I don't think there was any rush to judgment." Perhaps. But there certainly was a rush.

So intense was the push for confessions that Fairstein, who had sought and achieved celebrity from her sex-crime prosecutions, bullied and stalled and blocked the mother and two friends of one suspect, Yusef Salaam, from gaining access to him. Fairstein's apparent purpose was to keep the suspect under wraps because she had been informed by the interrogating detective that the questioning was in a delicate phase where Salaam had begun to make some admissions. A short while later, Fairstein realized she could not bar the mother any longer, and the angry parent halted the interrogation.

Thus, unlike the four others charged with the rape, Salaam had not signed any written statement nor given a videotaped confession. The prosecution's only evidence of what he said at his interrogation came from the detective, Thomas McKenna, who testified at Salaam's trial a year later. (The case was split into two trials, with three of the defendants grouped in the first one—Antron McCray, fifteen, Yusef Salaam, fifteen, and Raymond Santana, fourteen—and the remaining two accused—Kevin Richardson, fourteen, and Kharey Wise, sixteen—in the second. These groupings were largely maneuvered by the prosecution so as to get information to the juries in the order the district attorney's office preferred. Both trials were held in 1990, and both lasted two months.)

On the stand, McKenna, a detective for twenty years, openly acknowledged that he had used a ruse on the night after the rape to get Salaam's "confession." The boy, McKenna said, at first repeatedly denied having been in Central Park. Then, went McKenna's testimony, he, the detective, made the following untrue statement to Salaam: "Look, I don't care if you tell me anything. I don't care what you say to me. We have fingerprints on the jogger's pants. They're satin, they're a very smooth surface, and we have been able to get fingerprints off of them. I'm just going to compare your prints to the prints we have on the pants, and if they match up, you don't have to tell me anything. Because you're going down for rape."

At this, according to McKenna's testimony, Salaam blurted, "I was there but I didn't rape her." And then, said McKenna, the boy calmly proceeded to admit that he had hit the downed jogger twice with an iron bar and felt her breasts, but said it was four other boys who actually "fucked her." Salaam identified two of them, Kevin Richardson and Kharey Wise, McKenna testified. He said he didn't know the other two.

There never were, of course, any fingerprints on the jogger's running pants.

As described by McKenna, his trick-playing on Salaam is, under present case law, quite legal. As are many other kinds of law enforcement distortions, misdirections, and veiled (and sometimes not so veiled) suggestions that leniency will be granted if the witness is forthcoming. The justice system's premise for accepting these stratagems is that an innocent person will not falsely incriminate himself.

After the trial, some jurors said the detective had gained credibility with them by being so candid about his methods.

Probably the most blatant example of the prosecution's contortions under pressure had to do with distorting the meaning of critical evidence—the DNA. To wit, the district attorney's office all along, right up to the first trial in 1990, had told the press, and therefore the public, that the DNA results were "inconclusive" because they showed only a "weak" or "faint" pattern—leaving the impression that, while there was no match, the samples likely did belong to one or more of the indicted five, but were merely of poor quality. In fact, the semen samples taken from the victim were absolutely conclusive in ways important to the defense.

The prosecution never did reveal the true DNA results and analysis. The FBI did—at the first trial, more than a year after the crime. The disclosure was made by the witness from the FBI laboratory, Special Agent Dwight Adams. And it didn't come in his direct testimony as a witness for the prosecution, because Assistant District Attorney Elizabeth Lederer avoided any question to him that might lead to the whole truth. However, Adams told the story openly, with no reluctance, in his cross-examination by defense attorney Mickey Joseph.

Adams's testimony was a major departure from the line the prosecution had spun. Answering Joseph's questions, the FBI expert said that while there was no DNA match with the blood samples from any of the defendants or possible suspects in the wilding, or the sample from the jogger's boyfriend, some firm conclusions could be made. True, there was no match, Adams said, but all fourteen of the DNA samples could be excluded as belonging to the person or persons who penetrated the victim in Central Park that night. Answering Joseph's questions matter-of-factly, the FBI expert explained that in DNA testing, it is easier to exclude than to match. He said the weak pattern obtained from the cervix and the stronger pattern found on the sock, though not as complete as needed for a match, were nonetheless clear and strong enough to determine that they definitely did not belong to any of the fourteen people whose blood was tested.

The prosecution had known all along that the tests were not "inconclusive." They knew the results proved that the semen could not have come from any of the five defendants. And yet the prosecution stayed mute.

Adams revealed one more thing on the stand that the prosecution had never told the public: the FBI lab had compared the semen from the cervix and the semen from the sock—and they were from the same person. "They seemed to match," he said clearly.

In hindsight, the FBI disclosures should have exploded a bomb in the heart of the prosecution case. But the testimony set off no fireworks. The disturbing confessions were what had captured the minds of the jury—and the press.

What Adams's testimony meant was that only one person, still at large, had ejaculated inside the victim—while keeping in mind that since some rapists are not able to function sexually during the attack, the possibility that both Reyes and a temporarily impotent group assaulted her cannot be absolutely ruled out. (The police have lately been searching for possible evidence of a link between Reyes and the five who were convicted.)

But the theory of the crime that the hard, forensic evidence most supports is that the group of five, or some of them, took no part, or no significant part, in the sexual assault. This raises the further possibility or likelihood, as counterintuitive as this may seem given the confessions, that the five defendants were indeed "coerced" as the law defines the word—which would support their charges that they were intimidated, fed details about the rape, told that their friends had informed on them, and prodded with subtle hints that if they confessed about the others they would help themselves.

Penetration of the victim is a corollary legal issue here. Under the law, penetration is necessary before the crime of sexual assault rises to that of rape. In the case of a group of attackers, penetration by only one person (though, again, not necessarily ejaculation) is enough to implicate the rest of a group in a rape. Otherwise, in this case, the five could only be charged with other crimes committed during the wilding. The indictments did charge them with several other crimes, such as assault, robbery, and riot, but the pivot of the prosecution's case—and the primary focus—was always the rape.

At the same time, it is important to remember, in any examination of the public record of this flawed investigation and prosecution, that even if these five youths, or at least some of them, were not guilty of rape or sexual assault, they were not innocents—having been convicted of a whole series of other crimes committed in the rampage that night. One need only recall that among those crimes, two men, John Loughlin and Antonio Diaz, were horribly beaten and left bleeding and unconscious.

Timothy Sullivan, then the editor of *Manhattan Lawyer* and now news editor of the Courtroom Television Network, wrote a book in 1992 titled *Unequal Verdicts*, the most authoritative account of the trials and the case as it stood at that point.

Sullivan's book provides most of the now-forgotten details, and he goes behind the scenes a lot. He recounts several instances where the pressure and urgency felt by the prosecution showed through. Here are two of them.

1. Sullivan writes that Elizabeth Lederer, a respected assistant district attorney whom Linda Fairstein had named as lead attorney for the trials, was fully aware of all the pieces the prosecution was missing, one of which was proof or a statement that penetration had taken place. The following excerpt shows some of Lederer's questioning of Raymond Santana on videotape. Santana has told her that Kevin Richardson, fourteen, was the only one he had seen "having sex" with the victim.

> "Did he penetrate her?" she asked, referring to Richardson. "Did he put his penis inside of her?" "Um hmm," he confirmed. "Did he say that he had?" "No, he didn't say it." Santana scoffed. "But you could tell?" "Yeah." "How could you tell?" "Because he was

havin' sex with her! That's what you're supposed to do when you havin' sex!"

Lederer persisted. "Well, when he was doing that, was he moving up and down?"

"Yeah," Santana replied and, rather than wait for her to ask again how he could tell, added: "'Cause I seen it."

"And so you could see that he was moving," said Lederer, "thrusting up and down . . . thrusting into her?" "Yeah," said Santana. "That's how I knew he was havin' sex with her."

What leaps out from this interview is how Lederer, very frustrated, lapses into badgering to try to drag the information she needs out of him. Equally revealing is that Santana never actually says he saw Richardson's penis inside the victim.

2. In late November 1990, on the ninth day of deliberations in the second trial—of the two remaining defendants, Kevin Richardson and Kharey Wise—the press and players anxiously awaited the verdict (which didn't come until December 11).

Sullivan writes: "'If we don't get a rape conviction,' said Detective McKenna, 'we lost the case.' A reporter asked whether a conviction on attempted murder, technically a higher count, would not be considered a victory. No, said McKenna, it had to be a rape conviction. Detective John Taglioni nodded in agreement."

Today, none of the players are talking. The district attorney's office says that the judge handling the reopening of the case, State Supreme Court Justice Charles Tejada, has asked them to make no further public comments until the December 5 hearing before him, when Morgenthau will produce his report and make his recommendations.

One central unanswered question about the rape case falls completely on Morgenthau's office. Why didn't he and his people—when they received the FBI's final DNA results, just before the first of the two trials—ask the judge for a postponement? They could simply have told him they needed more time to identify and arrest the missing man they had now determined, from the semen tests, had penetrated the victim. The judge may have been annoyed with them and chewed on them a bit, but he would almost certainly have recognized the legitimacy of their request and granted it.

Matias Reyes has now confessed to being that missing man, and his DNA shows him to be right. He has also confessed to the rape and beating of another woman two days earlier—on April 17, 1989—in the same northern quadrant of the park. The authorities reportedly have tied Reyes to that April 17 rape as well.

Why, back in 1989, didn't the authorities look into a possible link between the April 17 and April 19 rapes? If they had, the April 17 victim, a twenty-six-year-old woman who had full memory of the assault, could possibly have identified her attacker early on or provided other critical information.

Was it simply human oversight, to which we are all susceptible, or were they in too much of a hurry? Or was the district attorney's office actually aware of the April 17 rape, which happened in daylight, and simply dismissed it as different in pattern?

In any event, the prosecutors cannot argue it wasn't right in front of their collective noses. On April 29, 1989, ten days after the jogger rape, the *New York Times* ran a long story about the twenty-eight other first-degree rapes or attempted rapes reported across New York City during the week of the Central Park crime. Fourth on the list was the following entry for April 17, now tied to Reyes: "3:30 P.M. As she walked through the northern reaches of Central Park on the East Side, a woman, twenty-six, was hit in the face, robbed and raped. The suspect escaped."

It's not uncommon for criminal cases to have a few unknown elements, inconsistencies, or gray areas. But the jogger case was shot through with them. Portions of the defendants' statements, for example, were flat-out contradictions of the accounts given by their codefendants.

If the authorities had just paused somewhere along the way and expanded the investigation to deal with some of these gaps, the case would likely have been turned upside down. What really explains the failure to delay the trials? Was it the pressure for quick results? Or the public embarrassment of having to admit gray areas and missing pieces after going too far? Whatever the explanation, the failure to pursue the loose ends surely altered the outcome.

Now there will be a second outcome. And a number of human dramas are playing out in the background.

The five convicted youths, now in their late twenties, and their families are obviously hoping their rape convictions will be set aside. They want to remove the stigma of being listed as sex criminals in the government registry and being required to report their whereabouts to the authorities every three months. They're surely also hoping their convictions on all the other charges—assault, robbery, attempted murder, and riot—will be vacated as well. City officials are bracing for huge damage suits should any of the counts be overturned. It bears repeating that, even if the five are found not guilty of involvement in the rape, we may never know the full story of what happened that night. It's not likely we'll hear any more confessions from the young men or any admissions of wrongdoing from the players on the prosecution side.

The rape victim has said that though she has no memory of the awful attack, she would like to know who did this to her. Her wish for all the answers may not be granted, either. She fought her way back from near-death to resume her post at Salomon Brothers, more quickly than anyone predicted. She's not the same, though, and won't be. She suffers from double vision and is wobbly on her feet. She has a hard time walking in a straight line. Of late, she is said to be writing a memoir.

Linda Fairstein, a fiercely competitive, driven professional who was forty-one at the time of the jogger rape, has since left the district attorney's office to write novels about an assistant district attorney who prosecutes sex crimes. When the rape occurred, she raced into the fray to wrest the case away from Nancy Ryan, thirty-nine, who was Fairstein's chief rival in the Morgenthau constellation. Now, Morgenthau has put Ryan in charge of his reinvestigation of the case. Those who know Fairstein say she harbors a dream of succeeding Morgenthau as Manhattan district attorney. The latest developments could wreck that dream.

Nancy Ryan is said to be under lobbying siege now from police and prosecutors, former and current, who believe her report will call for the rape verdicts to be vacated. With their reputations at stake, they're trying to talk her into a less drastic decision. Fairstein is reported to be lobbying Morgenthau. If it all weren't so real, it would be a soap opera.

Robert Morgenthau, it is fair to say, is a haloed icon in the New York establishment. At eighty-three, he has probably spent more years in public service here than any other active government official. For the past twenty-eight years (he began his eighth consecutive term in January), he has been the Manhattan district attorney. Some admirers call him "America's D.A." He has been an advocate for good government and has lent his name and time to many worthy causes. That said, he is, like all the other players in this story, a mortal being, not a deity. Like any district attorney, he has in his time covered up lots of his office's mistakes. Like other big-city district attorneys, he has also swept under a large carpet the misdeeds of myriad well-known personages. They owe him. Not long ago, his office buried an investigation into Charles Gargano, the state's economic czar, who has a recurring habit of giving big state contracts to people who make big campaign contributions to his friend Governor George Pataki. Some Morgenthau watchers think that he may have been too long with power and that with age, he may have lost his touch.

People sometimes use the phrase "the game" to describe how big systems like government and multinational corporations often get manipulated not for the common good but for the good of the people who run them. It's not a description of evil, but rather of human nature. It explains what happens when individuals have been doing things a certain way for a long time and come to believe this is always the right way. One symptom is when a player begins to focus only on winning, on trouncing the opposing side. Another is when people become so habit-formed and sure of themselves that they stop asking the question: "Could I possibly be wrong about this?"

The story of the Central Park jogger case may be in large part a story about people in the justice system playing the game—when they should have been doing the right thing.

Epilogue

On December 5, 2002, after an eleven-month investigation headed by Nancy Ryan and Peter Casolaro, Morgenthau released a report stating that DNA and other persuasive evidence indicated that the Central Park jogger had been beaten, raped, and left for dead by a single perpetrator—Matias Reyes. Two weeks later, on the recommendation of Morgenthau's office, Manhattan Supreme Court Justice Charles Tejada threw out the convictions of Antron McCray, Yusef Salaam, Raymond Santana, Kevin Richardson, and Kharey Wise.

The following month, a three-officer panel of the New York Police Department appointed by Police Commissioner Raymond Kelly issued a report—as Sydney Schanberg predicted—contending that the five exonerated men "most likely" participated in the crime with Reyes.

In March 2003 the Central Park jogger shed her anonymity, identifying herself as Trisha Meili, forty-two, as Simon and Schuster released her autobiographical account of her ordeal, *I Am the Central Park Jogger: A Story of Hope and Possibility*. Meili, who still had no recollection of the attack, wrote that she was "too stunned to respond" when she learned of Reyes's confession, but that "Reyes became real to me in a way the five had not."

The five exonerated men filed federal civil rights suits seeking $50 million in damages each from the NYPD. The suits were pending when this anthology went to press.

MELVIN DEAN NIMER

After falsely confessing, the eight-year-old "re-enacted"
the murder of his parents

FRED J. COOK AND GENE GLEASON
STATEN ISLAND, NEW YORK

A light flashed on the central switchboard of the New York Telephone Company office at precisely 2:04 A.M., September 2, 1958. Mrs. Catherine B. Thompson, one of the operators on duty, plugged in on the line. She heard the sound of heavy breathing. "Hello," she said, "hello." There was no answer, just that heavy, breathing sound. Mrs. Thompson turned to another operator, Mrs. Florence Parkin, and asked her to trace the call. Mrs. Parkin quickly found that it was coming from a house at 242 Vanderbilt Avenue. Then she cut in on the line, holding it open, while Mrs. Thompson notified police that something appeared to be wrong.

Even as Mrs. Thompson was speaking to the desk sergeant at the St. George police station, Mrs. Parkin heard the labored breathing on the line turn into a voice. A woman gasped: "I've been stabbed."

The operator immediately cut the police in on the conversation, and both she and the desk officer heard the woman repeat: "I've been stabbed. I've been attacked with a knife." A second later, the voice added: "My husband has been stabbed too."

Then there was silence. It lasted only a second. Then a new voice, a little boy's voice, came on the wire.

"My mother is bleeding," the voice said.

Mrs. Thompson told the boy police already were on the way.

"I'll wait for the police outside," he said.

"No," she told him, "you better stay with your mother."

Just six minutes later, Patrolmen Vincent J. Meli and Henry Tyson pulled up before the two-story house at 242 Vanderbilt Avenue in the Fox Hills section, an area that in olden days had been known as "The Witches'

From "The Shame of New York," *The Nation*, October 31, 1959. Copyright © The Nation. Adapted with permission.

Field." The house sat on a steep little hill. The patrolmen climbed seven steps, went up a ten-foot walk, climbed three more steps and entered the front door. Waiting to greet them, clad only in pajamas, was a small, slender, tow-headed boy, Melvin Dean Nimer, aged eight. Behind him in the silent house was a scene of blood and brutality.

The patrolmen found the boy's father, Dr. Melvin A. Nimer, thirty-one, a physician at the nearby Marine Hospital of the U.S. Public Health Service, sprawled on the kitchen floor, covered with blood from deep stab wounds. In the master bedroom upstairs, they found Mrs. Lou Jean Nimer, thirty-one, slumped on the floor between the bed and the wall where she had collapsed while telephoning. She, too, had been badly stabbed.

An emergency call went out for an ambulance and detectives. The ambulance arrived promptly, and at 2:18 A.M., Mrs. Nimer was placed in it to be taken to the Marine Hospital, just three blocks away. She was still conscious. Significantly, in the light of future developments, she still retained her presence of mind. As she was being placed in the ambulance, her thoughts obviously turned to her younger children still asleep in the house—Melvin Dean's brother, Gregory, two, and his sister, Jennifer Jean, just five months. The baby especially was on the mother's mind, for she told police: "Please feed the baby plain milk. No formula."

Even as the ambulance left, in the house, on the kitchen floor, Dr. Nimer was dying. Blood was welling up from his wounds. "I'm choking, I'm choking," he moaned. But he, too, still retained his faculties. He warned police against moving him or raising his head, and told them simply to brace his feet against the wall until the ambulance returned. When it did, within a few minutes, he too was rushed to the hospital and there he died shortly after he was admitted.

Mrs. Nimer lived a few hours longer. An emergency operation was performed in a desperate attempt to save her life, but at 5:30 A.M. she died while still on the operating table.

Staten Island authorities had a sensational double murder on their hands, and investigative forces were quickly marshaled. Staten Island District Attorney John M. Braisted Jr. and his assistant, Thomas R. Sullivan, were notified. Deputy Chief Inspector Edward W. Byrnes and Inspector Carl I. Blank assumed command of the police investigation. Detectives and technical experts swarmed over the house at 242 Vanderbilt Avenue. From the outset, they had one thing going for them.

They had an eyewitness—Melvin Dean Nimer, known as Deany, who told the police he had been asleep in his bedroom across the hall from his parents' room when he was awakened by something touching the bed, disturbing the bed clothing. Startled, Deany woke, looked up, saw a man looming above his bed. The man, he said, wore a white mask, like a sheet, that covered his entire head. Deany screamed.

The masked man grabbed him by the throat, tried to choke him. Across the hall, Mrs. Nimer, hearing her son scream, rushed to his aid.

"Mommy came and the man hit her with something and she started bleeding," Deany told police. "Then Daddy ran in and they started fighting and Daddy started bleeding."

The struggle between his father and the masked intruder took place in the hall outside his bedroom, at the top of the stairway, the boy told detectives. The prowler, he said, was "a little bigger than Daddy," and he broke away and ran downstairs with Dr. Nimer in pursuit.

Mrs. Nimer had gone to her bedroom and sat down on the edge of the bed to use the telephone and call for help. She slid off the bed, moaning faintly, "I'm dying. . . ."

This was Deany Nimer's story. Based upon it, police sent out a thirteen-state alarm for the prowler who had slain Dr. Nimer and his wife: "Unknown male, white, wearing blue dungarees and blue-striped shirt. May have blood on his clothing."

Right at the start there was one bit of undeniable physical evidence that seemed to lend substantiation to the story Deany Nimer had told. Only vague hints of this appeared in the press at the time, and its significance was quickly forgotten. It was mentioned that police had found a piece of cloth (some accounts said two pieces) that had been left folded on the boy's bed. Actually, we are told, there were about half-a-dozen strips of cloth torn into handy lengths that suggested they had been intended for gags or bonds. The cloth was a faded, odd-colored, cotton ticking—the kind of coarse, heavy material that was often used for old mattress covers—and the strips, according to those who tested them, were strong. The material matched nothing else found in the house, and police at first thought that the strips might have been ripped from an old hospital mattress. The nearby Public Health Service Hospital was checked on this supposition, but the cotton ticking evidently hadn't come from there. It never was traced and identified.

Indeed, the mysterious cloth strips soon were forgotten as investigators concentrated on two other elements of the mystery. How had the prowler entered the home? And where was the murder weapon?

Again these key questions were never to be answered, but the first one, from a combination of circumstances at the murder scene, appears to have assumed from the early moments of the investigation an exaggerated importance in official minds. An examination of the house showed that a cellar window had been left open. A water hose led out the window into the driveway, where Dr. Nimer had washed the car the day before he and his wife were murdered. An intruder could have slipped into the house through this window, but technical experts examined the windowsill and quickly discounted the possibility. Minute particles of dust and dirt on the sill had been undisturbed, and this would hardly have been possible had a full-grown man squeezed through the comparatively narrow opening.

Yet this appeared to be the only easy means of entrance. Elsewhere in the house, a screen on one of the downstairs windows was unhooked, but again there was nothing to indicate an intruder had crawled through the window. The inside front door had been partially open when the first patrolmen arrived, but the aluminum screen door had still been latched and Deany himself had released the catch to admit police. It almost seemed as if no one could have entered the house—and, especially, that no one could have departed in the kind of hasty flight that Deany Nimer had described, if Deany's story were true.

This, it became obvious later, was the first fork in the road the investigators were to take. A second element involved the location of Deany's Boy Scout knife. In searching the house for the murder weapon, detectives discovered that apparently none of the kitchenware had been used. But Deany's Boy Scout knife was missing. The boy was positive it had been in a pocket of his trousers, hanging on the knob of his bedroom door. Detectives looked, but the knife wasn't where Deany had said it was. A thorough search of the house finally turned up the potential weapon, hidden between the covers of the Mormon magazine *Era*. A laboratory analysis—the kind of minute examination that can reveal droplets of blood not perceivable by the human eye—soon established that the knife was absolutely unstained. Still, could the knife have been cleaned? Could it still be the murder weapon?

These questions were hovering unasked in the air, unknown as yet to press and public, when the first reporters converged upon the murder scene. Even though the early roadblocks, the early forks in the investigative pathway, were not clear, there was about this investigation from the start a disturbing overtone. One of the first reporters on the scene was scrambling for information when he was elated to receive a high-sign from a high-ranking detective whom he knew. The detective drew him aside, and the reporter was all anticipation.

"I thought he had something he wanted to tell me," the reporter recalled later. "But do you know what he said? He pointed to District Attorney Braisted, and he asked me: 'You've been around quite awhile. You've seen Hogan work. How do you think he compares with Hogan? Is he as good?'"

This early, it would seem, some minds were already more preoccupied with the question of the reflected public image, the question of their own reputations, than they were with the baffling details of the horrible crime that cried out for solution.

In the succeeding days, the investigation followed the usual frenetic course of sensational headline crimes. A number of suspects were picked up, questioned, released. The ground around the Nimer house, the streets in the area, were searched and searched again. In all of this just two discoveries were made that seem of significance now. Detectives disclosed that they had found two footprints—the footprints of a man—in the soft earth at the left rear side of the Nimer house. Plaster casts were taken of them in the hope that they might ultimately serve to identify the foot that had made them. The second discovery involved a knife. About 6:00 P.M. on September 3, the day after the murders, two patrolmen found a sharp-pointed knife, with a five-inch blade and a wooden handle, in a hedge about one thousand feet from the Nimer home. Under laboratory analysis, the knife revealed traces of blood, but they were so faint that it could not be scientifically determined whether the blood was animal or human.

Both of these discoveries, if they meant anything at all, seemed to point away from the suspicion that already had taken root in the minds of officials. This suspicion involved Deany Nimer. Newsmen, under a pledge of confidence, were told that the boy was a suspect in the murder of his parents. He was undergoing psychiatric examination.

While the public still had no suspicion of the sensation that was about to burst, journalists who had been given the tip dug energetically into the background of the Nimer family. The parents had been Mormons. They had been married in September 1946, in the culmination of a childhood romance that had begun back in their home town of Orem, Utah. Dr. Nimer had received his medical degree from the University of Utah, had served in a Public Health Service Hospital in Seattle, and had come to Staten Island only a few months before to start a three-year surgical residence at the Marine Hospital. Intimates of the family had considered their home life ideal. There had never been a hint, prior to the murders, of any mental problem involving Melvin Dean Nimer. He was an open-faced, smiling, attractive boy. Indeed, he and his father had seemed to have great affection for each other. Neighbors recalled how, when Dr. Nimer came home from the hospital, Deany would run up to him and throw his arms around him.

Was it possible that such a boy, at so young an age, could be a veritable Dr. Jekyll and Mr. Hyde? Even if he were possessed by a dark soul-demon hiding under the smiling face, was it physically possible for such a tiny lad to murder both of his parents? After all, Deany was only four feet four; he weighed only sixty pounds.

The authorities obviously decided that he could. Relatives of the Nimers had been notified promptly of the tragedy. Mrs. Bertha Park, mother of Mrs. Nimer, and Dr. Harold Nimer, Deany's uncle, had flown to New York immediately. With Dr. Harold Nimer's consent, District Attorney Braisted sent the boy on Friday, September 5, three days after the murders, to the Staten Island Mental Health Center for analysis. The clinic, under the direction of Dr. Richard M. Silberstein, examined the boy on just two days, Friday and Saturday. It was after these examinations, it was to be disclosed later, that Deany changed his original story and gave a statement confessing that he had committed the murders. This was still not known, even to reporters, when Deany left on the weekend, accompanied by his uncle and Detective James Cox, to fly to the funeral of his parents in Orem, Utah.

The funeral was held on Tuesday, September 9, and on Wednesday, September 10, as Deany was returning to New York with his uncle and Detective Cox, the *New York Journal-American* broke the story and announced in sensational headlines that the boy was a suspect in the murder of his parents. What happened next has to be considered of the greatest significance. For this was the crossroads, the point at which the life and the future of an eight-year-old boy were going to be protected—or he was going to be pilloried in public.

The *Journal-American*'s story was damaging, but it was not official. Other newspapers did not touch it until District Attorney Braisted had been given an opportunity to comment, and on what he said depended the extent to which the story would be used, the credibility that would be attached to it. The district attorney, quite obviously, had several courses of action open to him. He could have denounced the published story as a violation of confidence and refused to confirm it; he could have refused flatly to comment, as district attorneys often do, because the case was under investigation and still unsolved; or he could have confirmed the fact that the boy had been under suspicion—and at the same time pointed out all of the solid facts in the case (as yet unknown to the public) that seemed to negate that suspicion.

The district attorney did none of these things. Braisted gave the impression of a public official who was glad the story was out. He refused to be quoted on the fact that he had required a pledge of silence from newspapermen about the suspicions that had been focused on Deany; he refused to criticize publication of a story that had tarred an eight-year-old boy as a suspect in the murder of his parents. He said, on the contrary, that preliminary psychiatric examination to which Deany had been subjected had shown the boy was suffering "from a paranoid type of schizophrenia and that the boy's illness and basic personality were compatible with the commission of a crime of violence."

While thus throwing the prestige of his office behind the most horrible and harrowing suspicion that could be leveled at a child, the district attorney left himself an out in carefully expressed reservations. He pointed out that the boy's uncle, Dr. Harold Nimer, was not satisfied with "the statement"—he refused to say confession—that Deany had made. He added, "I am not satisfied, either," and said the boy would be subjected to more extensive and more thorough psychiatric tests.

The district attorney's statement made the story official. Press services spread it nationwide. And in the next hours it seemed that the last room for doubt had been banished. On the evening of this day of horrible revelation, little Deany was taken back to the house of tragedy on Vanderbilt Avenue, and there, in a pattern reminiscent of the one followed with all-but-convicted criminals, he "re-enacted" the crime, authorities said. The next day, Thursday, September 11, he was sent to Bellevue Hospital in New York for psychiatric examination. And that same day, in an extended press conference, Braisted was subjected to searching questions by reporters about the circumstances that pointed to young Deany Nimer's guilt or innocence.

On the side of innocence, Braisted listed just one theoretical proposition. "The one important thing that would negate" the idea of guilt, he said, was that the statement came from an eight-year-old boy. On the side of guilt, he listed an impressive array of supposedly solid facts.

The most important factor pointing to the boy's guilt, he said, "is the statement by the Medical Examiner that the wounds, their location, etc., could indicate they were received while the victims were in a [supine] position in bed." The first autopsy report (it was later revised) by Assistant Medical Examiner Dr. Dominick DeMaio disclosed that Dr. Nimer had a superficial wound on the back of the left shoulder and a fatal wound "in the upper abdomen under the left chest cage." Mrs. Nimer, Dr. DeMaio's report said, had a superficial wound of the right breast and "a lethal wound of the upper abdomen under the right chest cage." The medical report added that "the thrusts all were direct downward thrusts," supporting the theory that the Nimers were surprised and stabbed while lying "in a [supine] position in bed."

This scientific documentation seemed to offer a rational explanation for the incredible. Conceivably, even an eight-year-old, four foot four, sixty-pound boy *could* stab both of his parents to death if he surprised them as they slept and stabbed them in the soft flesh of the abdomen before they were aware of what was happening. The medical report seemed almost to explain how the crime *had* happened; but even so—and even though there were vital facts in this case that were still being kept from the press and public—there were a few obvious pieces that did not fit into this almost-final solution.

One dealt with Deany's person. Authorities said he had admitted he had washed his hands, and so, of course, there was no blood upon them. But what of his pajamas? They had, according to Dr. DeMaio's report, only "one or two" small bloodstains on them. Then there was the peculiar matter of the bed clothing. The murder night had been an exceptionally cool one when, almost certainly, the Nimers would have had covers over them. Yet there were no knife rips, no tears at all in the bedsheets.

These minute flaws in the case did not seem too significant at the time, but reporters questioned Braisted closely. And everything he said built one picture, a dark picture for Deany Nimer.

Asked about reports that the boy had changed his confession, the district attorney said: "No, he has not changed his story." Then he admitted that the boy, in answer to a question from his uncle, had said that his original story about an intruder was the true one. The district attorney was asked whether there were discrepancies in the boy's story. He said flatly: "No discrepancies." He added that Deany had had a motive and that it lay in "an attitude he had toward his parents." He explained, "I would be inclined to say they [the Nimers] were very strict." Of Deany, he said: "He has never shown any remorse."

Braisted was questioned about the absence of blood on any of the knives in the house, especially on Deany's Boy Scout knife. Assuming that the knife had been washed off, had detectives examined the drain traps to see if they could find any traces of blood? They had—and they found no blood. Only six minutes had elapsed between the first winking alarm light on the telephone switchboard and the arrival of police. Could Deany have rushed downstairs, washed off the knife so perfectly that it retained no trace of blood, and hidden it in that short time? "It is possible," said District Attorney Braisted. "The time limit is conceivable?" he was asked again. "It is possible," he said.

The effect of all this was to accuse and damn Melvin Dean Nimer in the public eye without accusing him in court. The story touched a sensitive nerve of the times and was a sensation across the nation. Parents everywhere have been concerned in recent years about the increasing frequency of violent and bloody youth crimes, and the case of Melvin Dean Nimer seemed to touch a new nadir. If so young and so attractive a boy could have committed so heinous a crime, then there were no limits to youthful depravity. No New York crime case in our experience caused such deep and widespread agitation among parents.

Yet all the time there were vital elements of the case that had been kept secret—elements that did not fit into the picture of a little boy's seemingly almost-certain guilt. They were vital facts that supported the story Deany originally had said about a masked intruder. For the plain truth was this: *virtually every word that he had uttered had been corroborated from the mouths of his dying parents.*

Though reporters questioned Braisted with the utmost thoroughness, he had given no hint of this. The district attorney had insisted there were "no discrepancies" in the boy's confession—nor, presumably, in the case against the boy. It was left for newsmen to drag the truth out into the light of day. On Friday, September 12, Vincent E. Sorge, a painstaking and tireless reporter for the *New York World-Telegram and Sun*, broke through the veil of official reticence. He revealed the verbatim question-and-answer exchange between a detective and Mrs. Nimer before Mrs. Nimer died:

Q: Can you tell me anything about the case?
A: A mask . . . a mask.
Q: Can you tell me anything else?
A: A hood . . . a hood.
Q: What kind?
A: White.
Q: Slits in the eyes?
A: Yes, covered full head.
Q: How tall?
A: Tall as my husband, same build.
Q: Why did you get up?
A: Heard boy scream.

Braisted was in the midst of another press conference, discussing Deany's motives, when the *World-Telegram and Sun* broke the story. Asked if Mrs. Nimer had made a statement before she died, Braisted said he understood she had described the killer as about the size of her husband and added: "We believe she might have seen her husband and no one else, but this matter is still being investigated."

Thomas Sullivan, Braisted's assistant, came into the room at this point, leaned over and whispered into the district attorney's ear. Braisted paled noticeably. Then he turned to reporters and said: "Mrs. Nimer did mention the words 'white mask and hood' to Detective John Morgan, but you must remember that she was in shock and was put under sedation . . . and [her statements] were made in dribs and drabs. . . . She also said, 'tall as my husband, same build.'" Pressed for further details, he said abruptly: "I will make no comment on any published statement attributed to victims of this crime. I am declining comment because I sincerely believe that comment would impede our investigation."

The lid had been lifted. Answers that did not answer no longer satisfied. More and sharper questions were asked. What about Dr. Nimer? He had lived for some time after the stabbing. Had he, like his wife, identified his assailant? "He didn't give us anything you would call useful information," one high police source said. "He made no positive identification of the assailant," said Braisted. It took reporters three days to pierce this screen of non-answering answers; but finally, on Monday, pressed again and pressed harder, Braisted admitted that Dr. Nimer, too, before he died, had used the words "prowler" and "mask."

The picture that then developed was this: Little Melvin Dean Nimer's first story that he had been awakened by a masked prowler, that he had screamed, that his parents had come to his aid—all of this had agreed in exact detail with the statements his dying parents had made to police. His description of the mask, his description of the intruder as a man "about Daddy's size," agreed perfectly with his mother's dying statement. Why, in the face of all this, had authorities concentrated such strong and harrowing suspicion upon the boy?

The answer may be found, perhaps, in District Attorney Braisted's admission of official investigative frustration. Three things, he said, led authorities to suspect Deany, and he listed them: "One, our inability to establish with any certainty that there had been an entrance to and an exit from the house. Two, motive—we couldn't settle on a motive. Three, a few statements by the boy which did not conform to the facts. Adding it all together—though we, like many other people, just couldn't believe it—we had no choice."

The only way, seemingly, that the positive statements of the dying parents could be explained away lay in the assumption that, to protect the son who had stabbed them, they had conferred and concocted the story of the masked intruder. Yet Mrs. Nimer had collapsed in the upstairs bedroom, Dr. Nimer in the downstairs kitchen, and there was absolutely no proof that they could have talked with each other in those six short minutes before police arrived. Anyway, in logic, the whole idea appeared preposterous, and in an analytical article on September 19, 1958, we tore into the case against Deany Nimer and asked this question: "Is it conceivable that a dying mother who thought enough of her children to warn about her daughter's formula would make up a story about a prowler and a mask to protect her son—and endanger the other two children—if he were a killer?"

The day we asked that, Braisted was not available to reporters, and Sullivan, his assistant, said: "No comment."

And with that story, the Nimer case virtually died. Melvin Dean Nimer's psychiatric examination at Bellevue was concluded. The report, as relayed to the public, was vague. Psychiatrists said they found evidence of "a personality disorder pre-dating the tragic occurrence on Staten Island." Deany needed continued psychiatric treatment, they said; but clear evidence that the boy was not considered dangerous was seen in the fact that he was released and allowed to go to his grandparents' home in Orem, Utah, there to attend school and mingle with other children. Deany left New York for Orem on October 23, 1958, and on November 3, the forty detectives who had been working on the mystery were called off. The case was as good as dead.

But the damage had been done, and a haunting, horrible suspicion still remained—the suspicion that Melvin Dean Nimer, only eight, might have committed one of the most horrible crimes of the century. Everywhere a reporter went, even in towns and away from New York, he was asked: "What is the truth about the Nimer case? Did the boy really do it?" It was a question to which there was no official answer, but one to which we can, we feel, give a positive answer now.

It is an answer that was obtained by the reporting half of this team only after weeks of exhausting and meticulous legwork. Every inch of the murder scene was reexamined. Every person who would talk, even many who didn't want to talk, was questioned. The picture that emerged grew more shocking every step of the way. For as we dug more deeply into the mystery, it became apparent that there wasn't a chance, *there never had been a chance*, that Melvin Dean Nimer could have committed the murders. Only the most incredibly slipshod investigation that proceeded in blind defiance of some facts and in blind ignorance of others could have resulted in even the vaguest suspicion being cast upon the boy.

We began with the house at 242 Vanderbilt Avenue. Any supposition of Deany's guilt rested upon the belief—in all logic, the only possible belief—that he had surprised his sleeping parents in bed and stabbed them there. But once we got into the master bedroom and examined the mattress on the bed, we found this: there was just one splotch of blood on the entire mattress and that was on the side of the bed on which Mrs. Nimer sat when she used the telephone.

The traces of blood still discernible in the house indicated clearly that the crime had been committed elsewhere. Across the hallway, there was a splash of blood on the doorjamb of Deany's room, and there was a large amount of blood around the light switch in the hall nearby—an indication perhaps that Dr. Nimer, his hands already bloody from his wounds, had fumbled desperately for the switch in an effort to turn on the light so that he could see his assailant already fleeing down the stairs. It was significant to us that signs of blood in massive quantities appeared first in the hallway and trailed down the stairs through the house—just as would have been the case if the first story Deany had told were the right one.

Downstairs, we faced the problem of the front door. It had been the conclusion by the police and the district attorney that no one could have come in—or, even more significantly, could have left in haste—through the aluminum door with its spring lock. Yet aluminum doors with this kind of latch often give under pressure. Gene Gleason set the catch, then gave the door a slight tug—and open it came, easily, without damaging door or lock.

Turning from the mute evidence of the house, we sought information of a more positive kind in the records of the Marine Hospital, where the Nimers had been taken. Mrs. Nimer, the records showed, had been placed in a recovery room at 3:04 A.M. Personnel of the hospital who knew her had talked with her. She was fully conscious, fully coherent. When a nurse giving Mrs. Nimer oxygen mistakenly placed the mask on backward, Mrs. Nimer reached up with one hand and said: "It's on backwards." This was not a woman, obviously, who was in such a state of shock or under such sedation that she did not know what she was saying when she talked about a prowler and a mask.

The vital questioning of Mrs. Nimer had been overheard by hospital personnel. Two detectives were present, and they questioned her gently. They heard her tell about the mask-hood, the slits for the eyes, and heard her describe the intruder as "about the size of my husband." And they heard her say: "I met the man in the hall."

Every effort was made to save Mrs. Nimer's life. Dr. Norman Tarr, deputy chief of surgery, was summoned to perform an emergency operation. He knew Mrs. Nimer personally, and she recognized him. Before he operated, the records show, he examined her carefully and turned her body over gently so that he could see if she had any wounds on her back. Mrs. Nimer told him that she had not been stabbed there and, indeed, she had not—a sequence again that seems to demonstrate that this was a woman still in possession of her faculties.

In his examination of his patient, Dr. Tarr discovered that she had three wounds. There was a slight knife wound on the heel of her right hand, received apparently when she had tried to ward off a blow. She had a one-inch stab wound in the upper right chest above the breast. And she had a mortal wound, not in the abdomen as the official medical examiner's report had said, but in the right chest between the sixth and seventh ribs.

The location and nature of this last wound assume vital importance. The presumption of Deany Nimer's guilt had been based to a large extent upon the autopsy report that placed the wound in the abdomen and described it as a direct downward thrust. This enabled officials to envision a boy stabbing his parents in bed, but Dr. Tarr's reports show conclusively that this was a completely inaccurate impression, that the stabbing did not and could not have happened that way at all.

The knife of the blade had been driven through the rib cage and muscles with terrific force. It had gone in at an angle, slanting down and toward the center of the body. So vicious was the thrust that the blade had penetrated about five inches, and there was evidence that the blow had been struck by an experienced knife-wielder. The wound on the outside was small, only about the width of the knife blade; but there was evidence that the knife tip had been flicked on an arc inside the body, the trick of an experienced killer. The flicking tip had slashed through the diaphragm, had severed the major blood vessel going into the vena cava, and had inflicted a cut about five inches long and very deep in the liver.

Dr. Tarr knew that only a miracle could save Lou Jean Nimer, but he attempted to perform that miracle. He made an incision, beginning approximately at the navel and proceeding upward to the bottom of the breast plate. He mopped up the blood and tried to staunch its flow. His patient was sinking fast. Her pulse and breathing faded. She was only a whisper away from death. Dr. Tarr reached into her chest cavity and tried frantically to massage her failing heart. He tried for twenty minutes, but he failed as he had known, almost from the first, that he must fail.

All during this grim drama of the operating room, Dr. Tarr detailed every step in operative notes that he dictated as he went along. Realizing that he would have to cut through the original wound, he was careful to describe its location, its size, its depth. All of this detail, so vital to any understanding of the murder case, was in Dr. Tarr's operative notes when Mrs. Nimer's body was released to the city morgue for autopsy at 7:05 A.M., September 2, 1958.

What happened next seems fairly obvious. The medical examiner, Dr. DeMaio, confused the incision which Dr. Tarr had made with the fatal wound. Only so could the wound have been erroneously located in the abdomen instead of between the sixth and seventh ribs; only so could it have been described as a direct downward thrust when Dr. Tarr, the only man who could know, described it emphatically as an angled, downward-slanting blow. How could this confusion have occurred? Quite simply. The autopsy report was ready the day after the murders, but Dr. Tarr's operative notes were not transcribed and forwarded to authorities for four days! And in the meantime, nobody asked. It was not until "about ten days" after Mrs. Nimer's death that detectives came around to question Dr. Tarr and hospital personnel—and learned, presumably for the first time, one of the most elemental facts about the crime they were investigating: the nature of Mrs. Nimer's fatal wound.

This sequence, revealing enough, is not quite so shocking as one other medical fact that until now has been buried from the public. Deany, it will be remembered, had told authorities originally that the intruder had grabbed him by the throat and tried to strangle him. During the period when suspicion was being focused on the boy, District Attorney Braisted had been asked about this. Had there been marks on Deany's neck? He had replied: "There might have been one or two little marks on the boy's neck. There were no lacerations or deep marks. The boy was examined superficially on the night of the murders, but was not given any medical treatment."

This account simply does not agree with specific reports that show conclusively that a man *had* tried to strangle Deany Nimer.

The story of the evidence that was plainly visible on Deany's throat comes from Dr. William Smith, an associate of Dr. Nimer and a neighbor and friend of the family. He hurried to the Nimer house early on the morning of the tragedy. Deany had already been questioned, had been sent back to bed to sleep, and had only just reawakened. Dr. Smith and Ralph L. Perkins, administrator of Marine Hospital, were present when detectives began to question the boy again about 6:00 A.M. Even then, police were saying that the boy's "story doesn't conform with the facts." And even then the trend of the questioning indicated that they suspected Deany. The questioning went on and on for nearly two hours, and considering the circumstances, the age of the boy, and the horror of the night, it impressed observers as excessive, as constituting a virtual verbal third degree.

Finally, about 8:00 A.M., in the kitchen of the Nimer home, police asked Dr. Smith to examine Deany's throat. The doctor turned a sunlamp on the boy, and this is what he found: "On the right side of the boy's neck—to the rear of the midway point—four fingerprints. On the left side, in approximately the same position, a thumb print and the curvature of a thumb nail mark. Clusters of petechiae, more commonly known as pinpoint hemorrhages caused by the rupturing of the capillaries."

Dr. Smith said he told police and the district attorney's men present: "The marks are more than halfway back. He could not have done it himself. The hand was too big."

This positive finding, it would seem, should have put an end to all suspicions of Deany Nimer. But as the sequel was to show, it did nothing of the kind.

Obviously, police and investigating officials were not listening to facts that they did not want to hear. Their attitude even at the time, even when one could not know what was to come, must have been obvious; for Dr. Smith, when he left the house and took Deany home with him, was so worried that he did an unprecedented thing. He discussed the situation first with his wife, then he called in a second doctor to examine Deany's throat again. This second examination corroborated Dr. Smith's findings, and both doctors wrote out formal reports of what they had found and filed them in the hospital records.

It was not until some weeks later that Detective James Cox, who appears to have taken a more realistic view of the case than some of his superiors, came around rechecking evidence and discovered that two formal medical reports establishing beyond doubt Deany Nimer's innocence, showing that a man *had* tried to strangle him, were reposing in hospital files like a couple of concealed time bombs. Cox was visibly disturbed. But no one else appears to have been. At least no one in official position to this day has had the grace publicly to admit the horrible sequence of blunders that ended in the pillorying of an eight-year-old boy. The pretense has been maintained publicly that the investigation is still open; that anyone, including Deany Nimer, could conceivably still be a suspect. But privately a high police official has since admitted to us, "We know that the boy could never have done it."

Out in Utah, Deany went back to school last winter like any other eight-year-old boy. According to his grandfather, Dean E. Park, he appeared normal and bright in every way. There had been no trouble, no need even for Deany to make regular trips to a psychiatrist. But, understandably, there was bitterness. Dean Park, speaking of New York, put it well: "We think we got a rotten deal back there."

Epilogue

The Nimers' killer was never caught. Melvin Dean Nimer declined all requests for interviews until late 2006 when he broke his silence to speak with Frank Donnelly, a *Staten Island Advance* reporter who had covered the case forty-eight years earlier. Nimer, who had spent most of his adult years in Utah working as an accountant and entrepreneur, told Donnelly he was still dogged by suspicions that he had murdered his parents.

MENTAL FRAGILITY

Persons of below-normal intelligence or suffering from mental illness tend to be especially susceptible to suggestion and manipulation, deferential to authority, and prone to confabulation—a combination likely to render statements they make under stress unreliable.

Separating true from false confessions in this category isn't easy because mentally fragile adults often are very good at concealing their conditions—an art they've been practicing much of their lives. Thus, police interrogators and, of course, prosecutors, judges, and jurors are likely to perceive them as normal and, consequently, scoff at claims that their statements were false or involuntary.

But it is clear that confessions by the mentally fragile ought never to be taken at face value because, absent substantial corroboration by independent evidence, they may very well be false.

Any number of clichés describe the not-so-arduous task of eliciting confessions from suspects in this category—piece of cake, duck soup, easy as pie, shooting fish in a barrel, falling off a log, striking out the pitcher.

But one describes the outcome better than any other—good enough for government work.

The articles that follow vividly illustrate the problem.

The story of Richard Lapointe in the "Unrequited Innocence" section of this anthology (page 469) is another example of a confession by a mentally fragile adult.

OZEM GOLDWIRE

His cognitive and developmental disabilities made him
especially susceptible to coercion

JIM DWYER
NEW YORK, NEW YORK

Because of the wiring of his brain, Ozem Goldwire must account for every
minute in an hour. Asked what happened on the day he came home from
work in January 2006 and found his sister, Sherika, dead in bed, Goldwire
responds that his alarm went off at 5:00 A.M. and he took the B-20 bus at
6:18. "I got to work at 7:04," he says, and so his narrative spools, one precise
moment after the next, until he gets off the bus at night and opens the door
to his house in Brooklyn.

A man possessed of normal intelligence and above-normal politeness,
Goldwire, twenty-eight, has a "developmental disability with autistic features," his school records show. Though he now speaks in the deep tones of
an old-time broadcaster, at the age of six he had not yet uttered a complete
sentence.

On January 3, 2006, after seventeen hours in custody, he confessed to
strangling Sherika, an act of violence that all who know him say would
have been completely out of character, had he really done it. In June 2007
a judge dismissed the case at the request of his lawyer, Gary Farrell, and
a Brooklyn assistant district attorney, Robert Lamb.

"Here we had the ingredients of the perfect storm for false confession,"
Judge Gustin L. Reichbach said. "You're actually innocent of this crime."

How did an innocent man come to confess, and conversely, how has the
guilty person gotten away with murder?

As he recounts the day, Goldwire sits erect. The strap of a computer bag is
looped over his shoulder. The bag rests on his stomach as he speaks, and he
never moves it during two hours of conversation. His voice is deep, the words
uninflected. Not surprisingly, he was the valedictorian of his eighth-grade
class.

From "Considering the Crime, Not the Suspect," *New York Times*, June 16, 2007. Copyright
© New York Times. Adapted with permission.

On the evening of January 2, 2006, this man—who has been described his entire life as polite and meek, who survives in the world through rigorous routines—returned from his job in a food-processing plant to find a barrage of disorder in his home. One of two locks on the door was open. Lights were on in the bedroom, living room, and basement. A closet was open and ransacked; the top drawer of his desk had been jimmied.

He went to the second floor, saw Sherika under a sheet on her bed, saliva and blood around her mouth. He called 911 around 8:00 P.M. On the tape, Goldwire can be heard struggling to calm his voice.

"Huh-huh, this is Ozem Goldwire of 72 Rockaway Avenue," he says, between gasps. "It's between Sumpter Street and Marion Street. Somehow, my home had been wrecked a bit and when I went upstairs to check—to see my sister—and I saw her lying in bed and her mouth full of blood."

When the authorities arrived, Goldwire went to the Seventy-Third Precinct station house. At 3:00 A.M., he gave detectives a statement about finding her. He gave the same account at 1:00 P.M. Two hours later, though, he wrote out a different version, saying that they had argued two nights earlier over the television volume, that he had hit her with a cookie tin, then strangled her. The next morning, he wrote, he had gone to work, thought he had dreamed it all, and came home to find the house rummaged.

"She remained dead—this was a bad accident," he wrote.

There is no recording of the interrogation of Goldwire, but these facts are undisputed: He was in custody for seventeen hours and questioned by six detectives before he gave the incriminating statement. Only then was a prosecutor called to videotape him.

During the early questioning, Goldwire recalled, a detective said to him, "You think you're a genius," perhaps a reaction to his sonorous speaking style.

"I told her that I was just only human," Goldwire said.

Some of the detectives later described him as a "Rain Man" character, invoking the movie starring Dustin Hoffman. He was asked about his religion, his sex life, and if he had intimate relations with his sister, who was a year older than he was and who also had developmental disabilities. Goldwire screamed that he had not.

At one point, Goldwire remembered, "I put my head down into my hands to try to marshall-ize my thoughts." A detective sergeant, he said, shoved him upright. "He was yelling, 'Look at me, look at me!'" Goldwire said. Later, two detectives ordered him to stand in a corner and face them.

When a prosecutor arrived and the video camera was, at last, turned on, Goldwire never admitted to hurting his sister, instead beginning his narrative once again with the 6:18 A.M. bus. Asked why he had told the detective that he killed her, he said that the detectives had been "tough" on him, though not physically.

Detectives often use psychological pressure on suspects, including outlandish allegations, like the suggestion that he had been having sex with his sister. Criminals will concede that they might be killers, but not perverts.

Such techniques help solve many crimes. They also snare the wrong people. Among the most startling revelations of the DNA era is the prevalence of false confessions by people who are proven unequivocally innocent. In recognition that the interrogation can be as revealing as the confession, police departments across the country are beginning to tape the questioning of suspects.

Not in New York City. The police commissioner, Raymond W. Kelly, who has championed widespread police videotaping of public activities, does not see the need for similar documentation of what happens inside interrogation rooms. Kelly sees enormous logistical problems, a spokesman said yesterday.

What saved Goldwire from a murder trial was the willingness of the Brooklyn District Attorney's Office to hire a psychologist to study the confession and his background. Some victims' families might oppose such a study, creating a political problem for the prosecutors, but Sherika Goldwire's mother—who is also Ozem's mother—supported it.

The psychologist, Kathy Yates, found that not only had there never been a hint of violence in his life, but even some of the detectives had doubts. She concluded, "It is likely that the interrogative techniques used by the officers over an extended period of time were coercive in nature for Goldwire, given his cognitive and developmental disabilities."

A tape of the interrogation might have been a special educational tool for everyone involved. Instead, Goldwire bided his time in jail, awaiting trial. "One year," he said. "And eleven days."

Epilogue

Although authorities said they had a strong suspect in the case, no charges had been brought when this book went to press. A federal civil rights suit brought on Goldwire's behalf was pending.

BARRY LAUGHMAN

Low IQ and wrong blood type didn't deter the prosecution

PETE SHELLEM

HARRISBURG, PENNSYLVANIA

In the summer of 1987, eighty-five-year-old Edna Laughman spent her days on the porch of a ramshackle house in Oxford Township, watching the world go by on Route 94. She liked living alone, but would move in with her niece during the winter because her wood-frame house had no heat other than a small wood-burning stove. Edna's house also had no running water and only one light bulb, in the kitchen. She used a chamber pot. The house was so cluttered that it could be navigated only by using eighteen-inch pathways among boxes and other junk.

During the summers, Edna would eat dinner almost every night two doors away, where twenty-four-year-old Barry Laughman lived with his parents and a brother. Barry and his family were distant relatives of Edna. As Edna watched the world go by, the world was passing Barry by. With an IQ of about seventy, Barry was a "moron" under then-existing mental health classifications, functioning at the level of a ten-year-old. He had dropped out of special education classes in eleventh grade and was scared of the dark. He flunked a National Guard entrance test and got a job stacking skids at a local chemical company, where he was barely able to complete the job application. He rode his bike to work because he couldn't pass the driver's license exam.

On the afternoon of August 13, Barry's mother, Madeline Laughman, became concerned when Edna didn't show up to watch soap operas that they usually watched together. When Edna didn't arrive for dinner, Madeline became more concerned. She and Barry went to Edna's home. Another son, Larry, and his wife, Ruann, joined them. There was no response at the door, so they pried it open. Madeline and Ruann went inside the dark home where they found Edna's body, naked except for a bra pulled up

From "Who Killed Edna Laughman?" *The Patriot-News*, June 1, 2003. Copyright © The Patriot-News Company. Adapted with permission.

above her breasts and a dress covering her face. Her upper body was on the bed and her feet were on the floor. The place had been ransacked. She had been beaten. Bruises covered her arms, legs, and nose.

Crime scene investigators found three safety pins in Edna's bra, one of which was open. Edna had pills stuffed in her mouth and a pill bottle in her right hand. A Marlboro cigarette had been extinguished on a chair next to the bed, and four more butts plus a Marlboro box lid were found in the home. A shoeprint impression—of a sneaker evidently worn by the killer—also was found.

A neighbor, Royce Emerson, who knew Barry, told police he had encountered a stranger walking behind his home around 7:00 or 7:30 A.M. When Emerson asked the man what he was doing, he pointed toward fields behind the homes and said he was coming from there. The man had reddish brown hair and a mustache, was wearing a blue work suit, and pulled a cigarette from a red-and-white flip-top box—it looked like a Marlboro box. After lighting the cigarette, the man walked off in the direction of Edna's home. State police drew a sketch based on Emerson's description and began stopping cars on Route 94 and asking whether anyone had seen him, but no one had.

An autopsy determined that Edna had been struck on the head with a blunt object and raped, either before or after death, but the blow didn't kill her. She had choked to death on pills that had been rammed down her throat. Semen was recovered and from it Janice Roadcap, a Pennsylvania State Police chemist, concluded that Edna's assailant had type A blood.

On August 18, with little progress in the investigation, Trooper John J. (Jack) Holtz was assigned to the case. Holtz had been instrumental the previous year in the conviction of Jay C. Smith, a suburban Philadelphia high school principal sentenced to death in a sensational murder case, and was basking in his favorable portrayal in *Echoes in the Darkness*, a book by Joseph Wambaugh about the case.

The very day Holtz received the Laughman assignment, he cracked the case—or so he would claim. While interviewing members of the Laughman family, he noticed that Barry's little finger did not bend properly—the result of a childhood injury—and recalled that he'd seen three bruises that he presumed were grip marks on Edna's arm. Since there were three marks, according to Holtz, he inferred, a la Sherlock Holmes, that they had been left by someone who had a problem using one of his fingers—namely Barry Laughman.

In addition to Holtz's amazing flash of deductive reasoning, he apparently had eyesight to match. No one else ever noticed the grip marks, nor were they visible in the autopsy photos. And despite Holtz's supposed high degree of certainty on August 18, he didn't arrange for Barry to come into the Gettysburg State Police Barracks for an interview until nine days later, August 27.

Under questioning that day by Holtz and Trooper Donald Blevins, Barry said that the night before Edna's body was found he drank beer with his brother David in their yard. Barry could not go to bed, he said, because another of his brothers, Tim, was entertaining his girlfriend in the bedroom. Barry fell asleep on a couch and didn't get up until the next morning. Asked if he owned "tennis shoes," Barry replied that he didn't. During the session, Barry smoked two Marlboros, which the troopers kept for testing.

In another session at the Gettysburg Barracks twelve days later, Holtz told Barry that David and other family members said he had not been in the yard drinking beer on the night in question. Holtz quoted David as saying he was taking medication at the time and could not drink alcohol. Moreover, said Holtz, the family claimed, contrary to Barry's August 27 statement, that he had gone to bed after Tim's girlfriend left at 11:00 P.M. Holtz also told Barry that the killer smoked Marlboros, adding that a fingerprint with a whorl pattern had been found on a Marlboro box top recovered from Edna's house. Holtz instructed Barry to look at his right index finger, which had a whorl pattern, as do 25 to 35 percent of all fingerprints. Then, showing Barry a plastic bag containing a Marlboro top, Holtz asked what really happened that night. At this point, according to Holtz and Blevins, Barry agreed to tell them what happened, but only on condition that they wouldn't tell his parents. Then, he allegedly proceeded to confess, saying he committed the crime "cause I never could get a girl."

The troopers would claim that Barry provided details of the crime that only the killer would know—that he struck her on the head with a flashlight, stuffed pills into her mouth, pinched her nose shut and stroked her throat to get her to choke on the pills, raped her, and stole four hundred dollars from a bag she kept pinned to her bra. He added that he disposed of the bag the next day in a dumpster at a furniture store and spent the money on beer and food, according to Holtz and Blevins.

At the end of the session, Holtz turned on the tape recorder and read Barry a statement purporting to memorialize the admissions he had just made and asked whether it was accurate. "Yes," Barry replied, softly. Based on the statement, Barry was charged with murder, rape, robbery, and burglary—offenses that made him eligible for the death penalty.

The next day, September 9, Blevins and Holtz obtained a warrant to search Barry's home and take blood samples for testing. In the home,

searchers found a flashlight—a light plastic one that authorities would contend was the weapon that knocked out Edna, leaving a two-inch bruise on
the back of her head. The police also found a pair of high-top sneakers.
The sneakers did not match the shoeprint found in Edna's home, but their
discovery led Holtz and Blevins to conclude that Barry had been deceptive
when he denied having any tennis shoes.

The flashlight and the sneakers aside, Barry's blood samples presented
a serious problem. When analyzed, it turned out that Barry had type B
blood—but Janice Roadcap, the state forensic chemist who analyzed the
semen recovered in the case, had concluded that Edna's assailant had type
A blood. Upon learning of the problem, Roadcap made a notation in the
margin to her lab notes stating that the seminal swabs "were moist when
placed in vials. Breakdown of B antigens could have occurred."

Laughman's attorney, Adams County Public Defender Jack Cook, filed a
pretrial motion to suppress the alleged confession on the ground that his
client was retarded and incapable of understanding his rights, but the trial
judge, Oscar Spicer, denied the motion.

When the case came to trial before a death-qualified jury on December
12, 1988, District Attorney Roy Keefer relied heavily on the confession
and inconsistencies in Laughman's and his family's statements, while Cook
hammered away at the scientific evidence and the contradictions between
the confession and the physical evidence.

Keefer's star witnesses were Troopers Holtz and Blevins, who testified
that Laughman had told them details of the crime that only the killer
would know, that his motive was not robbery but to have sex with Edna
because he couldn't get a girl, and that he killed her because if he didn't
she would tell his parents. The robbery, they quoted him as saying, was just
to cover up the murder.

Janice Roadcap offered various explanations for why no B antigens had
been detected in the semen samples she examined: perhaps the B antigens
simply had been too weak to detect, perhaps they had been devoured by
bacteria, or perhaps they'd somehow been changed to A antigens by an
antibiotic Edna was taking for a urinary tract infection.

The trial appeared to turn in favor of the prosecution when Trooper
Holtz took the stand and dropped his three-finger bruise bombshell, blind-
siding Cook, since none of the reports Holtz had filed had suggested a link
between Barry's injured pinkie and the grip marks on Edna's arm.

In a move he would regret, Cook responded to Holtz's surprise by putting Barry on the stand. After Barry testified that his confession had been

false and denied committing the crime, Cook instructed him to demonstrate his grip on a piece of clay. The demonstration backfired. Only three of Barry's fingers left marks in the clay. "In hindsight," Cook would say in an interview, "I shouldn't have put him on the stand."

Keefer regarded the demonstration as pivotal. "He sat there on the witness stand and squeezed so hard that his arm was shaking," he would tell the *Patriot-News*. "When we walked up and saw what he had done, there were three marks and not four—exactly the same type of pattern on the victim. It was pretty clear."

On December 16, 1988, the jury found Laughman guilty of first-degree murder, rape, robbery, and burglary, and he was sentenced to life in prison.

In interviews, jurors indicated that they had been leaning toward acquittal until Laughman took the stand. Their change of heart was based not so much on the ill-conceived demonstration with the clay, but rather on Laughman's demeanor and seemingly normal appearance.

"The defense portrayed this young man as very excitable and nervous," one juror, who asked that his name not be used, explained, "but when he took the stand, he was calm, cool, and collected. He was portrayed one way and came off as another." The juror added, "The police bungled this thing so badly [that] if we had to depend on [their investigation], we would have had to let him go."

Skip Gochenour, a private detective who worked for the defense, understood how jurors could overestimate Barry. On first impression, Barry had seemed normal to Gochenour as well. But it soon became clear to Gochenour that Barry was unable to grasp what was going on. He couldn't even make out or understand the meaning of the word "bra" when asked to read his own confession.

"Do I question whether Barry said some of the things that are in that statement?" Gochenour asked rhetorically. "No, I don't. But I think he was just responding. I could have gotten him to confess to being Jack the Ripper."

When Cook filed a post-verdict motion asking Judge Spicer to set aside the verdict on the ground that Barry's confession should have been suppressed because his "mental acuity prevented him from understanding his rights or making a voluntary statement," Spicer promptly denied it. Aside from Barry's low IQ, Spicer wrote, there was "absolutely nothing" to require excluding the confession. "He is a miserable reader," Spicer added, "but otherwise gives the appearance of competence."

After Barry exhausted his state appeals in 1992, the aura of stardom around the star witness against him, Trooper Holtz, began to fade when it was disclosed that he had accepted payments totaling fifty thousand dollars for information he provided to Joseph Wambaugh for *Echoes in the Darkness*—payments conditioned on Jay C. Smith being brought to trial in the case.

The Smith case was so riddled with official misconduct that the conviction had been overturned and the Pennsylvania Supreme Court had just barred retrial on double jeopardy grounds. A junkman removing trash from Holtz's home had found his agreement with the author, which they had entered into before Smith had even been arrested. The junkman also found notes contradicting some of Holtz's testimony at the Smith trial. In light of the disclosures, Holtz would retire under fire.

Richard Ofshe, a professor of sociology at the University of California, Berkeley, and an expert in false confessions, told the *Patriot-News* that Trooper Holtz's rendition of Laughman's confession was "useless and dangerous." "Someone who wants to get to the truth can't tell whether the suspect knew crucial information or whether the police contaminated the person by providing him crucial information," Ofshe said. "We now have a long, long list of innocent people who were made to seem to knowledgeably confess to crimes—and we know that the only way these individuals could have gotten much of the detailed information that they included in the confessions is from the police."

The credibility of Janice Roadcap also began to crumble under scrutiny. Two independent experts who reviewed her testimony at the request of the *Patriot-News* disputed the theories she advanced to explain how it could have been possible for semen to come from Laughman and yet contain no detectable B antigens.

One of the experts, Richard Saferstein, former chief forensic scientist for the New Jersey State Police who holds a Ph.D. in chemistry from the City University of New York and is the author of textbooks on forensic serology, said there is no basis in science or fact for Roadcap's conclusions. "She keeps saying it's possible," Saferstein said. "Well, anything's possible [but] we have to talk in terms of reasonable probability. These are outrageous statements."

The second expert, Dr. Cyril Wecht, former Allegheny County Medical Examiner and past president of both the American Academy of Forensic Science and the American College of Legal Medicine, scoffed at the notions that antibiotics could alter a blood type or that the B antigens were weak. "I think what's weak here is her whole argument," said Wecht, who is nationally known for his work on such cases as the John F. Kennedy assassination, Elvis Presley's death, and, more recently, the slaying of Washington intern Chandra Levy.

Moreover, Wecht added, it would have been easy to test for bacteria or other contamination, but Roadcap did not perform such tests. "It was her scientific duty to see to it that [the semen samples] were tested to confirm her findings," Wecht said. "Instead of having this be exculpatory, they come up with these totally scientifically unfounded reasons. [It's] just a disgrace that they proceeded with [the prosecution] without further testing. The first tragedy is [what] happened to an eighty-five-year-old woman. The second tragedy here is what happened to this case."

In addition, the claim of Troopers Holtz and Blevins that Barry couldn't get a girl—his purported reason for desiring to have sex with Edna—was called into question by the fact that he had a girlfriend at the time. She was never questioned by the authorities, but she confirmed to the *Patriot-News* that she and Barry had been intimately involved.

At the time of the trial, DNA testing was in its infancy, and substantial amounts of genetic material were needed for accurate results.

Public Defender Jeff Cook had unsuccessfully pursued DNA testing, but the quantity of material had been insufficient to test with then-existing technology.

After the trial, Judge Spicer ordered the biological evidence—eighteen swabs and six microscope slides—turned over to Cook and, for the next five years, until a new attorney was appointed to represent Barry, the evidence sat in a refrigerator in Cook's office.

In 1994, Barry's new lawyer, Mark D. Beauchat, who is now an Adams County district justice, said he sent a sealed box containing the evidence to a DNA expert whom he characterized in an interview as "some nutty professor" whose name he claimed he couldn't recall. According to Beauchat, the nameless expert informed him that conclusive tests could not be performed on the samples and neither wrote a report nor returned the samples.

A few calls by the *Patriot-News* soon identified the expert as Mark Stoneking, a Pennsylvania State University anthropology professor who in 1994 headed the university's Institute of Molecular Evolutionary Genetics. In 1998 Stoneking moved to the Max Planck Institute for Evolutionary Anthropology in Leipzig, Germany, where the *Patriot-News* found him.

Stoneking's recollection, alas, differed from Beauchat's. In fact, Stoneking told the *Patriot-News*, he had extracted DNA from the semen swabs, but needed comparison samples from Barry and Edna Laughman to draw any conclusions. Stoneking said he informed Beauchat of this in writing, but Beauchat didn't respond. Stoneking said he wasn't surprised because "there are all sorts of reasons why they don't follow up."

But Stoneking preserved the samples and took them with him to Leipzig—along with correspondence backing up his version of events.

"I consider this statement [Barry's confession] to be largely uncorroborated and in need of corroboration," Adams County Detective Frank Donnelly, a former Pennsylvania State Police cold-case investigator who is now reviewing the Laughman case for the prosecution, told the *Patriot-News*. "That's as I sit here now having read everything and looked at everything."

He drew an analogy: "If you're fixing a car, if you have it right, the part should slide into place. A lot of time if you're jamming the parts in, you either have the wrong parts or you're putting them in wrong. Do we have the wrong parts in this case because we have the wrong guy?"

"I know firsthand how, in a police custodial interrogation, a retarded man can be led into making a false confession, which may very well be what happened here," said David J. Foster, a Cumberland County lawyer who took up Barry's defense last month. "I'm very new to the case, but from everyone I've discussed this with, there's a general consensus that he's an innocent man."

Three years ago, Foster represented William M. Kelly Jr., a twenty-eight-year-old borderline retarded man who repeatedly confessed to the rape and murder of Jeanette Thomas, whose body was found in a landfill near Harrisburg the previous year. Investigators claimed that Kelly described in detail how he bludgeoned Thomas with a tree branch. Kelly was absolved of the crime while awaiting trial in 1992 when DNA linked serial killer Joseph D. Miller to the crime.

In the hope that DNA will do for Barry Laughman what it did for William Kelly, Foster said he will ask Adams County Presiding Judge John D. Kuhn to order the crime scene samples currently in Mark Stoneking's possession in Germany to be returned for testing with state-of-the-art technology.

Epilogue

Within days of the publication of Pete Shellem's article, Judge Kuhn approved the requested DNA testing. Five months later, on November 21,

Barry was released on his own recognizance when the results appeared to exonerate him. On August 26, 2004, Adams County District Attorney Shawn C. Wagner dropped the charges. In September 2007, a federal civil rights suit brought on Barry's behalf against Troopers Holtz and Blevins and Janice Roadcap was settled for an undisclosed amount.

Barry's exoneration was among several journalistic triumphs in wrongful conviction cases for Shellem, whom former Pennsylvania Attorney General Ernie Preate characterized for a 2007 *American Journalism Review* profile as "a one-man Innocence Project."

The murder of Edna Laughman remained unsolved when this anthology went to press.

EARL WASHINGTON JR.

He promptly confessed to every crime the police asked him about

MARGARET EDDS

CULPEPER, VIRGINIA

Melissa Marie was late for the school bus again. Her mother, Rebecca Lynn Williams, barefoot, tousled, wearing blue jeans and a red-and-white football jersey, flung open the front door of 682 Willis Lane in the Village Apartments and signaled to the bus driver that Missy was coming.

Moments later, the preschooler straggled out, stopped for a hug, and disappeared onto the bus. Once Missy was off to school, there were still Melinda May and Misty Michele to feed and dress. Becky had been little more than a child herself when her oldest was born, and now, at just nineteen, she was already a mother of three. The responsibility was more than she had bargained for, but little else in life had given her as much satisfaction as the girls. She felt a small swell of pride when relatives commented that she was a "good mother."

But on this morning—June 4, 1982—her mind was less on the girls than on Clifford, her childhood sweetheart, now her husband. There was no question that she loved Clifford, had almost from the moment a mutual friend had brought him by her house six years earlier. She was just thirteen then, tall, with lank, shoulder-length blond hair and a full-cheeked face. Clifford was fifteen, large for his age, crazy about engines and hot rods. Neither cared much for school. Clifford knew how to have a good time, and Becky was interested in learning. Their romance ignited like a firecracker. It wasn't long before Clifford had moved into Becky's family home and Melissa Marie was on the way.

There were plenty of happy memories from those first few years. Becky's passion was baton twirling; Clifford's was motorcycles. When she traveled to parades in Flint Hill or other Piedmont towns, he would hop on his bike, pick her up at the finish, and they would speed away. Sometimes they went

From *An Expendable Man* (New York: New York University Press, 2003). Copyright © Margaret Edds. Adapted with permission.

fishing at Lake Anna. Other times, they joined the parade of young people driving up and down the main streets of Culpeper on a Saturday night. School was a nuisance. Clifford dropped out to work at a gas station, Becky to care for Missy. He went back for a while, but then gave it up. She never went back. The babies kept coming. "I think she could walk past Clifford and get pregnant," Helen Richards, Becky's mother, would say ruefully.

There were arguments, driven by financial instability and emotional immaturity. At times, Clifford drank heavily and dabbled in drugs, and the bickering ran in cycles. A year and a half or so ago, Becky and Clifford seemed to have their problems in check. They took out a marriage license and made their union official. But now the old troubles were resurfacing. Clifford was drinking too much and spending time away from home. Becky, frustrated and angry, was thinking of doing something about it.

It was 8:05 A.M. when Missy told her mother goodbye and climbed onto the school bus, according to the next day's *Culpeper Star-Exponent*. Retracing Becky's steps the rest of the morning was not complicated. Sometime between 9:00 and 10:00 A.M., she placed the first of two collect calls to her mother, who managed an apartment complex in the Washington, D.C., suburbs. Becky was angry that Clifford had not come home after work. "She asked me to come pick her up," Helen Richards would recall. "He was drinking, back doing drugs. She did love him, but she was not going to let her babies live like that." Helen told her daughter she would try to come later in the day.

A neighbor saw Becky and her two youngest girls at a nearby 7-Eleven at about 10:30 A.M., according to the *Star-Exponent*. Nothing seemed amiss. Two other witnesses saw the trio as they headed back to the apartment complex. Eleven-month-old Misty was in a stroller. Two-year-old Mindy was walking at her mother's side. Neighbor Doris Campbell, who was on her way to an 11:00 A.M. job interview, drove past them moments before she was due at her appointment. Jerry Lane was headed out of the complex as well and stopped to chat with Becky near the apartment office, a few hundred yards from her home. He figured that was around 11:00 A.M.

According to Helen's telephone bill, Becky's second collect call was placed at 11:09 A.M. She was speaking from a neighbor's apartment because the Williams's phone wasn't operating. Again, Becky expressed her frustration with Clifford and her desire to leave once Missy was home from school. Helen promised to be there later in the day. It was the last time she heard her daughter's voice.

Whatever awaited Becky back at her apartment occurred quickly and brutally. There was no sign of forced entry. It is impossible to know whether

her attacker followed her into the apartment or was waiting when she and the children returned. But there is no question that Becky met her death in a frenzied spasm of violence. Blood spattering on the bed and wall suggested that much of the attack, if not all, occurred in a back bedroom. Becky was stabbed thirty-eight times. Incredibly, Becky did not die on the spot. Rather she made her way, wounded and bleeding, to the front door.

Shortly before noon, Paul Brundage and his wife, who were in the process of moving into the Village Apartments, saw what they thought was a mannequin lying in the doorway of 682 Willis Lane. They quickly realized that it was not a mannequin but a naked, bleeding woman, lying on her side and calling softly, "Please help me. I've been raped."

Moments later, Culpeper Police Patrolman J. L. "Scoobie" Jackson, who lived in the apartment complex, looked out of his second-floor apartment and saw the woman lying in the doorway. As he rushed to investigate, he saw blood and heard her cry, "He hurt me. He hurt me." Jackson saw Mindy standing just inside the apartment door, called to her, and she walked toward him. He handed her to a woman in the gathering crowd. Peering into the living room, Jackson saw Misty in a playpen. "I just reached in and picked her up and handed her to another one of the females that was outside," he said.

Answering the police dispatcher's call, Kenneth Buraker, a Culpeper police investigator, arrived on the scene at 11:57 A.M. "I stood directly over the top of her, so she could see me," Buraker would testify. "I asked her if she knew who her attacker was. She replied, 'No.' I asked her if the attacker was black or white and she replied, 'black.' I then asked her if there was more than one and she replied, 'no.'"

As Becky was lying there, her husband drove up. Pushing past the police cars and neighbors, Clifford knelt by her. "I tried to tell her that the ambulance was on the way, that she'd be all right, you know, that everything would be OK," he would say, choking back tears, "and I asked her, you know, who did it, and the only thing she replied to me was, 'a black man.'"

As Becky was being moved to the Culpeper County Volunteer Fire Department rescue vehicle, the fifth member of the Williams family, Missy, arrived home. She climbed down from the school bus and began running toward the apartment. Neighbors blocked her path, guiding her instead toward her sisters. According to a newspaper account, "Seeing her mother being placed in the ambulance she cried, 'My mommy. My mommy. What's happened to my mommy?'"

At Culpeper Memorial Hospital, there was a gallant effort to save Becky's life, but the wounds were too severe. At 2:05 P.M. she was pronounced dead.

Special Agents Curtis Reese Wilmore and Frank Lasley, of the Bureau of Criminal Investigation, Virginia State Police, worked methodically, first canvassing the area outside the apartment, then moving indoors, measuring, photographing, and preserving clothing, fingerprints, hairs, blood samples, anything that might be of use in tracing the killer. It was 8:30 P.M. when they finished.

Three days after the crime, fifty-eight items—including a plastic rug runner, a wooden match, a table knife, a pocketknife, a light blue baby's blanket, a royal blue blanket, fingernail scrapings from Becky's hands, samples of her pubic and head hair, a floral sheet, a green and white pillowcase, on and on—were shipped to the state Division of Forensic Science lab. In ensuing weeks, blood samples, saliva swabs, and hairs from some initial suspects also showed up at the lab.

On June 9, Culpeper Police Chief C. B. Jones, while assuring the public that his office was hard at work on the case, admitted that numerous interviews with friends, neighbors, and relatives of Becky Williams had produced no concrete leads. "If there's a witness, we haven't talked with them yet," he said. Three days later, John C. Bennett, the Culpeper County commonwealth's attorney, reported that "there have been developments" and "they are being evaluated." He declined to elaborate. But on June 16, twelve days after the murder, a headline in the local paper summed up the situation: "Murder Remains a Total Mystery."

It was as if the murderer had evaporated as quickly and stealthily as he had appeared. To investigators, failure to wrap up the case was embarrassing. But a year later, out of nowhere, an answer arrived, or so the authorities thought.

In the early morning hours of Saturday, May 21, 1983, Hazel Nancy Weeks heard a crash and sat up in bed. It sounded like glass breaking. Most likely, a storm was brewing and the wind had knocked a branch into the front of the house. A more timid or less practical soul might have burrowed under the covers. But Hazel had not spent her seventy-eight years as the daughter of one farmer and the wife of another for nothing. If there was a broken window, it needed to be covered before the rain started.

Two years earlier, her husband James would have done the fixing. Now he was gone. Their son, Jimmy, who lived not far down the road, would have taken Hazel in gladly. But she preferred her independence and had chosen to remain alone in her house a few miles outside Bealeton, in Fauquier County, east of Culpeper.

Hazel lifted the covers and gingerly swung her legs out of bed. After two knee replacements, she was walking well, but she had to be vigilant against falling. She clicked on the bedroom light and, barefoot and without her robe, headed toward the front door. Halfway down the hall she realized that she wasn't alone.

A man was standing just inside the living room archway. Hazel couldn't see him clearly. All she could tell was that he was black. Instinctively, she lifted her cane and ordered him away. "Get out of here," she demanded. His response was swift and violent. Whirling, he lifted a wooden armchair from the end of the dining room table. Within seconds, it came crashing into Hazel's head, then again, and again.

Stunned, Hazel felt her grasp slipping and wondered if she was about to die. Then it occurred to her that if she offered the man money he might stop hitting her. "Evidently, I was asking the Lord for help and I think that the word 'money' must have been put into my mind by the Lord," she would testify a month later.

"I don't have very much money, but what money I have, I'll give it to you, if you'll take it and let me alone," she told him. When he asked where her money was, she replied that it was in her purse in the bedroom. Her memory of what happened next was blurred. Either she was pushed or dragged to the bedroom, probably pushed—she thought—because she was still standing. The man asked where her purse was and she pointed toward the closet.

As the man searched for the purse, Hazel edged her hand toward the telephone, thinking that she might be able to signal for help. But the man saw her and knocked her hand down and her with it to the floor. Then he told her, "Take off your gown." She was a small woman, about five feet two, not frail, but not stout. She stood no chance of defending herself against the man, but she was not going to be violated without a struggle. "So when he told you to take off your gown, what did you do?" Assistant Common-wealth's Attorney John Inger would ask, replaying the moment in court. "I didn't do anything," she answered. "I didn't have any idea of taking my gown off. . . . He took the money and left and closed the bedroom door behind him as he went out."

Hazel inched across the floor to the phone and dialed her son, Jimmy. She told him an intruder was in her house. He scrambled into his clothes and raced to his car and down the road to her house, entering quietly through the kitchen door. Thinking a gun might be useful if the intruder was still in the house, he rummaged the top of the refrigerator, where a .22-caliber pistol had been kept for years. The gun was gone.

Jimmy switched on a light illuminating the living and dining room areas. Blood was everywhere. A broken dining room chair lay on the floor.

Items were scattered out of place. Hurrying down the hall, he found Hazel on the bedroom floor. She had taken some pieces of used bedsheet that she kept for rags and was pressing them against her skull to stop the bleeding. Jimmy helped her to the bed. His wife arrived and began tending to Hazel. Jimmy went out to wait for the rescue squad and the sheriff.

Deputy Denny Zeets of the Fauquier County Sheriff's Department was patrolling nearby at about 3:25 A.M. when the break-in at Hazel's home was reported. He sped to the site and found Jimmy Weeks waiting. Moments later, there was a gunshot. It seemed to come from a ramshackle dwelling across the road—the home of a woman named Nellie Mudd.

Zeets ran to the house, where he found Robert Washington nursing a gunshot wound to his foot, inflicted, according to the witnesses, by his brother, Earl Washington Jr. Just then, a second shot was fired outside the house. Zeets dashed outside. He saw no one, but lying on the ground there was a brown purse, which papers inside identified as Hazel's. As Zeets sifted through the purse, there was a third shot, this one from the opposite side of the road, back toward the Weeks home.

Reinforcements were arriving as Zeets hurried back across the road. A group of county and state officers assembled in Hazel's yard and fanned out to search the area. At dawn, Deputy A. L. Robinson spotted the suspect in three-foot grass in a nearby field. Service revolver drawn, Robinson ordered the man to come out with his hands up. Earl surrendered peacefully. Hazel's .22 was nearby. Robinson advised Earl of his Miranda rights and drove him to the Fauquier County Sheriff's Department in Warrenton, where he was charged with attempted rape, robbery, breaking and entering, and malicious wounding.

At 8:30 A.M., two hours after the arrest, Deputy Zeets put down on paper the first of several confessions Earl would make to the Weeks crime. Taken at face value, Earl's statement—which was not electronically recorded or taken down by a stenographer—seemed damning: "I was at [Nellie Mudd's] house. I found my girlfriend with my brother. We argued. I told him I was going to get a gun and shoot him. I went to Mrs. Weeks [sic] house to get gun, broke out the window and opened the door. I went to the kitchen, got gun from over refrigerator and started back to the door. I saw her coming down hall. I hit her with the chair. She fell to the floor. I keep hitting her untell [sic] the chair broke apart. That's when I decided to fuck her. I got on top of her but she started to move and then told me to leave her alone. I told her I want your money. She said it was in her purse. I got up [sic] took her purse from a chair in the living room. I went out the door and back to [the Mudd] house. I went around back and stopped for a time. I went in the house and shot my brother. I got scared and ran away."

Whatever Earl actually did, or intended to do, that fateful night, his life came spiraling down to a single, distilled sentence, heard during a drunken break-in: "Take off your gown." From those four words, misunderstandings, errors, and deceptions emerged that would bring him within nine days of execution.

Investigator Terry Schrum hadn't planned to stay when he walked into the Fauquier County Sheriff's Department that morning. It was Saturday, and he was off, and he had plenty to do at home. But the office was abuzz with news of the Weeks crime and the confession Earl Washington Jr. had just given.

"I knew Mrs. Weeks, didn't know her personally. I knew her son Jimmy and I knew she was an elderly woman. I was told he had gone in, hit her with a chair, violent, he's looking for the gun, and that he had got on top of her and tried to take her underpants off," Schrum would recall years later. "So, based on that, him being a young guy . . . I asked 'em, 'Did anybody interview him about the other cases we had outstanding?' And they said, 'No.'"

Violence was rare in Fauquier County in the early 1980s. But lately, there had been a string of assaults on females in Warrenton, the county seat. Residents were jittery. Now here was a suspect who—according to what Schrum was hearing—had broken into a house, committed an assault and robbery, and tried to rape an elderly woman. The details were being embellished, but Schrum had no way of knowing. The Warrenton assaults, unlike this one, had involved young women. And the Weeks attack had taken place not in Warrenton but twelve miles away, outside Bealeton. Still, there might be a connection, and Schrum thought Washington at least should be questioned about the other attacks.

The prisoner had spent the previous night drinking heavily, then broke into a neighbor's house, evaded police, and, shortly after his capture, sat through an interrogation by Zeets. If Earl had slept at all, it had been on the ground or in brief interludes after his arrest. Still, when Schrum began questioning him at 9:40 A.M., Earl seemed more expectant and fidgety than tired. Schrum thought he had a wide-eyed look and a half-smile on his face, nothing belligerent, and a sort of nervous twitching.

Schrum was no expert on mental retardation—his police training had barely touched on it—but his gut told him that Earl was slow, but "not pathetically slow." In fact, when tested on the Wechsler Intelligence Scale

shortly after his eleventh birthday, Earl had shown an IQ of fifty-eight, placing him in the lowest 1 to 2 percent of the population. When he was fourteen, his perceptual-motor skills were poorer than would be expected of
an eight-year-old. But a school psychologist noted that Earl had "obviously
built up a defense system to help him 'save face' in this difficult situation."

Zeets sat in on the session, which, like his earlier interview, was not
recorded. In giving the Miranda warning, Schrum said later, "I recited
what we're supposed to recite. Then I'd explain what each one meant to
him, like, 'You have the right to remain silent. Now, Earl, we're sitting here
talking to you. You don't have to talk to us if you don't want to.'" When
Zeets asked Earl if he understood, he replied, "Yes, sir."

After reviewing the Weeks case, the interrogators turned to the most
recent rape—that of Lynn Ellen Rawlings, twenty-three, on April 12, 1983,
on Culpeper Street in downtown Warrenton. At first, according to Schrum's
report, Earl "wouldn't deny or admitt [sic] it, hung his head." When Earl
finally did deny the crime, Schrum found the denial unpersuasive—Earl
somehow radiated guilt. The interview continued for two hours without an
admission. Then, according to Schrum's notes, "we told Earl to go back to
his cell and think about it. We told Earl that if he wanted to talk to us and
changed his mind, to tell the jailer and he would tell us."

About an hour later, a jailer told Schrum, "Earl wants to talk to you,"
and the questioning resumed, again without a recording. When Earl was
asked about the Rawlings rape, to quote Schrum's notes, "He said, 'I don't
know anything about it,' and smiled." Schrum was so struck by the inappro-
priateness of the smile that he underlined the word three times in his notes.
To him, the crime was no smiling matter. "OK, Earl, you're not telling us
the truth, are you?" Schrum demanded. "Earl, you are the one that raped
that girl . . . aren't you?"

After a few seconds, Earl nodded yes. He was starting to look nervous
again, and to Schrum, who had done many interrogations, the prisoner's
anxiety was a signal that he still had something festering inside.

Schrum knew that police in Culpeper had been wrestling for almost
a year with the unsolved murder of a young woman. He was sketchy on
the details—he didn't recall the victim's name or whether she had been
raped—but the thought struck him that Earl might have been involved in
that, too. This was the time to ask. "We told Earl that we now wanted to talk
to him about an incident in Culpeper in which a girl was stabbed." Schrum
wrote in his notes. "Earl didn't look at us, but was still very nervous." Then
Schrum asked, "Earl, did you kill that girl in Culpeper?"

For about five seconds, Earl was quiet. His shaking was the only movement in the room. Then his head moved up and down, yes, and he began
to cry. "To clarify things a little," Schrum wrote in his notes, "I told him
that I was talking about the one found laying [sic] outside the apartment
or townhouse with no clothes on in Culpeper and asked if that was the
one. Earl said yes." There was no mention that the victim had been raped.
Unsure whether there had been a rape, Schrum didn't ask about that.

The next step was to get the Culpeper officers to Warrenton for a full interrogation. But as for the prisoner, the confession appeared to have boosted
his spirits. "Earl stated that he felt better after admitting that he killed the
girl," Schrum wrote. "I asked him if it had been eating at his insides."

His answer was yes.

The next morning, Sunday, May 22, Culpeper Police Lieutenant Harlan
Lee Hart and Virginia State Police Special Agent Curtis Reese Wilmore
questioned Earl—once again without an electronically recorded or steno-
graphic record.

After Earl signed another Miranda waiver, according to the officers, Wilmore began, "I understand that you made some statements about stabbing
a woman in Culpeper. Did you stab the woman? Did you tell the truth?"
When the question was greeted with silence—Earl just hung his head and
pressed his hand to his forehead—Wilmore switched to more general questions to get him talking, and then asked again, "Did you stab a woman in
Culpeper?" This time Earl nodded yes, but he couldn't say where the stabbing occurred. When asked if he could show the officers, he said, "I don't
know. I think I can."

When Wilmore asked if the victim was white or black, Earl erroneously
said she was black. When Wilmore repeated the question, Earl amended
his answer to correctly say she was white. Police notes failed to mention
this, and it probably would never have come out if Wilmore hadn't voluntarily brought it up much later in testimony.

After a lunch break, Earl found himself in a car with Hart and Wilmore—Schrum and another investigator brought up the rear in another
car—en route to Culpeper where he would be asked to re-create his steps
the day Rebecca Williams was slain.

The re-creation began on a bridge along a state road not far from Bealeton where Earl said he was picked up by a couple of men whom he had
met the previous day. One was named Billy; he didn't know the name of
the other. When they arrived in Culpeper, the officers asked Earl to lead

them to the murder scene. Obligingly, he directed them to the Culpeper Town House Apartments—the wrong place.

Undaunted, the officers took him by other apartment complexes, instructing him to speak up if he saw anything that looked familiar. They went to the Catalpa Hill Apartments, Mountain View Apartments, Stuckner's Apartments, Redbud Apartments, and Westminster Square townhouses, but nothing registered with Earl. When they drove into the Village Apartments—the actual crime scene—he again recognized nothing. But on the way out, according to Wilmore, he hesitated. They turned back, but after another swing through the complex, Earl still recognized nothing. On the way out this time, however, he said Route 29, which ran beside the complex, separated by a wire fence, looked familiar. At this point, Wilmore asked him to point out the apartment where the assault occurred. "He pointed to an apartment on the exact opposite end from where the Williams girl was killed," Wilmore would contend—although there was no "exact opposite end" because the complex wasn't symmetrical.

On the return trip to Warrenton, Earl pointed to a spot where he supposedly threw the murder weapon out of the window of the car in which he was hitchhiking. Officers scoured the location up and down for about a mile but found no knife.

The next day Earl's confessions continued. He admitted the malicious wounding of Eugina Hecker in a nighttime attack outside her Warrenton home on November 12, 1982, and two separate break-ins at a house in Warrenton. Like the other interviews, this one was not recorded, but events were now set in motion from which there would be no turning back.

Until his arrest for the Weeks crime, Earl's most serious adult charge had been driving under the influence of alcohol. When the interrogations ended, he had confessed to three break-ins, two malicious woundings, one attempted rape, two actual rapes, two robberies, burglary, and capital murder—every crime about which he was asked.

Any notion that the Warrenton rape problem had been solved with the arrest of Earl Washington Jr. was short-lived. On July 21, 1983, less than a month after charges were certified against Earl, the *Fauquier Democrat* reported that a twenty-four-year-old woman who had been parked with her boyfriend on a street in downtown Warrenton at 4:30 A.M. was raped after the pair got into an argument and he left. About three weeks after that, a nineteen-year-old woman was raped as she walked alone on her way to a friend's house in downtown Warrenton. On January 19, 1984, the day testimony began in Earl's trial for the rape and murder of Becky Williams, the

Democrat reported that from July through September, five women were raped or assaulted in the Broadview Avenue vicinity of Warrenton. None of these crimes, obviously, could have been committed by a man who had been under lock and key since May.

Detailed knowledge of the case was not a bar to serving on the jury at Earl's trial before Culpeper County Circuit Court Judge David F. Berry for the Williams crime. A pharmacist selected for the jury knew, for instance, that the break-in at the Weeks home had triggered Earl's arrest, even though Judge Berry ruled against admitting evidence of any of the alleged crimes in Fauquier County.

Earl was entitled to court-appointed counsel, but his family pooled its meager resources and hired John Scott, who years earlier had come to prominence in the region as one of four black students who were plaintiffs in a federal suit that desegregated the Fredericksburg schools and was among the first several dozen black graduates of the University of Virginia School of Law. In 1974 he opened a Fredericksburg office of the Richmond firm of Hill, Tucker & Marsh, one of the South's premier practitioners of civil rights law. Earl's case was Scott's first capital murder trial.

Commonwealth's Attorney John Bennett dominated the trial from the opening moment, and Scott let pass comments that created an air of inevitability about Earl's guilt and conviction. Describing the confession in his opening statement, Bennett said that Earl had summoned officers at the Fauquier County Jail and "stated that he had killed a woman some time ago in Culpeper County." That wording implied that Earl had raised the matter unprompted, and the jury never heard an accurate version from Scott. Nor did Scott challenge Bennett's assertion that Earl had told the authorities "a number of different things that could only have been known by someone who had actually committed the offense."

Scott found Earl's incapacity to make a legitimate confession or to understand his legal rights so obvious that he believed the jury would as well. In his opening statement, Scott exhorted the jury to "listen to the circumstances surrounding the interrogation of Earl Washington Jr. by the law enforcement officers of this county."

In virtually every aspect of the trial, Earl's side of the story was inadequately told or never told at all. Bennett's opening statement took up eleven pages of the transcript, Scott's three. Bennett called fourteen witnesses whose testimony and cross examination filled 162 pages. Scott called two witnesses—Earl and his sister, Alfreda Pendleton—whose testimony was twenty-seven pages long. Bennett's closing statement covered nine pages,

Scott's two. Bennett's rebuttal was nearly four pages—almost twice as long as the statement he was rebutting.

Although someone had helped police prepare a composite drawing of a stranger who might be the killer, that person was not (or those persons were not) called to testify. Earl, presumably, either was not the man the unidentified witness or witnesses had seen or was not positively identified. Scott never established that his client had supplied no detail of the crime that was not known to the authorities in advance.

The jury of ten whites and two blacks began deliberations at 10:35 A.M. on January 20 and took just fifty minutes to reach a verdict—guilty, as charged. There was no dissent. After lunch, the trial moved directly into its penalty phase. For Earl to be sentenced to death, Virginia law required that the jury find one of two conditions—either that the crime was "outrageously or wantonly vile, horrible, or inhuman" or that there was clear evidence of the defendant's future dangerousness.

The jury deliberated ninety minutes before returning a verdict, which the foreman read: "We the jury . . . having unanimously found that his conduct in committing the offense is outrageously or wantonly vile, horrible, or inhuman . . . unanimously fix his punishment at death."

Epilogue

After the Virginia Supreme Court affirmed Washington's conviction in November 1984, his execution was set for September 5, 1985. Less than a month before he was to die, lawyers from the New York law firm of Paul, Weiss, Rifkind, Warton & Garrison led by Eric M. Freedman, a senior associate, took the case pro bono. On August 27, with just nine days to spare, they filed a petition for a state writ of habeas corpus and Culpeper County Circuit Court Judge Lloyd C. Sullenberger immediately granted a stay of execution.

While the petition was pending, Robert T. Hall, a Fairfax lawyer, joined the pro bono team. In a review of official documents pertaining to the case, he discovered a report showing that, before Washington's arrest, the Virginia Division of Forensic Science had analyzed semen stains on a blanket recovered from the Williams crime scene. The stains, said the report, had come from someone with type A blood. Neither Washington nor Clifford Williams, the victim's husband, could have been the source of the stains—both had type O blood. Prosecutors had dutifully turned the report over to

John Scott, Washington's defense lawyer, prior to trial, but he apparently didn't understand its significance and didn't raise the issue.

If Washington's jury had known about the forensic report, his lawyers now argued, it could have changed the outcome of the trial. Sullenberger disagreed, however, and denied the state habeas without a hearing in December 1986. After the Virginia Supreme Court affirmed Sullenberger's holding, Washington's legal team filed a petition for a federal writ of habeas corpus alleging, among other things, that their client had been denied his constitutional right to effective assistance of counsel. In July 1988, U.S. District Court Judge Claude M. Hilton denied the petition without a hearing. On appeal, the U.S. Court of Appeals for the Fourth Circuit remanded the case for a hearing on the ineffective assistance issue, but, in July 1992, after conducting the hearing, Hilton again denied relief. The Fourth Circuit affirmed Hinton's decision, holding that, while Scott's representation of Washington had been ineffective, it was harmless in light of the other evidence in the case—namely Washington's confessions.

Meanwhile, attorneys Barry C. Scheck and Peter Neufeld of the Innocence Project at the Cardozo School of Law had entered the case. In consultation with them and Washington's pro bono team, the state agreed to subject the biological evidence in the case to DNA testing. In October 1993 that testing confirmed, as the pretrial blood testing had indicated, that the semen stains on the blanket couldn't have come from Washington.

The DNA testing, however, came too late to be introduced into a legal proceeding under Virginia law, which afforded defendants only twenty-one days after sentencing to present new evidence. Thus, Washington's best hope to escape execution at this point resided with Governor L. Douglas Wilder, a popular African American Democrat, who, as a result of Virginia term limits, would leave office on January 15, 1994. On the day before he relinquished his office to Republican George Allen, Wilder removed the specter of death from the case by commuting Washington's sentence to life in prison.

In 2000, Allen's successor, Republican James S. Gilmore III, ordered additional DNA testing on other items. When the tests left virtually no doubt of Washington's innocence, Gilmore granted him an absolute pardon for the Williams murder. On February 12, 2001, Washington was released after seventeen years, thirty-eight weeks, and six days in custody. In response to his exoneration, the Virginia General Assembly promptly abolished the twenty-one-day restriction on new evidence, allowing biological evidence to be brought forth at any time

After a federal civil rights suit was brought on Washington's behalf in 2002, files turned over in discovery revealed that Special Agent Wilmore had provided details contained in Washington's confessions that the prosecution had contended only the killer would know. In 2004 a federal jury awarded Washington $2.25 million in damages, but the commonwealth appealed the verdict.

Meanwhile, DNA testing positively identified the man whose semen was found on the blanket from the Williams home as Kenneth M. Tinsley, a serial rapist serving a life sentence in Virginia for a 1984 rape. In April 2007, Tinsley pled guilty to the Williams murder and was sentenced to two additional life terms. Three months later, the commonwealth settled Washington's federal civil rights suit for $1.9 million.

INFERENCE

If you have a dream about a crime, it would be unwise to mention it to police.

Doing so may land you in prison—even if the details of the dream bare scant resemblance to the facts of the crime.

Similarly, an unguarded remark from which an inference of guilt can be drawn may bring the same result—even if the remark lends itself to an innocent construction, and even in the face of an unequivocal denial of the crime.

The goal of interrogation, of course, is to secure a straightforward admission of guilt that includes corroborating facts that only the perpetrator would know—preferably facts previously unknown even to the police.

But if the police believe you committed a crime and if an admission is not readily forthcoming, a dream statement or other ambiguous statement may suffice.

Anything you say can—and often will—be used against you.

The first three of the following articles illustrate how inferences drawn from dreams led to wrongful convictions. The fourth and final article in this section features a wrongful conviction that stemmed not from a dream but from an unguarded utterance that lent itself to diametrically opposed inferences—one consistent with innocence, the other suggestive of guilt.

The authorities built their case on the latter.

The story of Tommy Ward and Karl Fontenot in the "Unrequited Innocence" section of this anthology (page 453) is a further example of a dream confession.

ROBERT LEE MILLER JR.

His journey to death row began when he said he'd had a dream

BARRY SCHECK, PETER NEUFELD, AND JIM DWYER

OKLAHOMA CITY, OKLAHOMA

When ninety-two-year-old Zelma Cutler was found dead in her bed on September 2, 1986—apparently suffocated by the weight of the man who raped her—the Military Park section of Oklahoma City already was reeling with fear for its elderly neighbors. Four months earlier, in the house catty-corner to Cutler's, the same thing had happened to Anna Laura Fowler, eighty-three. In between the two murders, a man had been seen on the back porch of a third elderly woman, unscrewing a light bulb and trying to force his way inside. He was chased off before he could do any violence.

Now, Zelma Cutler had been killed. Both dead women were widows who lived alone in corner houses. No property was taken, and there was no sign of ransacking. Knotted rags were found at both crime scenes. Telephone lines were wrenched from the ground in both yards. The circuit boxes at both houses were switched off. In the semen left by the rapist in both victims, blood type A positive was detected. Three Negroid hairs were found on the gurney sheets that were wrapped around Mrs. Cutler's body. "My grandmother lived out there," recalled one young woman, Lee Ann Peters. "I was among many citizens wanting the police to get this case solved."

The city put twelve detectives on a task force. They swept the streets of the Military Park neighborhood. "There was mass hysteria," Ray Elliott, an assistant district attorney involved in the case, would recall. "Especially in that neighborhood. A lot of old-timers there. One victim had lived in her house for sixty years. The city police stopped everything that breathed or moved." Some 173 black men were questioned and listed as suspects. Of these, twenty-three gave blood samples. Among those whose finger pricks showed A positive blood was Robert Lee Miller Jr., a twenty-seven-year-

From *Actual Innocence* (New York: Doubleday, 2000). Copyright © Barry Scheck, Peter Neufeld, and Jim Dwyer. Adapted with permission.

old unemployed heating and air-conditioning repairman. He lived three blocks from the scenes of the murders.

On February 23, 1987, detectives visited Miller and asked if he could help. Miller felt unwell. He was a regular user of drugs, and he believed that someone had slipped PCP into something he had ingested. But, he said, he too sensed the unease heaving along the streets following the murders. Anything he could do to help, he would. He rode to the police station with the detectives, and they sat him in an interview room, where Detective Jerry Flowers asked him what he had to offer.

"I've got these powers," said Miller. "I can see things through the killer's eyes."

With that, Flowers made a signal. Watching through a mirror, his partner, David Shupe, switched on a hidden video camera.

"I was dreaming about it one night and you know, probably almost the same night it happened," Miller said. "You know I have dreams like that, you know, come to me all the time."

The next twelve hours were a numbing drone of hallucination, interrogation, exorcism, revival, and nonsense. The detectives held a Bible. They prayed. They cast out demons. They coaxed Miller, accused him, walked out on him, begged him to peer deeper into his visions. Miller spoke of enemies who stole his hair from garbage cans, pilfered his clothes, poisoned his days. An ancestor had predicted that he would be a great federal lawman, perhaps another Marshal Dillon, perhaps the Lone Ranger, he told the police. At times, he invoked the memory of his hero, Bruce Lee. He concentrated ferociously when asked to envision the killings, and what the murderer *was* doing. Like a TV set with a weak antenna, Miller's details were fuzzy, and sometimes he changed channels without warning. The detectives played with his mind-set and prayed with him to get him back in tune.

At the end, the detectives decided they had their man. With a flourish, Robert Macy, the district attorney of Oklahoma City, announced that he was moving quickly to file capital murder charges against Miller.

He had committed "incomprehensible crimes," said Macy.

"I want to let the public know this man is in custody, and the danger has been removed," said Macy.

Miller never actually admitted the crime, but he didn't have to. In the prosecutor's telling, he had coughed up inside details, fine points that would be known only to the investigating detectives—and the killer. A few months later, District Attorney Macy would tell a jury that Miller put himself into deep trouble with his own words, even if the videotapes were a lengthy display of "mind games" between the detectives and their quarry.

"You may not approve of the techniques, but you've got to remember what was going on," said Macy. "You have two cops sitting in there who knew very early on, before they got too far in there, they knew that they had the killer, these two men sitting across the table from him. And they knew it was their job, if they could, to get incriminating statements out of him that would identify him as that killer. And they did. He may have got tired. They got tired, too. They worked real hard at it, and they got damning—they got evidence that only the killer knew."

What was that evidence?

"He knew what rooms they were in. He knew how the rooms were decorated. He knew precisely how the killer got into the houses. He knew how the killer and why the killer disconnected the telephone lines so they wouldn't, couldn't call out. And he told you exactly what the killer was feeling and thinking. And there's only one person on the face of this earth that knows that, and that's him right there."

At trial, the jury heard the videotapes of Miller's interrogation running nearly twelve hours. They were often indistinct or incoherent. Miller had been a drug user, and he would later say that he thought someone in his household had doped his food or drink on the day the detectives came for him. The tapes sounded bad, even if Miller denied over and over having anything to do with the crimes and insisted he was merely channeling a vision, a power sent him by his deceased Choctaw grandmother.

Then there were a few hairs, described by the state's so-called hair expert as Negroid and supposedly consistent with Miller's hair. Then there was the ample residue of semen found at both crime scenes. "He put Mrs. Cutler through a sexual nightmare," Macy declared. "He climaxed more than once." And the blood type showed that his A positive was the same as that found in the rapist's semen.

Still, for drama, nothing beat the tapes. One of the detectives even claimed to have counted the number of times that Miller slipped and used the term "I"—gutting the defense claim that the killer was a "he," a character who dwelled within Robert's mind only in the third person.

When the defense had its turn, Miller denied having anything to do with the killings, just as he had on the tapes. All the details he discussed with the detectives were simple rumors he had picked up in the neighborhood—he lived only a few blocks from the murdered women—and from news accounts, including a TV broadcast of *Crimestoppers*. His discussions with the detectives were not based on any firsthand knowledge of the crime but on a mystical experience.

"I had visions from the Lord. An angel came to me—I assume it was my grandmother—warning me someone was trying to frame me," Miller swore.

Another defense witness, a neighbor, described Miller as a "peaceful" man who often helped with chores. The murders had been the talk of the neighborhood, she said, and many people knew that the killer had gone in the back door—one of the details that the prosecutor claimed only the killer would have known.

None of that could match the closing arguments of District Attorney Macy, who silenced the courtroom with supreme stagecraft. He paraded along the jury box, holding an elastic band from a pair of men's underpants. As he walked, Macy remembered aloud something Miller told the detectives. They had wanted to know if he could see that the killer had left something behind.

"It might have been underwear or something, he left something in the house," Miller had said.

And there was Macy, holding an underwear band in his hand. It was Fruit of the Loom, the same brand worn by Miller, and it had been found near the body of Anna Laura Fowler. "As I recall, well, he [said he] may have left a shoe, he may have left a glove, and then he said, no, he may have left his underwear," thundered Macy.

And there was the foul little piece of cloth, the band of the underwear. He approached the jury and displayed it.

After the fierce power of this relic had settled on the jury, Macy continued with other incriminating evidence. It was Miller's blood type in the semen. His type of hair on the bed. His knowledge of secret details of the murder.

"And he sat there and he laid it out without one tear, without one sign of remorse. Did you ever see one sign of remorse? Instead, he was able to tell you the killer felt good, that he didn't like white women. How does he know that he didn't like white women? How does he know—if he's not the killer—that the killer doesn't like white women but he likes to have sex with them?"

As Macy said this, Robert Miller, a dark-skinned man of African American and Native American lineage, sat at the defense table in front of an all-white jury. What Macy said was not even remotely related to proof that Robert Miller knew about the crime. In fact, no one knew what the killer liked sexually, or disliked socially, so there was no way of knowing whether

Miller's statement was true. Macy, however, had managed to end up with a jury of twelve whites, and it was more than likely that among those twelve would be at least one person stirred by some primal fear of black men as sexual predators.

High-octane prosecution was Macy's specialty. He wore string ties and Stetson hats, in the manner of the old western lawman, and it was his frequent boast that he personally had brought more death penalty cases to verdict than any other prosecutor in the country. As of early 1999, that figure was fifty-three. Now and then, he would lose a case on appeal or be slapped on the wrist for some extraordinary excess—withholding exculpatory information, playing fast and loose with the facts, or using rhetoric that perverted justice—but Macy said he never strayed from honest prosecution of people he believed were guilty. In the Miller case, he held back nothing. He told the jurors that they would be shirking their duty if they did not convict Robert Miller.

"We're not burning witches at the stake," said Macy. "We're not seeking out Communists. We're trying to seek justice. We're trying to bring a killer before the bar of justice. And that's why the twelve of you are sitting there, because a man who committed these crimes has got to be brought to justice. He sits right there. Only the twelve of you can do it. You can do it by going up in that jury room and finding him guilty as charged on all seven counts. Because if you do anything less than that, it's an assault to the memory of these two little ladies and everybody that cares about them."

In the days running up to the trial, an Oklahoma television station had done a poll on the case. Before a single word of evidence had been heard, 68 percent of the viewers voted that he was guilty. The jury, having heard the videotapes and the forensic evidence, convicted him of two murders, two rapes, two burglaries, and one attempted burglary. After that, a minitrial was held on the suitable penalty. A man who came to court reported that he had surprised a black man wearing a bandanna trying to break into his house in the Military Park section of town. Months later, when he saw Robert Miller's face in the news, he felt that this was the same man.

The judge sentenced Miller to two death penalties, plus 725 years. "I couldn't do none of it. I needed me a little red wagon to pull all that time out of that courtroom, it was so heavy," said Miller.

On his first night on death row, he listened to the howling and chaos and wondered if he had been born to suffer this hell.

Lee Ann Peters once had fretted for the safety of her grandmother while the Military Park murderer was at large. Now, as an appellate lawyer for the

Oklahoma City Public Defender's Office, she was trying to save the life of the very man convicted of being the fiend. Her tools were a sharpened pencil and an even sharper mind. And in the trial record, she discovered a peculiar fact.

The state's serologist had provided the names of twenty-three black men whose blood had been tested as part of the investigation. Then the serologist gave the names of all the men whose hair had been microscopically examined. Peters made a list of all the names, checking them off. Suddenly, she stopped. There had been twenty-three blood tests, and twenty-four hair checks. That meant there was one extra name on the hair list. Someone's hair had been examined but not his blood. Why?

The one extra man was named Ronald Lott, a name unknown to Robert Miller. In a few days, Peters and a retired homicide detective, Bob Thompson, would learn some astonishing details about the crime spree in the Military Park neighborhood.

It had not stopped with the arrest of Robert Miller.

After Miller was taken into custody, after he had made the twelve hours of videotapes, after District Attorney Macy announced that "the danger has been removed" from the community, similar crimes were continuing.

Two other elderly women who lived in corner houses were attacked by a man who broke in their back doors. Knotted rags were left at the scenes in these cases, too. The electricity and phone lines were disabled just as they had been in the two murders. Once again, it seemed that the point of the crimes was not robbery but rape, as little property had been taken. These two women, in their seventies and at least a decade younger than the earlier victims, had survived the rapes, not suffering the crushed chests of the two older women. One woman actually pulled a handgun on the attacker and bopped him on the head. He then wrested the gun away from her.

A few days after the second of these rapes, Ronald Clinton Lott was stopped on the street and found with that very gun, registered to the victim. His fingerprints were found at the other victim's home.

In August 1987, six months after District Attorney Macy had announced that Robert Miller was the Military Park rapist and killer, secret tests were done on Ronald Lott's blood to see if he could be linked to the crimes. Police reports found by Peters and Thompson showed that the detectives considered Lott a strong suspect not only for the rapes but also in the two murders charged to Miller.

As the lawyer and the investigator dug into details about Lott, they learned even more remarkable facts. One of the prosecutors initially assigned to the Miller case also was handling the Lott case. One Friday afternoon, that prosecutor, Barry Albert, had asked for a recess during a hearing on the Miller case because he had to go across the hall to another courtroom. There, Lott was pleading guilty to the two rapes that bore such similarity to the Miller case. And that very day, Albert would say later, he realized that Lott could be a suspect in the crimes that Miller had been charged with.

"This is déjà vu," Albert said he told the judge and bailiff in the Lott case. "This is exculpatory information [for Miller]."

Did he walk across the hall and share this information with the lawyer defending Robert Miller? Albert claims he did.

Never happened, insists Miller's lawyer, Ron Evans.

In any event, Albert withdrew from the Miller case, turning it over to Macy and Ray Elliott. And during the Miller trial no mention was made of Ronald Lott or his involvement in these amazingly similar crimes. The jurors never heard that Lott had admitted to doing identical crimes in the same neighborhood or that Lott had the same blood type as Miller. The jurors never learned that Lott had a record of felonies, unlike Miller, whose biggest crime was not paying parking tickets.

Instead, they had heard Ray Elliott argue passionately: "We have a semen donor of an A blood type secretor status. [Miller is] A blood type secretor status."

Many years later, Elliott would say that he knew Lott also had the blood type of the man involved in killing the old ladies, but believed that more sophisticated tests had ruled out Lott. The prosecution and Miller's appellate lawyers argued for years about whether the defense also knew of Lott and had been deprived of a chance to name him as a better suspect during Miller's trial. Certainly, the prosecution gave no hint at trial that anyone other than Miller could be responsible.

Robert Macy told the jurors they would have little to ponder if they merely reviewed all the physical evidence suggesting that the killer was black, wore a baseball cap, stood about the same height, had A positive blood, and so on.

"There can be only one man, only one person that fits all of this criteria, and he's sitting right there," said Macy, pointing at Miller. "He fits every one of them, and he's the only man in the state of Oklahoma, or maybe in more, that would fit all those criteria."

In short order, Lee Ann Peters would prove otherwise. She sought DNA testing of the evidence. Not surprisingly, the first results, based on the RFLP technique, were inconclusive. So much time had passed that the semen samples had started to degrade. Then PCR tests were done, and they clearly excluded Miller.

He had not been the rapist of either dead woman.

"We'd be waiting outside a judge's chambers, and Ray Elliott would say: 'It's a damn shame they didn't kill him before this DNA testing.'" Peters recalled. "I would get sick to my stomach."

Not only had the DNA cleared Miller, but it pointed directly at Ronald Lott.

The first argument made by Peters—that Robert Miller had been denied a fair trial because his attorney didn't bring up Ronald Lott as an alternative suspect—now took on even greater weight. But the district attorney had a strong-sounding rebuttal. So what if Lott raped and killed the women? All that meant was that there had been two rapists at the scene. After all, Robert Miller himself had confessed. It was there on the videotape.

Faced with DNA tests that showed Robert Miller had not raped Zelma Cutler or Anna Fowler, prosecutors at first disputed their validity. More tests in 1993 came back with the same results—indisputable proof that Miller had not raped the two dead women. "I thought he would be home by Christmas," said Lee Ann Peters, who had left the legal aid agency that represented Miller but continued to follow the case. Not a chance.

Prosecutors clung to the Miller conviction. "The bulk of the evidence presented against Mr. Miller was Mr. Miller's own videotaped statement to police detectives," Ray Elliott wrote to a member of the public who protested the continuing incarceration of Miller. "The DNA tests have proven only one thing, that is, that Robert Lee Miller Jr. was not the donor of the semen left at the crime scene. The DNA tests do not prove that Mr. Miller was not present during the commission of these crimes. The DNA tests do not prove that Mr. Miller did not commit murder. Furthermore, the DNA tests do not erase the statements given by Mr. Miller himself concerning these crimes."

Indeed, the DNA did not erase the videotapes.

And for the first time, people took a very close look at what Miller had said.

Miller told the detectives things about the murders that were so knowing that he had to have been involved, Elliott argued in public and in the press. During the questioning, Miller was brought to the scenes of the crimes, which included the two murders and a third case, an attempted break-in on Thanksgiving Day 1986 that was thwarted when the police arrived and the burglar fled. At the scene of the break-in, Elliott said, Miller showed the detectives the escape path. "He was like a bird dog on point," said Elliott.

Yet on the transcribed tape, Miller seems to know little about the flight of the burglar until he is prompted by the detectives. Asked about the events of Thanksgiving 1986, Miller says he ate turkey dinner with his sister. The detective, Jerry Flowers, lays out the basics.

> FLOWERS: Think . . . Go into your vision, I wanna see this, I wanna hear it, this is real important, by that church Thanksgiving morning, it's a full moon, something happened up there around one of those churches, or up around that church.
> MILLER: That must have been when this stuff happened.
> FLOWERS: What happened?
> MILLER: Something happened up that way.
> FLOWERS: Did this demon, did this demon, working through this body, this person, try to do something that day or that night?
> MILLER: Maybe.
> FLOWERS: What?
> MILLER: Did something, I can't, I can't recollect. They did something.
> FLOWERS: What?
> MILLER: 'Cause that was when I left my sister's house. . . . Naw, I was with my parents, my brother came for Thanksgiving from the penitentiary, and we had dinner with him.
> FLOWERS: OK. Now let me ask you this, is that the day that this demon-possessed person nearly got caught, that morning, early that morning?
> MILLER: I think so.
> FLOWERS: How did he nearly get caught? Look through your eyes and see.
> MILLER: I think the police was chasing him, somebody was chasing him.
> [In this exchange, Miller says nothing about an escape until Flowers tells him about it. A few minutes later, they return to this attempted break-in.]
> FLOWERS: You're there, you're there right now, you're there at the back door, looking through the eyes of the person kicking on the back door, trying to get in, you see that? You're there, you see the police, you hear the police coming up here, you're scared, you want to run away.
> MILLER: It's not me.

Some 130 times during the tape, when detectives switch from the third person to the second—from "he" to "you"—Miller cuts off the conversation and denies that he is present.

There was the matter of the underwear. No one could forget the dramatic presentation by District Attorney Macy of the underwear band dropped at one of the murders. Fruit of the Loom, the same as that worn by Miller.

That Miller had a "vision" of underwear left at the scene was not surprising at all because, early in the interrogation, he was asked repeatedly what the killer had left at the scene. Miller guessed about articles of clothing and tools until he at last hit on the underwear. Then the detectives locked in on that detail.

> FLOWERS: When the man got through doing what he was doing to the woman, think really hard 'cause this is really important. Did he leave anything with her?
> MILLER: He might have.
> FLOWERS: What would he have left, look into your dreams and tell me what he would have left. Did he leave any articles?
> MILLER: Yeah, something.
> FLOWERS: What did he leave?
> MILLER: 'Cause he was in a hurry.

Miller is on a verbal wander. The help of a Higher Power was summoned.

> FLOWERS: Jesus, help this man to recall. . . . What would he have left there with that woman? . . .
> MILLER: He left something.
> FLOWERS: Was it some type of article . . . was it, a rock, was it some type of object, was it a clothing item?
> MILLER: Maybe.
> FLOWERS: Maybe what?
> MILLER: 'Cause I have some clothes missing, too.

What kind of stuff? Flowers wanted to know. Pants, said Miller. Tools. Coats. Slacks. Shirts. Many things. He would have to go through it all.

> FLOWERS: What did—look at me, Robert. Let's go back in your dream. Let's go back in your dream. What did this person leave inside that house, that maybe it was stolen from you? What was left in the house?
> MILLER: Might have been something of my hair. I don't know.

Frustrated, the detective returned to the subject of clothing. Close your eyes. What kinds of clothes would he have left?

MILLER: Maybe a shoe or something. I don't know. I'll have to check
    my shoes again.

That wasn't the right answer. Look in the dream and see what the killer
was holding in his hand. Or did he forget something?

MILLER: He might have left that knife or he left something out of his
    pocket.

That wasn't it, either. The detectives pressed on. What would he have
left to set you up, Robert? Miller suggested hair.

FLOWERS: Look at this person's body, what's this person missing off of
    his body. Does he have his shirt on, what is he missing?
MILLER: It might have been the shirt.
FLOWERS: What is he missing, look at the person.
MILLER: She tore something off of him. . . . She tore some of the
    clothes. Probably the knife.
FLOWERS: Does he have shoes on?
MILLER: I don't. . . . He might have left one.
FLOWERS: Does he have pants on?
MILLER: Uh-huh.
FLOWERS: Look at this person, he's fixing to leave, but he realizes he's
    leaving something. What is it he's leaving?
MILLER: It might have been underwear or something, he left something
    in the house.
FLOWERS: Did he intentionally leave it in the house?
MILLER: Un-huh.
FLOWERS: Accidentally?
MILLER: Uh-huh. Didn't know he left it. He left it, but he didn't know
    he left it.
WOODS: What is it? Look at your dream. What is it?
MILLER: When he raped her, he took his clothes off, he might have left
    his underwear or something, but he left something I know, he didn't
    know he left it, though, but he left it.
FLOWERS: He left what?
MILLER: He, uh, when he took his pants off and raped her, I don't
    know.

What, what, what, they demanded.

> MILLER: He might have left his hat, ski mask, or something he left because
> . . . he forgot to put something back on because he was in a hurry.
> FLOWERS: What would it be?
> MILLER: I don't know.

A moment later, Miller suggests it was gloves. By that point, he had suggested virtually every stitch or tools that a rapist might have carried.

Many hours later, the interrogation returns to the underwear. This time, the police deal with it as an established part of Miller's memory.

> FLOWERS: You know, you told me a while ago that uh, this guy that's in
> this vision that you see, even left some clothing articles, either he
> brought them or forgot to, forgot to, take them.
> MILLER: Maybe.
> FLOWERS: And you told me that, ah, you this uh, was his underpants,
> his shorts, that he left at one of them, which one did he leave that at,
> the first one or the second one?
> MILLER: I was trying to tell you then, did you write it down?
> FLOWERS: Yeah, we was trying, we was doing it, but you never really
> elaborated on it that much. Did he leave that at the first one or the
> second one?
> MILLER: I don't know for sure right now.
> FLOWERS: What kind, what kind of underwear was it?
> MILLER: I don't know. I don't know exactly.
> FLOWERS: Are you hungry?
> MILLER: Yes.

They discuss getting hamburgers.

> FLOWERS: What kind of underwear do you have on?
> MILLER: I think they're Fruit of the Loom.
> FLOWERS: Let's see.

The detectives inspect his underwear—Fruit of the Loom, size thirty to thirty-two.

The final hours of the interrogation continue to focus on the underwear.

> FLOWERS: What does he do now?
> MILLER: Leaves the room.

FLOWERS: Did he put his clothes on?

MILLER: Some of them.

FLOWERS: What did he not put on?

MILLER: I don't know.

FLOWERS: Did he forget to put something on?

MILLER: I think so.

FLOWERS: What? You're there, you can see him, Rob, now tell me, he wants you to tell me.

MILLER: He left something.

FLOWERS: He's wanting you to tell me, Rob. This is it, he's wanting you to tell me. What does he leave in that room? . . . Look real close. . . . Where does he leave this item in the room, where is it?

MILLER: He forgot something, either his underwear or a glove.

Another powerful detail cited by the prosecution was Miller's supposed knowledge of the method of entry into the women's homes. "He picks the glass out of the frame and stacks it in a sack next to the trash—in the trash next to the door," Ray Elliott told the jury.

"Now who knew that trash—that glass—had been stacked in the trash? The police detectives that were there. Who else? The defendant."

In fact, Robert Miller didn't quite describe the glass going into a sack. But he did describe the killer removing the glass with some care. With the cheerleading Detective Flowers pushing for more and more details from the "vision" of the killing, Miller described the burglar's entrance to the Cutler residence.

FLOWERS: What's he doing, what's he doing?

MILLER: Trying to get in the back door.

FLOWERS: He's cut the lights off, what's he doing to that back door?

MILLER: Broke the glass.

FLOWERS: He broke the glass, how did he break the glass?

MILLER: Some kind of object.

FLOWERS: What's he using?

No answer.

FLOWERS: What's he using on that back door?

MILLER: Tools.

FLOWERS: Has he broke the glass? What's . . . he doing with that glass. Where is it? Where is the glass?

MILLER: Takes it out.

FLOWERS: What's he doing with it, he's taking it out of what?

MILLER: Out of the frame.

FLOWERS: He's taking the glass out of the frame, what's he doing with it?

MILLER: Put it somewhere.

FLOWERS: Where's he putting that glass? Look at him, Robert, you seen him. . . . What's he doing with that glass?

MILLER: I don't know. . . .

FLOWERS: Look, Robert, he's taking it out of the frame, what's he doing with that glass?

MILLER: Puts it somewhere.

FLOWERS: Where's he putting it, Robert, what's he doing with it? You see him, don't you?

MILLER: He lays it on a back porch somewhere.

FLOWERS: He's laying that glass on the back porch. . . .

MILLER: Somewhere.

FLOWERS: What's he doing with that glass?

MILLER: He takes it out.

FLOWERS: Is he just throwing it down, what's he doing with it?

MILLER: He's removing it.

FLOWERS: He's removing it from the frame.

MILLER: Uh-huh.

FLOWERS: Now what's he doing? You see him, what's he doing?

MILLER: He puts the glass somewhere.

FLOWERS: Puts the glass on somewhere.

MILLER: On that back porch. . . .

FLOWERS: How's he put it down, what's he doing to it?

MILLER: He's trying to be quiet.

FLOWERS: He's trying to be quiet, now then the glass is broke, he's removed the glass from the frame, what's he doing? You see him. . . . Look through his eyes.

MILLER: He sticks his arm through.

FLOWERS: He sticks his arm through the door. What's he doing?

MILLER: Trying to unlock the door.

As Ray Elliott said, the DNA did not erase the videotape. But Miller's so-called insider revelations were, in fact, buried under piles of mistaken information. For every flimsy statement that could be tied to the crime, there were dozens of details that were simply wrong. Miller said that the killer stole jewelry, a TV, a radio. Nothing was stolen from any of the homes. He

said the murderer stabbed one victim numerous times until she was covered with blood. That did not happen. He described one victim as being
middle-aged—a few years older than he was himself. At the time, Miller
was twenty-seven. The victim was eighty-three. He said the killer had left
his knife on the floor of one house, had left a shoe behind, had torn all the
victim's clothes off. All untrue. He said the victims were strangled with
lamp cords. There was no sign of ligature.

"He has done so many of these crime scenes, he gets confused," Ray
Elliott would say in 1999, by way of explanation. "At a minimum, he was
the lookout for Ronald Lott."

By the time Lee Ann Peters left the agency that was defending Robert
Miller, she had filed a potent appeal arguing that the defense either should
have been told about or acted upon the suspicions relating to Ronald Lott.
She also had arranged DNA tests that cleared Miller of the rape and implicated Lott. The case then languished as the prosecutors disputed the
validity of the results and new tests were arranged. In 1994, Miller's new
public defenders encouraged Miller to accept a deal with prosecutors that
offered him life without parole. He declined. He remained on death row
from 1988 to 1995, when the district attorney agreed that he should have
a new trial. Simultaneously, his new appellate lawyers dropped the claim
that Miller was denied information about Lott. The shift greatly troubled
Peters and Miller, but they had been waiting seven years—from the first test
results exonerating Robert—for the prosecutors to give any ground.

After Miller was moved from the state penitentiary to the Oklahoma
County Jail, he was visited by a young nurse, Kim Ogg, who had befriended
his brother. "I need help," Miller told her.

By 1997, a judge held a hearing to decide if there was any basis to keep
Miller for a new trial. The state had thrown out all its forensic testimony,
conceding that the DNA showed that Miller was not the source of the
sperm. A jailhouse snitch who testified at the trial had recanted and then
disappeared. Only Miller's interrogation remained.

"There is nothing in these statements by defendant which would in any
way be considered a confession," ruled District Court Judge Larry Jones.
He then talked about a lower standard for an "admission," in which a suspect reveals some guilty knowledge of a crime, as opposed to a full-fledged
confession.

"In my view," said Judge Jones, "the statements made by the defendant
in the taped interviews taken as a whole, or even divided into parts, do not
constitute an 'admission' either. Mr. Miller's statements come to the detec-

tives as visions and dreams—even images he receives from deceased grand-parents and so forth.

"Virtually every item of information is hedged with 'maybe' this hap-pened, 'probably' this occurred. Admittedly, after some prompting, he be-comes more definite in certain answers. I get the impression, however, taking the statements as a whole, that Mr. Miller was attempting to tell the detectives what he believed they wanted to hear. And it is evident from the video that the detectives are directing many of his responses.

"To the extent defendant's statements are consistent with known facts, the consistencies are not such as to compel even probable cause to believe he committed these crimes."

The prosecutors immediately appealed to a Judge Karl Gray, higher-ranking and far more sympathetic to the prosecution than Larry Jones. Even Judge Gray granted that the confession wasn't worth much—but said some of his accurate statements "might be deemed to be admissions or at least evidence which could be considered in making a probable cause determination."

Miller, Gray maintained, could be held for a new trial.

Garvin Isaacs, a veteran Oklahoma City defense attorney, agreed to rep-resent Miller, but prosecutors dropped the charges a few weeks later. The case had been disintegrating in public, but there was another, secret ele-ment in the prosecutors' decision.

Ray Elliott had been negotiating with the attorney for Ronald Lott, who already was doing forty years for the two rapes of the two old women who did not die. Lott was likely to face the death penalty based on his semen being found at both murders.

Lott was presented with the following offer: If he could implicate Robert Miller in the crimes—as a lookout or participant—Lott would not have to face any additional time. The prosecutors would agree that any sentence for the two murders could run concurrently. It was a tremendous deal, basi-cally, a chance to be given a free pass for two murders that would ordinarily send him off for a lethal injection.

"I offered him a straight life sentence, which meant he would have been out in thirty or forty years, and saved his life—if he would finger Miller," said Elliott. "He sat right there in my office and shook his head. Just shook his head."

Although Elliott continued to insist that Miller had guilty knowledge of the crime, Lott's refusal to take a plea deal did raise strong questions in the prosecutor's mind.

"It's clearly a good argument that if Miller really were involved, to save his own life [Lott] would take the plea. It's a damn good argument," said Elliott. "I gave him that out. I gave him that option."

With Lott's rejection of the deal, Elliott decided that Miller should not be tried again.

Miller was released on Thursday, January 22, 1998.

Epilogue

On November 3, 1998, Ray Elliott was elected as a judge of the Oklahoma County District Court, having been endorsed by District Attorney Robert Macy, who, until his retirement on June 30, 2001, continued to boast of holding the record for the most death penalty cases tried to verdict. Macy retired on June 30, 2001, and six months later an Oklahoma County jury gave Ronald Lott two death sentences, one for each of the elderly victims for whose murders Robert Lee Miller Jr. had been wrongfully convicted and sentenced to death.

DAVID VASQUEZ

His dream fit some of the facts—the ones the detectives fed him

DANA L. PRIEST
MANASSAS, VIRGINIA

David Vasquez is not at ease in the world. At forty-two, he clutches his mother's hand as they stroll the Manassas Mall. When a neighbor invites him to a local bar, he sits through happy hour, but his insides churn and he can't wait to leave.

Since January, when Virginia Governor Gerald L. Baliles pardoned him after he spent five years imprisoned for a murder he did not commit, Vasquez has spent most of his time inside his mother's Manassas town house. In June he got a part-time, nighttime janitorial job, but the only time he's out in public is the van ride to and from work.

"I just sit here or get the vacuum cleaner and vacuum clean, or whatever," Vasquez said. "Five years in there, it's hard. I don't know what the situation out here will be for me. . . . I'm afraid maybe somebody might try to accuse me of something else."

Vasquez wants to blame someone, everyone—the Arlington detectives who interrogated him, the prosecutor who took him to court, the judge who ruled that one of his three confessions was admissible, the defense attorneys who suggested he plead guilty, the prison officials who placed him in a hostile cellblock, the Prince William County social worker who said he was ineligible for financial assistance, and Timothy W. Spencer, the four-time convicted murderer whom Arlington police ultimately linked to the murder of lawyer Carolyn Jean Hamm, though they did not charge him.

The system, with all its parts functioning, with all its checks and balances in place, failed David Vasquez.

"I think everyone involved tried to do the right thing," said Arlington Commonwealth's Attorney Helen F. Fahey, who asked Baliles to pardon Vasquez. "I think people should know that; that even when the system

From "At Each Step, Justice Faltered," *Washington Post*, July 16, 1989. Copyright © Washington Post. Adapted with permission.

didn't work, people were doing their job and worked hard. It just didn't work."

This story starts sometime after 8:00 P.M. on January 23, 1984, when someone slipped through the basement window of Hamm's two-story white shingle house in south Arlington. Hamm, a thirty-two-year-old lawyer with the Washington firm of Wilkes, Artis, Hedrick & Lane, had just returned from a game of squash. Two days later, a friend, concerned that she had not heard from Hamm, discovered her nude body in the basement garage. According to police and the autopsy report, Hamm had been assaulted in her home and raped shortly before or just after she was hanged with a length of rope from a water pipe.

On January 29, police received a call from Joan Wells, whose brother lived across from Hamm. Wells said that at about 8:00 P.M. the day of the murder she parked her car in front of Hamm's home and she had seen Vasquez walking along the sidewalk in front of the house. It was a cold, clear evening and the path was illuminated by a street lamp. Another neighbor, a retired Army colonel, told police he also had seen Vasquez near Hamm's home on the day police discovered Hamm's body.

Vasquez had lived in the Arlington neighborhood with surrogate families for seventeen years until May 1983, when he moved to Manassas to help his mother, Imelda Shapiro, care for her third husband, who had had a stroke. Vasquez has maintained that he was at home or with a friend the night of the murder.

On February 4, ten days after Hamm's body was discovered, four plainclothes police officers walked into a Manassas McDonald's, where Vasquez was employed cleaning tables, and asked him to go with them to the Manassas police station.

He agreed—it was the last decision he would make outside the custody of the criminal justice system for five years.

Arlington detectives William Shelton and Robert Carrig took Vasquez to a tiny, hot, smoke-filled interview room at the Manassas police station. They did not read Vasquez the Miranda warning.

Henry E. Hudson, now the U.S. attorney for the Eastern District of Virginia and then the Arlington commonwealth's attorney who prosecuted Vasquez, argued in court that the warning was unnecessary because, at the time of the interview, Vasquez was considered a potential witness, not a suspect, and was not under arrest.

According to tapes and transcripts of the interrogations obtained by the *Washington Post*, Shelton and Carrig told Vasquez during this first ninety-minute session that they had found his fingerprints at the crime scene. That was not true, according to the detectives' later testimony. They yelled at Vasquez when his answers did not fit the facts of the crime. They told him dozens of details about the crime, then encouraged him to restate them.

With twenty-nine years of police work between them at the time, the detectives made a formidable team. Carrig, then thirty-nine, is a tall man who sounded demonstrative and gruff during the interrogations. Shelton, then thirty-six and diminutive in comparison, was often soft-spoken and gentle with Vasquez.

Vasquez is a slim man at five foot eight who walks with a slight hunch and wears awkward-looking, thick-rimmed glasses. He talks in short, often half-formed sentences. Friends and acquaintances say he reacts to the world like a young child and that he is easily flustered under pressure. He was described in court as having "borderline retarded/low normal" intelligence.

According to Hudson, what made the detectives suspicious in that first interview was that Vasquez denied even being in Arlington the night of the crime. Given what Joan Wells had said, that denial suggested that Vasquez had something to hide.

It took Carrig and Shelton about thirty minutes to get Vasquez to change his story, and they succeeded only after falsely telling him they had found his fingerprints in Hamm's house and that someone had seen him through her window.

"That's what set him off," according to Richard J. McCue, his former defense attorney. "He deteriorated after that. He couldn't fathom how they could have his fingerprints if he wasn't there. He was too naive to know they were lying to him."

Vasquez became frustrated and distraught, crying and pleading for his mother. "She's the only one that can help me. I know she can," he cried.

"The question is, why were you there, OK?" Shelton asked. "That's the only question to deal with."

Vasquez finally said he might have helped Hamm "move something. I don't remember."

In soliciting answers to their questions, the detectives told Vasquez about many details of the crime scene, including that a rope that had been wrapped around a rug was used to hang Hamm, Hamm's hands were tied behind her back with venetian blind cord, and a dryer vent was attached to the basement window through which the assailant entered.

Vasquez began to incorporate into his responses these and other details Shelton and Carrig had supplied. But the conversational flow was uneven, and Vasquez did not always provide answers that corresponded to the facts.

For example:

> SHELTON: Did she tell you to tie her hands behind her back?
> VASQUEZ: Ah, if she did, I did.
> CARRIG: Whatcha use?
> VASQUEZ: The ropes?
> CARRIG: No, not the ropes. Whatcha use?
> VASQUEZ: Only my belt.
> CARRIG: No, not your belt. . . . Remember being out in the sun room,
>   the room that sits out to the back of the house? . . . and what did you
>   cut down? To use?
> VASQUEZ: That, uh, clothesline?
> CARRIG: No, it wasn't a clothesline, it was something like a clothesline.
>   What was it? By the window? . . . Think about the venetian blinds,
>   David. Remember cutting the venetian blind cords?
> VASQUEZ: Ah, it's the same thing as rope.
> CARRIG: Yeah.
> SHELTON: That's what you're talking about?
> VASQUEZ: Um.

Moments later, Carrig and Shelton asked Vasquez specifically about the murder for the first time.

> SHELTON: OK, now tell us how it went, David . . . tell us how you did it.
> VASQUEZ: . . . she told me to grab the knife and, and, stab her, that's all.
> CARRIG [*raising his voice*]: David, no, David.
> VASQUEZ: If it did happen, and I did it, and my fingerprints were on it . . .
> CARRIG [*slamming his hand on the table and yelling*]: You hung her!
> VASQUEZ: What?
> CARRIG [*shouting*]: You hung her!
> VASQUEZ: OK, so I hung her.

Before the first interview ended, Vasquez, trying to speak through sobs, said once more that he had not been in Arlington, much less in Hamm's home, but that he "had to say this because you tell me my fingerprints were there."

Carrig yelled at Vasquez about how only he could have known all the details of the crime.

Then:

> CARRIG: You're two people, you're two people, David.
> VASQUEZ [*crying*]: How could I be two people, I can't.
> CARRIG: Mind, your mind.
> VASQUEZ: No. No.
> CARRIG: Your mind, David, your mind.
> VASQUEZ: No. I need my mother now.

Carrig and Shelton asked Vasquez if he wanted to go to the Arlington police station with them. He said no, but they drove him there anyway.

In Arlington, the detectives finally read Vasquez the Miranda warning, which he signed. They did not arrest him, but asked him to recall their conversation in Manassas.

"OK, earlier you mentioned to us a rope, do you recall a rope?" Shelton asked at one point.

"I recall the rope," Vasquez responded, "but I don't remember using it."

Later, Shelton and Vasquez sat alone in the interrogation room, without a tape recorder or a stenographer, for an hour and a half. "David and I sat and talked just generally about himself and where he went on the weekend, that sort of thing," Shelton testified.

Toward the end of that conversation, Vasquez inexplicably began to recount "a horrible dream," to use his words, that coincided almost identically with the facts of the case that he and the two detectives had discussed in Manassas.

Shelton found a tape recorder and captured the last eight minutes of the "dream," a rambling monologue in which Vasquez's voice sounds deep and clear, in contrast to the meek, pleading tones of the Manassas statement.

In court, Shelton described Vasquez's state. "I don't know the proper word but he became still, his eyes more or less became fixed on a table in front of him and his voice became lower," he said. "He became totally absorbed in what he was doing and what he was relaying to me. There was no distraction."

That scene has perplexed lawyers, detectives, and psychiatrists.

"I hypnotized myself, I think," Vasquez said after his release. "I just stared at something outside. There was kind of like a window, and I could see outside and I just kept staring and staring. . . . It was a shock to me and I just directed at that, what was in front of me."

Police arrested Vasquez that afternoon and charged him with capital murder, rape, burglary, and robbery. At eight forty-five the next morning, he appeared in Arlington General District Court, where the charges were read. A court-appointed lawyer was named, but not before Vasquez signed another Miranda waiver and Carrig and Shelton questioned Vasquez a third time.

Shelton asked Vasquez to "just kinda get yourself into a state where you can really think about your dreams, ah, you know, that feeling you get when you think about your dreams?"

What followed was a shorter version of Vasquez's previous "dream," but the only version that was admitted as evidence.

"It was just horrible, that's all," Vasquez said, his voice groggy and low. At times he panted. "I startled her and she startled me. . . . We stared at each other for a while. . . . Got some knife in the kitchen, went to the back, cut some venetian blinds. . . . Tied her with it . . .

"Too horrible, tied the rope underneath the car and threw it over the beam, and then she said to me, 'Now you can tie it around my neck.' I says, 'Why?' "

Shelton said, "OK, David. Stop thinking about your dream and relax. Here, have some, take some coffee."

At the request of Arlington Circuit Court Chief Judge William L. Winston, Vasquez was examined by a psychiatrist to determine if he was competent to stand trial. In Virginia, competency means defendants understand right from wrong, are capable of understanding the charges against them, and can assist in their defense.

A court-appointed psychiatrist concluded that Vasquez was competent and the judge concurred.

On May 7, the state forensic lab concluded that the blood type in semen stains found at the crime scene and on vaginal swabs from the victim did not match Vasquez's blood type—a development that the police interpreted as meaning only that someone else had been involved in the crime with Vasquez.

No second suspect emerged during the year Vasquez waited in jail for trial.

The prosecution had Vasquez's statements and Wells's testimony that he had been in the neighborhood. It also had hair found on Hamm's robe and on two blankets that exhibited "the same visual and microscopic characteristics" as samples of Vasquez's pubic hair.

The defense could show that footprints found outside the basement window entered by the presumed assailant did not match the soles of the shoes the police had confiscated from Vasquez. Vasquez did not drive a car, so how did he get from Manassas to Arlington and back? His coworkers would testify that he appeared the same as usual when he showed up for work at 6:00 A.M. the next day.

Vasquez's court-appointed attorneys, Richard McCue, then thirty-four, and Matthew Bangs, then thirty-two, were well respected around the Arlington courthouse, but neither had tried a capital murder charge.

They asked the judge to rule the confessions inadmissible. McCue argued that the first confession was inadmissible because no Miranda warning had been given and that the two subsequent confessions were "tainted" by the illegality of the first because the "three statements are so closely interconnected."

McCue also argued that the confessions were not voluntary because Vasquez was incapable of making a voluntary decision about whether to talk to detectives because of his low intelligence and his state of mind, particularly the trance-like behavior he exhibited while talking about his purported dream.

Prosecutor Hudson argued that any taint from the first statement, without the Miranda warning, "had been purged" by the time Vasquez met with detectives the third time. Hudson also argued that the confessions were voluntary and cited a Virginia Supreme Court case in which the court held that a suspect with an IQ lower than Vasquez's was capable of voluntarily waiving his rights.

"There is no question that Detective Shelton was persistent," Hudson told the court, "but there is no indication that Detective Shelton overbore the will of the defendant, that there was anything done contrary to his will, and given the circumstances and the setting, the decision that [Vasquez] made in this case was his own."

Three psychiatrists, two for the defense and one for the prosecution, examined Vasquez, but, in the words of Arlington Commonwealth's Attorney Helen Fahey, "the psychiatrists ran from one end to the other, which left everybody nowhere."

Without explaining his reasoning, Judge Winston held that the prosecution could introduce only the third confession, but that McCue and Bangs could introduce the other interrogations in hopes of showing that the detectives had put words in Vasquez's mouth.

Three days before the trial, the defense made a last-ditch attempt to find something that would exonerate Vasquez. He was administered amobarbital sodium—truth serum—at Mount Vernon Hospital, but continued to reiterate the dream at the core of his purported confession.

Seeing themselves with few options and the death penalty a possible result of failure, McCue and Bangs discussed a possible plea agreement with Vasquez. They explained that he could enter an Alford plea, which allowed him to maintain his innocence while conceding the evidence might be sufficient to convict him. He didn't understand, but agreed. He explained recently, "I think when they said you'll have the chair, that scared me and everything."

Under the Alford plea agreement, Hudson reduced the capital murder charge to second-degree murder, carrying a twenty-year sentence. Counting time already served and day-for-day good time, the plea would result in his release in about five years. Hudson said he agreed to the deal believing that Vasquez had not acted alone. "What he pleaded to was consistent with him being the lesser of two participants," said Hudson.

On February 4, 1985, Vasquez stood for the last time before Judge Winston, who asked, "Do you read English?"

"Yeah, but not too good," Vasquez replied.

"Not too good. Did you read this memorandum [the plea agreement]?" Winston asked.

"I had them read it to me," Vasquez responded.

Again and again, Winston asked Vasquez if he understood the plea, if he understood that he waived his right to a jury and to an appeal.

Solemnly, again and again, Vasquez answered yes.

Epilogue

On December 1, 1987, when Vasquez was a little more than three years into his sentence, a murder eerily similar to the Hamm murder occurred in the same Arlington neighborhood. Forty-four-year-old Susan Ann Tucker was raped and murdered and, although not hanged, she had been strangled with a noose of white thin nylon cord like that with which Hamm's hands had been bound.

Arlington County detectives surmised that the similarity of the crimes was not coincidental—but they were still operating on the erroneous theory that Vasquez had not acted alone in the Hamm case. In the company of Richard McCue, Arlington Detective Joe Horgas approached Vasquez in prison with a straightforward proposition—he could go free in short order if he would identify his furtive co-conspirator. But Vasquez only reasserted his innocence.

Horgas left the prison believing him—raising the specter that a serial killer was on the loose. Indeed, checking recent records, Horgas discovered that in the months preceding the Tucker crime, three similar murders had occurred in Virginia. Each victim had been raped, bound, and strangled with a ligature tied like those used to kill Hamm and Tucker.

A possible explanation of why no crimes had occurred between late January 1984 and September 1987 was obvious to Horgas—the perpetrator might have been in prison. On a hunch, Horgas checked the records of Terry Wilson Spencer, a burglar he had arrested several years earlier. It turned out that Spencer had been arrested on January 29, 1984, for an Alexandria burglary and released to an Alexandria halfway house on September 4, 1987. Moreover, Horgas found, Spencer had been signed out of the halfway house at the times of all of the 1987 murders.

It had recently been widely reported that a new forensic technology known as DNA fingerprinting had led to the arrest of a man named Colin Pitchfork for the rape and murder of two young girls in England. Wondering if DNA might solve the Virginia crimes—biological evidence had been preserved in most of them—Horgas contacted a New York laboratory called Lifecodes, which had been doing DNA paternity testing. He was told that if semen recovered from the victims contained enough DNA to test, it indeed could link a particular suspect to the crimes—provided, of course, that the suspect's DNA was available.

At Horgas's request, Spencer voluntarily provided a blood sample, which was sent to Lifecodes along with the semen samples recovered from the Virginia victims. It turned out that the sample from the Hamm case was not sufficient to test, but the other samples were. And Lifecodes (subsequently part of Orchid Cellmark, Inc.) determined that Spencer was in fact the source of the biological material in those cases.

On July 16, 1988, Spencer was convicted of the Tucker murder—the first U.S. conviction based on DNA. In succeeding months, he was convicted of the other 1987 murders. But there was only circumstantial evidence that Spencer had also killed Hamm. As a result, Vasquez had no judicial remedy for his wrongful conviction. He could only apply for a pardon, which he did.

Governor Gerald L. Baliles granted the pardon on January 4, 1989, and Vasquez was freed the same day. In 1990, the Virginia General Assembly approved special compensatory legislation awarding Vasquez $117,000. In 1994, Spencer went to his death in the Virginia electric chair.

STEVEN PAUL LINSCOTT

What he called a dream, the police called a confession—to a murder

ROB WARDEN

OAK PARK, ILLINOIS

Karen Ann Phillips, a twenty-four-year-old nursing student, was beaten to death in her Oak Park apartment on the night of October 3 or early morning of October 4, 1980. It was possible that she was raped, although it was equally possible that she had consensual sex a day or more before she was slain.

On October 6, Steven Paul Linscott, who lived nearby with his wife and two children, contacted Oak Park police and said he had a dream that might help solve the crime.

During the next few days, Linscott, then twenty-six, provided detailed accounts of the dream. On October 10, the police told him they didn't believe he had a dream. They said they thought his descriptions of the dream were really a confession to the murder.

This theory was not overwhelmingly persuasive because the similarities between the dream and the murder were vague and might have been coincidental—a stereo in the room, where the victim lived alone, much blood. The dissimilarities seemed more striking—the dream victim was black, the real victim white, their apartments were different, and the dream killer was much smaller than Linscott. Nonetheless, Linscott was indicted for murder and rape.

At Linscott's trial in 1982, a state forensic witness testified concerning semen found in the victim's vagina. Mohammed Tahir, of the Illinois State Police crime laboratory, told the jury that 20 percent of the population are "non-secretors"—meaning that they do not secrete their blood group substances into their bodily fluids. Linscott, said Tahir, was a non-secretor.

The only blood group substances found in the semen, Tahir continued, came from type O blood. Phillips had type O blood and, thus, the blood

From *Chicago Lawyer*, August 1987. Copyright © Chicago Lawyer, Ltd. Adapted with permission.

279

group substances in the semen could have been hers, since the semen had mixed with her vaginal fluids. It followed, said Tahir, that the semen probably came either from a non-secretor or from a man with type O blood. Those two groups comprise approximately 60 percent of the male population.

Tahir continued that he could not determine when Phillips had intercourse. If it had been more than a day before her death, he testified, it was possible that the semen might have come from absolutely any healthy male because, as time passes, blood antigens disappear.

Hence, according to Tahir, Linscott was among the 60 percent of the male population who could not be excluded as sources of the semen if Phillips indeed had been raped by her killer. If the intercourse occurred more than a day earlier, he said, no healthy male could be excluded.

Tahir's testimony notwithstanding, the prosecutors—Assistant Cook County State's Attorneys John E. Morrissey and Jay C. Magnuson—each told the jury at different times that Phillips had been raped by a non-secretor and that Linscott was a non-secretor. They thereby reduced the pool of Phillips's possible sex partners from 60 percent or 100 percent of the male population to only 20 percent.

Evidence also was introduced concerning several hairs found on Phillips's bed, carpet, and body. Some of these were Caucasian head and pubic hairs, which Tahir claimed were "consistent" with Linscott's hair. He added that hair comparisons are never positive and that he could not say that the hairs were Linscott's or matched Linscott's. The most he could say was that he could not exclude the possibility that some of the hairs were Linscott's. A defense expert, Dr. Kenneth Siegesmund, associate professor of anatomy at the Medical College of Wisconsin, claimed that none of the hairs was Linscott's.

On cross-examination, Magnuson asked Siegesmund if he was familiar with a Canadian study indicating that the probability of two head hairs from different people sharing twenty-three of the same characteristics is only one in forty-five hundred and that the probability of two pubic hairs from different people sharing twenty-three characteristics is only one in eight hundred. Siegesmund said he was familiar with the study, although it had no application to the hair comparisons made in the Linscott case.

In closing rebuttal argument, Magnuson told the jury that the hairs "matched" Linscott's, although the state's own expert, Tahir, had testified that they did not "match." Magnuson added, "A scientist will state that [in] every aspect that I examined they were consistent. And what does that mean? There was nothing different. And to a layman it means identical."

Magnuson also referred to the Canadian study, saying that the probability of Linscott coincidentally having both scalp hair and pubic hair that were the "same" as those found in Phillips's apartment was not high. "I leave it to you, ladies and gentlemen of the jury, to figure out the probability or likelihood of anybody having the same head hair and the same pubic hair. It is a figure of one out of every forty-five hundred and one out of every eight hundred."

The jury found Linscott guilty of rape and murder, and Judge Adam N. Stillo sentenced him to forty years. Church and community groups raised funds enabling Linscott to retain Chicago attorney Thomas D. Decker, who handled his appeal.

In 1985, after Linscott had served three years of his sentence, the Illinois Appellate Court reversed his conviction on the grounds that the state had failed to prove him guilty beyond a reasonable doubt. At that time, the court did not reach other issues raised by Linscott, who was released from prison on a $450,000 appeal bond posted by supporters.

However, the state's attorney's office appealed to the Illinois Supreme Court, which in 1986 reversed and remanded the case to the appellate court, forcing it to consider issues it had not dealt with in 1985.

In a two-to-one opinion handed down on July 29, 1987, the appellate court again reversed Linscott's conviction, this time on prosecutorial misconduct grounds. The majority opinion, written by Judge Dom J. Rizzi with William S. White concurring, said that the prosecutors' statements that Phillips was raped by a non-secretor were "simply made up" and were "a false and a stark distortion of the possibility that the defendant was the assailant. . . . The made-up evidence was doubly devastating because not only was it false, but it reduced the pool of possible assailants from a substantial percentage of the male population, or even the entire population, to just the males in 20 percent of the population." Magnuson's reference in rebuttal argument to the Canadian hair study "appears to have been a calculated, rank misrepresentation," said the opinion.

In reversing the case, the majority said, "We believe that the prosecutor's misrepresentations relating to the blood and hair comparisons were egregious. Defendant was entitled to a trial that comports with prevailing notions of fundamental fairness. Here the American ideals of fairness in our system were not just ignored, they were trampled upon."

Judge Daniel J. McNamara dissented, saying that he did "not believe that any of the claimed errors warrant reversal. . . . The prosecutorial comments at issue here go to the weight of the state's evidence and arguments.

The jury, as the trier of fact, is the proper forum to resolve factual questions such as whether the evidence supported inferences on which the prosecutor commented during closing arguments. Furthermore, I would find that even if the prosecutorial comments . . . were improper, the remarks did not substantively prejudice defendant."

The state's attorney's office plans to appeal the case to the Illinois Supreme Court. Meanwhile, Linscott is completing requirements for a bachelor's degree in psychology at Southern Illinois University.

Epilogue

On January 31, 1991, the Illinois Supreme Court affirmed the most recent appellate court decision, setting the stage for a retrial in the Linscott case. Cook County State's Attorney Jack O'Malley then agreed to DNA testing, which was performed by CBR Laboratories of Boston. When the results excluded Linscott as the source of the semen recovered from Phillips, O'Malley dropped the charges on July 15, 1992. Linscott completed his degree and went to work as a counselor in Springfield. On December 19, 2002, Governor George H. Ryan gave him a pardon based on innocence. The pardon cleared the way for Linscott to receive $60,150 through the Illinois Court of Claims in 1993 for his three and one-half years of wrongful imprisonment.

THOMAS M. BRAM

An unguarded remark was construed as a confession
to a triple ax murder

WILLIAM S. WARDEN

BOSTON, MASSACHUSETTS

What was deemed an "inferential confession" to a gruesome triple murder aboard a U.S. merchant ship on the high seas sent Thomas M. Bram to federal death row in 1896—even though he emphatically denied that he had committed the crime.

A little after 2:00 A.M. on Tuesday, July 14, 1896, the *Herbert E. Fuller* was 750 miles and five days into a voyage from Boston to Argentina with a cargo of lumber when the captain, Charles I. Nash, his wife, Laura A. Nash, and the second mate, August W. Blomberg, were hacked to death with an ax in the vessel's after house, the structure housing a chart room and officers' quarters near the stern.

Lester H. Monks, a Harvard University student who had joined the voyage as a passenger, was awakened by a woman's scream. Armed with a revolver, he rushed to Mrs. Nash's cabin, where he found the door ajar and her lying dead in a pool of blood. In an adjoining room, he found the captain, not yet dead but unable to speak.

Monks cautiously made his way forward, emerging onto the deck through a hatchway near the mainmast, where Bram, the first mate, was on duty. Seeing Monks holding a revolver, Bram picked up a plank and threw it at him. The plank missed Monks, who shouted, "Come below, the captain has been murdered! Come below, for God's sake!"

Bram and Monks went below, examined the bodies, and returned to the deck, where they stood back to back, each armed, ostensibly in fear of mutiny. The only other man on deck was Francis M. Loheac, who was at the wheel of the ship. Just minutes before Monks discovered the bodies,

From a case summary posted by the Center on Wrongful Convictions at www.law.northwestern .edu/wrongfulconvictions/exonerations/FedBramSummary.html. Copyright © William S. Warden. Adapted with permission.

Loheac had relieved the man who would become Bram's principal accuser—
a seaman who went by the name Charlie Brown but whose real name was
Justus Leopold Westerberg.

As daybreak approached, the ship's steward, Jonathan Spencer, emerged
from the forecastle, where the crew was quartered. When Monks and Bram
told him that the captain and Mrs. Nash had been slain, Spencer ventured
into the after house, where he discovered Blomberg's body.

Spencer, Monks, and Bram questioned Loheac, who said he had heard
nothing out of the ordinary during his turn at the wheel. Suddenly, Bram
pointed across the deck and exclaimed, "There is an ax. There is the ax that
done it." Spencer picked up the ax, but Bram took it from him. "Shall I
throw it overboard?" Bram asked. "Yes," Monks replied, as he would explain
under oath, "for fear the crew may use it against us."

"No," Spencer shouted—but it was too late. Bram had thrown the ax into
the ocean. "You shouldn't have done that," said Spencer.

The crew then was summoned to the deck. Although the killer presumably would have been splattered with blood, none was found on anyone.
Bram placed Westerberg second in command and set sail for Halifax, Nova
Scotia, which was not the nearest port but was favored by the prevailing
winds.

The next day, Westerberg came under suspicion when crew members
reported that he had changed clothes after leaving the wheel. When questioned, Westerberg acknowledged that he had changed, but insisted he
had done so only because he was cold. Bram, professing disbelief, ordered
Westerberg manacled and proclaimed that the killer was in custody.

Four days later, Westerberg accused Bram of the crime. Westerberg
claimed that while at the wheel, which was directly behind the after house,
he had heard a noise in the chart room and, peering through a skylight
window, had seen Bram strike Captain Nash with what was now presumed
to be the ax Bram had thrown overboard.

As dubious as Westerberg's accusation might seem—coming as it did
from an accused man five days after the fact—the crew seized and shackled
Bram. Spencer assumed command, and the *Herbert Fuller* proceeded to
Halifax, arriving on July 21 with both suspects in irons and the victims'
bodies in a small boat towed astern.

Westerberg's version of events apparently rang true to Halifax Police
Detective Nicholas Power, who led the investigation. Power's suspicion of
Bram may have been heightened by his pernicious disposal of the murder
weapon, which of course might have borne fingerprints.

Although fingerprinting had yet to be employed forensically, the potential had been popularized by Mark Twain's *Life on the Mississippi* and *Pudd'nhead Wilson* in the 1880s. Racism also may have been at play. Bram was of mixed race and had a swarthy complexion darkened by exposure, whereas Westerberg was white, as were the victims.

In any event, whatever Power's considerations may have been, by his own account he presumed Bram guilty from the start. Power would testify that he prefaced his interrogation of Bram: "Your position is rather an awkward one. I have had Brown [Westerberg] in this office, and he made a statement that he saw you do the murder. . . . Now, look here, Bram, I am satisfied that you killed the captain, from all I have heard from Mr. Brown."

According to Power, Bram responded, "He [Westerberg] could not have seen me; where was he?" "He states he was at the wheel," said Power, and to that Bram was quoted as replying, "Well, he could not see me from there"—an assertion that lawyers in the case would call an "inferential confession."

Power related the substance of what Bram allegedly had said to the U.S. consul in Halifax, who transferred jurisdiction of the case to Boston. There, on October 29, 1896, a grand jury—relying solely on Westerberg's purported eyewitness account—returned an indictment charging Bram with the three murders.

Bram's trial opened on December 14, 1896, before a jury and, under a procedure peculiar to maritime cases, two federal judges, Le Baron B. Colt and Nathan Webb. The prosecutors were Sherman Hoar, the U.S. attorney for Massachusetts, and his assistants, Jonathan H. Casey and Frederick P. Cabot. Two able court-appointed attorneys, James E. Cotter and Asa P. French, defended Bram, who was indigent.

The prosecution case relied primarily on Westerberg's purported eyewitness account, which the defense attempted to undermine by eliciting on cross-examination that Westerberg had been confined to a mental institution in Rotterdam five years earlier following a violent psychotic episode. The prosecution of course also called Spencer and Monks, who described how Bram had thrown the ax overboard. And Monks described how Bram had thrown a plank at him, although this hardly seemed sinister, given that Monk was pointing a revolver at Bram.

The only other prosecution witness of consequence was Detective Power, who described what he said to Bram and what Bram said to him during the interrogation in Halifax. On cross-examination, Power acknowledged that Bram's words could be construed innocently—Bram might have been saying simply that it was impossible to see into the after house from the wheel.

When the prosecution rested, Bram took the stand to deny the crime.

Bram was followed on the stand by an expert witness—Hugh G. Messenger, a ship carpenter, who testified that he had examined the *Herbert Fuller* at the behest of the defense and determined that Westerberg, from his vantage point behind the wheel, could not have seen what he claimed to have seen.

The prosecution had not arranged an inspection of the ship, which was at sea during the trial, and thus had no expert to counter Messenger. The defense also recalled Monks to the stand to testify that, in the seconds between Mrs. Nash's scream and his encounter with Bram on deck, Bram would not have had an opportunity to change clothes—a crucial point, given that the killer's clothes would have been blood-splattered.

The case went to the jury on New Year's Day 1897. That evening, the jurors conducted an experiment, ostensibly to verify Messenger's claim that Westerberg could not have seen the attack. Using napkins to cover parts of a window in the jury room, they created an opening the size of the skylight through which Westerberg would have peered. Then, guided by a diagram prepared by Messenger, the jurors looked through the window from the approximate distance of the ship's wheel to the after house and concluded that it would have been possible for Westerberg to have seen what he described.

Some jurors continued to harbor reasonable doubt, however. It took several ballots for the jury to agree on a guilty verdict, which was returned on January 2. When Bram's lawyers learned of the unauthorized experiment, they moved for a new trial, but on March 9 the motion was denied and Bram was immediately sentenced to death by hanging—the only sentence permissible for murder under federal law at the time.

"If I have to die," Bram tearfully told the court, "I thank God I shall die an innocent man."

Bram's execution was set for June 18, but it was stayed pending appeal directly to the U.S. Supreme Court. The oral argument spanned two days, October 18 and 19, 1897, with French arguing for Bram and U.S. Solicitor General John K. Richards for the government.

Of sixty-seven issues aired in the appeal, by far the most extensively briefed and argued was the admission of Power's testimony. And it was based on that issue that the court, by a six-to-three vote on December 13, granted Bram a new trial. The majority held that Power's confrontation of Bram had called "imperatively for an admission or denial" by Bram, thereby rendering his response involuntary.

"A plainer violation . . . of the letter and spirit [of the Fifth Amendment] could scarcely be conceived of," Justice Edward Douglass White wrote for the majority.

Bram's second trial opened on March 16, 1898, before the same judges and with the same lawyers and same witnesses as the first trial, except, of course, for Power, whose testimony had been barred by the Supreme Court.

There were two other differences between the trials. First, shortly after the first trial, Congress had approved an act authorizing juries in federal murder cases to find a defendant guilty but to specify "without capital punishment." Second, the *Herbert Fuller*, which had been at sea during the first trial, was anchored in Boston Harbor for the second and, on the motion of the defense, the jury toured the vessel.

On April 20, the jury found Bram guilty, but spared his life. Bram was sent to the federal prison in Atlanta. He did not appeal the verdict, but was released on parole on August 27, 1913.

Meanwhile, Mary Roberts Rinehart, an acclaimed mystery writer, had become convinced of Bram's innocence. She based a 1914 novel, *The After House*, on the case, portraying Westerberg—"Charlie Jones" in the novel— as "a madman, a homicidal maniac of the worst type."

Rinehart's advocacy was instrumental in persuading President Woodrow Wilson to grant Bram a full pardon on April 22, 1919. Although the pardon was not expressly predicated on innocence, it is hard to imagine any other basis for pardoning a man twice convicted of a triple ax murder.

Epilogue

Under *Bram v. United States*, the Fifth Amendment protection against self-incrimination applied only to suspects in federal criminal cases. But thirty-nine years later, in a case known as *Brown v. Mississippi*, the Supreme Court held that the due process clause of the Fourteenth Amendment extended the protection to state cases. Thirty years after that, in 1966, *Miranda v. Arizona* required police to inform suspects of their rights to remain silent and to have counsel prior to questioning. Despite these celebrated holdings, however, the tide of false confessions continued.

FABRICATION

*"All Crimes against the State are punished here with the utmost Severity; but
if the Person make his Innocence plainly to appear upon his Tryal,
the Accuser is immediately put to an ignominious Death;
and out of his Goods and Lands, the innocent Person is quadruply
recompensed for the Loss of his Time, for the Danger he underwent,
for the Hardship of his Imprisonment, and for all the Charges
he hath been at in making his Defense."*
—GULLIVER'S TRAVELS

When there's no solid evidence, the easiest way to solve a crime—or,
more precisely, to create an appearance of solving one—is to invent a
confession.

Although it's impossible to know their prevalence, fabricated
confessions probably are rare and only a last resort in the station house,
following the failure of hours of grilling and lying to the suspect and,
sometimes, the threat, or even the infliction, of violence.

Other than torturing suspects, there's no degree of police misconduct
worse than framing someone—if ever there were a crime deserving of
Lilliputian justice, this would seem to be it.

In death penalty jurisdictions—where the cases described in the
following articles occurred—fabricating a confession is tantamount to
attempted murder or, in the worst case, murder itself.

Yet, it's important to note, law enforcement authorities who fabricate
confessions don't always do so with the murderous intent one might
imagine.

In some cases, interrogators may simply imagine, and ultimately come
to believe, that something incriminating was said during interrogation
that wasn't. In other cases, interrogators may be so certain of the suspect's
guilt that a little fudging seems morally justified—otherwise a dangerous
predator may be put back on the street. And in some cases those factors
may work in concert.

Even if there are mitigating circumstances, however, that's little comfort to those who were falsely accused and sent to death row or unjustly deprived of their liberty.

KEITH LONGTIN

His denial that he'd confessed rang true when DNA cleared him

APRIL WITT

PRINCE GEORGE'S COUNTY, MARYLAND

The room is cramped and cold. The floor and walls are carpeted to muffle sound. A small table and two chairs are the only furnishings. There is no window, no clock, no clue to when night becomes day.

After twenty-eight hours in that interrogation room, Keith Longtin was so exhausted he wondered if he'd lost his mind.

"The detective said, 'Well, thanks for making a confession,'" Longtin recalled. "I'm like, 'What? I didn't admit to anything.' He said, 'Yes, you did.'"

Longtin spent the next eight months in jail, charged with the 1999 slaying of his wife while Prince George's County homicide detectives overlooked DNA evidence that would set him free.

Eventually, other investigators—not the homicide squad—linked the DNA to the real killer, Antonio D. Oesby. While Longtin sat in jail, Oesby allegedly sexually assaulted seven women.

Longtin said that when Prince George's homicide detectives couldn't get a confession from him, they simply twisted his words to concoct one. "They tried to frame me," said Longtin, now forty-five. "The police lie, and nobody holds them accountable for their lies."

He said that when a homicide detective walked into the interrogation room and placed a stack of photographs face-down on the small table, he feared that his wife was dead, although he was not told that immediately. He said he answered questions, waived his right to a lawyer, and volunteered to provide blood and hair samples.

"They asked me different questions like, did I carry a knife," said Longtin, a welder who identifies himself as a born-again Christian. "I said yeah, I did. For my work. I didn't have anything to hide. I didn't fear I'd be implicated. You don't think something like that. All I'm doing is telling them the truth."

He had been given a tag that said "visitor" when they took him into the room about 1:30 P.M. on a Tuesday, October 5. He didn't emerge until Thursday, October 7.

He began to fathom the depth of his troubles when a detective flipped the photographs. They showed the brutalized body of his once-beautiful wife.

"To see her like that, it looked like someone took a Skilsaw and went across her nose," Longtin said. "It was just wild to me. She's nude. She only has a top on. . . . Her eyes were open. I got broke down."

As he laid his head on the table and wept, he said, two detectives began accusing him and taunting him. While one detective shoved the hideous photos in his face, the other mocked his grief as phony and said he'd killed her.

The detectives believed they had reason to suspect Longtin. They knew that his brief marriage to Donna Zinetti had been in trouble. They knew that Longtin and Zinetti were living apart and that a church elder had separated them during a bitter argument in their Laurel church before she died. They knew that he had a bad temper and an arrest record for assault.

And they knew that he had shown up—tearful and hysterical—as police worked the crime scene in a wooded area near her apartment complex. The thirty-six-year-old Zinetti had been found strangled and stabbed to death, with her jogging shorts down around her ankles. The detectives knew that the medical examiner recovered semen during her autopsy.

When detectives briefly left Longtin alone in the interrogation room, he said, he made a futile attempt to call a lawyer on his cell phone. The detectives confiscated his cell phone when they returned.

By late Tuesday, reporters who had seen detectives hustle Longtin from the crime scene asked whether he was a suspect. No, said a police spokesman; Longtin already had gone home. Later, a spokesman would say he had been given "misinformation" by homicide detectives.

Longtin said there was no misunderstanding inside the interrogation room. He wasn't allowed to use the bathroom without two detectives escorting, records show.

"They wouldn't let me leave," Longtin said. "They wouldn't get out of the way and let me out of the room. They said later that they offered to let me go. That's a lie. I'd have left, believe me."

Longtin said one detective became angry when he stood up and asked to leave.

"He said he was going to handcuff me to the wall and beat the crap out of me if I didn't sit down," Longtin said.

As the questioning continued through a sleepless night, Longtin grew wearier. The police interrogation log shows that fresh rounds of detectives came in and out of the room to question him.

The interrogators dropped ever more details of the crime into their comments until he developed a pretty good idea of just what had happened to his wife, Longtin said.

"There were so many of them," Longtin said. "One detective would leave and another one would come in. He would say, 'Well, what do you think happened? This is what I think happened.' He would give me a clue or information. Then another one would come in and ask me what happened, and I'd say things that I'd heard [from the detective] before."

One detective told Longtin that his wife had sex before she died.

"She had a boyfriend," Longtin recalled the detective taunting him. "You killed her because you caught her with him, and that's why she had semen in her. It was consensual sex."

"I kept telling him, 'Look, my wife walked with the Lord. She walked with Jesus. She wouldn't do that.'"

He said one detective barked, "You did it!" over and over.

"I'd say, 'No,'" Longtin said. "He'd say, 'We know you did it.' He was hammering at me, just constantly. Every time I would say something: 'You did it.' That's all he would say. 'You did it. You did it.'"

The next day—more than twenty-four hours after the interrogation began—a police spokeswoman acknowledged that Longtin had not left the police station.

"I understand that he's here of his own free will," Corporal Irene Huskens told a reporter.

Inside the interrogation room, Longtin said, he continued to insist that he had nothing to confess.

Late Wednesday afternoon, about twenty-eight hours into the questioning, one detective suggested he was insane and just couldn't remember that he had murdered his wife, he said.

Longtin said he began to question his own sense of reality.

"I didn't have no sleep from Sunday," he said. "I was burned out—period. With all the back-and-forth, my mind wasn't right. I remember him at one point saying, he said to me, 'You have a split personality.'

"I said, 'No, I don't think so.' But I thought about it. At that point, when you are tired like that, I thought, 'Well, maybe I do.'"

Longtin said the detective asked: "Didn't you go over to her house and have an argument with her, and she ran out of the house and you grabbed a knife? How big was the knife?"

The detective "was trying to catch me that way," Longtin said.

"I'd say, 'Well, if I did that in my other self. . . . But I couldn't have done it because I had no blood anywhere. I had no blood anywhere on my clothes or on me.' I'd say, 'It wasn't me. It wasn't me.' We went around with that for like fifteen minutes. Then I remember saying something like, 'The guy who killed her, if he goes there and he grabbed a knife from the kitchen drawer, and he ran after her and he stabbed her. . .' The detective said, 'Well, thanks for making a confession. What can I do for you?' I'm like, 'What? I didn't admit to anything.' I said, 'No, I didn't do it.' He said, 'Yes, you did.'"

The police log indicates that Detective Bert Frankenfield was the only interrogator in the room between noon and 5:00 P.M. that Wednesday. His notes say that over those five hours, Longtin both maintained his innocence and "remembered" his wife being chased down her apartment hallway with a kitchen knife and grabbed from behind. Detective Glen Clark relieved Frankenfield and remained in the room until 10:00 P.M., the log shows.

In his notes, Clark boiled that into five spare sentences: "Defendant goes to victim's house on Sunday night. They have an argument. She leaves to go run. He goes to kitchen, grabs a knife to follow her. Defendant will not talk any more."

Longtin never wrote or signed any statement incriminating himself, records show. He said he didn't go to his wife's apartment, he didn't grab a knife and chase her—and he never told detectives that he did.

The police log indicated he slept about fifty minutes in more than thirty-eight hours in the interrogation room. He said he hadn't slept at all. On Thursday afternoon, two days after he arrived at police headquarters, Longtin was taken before a magistrate.

"The defendant admitted to having a verbal and physical altercation at the victim's apartment," Detective Ronald Herndon wrote in a sworn charging document. "The defendant gave details about this case that had not been released to the media and only the perpetrator would have known. He stated that during the altercation the victim ran out of her apartment and that he ran after her with a knife. The defendant knew that the victim had been stabbed several times and that the stabbing occurred in the wooded area near the victim's apartment."

The case against Longtin began to unravel when a Prince George's County detective—from the sex crimes unit, not homicide—and a District detective noticed similarities between the Zinetti case and a series of unsolved sexual assaults. Three days before the Zinetti slaying, a Howard County woman was abducted at knifepoint, forced to drive to a secluded spot, and raped in front of her toddler. Ten days after Longtin's arrest, a man with a knife sexually assaulted a Laurel woman in the stairwell of her apartment building.

Twenty days after Longtin went to jail, a man grabbed another woman in the stairwell of her Laurel apartment building, threatened to kill her, and held a knife to her throat while he sexually assaulted her.

The next day, a man assaulted a woman carrying groceries into her District apartment complex, raped her, and threatened that he'd kill her like he did that "other woman."

Three days later, a well-spoken man helped a woman carry her groceries, followed her into her New Carrollton apartment, and held a knife to her throat as he raped her.

Three days after that—and twenty-seven days after Longtin went to jail—a man with a knife sexually assaulted a woman outside her Laurel apartment building.

The following day, a man struck up a conversation with a woman entering her Laurel apartment building. He grabbed her from behind, put one hand over her mouth, and held a knife to her throat. He tried to steal her purse. She struggled and grabbed his knife, and he ran away.

In mid-November—more than five weeks after Longtin went to jail—a man with a knife forced a woman and her young child into a wooded area near her New Carrollton apartment complex, pulled down the woman's pants, threatened to kill her, and fled when a stranger approached.

The detective from the sex crimes unit took her suspicion that the knife-wielding rapist might have killed Zinetti to the homicide detectives, according to Assistant State's Attorney Tonia Belton-Gofreed.

"They ignored her and laughed at her," Belton-Gofreed said.

Confident that Longtin was the killer, homicide detectives had not sought to match the semen taken from Zinetti with DNA samples from the very similar Howard County rape three days before her death. Zinetti died with a clue in her hand, a single hair apparently torn from her attacker. Prince George's police lost it, records indicate.

On November 16, a woman walked into the London Fog shop at Union Station and was stunned when she recognized a new clerk, Antonio D. Oesby, as the man who had raped her about three weeks before, police said.

District police arrested Oesby, who had been released from prison in Maryland six months earlier after serving three years for the attempted kidnapping of a woman from her Columbia apartment building in 1996.

Within days, police said several Maryland women who had been accosted at knifepoint identified Oesby as their attacker.

A District prosecutor won a court order to draw blood from Oesby. A DNA analysis showed that the semen recovered from Zinetti's corpse was Oesby's.

The Prince George's sex crimes investigator's hunch had proved right.

"I remember her saying later when we got the [DNA] hit, 'I told you so,'" Belton-Gofreed said.

On June 12, more than eight months after his interrogation by Prince George's homicide detectives, Longtin was released from jail. The state dropped all charges against him.

During the eight months Longtin spent in jail, he missed his wife's funeral. His bills went unpaid. His credit rating was destroyed. He said police sent his truck to a junkyard. They gave the wedding ring he'd bought for his wife to in-laws who never liked him.

Longtin said all he had left was his faith. "I stood on the Lord," he said, "and He delivered me out of the mouth of the lion."

He still struggles with depression. He finds it hard to get out of bed to go to work. A lot of days, he doesn't.

Epilogue

Two months after the foregoing article appeared, Nathaniel Donnell Oesby was sentenced to two life terms for the murder of Donna Zinetti. In 2001, a civil jury in St. George's County awarded Keith Longtin $6.4 million for the violation of his civil rights.

MADISON HOBLEY

When torture didn't work, they made up a confession

JOHN CONROY

CHICAGO, ILLINOIS

Madison Hobley is on death row because he had an affair. At age twenty-five, Hobley, an installer of medical equipment and a religious man, gave in to his temptation to sleep with another woman. It proved to be a short-lived relationship. He met his lover at a party in mid-October 1986. On November 12, he rented her an apartment at 1121–23 East Eighty-Second Street. Hobley later explained that he did so because his girlfriend had no credit, but the landlord was under the impression that Hobley would be living there too. Hobley's wife, Anita, soon discovered that her husband had strayed, and she told him to leave and not come back until the affair was over. Hobley moved into the Eighty-Second Street apartment but moved out four days later, and it was a bitter parting. He returned to his wife and year-old son, and the couple set about trying to repair their relationship.

In December, Hobley's lover vacated the Eighty-Second Street apartment, unable to afford it on her own. Hobley later testified that she was angry, that as a result of the coming and going she was out $590. During the week before Christmas the Hobleys moved into the unit, which was far nicer than where they had been living. Their new home was in a long, narrow twenty-two-unit building with a garden-level basement and three upper floors. The Hobleys lived on the top floor in Apartment 301, which was just off the front stairway.

On the night of January 6, 1987, the building caught fire.

Hobley later testified that he was awakened by what he initially thought was his watch alarm. After a short time he realized it was a smoke alarm, and he moved quickly to investigate. The apartment was normally so warm that they kept a window open even though it was January, and Hobley slept in his briefs. He threw on a pair of gym shorts and one of his wife's T-shirts. When he opened the apartment door he saw and smelled smoke. He told his wife there was a fire and to get the baby, and then he went to investigate, leaving his front door open. He thought the fire might be coming from Apartment 304 because the smoke was low in the hallway outside that apartment. He walked down the hall to knock on the door and then heard a popping noise. He turned around to see that the fire had come up the stairwell and the doorway to his apartment was in flames. He pounded on the wall and yelled to his wife to shut the door and go to the window, and then he ran down the back stairs and out the back door.

Outside, he stood below his bedroom window. He could see smoke coming out the open window, but never saw his wife or baby. He ran to the front of the building to get help from some people gathered there. A man gave him some oversize pants to wear. After he put the pants on, fire trucks drove past. Hobley, a good athlete, gave chase but failed to catch them. He ran back to the building and saw Althea Tucker, who lived beneath the Hobleys, standing in the window of Apartment 203. Althea's brother Curtis was outside, calling for her to throw her children down. Althea later said that she dropped her infant son and that Hobley and her brother caught him. Hobley, she said, was wearing a T-shirt and pants but no shoes and no jacket.

Firemen arrived. Hobley could see flames coming out of his bedroom window. He went to the front of the building to get help. A woman gave him a coat. He saw Debra Bedford, who lived across the hall from the Hobleys in Apartment 302. She had awakened to a smoke alarm, but hadn't opened her front door because it was hot to the touch. She sat in her window for ten to fifteen minutes, her apartment filling with heat and smoke, until finally firemen arrived and rescued her with a ladder. She later testified that Hobley was upset, that he said he thought his wife and baby were still in the apartment but might have come out behind him down the back stairs. She said that Hobley was wearing a short jacket, like a peacoat, and pants, but no shoes. The coat proved to have its buttons on the wearer's left—it was indeed a woman's coat.

At about this time Hobley went into the home of Georgia White, who lived in the house next door to the building. He called his mother, asking her to bring clothes for the whole family. Mrs. White gave him a pair of gym shoes to wear. Hobley went back outside and asked a fireman to save his wife and baby. The fireman said that some people had been rescued from the third floor and he should go around back. A policeman there told him to check the trauma units in front, but all was confusion there.

Hobley's mother arrived. She later testified that her son was shaking and crying, and she took him home to calm him down. Hobley's sister Robin called paramedics because her brother was "hysterical," and at Saint Bernard Hospital she asked that he be given a sedative. The doctors indicated that tests would have to be performed first, and she took her brother home rather than have him sit around and wait for them.

Hobley's wife and son never escaped their apartment. They were among seven persons who died in the fire, which police and fire investigators would determine had been started with an accelerant. Detectives immediately began interviewing tenants. Detectives Robert Dwyer, James Lotito, and Daniel McWeeney arrived at Hobley's mother's home at about 9:00 A.M. The detectives would claim that Hobley spontaneously offered them the clothes he had been wearing at the fire, but Hobley's mother testified that the detectives asked for them and that she provided them with everything but his peacoat, which she forgot about and handed over to Hobley's public defender two days later. The detectives asked Hobley if he knew anyone who might have had a motivation to torch the building and how he'd been fortunate enough to escape the fire that had killed his wife and son. He mentioned his former lover, saying she had sworn to get back at him.

The detectives took Hobley to Area Two headquarters. He agreed to submit to a polygraph test, and arson investigators took him to police headquarters at Eleventh and State streets for that purpose. In the meantime Detectives Dwyer, Lotito, and McWeeney tried to locate Hobley's girlfriend. "We spoke to her first on the telephone at her employment," Dwyer would testify, "and she indicated to us that she would be glad to meet us, that she was soon to be on a lunch break and that is in fact when we located her and interviewed her." According to Dwyer, the woman was brought to Eleventh and State and interviewed for about a half hour. In his police report, Dwyer noted that she said Hobley had expressed a desire to reconcile with her and had even suggested that she move in with his wife and son. She denied having anything to do with the fire.

At some point that afternoon, Hobley allegedly confessed, first to a polygraph officer and then to Dwyer, Lotito, and McWeeney. According to the police report, Hobley said he'd started the fire because he wanted to leave his wife and be with his girlfriend. According to the detectives, Hobley said that he'd gone to a gas station with a can, purchased gasoline, poured it in the stairwell and in the hallway outside his apartment, lit it with a match, and pitched the can down the second-floor hallway.

In response to this information, Area Two Violent Crimes detective John Paladino was sent to the building to look for the can. He got there about

5:00 P.M. In the thirteen hours since the start of the fire, many police and fire personnel had been through the building, but none had seen a can. Paladino found one relatively quickly, under a sink in Apartment 206.

It was a great coup for the Area Two Violent Crimes Unit. They had walked onto the scene of a horrendous crime at 2:00 A.M. With twenty-two sets of tenants, an owner, a building manager, and all the suspicious friends and associates that those people might have had, the avenues of inquiry had been innumerable. And yet the Area Two detectives had found their man and the key piece of evidence before the day was out.

Hobley was charged with seven counts of murder, one count of arson, and seven counts of aggravated arson. The case came to trial on July 18, 1990. Prosecutors opened with various accounts of the horror of the fire. One tenant testified that she heard a mother screaming "Someone catch my baby!" just before the woman dropped the child out the window. The witness caught the infant girl by a leg. Another tenant told how she climbed out her third-floor window and clung to the roof until she could do so no more, whereupon she fell, landing on a car windshield, suffering severe injuries.

Andre Council was the first witness to finger Hobley. Council testified that he had stopped by a Union 76 gas station at Eighty-Third Street and Cottage Grove Avenue on the night of the fire. Council said he was visiting Kenneth Stewart, who was working at the station, and sometime after midnight a man walked up and bought a dollar's worth of gasoline, which he pumped into what looked like a one-gallon gas can. Council pointed to Hobley as the man who had bought the gas. He said that Hobley had been wearing a navy blue or black peacoat, a hat, and jeans at the time of purchase, and that he walked off in the direction of the building that later was torched. Council said that thirty to forty-five minutes later fire trucks drove by, and as they were headed toward his house he left the station. When he got home he could see that the fire was a block away, and he walked to the fire scene. Council said he saw Hobley about two houses away from the burning building, wearing the same outfit he'd had on at the gas station. While watching television the next day, Council saw Hobley on a news report that identified him as a suspect in the fire, and Council then phoned the police to report what he knew.

Kenneth Stewart followed Council to the witness stand. He recalled that on the night of the fire a short man with a standard red-and-yellow one-gallon gas can had purchased a dollar's worth of gas. Stewart said that before the day ended he was brought in by police to view a lineup. After viewing five men through a one-way mirror, Stewart said he could not identify anyone as the purchaser. He was taken into the lineup room to get a better look, but even then he declined to identify anyone. The men in the lineup were told to ask for $1.50 worth of gasoline (though the man who came to the station had asked for a dollar's worth), and Stewart still declined to pick anyone out. Finally, the police asked if any of the men in the lineup could have been the man who bought the gas. Stewart said the short man in the lineup "favored" the man who purchased the gas, but he could not point to him with "any degree of certainty." The short man was Hobley.

At the trial, Stewart was certain one minute, uncertain the next. When prosecutor Paul Tsukuno asked Stewart to apply a percentage to his degree of "favor" that Hobley was the man who bought gas, Stewart said 99 percent. On cross-examination, Stewart said forthrightly that he could not identify Hobley at the lineup even after he'd finally picked him out. He said police had asked him to state his certainty on a scale of one to ten, and he'd replied, "I can't even tell you any degree of certainty."

A fire marshal testified that the damage sustained outside Apartment 301 was evidence that an accelerant had been poured on the floor there, but he also acknowledged that if the door to Apartment 301 had been left open and a window inside the apartment was also open, fire would have been drawn to that location because fire seeks oxygen. Detective Virgil Mikus of the Chicago Police Bomb and Arson Unit testified that a flammable liquid had been poured in front of Apartment 301. He drew this conclusion from the burn pattern on the floor. Tests of the area revealed no traces of gasoline, but Mikus contended that water from the firemen's hoses could have washed it all away. Mikus's testimony, however, differed from his initial report. In his first report, written the day of the fire, he said that the fire had started on the stairwell and traveled up. At trial he said that the fire probably started at Apartment 301.

Detectives Dwyer and Lotito testified about meeting Hobley, bringing him to the police station, and getting his confession. Detective Paladino said he had found the gas can under a sink in Apartment 206, and the tenant of that apartment testified that although she had a gas can, the can Paladino found was not hers.

There were, however, certain problems with the detectives' testimony. Paladino's discovery of the can was curious. Though the state contended that it supported Hobley's confession, it seemed actually to raise questions about it. Hobley allegedly confessed to throwing the can down the second-floor hallway. Paladino found the can not in the hall but inside an apartment whose tenant said that her door onto the hallway was locked. No one explained how the can got from the hall into the locked apartment.

The detectives' treatment of Hobley's supposed confession also seemed peculiar, given the enormity of the crime at hand. Dwyer said he took notes of Hobley's confession but threw them out because they had gotten wet. Lotito's notes of the interview do exist, but they indicate that Hobley denied setting the fire, not that he had confessed to it. The first existing written account of the alleged confession is in a typewritten report dated January 31, 1987, fifteen days after the fire.

When the defense presented its case, Hobley took the stand and said there never was a confession. He claimed the detectives had suffocated him with a plastic typewriter cover until he blacked out. He claimed that they also pushed in his Adam's apple with their thumbs, kicked him in the shins and in the groin, beat him about the stomach and chest, and placed handcuffs on his wrists so tightly that they caused considerable pain and left marks. In court and in an interview with an investigator from the police department's Office of Professional Standards, Hobley said that Dwyer called him a "skinny little nigger," and that Lotito also made racial remarks, including one comment about blacks favoring pork chops.

Photographs taken the day after Hobley allegedly received this treatment showed scrapes on his wrists and a bruise on his chest. At trial, Dwyer testified that the wrist wounds were self-inflicted, caused by Hobley pulling on his handcuffs. But Steven Stern, a lawyer who showed up late on the day of the fire to represent Hobley, testified that Hobley immediately told him that he had been beaten and bagged, and that he noticed injuries on Hobley's wrists.

Hobley's public defenders presented their own fire expert, John Campbell, a consulting engineer who had been involved in the field of fire and explosion since 1953 and who had once worked for NASA doing aircraft fire and explosion research. Campbell testified that gasoline could not have caused the damage outside Apartment 301. That damage, Campbell said, was the result of the "chimney effect." Given the shape and structure of the stairway, Campbell said, it became a fireplace, flue, and chimney for the flames. "Fresh air would come in at the lower level. It would burn in the hot, superheated gases which expand about three times that of the initial air volume, then force their way out the top and effectively mushroom out at the upper level," Campbell said. He said the flames at that point would be like those on a blowtorch. "The fire would go just out of the stairway and just shoot across the hall and hit the upper part of the wall which would include the upper part of [the Apartment 301] door."

Campbell testified that the heat from the burning wooden door and the radiant heat from the hot gases coming up the stairway would then ignite and destroy the floor covering outside the apartment, and those flames could ignite the wood underneath, and in a few minutes the plaster ceiling would be destroyed and the roof would burn. Campbell's theory was consistent with the absence of gasoline outside Apartment 301. Campbell argued that accelerant was poured only in the stairwell above the entrance to the building, and that the resultant path and intensity corresponded "exactly" with Hobley's description of events.

Campbell was attacked by prosecutors because he had drawn his conclusions from photographs and investigative reports, not from a site visit, not from interviews with fire personnel, tenants, and police. The state's attorneys also implied that Campbell's conclusions were hastily drawn, as he had been hired to review the case the day before he testified.

Hobley's clothes, however, seemed to speak clearly of his innocence. The state stipulated that it had tested Hobley's T-shirt, shorts, oversize pants, and gym shoes and could detect no traces of any identifiable accelerant. The flimsiness of this attire seemed to raise the question: would someone planning to burn down a building in the middle of winter not be a little more prepared for the weather?

Surely no one would have looked askance at a bathrobe, or a pair of shoes or slippers. Tenants Althea Tucker and Debra Bedford, who saw Hobley at different stages during the fire, seemed to contradict Andre Council's testimony about Hobley's attire. Council said that when Hobley came to the gas station he was wearing a peacoat, blue jeans, a hat, and shoes, and that he was wearing the same outfit a short time later at the scene of the fire. When Tucker saw Hobley, however, he was coatless, shoeless, and hatless, and Bedford, running into him some minutes later, said he had neither shoes nor hat.

The case went to the jury on the evening of August 1, 1990. The jury was made up of six women and six men, only one of them African American. Hobley's public defenders had inexplicably not objected to the seating of Matthew Evans, a white suburban policeman, and he was elected foreman. On December 30, 1990, six months after the trial, *Chicago Tribune* reporter Barbara Brotman described the jury deliberations in an article headlined "The Verdict" on which the following account of the deliberations is based.

Postmortem photographs of the victims were viewed for the first time. "They were like charcoal," one juror said. "Their skin was completely gone." Afterward, the jurors cast their first ballot. The six men voted to convict, and they were joined by Janice O'Neil, a thirty-year-old cosmetics saleswoman from Schaumburg. The five remaining women either voted to acquit or hadn't made up their minds. Two of the women believed Hobley had been abused by the police.

In the next hour and a half, two of the women changed their minds and were willing to say Hobley was guilty. The jury adjourned and spent the night in a hotel. In the morning a third woman also capitulated, reasoning that "there was no way that he could have gotten out of that apartment without being burned." One of the women who believed Hobley had been beaten also switched sides. Hobley had testified that when he left his apartment to investigate he did not feel moisture beneath his bare feet, and the woman believed the prosecution's theory that gasoline had been poured there, and thus that Hobley should have felt it.

One woman remained, and she held out for six hours. Nancy Crandall argued for acquittal, troubled that there was no consensus as to where the fire had started. Crandall believed that some of the other women had been intimidated into changing their minds, and she later said that she wanted to free other jurors to go against the majority. But finally she concluded that the fire was so intense on the third floor that it probably had been ignited there. She still believed that Hobley had been beaten, but she told Brotman, "I wasn't sure if he was beaten because he did it or because he didn't do it." Knowing Hobley was likely to get the death penalty, she nonetheless cast her vote with the others. Then she went to the bathroom and cried. "I said a prayer to God that I had made the right decision," Crandall said. "God help me, and God help him."

The jurors delivered their verdict. All six women were crying, though O'Neil, the cosmetics salesperson, later said she was crying for the victims, whose portraits had been displayed in the front of the courtroom during the prosecution's closing arguments.

The trial then entered the death penalty phase, during which the prosecution presents witnesses in aggravation and the defense presents witnesses in mitigation. The state's attorney offered evidence that in the wake of the Hobleys' reconciliation, the couple had had a fierce argument that resulted in Anita staying briefly at a friend's apartment, and the friend contended that Hobley had thrown a brick through her window and threatened to set her apartment on fire if he did not get to see his wife. Hobley's public defenders argued that the police report on the incident "had been doctored."

Hobley's lawyers then presented their mitigation witnesses. Most defendants in capital cases produce four or five character witnesses. Hobley produced twenty-seven. Family members testified that he had supported his mother and sisters from a young age after his father left home. Former high school teachers testified that he had been a good student who never caused problems in class. His former coaches said he was a fine athlete who played unselfishly. Coworkers testified that Hobley, an installer of medical equipment in the homes of the elderly, was a quiet man who seemed to enjoy helping people, and they said that some of the senior citizens for whom he worked were praying for him. Hobley had never had a serious run-in with the police before the fire. Employees of Cook County Jail, where Hobley had been awaiting trial, testified that although 85 to 90 percent of the inmates had some gang affiliation, Hobley did not. They described him as a respectful person who did not give the guards any trouble, and a Presbyterian pastor testified that Hobley regularly attended Bible study classes in the jail and that he seemed to have sincere religious beliefs.

The jury's first ballot went seven to five in favor of execution. Surprisingly, Nancy Crandall, who had been the last to vote to convict, was among the first to vote to execute, while policeman Matthew Evans, her nemesis during the guilt phase, voted against the death penalty. Also opposed was the saleswoman O'Neil, who alone among the women had voted to convict on the first ballot during the guilt deliberations. After the first ballot, a juror who worked as a security guard argued that they had a moral obligation to kill Hobley, that the relatives of the victims were counting on them, and that the jury should show solidarity with those who had lost loved ones. One by one the opponents caved in until Carmen Sanchez, a computer programmer, was the last holdout. She said that, as she signed the verdict form, she thought of the photos of the victims when they were living and then went to the bathroom and threw up.

The debate had taken only two hours.

What the jury did not know, and what has been discovered in the ten years since their departure from the case, would seem to be enough to make even the hard-hearted among them reconsider. There are five components to the case against Hobley—the Kenneth Stewart identification, the Andre Council identification, Hobley's alleged confession, the gas can that allegedly supports the confession, and the evidence of Hobley's affair, which provided the prosecution with a motive. Hobley admitted the affair during his very first conversation with police. The other four elements have been undermined considerably in the last decade, thanks in large part to the work of the private attorneys who have handled his case on appeal—Kurt Feuer, Jon Stromsta, and Kelly Elvin of Ross & Hardies and Andrea Lyon, a legendary Chicago defense lawyer now on the law faculty at the University of Michigan, who joined the team in 1996.

Stewart's identification of Hobley, made with no degree of certainty at the lineup and moving up to 99 percent at trial, became even more questionable after an investigator working for Hobley visited him in 1995. In a notarized affidavit, Stewart said that the lineup was made up of five men, with Hobley the only short man among them. He said he felt pressured to make a positive identification, and so finally said that the short individual looked somewhat like the man who had bought the gas. "However, if any of the other four black men in the lineup had been closer to that person's height," Stewart said, "it would have been very difficult for me to pick out that person." He indicated that his much more certain identification at trial was the result of his again feeling pressured by a prosecutor, and he went on to say that he had never been positively sure that Hobley was the person who bought a dollar's worth of gas that night.

Andre Council's identification was troubling for reasons other than the fact that he saw Hobley in different clothes than other witnesses did. He seemed to have changed his account between the time he first told it to police and the time he told it on the witness stand. On the witness stand he said he saw fire trucks go past the gas station and then went home and on to the fire scene, but the police report has him saying that he went home directly after Hobley bought the gas, and that he was home for thirty to forty-five minutes before he heard the fire trucks arriving.

This discrepancy takes on some significance in light of the fact that on March 17, 1987, two months after Hobley's building burned, Council was arrested for arson.

Council's arrest came in the wake of a 1:00 A.M. fire at an apartment building at 8216 South Dobson, about a block from Hobley's apartment. Council lived at 8212 South Dobson. The fire was started on the basement steps and spread directly to the top floor and ceiling. According to the arresting officers' report, Council had been seen in the alley about the time the fire was started. The Fifth District officers who made the arrest also noted that there'd been an arson at 8204 South Dobson one day earlier, and their report indicates that Council was "named by citizens as possible offender."

On the Dobson Avenue fires, however, Council was released without charge five hours after being taken into custody. The Bomb and Arson detective assigned to the case noted that the "investigation failed to develop any evidence that could link [Council] to the fire at this time." At Hobley's trial, Judge Christy Berkos refused to allow Hobley's public defender to question Council about those two arsons because he had not been convicted of them.

Two weeks after Council's release, on March 30, 1987, he turned himself in to answer to charges of criminal damage to property, the result of accusations that he had smashed a car window with a tire iron on March 1. Normally a suspect is held in a police lockup until the results of a fingerprint check come back, a period that can last anywhere from three to twelve hours. The paperwork filed by Area Two Property Crimes detectives notes that after his arrest, Council was released on personal recognizance on the orders of Bomb and Arson Unit Commander Jon Burge, who waived the normal requirement that fingerprints be checked before the release of an arrested person.

It is extremely rare for the commander of one unit to directly intercede in an arrest made by another unit on behalf of the man charged with the crime. "I've never heard this one before," one veteran Chicago police detective told the *Reader*. "I would have been extremely surprised to have received that request from a high-ranking commander, and even more surprised to get it from a commander who wasn't from my unit." Fingerprinting is a necessary step in determining whether there are outstanding warrants against a suspect. "Waiving the results puts this in a different dimension," the detective said. "Perhaps the subject had an active warrant that they did not want brought up and have him incarcerated for. . . . But then Burge walked on water. He could do whatever the fuck he felt like without ever answering for it."

The interference of Commander Burge in a Property Crimes case raises the question of whether he might do the same in an arson case, specifically in the cases of the Dobson Avenue fires. Burge's intercession in the case of the smashed car window was only recently discovered by Hobley's lawyers. Documents pertaining to that incident were not turned over to Hobley's public defenders prior to trial. This seems to be a violation of the Brady rule, named for a 1963 U.S. Supreme Court decision in *Brady v. Maryland* requiring prosecutors to disclose exculpatory evidence. In their most recent petition for post-conviction relief, Hobley's attorneys argue that Council's testimony would have been impeached at trial because the documents imply that he "received consideration from the prosecutor's office and the Chicago Police Department in exchange for his agreement to testify at Madison Hobley's trial."

The third component of the state's case—Hobley's alleged confession— could cause the prosecution great problems should he someday get a new trial. Aside from the fact that Hobley neither wrote nor signed it, that it was not tape-recorded, that no state's attorney or court reporter was present, and that the only purported copy, in Detective Dwyer's hand, was dispatched to the garbage can, the confession is tainted simply because of the men who took it.

When Hobley was tried in August 1990, it was not commonly recognized, as it is today, that during the 1970s and 1980s a group of Area Two Violent Crimes detectives engaged in torture on a regular basis. Attorneys from the People's Law Office, known as the PLO, were the first to recognize the pattern and the potential extent of the practice. They represented Andrew Wilson, a convicted cop killer, in a civil suit in 1989. In the wake of his arrest Wilson claimed that he'd been suffocated with a plastic bag, burned against a radiator, and given electric shock on his ears, nose, and genitals, all at the hands of Jon Burge, who was then Area Two Violent Crimes commander, and detectives working under him. As Wilson's trial proceeded, his attorneys began to receive anonymous letters from within the police department indicating that Wilson was not the first to have been given such treatment and suggesting that the lawyers might want to speak to Melvin Jones, another victim, then in Cook County Jail. Jones verified that he had been given the electric shock treatment, and through Jones and his former attorney the PLO found other victims. Over the last ten years the PLO has compiled a list of more than sixty people who claim to have been tortured at Area Two. No one in any position of authority has ever made a systematic attempt to find the total number of victims.

When Hobley went to trial ten years ago, however, the PLO's ongoing research was not widely known, nor did it carry much credibility. In January 1990 the *Reader* reported some of what the PLO had discovered, naming a few victims and making it plain that the torture had been extreme, including electric shock, burning, suffocation, and standing on a man's testicles. None of the city's mainstream media picked up on the story, but David Fogel, chief administrator of the Chicago Police Office of Professional Standards, did. In March 1990, Fogel ordered two investigators to examine the Area Two allegations. The investigators eventually concluded that abuse had been "systematic," that it had included "planned torture," that the violence against suspects had taken place over more than a decade, that command personnel had known what was going on and had done nothing to stop it, and that Burge had used an electric shock device on Andrew Wilson. The investigation led to Police Board hearings that resulted in Burge being thrown off the force in 1993, but when Hobley went to trial in August 1990, the investigators were still working on their pivotal reports, and those reports, suppressed by the city, were not released until U.S. District Court Judge Milton I. Shadur ordered the city to make them public in February 1992.

Today, attorneys at Schiff, Hardin & Waite, who represent death row inmate Stanley Howard, and the PLO attorneys have computerized data banks matching Area Two perpetrators, techniques, and victims. Presented with someone who claims abuse at the hands of, for example, Dwyer, Lotito, McWeeney, or Paladino, they can print out the cases each was involved in and the techniques that were allegedly deployed. In their post-conviction petition, Hobley's current attorneys submitted a list of thirteen men who alleged brutal treatment at the hands of those four detectives.

When Hobley was charged, those data banks did not exist. By sheer coincidence, however, Hobley's public defenders knew of the case of Stanley Howard, whose accusations about his treatment by Lotito, Dwyer, McWeeney, and two other Area Two detectives were remarkably similar to the allegations made by Hobley. Both Hobley and Howard say that they were choked, beaten about their midsections while simultaneously being suffocated with a typewriter cover, and kicked in the legs, and that their handcuffs were applied so as to cut into their wrists. Howard says he was beaten about the face and suffered a bloody nose, but that the officer administering this treatment was told by Sergeant John Byrne to "lay off the head." Denying that any brutality took place, Area Two detectives said that their suspect confessed voluntarily to murder. The judge gave Howard's claim no credence, and he was convicted and sentenced to death.

Strangely, the striking similarities between Howard's allegations and Hobley's moved Judge Berkos not to certainty but to doubt. At a hearing on a motion to suppress Hobley's confession, Berkos speculated that Howard's story could have somehow reached Hobley in the years between their two cases, though there was no evidence that the two had anything to do with each other. (Howard had a lengthy felony record, including rape, home invasion, and armed robbery, while Hobley had no record.) Saying that Howard's reputation made his claims suspect, that there was "no indication of reliability or truthfulness" in Howard's claim, and that the case was "entirely too remote," as thirty-eight months separated Howard's alleged mistreatment from Hobley's, Berkos refused to allow Howard's story to be presented at trial. Berkos's decision was upheld by the Illinois Supreme Court, which has yet to acknowledge that torture was common at Area Two, even though U.S. District Court Judge Milton I. Shadur has branded it "common knowledge."

Nonetheless, if Hobley were to get a new trial, a prosecutor could feel no glee in working with Dwyer, Lotito, and McWeeney. Howard's lawyers at Schiff, Hardin & Waite have developed strong medical evidence in support of their client's claims and have found a witness who saw a detective leave Howard's interrogation holding a typewriter cover. Furthermore, an Office of Professional Standards investigator has concluded that it was the detectives, not Howard, who were lying. Howard's case has been remanded back to the trial level so that a judge can hear the convict's claims of torture in greater detail. If Howard's claims are found credible by one criminal court judge, it will be much harder for a judge in Hobley's case to dismiss them simply because they are "remote."

And at a new trial, the credibility of Detectives Dwyer, Lotito, and McWeeney would likely come under attack from another quarter as well. Hobley's girlfriend, whom the prosecution claimed they could not find at trial, and whom his public defenders made no attempt to locate, has been found by Hobley's current legal team. She has signed an affidavit detailing not the cooperative half-hour lunch break conversation portrayed in the detectives' report but an abusive session that lasted twelve hours.

In her affidavit, the woman said that on the morning of the fire she received a call from a police officer who said he was standing in the lobby of the building where she worked. The officer asked her to come down to talk about Madison Hobley. When she came to the lobby, the police asked her to go to police headquarters at Eleventh and State to answer questions. When she said she could not simply walk out of her job, the officers allegedly threatened to go up to her office and embarrass her.

Her affidavit claims that at police headquarters she was taken to an interrogation room and the officers then asked if she had ever played the game fifty-two pickup, whereupon they began to bombard her with photographs of the burn victims. "They then started calling me a 'bitch' and a 'ho' and stating that I took part in setting the fire at the apartment building," she said. She was handcuffed to a ring in the wall and was told that a person behind the tinted window had seen her at the fire. "I broke down and cried. They made me take several lie detector tests, during which the police officers were calling me a liar. . . . They held me at the police station at Eleventh and State from about noon to midnight." Her affidavit added that she was willing to testify at any hearing or trial.

The final component of the state's case against Hobley is the gas can that the prosecution contends supports his confession. At trial, Assistant State's Attorneys Tsukuno and Velcich argued that when Hobley confessed to the crime, he said that he had pitched the can down the second-floor hallway. As the can was found on the second floor, the prosecution now contends, the confession must be a true accounting of events. And yet it might equally be argued that the can contradicts the prosecution's evidence. It was a two-gallon can, but both Council and Stewart testified that the can filled at the filling station was a one-gallon can. As Council and Stewart had worked at gas stations, it might be assumed that they knew a one-gallon can from a two-gallon can, and there was no doubt that they got a close look, as both testified that the can was filled just a few feet from where they stood.

The can, which was introduced at Hobley's trial as People's Exhibit 8, was troubling for other reasons. If Hobley threw it down the hall, how did it get inside Apartment 206, the door of which was locked at the start of the fire? Firemen eventually smashed in the door, as they did doors throughout the building to make certain that no one was left inside. None of the firefighters ever claimed to have kicked a can into an apartment. Based on his observations of the can and crime scene photographs, fire expert John Campbell concluded that there was no way that the two-gallon can could have been outside the door of Apartment 206 or anywhere in the hallway leading to that apartment—the fire and smoke were too intense to leave the can in such fine condition. Judge Berkos, however, decided those conclusions were too speculative, and barred Hobley's attorneys from pursuing that line of questioning before the jury. The prosecutors argued that Hobley had "chosen not to leave his fingerprints anywhere on the can."

Hobley's attorneys remained suspicious of the can, and in a deposition taken on February 25, 1999, Velcich, now in private practice, made a startling statement. He said three times that the can presented at the trial was not the can used in the arson. This was a stunning admission, casually delivered. It meant that the prosecution had openly displayed a murder weapon that had nothing to do with the murder. Three months after giving his deposition, Velcich wrote a letter saying that he had made a mistake, that his memory had lapsed in the eight years since the trial, that he had recently reviewed the trial transcript and found that he and co-prosecutor Tsukuno had indeed argued that—to quote the letter—the can "could have been utilized to commit the crimes charged."

In support of their contention that the can used at trial had been planted by police, Hobley's attorneys offer an affidavit from Donnell McKinley, who was arrested for arson a few weeks before Hobley's fire. McKinley pleaded guilty to setting a fire at 8308 South Paulina on December 16, 1986, and thereafter served eighteen months in a juvenile detention center. In his affidavit, he states that in starting the fire, he used a scratched and dented two-gallon gas can that he had borrowed from a friend who had a neighborhood lawn-mowing business, and the can was confiscated by police when they arrested him. The Bomb and Arson detective who recovered McKinley's can was Virgil Mikus, who later investigated the Hobley case and testified against him at trial. In McKinley's affidavit, he says he recognizes the scratched-up can used in Hobley's trial as the one formerly used in his neighbor's lawn-mowing business. In a deposition given April 14,

1999, Mikus, now retired, said he could see no connection between the gas can taken from McKinley and the one attributed to Hobley. The state's attorney's office argues that McKinley's identification of the container is not only erroneous but preposterous.

The competing claims about the can are being heard by Circuit Court Judge Dennis Porter, who inherited Hobley's case after Judge Berkos retired. Thus far, Porter has shown no inclination to do anything to disrupt Hobley's steady progress toward an early death. Porter has been unmoved by the claims of torture at Area Two. In a ruling handed down on July 1, 1996, he dismissed the accounts of twelve victims who alleged they had been tortured by the same group of detectives who interrogated Hobley. Most of the cases were "unduly remote," he said, meaning they did not occur within three years of Hobley's, and the others should have been discovered by Hobley's trial attorneys and therefore were barred from consideration at the post-conviction stage of this particular appeal. Furthermore, Porter wrote, they would not have changed the result at trial.

Porter also was unmoved by Hobley's arguments about various alleged Brady violations having to do with the gas can or cans found at the fire scene. Later, the Illinois Supreme Court upheld Porter's decision on the brutality claims, but the judges were "deeply troubled" over the alleged Brady violations, and in a ruling dated May 29, 1998, they ordered Porter to conduct a hearing into the matter. The hearing will begin on May 31, and it is expected that the prosecutors, policemen, and defense lawyers who appeared at the original trial will take the stand in an attempt to determine what was turned over to the defense and what was not.

For Hobley, the best outcome would be to have his conviction overturned and then, in light of what is now known about the methods of Jon Burge and his detectives and about the reliability of the testimony of Andre Council and Kenneth Stewart, for the prosecution to drop the charges.

If Porter's record in the case is any guide, however, the hearing will end with Hobley another step closer to lethal injection.

Epilogue

Judge Porter took two years to rule, but, as predicted, denied relief. Porter's decision was appealed to the Illinois Supreme Court, which had not ruled by January 2, 2003, when Hobley and three other Chicago police torture victims—Stanley Howard, Leroy Orange, and Aaron Patterson—were granted full pardons based on innocence by Illinois Governor George H.

Ryan. The following May, Hobley filed a federal civil rights suit accusing the detectives involved in his case of manufacturing the confession, planting the gas can at the crime scene, and committing perjury at the trial. The suit was consolidated with civil rights claims brought by three other victims of Chicago police torture. In early 2008, the City of Chicago settled the claims for $19.8 million.

OPPORTUNISM

It's hardly surprising that some suspects and prospective witnesses in high-profile criminal cases see opportunity—a chance for a reward, perhaps, or leniency in an unrelated criminal matter, or simply the fifteen minutes of fame Andy Warhol promised everyone.

The opportunistic pretender, whatever the motive, naively thinks he's clever enough to convince the authorities that he possesses valuable information about how the crime in question occurred and who committed it.

The authorities would be remiss not to listen, so they eagerly lead him along.

He lays out elaborate, ever-evolving scenarios of the crime and, perhaps, names perpetrators who eventually prove to be either fictional or clearly innocent.

But the authorities construe various bits of his scenarios as guilty knowledge—facts that only someone with intimate knowledge of the crime would know. Once all of the purported perpetrators have been eliminated, the authorities conclude that the person with knowledge of the crime must have committed it.

But the conclusion is erroneous.

The flaw in the process that produced the wrong result was in its factual underpinning—the purported guilty knowledge. It actually was only a mixture of information that was publicly known, imparted by the authorities during the interrogation, or simply the product of guesses that turned out to be right.

Opportunistic suspects and prospective informants, as the following articles illustrate, are not sympathetic characters. Their deceptions are unconscionable, distracting authorities from legitimate paths of investigation and callously inflicting psychological pain on victims' loved ones and friends.

The police, however, share responsibility for the unfortunate outcome. If they were more professional in their factual analysis—and less gullible in their rush to judgment—much of the distraction and most of the pain associated with such cases could be avoided.

The story of John George Spirko Jr. in the "Unrequited Innocence" section of this anthology (page 483) is a further example of an opportunistic effort to scam the system that backfired.

ALEJANDRO HERNANDEZ
AND ROLANDO CRUZ

Tempted by a reward, they talked their way right onto death row

THOMAS FRISBIE AND RANDY GARRETT

NAPERVILLE, ILLINOIS

It was Friday, February 25, 1983, a bright winter afternoon. The sputtering Plymouth Volare irritated the scruffy young man behind the wheel, like a stubborn lock that wouldn't give in during a break-in. Brian Dugan had started the day in a sullen mood, skipped work, and was driving aimlessly and smoking marijuana. He wanted to forget that his girlfriend had broken up with him, forget that he had no money, and forget that nothing seemed to be going right. But the Volare wouldn't let him. It coughed at stoplights and hiccupped during low-speed turns, threatening to die. Something was wrong, probably the carburetor.

For the last three months, Dugan had been working at a tape and label manufacturing company while living in Aurora, an old river town being engulfed by the metropolitan sprawl of Chicago, thirty-five miles to the east. Although it wasn't a bad job for an unskilled laborer, especially one who, like him, had a criminal record, Dugan detested it. He'd always resented being told what to do, and the pay wasn't enough to solve his financial problems.

The job had made it possible for him to buy the 1980 Volare on credit for fifty-six hundred dollars, but he hadn't made a single payment on the loan, nor did he buy the required insurance. He was in debt to just about everyone, including both his girlfriend's mother and his own—the latter for her contributions to his legal bills and fines.

He had broken virtually every promise he'd made to his girlfriend, including that he would stop smoking and using drugs. A week earlier, she had ended their relationship, after it finally had become obvious to her that he'd never amount to anything. But the reality was far, far worse than she suspected. He wasn't just your run-of-the-mill, drug-abusing deadbeat. He'd become a habitual criminal, specializing in kicking down doors and grabbing what he could. Occasionally, when he was feeling angry or depressed, he also attacked women and children. He was, in fact, a serial killer in the making.

In a better-run criminal justice system, he would have been in prison, where he'd already done three stints. Six months ago, on August 23, 1982— ten days after his most recent parole—he'd attacked a twenty-year-old woman, a filling station clerk, in Aurora. He'd grabbed her late at night, after she'd locked the station. Covering her mouth with his forearm, he'd tried to drag her behind the building. She'd struggled, kicking and biting him, and managed to escape. Police arrested him, but the case was dismissed. Had his parole been revoked then, or had he been convicted of attempted sexual assault, as the facts appeared to warrant, Brian Dugan wouldn't have been driving around on this winter day in Naperville, a thriving, tranquil town bordering Aurora on the east.

Ten-year-old Jeanine Nicarico was home alone, at 620 Clover Court in Naperville, recovering from a bout with the flu. The youngest of three children of Thomas and Patricia Nicarico, Jeanine was cheerful, dimpled, and pretty, the darling of the neighborhood and popular at Elmwood Elementary School, where she was an average student in the fifth grade. She had shoulder-length brown hair, large brown eyes, and a bright smile. She loved horses, and her academic performance had improved after her fourth-grade teacher found a way to work horses into her studies.

Tom Nicarico had left early in the morning for his engineering job in downtown Chicago. Patricia, a secretary, also was at work. She'd felt obligated to go because surgery had sidelined her recently for almost a month. But at noon she'd come home to check on Jeanine and make her a grilled cheese sandwich. The other children, Kathy, thirteen, and Christine, sixteen, were at school.

Meanwhile, Brian Dugan was cruising the area in his green Volare. He was, according to an account he would provide to authorities two years later, looking for a place to break into. His method was to ring the doorbell. If someone answered, he'd ask if they needed yard work done or if he could use the phone. If no one answered, he'd kick in the door and take whatever he wanted.

Shortly after noon, Dugan stopped at a church less than a mile from the Nicarico home and asked the secretary, Eloise Suk, about a job. His appearance made Suk nervous. She told him there were no openings, and was relieved when he left. She wrote down his name and, although she wouldn't keep the piece of paper, it was indelibly etched in her mind. She'd remember that it was spelled with one "g" because she had friends with the same name who spelled it "Duggan." After leaving the church, Dugan stopped at a nearby home and rang the doorbell. The occupants were home, so he borrowed a screwdriver.

His next stop was 620 Clover Court, a yellow split-level house on a half-acre lot. He parked in front, where a rural-style mailbox with the name Nicarico on it stood at the curb. He kicked in the front door, splintering the jamb. Minutes later, the green Volare was gone—and so was Jeanine.

Louis Jerman, a motorist, had to brake to avoid a collision with a dark, medium-size car that ran a stop sign at the intersection of Clover Court onto Aurora Avenue. Jerman watched through his rearview mirror as the car headed west on Aurora Avenue, swerved around two cars stopped at a traffic light, ran the light, and continued west. Jerman wasn't certain, but he thought there might have been a small person pushed against the passenger door.

At the DuPage County Sheriff's Office in Wheaton, the county seat, the five detectives assigned to the sheriff's violent crimes unit were at their desks at 3:30 P.M., a half hour before their shift ended, when the missing-child report came in from Naperville. The detectives weren't particularly alarmed—the little girl probably was playing at a friend's house—but they piled into a squad car and headed toward Clover Court, eight miles to the south. Before they got there, they figured the radio dispatcher would notify them that the child was safe at home. But when they arrived, it was immediately obvious, from the kicked-in front door, that this was no routine case.

Naperville police had received the first report of Jeanine Nicarico's disappearance and had been the first to arrive at the home. They'd discovered a shoeprint on the door, which they cordoned off with chairs. But 620 Clover Court was just outside of the Naperville city limit, giving the sheriff's office jurisdiction in the case. Before the violent crimes detectives arrived, other sheriff's officers had gotten there and curtly informed the Naperville police that their services wouldn't be needed.

At 5:00 P.M., an evidence technician from the sheriff's office arrived and took photographs of the door with a special laser camera. He also dusted the door for fingerprints and photographed what appeared to be small fresh footprints on the ground outside the dining room window. Two bloodhounds tracked the child's scent across the front lawn.

Investigators canvassed the neighborhood, finding no one who'd seen anything that seemed relevant. But, with the Naperville police banished, the county investigators could cover only a limited area. They made it as far as the church where Brian Dugan had given his name to Eloise Suk, but they didn't go into the church. Nor did they find Louis Jerman who, unaware of Jeanine's disappearance, had headed out of town on a business trip.

On Sunday afternoon, two days after Jeanine Nicarico disappeared, a couple of hikers reported that they'd spotted what they at first thought was a mannequin near a nature trail known as the Prairie Path west of Naperville and north of Aurora.

It wasn't a mannequin—it was the brutally beaten corpse of the little girl.

Patricia and Thomas Nicarico were at home, while scores of Jeanine's friends, neighbors, and classmates had gathered at St. Raphael's Catholic Church in Naperville to pray for her safe return. Jeanine was a popular girl, and many of the pews were full, when the young pastor, the Reverend Michael O'Keefe, left the church with officers who wanted him to be with the Nicaricos when they were informed that their daughter's body had been found.

As Father O'Keefe consoled the family, the Reverend Richard Bennett, an assistant pastor, told the congregation at St. Raphael's, "I'm afraid our prayers are not going to be answered. The police have found a body. They are 99 percent sure it is Jeanine's."

A task force comprised of members of the FBI, DuPage County Sheriff's Office, Naperville Police, and other area law enforcement agencies was formed to investigate the crime.

Jeanine's body wasn't moved until the following afternoon, Monday, February 28, after officers on their hands and knees searched the Prairie Path and surrounding area for evidence. They found splatters of blood and made plaster casts of tire tracks and two footprints near the body. An autopsy performed that afternoon determined that Jeanine had been sexually assaulted and had suffered a number of severe blows to the head, any one of which could have killed her—although these facts were not made public.

Later in the afternoon, two Illinois Tollway workers reported that they'd seen a dark green car with Illinois license plates turn around on the Prairie Path between 2:45 and 3:00 P.M. the previous Friday. Both described the driver as a clean-shaven white man in his twenties or thirties, with medium-length, dark brown or black hair. They differed on the make of the car—one thought it might have been a Ford Granada, the other a Ford Fairlane or Mercury Monarch—but both recalled that it had a missing hubcap, a detail that would prove significant.

On Thursday, March 3, after a mass for Jeanine at St. Raphael's, a task force spokesperson announced that a dark-colored car, possibly missing a left front hubcap, was being sought and that a shoeprint "significant in the investigation" had been made by a type of hiking shoe called a Cloud Climber, which was sold at Fayva shoe stores.

An FBI psychologist, meanwhile, was developing a profile of the killer that would prove prophetic: "On or about February 25, 1983, [the killer] reached a point of anger that drove him to rage. A continuing problem with his life, possibly associated with a significant female . . . reached its peak."

Two weeks into the investigation, the authorities received an anonymous tip that an Aurora youth named Alejandro Hernandez had been talking as if he knew who committed the crime. Hernandez was a nineteen-year-old high school dropout and native of Puerto Rico who lived with his parents. He had a fondness for smoking marijuana and sniffing glue, and a rap sheet with several minor arrests, and a conviction for stealing an air conditioner. His IQ had been measured in the low- to mid-seventies, and he had a tendency, as a social worker once put it, "to tell tall tales in order to make you feel that he was someone special."

Detectives John Sam and Dennis Kurzawa went to interview Hernandez. They found him wary of talking at first, but, after learning that he had an ambition to become a police officer, they drove him around in their squad car and he became quite garrulous. In fact, he made a startling claim—that an acquaintance of his named Ricky had admitted the Nicarico crime. Hernandez initially said he didn't know Ricky's last name, but with a little prodding said it was Benevides. Asked what kind of car had been used in the crime, Hernandez said it was a green Oldsmobile Cutlass, like a car they happened to be passing at that moment. He added that two other young Aurora men, Mike Castro and Stephen Buckley, had been in the car with Ricky.

Sam had been in police work too long to put much faith in stories from those of Hernandez's stripe. Whenever there was a big case, especially one in which a reward had been offered—recently increased in this case from five thousand dollars to ten thousand dollars—there inevitably were people willing to string police along with fabricated stories. Still, Sam found it curious that the quotes Hernandez attributed to Ricky were in the first person, sounding almost as if Hernandez were making the statements himself.

Over the next few days, John Sam, Dennis Kurzawa, and other task force members searched in vain for Ricky. No such person would be found—because, in fact, Ricky was fictitious. But Mike Castro and Stephen Buckley, the young men Hernandez had placed in the car with Ricky, were real.

Asked to come to sheriff's headquarters, Castro and Buckley promptly agreed. They appeared at the appointed hour on March 21 and, in separate interviews, adamantly denied knowing the purported Ricky and, equally adamantly, ever having been in a car with anyone discussing any murder. When asked where he'd been on Friday, February 25, Castro said he'd been at work until 5:00 P.M. at a West Chicago manufacturing company—a fact that was soon verified, eliminating Castro as a suspect.

Buckley, however, was unemployed, and had no alibi. Sam showed him a hiking shoe with a heel pattern similar to that on the Nicarico door. To Sam's surprise, Buckley said he had a similar pair of shoes, and agreed to show them to Sam. That afternoon, Sam picked the shoes up at Buckley's home and took them back to Wheaton for forensic testing.

The next day, John Gorajczyk, the DuPage County crime lab's shoeprint expert, found significant differences between the sole pattern of Buckley's shoes and the print on the door. And Philip Gilman, the crime lab chief, tested the shoes for signs of blood, but found none.

Sam wasn't surprised by the results, figuring that, if Buckley had kicked in the Nicarico door, he wouldn't have surrendered the shoes so easily.

All in all, the investigation wasn't going well. Hundreds of interviews with potential suspects, witnesses, and informants had uncovered no other strong leads, and the task force was on the verge of disintegrating.

At this point, the authorities decided to try a subterfuge.

Armindo Marquez, a friend of Alex Hernandez since childhood, had been part of a burglary ring that had recently been smashed in neighboring Kane County. Facing scores of felony counts, Marquez made it clear that he was ready to help with the Nicarico case.

On March 17, Marquez and Hernandez were brought face-to-face in a partitioned area of the DuPage County Jail. Their conversation wasn't recorded—it is illegal in Illinois to record a conversation without consent of all parties—but DuPage County Detective Albert Bettilyon was in a position to overhear what was said. Unfortunately, Bettilyon understood only bits of what was said—because Marquez and Hernandez alternated between English and Spanish, and Bettilyon wasn't fluent in the latter.

Marquez had been instructed to say that he knew who'd killed a boy in the nearby suburb of Bolingbrook and was going to collect a ten-thousand-dollar reward in that case. As a prop, there was a box full of cash in the room. When Hernandez heard that, he said that he had been present at the Nicarico murder.

"All I did was hold her down," Bettilyon heard him say.

Hernandez would say years later that he'd been tricked—that DuPage detectives had told him to say those words in order to elicit incriminating information from Marquez about the Bolingbrook murder. But when Bettilyon repeated what he heard Hernandez say, the reaction of task force members was primal.

"Let's kill that little son-of-a-bitch," John Sam said to himself. "Let's take him and throw him out the fucking window. . . . Now we're all motivated. We want that little bastard. He just said the key words, 'I held her down.'"

At the end of March, the task force was disbanded, and the DuPage County Sheriff's Department assumed full control of the investigation.

Detectives continued to pursue potential suspects and informants, among whom was a twenty-year-old street gang member—a Latin King—named Rolando Cruz. Initially, when interviewed in mid-April by Detectives Thomas Vosburgh and Dennis Kurzawa, Cruz said he knew nothing about the Nicarico crime. After the detectives mentioned the ten-thousand-dollar reward, however, he said he'd check around. Over the next several days, he met with and had several telephone conversations with Vosburgh and Kurzawa and, from these encounters, apparently discerned that Alejandro Hernandez was a suspect.

On April 29, Cruz contacted the detectives and told them that an acquaintance of his, Ray Ortega, had told him that Hernandez had killed the little girl. In a tape-recorded interview with a group of DuPage detectives that afternoon, Cruz added a few vague details of what—he claimed—Ortega had said. Cruz didn't exactly come across as a person worthy of belief. Asked about his own background, he claimed to be an ex-Marine—yet he wasn't familiar with *Semper Fidelis*, the Marine Corps motto, or with Lewis (Chesty) Puller, the most decorated man in the history of the corps. Cruz also lied about his age and claimed to be of Native American descent, although his forebears were Mexican.

John Sam, who participated in the taped interview, concluded that Cruz was probably nothing more than an impudent liar with a craving for attention and a naive notion that he could con the authorities out of the reward money—an assessment that would prove correct, although not until a decade later.

In the meantime, Cruz's blabbering and insolence had thrust him right into the middle of the Nicarico investigation.

Detectives Sam and Warren Wilkosz Jr. took another crack at Stephen Buckley on April 20. Thinking that he'd be more likely to agree to meet them at a neutral site than at sheriff's headquarters, they invited him to breakfast at a Denny's near his home. Their intent, however, was to take him to headquarters, where they planned, in Sam's words, to "bust his balls."

Once at headquarters, Sam and Wilkosz told Buckley that forensic tests had proved that his shoes had left the mark on the Nicarico door. That, of course, was contrary to the actual findings of John Gorajczyk and Philip Gilman, but police interrogators are permitted to lie to suspects. To bolster their deception, Sam and Wilkosz displayed inked impressions of the soles of his shoes and diagrams of the mark on the door.

Glaring at Buckley, Wilkosz told him, "Your shoeprint is on the door. You know that. We know that. Tell us how it got there."

"I don't know," Buckley pleaded meekly. "Maybe somebody took my shoes, I don't know. All I know is that I wasn't there. I didn't hurt anybody."

Sam then took a slightly different tack. "Your friends, these mutts, what do you think they're going to do? Did you think they're going to sit in jail and take all the heat? No fucking way. They'll say, 'Get your ass right down here with us, buddy. You come down here with us.'"

"I didn't do it," Buckley insisted. "I know you don't believe me, but I didn't do it."

Sam yelled at him, "Don't you understand? This is a death case. The state's attorney will deal with the first person who talks. The others are . . . going to kill you."

The detectives then brought out photos of Jeanine's body and told Buckley, "Look at your handiwork. This is the result of what you did."

Buckley wouldn't budge.

Finally, late that afternoon, Sam and Wilkosz drove him back to the Denny's and released him.

"He never got off the story," Sam would recount years later. "He just said, 'I didn't do it, I know I didn't do it, someday you guys will know I didn't do it. If you're going to kill me, kill me. If you're going to put me in jail, put me in jail. I didn't do it.' He's crying and everything. The guy's very emotional, but nothing changes. Nothing changes. All those hours, he never changed his story, he never changed his attitude. Nothing. He had me totally convinced that he didn't do it."

On May 6, Rolando Cruz received a subpoena to appear the following week before a DuPage County grand jury. Three days after that—May 9, a date that would become important—he called the sheriff's office and claimed that someone had shot at him.

Detective Vosburgh promptly picked up Cruz and took him to sheriff's headquarters, where he proceeded to allege that the shooting had followed a warning from Alex Hernandez that he knew "way too much." In conveying that threat, according to Cruz, Hernandez made an incriminating statement—that Jeanine had been hit with a bat and that he "didn't do it . . . [but] just finished it 'cause [he] was getting blamed for it anyhow."

After spending the night of May 9 in the DuPage County Jail, ostensibly for protection, Cruz gave another tape-recorded statement. He now claimed he'd learned some things about the crime from an acquaintance named Emilio Donatlan. According to Cruz's new scenario, Hernandez had brought the kidnapped child to a birthday party Donatlan was hosting for Ray Ortega. Donatlan raped the little girl and, when she wouldn't shut up, hit her with a bat or club. Although the blow rendered her unconscious, Donatlan continued to rape her. When she regained consciousness, she resumed screaming. Donatlan hit her again and Ortega kicked her down a long stairway, breaking her nose. When she got up, Hernandez walked her to a car and drove her to the Prairie Path—where he killed her.

John Sam didn't think much of Cruz's latest scenario, for several reasons. First, according to the medical examiner, Jeanine had died two to four hours after she'd eaten the grilled cheese sandwich her mother had fed her in the early afternoon. Thus, the killer almost certainly had taken Jeanine straight to the Prairie Path, not to an apartment. Second, Jeanine's head wounds had been too brutal for her to have awakened, much less to have walked to a car. Third, it was highly unlikely that a group of youths at a birthday party would have committed such a crime in concert. Surely not everyone there could have been that depraved.

After detectives questioned Donatlan and searched his small second-floor apartment, Sam became even more skeptical of Cruz's tale. Not only did Donatlan deny the crime, as would be expected, but there was no sign of violence. A couple living on the first floor had heard nothing. And the flight of stairs Jeanine supposedly had been kicked down was an exterior staircase, which was visible for a long distance in a busy area. If Cruz's account had been true, surely somebody would have seen or heard something.

"I thought Cruz was just a bullshitting asshole," Sam eventually would reflect. "That's all I ever thought he was—that, and someone looking for a free ride."

Despite John Sam's misgivings, the DuPage County State's Attorney's Office put Cruz into a witness protection program—giving him spending money and paying for him to stay in a motel and, later, in apartments in the towns of Glen Ellyn and Wheaton. The county even footed the bill for classes in cable-TV installation Cruz was taking at the College of DuPage. Plus, Cruz had a shot at getting that ten-thousand-dollar reward.

On May 12, Cruz appeared before the grand jury. Assistant State's Attorney Thomas Knight, the county's chief criminal prosecutor, took Cruz again and again over the story he had told detectives, probing for any new facts that might bolster the prosecution theory. Cruz, alas, didn't provide any more facts. The grand jury met again the following week and each Thursday throughout the summer, fall, and winter. Cruz appeared five times in all and, as time passed, the prosecution theory gradually became that he had been a co-conspirator in the crime, with Hernandez and Buckley.

Hernandez appeared twice and both times much of his testimony was disoriented and incomprehensible. At his second appearance, on January 12, 1984, he said he'd appeared before the grand jury several times, although he'd actually been there just once.

Buckley didn't testify before the grand jury, but was implicated by forensic evidence that emerged somewhat belatedly. Despite the conclusion of the DuPage County's forensic expert, John Gorajczyk, that the shoeprint on the Nicarico door didn't match Buckley's shoes, the prosecution had found a self-styled "forensic anthropologist" named Louise Robbins who was willing to say, categorically, that they did match.

Robbins was an assistant professor of physical anthropology at the University of North Carolina at Greensboro who'd begun studying footprints in the 1970s. She had attracted the attention of Mary Leakey, a renowned anthropologist who was working in Tanzania. Leakey had found some ancient footprints and sought Robbins's help in identifying them. Robbins flew to Tanzania and concluded that one of the prints had been made by an even-toed, hoofed mammal. A maintenance man working with Leakey soon discovered additional prints and it was eventually determined that they were in fact prints of ancient human ancestors. Robbins had, as it were, put her footprint in her mouth, but she soon learned that it didn't matter in the world of forensic testimony—where she would carve out a quite lucrative sideline.

Because people walk differently and have different bone structures, Robbins had noticed, they wear down the soles of their shoes differently. Some people wear down the outside of the heel first, for instance, while others rub away at the inside. That much was self-evident, but Robbins went further, concluding that each individual has a unique wear pattern. Carried away with this notion, she claimed that she could determine with absolute certainty—without high-tech instruments, just a ruler and a protractor—whose shoes had made a particular shoeprint. And, she told the grand jury, she had determined that only a shoe worn by Stephen Buckley could have made the print on the Nicarico door.

The only evidence to support the theory that Hernandez and Cruz were involved in the crime were their vague statements, which didn't jibe with the facts of the crime, and the testimony of several witnesses of extremely dubious credibility that they'd heard one or the other of them make an incriminating statement. The case was so weak that Tom Knight kept the grand jury investigation going for nearly ten months without seeking indictments.

Finally, on March 8, 1984—twelve days before his boss, DuPage County State's Attorney J. Michael Fitzsimmons, faced a hotly contested primary election—Knight obtained true bills charging Hernandez, Cruz, and Buckley with murder, rape, kidnapping, deviate sexual assault, aggravated indecent liberties with a child, home invasion, and residential burglary.

Although the indictments were a political plus for State's Attorney Fitzsimmons, he was narrowly defeated in the March 20 Republican primary by an ambitious young opponent named James Ryan, who proceeded to run unopposed in the November general election.

Jim Ryan and Tom Knight were anything but mutual admirers—the friction between them, it was said, could split atoms at nearby Fermilab—so it wasn't surprising that Ryan promptly replaced Knight as chief of criminal prosecutions and announced that the new chief, Brian Telander, was taking over the Nicarico case.

By this time, however, the Nicaricos, their friends, and neighbors had become a political force in Naperville. Fearing that the new prosecutor might take the case in a different direction and perhaps lose it, or even drop it, they collected thousands of signatures on petitions demanding that Knight be retained.

Ryan quickly capitulated, agreeing to keep Knight on as a special prosecutor to handle the Nicarico case.

Morally certain that Hernandez, Cruz, and Buckley were innocent, John Sam continued to pursue an alternative suspect—the son of a prominent lawyer who lived near the Nicaricos. Although the young man was innocent, circumstantial evidence pointed in his direction. He'd slipped away from Naperville Central High School the day of the crime and claimed to have spent the afternoon with his girlfriend. She backed his story—but she'd torn that day's entry out of her diary. And the young man reportedly had once owned a green Granada.

When a lawyer for the young man complained that his client's reputation was being sullied by Sam's poking around, DuPage County Sheriff Richard Doria demanded that Sam explain himself. As Sam would recall the conversation, Doria asked him, "Why are you doing this?" And Sam responded to the effect, "Because these guys in jail didn't do it."

After further back and forth, Doria reassigned Sam from the violent crimes unit to patrolling convenience stores to make sure minors weren't buying liquor.

That was it for Sam. He resigned, effective December 1, 1984.

Anyone facing a felony charge is in a precarious position, but Hernandez, Cruz, and Buckley were particularly vulnerable. Juries everywhere tend to lower the conviction threshold for horrible crimes—rarely had there been one more horrible than the abduction, rape, and murder of Jeanine Nicarico—but a jury in conservative DuPage County was likely to be especially conviction-prone. Also, as usual in cases arousing strong public passions, the prosecution could count on favorable rulings from the judge on evidentiary and procedural issues.

Judge Edward W. Kowal, to whom the Nicarico case had been assigned, was a former DuPage County assistant state's attorney who would be up for reelection in less than a year. The most important pretrial issue he had to decide was whether the defendants would be tried together, as the prosecution wanted, or separately, as the defense wanted. Normally, when one defendant has made statements implicating another, the trials are severed. Defendants have a constitutional right to cross-examine their accusers, but that isn't possible when the accusers exercise their constitutional right not to testify. Such was the situation in this case—Cruz had made statements implicating Hernandez, and Hernandez had made statements implicating Buckley.

Most often, the solution is separate trials. Another solution is to empanel a separate jury for each defendant, but to try the defendants simultaneously—when evidence admissible against only one defendant was presented, the codefendants' juries would be excused from the courtroom. But in this case, Tom Knight proposed a third solution—to redact, or edit out, all of the names in the statements. Defense lawyers argued that the jury would assume that it was the defendants' names that had been redacted, even in statements in which they had not actually been named. Kowal, however, sided with Knight. The defendants would be tried jointly, before a single jury.

The denial of severance was devastating for the defense, but an issue even more devastating arose when Knight revealed that he planned to introduce a previously undisclosed oral statement that Cruz supposedly had made to Detective Thomas Vosburgh on May 9, 1983.

During the trial, Vosburgh would claim that Cruz had told him of a "vision" that he had had—a vision in which he'd seen a girl dragged from her home, sodomized, and beaten so badly while lying on the ground that her head left an indentation in the mud. Because the alleged vision included information that had never been made public, Vosburgh's testimony suggested that Cruz had actually witnessed the murder. Then the defense was in for another shock—Vosburgh's partner, Detective Dennis Kurzawa, took the stand and claimed that he, too, had heard Cruz describe the vision on May 9.

The detectives' account was dubious because they had made no contemporaneous record of such a statement. Nor, in a tape-recorded interview the following day, did they inquire about the supposed vision. In explaining why they hadn't written a report, the detectives said they'd called Tom Knight, the prosecutor, and he'd told them not to because he was going to question Cruz before the grand jury in the coming days.

Cruz wasn't asked about it, however, at any of his grand jury appearances.

As preposterous as the detectives' testimony seemed to the defense lawyers, they were aware that the jury was likely to find it quite credible. The defense, of course, could have called Knight to testify, but if he corroborated the detectives' claims it would only make matters worse.

The balance of the prosecution case against Cruz was not much stronger. It was comprised of the introduction of the tape-recorded statement he'd made on May 10—the day following the supposed vision statement—the testimony of informants with criminal records who attributed damning admissions to Cruz, and the testimony of a jailer who said Cruz had made admissions about the crime. While the May 10 statement was horrifying, it contained no admission that Cruz had been involved in the events he described.

Typical of the informant witnesses was Dan Fowler, who testified that in the spring of 1983, after drinking beer, Cruz had broken into tears and admitted having been present when Jeanine was murdered. "He said he was there, but he wasn't involved in what happened," said Fowler, who'd told the grand jury the previous year that Cruz had said only that he knew people involved in the crime. Fowler's explanation for the contradiction was that, "I was holding back. I didn't want to get so involved, like, so I'd end up here today."

The case against Hernandez was similarly weak, resting principally on the testimony of several witnesses. One was Armindo Marquez, who told the jury about his conversation with Hernandez in the room with the box of money. Another was Arthur Lee Burrell, who said he and Hernandez were "like brothers" and that they'd often gone to the Prairie Path and had built a clubhouse there. It was a popular place for parties, Burrell continued, and he'd seen Cruz and Buckley there as well. Hernandez's cousin, Jackie Estremera, said Hernandez had told him of a longtime plan to burglarize the Nicarico home. And a deputy sheriff and a sheriff's lieutenant each testified Hernandez had made incriminating comments to them.

The case against Buckley relied heavily on Louise Robbins's testimony that one of his shoes—to the exclusion of all other shoes in the world—had left the print on the door. But the prosecution also sprang a surprise on Buckley—an in-court identification of him by a woman named Joann Johannville, who'd reported seeing a rusty, light-colored car on Clover Court about the time Jeanine disappeared. The surprise apparently backfired, however, when the defense forced her to admit on cross-examination that she'd initially told the authorities that the driver of the car was smooth-complexioned, had no facial hair, and wore glasses. Buckley's complexion was severely pitted, he had bushy muttonchops, and he had never worn glasses.

Robbins and Johannville weren't a winning combination. At the conclusion of the seven-week trial the jury could not reach a verdict on Buckley, but found Cruz and Hernandez guilty as charged. Three weeks later, after a sentencing hearing for which Cruz and Hernandez waived a jury, Judge Kowal sentenced them both to death.

The trial was over, but John Sam wasn't satisfied. He didn't believe Cruz had made the vision statement. Almost every day during the grand jury investigation, the detectives involved had discussed the case, brainstorming and talking about leads. Not once had anyone mentioned Cruz's vision.

"I remember we'd sit and drink sometimes," Sam recalled in an interview years later. "Vosburgh and Kurzawa would say, 'Oh, I really think he knows something.' They really did believe that either he had something to do with it or he knew about it. But never once did they talk about this goddamned vision."

Even before Cruz and Hernandez's appeal was filed, another child rape and murder rivaling the Nicarico crime in horror occurred, this one in Somonauk, Illinois, in LaSalle County, about twenty-five miles southwest of Aurora.

There, on Sunday, June 2, 1985, Brian Dugan was cruising along U.S. Route 34—he now had a blue Gremlin, his green Volare having been repossessed in October 1983—when he spotted two girls, ages seven and eight, riding their bicycles on a gravel road at the southern edge of the village. Pretending that he needed directions, he got out of his car, grabbed the eight-year-old, and threw her into his car. The seven-year-old ran, but he chased her down, as the child in the car frantically struggled to get out. Dugan had removed the inside lock knobs, so she couldn't open the locked doors, but she squeezed through the open window on the driver's side and ran before Dugan returned with the other child.

The terrified eight-year-old, her clothes torn, ran a half mile to the home of a family she knew. She was so hysterical that the people had a hard time figuring out what she was saying, but when they finally did, they called the police to report that a man had taken her friend and second-grade classmate, Melissa Ackerman.

The LaSalle County sheriff and Somonauk police set up a command post in the local volunteer fire station and, based on information provided by the child who escaped, bulletins were issued to the state police and law enforcement agencies in surrounding counties to look for a battered blue car driven by an unshaven man with brown hair and a mustache.

That evening, the LaSalle sheriff's police were notified that a car and driver meeting the description had been stopped in Mendota, a village in Kane County about twenty-five miles southwest of Somonauk. A Mendota officer on patrol had followed the car, a Gremlin, into a filling station only because it lacked a current vehicle identification sticker. When the officer asked the unshaven man for his driver's license, he couldn't produce one, but showed the officer an expired fishing license. The officer let the man go, but made a note of his name—Brian Dugan—and license plate number.

A records check revealed that five days earlier a nineteen-year-old woman in Geneva, Illinois, had reported that a man had attempted to force her into a car bearing the same license number. Dugan, who was employed as a stock handler at an equipment supply company in Geneva, had been on a week's vacation, which was scheduled to end the next morning.

When he arrived for work at 6:45 A.M. on Monday, June 3, Dugan found himself surrounded by a team of Geneva police and Kane County sheriff's officers with guns leveled at his chest. He was charged with the attack on the Geneva woman and a similar attack on a twenty-one-year-old woman from the village of North Aurora.

Two weeks later, on June 17, two LaSalle County deputy sheriffs were checking a secluded spot five miles east of Mendota for underage drinkers when one of the officers caught a glimpse of some clothing beside an irrigation ditch. Upon closer inspection, they discovered a decayed, bloated, and unrecognizable corpse partially submerged in the ditch. The next day, the body was identified from dental records as Melissa Ackerman's. She'd died of asphyxiation.

Meanwhile, Kane County authorities were building a case against Dugan for the murder eleven months earlier of a twenty-seven-year-old nurse, Donna Schnorr. Around 4:00 A.M. on July 15, 1984, Schnorr was driving home from a party in Oswego, Illinois, when another car knocked her 1979 Chevrolet Monte Carlo off the road outside of Aurora. She was abducted, taken to a quarry eleven miles away, raped, and drowned in a water-filled gravel pit. At the time, Dugan owned a brown and gold 1974 Chevrolet Impala, which he'd reported stolen shortly after the Schnorr murder. The car had been recovered in neighboring Will County, where it remained. Now it was towed to the Kane County jail and parked conspicuously where Dugan could see it—just to let him know that he was likely to be linked to a capital murder.

On June 25, Dugan was charged with the murder of Melissa Ackerman, and LaSalle County State's Attorney Gary Peterlin announced that he would seek the death penalty. Facing two potential death penalty offenses, Dugan concluded it was in his interest to enter into plea bargaining. Through his lawyer, LaSalle County Public Defender George Mueller, Dugan offered to plead guilty not only to the Ackerman and Schnorr murders but also the Nicarico murder in exchange for a sentence of life in prison without the possibility of parole.

Nothing happened, at least officially, for nearly five months, but finally on November 16 prosecutors in LaSalle and Kane counties, the jurisdictions of the Ackerman and Schnorr cases, took the deal. For DuPage County prosecutors, however, Dugan's offer posed a problem—they'd sent two men to death row for a crime he was claiming he, and he alone, had committed. They weren't about to accept his terms.

Illinois State Police Lieutenant Edward Cisowski, who'd worked on the Ackerman and Schnorr investigations, was at the LaSalle County Jail on November 16 when the deal was struck on Dugan's pleas in those cases.

Cisowski was aware that Dugan had confessed to a third murder, but knew nothing more. In fact, he assumed, incorrectly, that it was a Kane County murder in which the adult victim, Linda White, had been abducted and drowned—a modus operandi similar to that of the Ackerman case.

When Dugan denied the White murder, George Mueller, the public defender, promptly made it clear that the third victim was Jeanine Nicarico. Dugan was prepared to discuss the crime in detail, Mueller said, but only if he were guaranteed immunity from the death penalty—a condition that would require the approval of DuPage County prosecutors. Meanwhile, however, Mueller was willing to allow Dugan to answer hypothetical questions about the case, and Cisowski was fine with that.

Cisowski lived only about seven blocks from the Nicaricos and had gone there on the day of the crime. He hadn't followed the case closely, but was aware that there had been convictions and that Tom Knight, the prosecutor, had attributed the crime to a gang of burglars. Hence, Cisowski thought it quite possible that Dugan had been a participant. But Cisowski was puzzled that Dugan would confess. It made sense for him to confess to the Ackerman and Schnorr murders—that was his best hope of avoiding death sentences in those cases. But why would he confess to a third capital murder in which he wasn't a suspect?

Three possibilities occurred to Cisowski. The first was that Dugan had committed the crime with Hernandez, Cruz, and Buckley. Since they hadn't ratted on him, now that he was going to prison for life anyway, maybe he was returning the favor. The second was that he was just toying with the system—trying to muck up the works for whatever reason. The third, of course, was that he was telling the truth—in which case the two men on death row and their codefendant then awaiting retrial were innocent.

Dugan, speaking only hypothetically now, said he'd been driving aimlessly through Naperville on the day of the crime. After stopping at a house to borrow a screwdriver, he stopped at the Nicarico home. When he realized that Jeanine was home alone, he kicked in the door, abducted her, and took her to the Prairie Path, where he assaulted and killed her. Cisowski wasn't impressed. Dugan could have gleaned that much from the news media.

But Cisowski, having been at the Nicarico home the day of the crime, knew something he felt certain the killer would know—that a twenty-two-foot-long yellow sailboat had been parked at the edge of the driveway. So Cisowski asked Dugan what was in the driveway. Nothing, said Dugan. Based on that wrong answer, Cisowski figured that Dugan's whole story was bogus.

"With all due respect," Cisowski told Mueller, "your client is full of shit."

In the ensuing weeks, Cisowski had to reconsider his snap judgment that Dugan was lying.

After Dugan passed a polygraph test, which he'd volunteered to take, the state police arranged to take Dugan out of jail to see if he could lead them to the Nicarico home and the Prairie Path. Two officers who didn't know where the Nicaricos lived took Dugan on the outing. Cisowski didn't go along, thus avoiding any possibility that he might unconsciously tip Dugan. And, because Cisowski had mentioned the sailboat to Dugan, it was moved.

The officers drove Dugan to an Aurora shopping mall and told him to lead them from there. He directed them straight to the correct subdivision—one of 125 Naperville subdivisions at the time—and easily found the Nicarico home. Then, after a couple of wrong turns, he took them to the Prairie Path. He couldn't pinpoint exactly where the body had been left, but neither could county officers who'd spent more time there than he had.

In continuing discussions with Cisowski, Dugan provided accurate, significant details of the crime, on the condition that nothing he said could be used against him. Although some of the details weren't accurate, Dugan tellingly described a towel with which Jeanine had been blindfolded. He described how he'd folded the blindfold and secured it with an uncommon type of medical tape with a serrated edge—correct information that had never been made public.

Cisowski also deduced why Dugan, immediately after his arrest, had been so eager to negotiate a deal to shield him from a death sentence in the Nicarico case—he had in fact been investigated as a suspect in that case soon after he'd been charged with the Ackerman and Schnorr murders. Detective Warren Wilkosz had learned that Dugan ditched work the day of the crime and owned a green Volare, which was similar in appearance to the car the tollway workers had described. Dugan had refused to talk to Wilkosz, but certainly was aware of the possibility that he would be charged in the case.

As Cisowski's discussions with Dugan continued, other state investigators learned that Dugan's green Volare, which had been repossessed in 1983, was missing a front hubcap—like the car the Illinois Tollway workers saw turn around on the Prairie Path the afternoon of the crime. Dugan also fit the description the workers had provided of the driver.

As stories about Dugan's confession began appearing in the newspapers and on television, Eloise Suk came forward to report that, on the day of Jeanine's murder, a young man had come to the church where she worked and inquired about work, giving his name as Brian Dugan.

To Cisowski, the possibility that Dugan had committed the crime with others was appearing increasingly unlikely. Dugan had been alone at Suk's church. The tollway workers had seen just one man in the car with the missing hubcap. Neither a computer search of police records nor interviews with some seventy-five of Dugan's friends and relatives, whose names were in an address book at his apartment, hinted at a link between him and any of the three young men who'd been tried for the crime.

On top of that, Dugan's shoe size was consistent with the print on the Nicarico door and he described hiking shoes he claimed to have worn when he kicked in the door, saying he'd thrown them into a farm field after the crime. A farmhand who'd worked the field told investigators that he'd seen one such shoe as he turned over soil that spring. And Dugan said he bought the shoes at Fayva, which carried shoes of the type that had left the print.

As Cisowski's investigation continued, moreover, the case against Buckley suffered a devastating blow when the nation's leading shoeprint expert, William Bodziak, of the FBI, issued a report concluding that Buckley's shoe couldn't have made the print on the Nicarico door.

As evidence continued to pile up corroborating Dugan's claim that he—and he alone—had killed Jeanine Nicarico, Tom and Pat Nicarico grew angry and resentful, stoutly maintaining that the original three defendants were guilty.

For a year after the crime, they'd hoped that their daughter's killer or killers would be caught and indicted. For another year, they'd hoped that the young men who were indicted would be convicted. They'd attended every pretrial hearing, every day of the trial, every day of the death penalty hearings, and every day of the pretrial motions for Buckley's scheduled second trial.

When Cisowski began investigating Dugan's claims, they'd been supportive. "Early on, the Nicaricos thought I was the greatest thing since sliced bread because I was putting another guy on death row," Cisowski would recount years later. But they soon realized that if Dugan's story were accepted as part of a plea bargain, the original defendants would be freed and Dugan would get only a life sentence—meaningless because he already was serving two of those. "Once the Nicaricos found out there was no death row," said Cisowski, "everything changed."

In early 1987, State's Attorney Jim Ryan faced a tough choice. Should he drop the charges against Buckley? Should he move to free Hernandez and Cruz?

If ever there was a time when Ryan could walk away from the case, this was it.

That option, however, wasn't hazard-free. He'd carefully cultivated an image as a committed crime-fighter, and opening jail and prison doors wouldn't fit that image. Even though the case had been initiated by his predecessor, Ryan would have some explaining to do. How could he defend the decision to use Louise Robbins as an expert witness? How could he explain the county's failure to pursue Dugan initially—before he went on to rape and kill Donna Schnorr and Melissa Ackerman?

Ryan also had to consider the sheriff's office and the Nicarico family. If he accepted Dugan's story as true, how could Cruz have made the vision statement, including information that, supposedly, only someone involved in the crime would know? And the Nicaricos knew how the news media worked. They could make quite a splash if they ripped Ryan publicly for changing course, making him look like an inept politician who'd blown the biggest case in the history of DuPage County.

As Ryan pondered the predicament, Judge Robert Nolan, who had taken the Buckley case over from Kowal, gave the prosecution a tremendous boost when he held that the jury wouldn't learn of Dugan's "totally unreliable" statements. "For a while, he has been Mr. Big," said Nolan. "Maybe that's why he said what he did. He certainly has been the center of attention. Maybe if he could throw a monkey wrench into the case, he would be an even bigger Mr. Big. Whatever his motives, it is clear he was fabricating. . . . Perhaps he was gratifying some impulse or need. . . . Perhaps this was his idea of fun."

Ryan decided to proceed with the Buckley retrial, even though the case was incredibly weak, resting as it did principally on Louise Robbins's testimony, which the FBI had thoroughly discredited. But on the opening day of the trial—September 19, 1986—after jury selection had begun, the prosecution produced an astounding surprise—a jailhouse informant was prepared to testify that he'd heard Buckley admit the crime.

Buckley's lawyers, Carol Anfinson and Gary Johnson, moved for a continuance so that they could investigate and interview the informant, who was then in prison in Indiana. Judge Nolan could hardly deny the request.

He aborted the trial, dismissing the prospective jurors. Johnson went to interview the informant, and concluded that he wouldn't be a problem—he couldn't identify Buckley. Thus, at the next hearing before Nolan on November 12, Anfinson and Johnson said they were ready for trial. That surprised Nolan, who'd expected them to ask for more time.

Illinois law guarantees a defendant in custody a trial within 120 days, not counting time that lapses during continuances requested or agreed to by the defense. Given the long history of the Buckley case, it wasn't clear how much time remained. Nolan asked Anfinson and Johnson to calculate it, but they refused. To do so would waive the issue on appeal. Nolan angrily ordered Anfinson and Johnson shackled and jailed for contempt of court. They sat in jail until Anfinson's husband arrived to post bond, which Nolan had set at one thousand dollars each. Although the speedy-trial issue remained unresolved, the case continued to move slowly, dragging on for months.

On February 22, 1987, Louise Robbins's technique for evaluating shoewear patterns was discussed at the annual convention of the American Academy of Forensic Science by a panel including three anthropologists, two criminologists, and a judge—all of whom agreed that her method was unsound.

Meanwhile, Anfinson and Johnson had filed a motion to dismiss the charges against Buckley, accusing Ryan's assistants of a pattern of misconduct, including having withheld the fact that—before the shoeprint evidence had been sent to Robbins—the DuPage County shoeprint expert, John Gorajczyk, had concluded that the print on the door hadn't been left by Buckley's shoes.

On March 5, the day the motion to dismiss was to be argued, prosecutors dropped all charges against Buckley, and he was freed, three days short of the third anniversary of his arrest. At a press conference, Jim Ryan said the charges were dropped primarily because Louise Robbins had been stricken with cancer and was too ill to testify. "In the original trial, the testimony of Dr. Robbins, that the boot print found on the front door of the Nicarico home was that of the defendant Buckley, was critical to the state's case against him. Without that testimony, the evidence [is] insufficient to proceed to trial."

Ryan added, "Today's action was in no way influenced by the statements attributed to Brian Dugan. Those statements have been judicially determined to be unreliable, and I concur with that finding. Likewise, today's action has no bearing on the convictions of Cruz and Hernandez. Today's decision to [dismiss] the case against Stephen Buckley is necessitated by the current state of the evidence. In the absence of sufficient evidence, it is my duty to dismiss the prosecution."

The Nicaricos also held a press conference. "I'm frustrated with the state's attorney's office," Pat Nicarico told reporters. "I just watched the case disintegrate in the last two years. . . . It didn't seem like they were doing much to make the case stronger."

Five weeks later, the Nicaricos held another press conference, this time to charge that the accurate details of the crime Dugan had provided had been fed to him through a conspiracy that might have involved the state police—implicitly Ed Cisowski—and defense lawyers. "It's a pretty darn good story that matches the facts pretty well," Tom Nicarico said. "But for [the first] three weeks, it didn't match the facts. Somebody has been helping him fabricate a story."

Prosecutors knew full well that Cisowski was being unfairly maligned, but said nothing. The truth, which wouldn't emerge until years later, was that Dugan's public defender had met with two of Jim Ryan's top assistants—Robert Kilander and Patrick King—on November 13, 1985, two days before Cisowski was assigned to the case, and related some of the same facts that the Nicaricos were accusing Cisowski of feeding Dugan.

On January 19, 1988, the Illinois Supreme Court reversed the convictions of Hernandez and Cruz and remanded their cases for separate trials on the ground that their constitutional right to confront witnesses had been violated by trying them together. Although Hernandez's name had been redacted from Cruz's statements, the court said, it was obvious that some of the references were to him. And even though Hernandez had never mentioned Cruz's name, the redaction of his statements "rendered it impossible for the jury to conclude" that he was referring to someone other than Cruz.

While the retrials were pending, the DNA forensic age was just dawning and, in April 1989, blood samples from Dugan, Buckley, Cruz, and Hernandez were submitted to the nation's leading forensic geneticist, Edward T. Blake, for comparison with semen recovered from Jeanine Nicarico. At this early stage of its development, DNA technology couldn't link one sample to another with certainty. Rather, it could only divide genetic profiles into categories. As it turned out, the profile of the semen recovered in the case fell into a category that included roughly 10 percent of the population. Neither Hernandez's nor Buckley's DNA fell into that category, but Dugan's did—and Cruz's was close enough that it wasn't possible to exclude him.

If Dugan hadn't raped Jeanine—as the prosecution had recently argued in pretrial hearings in the Buckley case—it would have to be only happenstance that, against ten-to-one odds, his DNA was in the same category as that of the semen. Other than that, however, the test results weren't edifying. The prosecution had never contended that all three of the original defendants—or any of them, for that matter—had raped Jeanine. The possibility had always been left open that someone else, someone unknown, had been involved in the crime; the semen could have come from such a person.

The centerpieces of the cases against Cruz and Hernandez, as at the first trial, remained the words attributed to them by the authorities—Cruz's purported vision statement and Hernandez's assertion, in his conversation with Armindo Marquez at the DuPage County Jail, that he'd held Jeanine down.

At Cruz's retrial, Detective Vosburgh, who'd reported the vision statement just before the first trial, added a detail he hadn't mentioned before— that before they and Detective Kurzawa called Tom Knight, they'd called their supervisor, James Montesano, and he'd instructed them to call Knight. The defense could have called Montesano, or even Knight, but if they corroborated the detectives' claims it would have only made matters worse.

Dugan offered to testify at the retrials, but only if guaranteed immunity from the death penalty. He was called to the stand in both cases, but, because Jim Ryan wouldn't agree to immunity, refused to testify, citing his Fifth Amendment right against self-incrimination.

The prosecution was no longer contending that Dugan hadn't been involved in the crime—but only that he hadn't acted alone. The prosecution, in fact, had come up with a new informant—Robert Turner, a death row inmate—who claimed that Cruz had admitted committing the crime with Dugan and Hernandez. Cruz, Turner testified, "told me they raped her, and after they got done, they drug her out to the car and Cruz told me, you know, they beat her in the head and killed her with a crowbar. . . . I remember him telling me that it was a shame he had to kill her, because it was the tightest little white bitch [he'd] ever had."

At the Hernandez retrial, the prosecution came up with yet another surprise—the testimony of two deputy sheriffs, Thomas Bentcliff and Howard Keltner, who claimed that when Hernandez was booked at the DuPage County Jail three years and nine months earlier, he'd admitted taking part in the crime. Neither deputy had filed a report at the time, but now claimed to recall Hernandez's exact words. "I didn't hurt anybody," Bentcliff quoted Hernandez as saying. "I just went [to the Nicarico home] to do a burglary."

Keltner testified he'd heard Hernandez say, "I went there to get money for drugs."

Both retrials ended in guilty verdicts, Cruz's on February 1, 1990, just three and a half weeks short of the seventh anniversary of the crime, and Hernandez's, after one mistrial, on May 16, 1991. Cruz again was sentenced to death, Hernandez to eighty years.

On March 6, 1992, beneath a banner headline, the *Chicago Sun-Times* reported a stunning development:

> A deputy to Illinois Attorney General Roland W. Burris quit Thursday because Burris refused to tell the Illinois Supreme Court that the wrong men might have been convicted for the 1983 murder of Jeanine Nicarico.
>
> In an impassioned letter of resignation, Mary Brigid Kenney said Rolando Cruz and Alejandro Hernandez, both twenty-eight, were unfairly convicted of murdering the ten-year-old Naperville girl. Their trials, she said, "were infected by many instances of prosecutorial misconduct."
>
> . . . Kenney said she is convinced the real murderer is convicted child-killer Brian Dugan, thirty-five, [who] has claimed since 1985 that he was the killer.
>
> Assigned by Burris to represent the state in Cruz's appeal, Kenney urged Burris to "confess error."
>
> "I cannot sit idly as this office continues to pursue the unjust prosecution and execution of Rolando Cruz."

Kenney had been assigned to the case after another attorney in Burris's office who'd initially been assigned to it said she didn't want her name on the brief. After reading the record, Kenney realized why. When she raised her concerns with other attorneys in the office, they advised her to write a weak brief—and hope for the best.

The next day, Burris called a press conference and vowed to continue the appeal.

"It's not for me to look at the record and make a ruling," he said. "[A] jury has found this individual guilty and given him the death penalty. It is my role to see to it that [the conviction and sentence are] upheld. That's my job."

Four assistant attorneys general had no compunction about having their names on the Cruz brief, and when the case was argued on June 22, 1992, one of them, Terence M. Madsen, ended the state's presentation with a standard request that the court "set a date certain for the execution of Rolando Cruz."

The following December 4, a divided Supreme Court affirmed the conviction. "The evidence adduced at trial implicating the defendant in the murder of Jeanine Nicarico was overwhelming," Justice James D. Heiple wrote for the four-to-three majority. "The State's case consisted of physical evidence linking defendant with the crime as well as testimony by several persons that defendant confessed to varying levels of involvement."

In fact, there had been no physical evidence linking Cruz to the crime, and Heiple's claim that there was dazed Lawrence C. Marshall, Cruz's lead appellate attorney. "It was just unbelievable," Marshall said later. "It was so hard to fathom. I never, ever had seen a case in which a judge made up devastating lies like that."

On December 7, three days after the Cruz opinion came down, the composition of the Illinois Supreme Court changed. Three new justices were sworn in, replacing two who'd been in the majority and one who'd been in the minority on the opinion. Given the backgrounds of the new justices, one appeared likely to support the majority opinion and one seemed likely to support the minority, but the third, Mary Ann G. McMorrow, might change the outcome by voting on Cruz's behalf.

McMorrow's swearing-in gave Lawrence Marshall a realistic chance of winning a rehearing in the case. Petitions for rehearing, although routine, are rarely granted. And, in the Cruz case, given that the reputations of Roland Burris and Jim Ryan were at stake, Marshall was painfully aware that political considerations were likely to overshadow the legal issues.

Consequently, he persuaded deans of six of the nine law schools in the state and twenty-four major religious leaders, including Chicago Catholic Archbishop Joseph Cardinal Bernardin, to file friend-of-the-court briefs in support of the Cruz petition for rehearing.

"The specter of Rolando Cruz's execution on the basis of the court's current opinion cannot help but erode the moral force of the law and the public's confidence in our criminal justice system," said the religious leaders' brief. "The planned execution . . . is fundamentally inconsistent with the requirement that only the clearly guilty be subjected to the ultimate penalty."

The court granted the rehearing, holding arguments on June 22, 1993—the anniversary of the original hearing. As Marshall addressed the justices, Heiple didn't look at him, staring instead at the ceiling. McMorrow asked several questions, focusing—disquietingly for Marshall—on the points Brian

Dugan had gotten wrong. The hearing took a positive turn, however, when Chief Justice Ben Miller, who'd dissented from the first opinion, asked Terence Madsen whether there was any physical evidence linking Cruz to the crime. It was a direct confrontation of Heiple. After a pause, Madsen acknowledged that there wasn't, despite the earlier opinion's assertion to the contrary.

While the court pondered the case, *Chicago Tribune* columnist Eric Zorn launched an intermittent series of columns focusing on the dubious testimony of the DuPage County detectives who claimed to have heard Cruz's so-called vision statement. Noting that the officers hadn't bothered to make a contemporaneous record of the alleged statement, Zorn chided, "Hey, it could have happened, right? The biggest break in the biggest murder case in DuPage County history could have slipped through the cracks for a year and a half." Zorn also blasted the prosecutors' reliance on jailhouse snitch testimony, asking rhetorically, "Is there a jailhouse snitch out there so vile and nakedly opportunistic that DuPage prosecutors would be embarrassed to put him on the witness stand?"

Justice McMorrow, alas, didn't see it that way—but it didn't matter. When the court issued its opinion on July 14, Bastille Day, one of the other new justices, John L. Nickels, joined with Ben Miller and two other justices to overturn the conviction.

In dissent, McMorrow wrote, "The record demonstrates that the defendant did receive a fair trial." Heiple, writing separately, declared that Dugan's admissions were "unquestionably false" and branded the six law deans who'd filed a friend-of-the-court brief a "questionable cabal," adding, "The twenty-four religious leaders who combined to use their names in a joint appeal to this court, even when considered collectively, do not have the knowledge of this case which is possessed by even one of the jurors who heard the testimony and received the evidence at the trial."

At the prospect of Cruz's third trial, Heiple concluded, ominously, "Even an acquittal is a possibility."

In November 1994, Jim Ryan was elected to succeed Roland Burris, who'd resigned as attorney general to run, unsuccessfully, for governor.

After the reversal of Cruz's second conviction, Assistant State's Attorney Joseph Birkett had met with a prospective new informant, Stephen Schmitt, a former DuPage County Jail prisoner who claimed that Cruz had admitted committing the Nicarico crime with Dugan and Hernandez.

Tom Breen, a former prosecutor whom Lawrence Marshall had recruited to lead Cruz's defense, didn't believe for a moment that Cruz had made any such admission. Nine years earlier, when Dugan arrived at the Joliet Correctional Center, other prisoners taunted him and dumped feces on him. Two years after that, Dugan was stabbed nine times by a prisoner who said he was offended by the nature of Dugan's crimes. So, even if Cruz were guilty, Breen thought, the last thing he'd do was tell another prisoner he'd been involved in the rape and murder of a little girl.

Breen sent an investigator to interview Schmitt, who admitted he'd lied— that Cruz hadn't told him anything. Schmitt signed an affidavit saying that sheriff's officers had threatened to send him back to jail if he didn't go along with what they wanted him to say.

While the recantation was embarrassing, the essential, albeit dubious, element of the prosecution case remained intact—Cruz's alleged vision statement. Yet, at the first two trials, neither side had called James Montesano, now a sheriff's lieutenant, to ask whether Detectives Thomas Vosburgh and Dennis Kurzawa really had told him about the statement, as they had testified.

It seemed to Breen and Marshall that there must have been a reason that Montesano hadn't testified. Could it be that the prosecution hadn't called him because he wasn't willing to lie? Montesano had a reputation as a straight-shooter. But what if he'd told the prosecutors, in effect, don't call me, but if push comes to shove, I'll stick with your story? In the latter event, calling him to testify could be devastating for the defense, but Breen decided to take the risk.

When Montesano took the stand at a pretrial hearing before Judge Ronald Mehling on August 31, 1995, Breen's worst fear was realized—Montesano testified that Vosburgh had called him at home and told him about the vision statement.

As the trial neared, though, there was good news for the defense. DNA testing had become much more discerning since it was originally done prior to the Cruz and Hernandez retrials. And on September 21, Edward Blake, the forensic geneticist who had performed the prior testing, reported that testing with the latest technology had positively excluded Cruz as the source of the semen recovered from Jeanine Nicarico. Dugan, however, was a match—and the chance was only three in ten thousand that the semen could have come from anyone else.

Of course, the DNA results didn't eliminate the possibility, as the prosecution was now contending, that Cruz had been involved in the abduction and murder, but not the rape.

During the second week of the trial, the prosecution made a belated disclosure of a document favorable to the defense. It was a memorandum stating that Montesano, who had previously testified that Vosburgh had called him at home to tell him about the vision statement, hadn't in fact been at home on May 9, 1983, the date of the purported call. He'd been on vacation in Florida.

The solid wall of prosecutors and sheriff's deputies who had steadfastly clung to their stories of what happened during their investigation had cracked.

The next day, November 3, 1995, Montesano, looking pale and extremely nervous, took the stand and said he'd been mistaken when he testified in August that he'd received the call.

Judge Mehling called a thirty-minute recess, after which he returned to the bench.

"Is there any physical evidence in connection with this case, anything at all, that connects this hideous crime to Mr. Cruz?" said Mehling. "Anything? Fingerprints, blood spots, blood, DNA, hair, fibers, clothes, something left there, something taken from the home that he had? Anything? Anything at all? Any item? There is none. There is absolutely none."

Then he concluded, "I'm sure the defense and the state realize what actually occurred here today. It was devastating. It was unique in the annals of criminal justice. . . . Did Cruz make the [vision] statement? I don't think I need to answer that, because I'm going to enter a finding of not guilty and he will be discharged today. Case is closed."

Five days after his acquittal, Cruz appeared at a forum at Northwestern University School of Law and apologized for the lies he'd told during the initial investigation.

"I'm real sorry I ever lied," he said. "I was just a smart-ass kid off the streets. That's the honest-to-God truth. It's hard to sit up here and admit this, but it's true. I didn't have respect for the law because they didn't have respect for me or my people when I was out there. I'm sorry to the Nicaricos that I ever lied and allowed myself to get caught up. I'm sorry the police did it to them, too."

On November 21, 1995, best-selling novelist and former Assistant U.S. Attorney Scott Turow, who'd taken on Hernandez's defense, secured his client's release bond. Finally, on December 8, the prosecution dropped the charges against Hernandez.

"I've always been innocent of my charges," a teary-eyed Hernandez told reporters. "I want to say that I just want to go home and be with my family now. . . . You know, we're going to celebrate Christmas together like a family should."

Epilogue

Judge Ronald Mehling called for an investigation of the police and prosecutorial misconduct in the case, and Judge Edward Kowal, who'd become the chief judge of DuPage County, responded by appointing a special prosecutor. On December 12, 1996, the special prosecutor, William J. Kunkle Jr., announced the indictments of three detectives, a jailer, and three assistant state's attorneys. On May 13, 1999, Judge William A. Kelly dismissed the charges against two of the prosecutors. Four of the remaining defendants were acquitted by a DuPage County jury on June 4 and the fifth, who'd waived a jury, was acquitted by Kelly.

On September 26, 2000, the DuPage County Board approved a $3.5 million settlement of civil claims brought by Cruz, Hernandez, and Buckley.

On November 29, 2005, more than two decades after Brian Dugan's initial confession, State's Attorney Joseph Birkett announced that a DuPage County grand jury had indicted Dugan for the Nicarico murder. As he had from the beginning, Dugan offered to plead guilty in exchange for immunity from the death penalty. But, intent on pursuing a death sentence, Birkett refused. The case was pending as this anthology went to press.

EUGENE EARL DYKES

Hoping for a break, he feigned knowledge of a ghastly crime

PAUL EDDY

EL PORTAL, CALIFORNIA

Approached from San Francisco, there are several ways to reach Yosemite National Park. But in the winter, before the snows melt, the only recommended route is the freeway to Modesto, a short diversion to Merced, and then Highway 140, which twists and turns for eighty miles through Mariposa County until it reaches El Portal, the gateway to more than one thousand square miles of spectacular California wilderness. On the western outskirts of that tiny town, set alongside the Merced River in a valley of breathtaking beauty, there is a motel that bears no resemblance to the Bates Motel of Alfred Hitchcock's *Psycho*, except for the sheer horror of events that happened there.

On February 14, 1999, a Sunday, three women—Carole Sund, forty-two, her daughter Juli, fifteen, and Silvina Pelosso, a sixteen-year-old exchange student from Córdoba, Argentina—checked into the Cedar Lodge motel, paying just over two hundred dollars for two nights' stay. On Monday they explored Yosemite. That evening they ate supper in the motel's coffee shop and then retired to Room 509 to watch a video they had rented. Carole called her husband, Jens, to report that all was well. In the morning they were gone, as was their luggage and their rented car, an almost new Pontiac Grand Prix that was painted a strident red. There was no sign of disturbance in the room and the towels were damp, suggesting that they had showered.

They were never seen alive again (though many people thought they saw them over the next few days). Whatever terrible event had caused their disappearance, nothing suggested it had happened at Cedar Lodge—until, that is, March 5, almost three weeks after they vanished, when sheriff's deputies and FBI agents began making a series of arrests.

From "Murder Wore a Friendly Face," *Sunday Times Magazine* (London), November 21, 1999. Copyright © Sunday Times. Adapted with permission.

347

The first to be taken in was Billy Joe Strange, thirty-nine, a night cleaner at Cedar Lodge. Billy Joe, it emerged, had a criminal record for causing "great bodily injury and spousal abuse" and he was picked up for drinking a beer, a violation of his parole. The same day in Modesto, Eugene Earl Dykes, thirty-two, also was arrested for a parole violation—and now the pattern was emerging.

Dykes had spent most of his adult life in prison for sex, weapons, and drug offenses. His half-brother, Michael Larwick, forty-two (who was arrested after a fourteen-hour stand-off with police), had an even worse record, with convictions for, among other things, attempted manslaughter, kidnapping, rape, and "forcible oral copulation." Billy Joe's one-time roommate, Darrell Stephens, was arrested in El Portal for failing to register as a sex offender. So was Larry Duane Utley, forty-two, a giant of a man who was dragged naked from his house by the FBI.

Five more parolees also were picked up, and most of them, like the first five, had one more thing in common: they were "cranksters"—users or dealers of methamphetamine, the powerfully addictive stimulant made notorious by the outlaw motorcycle gangs of the 1960s who gave "crank" its street name by transporting it in the crankshafts of their Harley-Davidsons.

Encouraged by statements from the FBI, a terrifying scenario emerged: that Carole, Juli, and Silvina had fallen victim to a loose-knit gang of drug-crazed, violent ex-cons who sought out their victims in the isolated motels around Yosemite, aided, perhaps, by spotters like Billy Joe. The only comfort was the confidence of the FBI that the guilty men were now safely behind bars.

But what if the FBI was wrong?

After the snows were gone, after the fate of the three women had been determined but not explained, I arrived at Cedar Lodge to a hostile reception. They'd had enough of sheriff's deputies, federal agents, and nosy reporters invading their tranquil oasis, implying with their questions that something truly evil had happened at their motel.

In the car park, taking pictures of the red cedar cabins and their surroundings, I was approached by the motel's handyman, who, I now know, was Cary Stayner. He asked me to stop what I was doing and to leave them alone. He was a tall, athletic-looking man, but he was polite, not the least bit threatening; the very antithesis of a crankster. Even so, he made me edgy.

I had intended to spend the night at Cedar Lodge. But, unsettled by the encounter with Stayner, I set out on the long drive to Modesto, taking a route that led me past the thicket of poison oak where Juli's throat was cut and where her body was eventually found.

Standing on that spot, known as Moccasin Point, looking down on the broad reach of Lake Don Pedro, I pondered the curiosity that, for all of the FBI's public assurances, and though the cranksters had been in custody for weeks, none of them had been charged with the murders. Why not? I would like to claim that I realized then that the true killer was not behind bars, that, like the FBI, I had spoken to him and walked away. I would like to say I recognized a serial killer when I saw one. But, like the FBI, I was too naive.

On the evening of Wednesday, February 17, when Jens Sund called the highway patrol and the Mariposa County Sheriff's Office to report the trio missing, he could not shake their first assumption that he had had a fight with his wife and that she had gone off in a huff. To Jens, the notion was absurd. The last thing he'd done before Carole left, he said, was give her a Valentine's Day present. And whatever the state of their long relationship—they'd met in high school—she was an utterly devoted mother to Juli *and* their adopted children, who were waiting anxiously for her to come home.

If the authorities would not take Jens's alarm seriously, Carole's family certainly did. She was one of five siblings of the Carringtons, a northern California dynasty made wealthy through the development of shopping malls across America. In the small city of Eureka, where the Carrington Company has its headquarters, and near where Carole's parents maintain a four-hundred-acre timber and cattle ranch, the Carringtons have influence and means.

On Thursday, while Jens hurried back from Arizona and Carole's father set out at 4:00 A.M. to drive to Yosemite, a small army of volunteers traveled to Modesto to establish a search headquarters in the Sunrise Suite of the Holiday Inn. Wearing T-shirts emblazoned with photographs of the missing women, they printed and distributed hundreds of flyers and posters appealing for information, generating a flood of calls to their bank of mobile phones and a wealth of publicity.

There were dozens of reported sightings of the three women in their distinctive car, and the following morning, at a busy crossroads just a mile from the Holiday Inn, a student on her way to high school found an insert from Carole's wallet containing some of her credit cards. Here, finally, was evidence that something untoward had happened—or that was the view of FBI agents and, since kidnapping is a federal crime, the FBI had jurisdiction.

Yet it was not until the following Wednesday, a week after they were reported missing, and after the Carringtons had posted a reward of $250,000, that a comprehensive search and rescue operation was organized. Aircraft, ten FBI agents, thirty park rangers, and scores of deputies and police scoured Yosemite and the surrounding sierra as far as one hundred miles north of the park. They found nine abandoned cars, but there was no sign of the red Grand Prix or its occupants.

"Something has happened to them," said James Maddock, the FBI agent in charge of what was now a seven-agency task force devoted to what he christened the "Tournap" (for tourist kidnapping) case. "They're gone. They're victims." He warned their families to expect the worst.

So now it was a potential murder investigation and, going back to the beginning, FBI agents descended in force on Cedar Lodge to question all those who worked there, including Cary Stayner.

Interviewed by two agents on March 3, Stayner was amiable and calm and only sorry he couldn't help; he'd never seen the women, he said, and the agents believed him. They did not have the slightest suspicion that Stayner had bluffed his way into Room 509 on the night of February 15, claiming he needed to fix a leak in the roof; held the women at gunpoint; and bound them with duct tape. He had strangled Carole Sund and sexually assaulted Silvina Pelosso before strangling her, too. He carried the bodies to the car and hid them in the trunk, leaving Juli in the room, helpless but alive—for now.

It was Billy Joe Strange's violent criminal record that made him, rather than the clean-cut Stayner, the obvious suspect among Cedar Lodge's employees. Although Billy Joe denied ever seeing the women, his denial registered as a lie when he was strapped to a polygraph machine and asked, "Did you cause, or were you involved in any way with the disappearance of these three people?" And Eugene Dykes, with his appalling record and addiction to crank, perfectly fit the bill as Strange's accomplice. The investigators were convinced it must have taken more than one man to abduct three women and dispose of both their bodies and their car without leaving the slightest trace.

Dykes also protested his innocence, but he too failed a polygraph test when asked if he had harmed Silvina Pelosso. And when eventually questioned again and again, Dykes claimed his half-brother, Michael Larwick, had boasted of being involved in killing the women and had given Dykes some of their possessions.

Larwick did not come quietly. Pulled over in Modesto by a police officer on March 16 because the license plates of his car were out of date, he produced a semiautomatic pistol and fired ten shots. Then he broke into a nearby house and held off a SWAT (Special Weapons and Tactics) team for fourteen hours, until he was persuaded to surrender by thirty canisters of tear gas fired through the windows.

Unlike Dykes, Larwick would admit to nothing and stuck to his story, but evidence against the cranksters was steadily mounting. A teenage girl, a crank addict, was secretly taped by a police informant as she tearfully described how Dykes had admitted cutting the throats of the three women. Another addict reported that during a crank session two men had bragged to her of holding Juli prisoner in a house in Modesto, of force-feeding her methamphetamine, and of repeatedly raping her. More reliably, perhaps, the task force retrieved a ring that Larwick had given to a girlfriend, a ring that Juli's family was "ninety percent sure" belonged to her.

It seemed only a matter of time before the task force would build a murder case strong enough to take before a federal grand jury—if, that is, they could find the bodies and the car.

Back on the night of February 15 in Room 509, Cary Stayner had sexually assaulted Juli Sund on one of the beds, but still he did not kill her. Instead he wrapped her in one of the motel's dark pink blankets and carried her to the car, placing her in the trunk on top of the bodies of her dead mother and friend. Then he returned to the room to pack their belongings. He rumpled the beds to make them look slept in, and he dampened the towels to make them look used. Then he departed, taking their luggage and leaving the room key on the table.

It probably took him about an hour to drive the forty miles to Moccasin Point. He took Juli out of the trunk and forced her down a steep incline and cut her throat so deeply she was almost decapitated.

Stayner would have dumped the car and its grisly cargo in a nearby reservoir but, as he approached the boat ramp he intended to use, he saw an early-morning fisherman on the bank. He doubled back to Moccasin Point and then headed north, for another thirty miles, into what used to be gold country. Near a dot on the map called Long Barn, he found a disused logging road and drove the car as far along it as it would go.

After walking a mile and a half to the nearest village, Stayner called the Courtesy Cab Company in nearby Sonora and ordered a taxi to take him to Yosemite Lodge, the main tourist center for the park. From there, he took a bus to the motel and returned to Room 509. Worried that he might have left traces of hair or fluids on the bedspread during the assaults, he changed the bedding.

Stayner would later say that the hue and cry set off by the Carringtons alarmed him. He had not expected the flow of people who arrived at Cedar

Lodge asking questions. He said he spent most of the week in his room above the coffee shop, losing fifteen pounds through anxiety.

But he evidently lost none of his cunning. Two days after abandoning the Grand Prix, he returned to the disused road, driving his own pickup truck, and set the car on fire. First, however, he retrieved Carole's wallet, drove to Modesto and dropped it in the street, hoping to mislead the investigators.

And sometime in mid-March, as the task force's crankster theory gained public momentum, and the search got nowhere, he tore a page from a spiral notebook and wrote a taunting letter to the FBI's Modesto office, saying where Juli's body could be found. To provide a DNA sample that could never incriminate him, Stayner persuaded an unwitting acquaintance to lick and seal the envelope. He was over his anxiety, and the urge to kill again was building—an urge to bind and hurt women that he says he nurtured for thirty years, since he was seven.

In late March, Mary Ellen Geist, a radio reporter from San Francisco who was covering the story, stayed at Cedar Lodge and, late at night, encountered Stayner in the motel's hot tub. Their conversation was friendly, but something about the handyman gave her "the creeps." She suddenly excused herself and ran up the steps to her room, double-bolted the door, and pushed a table and chairs against it. Given what was to happen, her intuition may have saved her life.

Growing ever more frustrated at the lack of solid leads, the Carringtons offered a second reward. The first had carried the caveat that it would be paid for "information leading to the safe return" of the three women. Accepting now that the reward could never be claimed on that basis, they offered fifty thousand dollars to whoever found the car.

On March 18 the reward became due to a hiker who came across the Grand Prix by chance. It was no longer red—the fire had been sufficiently intense to remove all of the paint, leaving a shell that already had begun to rust. The task force sealed off the area around Long Barn, but did not open the trunk until the next day, when the FBI's Evidence Response Team arrived from Sacramento. The team found little to work with. Inside the trunk the two bodies were burnt beyond recognition, and it would be several days before they were positively identified through dental records as the remains of Carole and Silvina. Everything in the car had been destroyed, but lying on the ground nearby, untouched by the fire, was a roll of undeveloped film. All it provided was deeply poignant evidence of the lives that had been taken: Carole's pictures of two happy teenage girls in Yosemite, just hours away from annihilation.

The dramatic announcement that the car and two corpses had been found, but that the third body was still missing, must have puzzled Stayner, for it was Juli he wanted them to find. He had mailed his taunting letter to the FBI three days before, not mentioning the car. But the letter had gone astray in the mail and took nine days to reach the Modesto bureau, so it was not until the morning of March 25 that the Evidence Response Team carefully approached the thicket on Moccasin Point.

Now, at last, the task force had something to work with—a crime scene that had not been destroyed by fire, with its forensic clues intact, of which the most promising were tiny fibers found on and near Juli's body. To the huge satisfaction of the members of the task force, but not to their surprise, the FBI laboratory in Washington, D.C., concluded that these threads were microscopically identical to fibers found on a jacket belonging to Eugene Dykes, to fibers found in his Jeep, to more fibers found in his half-brother's car, and yet more fibers found in a car belonging to another of the cranksters.

Confronted with this evidence, Dykes confessed—sort of. His story changed constantly. At first he stuck to the line that he had merely taken the women's possessions. Then he admitted transporting the bodies. And finally he confessed to slashing Carole Sund's throat on "a remote mountain top." He agreed to show agents where that murder supposedly took place and he was taken out of jail several times to be driven around the sierra, but he never found a spot that "looked familiar." And, crucially, he could never provide the "how, when, and where" detail that the task force had held a close secret. Without corroboration his confession was worthless.

None of the cranksters was charged, though they all remained in jail on various unrelated charges while the task force continued the painstaking work of building a case against them. In May, FBI agents returned to Cedar Lodge, hoping to establish that the fibers found on Juli's body came from a blanket in which, they surmised, she might have been wrapped. They intended to seize every dark pink blanket in the motel, which meant gaining access to all 206 rooms. The amiable, ever-helpful Stayner unlocked the doors and helped the agents collect the evidence.

Stayner killed again on a Wednesday evening in late July. He drove his powder-blue, twenty-year-old pickup truck from Cedar Lodge to Yosemite, where he chanced upon Joie Ruth Armstrong, twenty-six, a naturalist employed by the park. She was going to and from her cabin, packing her car for a trip when Stayner attacked her. Judging by her injuries, she fought ferociously, but at five feet two and 110 pounds she was almost a foot shorter than Stayner and little more than half his weight. He bound her with duct tape and assaulted her inside the cabin. She may have already been dead when he cut off her head.

Her headless body was discovered at lunchtime the next day, July 22, lying half-submerged in a stream. When that shocking news began to circulate throughout Yosemite, a park fireman reported seeing a powder-blue pickup near Joie's cabin the previous evening. Yosemite's law enforcement department broadcast a BOL (Be On Lookout) for the truck, which was spotted three hours later parked by the Merced River.

Park Ranger Bonnie Schwartz and Detective Kathi Sarno of the Mariposa County Sheriff's Department found Stayner on what passes for a beach, naked and smoking marijuana, sitting by a backpack in which they feared they might find Joie Armstrong's head. For once, Stayner was neither amiable nor cooperative. He refused consent for them to search his backpack, but the two women seized it anyway, promising they would not open it until they had obtained a search warrant.

Their fears turned out to be groundless. Joie's head was later found submerged in the stream, about forty feet from her body. But among the personal trivia Stayner had taken to the beach, they found a paperback copy of *Black Lightning*, a novel that vividly describes the career of a serial killer who terrifies Seattle, slashing his victims—always women—with knives and power saws. The twist in the tale is that after the supposed killer is caught, convicted, and executed, the killings continue. A parallel? With all of the task force's suspicions in the Tournap case on the cranksters, was Stayner acting out a deadly fantasy?

Stayner was interviewed Thursday evening, this time at Cedar Lodge. He denied being near Joie's cabin and gave a detailed account of his movements. But the FBI was suspicious and after the interview one of its agents surreptitiously photographed the tires of his truck. By the next morning they knew that the tire prints found at Joie's cabin matched the tires on Stayner's truck. The next morning they found the treads matched tracks at the cabin. By then, Stayner had fled.

The FBI was the lead agency in the task force and James Maddock, the agent in charge, called the shots. He ordered that the hunt for Stayner would remain a closely guarded secret. But there were deep divisions within the task force. Maddock was regarded by some of the local investigators as dour and imperious. Behind his back they called him "Mr. Personality." Disregarding his instructions, they leaked news of the manhunt to the media, and by Friday evening Stayner's face was plastered on television.

Within minutes of the first news bulletins the task force learned that Stayner—and his truck—were at the Laguna del Sol nudist resort near Sacramento. On Saturday morning, while Stayner was eating breakfast, FBI agents arrived and impounded his truck for forensic examination. They told him he was not under arrest, but he insisted on accompanying them to the Sacramento bureau. There he was told that if he insisted on staying he must be read his rights.

He waived his rights and proceeded to confess—in chilling detail—to the murder of Joie Armstrong and to the murders of Carole and Juli Sund, and Silvina Pelosso. Taken back to Yosemite, placed before an FBI video camera, he reconstructed precisely how he had killed Joie. He told the FBI where to find the two blood-stained knives he had used to kill Juli and Joie, and where to find the clothes he had worn when he murdered them. The detail he provided matched every secret the task force knew. He was adamant that in killing the Sunds and Pelosso, and in disposing of their bodies, he had acted entirely alone.

Stayner's confession profoundly shocked members of the task force. They could not understand how they had been so misled by their crankster theory, and some of them refused to believe—and still will not accept—that Eugene Dykes and his cohorts were not involved in the first three killings. On October 20, however, three months after his arrest, Stayner was the only one charged with the murders of Carole and Juli Sund and Silvina Pelosso.

Dykes's explanation for his false confessions was that he hoped to cut a deal with the FBI. Given his record, and California's "three strikes and you're out" law, even the parole violation was sufficient to keep him in prison for life. He says he believed that if he helped the task force "solve" the Sund-Pelosso murders, he might get a break, but they were ultimately too demanding. He says: "I told them, 'I gave you guys eighty stories. I don't have any more.'"

James Maddock, appearing at a nationally televised press conference, said he had asked himself "whether we could have done anything differently that might have prevented the murder of Joie Armstrong." His answer was no. In investigating the Sund-Pelosso murders, he said, the task force had done "everything that reasonably could have been done."

But Francis Carrington posed awkward questions: "Apparently somebody made a mistake, didn't they?" he asked. "Even with the limited information that came out, it wasn't right, was it?"

The Carringtons cope with their grief by airing it, granting interviews, appearing on national TV shows, attending memorial services, and sponsoring a foundation that helps other families whose loved ones are torn away from them in similar brutal circumstances.

Jens Sund, on the other hand, has withdrawn into a mist of denial, in the sense that he protects himself and his surviving three children from further hurt by blocking out the details. Until the bodies were found and the last flicker of hope extinguished, he barely left the search headquarters in Modesto. Once the bodies were found, he left without visiting the touching memorials that the volunteers erected at Long Barn and Moccasin Point. He does not follow developments, nor will he attend Stayner's trial. He says he will not dwell on what he cannot change.

Standing with me at the graveside in a cemetery in Eureka where the remains of Carole and Juli are buried together, he seems distanced, shell-shocked, as though he can not quite remember why we have gone there. His house is crowded with memories of them: a painting of his Carole and Juli dominates the living room; Carole's vast collection of porcelain figurines; family photographs seem to line almost every wall; notes and schedules that Carole wrote still on the fridge. He insists that he is not maintaining a shrine. He simply has not yet put things away.

Juli's small bedroom is almost as she left it. Her clothes still hang in the closet, her things cluttering the dressing table and the chest of drawers, the walls covered with posters, most of which she made. There is one that is almost unbearable to look at.

A little more than a year before Juli died, Karen Mitchell, a sixteen-year-old fellow student at Eureka High School, vanished from outside the food court at the Bayshore Mall. She was most certainly abducted and no trace of her has ever been found. There then followed a series of attacks on other students. Two of them, including Juli's best friend, were raped on their way home from school, and the fear and panic that ensued were profound. Juli did not panic. Rather, she formed a rape-awareness group and, mature beyond her years, spent hours counseling victims of the attacks. In her giant scrapbook, among the memorabilia of a typical teenager's life, there is pasted a letter from her best friend that describes in touching detail the importance of what she did.

The poster on the wall shows the two of them together beneath a promise: "BFF—Best Friends Forever." When the girls had that poster made, "forever" had only a few weeks to run.

Epilogue

Under an agreement with federal prosecutors allowing him to avoid a death sentence, Cary Stayner pled guilty to the Armstrong murder on September 13, 2000, and was sentenced to life in prison without parole. The following October 9, a Santa Clara County jury found him guilty of the Sund-Pelosso murders and recommended a death sentence for those crimes. Judge Thomas Hastings accepted the recommendation on December 12, and Stayner joined 616 other prisoners on California death row (where he remained when this book went to press).

Stayner's defense was insanity. Psychiatrists, relatives, friends, and acquaintances told the jury that he had a long history of psychiatric problems and had been sexually abused by an uncle who showed him child pornography. When he was two or three, he developed a chronic habit of pulling out large chunks of his hair. At seven, he began imagining violent images and hearing imaginary voices. His psychiatric problems were exacerbated at age eleven when his younger brother, Steven, was abducted by a pedophile. (Steven was held for seven years, before his release in 1980. Nine years later, Lorimar/NBC-TV aired a two-part movie entitled *I Know My First Name Is Steven* based on his experience. Steven was killed in a motorcycle accident the same year.) In 1990, the uncle who had molested Cary was shot to death in the Stayner home, a crime that was never solved. Five years after that, Cary suffered a breakdown after fantasizing about burning down a glass shop where he worked and murdering his employers. He was taken to a psychiatrist, but he soon began skipping group therapy and stopped taking his medication. A positron emission tomography (PET) scan in 2000 detected brain abnormalities consistent with schizophrenia, psychotic disorder, and obsessive compulsive disorders.

The prosecution case rested on his tape-recorded confessions, which, unlike those of Eugene Earl Dykes, comported with the facts of the crimes. Before he confessed, the jury learned, Stayner had asked his FBI interrogators to show him child pornography. "It's sick, disgusting, perverted," he said. "I know that." Agents rejected the request, but before doing so asked him to state one fact that only the killer would know about the Sund-Pelosso murders. He responded by telling them about the anonymous note he had sent to the FBI with a map leading to Juli Sund's body. Then, without renewing the child-porn demand, he proceeded to describe each murder in chilling detail. When the tapes were played in the courtroom, the forty-one-year-old defendant covered his ears with his hands and closed his eyes. In the hope of undermining the power of the confessions, his attorney, Marcia Morrissey, sought to introduce Dykes's confessions, but Judge Hastings would not allow it.

There was no official inquiry into the circumstances that led to Dykes's false admissions.

PRETENSE

It is hardly unheard of for innocent men and women to come forward and falsely confess to crimes they were not suspected of committing. In fact, criminal pretenders abound, particularly in high-profile cases. Hundreds came forward in the Lindbergh kidnapping case, the Hollywood "Black Dahlia" murder, and the Simpson/Goldman murders.

Mental health experts say the pretenders' motives are elusive but no doubt varied—ranging from cravings for notoriety, to extreme guilt over something unrelated, to delusional beliefs that they had actually committed the crimes.

Because confessions of this sort occur with considerable frequency, they are not regarded as newsworthy, and thus individual examples rarely come to public attention. There are, however, exceptions, one of the most well-publicized being John Mark Karr's claim that he had been with Jon-Benét Ramsey when she died.

Also in the volunteer category, innocent persons occasionally come forward for the ostensible purpose of helping the authorities solve crimes and then either wind up confessing to the crimes or making statements that the authorities construe as confessions.

One such person was Laverne Pavlinac, who, in an ill-conceived and vindictive attempt to implicate her abusive boyfriend in a murder, wound up inculpating not only him but also herself. Both were convicted of the murder, which actually had been committed by a serial killer—as authorities were chagrined to discover five years later.

The bizarre stories of John Mark Karr and Laverne Pavlinac follow.

JOHN MARK KARR

A confession as confounding as JonBenét's murder itself

ALEX TRESNIOWSKI

BOULDER, COLORADO

It started with a stunning phone call: there was a new suspect in the case. Patsy Ramsey, her cancer spreading, her strength sapped, boarded a plane to Colorado last February and, with her husband, John, went to see Boulder County District Attorney Mary Lacy. There had been other suspects, and even a number of false confessions, but this time was different: this suspect seemed to know undisclosed details of the crime scene.

The Ramseys, who for many years had lived with widespread public perception that they might have been involved in or knew more than they were saying about the crime, left the meeting with Lacy feeling hopeful. "That trip to Boulder was very hard for Patsy physically," says her close friend Suzanne Goebel. "She came back, and the tumors in her brain were diagnosed, and it went downhill from there. But somehow she talked her body into not dying until she was pretty sure they had the killer. I think she concluded in her head and heart that this time they have the right one."

But do they? Just two months after Patsy Ramsey died of ovarian cancer and four months shy of the tenth anniversary of the murder of JonBenét Ramsey came electrifying news: John Mark Karr, a forty-one-year-old teacher with a history of bizarre behavior around children, had told police in Bangkok, Thailand, that the six-year-old had died at his hands in the basement of her Boulder, Colorado, home. But he also professed his love for her and calmly insisted that her death—she was strangled and suffered a skull fracture—was accidental.

The Ramseys "feel their daughter was brutally murdered, and she wasn't," Karr told a Thai official who spoke with *People*. "It looks like that but she wasn't. I want them to hear the truth. . . . I need closure and [JonBenét's] family needs closure . . . all of us have gone through enough pain."

Yet almost immediately there were troubling questions about Karr's strange confession. Not long after he was detained, U.S. investigators took a saliva swab from Karr to compare his DNA with that found in JonBenét's underwear and under her fingernails; the results of those tests have not been revealed. "Even as kooky as his confession was, if you pair it up with a DNA match, then it's game, set and match for the state," says former Denver prosecutor turned talk-show host Craig Silverman, an expert on the case. But without that, investigators will need to tie up a number of puzzling loose ends before one of the most infamous unsolved murders can, at last, be solved. John Karr "isn't normal, and he may even be a child molester," says Denver defense attorney Scott Robinson, who has followed the case from the beginning. "But at this point it's pretty hard to believe that he's a murderer who committed this particular murder."

Perhaps most puzzling of all is that Karr, the twice-married father of three teenage boys, has no apparent connection to the Ramsey family. Neither John nor Patsy had ever heard of him, and Boulder investigators did not have him on their radar until earlier this year, and then only after a University of Colorado journalism teacher who was corresponding with Karr brought him to their attention. What's more, Karr's second wife, Lara Knutson, thirty-three, says Karr spent Christmas Day 1996, the day before JonBenét's body was found, with her and their sons either at home in Alabama or with his family in Georgia.

So far, there is no proof to back that up, but "we've got a picture of his three children that was taken in his father's house on Christmas Day of 1996," says Georgia attorney Gary Harris, a spokesman for the Karr family. "The fact that his kids were there tells me he was there. His wife would not have come to the Christmas party without him." Karr was also known to be obsessed with the Ramsey case, reveling in its every detail. He was similarly fascinated by the 1993 murder of twelve-year-old Polly Klaas, even moving his family to her hometown of Petaluma, California.

Could he have confessed to a crime he didn't commit just to link himself to JonBenét? The idea that Karr killed her is "ridiculous," his brother Nate Karr, thirty-four, told *People*. "We have no hidden skeletons; there's nothing brutal in his background, nothing like that." Now the pressure is on Boulder officials to sort out fact from fiction in what in the past has been a horribly flawed investigation.

District Attorney Mary Lacy, who took over the case in 2002, admitted her investigation into Karr wasn't complete at the time he was picked up. So far, it's not clear if she has lined up basic evidence such as handwriting samples to match against the ransom note or proof that Karr was even in

Boulder at the time of the killing. At a press conference, Lacy suggested that Karr, who in 2001 was charged with possessing child pornography but had still recently managed to land three teaching jobs in Thailand, posed a serious safety risk, which would explain his sudden arrest.

The key evidence so far seems to be hundreds of e-mails Karr sent to journalism professor Michael Tracey, who produced three documentaries about the Ramsey case. In the e-mails, the Ramseys were told, Karr showed he knew things that "only people in the house or the killer would know," says Suzanne Goebel. "One was about a bracelet JonBenét had on and that Patsy evidently purchased and gave to her earlier in December." Boulder officials won't comment further, and the arrest warrant is under seal, but "I would be shocked if Mary Lacy made the decision to arrest this man on anything other than substantial evidence," says the Ramseys' friend and attorney Lin Wood. "The [arrest] document is eighty or ninety pages."

So is Karr a cold-blooded killer or just delusional? What's clear is that throughout his life he has struck many people as strange. His parents, Wexford and Patricia Karr, raised him in Georgia and divorced when Karr was nine. His mother, Karr once said, tended to raise him like a girl. Smaller and quieter than most boys, Karr went to live with his grandparents in Hamilton, Alabama, where "he was the neighborhood kid who wouldn't play with the rest of us," says Brenda Perham, who lived nearby. "We'd be in someone's yard and he'd come and sit with a book." The flip side to his shyness was an urge to stand out: When he was old enough to drive, Karr made the rounds in a DeLorean he painted fire-engine red. "He said, 'I don't want to blend in with everyone else,'" says Perham.

When he was nineteen, Karr married Quientana Shotts, then only thirteen; the marriage was soon annulled. Four years later, Karr took another young bride: Lara Marie Knutson, who was sixteen and pregnant with twins when she wed Karr in 1989. Karr insisted on delivering the twins himself in their home; the babies, named Angel and Innocence, died shortly after birth. In the next four years, the couple had three sons, John, Damon, and Seven Exodus.

In 1996 Karr began working as a substitute teacher at his alma mater, Hamilton High School, the first of more than a dozen teaching jobs in several states and at least three different countries, many of which ended with Karr being dismissed for erratic behavior. "He was scary," says one former student. "He had a very nice side, and if you forgot your lunch money he'd give you a dollar. But he was always yelling and he had a short fuse." At another school "there were reports that students were terrified of him," says a teacher. "One kid got so scared he wet himself."

After moving his family to Petaluma in 2000, apparently to get closer to the Polly Klaas case, Karr worked as a substitute teacher at a half-dozen elementary schools in the Bay Area. In April 2001 Napa County sheriffs summoned him from his classroom at Pueblo Vista Elementary School. He was arrested for possessing child pornography and served six months in jail before being released. "He was in correspondence with Richard Allen Davis [the man who murdered Polly Klaas] and that was disturbing," says Julia Freis, the former Sonoma County Deputy District Attorney who prosecuted Karr. "The whole case was strange and kind of twisted."

Karr lost his teaching credentials, and his wife filed for divorce and asked a judge to suspend Karr's visitation privileges. Karr soon skipped town, missing a court date relating to the child-porn charges and becoming a fugitive. But he wasn't done teaching young children. By 2004 he had turned up in Honduras, where he worked at two schools. In 2006 he taught at three schools in Thailand. A colleague at Bangkok Christian College says Karr "was famous for kicking chairs in class because the kids weren't picking up English fast enough."

A lax screening process for foreign teachers apparently wasn't the only thing that drew Karr to Thailand. Earlier this year he visited the Pruksa Laser Center to have his beard and sideburns removed. "He told me he was on medication to prepare for a sex change," says the center's Dr. Setthakarn Attakonpan. "He said, 'Don't take all of the hair, leave what a woman would have.'"

It was while he was out of the United States that Karr began his anonymous correspondence with Professor Tracey, whom he knew to be a strong advocate of the theory that an intruder killed JonBenét. According to the *Rocky Mountain News*, in one e-mail about JonBenét, Karr wrote, "I love you and shall forever love you. If there is to be a life for me after this one, I pray that it will be with you." Earlier this year, Tracey grew alarmed enough by something in an e-mail to contact the Boulder District Attorney's Office. Police then fooled Karr into thinking he was exchanging e-mails with Patsy Ramsey. On August 16, just a day after Karr began teaching at the New Sathorn International School in Bangkok, Thai police, acting on behalf of U.S. officials, picked him up in his apartment. During his interrogation, U.S. investigators brought up the Ramsey case, and Karr quickly confessed. According to Thai police, Karr admitted to having sex with JonBenét, but later insinuated he may have just kissed her.

On August 20, U.S. officials whisked Karr out of Bangkok on a commercial flight; during the fifteen-hour trip to Los Angeles, Karr ate the standard business-class meal of prawns and pâté and even sipped champagne. But once in Los Angeles he was locked in a six-by-nine-foot cell, where he awaited extradition to Colorado and formal charges in JonBenét's murder.

Ten years ago the Ramseys themselves were under an "umbrella of suspicion," as one law enforcement official put it, for the murder of JonBenét. Investigators made them the chief suspects after they quickly hired lawyers, refused police interviews for four months, and even engaged a publicist. Many saw their evasiveness as evidence they were involved, and they have never been officially cleared as suspects. But in 2003 Mary Lacy said, "the weight of the evidence is more consistent with the theory that an intruder murdered JonBenét." John Ramsey, in a statement, urged that Karr be spared "the type of media speculation that my wife and I were subjected to for so many years" until forensic tests are done. "John isn't getting all revved up about the arrest," says his friend Barney Way in Charlevoix, Michigan. "He's keeping level-headed, as always."

But with Karr's arrest, both John Ramsey and his son Burke, nineteen, will have to relive the horror of JonBenét's murder. Burke, a computer-programming major at Purdue University and a skateboarding whiz, was also once a suspect, particularly in the tabloids; he was officially cleared by the district attorney of any involvement. Today, if his sister's murder "does haunt him, he doesn't let it show," says a friend. "He tries to live like everybody else." Burke has been dating a college student he met in high school for a few years. "I asked him if he was excited [about Karr's arrest] and he said yes," says his friend. "But he didn't mention anything specific. He's learned not to say a whole lot."

Patsy Ramsey's sister Pamela Paugh says the accusations against the family have taken a heavy toll on them. "At one point or another, we all considered suicide," says Paugh. "Of course, John and Patsy thought about it at some point. But having a strong faith means you can stand in the fire." What the Ramseys need now, she says, is DNA evidence linking Karr to the murder: "JonBenét fought like a banshee. She tried to get that rope off her neck. She had somebody's DNA under her fingernails. And I'm a hundred percent certain that it belongs to the killer." But even if Karr's DNA isn't a match, says Paugh, "it doesn't mean he doesn't have intimate knowledge of the crime. Does he know who was there?"

Like so much about the murder of JonBenét Ramsey, the question of Karr's guilt or innocence may not be resolved quickly. "Closure in this case doesn't come with someone being arrested," says Lin Wood. "Closure for John and his family is when someone is found guilty in a court of law."

Epilogue

At a nationally televised press conference on August 28, 2006—after the foregoing story appeared, although six days before the cover date of the magazine—District Attorney Mary Lacy announced that DNA testing had absolved John Mark Karr of JonBenét Ramsey's murder. Lacy's announcement embarrassed handwriting experts who concluded that Karr had written the ransom note and an eyewitness who claimed to have seen Karr at the Boulder Greyhound station around the time of the crime. Lacy, of course, also drew a barrage of criticism for bringing Karr to the United States—he washed down giant shrimp with champagne on his business-class flight, courtesy of taxpayers—but she defended her action. "Frankly, it started out as a long shot," said Lacy. "We were always cautious and skeptical, but we could not ignore it." On July 9, 2008, Lacy announced that sophisticated DNA testing had absolved all close family members of the crime. "To the extent that we may have contributed in any way to the public perception that you might have been involved in this crime, I am deeply sorry," Lacy said in a letter to John Ramsey. "No innocent person should have to endure such an extensive trial in the court of public opinion."

LAVERNE PAVLINAC

She wasn't a suspect until she voluntarily implicated herself

PHIL STANFORD

WILSONVILLE, OREGON

On February 5, 1990, two weeks after twenty-three-year-old Taunja Bennett was raped and murdered, the Multnomah County Sheriff's Office received an anonymous telephone call. The caller said she'd overheard a man in a bar bragging that he had committed the crime. She gave the man's name, but it was misspelled in the report, and there was no follow-up by the sheriff's office.

A week later, she called the sheriff's office in adjacent Clackamas County and said the same thing. The victim's body had been found in Multnomah County, but the caller said the man was on probation in Clackamas County and she thought officers there might check him out. His name, correctly spelled, was Sosnovske—John Sosnovske.

The Clackamas County Sheriff's Office passed the information along to John Ingram, Multnomah County's lead investigator in the case. Ingram in turn called Steve Bracy, Sosnovske's parole officer. Bracy told Ingram that Sosnovske was a forty-three-year-old parolee with several DUI convictions and that the caller almost certainly had been his girlfriend, Laverne Pavlinac.

Pavlinac, who was eighteen years Sosnovske's senior, had lived with him off and on for about ten years. When Sosnovske drank, which violated the terms of his parole, he became abusive. Pavlinac then would call Bracy, urging him to come and take Sosnovske back to prison. Pavlinac also once called the FBI, claiming that Sosnovske was a bank robber depicted in a Crime Stoppers photo she'd seen. But the agent who took the call concluded, after a look at a photo of Sosnovske, that the tip wasn't worth pursuing.

At Ingram's request, Bracy called Pavlinac and asked her if she'd made the anonymous calls. When Pavlinac said she had, Bracy set up a meeting

From "The Happy Face Killer, a Five-Part True Crime Story," *The Oregonian*, May 22–26, 1994. Copyright © The Oregonian. Adapted with permission.

with her for the next morning at her apartment in Wilsonville. Pavlinac seemed a bit surprised when Ingram and Alan Corson, an Oregon State Police detective assigned to the case, arrived with Bracy. But she invited them inside, served them coffee, and told them what they had come to hear— later they would note how hospitable she was whenever they came to call.

She said that on February 1 or 2 she'd been with Sosnovske at J.B.'s Lounge, one of his favorite watering holes, which was at the Burns Brothers Truck Stop in Wilsonville. She excused herself to use the restroom and, when she returned, she heard Sosnovske say he'd "wasted" a woman. Sosnovske was confiding this to a man whose name Pavlinac didn't know. "I strangled her," Pavlinac quoted Sosnovske as saying, or maybe he said "We"—Pavlinac wasn't sure.

Based on Pavlinac's claim, Ingram and Corson obtained a search warrant for her home seeking items that might link Sosnovske to the crime— Taunja Bennett's missing purse and Sony Walkman, links of rope similar to that with which she had been strangled, and a piece of material that the killer had cut from her jeans. When the investigators returned with the warrant, Pavlinac was helpful, showing them where Sosnovske stored his personal possessions. Ingram and Corson found none of the items specified in the warrant, but they did find a shoe box containing a letter addressed to Sosnovske. On the back of the envelope, someone had written "T. Bennett—Good Piece."

Four days later, Pavlinac called Ingram and told him that in the trunk of her car she had found a purse that didn't belong to her. Not only was it a small black purse of the sort Bennett might have carried but inside it was a swatch of cloth that obviously had been cut from a pair of denim jeans. If the discovery seemed too good to be true, it was. Before the end of the day, Ingram and Corson were notified by the State Police Crime Laboratory that the piece of denim couldn't possibly have come from Bennett's jeans.

By then, however, Ingram and Corson had picked up Sosnovske and taken him to State Police Headquarters in Portland for questioning. He denied having anything to do with the murder. But at around 9:00 P.M.— after he had been in custody more than seven hours—he said something that seemed, in the minds of the investigators, to betray knowledge of the crime.

"At this time," Corson wrote in his report, "I asked Mr. Sosnovske to 'Give me a hypothetical answer.' I asked Mr. Sosnovske how he believed this homicide had occurred and what had happened to the victim's body. Mr. Sosnovske immediately stated, 'They took the body out to the gorge.' I asked Mr. Sosnovske, 'How did they do that?' He responded, 'in the car.'"

That much had been in the newspapers, but before the interrogation ended, almost eleven hours after it began, Sosnovske was telling the investigators that on the night of the murder he had gotten a ride home with a drinking buddy, Chuck Riley. "I believe I saw a body in the back of the car," Sosnovske allegedly said. "The body was wrapped in a blanket."

Ingram and Corson released Sosnovske, but not before arranging for Pavlinac to wear a recording device—a "wire," in the vernacular—hoping that alone with her he would say something more incriminating, which he didn't.

Within hours of Sosnovske's release, Pavlinac called Ingram and told him she wanted to change a few things about her story.

The next morning, Ingram and Corson returned to Wilsonville for a little talk with their star witness. When they confronted her with the phony pieces of evidence she'd tried to pass off, she readily acknowledged that the purse belonged to her daughter. And the piece of denim? She'd cut that from a pair of jeans belonging to one of her granddaughters. When asked if she had faked the evidence, she responded, "I wanted him caught. . . . I tried to make it easy so someone else would do it."

But now Pavlinac said she was ready to tell the truth about the death of Taunja Bennett. It wasn't true that Pavlinac had overheard Sosnovske bragging that he'd committed the crime. Rather, Pavlinac actually had seen the body.

The night of the crime, Pavlinac continued, she'd been at home watching television when Sosnovske called saying he was at J.B.'s—and he was in trouble. He told her to bring a blanket or plastic sheet to the truck stop. She did as he said and, when she arrived, she saw Sosnovske standing between two semi tractor-trailers. A woman was lying on the ground in front of him.

Pavlinac rolled down her window and asked, "What is wrong? Is she sick?"

"It's worse than that," Sosnovske replied. "She's dead."

Pavlinac had brought a shower curtain, onto which they placed the body. With Sosnovske in the back seat with the body, Pavlinac drove to the Columbia River Gorge in Multnomah County. On the way, Sosnovske cut a piece of material from Bennett's jeans, saying he wanted it as a souvenir. At the gorge, Sosnovske dragged the body into the woods as Pavlinac waited in the car. On the way back to town, they threw the shower curtain out the window.

After telling the new story, Pavlinac accompanied the investigators to the Burns Brothers Truck Stop, where she pointed to the precise spot where she said she'd seen Sosnovske standing over Bennett's body. Then they went to the gorge and she pointed to the spot where the body had been found, which was no secret—the *Oregonian* had reported the location and it was identified by bright red markers.

But, based on Pavlinac's evolving story, prosecutors in Washington County—where the truck stop was located—obtained a grand jury indictment charging Sosnovske with the murder of Taunja Bennett.

There were three problems with Pavlinac's confession. Two of them seemed fairly minor—crime laboratory technicians had found not a shred of evidence to corroborate the claim that a body had been transported in Pavlinac's car, and the shower curtain was nowhere to be found along the route Pavlinac claimed to have taken from the gorge back to Wilsonville.

The third problem, however, couldn't be easily dismissed. During the initial investigation of the crime, Multnomah County investigators had interviewed witnesses who on the night Taunja Bennett disappeared said they'd seen her partying at a tavern in the town of Gresham, a good twenty-four miles from J.B.'s Lounge at the Brothers Truck Stop. Neither Bennett nor Sosnovske had a car or, for that matter, a driver's license.

So how could Bennett have gotten to the truck stop? And weren't there witnesses who recalled seeing her there?

A week after Sosnovske's indictment, Ingram and Corson returned to Pavlinac's apartment to question her further, this time with a tape recorder.

"It's correction time," she told them—prefacing her third version of the murder of Taunja Bennett.

Now she said it wasn't true that when she arrived at the truck stop she'd found Sosnovske standing over the body. Rather, Sosnovske and Bennett were standing in the parking lot. They got into the car with her—Bennett in the back seat, Sosnovske in the front—and began to argue.

Pavlinac asked Bennett where she lived, planning to take her home. Bennett said she lived with her mother in northeast Portland, and Pavlinac headed north on Interstate 5. No sooner had they gotten under way when Sosnovske punched Bennett and said, "She's not going home." Sosnovske grabbed the steering wheel and forced Pavlinac to turn east onto Interstate 84.

In the gorge, they turned again, this time onto the scenic highway. They stopped at the old stone edifice, the Vista House. Sosnovske and Bennett went inside. Then Sosnovske came back alone, took a rope from the trunk of the car, and told Pavlinac to come with him. Inside the Vista House, Bennett was lying on the ground and moaning.

Sosnovske told Pavlinac to tie the rope around Bennett's neck and hold her down while he raped her. Pavlinac did as she was told, but closed her eyes so she wouldn't have to watch. "I hope I didn't kill her," Pavlinac now said. "I didn't plan to kill her. I was doing what I was told."

Suddenly the lack of an independent witness who could place Bennett at the truck stop was less of a problem. Now Ingram and Corson had something better—an accomplice.

On that basis—Pavlinac's third version of events—the pending Multnomah County indictment against Sosnovske was dismissed and he and Pavlinac were indicted in Washington County, where she said the murder had occurred.

Pavlinac's trial—their cases were severed because of their conflicting defenses—began on January 24, 1991, eleven months after she had implicated herself in the crime.

The principal prosecution evidence was her tape-recorded statement. She took the stand in her own defense, testifying that she had made the anonymous calls and fabricated the stories because she wanted to get away from Sosnovske because he'd been abusing her for ten years. When she had moved away, she told the jury, he had followed her, threatening to harm her children and grandchildren.

The jury didn't buy that, promptly returning a verdict of guilty.

Judge Robert W. Redding sentenced her to life in prison, with a minimum of ten years before she would be eligible for parole. Judge Redding said Pavlinac deserved some leniency because she had no criminal record and, when she became involved in the crime, had been under Sosnovske's influence.

Sosnovske, whose trial was set to begin the following week and who faced a possible death sentence, pleaded no contest to felony murder and kidnapping in exchange for a life sentence with a possibility of parole after fifteen years.

And that was the story of the case—except for one unsettling bit of information that had come to light. In the middle of Pavlinac's trial, police in Livingston, Montana, informed Oregon authorities that a custodian at the local Greyhound bus depot had discovered a disturbing message scrawled on the restroom wall.

"I killed Tanya Bennett Jan. 21, 1990, in Portland, Oregon," the message said. "I beat her to death, raped her, and loved it. Yes, I'm sick, but I enjoy myself too. People took the blame and I'm free." A few days later, a similar message was found in a restroom at a truck stop in Umatilla, Oregon. The messages were of no evidentiary value, since they were anonymous, and thus were not introduced at Pavlinac's trial.

But the messages became significant three weeks ago when the *Oregonian* received a handwritten letter from a person whom the newspaper deemed "the Happy Face Killer" because a smiling cartoon face appeared at the top of the first page of the six-page letter.

The writer, who used an odd mixture of capital and lowercase letters resembling the messages on the restroom walls, claimed to have raped and murdered five women, the first of whom was Taunja Bennett. "I want the world to know that it was my crime," said the letter. "It turned me on. I got high. . . . She was my first and I thought I would not do it again. But I was wrong. I went to truck driving school and learned to drive. While driving I learned a lot and heard of people that have gotten away with such a crime because of our nomad way of life."

The letter included details of the crime that were generally consistent with known facts of the Bennett crime. All of those facts were publicly known, but the descriptions of the other murders included details thought to be known only to investigators—and, of course, to the killer.

Murder number two: "On the way out of L.A. my mind went wild with the thought of a sex slave, and when I stopped at a rest area I took her. I taped her up and raped her again and again. I kept her for 4 days alive then I killed her and dumped her body about 7 miles north of Blythe on 95." In fact, on August 30, 1992, the body of an unidentified young woman had been found near Interstate 95 just outside Blythe, California, a small town east of Palm Springs near the Arizona border. The body was so badly decomposed that the cause of death could not be determined, but the victim had been bound with duct tape—a fact that had never been released.

Murder number three: "I stopped in Turlock, CA, rest area. A hooker became my next victim. This time I just strangled her right there without sex. She was in my truck only five minutes. . . . I dropped her body off behind the Blueberry Hill Cafe 10 miles south on 99. I placed her body in the dirt and stepped on her throat to make sure she was dead." Indeed, a body had been found at the location described and identified through dental records as that of a local prostitute.

Murder number four: "My next victim was a hooker I had used three weeks earlier. I summoned her on the C.B. She had a raincoat on. We went through the Normal procedure. . . . I felt so much power. I then told her she was going to die and slowly strangled her and dropped her off behind

GI Joe's in Salem [Oregon]. I put her against the fence under the black-berry vines and covered her with leaves." A woman's body covered with leaves was found there in November 1992. An autopsy determined that she had been strangled.

Murder number five: "I stopped at a rest area near Williams [in Santa Clara County, California] and had her. I put her body on or near a pile of rocks about 50 yards north of Highway 152 westbound, about 20 miles from Santa Nella." Detective Michelle Sandri of the Santa Clara County Sheriff's Department says there is no way anyone other than investigators and the killer would have known that the body found there, in July of 1993, was lying beside a pile of rocks.

Epilogue

In March 1995, ten months after publication of the *Oregonian* series from which the foregoing was adapted, the Happy Face Killer was identified as Keith Hunter Jesperson, a forty-year-old long-haul trucker from Selah, Washington. After writing to the *Oregonian*, he had murdered at least three more women. Taunja Bennett's missing purse was recovered after Jesperson revealed where he had left it. On November 2, 1995, Jesperson entered a plea of guilty to the Bennett murder and was sentenced to life in prison by Multnomah County Circuit Court Judge Donald H. Londer. Pavlinac and Sosnovske were released, belatedly, twenty-three days later. On March 4, 2003, Pavlinac died of heart failure. She was seventy years old.

There's an old story—apocryphal, perhaps—that circulates now and then in Chicago legal circles.

To evaluate the efficiency of crime-fighting agencies, the National Institute of Justice sponsored a competition. The final contestants were the Central Intelligence Agency, the Federal Bureau of Investigation, and the Chicago Police Department. Each was assigned to catch a rabbit that had been released into a forest.

The CIA dispatched a team of agents (operating undercover as State Department cultural attachés), paid millions of dollars (exact amount classified) to scores of informants (animal and mineral), surreptitiously intercepted millions of mysterious forest noises, analyzed thousands of satellite photographs, and concluded, after two years, that rabbits do not exist.

The FBI deployed its Critical Incident Response Group (CIRG), which ringed the perimeter with Light Armored Vehicles, waited patiently for two weeks, and then burned the forest down, killing everything in it, including the rabbit. No apologies—the rabbit deserved it.

The CPD put two detectives on the case. They went deep into the forest and emerged triumphantly in just two hours, dragging a badly beaten bear. "OK, OK," the bear was yelling. "I'm a rabbit, I'm a rabbit."

True or not, the story makes a valid point—even though it is unfair and misleading to suggest that physical coercion of confessions is a problem peculiar to Chicago. The brunt of the story could just as well be the police department of almost any large U.S. city or metropolitan area.

While police brutality has received a great deal of public attention (witness Rodney King and Abner Louima), jurors are inclined—even in defiance of competent evidence and common sense—to reject defendants' claims that their confessions were physically coerced.

As the following articles illustrate, however, defendants' claims that their confessions were physically coerced ought not to be rejected out of hand.

The article about Daniel Taylor in the "Unrequited Innocence" section (page 429) is another example of a case involving probable physical coercion.

COREY BEALE

When he asked for a lawyer, the cop "started getting violent"

APRIL WITT

BRANDYWINE, MARYLAND

Joanne Beale wasn't worried when she delivered her seventeen-year-old son to a detective at the Palmer Park headquarters of the Prince George's County Police at about 5:30 P.M. on Thursday, August 13, 1998. She waited inside the locked homicide unit for less than an hour, she said, before a second detective ushered her to the lobby, saying her son was free to go and was waiting there for her. As soon as the locked door slammed behind her, she realized she had been tricked and began to pound on the door. She would not see her son again for several days. By then, he was facing a first-degree murder charge.

Homicide detectives took turns questioning Corey Beale over three days. According to Corey, they slammed him against a wall, threatened him with execution, and deprived him of sleep—until he confessed to a slaying that evidence would show he did not commit.

"They just wore me down," Corey said.

He spent ten months in jail and missed his senior year in high school before detectives in adjoining Charles County—and not the Prince George's homicide unit—found evidence that convinced them he was not the killer.

"I never knew that police could do these terrible things," Joanne Beale said in a recent interview. "How many other Coreys are in prison right now for things they didn't do?"

Lieutenant Michael McQuillan, commander of the Prince George's homicide unit, said his detectives handled the questioning appropriately, but he declined to answer specific questions about the case. "Under no circumstance is a defendant, a witness—anyone—slammed against the wall in any of the interrogation rooms," he said. "It would not be tolerated. If it occurred, the department would take the necessary steps."

From "In Pr. George's Homicides, No Rest for the Suspects," *Washington Post*, June 4, 2001. Copyright © Washington Post. Adapted with permission.

It never occurred to Joanne Beale that anyone would suspect her son of murder.

She had heard that police wanted to talk to him about a body that had been found. His close friend, Michael Harley, had been stabbed to death. Harley's badly decomposed corpse was found under a pile of leaves in Brandywine. His jawbone was missing.

Harley had been with Corey and other pals at a party in a hotel room on the August night in 1998 when he disappeared.

Joanne Beale, a former deputy U.S. marshal, told the detectives that her son suffered from learning disabilities, comprehension problems, and a seizure disorder, and that she did not want the police to speak to him without her present. The police verbally agreed to her request, then separated her from Corey, and escorted her from the detective station into the lobby, where they told her that Corey was waiting for her. By that ruse they locked her out of the area where they were, in reality, holding and interrogating Corey.

She knew he ran with some tough kids. But she considered him a softy, a natural jokester who tended stray animals in their middle-class Clinton neighborhood. He was immature—at seventeen, he still asked for toys for Christmas—though he was about to become a senior at Gwynn Park High School.

Beale said she took her son to police headquarters at Palmer Park about 5:30 P.M. on Thursday, August 13, 1998. The following account of his interrogation is drawn from available police records, court files, and Corey Beale's recollection. After he was separated from his mother, Corey Beale found himself in a small, windowless room with carpeting up the walls.

"It was like being in a closet," he said.

There were a table, two chairs, and a metal fitting on one wall.

Almost three years later, Beale insists that the first statement he gave police was the truth: Harley, who was black, was talking to a white girl when Beale and his friends left the party.

"That was the last time I saw him," Beale's statement said.

Everyone who had been at the party in the hotel that night told detectives the same story, according to the police records that were turned over to Beale's defense attorney.

But in the confines of the interrogation room, Beale said, detectives first insisted that Harley must have gotten into a fatal fight after the party with another buddy, Jurwand "Posey" Riley.

No, Beale told them, Riley left the party with him.

"They kept trying to blame it on my friend Posey," Beale said. "They kept trying to say that he did the murder and they know that I know it. Just say it and they'd let me go."

Beale said he asked to see his mother.

"They wouldn't give me her," he recalled. "I asked for a lawyer. They wouldn't give me him. They kept saying I was a witness, not a suspect; when you are not a suspect you are not appointed a lawyer. I ain't never been in trouble. I didn't understand what they was talking about. I was like, 'I want a lawyer.' They were like, 'You don't need a lawyer.' "

After four and a half hours of questioning, Beale said, he was relieved when detectives said they wanted him to sign a "release form."

"They said, 'Initial here and here,' and I did it," Beale said. "Like a dummy. I thought it was a release form so I could go home."

He had signed a Miranda waiver form, the first of several he would initial in the days that followed, indicating that he was willing to give a statement without consulting a lawyer. He signed another form saying the detectives had not threatened him.

One detective gave Beale a test he called a Voice Stress Analyzer and told him it indicated he was lying when he denied knowing who killed Harley, Beale said.

"I was like, 'It should say I'm telling the truth, 'cause I don't know nothing,' " recalled Beale, who was unaware that police are allowed to lie to people under interrogation.

Around midnight, after more than six hours of questioning, Beale said he decided to appease detectives with something they wanted to hear: he said Harley and Riley got into a fight after they left the party. It was a lie, but the detectives wouldn't accept the truth, he said.

"I drove off, and they was still fighting," Beale's statement said.

The statement was taken by homicide Detective Troy Harding, who was hired by the Prince George's County Police Department in 1990 even though he had been arrested on charges of theft and battery in Anne Arundel County and assault in Montgomery County. He was found not guilty of the Anne Arundel charges. He was found guilty in the Montgomery assault, but the judge struck the guilty verdict and placed him on probation.

Harding did not respond to requests for an interview.

As the questioning continued through the night, Beale said, the detectives seemed to rethink their theory of who committed the murder.

"They started changing the story from [Riley] doing it, to I did it," Beale said. "They told me, 'We're trying to help you out. If you just say you did it, we can let you go right now on pretrial.' I didn't even know what pretrial was back then."

He said the tenor of the questioning grew more threatening when he again insisted that he knew nothing about Harley's murder.

"That's when they got all aggressive and started cussing and stuff."

At some point, Beale said, he again requested his mother and a lawyer and asked to use the phone.

"Then the cop started getting violent," Beale said. "He started jacking me up. He snapped me out of the chair and he threw me up against the wall. He was short and white. He was like, 'We ain't got time to be playing games with you. Just confess so we all can go home.'"

Through the night, detectives came and went from the interrogation room, Beale said. About nine hours into the interrogation, at 2:30 A.M., Detective Joseph McCann took a third statement from Beale that was at odds with the first two. This time, Beale said he became involved in the fight between Harley and Riley. That statement wasn't true either, but Beale was afraid not to write it, he said.

"I get out the car trying to break it up but Mike start to try to hit me and I swang, Then I told Posey lets go, and I drop him off at his house then went home," Beale's statement said.

The interrogation continued, and McCann later elicited a fourth version of events.

"After I get into my little fight I saw Mike go down and Posey had a knife in his hand with blood on it," Beale's statement said.

Based on statements McCann took from Beale, Detective Joseph Bergstrom typed out the paperwork to charge Beale with murdering Harley and to pick up his pal Riley on the same charge.

Beale was taken before a court commissioner, who assured him he was entitled to a lawyer. Then he was taken to the Upper Marlboro jail. He was offered food at the jail but said he felt too sick to eat.

When detectives picked up Riley, he refused to implicate himself in Harley's death. Riley told detectives Harley had been talking to the girl when he and Beale left the hotel. That was the last they saw of him, according to Riley's written statement.

Detectives retrieved a bleary-eyed Beale from jail and returned him to the interrogation room. He said they handcuffed him to the metal fitting in one carpeted wall.

"I was so tired I just wanted to lay down," Beale said. "But the way they had it, it's like you can't lay down, you've got to be up against the wall."

It was Saturday, his third day in the room, and the grilling had begun again. At 9:49 A.M., he initialed another form waiving his right to a lawyer.

He said the same detective who earlier had slammed him against the wall demanded a new statement: this time he was to say that he alone had killed Harley. Beale said he was assured that if he said Harley hit him first, he would have a solid claim of self-defense.

"It's not my words," Beale said. "That short, white dude. He was standing over top of me. Right on the side of me. He was telling me what to say so I could get off."

A little after 5:00 P.M. Saturday, the third day after his mother delivered him to the detectives, records show Beale confessed to murder.

"Mike picks up a tree branch and swang it at me and I took my knife and sta[b] him," Beale's statement said.

"They said they were going to send me home," Beale said in an interview. "They kept pressuring me: 'The only way you are going to get up on out of here is if you confess and say you did it.' Then after I done it, they were, 'OK, we're about to send you home now.' I guess by 'home' they meant 'jail.' Because that's where I went."

Fourteen months later, the case against Beale that began in the secrecy of a locked interrogation room ended with a courtroom whisper.

Assistant State's Attorney Frances R. Longwell asked if she could approach the bench. In a voice just audible on a court videotape, she told Judge C. Phillip Nichols that she needed to drop the charges against Beale.

"Because we found another defendant and [the murder] happened in Charles County on top of that," Longwell said on October 19, 1999.

While he was in jail, Beale had passed a lie detector test arranged by his attorney, but that's not what freed him.

Police in Charles County had found Harley's missing jawbone and determined that Beale was not the murderer, although they won't say how.

The Prince George's detectives who had won Beale's confession resisted dropping the charges, according to Louis Martucci, Beale's attorney.

"It was a nasty business," Martucci said. "I don't think the lead detective gave a damn. He told me to my face one day: 'He's it. He's been arrested, and we don't care if there are other suspects.' I found that rather shocking."

Prince George's State's Attorney Jack B. Johnson said last week that his office dropped the charges against Beale as soon as it received evidence from Charles County that he was innocent.

"The criminal justice system is not fair," he said. "My job as prosecutor is to make it as fair as possible."

Charles County detectives, still hopeful that they will gather enough evidence to make an arrest in the Harley case, decline to talk publicly about the facts that cleared Beale.

Beale, now twenty, recounted his story sitting in the living room of his mother's house. She said she took a second mortgage on her home—and so did her ex-husband, a retired District firefighter—to pay his legal bills. As Beale talked, his mother put her head down and pulled on her hair in anguish.

"He's not the same Corey," she said. "He doesn't laugh anymore. He doesn't trust anyone. He's just angry. He'll go into a rage and whoop and holler: 'I was locked up by the white man for eleven months for something I didn't do.' I know that's what's wrong with the boy."

Frustrated by trying to explain why he agreed to confess to a murder he didn't commit, Beale jumped up and raised his voice:

"I was in questioning for three days. Man, I was tired. I wanted to go home. If they tell me, 'Shoot this dude right here and you go home,' I'm going to do it if that's what it takes to go home.

"I would have said anything to get out of that room."

Epilogue

Michael Harley's actual killer, Kenneth Shirell Williams, pled guilty to the crime in July 2002 and was sentenced to thirty years in prison.

AARON PATTERSON

Coercion, Chicago style—third-world-quality torture

DON TERRY

CHICAGO, ILLINOIS

With a film crew from Germany right behind him on an afternoon last spring, Aaron Patterson pushed through the door of a low-slung building that houses the Area Two headquarters of the Chicago Police Department. It is where, in 1986, when he was twenty-one years old, he was questioned about a double murder that sent him to death row. Back then, Patterson was whisked into the station wearing handcuffs in the back of a police car, a detective on either side.

"I'm not used to coming in the front door," Patterson jokes with the crew as he strides up to the front desk, chest out, head high. "I want to see the watch commander," he announces. "Tell him Aaron Patterson is here. I was a visitor here seventeen years ago."

A detective passes by, leading a handcuffed prisoner up a flight of stairs.

"That's the interrogation room up there—the house of screams," Patterson says.

A lieutenant in a crisp white shirt comes out to see what Patterson wants.

"They want to film the interrogation room where I was tortured," Patterson tells him, in a voice that carries through the large lobby. The lieutenant stares at Patterson and says that could happen only with permission from the news affairs unit downtown.

"Please step away from the desk so other people can come up," the lieutenant says.

"Yeah, right," Patterson says. "I can see there's a long line."

There is no one else waiting.

About ten minutes later, the answer from downtown is no. Patterson pronounces the trip a success anyway.

"For them to know a European country is concerned about what's going on in this police station," he says, "it's a beautiful thing."

From "Aaron Patterson: 'Live from Death Row,'" *Chicago Tribune*, November 2, 2003. Copyright © Chicago Tribune. Adapted with permission.

Vincent and Rafaela Sanchez sold all sorts of things—television sets, radios, water heaters, maybe even guns—out of their home at 8849 South Burley Avenue, where police were summoned shortly before noon on April 19, 1986.

Responding to a call from neighbors, a police officer entered through the kitchen and found the floor covered with dried beans from an over-flowed pot on the stove—and a trail of blood. Vincent Sanchez, seventy-three, was found on the bathroom floor. He had been stabbed twenty-five times. Rafaela Sanchez, sixty-two, was lying on the dining room floor in a blood-soaked beige nightgown. She too had been stabbed.

Police Lieutenant Jon Burge, commander of the Area Two Violent Crimes Unit, arrived on the scene, and a short time later his detectives were round-ing up suspects and witnesses, including a young man named DeEdward White. A few days later, White's cousin, sixteen-year-old Marva Hall, told investigators that she had run into Patterson on the street the day after the Sanchez bodies were discovered. She said Patterson asked her if she wanted to buy a shotgun and a chain saw and told her that he and some friends had killed the Sanchezes.

Hall eventually recanted that story, saying prosecutors threatened her with jail if she did not cooperate. The authorities deny that.

The police already were familiar with Patterson, who led the Apache Rangers, a branch of the Blackstone Rangers, one of the city's most violent gangs, and was wanted in three cases of gang-related violence, including beating and pistol-whipping a fellow Apache Ranger suspected of stealing a gang gun.

Eleven days after the Sanchezes' bodies were found, the police found Patterson hiding in a friend's attic. Patterson says he assumed he was wanted for the gang violence and expected to get slapped around at the police station—that was just the way the game was played—and was stunned when the detectives started questioning him about the Sanchez murders.

As he sat surrounded by detectives, crowded into the small room at Area Two, the lights suddenly went out, Patterson says. Then someone threw a typewriter cover over his face. Desperate for air, he tried to bite through the heavy plastic, as he was punched in the chest. The cover was yanked from his face, the lights went on, and the detectives were back in their original places, pretending nothing had happened. Then they did it again.

After that, he says, he answered every question about the murders with "Whatever you say."

An assistant state's attorney soon came into the interrogation room and gave him a "confession" to read. Left alone, chained to a steel hoop in the wall, Patterson found a paper clip and an idea. He unwound the paper clip and scratched this message into the metal bench: "Aaron 4/30 I lie about murders. Police threaten me with violence. Slapped and suffocated me with plastic. No lawyer or dad. No phone. Sign false statement to murders."

Patterson changed his mind and refused to sign the statement. Since he didn't kill the Sanchezes, he now says, nothing was going to make him sign his name to a lie.

But in 1989, based on the testimony of Marva Hall, who had recanted but recanted her recantation, and the claims of detectives and prosecutors that Patterson had confessed, a jury found him guilty and Cook County Circuit Court Judge John E. Morrissey sentenced him to death.

A codefendant, Eric Caine, was convicted at a separate trial based on a confession he also claimed was beaten out of him. Because he said in his confession that he had fled when the killing started, he was spared the death penalty. He was sentenced to life in prison, where he remains today, still maintaining his innocence.

There was no physical evidence that Patterson was abused by police—he was not hospitalized and there were no obvious bruises when he appeared in court the day after his interrogation—but Caine had been treated for a broken eardrum immediately after he confessed.

Although police and prosecutors deny to this day that Patterson and Caine were mistreated, Jon Burge was fired by the Chicago Police Department in 1993 for his role in an unrelated beating at Area Two. An internal police investigation found that torture and abuse were systematic and common under Burge and other officers. The report documented five dozen brutality cases. Special prosecutors are investigating whether criminal charges can and should be brought.

In a sweltering cell in a prison on a hilltop in southern Illinois, Aaron Patterson stared at the walls and thought about the river.

Below him, during the sodden summer of 1993, the mighty floodwaters of the Mississippi raged, swallowing up farmlands and tiny towns, minor-league ballparks and cemeteries.

Lost in fear and frustration, Patterson was waiting for a sign. Finally, he thought, a higher power had heard his pleas from Menard Correctional Center.

Patterson prayed that the water would climb the hill and wash away death row, carrying him to freedom. "I was going to float all the way to the Gulf of Mexico," he says.

The river rose for weeks, then returned to its banks. And Patterson returned to his war inside the prison walls.

Believing he was innocent, seeing himself as a hostage and carrying himself as a warrior, he resisted relentlessly. He threw around his bitter words and his body wastes. "Sometimes the only way for you to get them to listen to you is to act the fool," he says.

He spent most of his time on death row in segregation. Instead of the bars of a regular cell that an inmate can see through, the segregation cells have a solid steel door that closes like a coffin. The prisoners are fed through a chuckhole.

Over the years, Patterson was slapped with about 125 yellow tickets for disciplinary violations. He had years and years to go in segregation at the time of his pardon. More than thirty of the tickets were for assaulting correctional officers.

Patterson's rage was so red-hot that even people sympathetic to his cause were afraid of getting burned. The Illinois Coalition Against the Death Penalty regularly sent visitors to the men on death row. In the early 1990s, Mary L. Johnson was one of the volunteers. For her it was personal. Her son could have easily been on death row. Instead he was serving a sentence of natural life in another prison.

She tried to treat the men, the ones she knew were guilty and the ones like Patterson who she believed in her heart were innocent, just the same— like sons. Johnson says she was assigned to visit the segregation unit, and at first she balked.

"I didn't want to go back there," she says. "They were throwing urine."

But another member of the coalition told her Jo Ann Patterson's son was there, and that persuaded her to give it a try. Jo Ann Patterson was also a member of the coalition.

Johnson put her face against the steel door of Patterson's cell. There were dried feces on the walls and what else she couldn't be sure. She put on her mama-knows-best voice.

"You can't get people to come back here acting up," she told him. "People are afraid. You have to cool down. It's disgusting back here."

Over time Patterson did calm down, at least with Johnson and a few others on the visiting team. His mother was a frequent visitor. For a time after her son's conviction, Jo Ann Patterson retreated from the world. But eventually she became a driving force in the movement to free Patterson.

Supporters unleashed a barrage of letters and pamphlets outlining his charges of torture and the weak evidence in the case. Patterson became the best known of a group of men called the Death Row Ten, all of whom claimed to have been tortured by Burge and his men.

From his tiny cell, Patterson called most of the shots, writing long letters to his supporters with detailed instructions. Contact this reporter, that preacher. Go see this state representative or that congressman. Do civil disobedience. Raise some hell.

Finally, the momentum began to shift. Not just for Patterson, but for the entire population of death row, when Governor George H. Ryan declared a moratorium on executions in 2000.

Last January, after Patterson had spent nearly seventeen years behind bars for the Sanchez murders, Governor Ryan freed him, part of a dramatic and sweeping condemnation of the Illinois death penalty system.

Saying he wanted to correct a "manifest injustice," Ryan granted Patterson a pardon based on innocence.

TV cameras were there to record Patterson's release from prison.

Out of bitter habit, Patterson says, he fought back the tears that were trying to burst out of him. But on his first day of freedom, his first glimpse of the Chicago skyline weakened his resolve. As he approached the city in a car crowded with family and friends, he says, it looked like the sparkling skyscrapers had tumbled out of heaven and landed upright and perfect on Earth: "It didn't look real."

The next day, January 11, 2003, Patterson spoke at an antiwar rally and then went to Northwestern University School of Law, where Governor Ryan was preparing to announce that he was commuting the death sentences of 167 men and women, when an aide rushed in.

"Governor, you can't go downstairs," Ryan recalls the aide breathlessly telling him. "Aaron Patterson is down there and he's raising hell."

"Get him and bring him up here," the governor said.

The former inmate came in. "I still got friends who are still in prison, who are innocent," Ryan said Patterson told him. "And nobody is doing anything about it."

Patterson had promised the men he had just left behind that he would plead for their pardons. And that's what Patterson did.

"After that," Ryan said, "he was a perfect gentleman."

Someday, Patterson wants justice—and lots of money for his suffering.

He has filed a multimillion-dollar lawsuit over his wrongful conviction.

But right now, all he's seeking is a discount.

"I just got off death row," he tells the attendant in the pay booth of a downtown parking garage a few months into his second shot at life. "Can I get the death row discount?"

The death row discount has worked before—Patterson got a couple of free dress shirts from a sympathetic salesman—but not this time.

The attendant doesn't crack a smile.

OK—you can't blame a broke brother for trying.

Patterson forks over the cash.

A few days later, Patterson tells a dancer-rapper at a nightclub that he's been on death row.

She gives him a wide smile, thinking he's from Death Row Records, the rap music label. Her big break has just walked through the door—next stop, Hollywood.

He can hook a sister up, right?

"No," he says. "I'm from the death row where they kill people, not make records."

"I ain't never met anyone from death row before," she says.

"I bet you haven't," he replies. "There ain't too many of us walking around."

Epilogue

In August 2004 Patterson was arrested on federal charges of running drugs and selling guns—offenses for which he was tried and convicted by a jury the following year. At Patterson's sentencing hearing, his lawyer, Andrea Gambino, argued that he deserved credit for the seventeen years he had spent behind bars for a crime he did not commit. "We owe this man time," Gambino told U.S. District Court Judge Rebecca Pallmeyer. Unmoved, Pallmeyer sentenced Patterson to thirty years. In January 2008, the City of Chicago agreed to settle the cases of four Burge torture victims, including Patterson, for $19.8 million.

GEORGE WHITMORE

"We got the right guy—no question about it. He gave us details
only the killer could know."

SELWYN RAAB

NEW YORK, NEW YORK

On the pleasant summer day of August 28, 1963, Janice Wylie and Emily
Hoffert were murdered in their apartment on Manhattan's fashionable East
Side.

In a corner of a bedroom, wedged between a bed and a wall, their bodies lay tangled together, their faces frozen in final grimaces of agony. They
were bound in death by bloody strips of sheets and bedspreads which had
been twisted around their bodies. Both young women were coated with
their own blood, both had been stabbed repeatedly. Janice Wylie died
nude, plastic curlers dangling incongruously from her blond hair. She had
been disemboweled. Her body bore marks of sexual abuse. Emily Hoffert
met death fully clothed. Her throat was sliced from ear to ear. The apparent
murder tools were nearby: two broken kitchen knives lay on a blood-soaked
floor, and a third weapon, a carving knife, was on the washbasin in the
bathroom across the foyer from the bedroom.

The savagery of the crime horrified even normally impervious police
officers. The police would consider any double murder of women an
important case. Yet there were additional reasons to put the Wylie-Hoffert
slayings in a special category. Both Janice Wylie and Emily Hoffert came
from fairly prominent families. Janice's father, Max Wylie, was a writer and
advertising executive, and her uncle was the author Philip Wylie. Emily
Hoffert's father, a surgeon, and her mother were influential figures in Minneapolis society. Janice, who was twenty-one, worked as a researcher at
Newsweek magazine, but dreamed of a career as an actress. Twenty-three-
year-old Emily Hoffert had an impressive academic record, and was about
to start her first teaching job. Neither of the women could be described as

From *Justice in the Back Room* (Cleveland: World Publishing Company, 1967). Copyright ©
Selwyn Raab. Adapted with permission.

an ordinary working girl. More important, the murders carried the trademark of an insane killer, a madman who had slipped into a well-guarded apartment building on a posh street off Park Avenue. Widespread publicity and a wave of public fear immediately combined to generate immense pressure on the police for a quick solution.

Patricia Tolles, the third roommate in the $280-a-month apartment on Eighty-Eighth Street, had arrived home early that Wednesday evening to find the apartment in disarray. After seeing a knife and blood-streaked strips of sheet in a bathroom, she was too frightened to inspect the rest of the apartment by herself. Instead, she got help by telephoning Janice Wylie's parents, who lived nearby. Max Wylie was the first to enter the bedroom.

The city's chief of detectives was assigned to the inquiry, along with some of the best investigators on the police force. Within hours, they had put in motion the largest manhunt in New York City's history, a manhunt that would produce repercussions for years to come.

A basic belief held by most high-ranking officials of the New York City police force is that all tough cases can eventually be solved if sufficient manpower is committed. Despite the publicity given to scientific criminology, the men who ran New York's Police Department in 1963 had been taught by their elders, and had learned through their own experience, to rely on legwork and tips. In the Wylie-Hoffert case, this approach was adopted fully.

The fifty detectives originally assigned to the case were a large number for even an important inquiry. When after one week they seemed stymied, police headquarters doubled the detective staff to one hundred, bringing in homicide squad experts from other precincts in the city. Even the most ordinary tasks of the investigation were carried out with unusual thoroughness and intensity. But nothing the police did, whether it was accepted or unorthodox procedure, brought them closer to a solution.

In Emily Hoffert's past, not a single person could be found who had the slightest motive for harming her. After graduation from Smith College in Northampton, Massachusetts, she earned a master's degree in English at Tufts University, near Boston, in the spring of 1963. Emily had spent July—the month before the murders—with her family in Minneapolis, returning to New York in early August to prepare for her first elementary-school teaching job, in Valley Stream, Long Island. The police profile of Emily Hoffert showed a quiet, bookish, unpretentious young woman, a woman who had dated little and was well acquainted with perhaps twenty-five people in New York City.

Janice Wylie's history gave police innumerable avenues to explore. Having lived most of her life in Manhattan, Janice knew hundreds of people in New York. Her address book was crammed with the names of men and women in the city and suburbs. Most of her schooling had been in New York, in the same neighborhood where she lived and died. She attended the exclusive Nightingale-Bamford School for Girls on Ninety-Second Street and Fifth Avenue. In her late teens she began thinking of a stage career, and her hopes had led her to a year of acting school and to a few seasons in summer stock companies before she decided to take a researcher's job. While at *Newsweek*, she still talked vaguely of another try at the theater, and she had retained her show-business friends.

Newsweek offered a ten-thousand-dollar reward for information leading to the arrest and conviction of the killer, but the reward did not produce any immediate leads.

One place the Wylie-Hoffert investigation did not meander toward was a slum section of Brooklyn called Brownsville. Almost in the center of Brooklyn, ten miles from the murder scene, Brownsville seemingly had no connection with either of the victims. There was no reason for any detective to believe a clue to the crime might be hidden somewhere in that drab neighborhood. Yet a peculiar axis was being welded to join the Wylie-Hoffert case with Brownsville.

In the first minutes of Thursday, April 23, 1964, Patrolman Frank C. Isola began walking his beat in Brownsville. His midnight to 8:00 A.M. shift was an unenviable one, a patrol through some of the most crime-troubled streets in the city. Armed with a .38-caliber service revolver and a lead-tipped nightstick, he walked warily across the scarred sidewalks and past the endless rows of garbage cans lined up outside apartment buildings.

At 1:10 A.M., Isola stopped in front of Junior High School 263, on Sutter Avenue, and used a green police telephone callbox to talk to the Seventy-Third Precinct, his home base. It was his second report to the station house that night, and again he had no news to pass on. All was quiet. Once more Isola began trudging past the tenements, now blurred in mist.

He was fifty feet beyond the callbox when a loud scream, clearly a woman's cry, stopped him. Scanning the streets, he saw a man and a woman, about seventy-five feet away, vanish into an alleyway on Bristol Street. As the couple entered the alley, he noticed the man had an arm around the woman's shoulders, as if embracing her. Isola did not run toward the alley. An occasional nighttime scream arising from an argument in the street or inside a tenement was not unusual, and Isola had become conditioned to remaining calm in such circumstances. He walked slowly toward the alley, not certain if the scream had come from that direction. As he reached the alley, he aimed his flashlight into the darkness.

As soon as the light clicked on, a woman began shrieking. Isola saw her backed against a wall, about fifteen feet away from him, with a man facing her, holding a pocketbook. The man gasped, "Oh, my God," and staggered away from the beam of the flashlight. Unholstering his gun, Isola shouted the customary, "Stop, or I'll shoot!" The man bolted out of the alley through a side door leading to the vestibule of an apartment building. Isola brushed past the woman and got off one shot as the man ran out the front door into the street. In the street, Isola fired three more times before the man swerved into Amboy Street and disappeared.

On the sidewalk in front of the building where the pursuit had begun, a dozen Puerto Rican tenants, many in their nightclothes, were chattering excitedly in Spanish and English. They told Isola that the woman in the alley, Elba Borrero, lived in the building, and that she had been helped upstairs by her husband and neighbors. Isola interviewed her in the third-floor apartment. She was a short, stout, twenty-year-old practical nurse from Puerto Rico. She said she had been on her way home from work when a man grabbed her from behind, put something sharp against her throat, and threatened to rape her. As he shoved her into the alley, she let out the scream that had alerted Isola.

Elba, who was unhurt, described the assailant as a light-skinned Negro, twenty-three to twenty-six years old, standing five feet seven or eight, and weighing 150 to 165 pounds. She said he wore a tan three-quarter-length coat and a green hat. She had torn off a button from his coat as he pulled away in panic. She also had snatched a mechanical pencil from his hand. Isola took the button, which he considered a potential clue, but left the pencil with her.

Isola's beat was quiet again. At 7:00 A.M., with an hour of his shift left, he was at Sutter and Hopkinson avenues, a major intersection two blocks from the attack, when he saw a young Negro standing in the doorway of a launderette, sheltering himself from the morning cold. Approaching the young man, Isola asked, "What are you doing here?"

"I'm waiting for my brother to go to work with him," the youth replied. He identified himself as George Whitmore and said he was staying with relatives in the area. Then he added, "I know why you're asking me all these questions." He said he had left his girlfriend's apartment several hours earlier when he heard shots and saw a man being pursued by Isola. The man ran up to him, pleading for help. "I told him there was nothing I could do for him and he ran away, into a building on Amboy Street." Isola jotted down the youth's name—incorrectly as "George Whitman"—and spent the final hour of his shift directing morning traffic.

Later that day, Detective Richard Aidala saw an item on the police blotter about the Borrero attack. It immediately occurred to him that there might be a connection between the attack and a murder case he was working on—the case of Minnie Edmonds, a forty-six-year-old Negro cleaning woman, who nine days earlier had been knifed to death in an alley a block from where the Borrero crime occurred. Aidala called Joseph DiPrima, another detective assigned to the Edmonds case, who agreed that there could be a connection. Elba Borrero was brought to the precinct, where she examined photos of suspected sex criminals, without identifying one, and gave Aidala the mechanical pencil she had seized from her attacker.

Although Isola had concluded that "Whitman" was not the person who had attacked Borrero, Aidala and DiPrima wanted to question him. Isola was scheduled to be off the next day, and he met DiPrima at 5:30 A.M. at the Seventy-Third Precinct. Playing a hunch, they staked out the launderette where Isola had encountered "Whitman" twenty-four hours earlier. Indeed, at 7:00 A.M., Isola spotted the youth walking down the street. Aidala and Isola got out of the car. Flashing his shield, Aidala asked, "Are you the fellow who spoke to this police officer yesterday and told him you heard shots and saw a man running into Amboy Street?"

The young man nodded. Aidala asked him for identification, and he produced a New Jersey driver's license, showing his name as George Whitmore, his age as nineteen, and his address as Wildwood, New Jersey. Without hesitation, Whitmore agreed to go with the officers to the Seventy-Third Precinct for questioning. Aidala took him into a room reserved for use by detectives, and told him to take off his coat and sit at a desk near the window. At this point, Aidala considered Whitmore a witness, not a suspect. But before questioning him as the former he wanted to eliminate him as the latter. The quickest way to do that was to ask Borrero. Aidala went into an adjacent room and called her. "We have someone we want you to look at." he said. "I'm sending Patrolman Isola over to drive you to the precinct."

The trip took only a few minutes, and Isola took Borrero into the squad commander's office, the door of which had a peephole. Aidala brought Whitmore to the center of the squad room, about five feet from the peephole. Elba, barely five feet tall, was unable to reach the peephole even on tiptoe. Isola placed two telephone directories on the floor as a makeshift stool. Standing on them, she appraised Whitmore for about thirty seconds before turning to Isola.

"This is the man," she said. To solidify her identification, however, she wanted to hear him speak. Isola went into the room with Whitmore, and told him to say, "Lady, I'm going to rape you. Lady, I'm going to kill you." Whitmore shrugged and agreed. Hearing the words, Elba began to tremble. "This is the man," she said. "This is the man."

Although Whitmore was considerably younger than Elba had indicated her attacker was, he matched other elements of her description: He was a light-skinned Negro, about five feet six inches tall, weighing no more than 150 pounds, and wearing a tan coat, which had tufts of thread in places where once there had been buttons. His face was pockmarked and pimpled—a feature that Elba and Isola later would insist she had mentioned in her initial description of the assailant, although Isola failed to note that crucial element in his report.

Isola stepped into the squad room and nodded to Aidala, indicating that Elba had made a positive identification. Aidala turned to Whitmore. "I'm placing you under arrest," he said. "A woman has identified you as the man who tried to rape her."

"You're making a mistake," Whitmore said. "I didn't do anything."

Aidala ordered him to empty his pockets. Whitmore pulled out a wallet stuffed with photographs and papers, a handkerchief, a black comb, and a pink-handled jackknife. From his coat pocket, Whitmore produced a paperback mystery entitled *The Tall Dark Man*. He had no money, not a penny.

Aidala and Isola told Elba that they needed her to make one more identification, this time face-to-face. She was visibly distressed, weeping and quivering. The officers assured her she had nothing to fear and that the face-to-face encounter would wait until she felt sufficiently composed. Twenty minutes later, Aidala brought Whitmore into the squad commander's office. When he entered, Elba trembled again.

"You're the man who tried to rape me," she said angrily.

"You're making a mistake, ma'am," Whitmore responded.

Now it was time for the police to question Whitmore. Aidala called Detective DiPrima and gave him a quick review of the arrest and identification. "I'm coming right over," said DiPrima, who had questioned thousands of suspects and was known as an "old pro" within the department. When he arrived shortly after 8:00 A.M., he had no reason to suspect that he was entering into the most important case of his career.

After introducing himself to Whitmore, DiPrima asked, "How about something to eat?" Whitmore said he would like rolls and coffee. DiPrima handed Isola two dollars and asked him to bring rolls and coffee from a delicatessen next door. Then, with Aidala sitting by quietly, DiPrima began asking Whitmore about himself. Whitmore said he had been born in Philadelphia. His family had moved to New Jersey when he was a small child. The family now lived in Wildwood, where his father owned an auto shop.

As Whitmore talked about his home life, Isola returned with breakfast. The delicatessen was out of rolls, so he had brought slices of buttered Italian bread instead. When the meal was finished, Aidala gave Whitmore a cigarette. DiPrima was now ready to question him about the Borrero case. He asked Whitmore to describe the attack.

"I didn't do it," was the answer.

"George, Mrs. Borrero identified you as the man," DiPrima said.

Whitmore inhaled the cigarette and reflected. The room was silent except for the street sounds that penetrated the screened window. Finally—all of the following dialogue and factual assertions relating to the interrogation are the police version of what transpired—Whitmore said, "You're speaking better to me than anyone else ever spoke to me in my life." He paused, and then asked: "How much time would I have to do?" "That would be up to the judge," said DePrima. "I can't make any promises. But the best thing to do is tell the truth." Aidala took out a yellow writing tablet, and DePrima said, "Start from the beginning, George. Tell us what you were doing and how it happened."

It took about an hour for Whitmore to relate what had happened. The sole question the detectives asked, or so they claimed, was: "What happened next, George?" With no other prodding, Whitmore allegedly said that he had left his girlfriend's house the night of the attack. It was late and he was without a place to sleep. He was wandering in the streets when he saw a woman walking and followed her. After several blocks of slow pursuit, he caught up with her and grabbed her from behind in a stranglehold. Jabbing a mechanical pencil against her throat to simulate a knife, he forced her into the alley and put his hand under her dress. "I wanted to feel her pussy, and I told her I wanted to fuck her," he said. At this moment the flashlight had burst upon him. He heard shots as he raced through the streets. After eluding the pursuing officer, he hid on the roof.

Aidala showed him the button Elba had ripped off her assailant's coat. "Is this your button?" he asked.

"I don't know, it might be. I lost the top button from my coat. I don't know where."

"What about this pencil, is this yours?" asked Aidala, showing him the mechanical pencil he had retrieved from Elba.

Whitmore nodded.

In the course of the interrogation, Whitmore had mentioned Chester Street, which was unrelated to the case but was the street where Minnie Edmonds had been found slain on April 14.

"What about Chester Street, George?" DiPrima asked. "Why'd you mention it?"

"Oh, that's the street where the fellows do a lot of bebopping."

"We know all about gangs fighting in the neighborhood," DiPrima continued. "Is there anything else you want to tell us about Chester Street?"

Whitmore was silent for several seconds before answering: "I heard a woman was hurt on Chester Street."

"What about that woman, George?"

"I was the one who hurt the woman."

While DiPrima continued the questioning, Aidala made a more careful examination of items found in Whitmore's wallet, including two photographs of young white women.

"Where'd you get these pictures, George?" Aidala asked.

"A girl in New Jersey gave them to me," he said.

Aidala did not pursue the matter, satisfied that the photos had nothing to do with the Borrero and Edmonds cases. He notified the district attorney's office of Whitmore's confession and was told that an assistant district attorney would be dispatched to the precinct to take a verbatim confession in front of a stenographer. Since it would take the district attorney at least thirty minutes to get there, Aidala and DiPrima decided to take Whitmore to the scene of the Edmonds murder and have him reenact the crime.

While they were gone, two detectives who had been sent in from nearby precincts to aid in the Edmonds investigation—Charles Fazio and Edward Bulger—went through Whitmore's possessions. Fazio and Bulger, who worked as a team, had been among the scores of homicide detectives from throughout the city who had been assigned eight months earlier to the Wylie-Hoffert investigation. Fazio fixed his gaze on one of the photos from Whitmore's wallet—a snapshot of two young women sitting in a convertible. One of the women was blond and appeared to be about twenty. When Fazio called the photo to Bulger's attention, he said what Fazio was thinking: "That girl resembles Janice Wylie."

When DiPrima returned to the station house with Aidala and Whitmore, Bulger took him aside. "Joe," Bulger said, "the girl in this picture bears an awful lot of resemblance to Janice Wylie. I'd like to talk to him about it." The assistant district attorney had not yet arrived, and DiPrima saw no reason why Bulger should not question Whitmore. They went into the squad commander's office.

"Where'd you get this picture?" Bulger asked.

"I found it in a junkyard in Wildwood, where I used to work."

"Are you sure that's where you got it?"

Whitmore did not answer. Bulger repeated the question.

"A girl I know in Jersey gave it to me," said Whitmore.

"What's her name?"

"Carol, I think."

"Remember, George, tell us the truth. We can always check. You've been truthful all day. Are you sure you're telling the truth?"

"This girl gave it to me, her father had a riding academy and he's let me ride the horses. That's how I knew her."

"Come on, George, tell us where you really got the photo. Did the girl really give it to you?"

Now Whitmore offered a different explanation: "I was in the girl's house once, and I took it from a drawer."

"We'll have to call the girl."

Once more, Whitmore said the photograph came from a house in Wildwood.

Noting that Whitmore had now offered three versions, Bulger asked: "Which one is true? Did you find it in a junkyard? Did a girl give it to you? Or did you steal it?"

"I stole it from a house in New York."

"Do you remember where in New York you got the photograph? What street?"

"It was Eighty-Eighth Street. I took it from a drawer."

Bulger asked when this had happened.

"About the end of August 1963, it was a weekday. I was in Brooklyn and felt like taking a train ride. It was almost ten in the morning. I took the 'A' train and rode to the Forty-Second Street station near the Port Authority building."

"What'd you do next, George?"

"I came to the street and did some window shopping. I walked uptown just to look around. At Eighty-Eighth Street, near Park Avenue, I saw a building with a canvas canopy out to the street; it looked like wealthy people lived there."

"What happened next, George?"

"I went into the building to go to the roof to look around. I went through the lobby and past the elevator and then an exit door to the left. There were concrete steps leading upstairs. I went up and I don't remember if it was three or four flights of stairs and I saw a door open a crack on the second or third floor landing leading to the kitchen of the apartment. I pushed open the door and stuck my head in and looked around."

At this point, the assistant district attorney arrived to take Whitmore's formal confession to the Edmonds and Borrero crimes. But when the detectives told him that they were in the process of obtaining a confession to a third crime, he left. Over the next two hours, Bulger did most of the questioning. He would report that Whitmore seemed remarkably calm and friendly. Whitmore repeated that he had traveled to Manhattan, aimlessly wandered the streets, entered a building, and walked toward the roof.

"What did you do inside?"

"I looked around and saw a carton with all the soda bottles in it."

"Do you remember what kind of soda bottles, George?"

"They were Coca-Cola bottles, I think, and they were empty. I took three bottles from the carton in case somebody walked in and caught me. Then I would have the bottles to protect myself."

"Go on, George, what happened next?"

"I walked through the dining room from the kitchen."

"Which way did you go?"

"I went to the right and into the front room and looked around. Then I picked up a picture off the end table in the front room parlor."

"What kind of table, do you remember?"

"I think the table is mahogany, and I think there was a lamp on it."

"What picture did you take from the table, George?"

"The picture of the blonde girl."

"What happened after you took the photograph?"

"Well, before I went into the front room, I set the bottles on the floor of the hall so I could get to them in case I needed them. I picked up quite a few things and I looked at them. I needed my hands free."

"OK, what then?"

"When I was leaving the parlor, I picked up the bottles and walked through the hall and looked in the first bathroom and no one was there. I looked in the bedroom and walked in and looked around."

"When did you see someone?"

"As I was coming out of the bedroom, I saw a girl with blonde hair coming out of the bathroom in the back."

"How was she dressed?"

"She was naked but she was holding a sheet around her hips and she was naked from the waist up."

"Did she say anything?"

"She got hysterical when she saw me and started to scream and I tried to stop her from screaming."

"How'd you try to stop her?"

"I set the bottles on the floor and grabbed her around the neck and, with my left hand, I pulled her left arm behind her back. I told her to shut up, 'I don't want to hurt you.'"

"Did she fight back?"

"She kept screaming. I dragged her into the bedroom, pushed her between the beds, but she wouldn't stop screaming. So I pushed her head towards the window and ran back, grabbed a bottle, and hit her on the head with the bottle. I hit her once and she just laid there. I think the bottle broke." He then tore sheets into strips and used them to bind her hands and feet. As he was leaving the bedroom, a second woman appeared. "She said, 'Who the hell are you? What are you doing in my house?' I ran towards her and told her to be quiet and she kept on screaming for help. She kept on making a lot of noise. I grabbed another bottle that was lying on the floor and hit her on the head."

He dragged her into the bedroom, placing her on the bed, and binding her hands and ankles, too. He was committing cunnilingus on her when she awoke and screamed. Panicking, Whitmore ran into the kitchen, brought back three knives, and plunged one of them into her. When she was quiet, he stabbed the blond girl, even though she had not cried out.

"What happened next, George?"

"I washed up and left the apartment."

That night, two assistant district attorneys—Saul Postal, from Brooklyn, and Peter J. Koste, from Manhattan—arrived to question Whitmore before stenographers. It was agreed that Postal would question Whitmore first about the Brooklyn crimes and Koste then would question him about the Manhattan double murder. As Postal questioned Whitmore, asking 120 questions over thirty-seven minutes, officers who had been dispatched to show the photo of the young women in the convertible to Janice Wylie's parents and sister reported that they could not identify the blond as Janice. Undaunted, Bulger, DiPrima, and Aidala assured Koste that they had no doubt that the photo had come from the Wylie-Hoffert apartment—as they claimed Whitmore had spontaneously blurted out—even if the blond was not Janice.

At exactly 2:00 A.M. on April 25, 1964, with Bulger, DiPrima, and Aidala watching, Koste began taking Whitmore's third confession of the night.

At 3:30 A.M., the Associated Press sent out a bulletin reporting that "a nineteen-year-old Negro has admitted slaying Janice Wylie and Emily Hoeffert [sic] in their East Side apartment last August 28." The bulletin identified the suspect as Whitmore, who was still being questioned by Koste. In fact, Koste did not finish until 4:12 A.M., forty-two minutes after the AP had issued the bulletin.

By 4:30 A.M. more than a dozen newspaper, television, and radio reporters had squeezed into the squad commander's office, which could hold only about six people comfortably, where Manhattan Chief of Detectives Lawrence McKearney held a press conference. After giving a brief narrative account of Whitmore's arrest and confessions, McKearney added, "We got the right guy—no question about it. He gave us details only the killer could know."

When transcribed by the stenographer, the confession was sixty-one pages long.

New York City awoke to immense headlines declaring, "Drifter Admits Wylie Murder" and "Accused Killer Called Animal by Girl's Dad." The stories under the headlines described Whitmore as a "lone-wolf burglar" and a "sadistic knifer."

Meanwhile, Whitmore was taken to Brooklyn police headquarters, where a full set of fingerprints and mug shots were taken. He was stripped and photographed nude, in accordance with a police policy, to provide rebuttal evidence against charges of brutality. Whitmore was arraigned a little later on charges of murder, robbery, and attempted rape before Supreme Court Justice James J. Comerford. "Without saying or implying any guilt in this matter," said Comerford, "the people of this town are pleased with the arrest for murder in which the citizens were very concerned. The police are doing a fine job."

Whitmore had no legal representation; New York did not have a public defender system. Comerford looked around the courtroom, spotting a young lawyer, Jerome J. Leftow, and asked him to represent Whitmore for his plea at the hearing. After a fifteen-minute consultation, Leftow told Comerford that Whitmore wished to plead not guilty and claimed that police had beaten the confessions out of him. Comerford accepted the plea and ordered Whitmore held without bail pending grand jury action.

The next day, Sunday, April 26, 1964, Leftow visited Whitmore in the Brooklyn House of Detention for Youth. In response to Leftow's questions, Whitmore repeated what he had said the previous day—that he was innocent and that the police "beat me and scared me into confessing." When Leftow asked Whitmore to talk about himself, he replied that he had dropped out of school two years earlier, after completing only the eighth grade, and that, because he lacked a trade, he had difficulties finding a steady job.

Leftow asked if he had ever been in trouble with the police.

"No, I swear I never have been," said Whitmore.

After about an hour, as Leftow rose to leave, Whitmore said gravely, "I want you for my lawyer. I trust you; you got a good face. I think you've been sent by God to help me."

Like every criminal lawyer in New York, Leftow was aware of the importance of the Wylie-Hoffert case and assumed that, in view of the attention the trial would attract, the police must have had a mountain of damning evidence before accusing Whitmore.

The following Tuesday, a Kings County grand jury indicted Whitmore for the murder of Minnie Edmonds. A week after that, another Kings County grand jury indicted him for the attempted rape and robbery of Elba Borrero. That same day, May 5, 1964, a New York County grand jury indicted him for the murders of Janice Wylie and Emily Hoffert.

After meeting with members of Whitmore's family, Leftow agreed to represent him without a fee and, at a hearing in the Edmonds case, made an unusual offer: Whitmore would be willing to take a lie detector test if the police officers who questioned him would do so as well.

It was an offer the police could and would refuse.

On Friday, May 8, Whitmore was taken from his Brooklyn cell to Manhattan, where he entered a plea of not guilty to the Wylie-Hoffert murders before Supreme Court Judge Charles Marks. Alluding to the brutality of the murders, Marks ordered a psychiatric report to be completed by June 12. Leftow did not object, and Whitmore was taken from jail to Bellevue Hospital.

Whitmore remained at Bellevue until October—inexplicably four months beyond the deadline set by Marks—when two psychiatrists pronounced him fit for trial, noting that he "steadfastly maintained his innocence." Their report concluded: "He is not in such a state of idiocy, imbecility, or insanity as to be incapable of understanding the charge, indictment, proceedings, or of making his defense."

Five days after the mental report was submitted to Judge Marks, Brooklyn District Attorney Aaron E. Koota announced that "in the best interest of justice" Whitmore would be prosecuted first for the attempted rape of Elba Borrero.

In early November, a week before that trial was to begin, the *New York Post* published an unconfirmed report that another suspect was under investigation for the Wylie-Hoffert murders. The suspect was said to be a narcotics addict who had been implicated in the crime by a fellow junkie under arrest for a murder in East Harlem.

Leftow went to the office of Peter Koste, the assistant district attorney who had taken Whitmore's confession to the Manhattan murders, and asked if there was any truth to the report. Koste would not answer, but took him to the office of an older assistant district attorney, apparently Koste's supervisor. Leftow said he thought that, if the Manhattan charges were being reconsidered, the attempted rape trial in Brooklyn ought to be delayed.

Both prosecutors remained still until Leftow demanded, "Either answer or I'll leave."

"Mr. Leftow," said the older man, "we know a great deal about this case, and we'll do the right thing."

Leftow dejectedly left, but just outside the building, he ran into two detectives whom he knew slightly.

"You're getting lucky, counselor," one of them said. "Your client is getting out of this."

"What do you mean?"

The detective looked perplexed, as if he had said too much, and refused to discuss the matter further.

Whitmore's trial in the Borrero case opened on November 9, 1964, before Kings County Supreme Court Justice David L. Malbin. It took two days to select a jury, which comprised twelve white men of middle-class backgrounds. Malbin then excused the jury for a voir dire hearing on whether the jury would be allowed to hear Whitmore's alleged confessions to the crime.

The first witness called by Leftow was Detective Aidala, who testified, as expected, that the confession had been voluntary. Leftow then called Whitmore, who testified that he had been beaten by Aidala and Isola. "They stood me in front of a chair," he said. "They called me a liar. I told them that if I said I did it, I would be lying. So, every time I said I didn't know what happened, I got knocked into the chair. Then they stood me up aside this wall and I continuously got beat until I couldn't take it no more. So I just broke down and shook my head." He said he had been hit in the back, chest, and stomach, but never in the face.

Assistant District Attorney Sidney A. Lichtman's first witness in the voir dire hearing was Elba Borrero. She testified that she had sat in the squad room while Whitmore was questioned in an adjoining room, and Lichtman asked, "Did you hear anybody yell or scream from inside that room?" She said she had not.

Malbin ruled that Whitmore's confession had been voluntary and thus would be admitted into evidence. The jury then returned to the courtroom to hear Aidala and DiPrima recount their version of what Whitmore had told them.

Borrero was the next prosecution witness. After she described the attack, Lichtman asked if she saw her assailant in the courtroom. "Yes," she said, without hesitation, pointing a finger at Whitmore.

On cross-examination, Leftow elicited that she initially had described her assailant as twenty-three to twenty-six years old, significantly older than his nineteen-year-old client. Leftow also established that at the police station she had identified Whitmore through a peephole, not in a lineup, and asked why she had requested that he speak—was it because she had not been sure he was the man? "No," she responded, "it was because I wanted to be sure beyond any shadow of doubt."

Leftow then switched to a topic that the prosecution may not have anticipated. "You have nothing to gain or lose whether this defendant is convicted or acquitted?" he asked. "Of course not," Borrero answered. With that on the record, Leftow asked whether she had consulted with two lawyers about the possibility of collecting the ten-thousand-dollar reward in another case. He was referring, of course, to the Wylie-Hoffert case and the reward offered by *Newsweek*, although the case was not identified to the jury. Borrero acknowledged that she had explored the possibility of collecting a reward.

The next witness was Patrolman Isola. On direct examination, he explained how he had interrupted the alleged attempted rape and stated that Whitmore fit the general description provided by Borrero, including that her attacker had a pockmarked face. The latter detail had not appeared in his report, however, and on cross-examination Isola was at a loss to explain how he could have failed to mention something so obviously relevant.

When the prosecution rested, Leftow called Whitmore, who testified that the night of the crime he had been with his girlfriend, Beverly Payne, and her eight-year-old sister until about 12:30 A.M. or a little later—he was unsure of the time. When he left, he walked down Amboy Street and about a block from the Payne apartment a man he had never seen before almost collided with him. Turning to what happened at the Seventy-Third Precinct, Whitmore testified that, once Borrero identified him, Aidala and Isola began punching him, although he insisted, "I never seen this lady before."

As he was about to begin cross-examination, Lichtman moved to introduce the confession Whitmore had made to Assistant District Attorney
Postal. After the judge, over Leftow's objection, held the statement admissible, Lichtman slowly read each question and answer to Whitmore, asking
after each, "Were you asked that question, and did you make that answer?"
Whitmore never replied affirmatively. Most of his answers were "No," but
several times he said, "I'm not sure," "I don't recall," or "I don't know."

When Lichtman finished, Leftow tried to spotlight Whitmore's limited
intelligence—his IQ was ninety—and possible mental confusion during the
interrogation. He asked Whitmore what day it was. Whitmore answered,
"I'm not sure." After calling Beverly Payne, who corroborated Whitmore's
testimony that he had been with her until around 12:30 A.M. the previous
April 23, Leftow rested the defense case.

After calling rebuttal witnesses, who added little of substance, Lichtman
began his summation. He scoffed at Whitmore's allegation that he had been
battered around and frightened, pointing out that the police photographs
of Whitmore in the nude failed to show a single bruise. Lichtman asked the
jury to picture what would have happened if Aidala, a two-hundred-pound
detective, had "belted this guy in the solar plexus five or six times."

Leftow began his summation by exhorting the jury not to be swayed
by publicity—even though the publicity stemmed from the Wylie-Hoffert
case, which the judge had forbidden being mentioned in front of the jury.
"Cases are decided in a courtroom, not in newspapers," Leftow said, urging
the jury to be "free of prejudice, free of bias." He also emphasized that Borrero's initial description of her assailant, as related in Isola's written report,
did not fit Whitmore, except for his being a slender Negro.

The jury deliberated nine hours before returning a verdict of guilty on
April 30, 1965.

Newsmen waiting outside the courthouse intercepted jurors as they left.
Most of them refused to say anything, but one stopped and spoke amicably
with reporters. He said he was certain that twelve men on the panel had
been aware that Whitmore was under indictment for the Wylie-Hoffert and
Edmonds slayings. As he was about to break away from the reporters, the
juror casually noted that one member of the panel had commented inside
the jury room, "This is nothing [compared] to what's coming to him."

Richard "Ricky" Robles had been a suspect in the Wylie-Hoffert case long
before Whitmore became enmeshed in it. In the frenzied early days of the
investigation, one of many probing rays emitted in the desperate search
for the killer rested on Robles. Plowing through thick files, detectives had

come across his dossier, which made interesting reading. He had a felony record of burglary and assault and a history of tying up victims. Also, unlike Whitmore, he lived nearby. He had been interviewed but dismissed as unworthy of attention based on an uncorroborated alibi provided by his mother. Logically, it would seem that he deserved considerably more scrutiny.

He had grown up in Yorkville, a neighborhood on the East Side of Manhattan extending from Eightieth Street north to Ninety-Sixth Street, with its other borders at the East River and Park Avenue. To Yorkville residents, Park Avenue is an important dividing line. The fabled thoroughfare and the numbered streets stretching westward from it to Central Park form the famed Gold Coast of ornate apartment buildings, expensive shops, and private schools—the section that was Janice Wylie's environment. East of Park Avenue is Yorkville, where the middle class and the poor live in scarred tenements.

The first ominous shadow in Robles's life materialized in 1956, shortly after his parents had divorced. He was a thirteen-year-old junior high school student, with an IQ of 130, when he took his first drag of a marijuana cigarette. When he was fifteen, in 1958, his twenty-year-old brother Michael, who had been his idol, was killed in a parachute jump with the 101st Airborne Division while on maneuvers in Kentucky. Michael's death apparently unloosed an inordinate emotional turmoil in Ricky, leading him into the midnight world of the junkie—heroin. His shocked mother and stepfather sent him to a psychiatrist, but to no avail. He was hooked on a twenty-dollars-a-day drug habit, and the only way for him to get that kind of money was through crime.

When the police caught up with Robles in 1960, he was a seventeen-year-old baby-faced bandit who, with gangster-film bravado, boasted of committing a hundred burglaries. The actual number was uncertain, given a police propensity for exaggerating the exploits of captured criminals—a convenient way to close otherwise unsolvable cases. But in one case Robles had pistol-whipped a woman after finding that she had no money in her apartment. In two burglaries, he had tied up his victims before ransacking their apartments. He was indicted in those cases and six others, but never tried. The Manhattan District Attorney's Office dropped all of the charges in exchange for a guilty plea to a single count of second-degree assault. He was sentenced to an indeterminate term of one day to five years at Elmira Reception Center, a prison for males under age twenty-one. He spent thirty-eight months in Elmira, where he obtained a high school diploma and learned the machinist's trade.

Robles was released on June 3, 1963, less than three months before Janice Wylie and Emily Hoffert were murdered in their apartment, a half-mile from where he was living in Yorkville. He was among hundreds of ex-convicts interviewed about the crime by detectives. He said that he, of course, had heard of the double murder, but all he knew was what he had read in the newspapers. He added that since his release he had kept away from his old associates, concentrating on his job as a machinist and doing his best to avoid trouble.

"I wouldn't ice two dames," he told the detectives who interviewed him.

On August 28, the day of the crime, the Bronx factory where he worked had been closed for the week. Since he was on vacation, he slept late—until noon—at his mother's apartment. After getting up, he puttered around the apartment most of the day, occasionally watching television. His mother corroborated his statement, and there were no clues pointing to him. Like a score of men interviewed the same day, he was regarded by the police as examined and cleared.

In December 1963, Robles went to his parole officer with an odd request—he wanted to return to Elmira. He said he was afraid of slipping back into drug addiction and needed the antiseptic harshness of prison—or "cold-turkey" life—to prevent a relapse. His request was granted. He stayed at Elmira for the next nine months, during which he read in newspapers that the Wylie-Hoffert killings had been solved with the arrest of George Whitmore.

On October 8, 1964, a month after Robles was released from Elmira and a day before Whitmore would go on trial for the attempted rape of Elba Borrero, a drug pusher named Roberto Cruz Del Valle was stabbed to death after a quarrel in the hallway of an East Harlem tenement—a crime that fell within the jurisdiction of the Twenty-Third Precinct.

Witnesses recognized the killer and without hesitation provided a name—Jimmy Delaney, whom police knew as a junkie and pusher from Yorkville. At his apartment, detectives were greeted by a man who identified himself as Nathan Delaney and produced an ID identifying him as such. He said Jimmy was his brother and, after he provided a snapshot of him. Detectives left, snapshot in hand.

In fact, Jimmy and Nathan were one and the same. That evening, at a friend's apartment, he gleefully told a group of friends—including Ricky Robles—how he had outwitted the police. The snapshot he had given them was of his dead brother-in-law. Delaney's glee was short-lived, however.

When he returned to his apartment that night, detectives were waiting to arrest him. Although he insisted that he had stabbed Cruz in self-defense, Delaney knew he was in serious trouble. He was a three-time loser who, even if convicted only of manslaughter, would face a life sentence.

The next morning, Detective Patrick Lappin was assigned to move Delaney from the Twenty-Third Precinct, where he had been booked for murder, downtown to the Tombs. On the way, Delaney made a startling claim: "You guys got the wrong guy in the Wylie-Hoffert job—it isn't Whitmore."

Delaney said the killer was a friend of his, who had come to his apartment the day of the murders and told him that he had just killed two women during a burglary. He said the murderer was a narcotics addict, who had said he slipped into an apartment to pull a burglary when he encountered a nude blond. He forced her to perform oral sex. Then another young woman came into the apartment. He tied up both women and, fearing that they would be able to identify him, stabbed them to death.

Delaney told Lappin that much—without identifying the killer. Lappin had not been detailed to the Wylie-Hoffert investigation and had no way of judging whether Delaney was speaking truthfully or just concocting a tale in the frantic hope it might help him with his own murder case. After depositing Delaney at the Tombs, Lappin returned uptown to fill out a report for his supervisors, Lieutenant Thomas J. Cavanaugh, head of the Twenty-Third Precinct detective squad, and Sergeant William Brent, second in command.

Cavanaugh and Brent were aware of a well-kept secret—that the evidence against Whitmore in the Wylie-Hoffert case had disintegrated to the point that his guilt was doubted at the highest levels of the police department and the Manhattan District Attorney's Office. For one thing, detectives had located the young blond in the photograph found in Whitmore's possession—the photo that had led police to suspect Whitmore of the crime in the first place. She was Arlene Franco, of Wildwood, New Jersey—where Whitmore initially had stated that he found the photo in a junkyard. Consequently, Manhattan District Attorney Frank S. Hogan had more than a passing interest in Delaney's tale when it came to his attention on October 10, while jury selection was underway for Whitmore's trial in Brooklyn.

On October 19, Delaney was taken from his cell in the Tombs to the office of Peter Koste, the assistant district attorney who had taken Whitmore's formal confession six months earlier—but who since had come to doubt its veracity. Delaney repeated essentially what he had told Detective Lappin, adding details about his friend's admission that seemed to make more sense than details in Whitmore's alleged confession. For instance, according to Delaney, the friend had said he entered and left the building through a basement window. In contrast, Whitmore's statement that he entered the building through a lobby door had been suspect because the door was always locked.

Delaney's story was persuasive, but he was not ready to identify his friend. He wanted something for that—immunity from prosecution for the murder of Roberto Cruz Del Valle. Koste left the room for several minutes, apparently to confer with District Attorney Hogan. When Koste returned, he told Delaney that the Cruz case would be dismissed if his identification of the Wylie-Hoffert killer proved accurate.

"His name," said Delaney, "is Richard Robles—Ricky Robles."

Detectives questioned Delaney's wife, Marjorie, who said she had heard the damaging admissions her husband had described.

Within hours, a detective found Robles at a girlfriend's flat on East Eighty-Ninth Street. He agreed—although he actually had no choice—to go "downtown," the police euphemism for a place of questioning. It was close to midnight when Robles was ushered into Koste's office and told that Nathan and Marjorie Delaney had accused him of the Wylie-Hoffert murder.

With no outward signs of emotion, Robles said they were lying. He calmly but adamantly insisted that he was innocent. Koste had little doubt that Robles was lying, but had no evidence to hold him. Thus, Robles walked into the somber early-morning silence a free man, as Nathan Delaney was returned to the Tombs.

A week later, during a party at his girlfriend's apartment, Ricky Robles collapsed from an overdose of barbiturates that almost killed him. After a day on the danger list at Metropolitan Hospital, however, he rallied. He remained in the hospital for eight more days, during which police and the district attorney's office devised a strategy for trapping him.

After obtaining court orders, the police planted miniature microphones in the Delaneys' apartments. Recordings of anything Robles might say of an incriminating nature could be used in court; New York was one of five states that explicitly sanctioned such evidence. Both of the Delaneys had agreed to cooperate in the investigation. After Nathan was released from the Tombs the day after Thanksgiving, the first step in the plan was for them to persuade Robles that they had talked to the police only to save Nathan from a life sentence. Now that that goal had been accomplished, they were back on his side—and in a position to pass along misleading information that would confound the investigation or lead the authorities to conclude that he had nothing to do with the Wylie-Hoffert crime.

Every time he visited—the visits were frequent because they were his drug source and they got high together—the Delaneys tried to get him to talk about the murders, hoping that he would say something that would betray him as the killer. As if engaged in macabre mental combat, however, he answered their questions with double entendres, grunts, or laughs—until the night of January 24, 1965, when he became careless.

As the three were getting high, the Delaneys told him that men from the district attorney's office were going to pick them up the next day for further questioning about the murders. The session, they said, would provide an opportunity for them to offer information that would prove false, thus damaging their credibility. As the conversation ensued, Robles said several incriminating things. For instance, when asked what they should say about how he left the building, he replied that they should say he used the service exit. "But that's the way you came out, man," said Marjorie, to which he replied, "So what?"

Two days later, Robles was arrested when he arrived at his girlfriend's Eighty-Ninth Street apartment, which detectives had been staking out in a police car disguised as a New York cab. They drove north, or uptown, stopping at Third Avenue and Ninety-Third Street, where Lieutenant Cavanaugh got into the back seat beside Robles.

"This is D-Day, Ricky," said Cavanaugh. "It's all over."

Robles was one day short of his twenty-second birthday.

On January 27, 1965, Manhattan District Attorney Hogan dismissed the murder charges against Whitmore and Robles was arraigned on the same charges. The Robles trial took place eight months later, in the summer-scented days of October and the raw, rainy days of November 1965. Robles appeared in court dressed like a college graduate seeking his first job, his blue suit offset by a white shirt and a properly conservative striped tie, his black shoes gleaming, his hair neatly trimmed. In the dimly lit courtroom, he watched and listened without a flicker of emotion on his prison-paled features as witnesses testified and lawyers argued. The trial lasted seven weeks; the jury of seven men and five women required only six hours of deliberation to convict him of two counts of murder in the first degree.

Supreme Court Judge Irwin D. Davidson sentenced him to life in prison on each count.

Epilogue

On March 19, 1965, after a post-conviction hearing, Justice Malbin reversed Whitmore's conviction in the Borrero case, holding that the jury had been influenced by prejudice and racial bias; one juror was quoted as saying during deliberations, "These guys are all the same, they have got to have it. They fuck like jack rabbits."

Although the veracity of Whitmore's confessions in both the Borrero and Edmonds cases was undermined (to put it mildly) by the obvious falsity of his confession in the Wylie-Hoffert case, Kings County District Attorney Aaron A. Koota plowed blithely ahead in both cases as if nothing had happened.

In April 1965, Koota took Whitmore to trial for the Edmonds murder before Supreme Court Justice Dominic S. Rinaldi, who had denied a pretrial defense motion to suppress the alleged confession in that case. The jury deadlocked, however, resulting in a mistrial. Then, in March 1966, Whitmore was again convicted of the Borrero crime, following a retrial before Supreme Court Justice Aaron F. Goldstein. Whitmore was sentenced to an indeterminate term of five to ten years in prison.

When the *Miranda* decision came down on June 13, 1966, Koota had no choice but to drop the Edmonds case, given that the confession—the only evidence purporting to link Whitmore to that crime—could not be introduced at a retrial. On Koota's motion, Supreme Court Justice Hyman Barshay dismissed the case on June 30. Two weeks later, Kings County Supreme Court Justice Philip M. Kleinfeld granted a motion to release Whitmore on five thousand dollars bond in the Borrero case. On July 13— two years, eleven weeks, and three days after Whitmore's arrest—a New York radio station posted the bail and he was released.

In April 1967, Whitmore's conviction in the Borrero case was overturned on the ground that Goldstein had erred in refusing to allow the defense to cross-examine police concerning the false confession in the Wylie-Hoffert case. The following month, Koota, declaring that he was acting "in the interests of justice," took Whitmore to trial yet again, this time before Supreme Court Justice Julius Helfand. With the confession inadmissible under *Miranda*, the prosecution case rested solely on Borrero's identification testimony. The jury found that sufficient to convict, returning a verdict of guilty on May 17. Helfand sentenced Whitmore once again to five to ten years in prison.

Whitmore proceeded to exhaust his appeals, but in December 1972, Selwyn Raab, author of *Justice in the Backroom* (from which the foregoing article was excerpted), obtained dramatic new evidence—an affidavit from Borrero's sister, Celeste Viruet, disclosing that before Borrero identified Whitmore, police had shown her an array of photos of other suspects—and she had positively identified another man as her assailant.

By this time, Kings County had a new district attorney, Eugene Gold, who confirmed the accuracy of the affidavit and agreed to reopen the case. On April 10, 1973, at Gold's request, Supreme Court Justice Irwin Brownstein vacated Whitmore's conviction, ordering his immediate release.

Whitmore sued for violation of his civil rights, but lost. He received no compensation for his wrongful prosecution and imprisonment. Neither detectives nor prosecutors involved in the case were disciplined or otherwise held to account for the misconduct that had put Whitmore behind bars for a total of eight years, five weeks, and four days for a crime he did not commit.

As a direct result of the fact that Whitmore had faced a death sentence for crimes he did not commit, the New York State legislature voted in May 1965 to abolish capital punishment; the vote was forty-seven to nine in the senate and seventy-eight to sixty-seven in the assembly. Governor Nelson A. Rockefeller signed the measure into law on June 1.

A year later, the U.S. Supreme Court cited Whitmore's false confessions in its landmark *Miranda v. Arizona* decision requiring police to advise suspects of their rights to remain silent and to consult with counsel before questioning.

The case also inspired a popular 1970s CBS television series starring Aristotle (Telly) Savalas in the title role of Kojak, a heroic character who was entirely fictitious; there was no police hero in the actual case. The series grew out of a two-part made-for-TV movie entitled *The Marcus-Nelson Murders* that aired in 1973.

UNREQUITED INNOCENCE

Once you've been wrongfully convicted of a crime, you'll find that the standard of proof necessary to set you free is considerably higher than that required to convict you in the first place.

As a matter of law, appellate courts must view the evidence in criminal cases in the light most favorable to the prosecution. The larger problem you'll confront, however, is that weighing the evidence in your favor against that against you is a subjective process affected by biases.

Unfortunately, the officials in whose hands your fate resides—judges, prosecutors, governors—are neither immune from bias nor prone to objectivity. To them, or so it often seems, admitting mistakes, much less malfeasance, is anathema.

Biases, of course, affect all criminal cases, but their impact is especially obvious in false-confession cases. The reason, no doubt, is simply that the power of confessions, even when they make no sense, is so overwhelming that they are all but exempt from the laws of logic.

Appellate judges and governors are not necessarily any more likely than lay jurors to overcome the unwarranted assumption that normal persons—absent physical abuse or extreme coercion—do not confess to crimes they didn't commit.

The point is vividly illustrated by the following articles about cases in which, despite strong evidence of actual innocence, relief has been denied.

JOSEPH DICK, DEREK TICE, DANIAL WILLIAMS, AND ERIC WILSON

The confessions were greatly at odds with the facts—but that didn't matter

ALAN BERLOW

NORFOLK, VIRGINIA

At the Keen Mountain Correctional Center, a gray complex of poured concrete in rural southwest Virginia, Joseph Jesse Dick Jr. sits behind the thick glass pane of a prison interview booth like a specimen in an oversize shadow box. A man of delicate bearing with receding reddish-brown hair, a sparse mustache, and rectangular prison-issue glasses a bit wide on his long, gaunt face, Dick is here because he pleaded guilty to the 1997 rape and murder of his neighbor Michelle Moore-Bosko—a crime he now says he didn't commit. And maybe he didn't.

Such proclamations of innocence are no longer surprising. The imprisoned man exonerated by DNA evidence or a belated confession by the actual killer or the emergence of a credible alibi witness is a narrative of increasing familiarity. But even in the upside-down world of wrongful convictions, the extravagant case of Joseph Dick and his supposed partners in crime is in a class of its own.

To conclude that Dick is innocent, you must believe, first, that the tape-recorded confession he gave to the police was untrue and, second, that three other men who said they committed the brutal crime with Dick also falsely confessed. In addition, you must believe that Dick perjured himself when he helped convict two of those codefendants by testifying against them at their trials for rape and murder, lied when he named five other accomplices, and lied moments before a judge gave him a double life sentence when he apologized to the parents of Moore-Bosko, declaring, "I know I shouldn't have done it; I have got no idea what went through my mind that night, and my soul."

From "What Happened in Norfolk?" *New York Times Magazine*, August 19, 2007. Copyright © Alan Berlow. Adapted with permission.

This is a lot to accept. But perhaps the most astonishing aspect of this case is that these may be the most logical conclusions to draw. When I met Dick, who is now thirty-one, at Keen Mountain in January, he told me that initially, for more than seven hours, he had proclaimed to investigators his innocence of any involvement in the crime. During that interrogation, he claimed in an affidavit, Robert Glenn Ford, a Norfolk police detective, taunted him incessantly, told him he was lying, shouted at him, threatened him with the "hoses," and told him he would get the death penalty unless he cooperated. Dick told me that he finally gave Ford the confession he demanded "to avoid the death penalty."

Dick did not have Detective Ford or any other detective breathing down his neck when he testified for the state against his two Navy colleagues. When I asked him what it was like to sit on the witness stand, knowingly fabricating a story that could have resulted in their executions, Dick let out an audible sigh that seemed to say, "I know you're not going to believe this," and, after an extended silence, replied, "It didn't cross my mind that I was lying. I believed what I was saying was true." By the time he became a witness for the state, said Dick, he had convinced himself he was guilty. Police officers, prosecutors, and even his own lawyer insisted that he had committed the crime. "They messed up my mind and made me believe something that wasn't true," he said. Michael Fasanaro, Dick's defense attorney at the time, says he still believes Dick is guilty. "I've seen nothing to convince me otherwise," said Fasanaro, who no longer represents Dick.

Three other men now say, as Dick does, that they falsely confessed to involvement in the rape and murder of Moore-Bosko under pressure from Ford. Damian J. Hansen, one of three assistant commonwealth's attorneys who prosecuted the so-called Norfolk Four and four other men for the murder, says these claims are nothing more than "sound bites" invented by "hired gun" experts and what he calls the "clemency gang," a team of high-powered New York and Washington attorneys who have asked Governor Tim Kaine to grant the Norfolk Four an absolute pardon. "There is no new evidence," Hansen says. "There are no unanswered questions."

Nevertheless, the Norfolk Four count a growing list of supporters, including four former Virginia attorneys general, one of them a Republican, who have no obvious motive for suggesting that the state perpetrated a major miscarriage of justice. Richard Cullen, who was appointed U.S. attorney for the Eastern District of Virginia under President George H. W. Bush and Virginia attorney general by former Governor George Allen, said the "totality of the scientific evidence" and "the crime scene being inconsistent with the prosecution theory" convinced him that the four are innocent.

Governor Tim Kaine, a Democrat, will be under enormous pressure to reject clemency for the three defendants serving life sentences and the fourth who was released after more than eight years in prison. Two of the defendants were convicted by juries, which governors are loath to second-guess (Dick and a second defendant pleaded guilty and were never tried), and the victim's family is adamantly opposed to a pardon. Moreover, a pardon would probably be seen as a tacit repudiation of the police and prosecutors. Cullen, who advised Governor Allen on clemency matters, said he decided to speak out in part because he believes that Kaine should be free to grant clemency without being attacked by Republicans.

Assuming Kaine can set politics aside and focus solely on the voluminous evidence, he is likely to find that the controversy turns on two complex and interrelated questions. First, did four grown men, three on active duty in the U.S. Navy and one recently retired, falsely confess to a horrible crime? Because the state had no outside witnesses and no physical evidence linking any of the four to the crime—no blood, saliva, hair, fibers, fingerprints, or DNA—the case rested almost entirely on the defendants' own confessions, all given in the absence of attorneys. Second, Kaine will have to decide whether the crime was committed by eight men, as the state maintains, or by one man, as is argued by Cullen and other defenders of the Norfolk Four.

Kaine might begin by looking not at the end result—the incontrovertible fact that the four men confessed to a crime—but at the investigative process that led to those confessions. More specifically, he might want to examine how the state's theory evolved from a crime committed by a single perpetrator to one involving two assailants, then three, six, seven, and finally eight men who the state says took turns raping and stabbing the eighteen-year-old victim. The man behind that tortuous investigative odyssey was Joe Dick's interrogator, Detective Ford.

The Gates of West Bay apartments are a modest collection of tidy, two-story red-brick buildings located only a short walk from Gate Four of the Norfolk Naval Station. They are a popular residence for Navy enlisted men and others with limited means—people like Michelle Moore-Bosko and Bill Bosko, the man she secretly married two months before the murder. According to Bill's testimony at the trials of two defendants, he and Michelle were planning to have a "really big wedding" for their families in Pittsburgh in October, but they eloped both because they wanted to be together and because he was going to be spending a lot of time at sea and wanted Michelle to have his insurance "in case anything were to happen." He said they settled on the apartment on West Bay Avenue because it looked like "a safe place" and was affordable.

On July 8, 1997, Bill returned from a week at sea aboard the USS *Simpson*, a guided-missile frigate, took a taxi home, opened the door, and went inside. He would later testify, "I got into the house, and the house was nice and clean," a point that police investigators also noted in their reports and that would take on increasing significance as the number of men charged grew from one to eight. "I didn't figure she was home," Bill testified, "so I decided I was going to shower and shave and get all cleaned up and go to her work and surprise her, and I walked into my bedroom and I found my wife butchered on my bedroom floor." Unable to find the couple's portable phone, Bosko ran across the hall and banged on the door of an apartment, shouting: "My wife is dead. My wife is dead." The door was opened by Danial Williams, who lived with his wife, Nicole, and a roommate—Joe Dick. Williams called 911. A few hours later, Williams was asked to answer questions at the police station after the victim's best friend, Tamika Taylor, told the police that Williams was "obsessed with Michelle."

Then twenty-five and on his second tour with the Navy, Williams had married Nicole eleven days earlier, after learning that she had ovarian cancer. Williams proclaimed his innocence to police investigators for more than eight hours before Detective Ford entered the four-by-seven-foot interrogation room at around 5:00 A.M. Less than one hour later, Williams began his confession. Now thirty-five and serving a life sentence at the Sussex II State Prison in Waverly, Virginia, Williams, like the other Norfolk Four defendants, had no prior criminal record. But he said in an interview (and in an affidavit) that Ford treated him like a criminal from the outset, poking him in the chest, yelling in his face, calling him a liar, and telling him, falsely, that he'd failed a polygraph test, and that a witness had seen him go into the apartment. The police got him to "second-guess" his memory, Williams said. "They wear you down to the point that you're exhausted. I just wanted the questioning to end."

Ford has testified on several occasions that he has never coerced or threatened witnesses, fed them information, or otherwise encouraged a false confession. Numerous requests to interview Ford, a twenty-nine-year police veteran, were declined by Chris Amos, the Norfolk Police spokesman. Two Freedom of Information requests for police records on the Norfolk Four case were turned down by Norfolk's assistant city attorney, Andrew R. Fox, who also represented Ford at a deposition for one of the Norfolk Four defendants. Ford retired on August 1.

It seems clear that Ford and the other investigators concluded that they had solved the crime. The Norfolk Four's new lawyers say they have found no record that the police searched Williams's apartment for evidence—blood from the crime scene, Williams's own blood, the victim's DNA on a towel, or an item of Williams's clothing. Instead, the investigation was effectively dropped for the next five months. It resumed on December 11, 1997, when Ford's office learned that DNA recovered from Moore-Bosko did not belong to Williams.

Ford seemed to conclude that Williams had an accomplice, and he turned his attention to Dick, Williams's roommate. Dick says he told his interrogators that he was on board the USS *Saipan* at the time of the crime. And Dick's immediate supervisor, Senior Chief Michael Ziegler, says that he has "no doubt" Dick was on duty the night of the murder. A decorated chief petty officer, Ziegler took a special interest in Dick because of what he described as his "diminished mental capacity." When Dick was questioned by the police, Ziegler says, he double-checked the *Saipan*'s records to confirm that Dick was assigned to the ship. Given the ship's rigorous security, it would have been virtually impossible for Dick to sneak off, commit the crime, and sneak back on board. "The Joseph Dick I knew couldn't chew bubble gum and tie his shoes at the same time," Ziegler told me. "There's no way in hell anyone can convince me Joseph Dick could pull that off."

Ziegler says that his superiors told him that the murder investigation was a "civil matter" and that the police would contact him if he was needed. Ziegler spent the next two years in Norfolk but says he never heard from the police, the prosecutors, or Dick's attorneys and that no one asked to view the ship's "muster," or attendance records, which he says would have proved Dick was on board. Commander Scott Rettie, who was Ziegler's superior at the time, told me that no police officers or defense attorneys interviewed him either. Dick's lawyer, and Hansen, the prosecutor, both insist Dick was not on board the ship. "It was clear he was not on duty," Fasanaro said in an interview. It "was confirmed through the Navy" and "Hansen had the same information."

For his part, Hansen said he never personally investigated Dick's alibi. "We don't go out and research people's alibis and where they possibly could have been," he told me, adding that he was "certain Dick's lawyer . . . would certainly have investigated that." Because Dick was never tried, the state was never forced to produce documentation to support the claim that Dick was not assigned to the ship at the time of the murder. The ship's records have since been destroyed.

Based on their statements to the police, Dick and Williams might seem an odd pair of accomplices. Each said, "I did it," but their confessions were inconsistent with the evidence and with each other's confessions. Williams said he committed the crime alone; Dick said they did it together. Dick said they entered between 9:00 p.m. and 11:00 p.m. But Michelle's friend Tamika Taylor had already told Ford and a second investigator that she and Michelle were out together from noon until 11:30 p.m. Williams knew the body was in the bedroom either because he was involved in the crime or because he saw it there when he entered the apartment with Bill Bosko just after calling 911. Dick said the body was in the living room. Williams said he beat Michelle's head with a shoe and hit her in the face three times. No shoe was found, and the autopsy showed no sign of a beating. Williams denied choking her and said he didn't use a weapon. But when the autopsy showed Moore-Bosko had been stabbed and strangled, Williams obligingly amended his confession, saying he may have grabbed Michelle's neck and that he had used a knife he found in the bedroom to kill her. Dick, meanwhile, said Michelle retrieved the knife from the kitchen while he and Williams were arguing, and that she was attacking him, Dick, when he stabbed her. Neither Dick nor Williams could accurately describe the knife. Williams said he was wearing the same underwear at the time of his arrest as he wore before the rape, but none of the victim's DNA was found on it. Dick said he ejaculated in the victim's mouth, but no semen was found there. He said he threw a blanket over the victim's legs before he left, but Bill Bosko had already told police he found his wife naked from the waist down and that he covered her with the blanket.

None of this seemed to trouble Ford or the prosecutors. The state argued that the defendants' accounts of what happened were consistent "at their core" and that guilty people often lie or change their stories before telling the truth while confessing. But Richard J. Ofshe, an expert on police interrogations who was hired by lawyers for the Norfolk Four, says the Williams and Dick misstatements and others that would follow are typical of a "classic false confession" and are evidence of the defendants' innocence. "On virtually every important detail," Ofshe wrote in his evaluation for the defense attorneys, Williams and Dick "got the facts of the crime wrong."

But there was a more fundamental evidentiary problem that should have leapt out at investigators as soon as the state's theory on the number of perpetrators rose from one to two. Or so says Dr. Werner U. Spitz, a medical doctor and professor of forensic pathology at Wayne State University's School of Medicine who has worked on nearly sixty thousand autopsies over fifty years. Spitz, who was hired by the Norfolk Four attorneys, says a careful examination of the victim's wounds makes it "extraordinarily unlikely that more than one person" wielded the knife and "even less likely that several people" stabbed her to death. When I interviewed Spitz in Richmond, he thumbed through the gruesome autopsy photos, pointing out that all of the knife wounds were clustered in an area two and three-quarter inches by two inches and that the three fatal wounds were all five inches deep and perfectly parallel to one another. Assuming the state's final theory, that eight men took turns stabbing the victim through her black T-shirt, Spitz wondered out loud, "How does the next guy know where to stab her?" to get this concentrated pattern with wounds at precisely the same angle.

The state's medical examiner testified in the cases that went to trial that the wounds were consistent with a single assailant, although it was "possible" more than one person was involved. This ambiguous conclusion was never challenged at trial by an outside expert like Spitz. I asked Dr. John E. Adams, a Maryland forensic pathologist who has testified in more than five hundred cases but not in the Norfolk Four case, to look at the autopsy and knife-wound evidence. He said that the wounds appeared to have been "made in rapid succession by one person." He added, "It's the only way you get a tight pattern like that."

Hansen, the prosecutor, is not swayed by the arguments raised by the new lawyers and experts. He points out that the wound evidence, the appearance of the apartment, and the inconsistencies in the defendants' statements were all thoroughly aired. "The juries heard everything," he told me, and they still voted unanimously to convict two of the defendants. (As mentioned previously, the other two pleaded guilty.) What the juries also heard, most convincingly, was the one thing that is almost impossible to rebut—a defendant's recorded confession. A confession, one legal scholar wrote, "makes the other aspects of a trial in court superfluous."

Eleven weeks after Dick's confession, his DNA analysis came back negative. At that point, Ford had to question the reliability of his confessions or look for another suspect. Once again, he chose the latter course. His notes indicate he returned to Dick, who "agreed to tell us the truth" about who was involved. This time Dick made a new claim, wholly unsupported by the evidence, that the men decided to dump the body and moved it from the bedroom to the living room and, when they heard a noise outside, back to the bedroom. Dick also named a new assailant, Eric Wilson, a twenty-year-old sailor and former Eagle Scout and friend of Williams's, who he said washed blood from the knife in Danial Williams's unsearched apartment.

There is no indication in Ford's notes that he asked Dick how they moved the blood-soaked body without leaving a trace on the floor, or how the knife got back into the Bosko apartment, where the police found it. Ford focused instead on Wilson, who was arrested and, after ten hours of questioning, gave a recorded confession. Wilson would later testify that Ford hit him several times and showed him photos of the crime scene and the victim and gave him details about the crime to include in his confession. At his trial in 1999, Wilson testified that he couldn't withstand Ford's pressure: "If they had told me that I killed J.F.K., I would have told them I handed Oswald the gun." A jury found Wilson guilty only of the rape, and he served eight and a half years in prison.

Wilson's DNA was tested, of course, but it, too, failed to match the crime-scene samples, so Ford returned to Joe Dick, who offered yet another version of events. This time, Dick said there were three others involved but that he could only remember a guy named George, whom he later identified in a Navy photograph. The man's name, however, was not George but Derek Tice. Ford personally went to Orlando, Florida, to pick up Tice. After fourteen hours in custody, Tice also confessed.

Now incarcerated in the same facility as Williams, Tice is a slight, soft-spoken thirty-seven-year-old who describes the same sort of belligerent, accusatory, and threatening style claimed by the others. He has testified that Ford fed him details that went into his confession. Although Ford recorded confessions from all of the Norfolk Four defendants, he recorded none of the lengthy interrogations, making it impossible to reconstruct what occurred.

As was the case with the earlier confessions, Tice introduced several glaring new inconsistencies, like his assertion that the men used a claw hammer to pry open the apartment door, despite no evidence of a forced entry. But the most explosive claim made by Tice was that seven men participated, including three new accomplices whose names he provided and whom the state subsequently indicted.

As this universe of conspirators expanded, so did the contradictions. Prosecutors had no choice but to concede that none of the seven indictees matched the DNA samples, but they argued, "the lack of DNA doesn't prove" that a defendant wasn't there, a claim that went largely unchallenged in court. More recently, the DNA and all other evidence in the case came in for a new level of scrutiny.

In the fall of 2004, after both Tice and Wilson were convicted and the other two men had pleaded guilty, the case of the Norfolk Four came to the attention of Peter J. Neufeld, a director of the Innocence Project at

Cardozo Law School in New York. Neufeld contacted George Kendall, one of the country's preeminent death-penalty lawyers, who examined the evidence and secured a commitment from his firm, Holland & Knight, to represent Dick pro bono. Kendall then asked two other firms—Skadden, Arps, Slate, Meagher & Flom and Hogan & Hartson—to examine the cases of Williams and Tice. Their lawyers also concluded the men were probably innocent and agreed to represent them at no cost. Wilson continued to be represented by his original trial lawyer.

The legal team, consisting of thirteen lawyers in all, in turn hired several outside experts to examine the crime-scene evidence and the DNA. For the latter they brought in Todd W. Bille, a forensic DNA analyst who developed a DNA-extraction method used to identify remains from the World Trade Center disaster. Bille concluded that given the number of men the state claimed were involved in the rape, it was "extremely unlikely" that DNA from at least one of the Norfolk Four would not have been found. Moreover, the DNA recovered at the crime scene—from a vaginal swab, fingernails, and a blanket—all came from only one source, which Bille suggested would be highly unlikely under the state's logic.

A second problem with the seven- or eight-man theory was the crime scene. The police department reported finding the tiny seven-hundred-square-foot apartment immaculate and almost totally undisturbed. Was this really possible if seven or eight men were involved? Relying on Tice's confession, Hansen argued at trial that "this gang, this pack, this crew pushed their way" into the apartment, carried the struggling young woman down a narrow, thirty-four-inch hallway, and "ravished" and stabbed her. Yet there was no evidence of a struggle. This "pack" didn't disturb papers that were jutting precariously into the hallway, didn't leave a single shoe print on the recently polished floor or any other evidence of their rampage.

The third problem raised by Tice was that the three men he named all denied any involvement, two with nearly airtight alibis. John Danser, an air-conditioning technician, recently retired from the Navy, had a worksheet showing he'd just finished a job at precisely the time Tice claimed the men entered Moore-Bosko's apartment, as well as an ATM receipt from a bank near his home in Warminster, Pennsylvania—three hundred miles north of Norfolk—showing a withdrawal ten minutes after Tice said they left the apartment.

A second defendant fingered by Tice, Richard Pauley, was represented by Jon Babineau and John R. Doyle, who now heads the Norfolk State Attorney's Office, which indicted the Norfolk Four. Babineau said he and Doyle found computer, Internet, and phone records proving that their client was talking and e-mailing with his girlfriend in Australia for more than three hours, starting at 11:00 P.M., shortly before Michelle's friend Tamika Taylor said she left her alone at her apartment.

Although charges against the three men named by Tice were eventually dropped, Ford and Hansen continue to insist that they were involved. "Charging it and proving it are two different things," Hansen says. But his continued insistence on the guilt of Danser and Pauley has raised more than a few questions about the credibility of the rest of the case against the Norfolk Four.

Ford certainly knew false confessions were possible. In 1990, the detective and two other officers were transferred out of the homicide division after three teenagers they interrogated confessed falsely to a murder. Ford has acknowledged that the three falsely confessed to being at the scene of the murder, but he insisted that they helped to plan the crime.

When the issue of Ford's earlier false confessions came up at Tice's second trial, Judge Charles E. Poston ruled that the evidence was inadmissible. Whether Ford "obtained a false confession or not seems to me to be relatively benign," Poston said, "because I suspect that many police officers have done that, because we have all seen people who confess to anything." Poston opined that it was neither "unusual" nor "rare" for people to confess to crimes "totally imagined."

But three jurors I interviewed from Tice's first trial were anything but blasé about his eighteen-minute taped confession. If I listened to it, they insisted, I'd understand why they felt compelled to convict him. The tape is, indeed, chilling. Tice describes calmly and methodically how seven men took turns raping Michelle Moore-Bosko, how one of them retrieved a knife from the kitchen and how Tice told him, "Just go ahead and stab the bitch."

"Just listen to his tone of voice," Prosecutor Valerie Bowen implored these jurors in her closing arguments. "Does that sound like someone who is being pressured into making a statement?" According to Randall Mc-Farlane, the jury foreman, "Nothing could blunt the force of that taped confession."

By December 1998, eighteen months after the murder, the state had seven men in custody but still no DNA match. Then, in February 1999, a woman named Karen Stover handed over to the Norfolk Police Department a letter from a Virginia prison inmate, Omar Abdul Ballard, in which Ballard not only threatened to have Stover murdered unless she sent him money and "nasty pictures" of herself but also confessed to the murder of Moore-Bosko. "And one last thing," Ballard wrote, "you remember that night I went to mommies house and the next morning Michelle got killed guess who did that, Me HA, HA."

Ballard, it turns out, was a childhood friend of Tamika Taylor's. Taylor introduced Ballard to the Boskos, and they had all socialized. It was Taylor who pointed police to Danial Williams the day Michelle was found dead and told police Michelle was afraid of him. But Taylor now claims she also told the police to "check out Omar Ballard." Taylor knew that Ballard had beaten a young woman with a baseball bat not long before the murder just down the street from the apartments where she and the Boskos lived, and he had been protected by the Boskos.

Bill Bosko testified that Ballard had been pursued by thirty or thirty-five men who "said they were going to kill" him, and that he and Michelle gave Ballard refuge in their apartment. Ten days after Michelle's murder, Ballard raped and beat a teenage girl one mile from the Boskos'. The girl survived, and Ballard was sent to prison for forty years. Curiously, a warrant for Ballard's arrest for the baseball-bat assault was issued the same evening the police were grilling their first suspect, Danial Williams, putting Ballard squarely on the police radar for a crime committed only a few hundred feet from the murder scene. Two weeks later, they arrested him for the rape of the teenager. By then, Ford had Williams's confession.

Once Ballard's DNA was tested and Detective Ford learned that it matched the samples recovered from the crime scene, he confronted Ballard. Unlike the four others, who confessed after seven to fourteen hours in custody, Ballard confessed in twenty minutes. He also accurately described the knife and the crime scene without prompting, gave details none of the others had mentioned, and provided a time frame for the murder consistent with Tamika Taylor's testimony. The only problem—from Ford's point of view—was that Ballard said he acted alone. At the end of his recorded confession, Ford asked Ballard, "Is there anything you wish to add to this statement?" Ballard replied, "No, just them four people that opened their mouths is stupid."

Ballard's confession complicated the state's case yet again. Under the new theory, Ballard, who has an extensive criminal record and a history of assaulting women, protected seven men he didn't know. According to the state, he did so because he was at the time serving a life sentence and feared being labeled a "snitch." Moreover, prosecutors argued, Ballard, who is black, was afraid people would know he'd committed a crime with "white boys." At the same time, the state's theory would mean that the white defendants, who didn't have criminal records, resolutely refused to name Ballard under grueling interrogations even though three of them were willing to incriminate other accomplices, simply because they were afraid of Ballard.

Lawyers for the Norfolk Four say the obvious reason Ballard didn't identify the seven whites was that he didn't know them, they didn't know him, and he committed the crime alone. He was trusted by Michelle; she let him in; he followed her to the bedroom and killed her. That's why the apartment is largely undisturbed, the knife wounds are in a tight pattern, and the DNA matches only Ballard's. Nevertheless, the state persuaded three separate juries to accept a different version: the seven whites went to Moore-Bosko's apartment, were told to go away, and gathered outside in the parking lot, where they chanced upon Ballard, whom Michelle trusted (but whom they didn't know). Ballard provided them "their ticket in," as Hansen put it.

Unlike the Norfolk Four, who claimed Ford gave them a Hobson's choice—confess or die—Ballard confessed without any threat. But Ballard, like the others, changed his story when, he says, Ford threatened him with a death sentence. A year after confessing and telling Ford he acted alone, Ballard was brought to the Norfolk Police interrogation room, where he claims Ford told him that in order to "escape the death penalty," he would have to sign off on "a version of the story that I never heard of before." Ballard says he agreed to incriminate the Norfolk Four in exchange for two life sentences. He now says the statement he signed was "totally false."

Ballard never testified before a jury against any of the Norfolk Four defendants. More important, he never testified for them.

In the end, five men went to prison. To avoid a possible death sentence at trial, Williams pleaded guilty and signed the state's "stipulation of facts," naming six accomplices. Although he tried to withdraw his plea when Ballard came forward, the courts turned him down. Ballard agreed to a similar plea but named only four accomplices. Dick's lawyer, Fasanaro, had him stick with his life-sentence deal despite Ballard's confession, and Dick became the state's star witness against Wilson and Tice.

In his little booth on the top of Keen Mountain, Joe Dick says he never should have named Eric Wilson and Derek Tice. He says he'd like to apologize to Wilson and that he was going to tell the truth at Tice's second trial but that Ford told him he would face the death penalty if he changed his testimony. For his part, Derek Tice, whose conviction was overturned but who remains in prison awaiting a third trial, says he feels "horrible" that in "trying to save my own life" he brought "three innocent people" into the case. "If I could talk to them, I would ask their forgiveness and hope that they would understand."

Senior Chief Michael Ziegler, now based in Nevada, says he regrets he didn't do more to save Joe Dick. "I wish I'd gone and forced someone to listen to me—Joe's lawyer, the police, the D.A.—to say something's wrong here." Ziegler says: "My biggest mistake was I trusted that the justice system was going to do the right thing. I couldn't conceive that someone who was obviously innocent was going to go to jail. That's where I was wrong."

Epilogue

In November 2008, thirty former FBI agents added their voices to the chorus of prominent persons calling on Governor Tim Kaine to grant the Norfolk Four full pardons based on innocence. Kaine, who had been considering the pardons for more than three years, had not acted when this book went to press.

DANIEL TAYLOR

He's doing the time—although he couldn't have done the crime

STEVE MILLS, MAURICE POSSLEY, AND KEN ARMSTRONG
CHICAGO, ILLINOIS

Early on a December morning in 1992, a seventeen-year-old gang member named Daniel Taylor sat in a windowless police interrogation room and confessed to a double murder that occurred two weeks earlier in Chicago's Uptown neighborhood.

With a detective, a prosecutor, and a stenographer in the room, Taylor said he and seven other gang members met in Clarendon Park to plot the crime and then walked to a nearby apartment building to carry it out. Four of the gang members waited on the street, acting as lookouts, while Taylor and three others went up to a second-floor apartment, broke down the door, and demanded money from one of the tenants.

When the tenant refused, a gang member "shot the guy on the left side of his head, around the temple area," Taylor said. Then they turned their attention to a woman who lived in the apartment, grabbing her arms.

"Please don't, please don't," she pleaded, according to Taylor's confession.

Twenty-nine minutes after Taylor began the confession, prosecutors had the evidence they would need to send him to prison for the rest of his life.

Just as he was going to be formally charged with two counts of murder, however, Taylor protested that he could not have committed the crimes because he had been in police custody when they occurred.

Indeed, within days, police found records showing that at the time of the crime—8:43 P.M. on November 16, 1992—Taylor had been under arrest for disorderly conduct. He'd been picked up at 6:45 P.M., just short of two hours before the crime, and released at 10:00 P.M., more than an hour after it occurred.

But instead of questioning how Taylor had come to confess to a crime that police records indicated he could not have committed, detectives and prosecutors set about discrediting the records. They found a witness—a drug dealer and rival gang member named Adrian Grimes—who claimed he'd seen Taylor in Clarendon Park at 7:30 P.M., and two police officers, Michael Berti and Sean Glinski, who wrote a report claiming that they'd seen Taylor half a block from the murder scene at 9:30 P.M.

A *Chicago Tribune* investigation has uncovered new evidence that supports Taylor's version of events and his contention that his confession was false. The witness who put Taylor in the park now says he lied at the request of detectives, and later was rewarded with leniency on a narcotics charge. Key portions of the chronology laid out by Officers Berti and Glinski are undermined by recent interviews and records obtained by the *Tribune*.

Raising further questions about Berti's credibility, the *Tribune* found a transcript of a pretrial hearing in an unrelated murder case. Four months before Berti and Glinski wrote their report belatedly claiming to have seen Taylor on the street after the murders, Cook County Circuit Court Judge Earl Strayhorn took the extremely rare action of interrupting Berti's testimony, ordering him off the witness stand, and declaring, "I don't believe a thing he says. He goes down in my book as a liar."

"I didn't do this and they know it," Taylor, now twenty-six, said in one of several interviews at Stateville Correctional Center near Joliet. "I was in jail when this happened. No way I could have committed those murders."

Seven other young men originally were charged along with Taylor in the case. The cases against three of the defendants fell apart—charges were dropped against two of those after their confessions were thrown out and the third was acquitted—but Taylor and four others were convicted.

Taylor's alibi raises troubling questions about all of the cases—because all of the defendants said in their confessions that Taylor was with them.

Jeffrey Lassiter and Sharon Haugabook were shot to death in their small second-floor apartment at 910 West Agatite Avenue on November 16, 1992. Lassiter, a crack-cocaine abuser with a string of arrests, rented the apartment and Haugabook, a drug abuser with a record of prostitution, had recently moved in with him.

At 8:34 P.M. on November 16, neighbors called police after hearing gunshots in the apartment. When Faye McCoy, a resident of the building, heard the shots, she looked out her window and saw four men walking out of the building. When the police arrived, they found the front door broken in and Lassiter and Haugabook on the floor, each shot in the head at close range. Lassiter, forty-one, was pronounced dead at the scene. Haugabook, thirty-seven, was taken to Illinois Masonic Hospital, where she died without regaining consciousness.

The investigation immediately focused on Dennis Mixon, a gang member whom Lassiter, in exchange for crack, had allowed to deal out of the apartment; the two had reportedly had "an altercation" over a VCR in recent weeks. When police showed Mixon's mug shot to Faye McCoy, she identified him as one of the men she'd seen leaving the building.

On December 2, while Mixon remained at large, patrol officers arrested Lewis Gardner, fifteen, and Akia Phillips, nineteen, for trying to sell drugs on an Uptown street corner. Gardner, whose IQ was seventy, indicating borderline mental retardation, told arresting officers that he'd gotten his drugs from Deon Patrick—and claimed that Patrick had been involved in the Agatite Avenue murders.

According to detectives who took over the questioning, both Gardner and Phillips proceeded to confess that they and two other youths, Joseph Brown and Phillips's brother Paul, had served as lookouts for four others who entered the apartment—Daniel Taylor, Dennis Mixon, Rodney Mathews, and Deon Patrick.

A few hours later—just after 2:00 A.M. on December 3—detectives roused a sleeping Taylor from a youth home where he was staying and took him to the area detective headquarters for questioning.

One way or another, Daniel Taylor has been in the custody of the State of Illinois for most of his life. One of four children of Debra Taylor, he never knew his father. In February 1986, at age eleven, he became a ward of the state, though the state first took him away from his mother three years earlier because of her cocaine use. His mother, now forty-four and working as a hospital records analyst, says he struggled with behavioral problems, particularly a temper.

As a ward of the state, he was shunted from one foster home or shelter to another. By his own count, he lived in more than a dozen different homes or facilities growing up. He was involved in a wide variety of incidents, large and small. One time he threw pepper at a girl. Another time he ran away and stole a car. He recalls those years as a time when he was increasingly angry and resentful at how his mother's drug use had shattered the family. "Being in the state, having no family that's your blood, it gets to you sometimes," he said. "It's almost like jail. It's not really home."

About three months before the Lassiter and Haugabook murders, Taylor joined the Vice Lords street gang. His friends were Vice Lords, so it made sense to him to join them. They sold drugs, mostly small amounts of cocaine and marijuana, and hung around Clarendon Park. In the weeks preceding his arrest for disorderly conduct on November 16, 1992, he'd been arrested five times, twice for theft and three times for mob action, but had never been convicted of anything.

Within hours of his arrival at the area detective headquarters in the early morning hours of December 3, Taylor gave a twenty-seven-page confession in the presence of a court reporter and an assistant state's attorney.

Detective Brian Killacky would testify that Taylor at first denied knowing anything about the crime, but, after being read his rights, "almost immediately" and without prompting, confessed.

Taylor's account differs dramatically.

After his initial denial, according to Taylor, Detectives Killacky and Anthony Villardita told him that Gardner and Phillips had implicated him in the murders. When he persisted in his denial, one of the detectives hit him with a flashlight. Then they yelled at him and told him they would let him go if he confessed, saying, "We don't want you. You're not the one. We really want Rodney Mathews and Deon Patrick."

Taylor said he concluded that continuing to resist would be futile, and believing that the detectives would make good on their promise to release him, he gave them what they wanted—a confession. It was made up of details he picked up from their questions, from information he had heard on the street, and from Akia Phillips's confession, which the detectives gave him to read. "I just sort of put it all together," he said.

In the confession, Taylor said that he, Mathews, Patrick, and Mixon went to the Agatite Avenue apartment to collect a two-hundred- or three-hundred-dollar drug debt Lassiter owed Mixon. Gardner, Brown, and Akia and Paul Phillips stayed outside as lookouts. When Lassiter said he did not have the money, Patrick shot him and then shot Haugabook.

At the conclusion of Taylor's confession, Assistant Cook County State's Attorney Joe Magats noted the time—5:52 A.M.

Taylor was then put into a lineup, which was viewed by Faye McCoy, the woman who had seen a group of men leaving the building after hearing the shots. McCoy said she'd seen Taylor in the neighborhood—and was certain he wasn't one of the men she had seen.

In an interview with the *Tribune*, McCoy said detectives pressed her to implicate Taylor and the other defendants, sometimes coming to her home in the middle of the night. "They told me, 'They say they did it,'" said McCoy, a neighborhood activist who has served on local school councils. "They kept on bringing me pictures and trying to get me to say it was them."

But she refused, and never identified anyone other than Dennis Mixon.

Taylor said that after he was charged with the murders, he searched his mind for where he'd been on November 16. He remembered being in court on November 19, and worked backward, recalling that he had been in custody at the time of the murders.

Even though detectives promptly found the records that appeared to confirm his alibi, Taylor continued to be held without bond.

When Dennis Mixon was finally arrested, he confessed as well, implicating all seven codefendants. According to detectives, Mixon claimed that, when the group met at Clarendon Park before going to attempt to collect the debt from Lassiter, Taylor mentioned that he had just been released from the police lockup.

Mixon's confession was the only one made after police learned of the lockup records corroborating Taylor's alibi—and it was the only confession that worked Taylor's time in police custody into the narrative of the murders.

By the time Taylor came to trial in late August 1995, three of his codefendants had been set free. In one case, Cook County Circuit Court Judge Thomas Hett held that the arrest had been illegal and threw out the confession. In another case, he ruled that a detective's promise to drop unrelated drug charges was an improper inducement for the defendant to confess. In the third case, a jury acquitted Rodney Mathews, who said that he confessed only because detectives mistreated him.

Taylor and Mixon were tried together before Hett with different juries. For Taylor's jury, the question was simply whether to believe his confession that he'd been in the Agatite Avenue apartment when Lassiter and Haugabook were shot or to believe the records and witnesses indicating he'd been in police custody at the time.

The prosecution was led by Assistant State's Attorney Thomas Needham, the son of a high-ranking Chicago police officer and later a top aide to Mayor Richard M. Daley. When Needham and second-chair prosecutor Jeanne Bischoff entered Hett's courtroom for Taylor's trial, their best piece of evidence against Taylor was his confession.

Fingerprints found in Lassiter's apartment did not match Taylor or any of the codefendants; no DNA was found that linked Taylor or the other defendants to the murders; and police never recovered the murder weapon.

To challenge Taylor's arrest and lockup records, the prosecutors called Adrian Grimes, the drug dealer who claimed he'd seen Taylor at Clarendon Park at about 7:30 P.M., or forty-five minutes after his arrest and more than an hour before the murders. Needham and Bischoff also offered the testimony of Officer Glinski, who, with Officer Berti, had reported seeing Taylor on the street shortly after the murders.

Glinski testified that he was among several officers who responded to a radio bulletin regarding the shooting. The officers tried to question a youth they spotted in an alley near the murder scene, but he fled into a nearby building. The officers followed him to a second-floor apartment. When they entered the apartment, the youth wasn't to be found. But the officers did find, or so they claimed, a small amount of cocaine in the possession of the occupant—Andrea Phillips, mother of Akia and Paul Phillips.

Phillips was taken into custody and, as the officers left the building, Glinski continued, they encountered Taylor, whom they asked to help them find the youth they'd followed to the apartment—one of Phillips's sons. Taylor agreed and rode around with the officers for ten or fifteen minutes without finding the youth. Then, at about 10:00 P.M., the officers dropped Taylor off at the shelter where he was staying.

Like the prosecution, Taylor's attorney, Nathan Diamond-Falk, relied on police testimony. Officer Terrence Duffy testified that he arrested Taylor for disorderly conduct at 6:45 P.M., took him to the district police station, handcuffed him to a metal ring on the wall, and moved him to the lockup at 7:25 P.M.—about the time the prosecution put Taylor in Clarendon Park. Lockup keeper John Meindl testified that he left for the evening at between 9:15 and 9:30, and that Taylor was still in the lockup. Officer James Gillespie testified he started work at the station's front desk at 9:30 P.M. and issued Taylor's bond slip, which showed Taylor's release time as 10:00 P.M.

In closing arguments, Bischoff sought to discredit the defense witnesses, accusing them of covering up sloppy record-keeping for fear they would be blamed for letting Taylor leave jail early to commit the murders. "Paperwork is not foolproof," Bischoff told the jury. "But I'll tell you what is foolproof. And what is foolproof are the defendant's own words."

Diamond-Falk argued that the arrest report and bond slip showed definitively that Taylor was in custody when the murders occurred. "There isn't one reasonable doubt in this case—the whole case is doubtful," he said. "The whole case is one big doubt despite the statement."

Jurors began deliberating late in the afternoon on September 7. By that evening, they had reached their verdict—guilty—having found it easier to imagine the records and defense witnesses being wrong than to imagine that Taylor would have confessed to a crime he didn't commit.

"A couple people were skeptical for maybe a couple minutes," juror Donald Borta said in an interview, "but once we figured it out, it was pretty easy." "The only piece that didn't seem to fit was that stuff that he'd been in jail at the time," said juror Daniel Cacchione. "He could have walked out the back door for all we knew. Who knew if he was really in jail?"

Mixon's jury also quickly returned a guilty verdict, and Judge Hett sentenced both men to life in prison.

In a *Tribune* interview at Stateville Correctional Center, Mixon insisted that all of the other defendants were wrongly charged. "The guys they had in this case with me," he said, "they never set foot in that apartment."

And Adrian Grimes, the prosecution witness who testified that Taylor was at Clarendon Park shortly before the murders, told the *Tribune* that he'd lied under pressure from detectives.

Earlier in the year, he said, he'd been picked up on a felony narcotics charge that was dropped for lack of evidence, but to force him to testify against Taylor prosecutors re-indicted him on that charge. Grimes said two police officers, whose names he could not recall, threatened to keep him locked up if he did not cooperate. "I wasn't even at the park," Grimes said, "but the police kept saying, 'If you testify this guy right here was at the park, we'll let you go.' They told me, 'Won't nobody care about him. He ain't got no family. It won't be nobody's loss.'"

Two months after he testified at Taylor's trial, Grimes pleaded guilty to the narcotics charge. Although he faced one to three years in prison, he was given two years' conditional discharge and was not even required to report to a probation officer.

"My intention wasn't to hurt no one," Grimes told the *Tribune*. "Only thing they wanted me to do is point him out and say he was at the park. But they used me to destroy a perfectly good young man's life."

Faye McCoy said the prosecutors showed her Taylor's confession to try to get her to testify against him. "They were giving me little things they wanted me to say," she told the *Tribune*. "And I wouldn't cooperate. I wouldn't lie. They said it's not lying because it's in the confessions. They just wanted the boys."

Andrea Phillips said in an interview that, contrary to Officer Glinski's testimony and the report Glinski and Berti filed following her arrest, the officers did not leave her apartment until after 10:00 P.M.—they stayed to watch a TV news report about police officers with criminal records. A report on that subject was the lead story broadcast on WMAQ-TV news the night of the murders. The *Tribune* also obtained a record from the shelter where Taylor was staying indicating that Taylor didn't arrive until 3:00 A.M., although Glinski testified that he and Berti dropped Taylor off there at about 10:00 P.M.

Taylor said that, after his release from the lockup, he walked to the Phillips apartment, arriving around 10:30 or 10:45 P.M., and that he did not encounter Glinski and Berti. Several hours later, he said, Andrea Phillips called him and said she had been arrested because he had left drugs in her apartment. She blamed him for her arrest and told him to leave her apartment. Police records show that Phillips called her apartment at 1:30 A.M., which was consistent with Taylor's 3:00 A.M. arrival at the shelter.

The *Tribune* also discovered two police reports identifying a man who— if Diamond-Falk had known he existed—very likely would have corroborated Taylor's alibi. Under the law, prosecutors are required to turn over evidence that could be favorable to the defense, but Diamond-Falk said he never saw the reports. The potential witness was James Anderson, a cocaine and marijuana abuser with a long record of arrests and convictions, who apparently had been in jail with Taylor at the time of the Agatite Avenue murders. The first report, dated December 29, 1992, stated, "Need to locate James Anderson concerning the Lassiter Homicide." The other, dated December 31, said that Anderson was still being sought.

In a recent interview at Champaign County Jail, where he was being held on a bad-check charge, Anderson told the *Tribune* that he in fact had been interviewed by detectives about being in the lockup in November. "I told them I remembered being in [the lockup] with a kid," said Anderson, who did not recall the names of the detectives. "I said I remembered the kid. But then they sort of lost interest."

Diamond-Falk conceded that he had made no effort to locate anyone who might have been in jail with Taylor at the time of the murders. Nor did he obtain the records of the youth shelter where Taylor was staying, which would have bolstered Taylor's alibi.

"I'm a . . . moron," Diamond-Falk said, shaking his head.

Taylor appealed his conviction, contending, among other things, that the state had failed to prove him guilty beyond a reasonable doubt, but in October 1998 the Illinois Appellate Court denied the appeal with an unpublished decision.

In April 2001, Taylor filed a petition for post-conviction relief alleging, among other things, that he had been denied due process of law. Normally such petitions are heard by the judge who tried the case. Because Judge Hett had retired the previous year, however, the case was assigned to Judge Bertina Lampkin. She dismissed the petition without a hearing, calling it "frivolous and patently without merit."

For Taylor, who completed his GED at Stateville and works as a teacher's aide, earning forty-five dollars a month, the situation is perplexing. "I don't understand how I can be in here," he said. "How many times can somebody say they can prove their innocence like me?"

Epilogue

After the *Tribune* article appeared, a volunteer attorney, Kathleen Zellner, brought another petition for post-conviction relief based on the new evidence uncovered by the reporters, but in November 2007 Judge Lampkin denied that petition as well. As this volume went to press, Taylor remained in prison, despite the veritable mountain of evidence that he could not have been in the Agatite Avenue apartment when Jeffrey Lassiter and Sharon Haugabook were murdered.

LEBREW JONES

Exculpatory testimony paled in the face of his confession

CHRISTINE ELLEN YOUNG

NEW YORK, NEW YORK

Salvation Army Major Betty Baker remembers riding on the big white canteen truck as it rumbled through Hell's Kitchen and seeing the sweet, troubled girl with long blond hair.

"Johnny, stop the truck," she said. "There's Blue Eyes."

As the girl climbed aboard, Baker stood up and offered her the passenger seat. Blue Eyes sat down, nodding toward the driver.

"He doesn't like me," Blue Eyes told Baker.

It was a cold November morning, but Blue Eyes didn't want hot cocoa or chicken broth. She seemed weary and sad. At twenty-one, she had been turning tricks since she was fifteen. She was getting tired of the streets, she told Baker, and was thinking of moving back home to Buffalo.

It was about 2:00 A.M., Baker remembers, when Blue Eyes said goodbye.

Five hours later, her mutilated, half-naked body was found bent over a metal bar in a walled-off construction site, face-down, an eight-inch section of scrap wood shoved inside her vagina. A second piece of wood, which had fallen to the ground, had torn a two-and-one-half-inch hole in her rectum. A two-inch piece of rock was embedded in her fractured skull. A blood-soaked white-and-yellow sock was jammed down her throat. Her muddy, blood-streaked white leather jacket was pulled over her head. Pinned to the lapel was a red button: "I can't be fired. Slaves must be sold."

Two days later, police arrested Lebrew Jones, a security guard who led a law-abiding life, and charged him with second-degree murder. It took a Manhattan jury about four hours in 1989 to convict Jones, now fifty, who is now serving twenty-two years to life at Otisville Correctional Facility, where his hair has turned gray and his behavior has been good.

The morning of Thanksgiving 2006, I met Jones for the first time, driven by a strange series of events that began almost two decades ago.

On February 16, 2007, I met with the Manhattan District Attorney's Office and explained why I believe that Jones was wrongfully convicted.

The district attorney has reopened the case.

Michaelanne Hall was a child who picked dandelions for her mother, had a contagious giggle, and never forgot a birthday. Known as "Micki," she was blond and blue-eyed, vivacious and bright. Growing up in a Buffalo housing project with her mother, Lois, and her older sister, Cindy, Micki excelled in school and talked of becoming a veterinarian.

"There was never a sweeter, nicer person in the world than my little Micki," said Lois. "Everybody loved her."

By the time Micki was fifteen, Lois had a difficult time keeping track of her. One day, a girl Lois didn't know showed up at her door in a panic. The girl told Lois that Micki was being kept in an apartment on Maryland Street by a man known as "Cain"—short for cocaine.

The frightened girl said she had escaped through a kitchen window, but Micki was locked in a closet. Frantic, Lois called the police, who went to the apartment and knocked. When nobody answered, Lois recalls, the cops said there was nothing they could do because Micki was probably just a runaway.

Three weeks later, Lois said, Cain took Micki to Manhattan. Get out on the street, he told her. You're gonna make me some money. Micki lived with Cain in a New Jersey motel outside the Lincoln Tunnel.

Each night, he would drive her into the city, where she would turn tricks until she earned her quotas—five hundred dollars on weeknights, one thousand dollars on weekends. At about 4:00 A.M., Cain would pick Micki up in his cream-colored Mercedes, take the cash, and then drive her back to New Jersey. Lois noticed bruises when Micki came to visit. Once, she had a black eye. She was hooked on heroin and booze.

"Micki, come home," Lois would beg. "There's a place for you here."

Micki always refused, insisting that she and Cain were in love. After six years on the street, however, it looked as though Micki had finally had enough. On October 28, 1987, her twenty-first birthday, she brought all of her clothes back to Buffalo. "I'm sick and tired of getting beat up," she told Lois. "I'm sick and tired of being called bitch. I want to come home."

Micki stayed with Lois for about two weeks. Then she got a phone call from Cain.

"I have to go back," she told her mother. "I have to say goodbye to my friends."

A couple of weeks later, on November 20, 1987, Micki went to Rudy's, a Ninth Avenue watering hole. She was already buzzed on rum and Coke when another working girl, Rachel Hayes, showed up at about 7:00 P.M. She needed a shower, having just been released from jail after getting arrested for loitering. They had a few drinks before going to the Elk Hotel, a nearby flophouse. Micki told Hayes she had been living there for a week, since leaving her pimp.

Hayes took a shower, got dressed, and told Micki to sleep off the booze. Hayes left the hotel at 10:20 P.M., and they agreed to meet at midnight. The clock struck 12:00, Hayes waited. Micki never showed up.

Lebrew Jones was about eight years old when his school, P.S. 257 in Brooklyn, invited parents to a daytime fund-raiser. Lebrew's mother had promised that his father would attend, but when Lebrew entered the auditorium, he was disappointed not to see him there.

The principal was on the stage next to a shiny, double-bass drum set. As the audience settled down, Lebrew's eyes widened. "This is Speedy Jones, Lebrew Jones's father," the principal announced. "He plays with Count Basie."

Lebrew nearly burst with pride as Rufus "Speedy" Jones showed the crowd why jazz dynamo Maynard Ferguson had called him "the most exciting drummer in the world." Like nobody else, Speedy could make thunder and lightning with a pair of sticks.

Afterward, Speedy smiled and gave a quick, bashful bow. He gestured toward Lebrew. "Do you want to play?" he asked his son. "C'mon. Show your stuff—you're good enough!" In the prison's visiting room more than forty years later, Lebrew smiled at the memory. "So I got up on the stage and started playing," he said. "It was nice."

Born in Fort Jackson, South Carolina, in 1957, Lebrew started learning the drums almost as soon as he could sit up. His father, a disciplined and accomplished musician, was a member of Lionel Hampton's orchestra before getting drafted. While stationed at Fort Jackson, Rufus played in a quintet every Saturday night at the black United Service Organization clubhouse in Columbia.

"Know your gift," Lebrew remembers him saying. "If you know your gift, you can succeed."

After Rufus's Army stint was up in 1959, he and Nora Jones moved their family to New York. A second son, Chanel, was born, and Nora was strict and protective with her adventurous little boys. "She was an educated mother," said Ada Davis, Nora's sister. "She cherished her boys."

Meanwhile, Rufus's career took off, and his musical gift took him all over the world, landing him long-term gigs with Maynard Ferguson, Count Basie, and Duke Ellington.

Years of playing and traveling, however, took their toll. When Lebrew was sixteen, Rufus and Nora, high school sweethearts, separated. Rufus moved to Las Vegas and developed crippling arthritis that prematurely ended his career.

Lebrew remained in New York with Nora, and after high school, he took care of his mother, eventually selling his Ludwig drum set to help pay the rent. He worked for two years as a stock clerk before going to work for Swingline, the stapler company. He was steadily employed to support his mother, eventually taking a job in security, protecting nurses while they visited patients' homes.

In 1985 Lebrew and Nora moved to California to be near Chanel, who had joined the Navy. In 1987 Lebrew returned to New York City and accepted a job with another security company, Patrol and Guard.

He could not have foreseen how this would change his life forever.

The cold morning air nipped at Lebrew's face as he walked toward the construction site on West Forty-First Street on Saturday, November 21, 1987.

He played drums occasionally in a club band, but his job as a security guard paid the bills. He had worked at Forty-First Street between Ninth and Tenth avenues until eleven thirty the night before, then he had gone straight to his other job site at Eighty-Sixth Street and York Avenue, where he had caught some sleep while covering the graveyard shift.

Now, at about 8:30 A.M., he was going to offer to take the day shift at West Forty-First Street. He was living with a friend in the Bronx. To save money for an apartment with his girlfriend, Lebrew went back and forth continuously between job sites, catching naps at work.

As Lebrew approached the plywood wall-enclosed work site, he saw flashing police lights. Two uniformed officers stopped him and asked where he was going.

"To see my partner, the guard," Lebrew replied. "I work here."

You can't go in there, one of the cops said. We just had a homicide.

"A homicide?" Lebrew said. "Whoa."

Showing up at a time that he was not scheduled to work would later arouse suspicion among investigators that Lebrew was returning to the scene of the crime. Police said they wanted to talk to him. Lebrew climbed into the back seat of a cruiser and told the officers he'd left the Forty-First Street construction site at eleven thirty the night before to go uptown.

No, he hadn't seen anything unusual.

After about an hour, two detectives showed up. James Lockhart was older and looked like the actor Stacey Keach, Lebrew thought, while the younger man, Paul Clermont, resembled John Travolta.

Lebrew agreed to answer some questions, and the detectives took him to the Tenth Precinct station, where he told Lockhart that on Friday he had worked from 3:00 until 11:30 P.M. His relief, Frederick Baddoo, had arrived half an hour late, so Lebrew hurried uptown and checked in at his other job, where he signed in. In the morning, he returned to the West Forty-First Street construction site.

Did you see a dead body before you left Friday night? Lockhart asked.

No, Lebrew replied. I didn't see anything.

Over the next forty-eight hours, police verified that Lebrew had signed in at his second job after leaving West Forty-First Street. They found no blood on any of his clothes or belongings. They learned that the lock on the site entrance was broken, and that Lebrew's relief, Baddoo, had fallen asleep in the guard shack until sometime after 2:00 A.M. They learned that Lebrew had no criminal record.

Yet when Lebrew told detectives he knew nothing about the body or the murder, they refused to believe him.

He was picked up at his job on Sunday night and questioned for eight hours into Monday morning. Lebrew gave five different statements before being informed of his right to remain silent, according to testimony by Clermont.

By 5:30 A.M. Monday, Lebrew found himself in front of a video camera, telling prosecutor Brian O'Donoghue a ludicrous tale: a young woman performed fellatio on Lebrew in exchange for being allowed to stay overnight at the construction site, but when he asked her to leave, she shoved a sock down her throat and committed suicide by hitting herself in the head with a rock.

O'Donoghue would occasionally challenge Lebrew's version of the facts, and Lebrew would then change his story accordingly. After the tape stopped rolling, according to court documents, Lebrew tried to recant his story but was hustled away by detectives.

Several hours later, he was charged with murder.

Lebrew's court-appointed lawyer, Robert Beecher, made a motion to suppress the videotaped statement and the earlier statements Lebrew had made, contending he had succumbed to sly and coercive police tactics.

Lebrew testified at a suppression hearing that his original story—that he knew nothing about the body—was the truth, but eventually he got "tired of the 'terrogation."

"I didn't do a good job of helping," he said. "All I wanted was my freedom out of there. I wanted to go home."

Lebrew's videotaped statement, while far-fetched, included details that only police and the killer should have known.

A clue as to how Lebrew might have learned those details emerged during the suppression hearing.

"Did you tell [Lebrew] why his stories didn't fit what you knew?" O'Donoghue asked Lockhart.

"Yes, sir," replied Lockhart.

"Did you tell him what actually had taken place, or what you had observed inside?" asked O'Donoghue.

"Yes, sir," Lockhart responded, adding that Clermont was present at the time.

Nevertheless, Judge Richard Andrias admitted Lebrew's statements into evidence.

During the jury trial a month later, both detectives would deny giving Lebrew any details of the crime.

In 1989 I was a journalism student at CUNY in New York City, researching a story about runaway kids who ended up as prostitutes. The project led me to Betty Baker, a feisty, fiercely devout Scottish woman of sixty-two who had arrived in America as a GI bride some forty years earlier and soon found herself divorced.

When we met sixteen months after the murder, she had become Major Betty Baker of the Salvation Army. Every weeknight at about eight thirty, Baker would leave her Gramercy Park apartment and head down to Booth House on the Bowery, where she and a driver would load hot cocoa, chicken broth, and sweets into a converted ice-cream truck and cruise the city's underbelly, sharing the mercy of Jesus with the destitute and despised.

Baker had witnessed the ravages of AIDS, the brutality of pimps, and the despair of the poor and forgotten. She was haunted by the savage death of a young prostitute from Buffalo whose street name was "Blue Eyes." Baker recalled how she had spoken with her only a few hours before she was found bludgeoned and defiled.

To me, Blue Eyes' story was a horrible example of the danger facing street kids, but I had no intention of delving into a homicide case.

It was only after I met Detective Paul Clermont, by sheer coincidence, that my interest in Blue Eyes took an uncanny twist.

Clermont worked at the Tenth Precinct, one block from my apartment. As a journalism student, I enjoyed chatting up the neighborhood cops and hearing their war stories.

When I met him in the spring of 1989, Clermont told me about a gruesome homicide case that was about to go to trial. He pulled a folder from his briefcase and began flipping through crime-scene photos, describing what had been done to the girl.

Suddenly, I realized who she was.

I told Clermont that I had recently interviewed an outreach worker for the Salvation Army. Betty Baker had seen Blue Eyes at 2:00 A.M., I told him, just a few hours before her body was found.

Clermont turned his head and raised his hand, as if telling me to stop.

I will always remember his words.

"Don't tell me that."

I was puzzled. Why not?

Clermont said, essentially, that if the information were true, his case would be ruined. If the victim were alive at 2:00 A.M., the man he had arrested could not have killed her.

I told Clermont I would double-check with Baker. Later, when I told Baker what Clermont had said, she got mad.

"I saw her!" she said. "I told them that when I called!"

You told who? I asked.

"A detective," Baker said, explaining that she had called Lockhart to make sure someone had claimed Blue Eyes' body and that she would have a proper burial.

Baker dug out her journal, a nightly log of her contacts on the street.

"Look!" showing me the page, she pointed to her entry for Friday, November 20, 1987. "'Saw B.E.' That stands for Blue Eyes."

Baker said she remembered it clearly because she had attended Friday evening services at the Salvation Army before starting her rounds. Also, her driver, Johnny Lancaster, had run a red light that night and nearly gotten them killed.

Afterward, he had shrugged with nonchalance.

"Johnny, what is wrong with you tonight?" Baker remembered saying. "Let's just run in early and go home."

The following Monday, Baker was without a driver because Lancaster never returned to work. That was OK with Baker because, she said, he was "too heavenly minded to do any earthly good."

With the trial only weeks away, I told Clermont what I had learned. He turned over the information to the prosecutor's office, which interviewed Baker several times before turning her over to the defense.

But neither side had spoken with Lancaster before the trial or called him as a witness to verify Baker's account.

Soon afterward, I left the city to start a job in New England.

Lebrew Jones's murder trial began at the Manhattan Criminal Court building on May 30, 1989, against a societal backdrop of frayed nerves and seething racial animosity. Only six weeks earlier, a twenty-eight-year-old white woman had been viciously raped and beaten into a coma while jogging in Central Park. Five black teenagers had been arrested, accused of participating in an all-night rampage of fiendish attacks.

Fear of violence was widespread among New Yorkers, who by the late 1980s had seen crime rates triple and courts so bogged down that half the criminal cases were disposed of in 3.4 minutes, according to the *New York Times*. Judicial expediency was explained as a necessary evil by a number of judges, including Andrias, who presided over Lebrew's two-week trial. Andrias told the *Times* in February 1987: "I'm not saying it's good what we do. I'm saying we have to do it."

Maybe so, but a careful examination of Lebrew's conviction raises troubling questions. As the trial unfolded, the following facts emerged, according to court documents:

- Despite the bloodbath at the scene, Lebrew had no blood on his clothes, shoes, gloves, or leather jacket. Police confiscated his belongings from both job sites, but did not submit them to the police lab for testing.
- Police verified that Lebrew checked in at his second job after leaving the construction site. There was no evidence presented that he had washed up or changed his clothing.
- None of the fingerprints collected at the scene matched Lebrew's.
- No evidence was presented that hair samples taken from Lebrew matched any found on the body or at the scene.
- The victim's fingernail clippings were sent to the medical examiner's office but were never tested.
- No medical examiner came to the crime scene.
- Detectives interviewed two men who had witnessed a nasty argument between Hall and a black man at the Elk Hotel shortly

before she was killed. The two witnesses viewed a lineup that included Lebrew. They did not pick him out.

I recently called Clermont, now retired, at his home in Mason, Ohio.

"I treated Lebrew very good," he said. "He's not innocent. He's guilty. . . . Talk to someone else, because I'm out of it."

Lockhart, who retired before Lebrew's trial, died in 1995.

The prosecution's theory, as O'Donoghue described it to the jury, was essentially this: Lebrew met up with Hall while taking a dinner break at about 10:30 P.M. Friday. He paid her to perform fellatio, and when he couldn't ejaculate, she mocked him until he "erupted" and killed her on the spot.

The prosecutor never explained why lab tests showed no trace of saliva on a condom found at the scene, a fact mentioned only briefly by the defense.

The jury would have to decide on two critical factors: whether Hall was killed while Lebrew was on duty and whether the police had fed Lebrew key details of the crime.

The prosecution strengthened its claim that the murder happened during Lebrew's shift by calling the Reverend Raymond Roden of Covenant House, who testified that he had thought he heard a woman "grunt" or "groan" while walking by the site at 10:30 P.M. Friday. But when Roden peeked through a crack in the plywood wall, he testified, he saw nothing.

Because the jury would see Lebrew's videotaped statement, Beecher knew he faced a formidable task—explaining why his client, if he were innocent, would tell such a ridiculous tale of Hall killing herself with a rock.

Before the trial started, Beecher hit the streets. He visited Covenant House, where outreach workers had seen Hall regularly over the last seven months of her life, sometimes with bruises that she said were inflicted by her pimp, according to the nightly logs.

Beecher asked the judge's permission to call the outreach workers as witnesses, and to argue during his opening statement that a violent pimp might be among the possible suspects. Andrias shot Beecher's argument down, calling it "wild speculation" and pointing out that beatings were among "several ways to keep a prostitute in line." The victim's complaints, the judge added, might have been "the typical grousing of a young woman . . . about her pimp."

In her opening statement, Assistant District Attorney Sandra Leung made claims that did not square up with evidence presented later. For example, she told the jury that Baddoo saw Hall's body only an hour after Lebrew left the construction site at 11:30 P.M.

In fact, Baddoo took the stand and admitted that after Lebrew left, he fell asleep in the guard shack for several hours. After Baddoo woke up, he saw the body, he testified, but he didn't call police until 7:00 A.M. because he thought it was a "toy." He also admitted that he had been fired from previous jobs for sleeping at work.

Leung also misinformed the jury that a "pick-type comb" was found in the victim's mouth, referring to a grooming accessory for African American hair. But it was a seven-inch rattail comb, not a pick, as the evidence photos and autopsy report clearly showed.

"The only way in and out of the construction site was through a door that was locked from the inside," Leung told the jury, failing to disclose that the lock was broken, as documented by police in a photo.

The other prosecutor, O'Donoghue, compounded this misconception by stating that Lebrew was "locked in there when Baddoo showed up." That, along with the videotaped statement, "is enough to convict him," O'Donoghue told the jury.

To explain the videotaped statement and the conflicting stories Lebrew gave police, Beecher relied on psychologist Sanford Drob, who testified that Lebrew, who had an IQ of sixty-six, was highly suggestible, obedient, and eager to please authority figures.

O'Donoghue told the jury to ignore Drob's testimony. "Drob is not worthy of any belief or credit," he said, pointing out that the detectives could not get Lebrew to say that he killed her. "Why didn't he confess? Why wasn't he suggestible to that?"

The prosecutor asked the jury how Lebrew could have known Hall was drunk before the toxicology report had been received. "If the detectives didn't know that she was drunk, how could they suggest it?" he asked, implying that Lebrew knew information that only the killer would have known. In fact, the detectives had interviewed the desk clerk at the Elk Hotel, where on Friday night a visibly drunk Hall had been involved in an argument so heated that police showed up to settle it.

O'Donoghue, now retired from the district attorney's office and practicing law in Huntington, Long Island, did not respond to numerous requests for an interview. Leung left the district attorney's office in 1992 and is now general counsel for Bristol-Myers Squibb. "I don't think that there was anything inappropriate that happened with respect to the prosecution of the case," she said by phone recently. Asked to discuss it further, Leung said she would think about it but has not called back.

Probably the most critical defense witness was Betty Baker, the Salvation Army worker who testified in detail about seeing Hall early Saturday morning. Calling Baker "a God-fearing woman," O'Donoghue told the jury that she had nevertheless "confused her days. . . . If there is any implication of some kind of unfairness here, it's taken away, cleared up, removed by the fact it was the prosecution that found Betty Baker." He never disclosed that I had brought Baker forward and insisted she be turned over to the defense.

Baker also testified that only four days after the murder, she had called a victim's services agency to inquire about funeral arrangements and was given Lockhart's name. When she telephoned the detective to offer assistance with the burial, she told him about her encounter with Hall, adding that she was probably the last person to see her alive.

Later at the trial, Lockhart denied that the conversation took place.

"I never received that call," he testified.

Baker testified that during her conversation with Lockhart, he had informed her that Hall's body would be shipped to her mother in Buffalo, which was true. But Lockhart had also mentioned something else, "that there was another girl who was killed," Baker testified. "I thought he had said in Brooklyn, and it was the same MO."

In fact, another prostitute had been killed in a very similar fashion less than twelve hours before Hall's death, but it had happened in Queens, about three miles from where Hall's body was found. The New York Police Department command center in Brooklyn had issued an internal bulletin stating that two females had been murdered by "one or several deviates."

At about 4:00 P.M. Friday, November 20, a man and a woman had checked into the Turf Club Motor Inn in Long Island City, Queens. About three hours later, Lorena Tourney, who was known to police as a prostitute, was discovered face-down, nude and beaten, penetrated with a foreign object.

Recently, I sent the Hall photos and autopsy report to Dr. Michael Baden, former chief medical examiner of New York City and now the chief forensic pathologist for the New York State Police. I also described the condition of Tourney's body. "It would sound like the same person did both," Baden said. "It's a very unusual way to kill somebody. I'd be very surprised if it was more than one person."

When Baker mentioned the Tourney slaying, the judge ordered it stricken from the record.

Today, that homicide remains unsolved.

On Monday, June 12, 1989, the lawyers rested their cases and gave their closing arguments. At 7:30 P.M., jurors went home. Shortly after 1:00 P.M. the following day, they came back with a verdict: guilty.

Andrias thanked the jurors and excused them. "Lebrew Jones, may I have your date of birth?" the judge asked. "I didn't do that murder," Lebrew replied. On July 5, 1989, he was sentenced to twenty-two years to life.

In early 1990, I moved to Maine and began working in television news.

Lebrew's conviction continued to gnaw at me. I often imagined him, handcuffed and bewildered, getting hauled into Central Booking in Manhattan. From time to time, I would drag out the dog-eared trial transcript that Lebrew's lawyer, Robert Beecher, had given me shortly after the trial.

Someday, I told myself, I would try to do something about this.

In late 2005, I accepted a position with the *Times Herald-Record* and moved to Hudson Valley. In November 2006 I went online and did an inmate search for Lebrew. To my amazement, he had recently been transferred to the medium-security state prison in Otisville, only twelve miles from my home. I immediately wrote him, "I've known about your case for almost twenty years. I would like to come and see you."

I received his reply, eerily, on the nineteenth anniversary of the murder. "First about me," he wrote. "I'm completely innocent of the crime and need some proof of my innocents [*sic*]. . . . You can come anytime on the weekend, holidays as well. . . . I hope to hear from you real soon. God bless you."

Two days later, on a rainy Thanksgiving morning, I entered the prison through a converted gymnasium overlooking breathtaking mountains through barred windows. A diminutive black man with curly gray hair entered the room and handed the guard a pass. He scanned the crowd. I stood up, and he smiled and walked my way. I introduced myself and studied him for a moment. We talked for hours.

Several weeks later I met with Beecher, a lively, dapper man of sixty who now spends most of his time defending federal criminal cases. He had discarded all of the Lebrew Jones files except the videotaped statement and evidence photos but agreed to get whatever files he could from the Manhattan District Attorney's Office.

In the meantime, I started researching prostitute murders throughout the country. I learned that in 2001, the FBI noted that local police departments were increasingly requesting consultations with the FBI on serial homicides of prostitutes. In response, the U.S. Department of Justice awarded a grant to researcher Jonathan Dudek to find distinctions between serial and one-time offenders. Dudek collected data on 123 murdered prostitutes, their killers, and the crime scenes using closed investigative case files and an FBI database.

Among Dudek's findings:

- Placing the body in a degrading position could signal the work of a "mission-oriented" serial killer who wants to rid society of prostitutes.
- Serial victims were nearly two and a half times more likely to be found partially undressed or nude than victims of one-time offenders.
- Serial killers engaged in necrophilia (such as postmortem penetration with foreign objects) significantly more frequently than did one-time offenders.
- Serial killers more often utilized weapons found spontaneously at the crime scene.

After studying the Hall crime-scene photos, autopsy report, and other documents from the case, Dudek called Hall's death "very sadistic and very, very provocative."

"That offender was trying to make a statement by the way that he left her," Dudek said. "There was meaning to this offender from what he's left us, whether that's a statement about his mission in life or him enacting his deviant sexual fantasies. . . . A lot of serial offenders have gone to great lengths with their victims to dehumanize them, to torture them, mutilate them. I think we see some of that here."

Next, I found news and law-enforcement reports of dozens of unsolved prostitute killings throughout the country, particularly in the Midwest since the early 1990s. Within days of some of the more recent murders, a hand-scrawled note was left at an Oklahoma truck-stop ministry, railing against pimps and "parking lot sin," and warning: "Better get busy for Jesus and clear the whores out of here."

The reports said police believed the killer was a truck driver.

I contacted Beecher with what I had found. On January 4, Beecher wrote a letter to the Manhattan District Attorney's Office requesting a "fresh look at the investigation of this homicide."

On January 30 Beecher called me, very excited. He said Assistant District Attorney Linda Ford wanted to talk to me. Two weeks later, I met with Ford and an investigator for the district attorney's office, Jerry Giorgio. Ford was friendly and approachable, while Giorgio, a thirty-eight-year NYPD veteran nicknamed "Big Daddy" for his legendary interrogation skills, assumed a tough demeanor. Nonetheless, he lit up when I told him my late grandfather was a retired NYPD cop, and that my dad retired from the FBI.

I told them about the Dudek study and mission-oriented prostitute killers. I pointed out how Hall's killer had engaged in necrophilia and displayed her in a degrading position. I also reminded them of the unsolved prostitute murder in Long Island City that took place shortly before Hall was killed.

Eleven days after my meeting with Ford and Giorgio, Beecher called with big news. The district attorney's office had assigned an additional investigator to the Hall murder.

"There's going to be some travel involved," he said. "They got approval to reinvestigate the whole thing."

On July 3, 2007, I tracked down Michaelanne's mother, Lois Hall. "Did you know the district attorney had reopened the case?" I asked her. Lois gasped. "No! And you know something? When they took that man to jail, I said, 'He didn't do it.' I have been on the computer talking with lawyers in New York City, trying to get them to tell me what to do about a guy that was wrongly convicted for my daughter's death."

Lois had a memorial service for Michaelanne, but there has never been a funeral. "I haven't been able to bury her yet," Lois told me. "I just have her remains here, and I haven't really been able to let go. For me to know her killer's been found. . . . I would have a huge sense of relief that they found this guy—and not just passed her off as another dead prostitute."

"Which is what you think has happened now?" I asked.

"Yeah," Lois replied. "I have thought that for many years."

Epilogue

Lebrew Jones remained in prison when this anthology went to press.

TOMMY WARD AND KARL FONTENOT

Their confessions unraveled—but their convictions didn't

JOHN GRISHAM

ADA, OKLAHOMA

Denice Haraway was a twenty-four-year-old East Central University student working part-time at McAnally's convenience store on the eastern edge of Ada. She had been married for eight months to Steve Haraway, also a student at East Central and the son of a dentist in town. The newlyweds lived in a small apartment owned by Dr. Haraway and were working their way through college.

Around 8:30 P.M. on Saturday, April 28, 1984, a customer was approaching the entrance to McAnally's when he was met by an attractive young woman who was leaving the store in the company of a young man. His arm was around her waist; they appeared to be just another pair of lovers. They walked to a pickup truck, where the woman got in first, on the passenger's side. Then the young man got in and slammed the door, and a few seconds later the engine started. They left going east, away from town. The truck was an old Chevrolet with a spotty, gray-primer paint job.

Inside the store, the customer saw no one. The cash register drawer was open and had been emptied. A cigarette was still burning in the ashtray. Beside it was an open beer can, and behind the counter was a brown purse and an open textbook. The customer tried to find the clerk, but the store was empty. Then he decided that perhaps there had been a robbery, so he called the police.

In the brown purse an officer found a driver's license belonging to Denice Haraway. The customer looked at the photo on the license and made a positive identification. That was the young lady he'd passed on the way into the store less than half an hour earlier. Yes, he was sure it was Denice Haraway because he stopped at McAnally's often and knew her face.

From *The Innocent Man: Murder and Injustice in a Small Town* (New York: Doubleday, 2006). Copyright © Bennington Press. Adapted with permission.

Detective Dennis Smith was already in bed when the call came. "Treat it like a crime scene," he said, then went back to sleep. His orders, though, were not followed. The manager of the store lived nearby and he soon arrived. He checked the safe; it had not been opened. He found $400 in cash under the counter, awaiting transfer to the safe, and he found $150 in another cash drawer. As they waited for a detective, the manager tidied up the place. He emptied the ashtray and threw away the beer can. The police didn't stop him. If there were fingerprints, they were gone.

Steve Haraway was studying and waiting for his wife to come home after McAnally's closed at 11:00 P.M. A phone call from the police stunned him, and he was soon at the store, identifying his wife's car, textbooks, and purse. He gave the police a description and tried to remember what she was wearing—blue jeans, tennis shoes, and a blouse he couldn't recall.

Early Sunday morning, every policeman on Ada's thirty-three man force was called in for duty. State troopers arrived from nearby districts. Dozens of local groups, including Steve's fraternity brothers, volunteered to help in the search. Oklahoma State Bureau of Investigation Agent Gary Rogers was assigned to lead the investigation from the state level, and once again Dennis Smith was to direct the Ada police. They divided the county into sections and assigned teams to search every street, highway, road, river, ditch, and field.

A clerk at JP's, another convenience store half a mile from McAnally's, came forward and told the police about two strange young men who'd stopped by and spooked her not long before Denice disappeared. Both were in their early twenties with long hair and weird behavior. They shot a game of pool before leaving in an old pickup truck.

The customer at McNally's had seen only one man leaving with Denice, and she did not appear to be frightened by him. His general description sort of matched the general description of the two weird boys at JP's, so the police had the first hint of a trail. They were looking for two white males, between twenty-two and twenty-four years of age, one between five feet eight and five feet ten with blond hair below his ears and a light complexion, the other with shoulder-length light brown hair and a slim build.

The intense manhunt on Sunday produced nothing, not a single clue. Dennis Smith and Gary Rogers called it off after dark and made plans to reassemble early the next morning.

On Monday, they obtained a college photograph of Denice and printed flyers with her pretty face and general description—five feet five inches tall, 110 pounds, brown eyes, dark blond hair, light complexion. The flyer also listed a description of the two young men seen at JP's, along with one of the old pickup truck. These were placed in every store window in and around Ada by cops and volunteers.

A police artist worked with the clerk from JP's and put together two sketches. When the drawings were shown to the customer at McAnally's, he said that one of them was at least "in the ballpark." The two composites were given to the local television station, and when the town got its first look at the possible suspects, calls poured in to the police station.

Ada had four detectives at the time—Dennis Smith, Mike Baskin, D. W. Barrett, and James Fox—and they were soon overwhelmed with the number of calls. More than a hundred, with about twenty-five names given for potential suspects.

Two names stood out. Billy Charley was suggested by about thirty of the callers, so he was invited in for questioning. He arrived at the police station with his parents, who said that he had been at home with them throughout Saturday night.

The other name given by about thirty concerned citizens was that of Tommy Ward, a local boy the police knew well. Tommy had been arrested several times for misdemeanors—public drunkenness, petty theft—but nothing violent. He had family all over Ada, and the Wards were known as generally decent folks who worked hard and tended to their own business. Tommy was twenty-four years old, the second youngest of eight children, a high school dropout.

He voluntarily came in for questioning. Detectives Smith and Baskin asked him about last Saturday night. He'd been fishing with a friend, Karl Fontenot, then they'd gone to a party, stayed out until 4:00 A.M., then walked home. Tommy didn't own a vehicle. The detectives noticed that Ward's blond hair had been cut very short, a hack job that was uneven and obviously unprofessional. They took a Polaroid of the back of his head and dated it May 1.

The suspects in the composites both had long, light-colored hair.

Detective Baskin found Karl Fontenot, a man he did not know, and asked him to stop by the station for some questions. Fontenot agreed, but never arrived. Baskin didn't pursue it. Fontenot had long, dark hair.

As the search continued with great urgency in and around Pontotoc County, Denice Haraway's name and description were broadcast to law enforcement officials nationwide. Calls came from everywhere, but not one was of any benefit. Denice had simply vanished without leaving a single clue.

When Steve Haraway wasn't handing out flyers or driving the back roads, he was secluded in his apartment with a few friends. The phone rang constantly, and with each call there was a moment of hope.

There was no reason for Denice to run away. They had been married less than a year and were still very much in love. Both were seniors at East Central, looking forward to graduation and leaving Ada for a life somewhere else. She had been taken against her will, he was certain of that.

Each passing day brought a greater likelihood that Denice would not be found alive. If she had been grabbed by a rapist, she would have been released after the assault. If she had been kidnapped, someone would have demanded a ransom. There were rumors of an old lover in Texas, but they came and went. And there were rumors of drug traffickers and such, but then most bizarre crimes had a few of those.

As weeks passed, the rumors died down but didn't stop altogether. A suspect in Texas boasted of killing ten women, and the Ada police raced off to interview him. A woman's body was found in Missouri, with tattoos on her legs. Denice had no tattoos. And so it went through the summer and into the fall. The police had nothing—no body, no witnesses, not a single solid clue.

The cops were due for a break, and it came out of nowhere early in October 1984 when a man named Jeff Miller walked into the Ada Police Department and said he had information about the Haraway case. Miller was a local boy with no criminal record, but the police knew him vaguely as one of the many restless young people in the town who kept late hours and moved from job to job, usually in factories. Miller pulled up a chair and proceeded to tell his story to Detective Dennis Smith.

The night Denice disappeared, there had been a party near the Blue River, at a spot some twenty-five miles south of Ada. Miller had not actually been at the party, but he knew two women who were there. These two women—and he gave Smith their names—later told him that Tommy Ward was there, and that at some point early in the party there was a shortage of alcohol. Ward, who did not own a vehicle, volunteered to go get some beer, and he borrowed a pickup truck from one Janette Roberts. Ward left by himself in the truck, was gone for a few hours, and when he returned without the beer, he was distraught and crying.

When asked why he was crying, he said he'd done something terrible. What? everyone at the party wanted to know. Well, for some reason he had driven all the way back to Ada, passing many beer stores along the way, and had found himself at McAnally's out east of town, where he snatched the young female clerk, raped her, killed her, disposed of her body, and now he felt awful about it. Confessing all this to a random group of hard drinkers and dope smokers seemed like the logical thing to do. Miller offered no clue as to why the two women would tell him and not the police, nor did he suggest any reason why they had waited five months.

As absurd as the story was, Dennis Smith quickly pursued it. He tried to find the two women, but they had already moved away from Ada. (When he finally tracked them down a month later, they denied being at the party, denied seeing Tommy Ward there or at any other party, denied ever hearing a story about a young female store clerk getting kidnapped and killed, or any other young female for that matter, and denied everything Jeff Miller had included in his tale.)

Dennis Smith located Janette Roberts. She was living in Norman, seventy miles away, with her husband, Mike Roberts. On October 12, Smith and Detective Mike Baskin drove to Norman and dropped in unannounced on Janette. They asked her to follow them down to the police station for a few questions, which she reluctantly did.

During the interview, Janette admitted that she, Mike, Tommy Ward, and Karl Fontenot, among many others, had often partied down by the Blue River, but she was almost positive they had not done so on the Saturday night the Haraway girl disappeared. She often let Tommy Ward use her pickup, but he had never left with it from a party at the river, or any other place, nor had she ever seen him crying and upset, nor had she ever heard him blubbering about raping and murdering a young woman. No, sir, that had never happened. She was quite certain.

The detectives were pleasantly surprised to learn that Tommy Ward was living with the Robertses and working with Mike. The two men were employed by a siding contractor and putting in long hours, usually from sunrise to dark. Smith and Baskin decided to wait in Norman until Ward came home from work and ask him to come to the local police station to answer some questions.

Tommy didn't trust the Ada police, who had interviewed him five months earlier about the Haraway case. He was reluctant to talk to Smith and Baskin, but, in Janette's opinion, if he had nothing to hide, then it was safe to go to the police station and chat with them. After wrestling with the issue for an hour, he asked Mike to drive him to the Norman Police Department.

Smith and Baskin took Tommy downstairs to a room with video equipment and explained that they wanted to make a tape of the interview. Tommy was nervous, but agreed. The machine was turned on, and they read him his Miranda rights, and he signed the waiver. The detectives began politely enough; it was just another routine interview, nothing important. They asked Tommy if he remembered the previous interview five months earlier. Of course he did. Had he told them the truth then? Yes. Was he telling the truth now? Yes.

Within minutes Smith and Baskin, going back and forth with the questions, confused Tommy with the days of the week back in April. On the day Denice Haraway disappeared, Tommy had worked on the plumbing in his mother's home, then showered and gone to a party at the Robertses' home in Ada. He'd left at four in the morning and walked home. Five months earlier he'd told the cops this had happened the day before the disappearance. "I just got my days mixed up," he tried to explain, but the cops' replies were, "When did you realize you hadn't told us the truth?" and "Are you telling us the truth now?" and "You're getting yourself into more serious trouble."

The tone became harsh and accusatory. Smith and Baskin lied and claimed to have several witnesses who would testify that Tommy was at a party by the Blue River that Saturday night and had borrowed a pickup truck and left. Wrong day, Tommy said, sticking to his version. He'd gone fishing on Friday, partied at the Robertses' on Saturday, and gone to a party at the river on Sunday.

Why were the cops lying? Tommy asked himself. He knew the truth.

The lying continued. "Isn't it true you were going to rob McAnally's? We've got people who are going to testify to that."

Tommy shook his head and held firm, but he was deeply troubled. If the police were willing to lie so casually, what else might they do?

Dennis Smith then pulled out a large photograph of Denice Haraway and held it close to Tommy's face. "Do you know that girl?"

"I don't know her. I've seen her."

"Did you kill that girl?"

"No, I didn't. I wouldn't take nobody's life from them."

"Who did kill her?"

"I don't know."

Smith continued to hold the photo while asking if she was a pretty girl. "Her family would like to bury her. They'd like to know where she is so they could bury her."

"I don't know where she's at," Tommy said, staring at the photo and wondering why he was being accused.

"Would you tell me where she's at so her family could bury her?"

"I don't know."

"Use your imagination," Smith said. "Two guys took her, got her in a pickup, took her away. What do you think they did with the body?"

"No telling."

"Use your imagination. What do you think?"

"She could be alive for all I know, for all you know, for all anyone knows."

Smith continued to hold up the photo as he asked questions. Every answer by Tommy was immediately disregarded, treated as if it weren't true or weren't heard by the detectives. They asked him repeatedly if he thought she was a pretty girl. Did he think she screamed during the attack? Don't you think her family should be able to bury her?

"Tommy, have you prayed about this?" Smith asked.

He finally put the photo aside and asked Tommy about his mental health, about the composite sketches, about his educational background. Then he picked up the photo again, thrust it near Tommy's face, and started over with questions about killing the girl, burying the body, and wasn't she a pretty girl?

Mike Baskin attempted a tearjerker when he talked about Denice's family's ordeal: "All it would take to end their suffering would be to tell where she's at."

Tommy agreed, but said he had no idea where she was.

The machine was finally turned off. The interview lasted an hour and forty-five minutes, and Tommy Ward never wavered from his original statement—he knew nothing about the disappearance of Denice Haraway. He was rattled by the meeting—the cops had accused him of the murder and repeatedly lied to him—but he agreed to take a polygraph test in a few days. He would tell the truth, the test would prove it, and the cops would stop hassling him.

Then he began having nightmares about the murder; the accusations by the police; the comments about his resemblance to the man in the sketch; the pretty face of Denice Haraway and her family's anguish. Why was he being accused? The police believed he was guilty. They wanted him to be guilty! Why should he trust them with a lie detector exam? Should he talk to a lawyer?

He called his mother and told her he was scared of the police and the polygraph. "I'm afraid they'll make me say something I'm not supposed to say," he told her. Tell the truth, she advised him, and everything will be fine. So on Thursday morning, October 18, Mike Roberts drove Tommy to the Oklahoma State Bureau of Investigation offices in Oklahoma City, twenty minutes away. The exam was to take about an hour. Mike would wait in the parking lot, then the two would drive to work. Their boss had given them a couple of hours off.

Dennis Smith met Tommy with a big smile and a warm handshake, then put him in an office where he waited, alone, for half an hour—a favorite police trick to make the suspect even more nervous. At 10:50 he was led to another room, and waiting there was Agent Rusty Featherstone and his trusty polygraph.

Smith disappeared. Featherstone explained how the machine worked, or how it was supposed to work, as he strapped Tommy in and hooked up the electrodes. By the time the questions started, Tommy was already sweating. The first questions were easy—family, education, employment—everybody knew the truth and the machine complied. This should be a cakewalk, Tommy started thinking.

At 11:05, Featherstone read Tommy his Miranda rights and began probing into the Haraway matter. For two and a half hours of tortuous questioning, Tommy gamely stuck to the truth—he knew nothing about the Denice Haraway matter.

Without a single break, the exam lasted until 1:30, when Featherstone unplugged everything and left the room. Tommy was relieved, even elated because the ordeal was finally over. He had aced the test; finally the cops would leave him alone.

Featherstone was back in five minutes, poring over the graph paper, studying the results. He asked Tommy what he thought. Tommy said he knew he'd passed the exam, the matter was over, and he really needed to get to work.

Not so fast, Featherstone said. You flunked it.

Tommy was incredulous, but Featherstone said it was obvious he was lying and clear that he was involved in the Haraway kidnapping. Would he like to talk about it?

Talk about what!

The polygraph doesn't lie, Featherstone said, pointing to the results right there on the paper. You know something about the murder, he said repeatedly. Things would go much smoother for Tommy if he came clean, talked about what happened, told the truth. Featherstone, the nice cop, was anxious to help Tommy, but if Tommy refused his kindness, then he would be forced to hand him over to Smith and Rogers, the nasty cops, who were waiting, ready to pounce.

Let's talk about it, Featherstone urged him.

There's nothing to talk about, Tommy insisted. He said again and again that the polygraph was rigged or something because he was telling the truth, but Featherstone wasn't buying it.

Tommy admitted to being nervous before the exam, and anxious while it was under way because he was late for work. He also admitted that the interview six days earlier with Smith and Rogers had upset him and caused him to have a dream.

What kind of dream? Featherstone wanted to know.

Tommy described his dream: He was at a keg party, then he was sitting in a pickup truck with two other men and a girl, out by the old power plant near Ada where he grew up. One of the men tried to kiss the girl, she refused, and Tommy told the man to leave her alone. Then he said he wanted to go home. "You're already home," one of the men said. Tommy looked through his window, and he was suddenly at home. Just before he woke up, he was standing at a sink, trying in vain to wash a black liquid off his hands. The girl was not identified; neither were the two men.

That dream doesn't make sense, Featherstone said.

Most dreams don't, Tommy retorted.

Featherstone remained calm but continued to press Tommy to come clean, tell him everything about the crime, and, especially, tell him where the body was. And he threatened again to turn Tommy over to those "two cops" waiting in the next room, as if a lengthy torture session could be in the works.

Tommy was stunned and confused and very frightened. When he refused to confess to Featherstone, the nice cop turned him over to Smith and Rogers, who were already angry and seemed ready to throw punches.

Featherstone stayed in the room, and as soon as the door closed, Smith lunged at Tommy, yelling, "You, Karl Fontenot, and Odell Titsworth grabbed that girl, took her out to the power plant, raped and killed her, didn't you?"

No, Tommy said, trying to think clearly and not panic.

Talk to us, you little lying sonofabitch, Smith growled. You just flunked the polygraph, we know you're lying, and we know you killed that girl.

Tommy was trying to place Odell Titsworth, a name he had heard but a man he'd never met. Odell lived somewhere around Ada, he thought, and he had a bad reputation, but Tommy could not remember meeting him. Maybe he'd seen him once or twice, but at the moment he couldn't remember, because Smith was yelling and pointing and ready to punch him. Smith repeated his theory about the three men snatching the girl, and Tommy said no. No, he had nothing to do with it. "I don't even know Odell Titsworth."

"Stop lying," said Smith.

Karl Fontenot's involvement in their theory was easier to understand because he and Tommy had been friends off and on for a couple of years. But Tommy was bewildered by the accusations and terrified of the smug certainty of Smith and Rogers. Back and forth they went with their threats and verbal abuse. The language deteriorated and soon included every profanity and obscenity on the list.

Tommy was sweating and dizzy and trying desperately to think rationally. He kept his responses short. No, I didn't do it. No, I wasn't involved. A few times he wanted to lash out with sarcastic comments, but he was scared. Smith and Rogers were erupting, and armed, and Tommy was locked in a room with them and Featherstone. His interrogation showed no signs of ending anytime soon. Tommy really needed a break. He needed to find a restroom and smoke a cigarette and clear his head. He needed help, to talk to someone who could tell him what was going on.

Can I take a break? he asked.

Just a few more minutes, they said.

Tommy noticed a video camera on a nearby table, unplugged and neglecting the verbal battering under way. Surely, he thought, this cannot be standard police procedure.

Smith and Rogers repeatedly reminded Tommy that Oklahoma uses lethal injection to kill its killers. He was facing death, certain death, but there might be a way to avoid it. Come clean, tell what happened, lead them to the body, and they would use their influence to get him a deal.

"I didn't do it," Tommy kept saying.

He had a dream, Featherstone informed his two colleagues.

Tommy repeated the dream, and again it was met with disapproval. The three cops agreed that the dream made little sense, to which Tommy replied again, "Most dreams don't."

But the dream gave the cops something to work with, and they began adding to it. The other two men in the truck were Odell Titsworth and Karl Fontenot, right?

No, Tommy insisted. The men in his dream were not identified. No names.

Bullshit. The girl was Denice Haraway, right?

No, the girl was not identified in his dream.

Bullshit.

For another hour, the cops added the necessary details to Tommy's dream, and every new fact was denied by him. It was just a dream, he kept saying over and over and over. Just a dream. Bullshit, said the cops.

After two hours of nonstop hammering, Tommy finally cracked. The pressure came from fear—Smith and Rogers were angry and seemed perfectly able and willing to slap him around if not outright shoot him—but also from the horror of wasting away on death row before finally getting executed. And it was obvious to Tommy that he would not be allowed to leave until he gave the cops something. After five hours in the room, he was exhausted, confused, and almost paralyzed with fear.

He decided to play along. Since he was innocent, and he assumed Karl Fontenot and Odell Titsworth were too, then give the cops what they want. The truth would quickly be discovered. Tomorrow, or the next day, the cops would realize that the story did not check out. They would talk to Karl, and he would tell the truth. They would find Odell Titsworth, and he would laugh at them.

Play along. Good police work will find the truth.

If his dream confession was sufficiently ridiculous, how could anyone believe it?

Didn't Odell go in the store first?

Sure, why not, Tommy said. It was only a dream.

Now the cops were getting somewhere. The boy was finally breaking under their clever tactics.

Robbery was the motive, right?

Sure, whatever, it was only a dream.

Throughout the afternoon, Smith and Rogers added more and more fiction to the dream, and Tommy played along.

It was only a dream.

Even as the grotesque "confession" was happening, the police should have realized they had serious problems.

Detective Mike Baskin was waiting back in Ada at the police department, sitting by the phone and wishing he was at the Oklahoma State Bureau of Investigation in the thick of things. Around 3:00 P.M., Gary Rogers called with great news—Tommy Ward was talking! Get in the car, drive out to the power plant west of town, and look for the body. Baskin raced off, certain the search would soon be over.

He found nothing, and realized he would need several men for a thorough search. He drove back to the police station. The phone rang again. The story had changed. There was an old burned house on the right as you approach the power plant. That's where the body is!

Baskin took off again, found the house, picked through the rubble, found nothing, and drove back to town. His goose chase continued with the third call from Rogers. The story had changed yet again. Somewhere in the vicinity of the power plant and the burned house there was a concrete bunker. That's where they put the body.

Baskin rounded up two more officers and some floodlights, and took off again. They found the concrete bunker, and were still searching when darkness fell. They found nothing.

With each call back from Baskin, Smith and Rogers made modifications to Tommy's dream. The hours dragged on, the suspect was beyond fatigue. They tag-teamed back and forth, good cop, bad cop, voices low and almost sympathetic, then bursts of yelling, cursing, threatening. "You lyin' little sonofabitch!" was their favorite. Tommy had it screamed at him a thousand times.

"You'd better be glad Mike Baskin ain't here," Smith said. "Or he would blow your brains out."

A bullet to the head would not have surprised Tommy.

After dark, when they realized that the body would not be found that day, Smith and Rogers decided to wrap up the confession. With the video camera still unplugged, they walked Tommy through their story, beginning with the three killers riding around in Odell Titsworth's pickup, planning the robbery, realizing Denice would identify them so they grabbed her, then decided to rape and kill her. The details on the location of the body were vague but the detectives felt sure it was hidden somewhere near the power plant.

Tommy was brain-dead and barely able to mumble. He tried to recite their tale but kept getting the facts mixed up. Smith and Rogers would stop him, repeat their fiction, and make him start over. Finally, after four rehearsals with little improvement and their star fading fast, the cops decided to turn on the camera.

Do it now, they said to Tommy. Do it right, and none of that dream bullshit.

"But the story ain't true," Tommy said.

Just tell it anyway, the cops insisted, then we'll help you prove it's not true. And none of that dream bullshit.

At 6:58 P.M., Tommy Ward looked at the camera and stated his name. He had been interrogated for eight and a half hours, and he was physically and emotionally wasted. He was smoking a cigarette, his first of the afternoon, and sitting before him was a soft drink can, as if he and the cops were just finishing up a friendly little chat, everything nice and civilized.

He told his tale. He, Karl Fontenot, and Odell Titsworth kidnapped Denice Haraway from the store, drove out to the power plant on the west side of town, raped her, killed her, then tossed her body somewhere near a concrete bunker out by Sandy Creek. The murder weapon was Titsworth's lock-blade knife.

It was all a dream, he said. Or meant to say. Or thought he said.

Several times he used the name "Titsdale." The detectives stopped him and helpfully suggested the name "Titsworth." Tommy corrected himself and plodded on. He kept thinking, any blind cop could see that I'm lying.

Thirty-one minutes later, the video was turned off. Tommy was handcuffed, then driven back to Ada and thrown in jail. Mike Roberts was still waiting in the parking lot of the Oklahoma State Bureau of Investigation building. He'd been there for almost nine and a half hours.

The next morning, Smith and Rogers called a press conference and announced they had solved the Haraway case. Tommy Ward had confessed and implicated two other men who were not yet in custody. The cops asked the press to sit on the story for a couple of days, until they could round up the other suspects, The newspaper complied, but a television station did not. The news was soon broadcast over southeastern Oklahoma.

A few hours later, Karl Fontenot was arrested near Tulsa and driven back to Ada. Smith and Rogers, fresh from their success with Tommy Ward, handled the interrogation. Though a video recorder was ready, no tape was made of the questioning.

Karl was twenty years old and had been living on his own since he was sixteen. He grew up in Ada, in wretched poverty—his father had been an alcoholic and Karl had witnessed his mother's death in an auto accident. He was an impressionable kid with few friends and virtually no family.

He insisted he was innocent and knew nothing about the Haraway disappearance.

Karl proved to be considerably easier to break than Tommy, and in less than two hours Smith and Rogers had another taped confession, one suspiciously similar to Ward's. Karl repudiated his confession immediately after he was placed in jail, and would later state: "I've never been in jail or had a police record in my life and no one in my face telling me I'd killed a pretty woman, that I'm going to get the death penalty, so I told them the story hoping they would leave me alone. Which they did after I taped the statement. They said I had a choice to write it or tape it. I didn't even know what the word statement or confessing meant till they told me I confessed to it. So that's the reason I gave them an untrue statement, so they would leave me alone."

The police made sure the story got to the press. Ward and Fontenot had made full confessions. The Haraway mystery was solved, most of it anyway.

They were working on Titsworth, and expected to charge all three with murder in a matter of days. The site of the burned house was located, and the police found the remains of what appeared to be a jawbone.

But in spite of the careful coaching, Karl's confession was a mess. There were huge discrepancies between his version of the crime and Tommy's. The two were in direct contradiction on such details as the order in which the three raped Denice, whether or not she was stabbed by her attackers during the rape, the location and number of stab wounds, whether or not she managed to break free and run a few steps before being caught, and when she finally died. The most glaring discrepancy was how they killed her and what they did with her body.

Tommy said she received multiple knife wounds while lying in the back of Odell's pickup during the gang rape. She died there, and they flung her body into a ditch near a concrete bunker. In Fontenot's version, they took her into an abandoned house where Titsworth stabbed her, stuffed her beneath the floor, then poured gasoline over her and burned down the house.

But the two were in almost complete agreement on Titsworth. He had been the organizer, the mastermind who rounded up Ward and Fontenot to go riding in his pickup, to drink some beer, smoke some pot, and at some point rob McAnally's. Once the gang had decided on which store to rob, Titsworth went in and stole the money, grabbed the girl, and told his buddies they would have to kill her so she couldn't identify them. He drove out to the power plant. He directed the gang rape, going first himself. He produced the weapon, a six-inch lock-blade knife. He stabbed her, killed her, and either he burned her or he did not.

Late on the afternoon of Friday, October 19, the police arrested Titsworth and questioned him. He was a four-time felon with a lousy attitude toward cops and far greater experience with their interrogation tactics. He didn't budge an inch. He knew nothing about the Haraway case, didn't give a damn what Ward and Fontenot said; he had never met either of the gentlemen.

No video was made of the Titsworth interrogation. He was thrown in jail, where he soon recalled that on April 26 he had broken his arm in a fight with the police. On April 28, when Denice disappeared, his left arm had been in a heavy cast. Yet he had been described, in both the Ward and Fontenot confessions, as wearing a T-shirt, with tattoos covering his arms.

Dennis Smith interviewed the treating physician, who described the break as a spiral fracture between the elbow and shoulder and very painful. It would have been impossible for Titsworth to carry a body or commit a violent attack only two days after the fracture. His arm was in a cast, and the cast was in a sling. Impossible.

The confessions continued to unravel. As the police sifted through the rubble of the burned house, its owner appeared and asked what they were doing. When told that they were looking for the remains of Denice Haraway, and that one of the suspects had confessed to burning her with the house, the owner said that was not possible. He'd burned the old house himself in June 1983—ten months before she disappeared.

And the state medical examiner completed an analysis of what had been thought to be a human jawbone found at the house.

It was not Denice Haraway's—it came from a possum.

Epilogue

Undeterred by the lack of credible evidence, Pontotoc County District Attorney William N. Peterson took Thomas Jesse Ward and Karl Allen Fontenot to trial in September 1986 for the robbery, kidnapping, and murder of Denice Haraway. Judge Donald E. Powers allowed the confessions of both men into evidence, and Peterson sponsored the testimony of two jailhouse snitches—a career criminal named Terri Holland, who claimed that Fontenot had admitted the crime, and a petty thief named Leonard Martin, who claimed to have heard Ward mutter to himself, "I knew we'd get caught. I knew we'd get caught." After brief deliberations, the jury found both men guilty and later sentenced them to death.

The Oklahoma Supreme Court overturned Fontenot's conviction in 1987 and Ward's in 1988 on the ground that the case against each had been prejudiced by the admission of the other's statement at their joint trial. The cases were remanded to Powers for separate retrials. After the prosecution agreed that impartial juries could not be impaneled in Pontotoc County, Powers granted changes of venue. Fontenot was retried in Hughes County in 1988 and Ward in Pottawatomie County in 1989.

Meanwhile, Denice Haraway's body had been found and it had been determined that she had died from a single gunshot wound to the head. She had not been burned and it was extremely doubtful, although not impossible, that she had been stabbed. Thus, the confessions were even less credible than they had been the first time around. Still, the juries convicted both men. Fontenot was again sentenced to death, but Ward was sentenced to life without parole. Fontenot's sentence was subsequently commuted to life without parole, but the convictions were left intact.

As this book went to press, volunteer lawyers, investigators, and law students were pursuing new evidence in the hope of exonerating Ward and Fontenot, who remained prime examples—victims, really—of unrequited innocence.

RICHARD LAPOINTE

"I killed her," he confessed, "but I don't remember being there"

TOM CONDON
MANCHESTER, CONNECTICUT

It was mid-afternoon on the Fourth of July 1989. Richard Lapointe was going to have a picnic with his wife and son when the phone rang. It was the Manchester police. Could he come down to the station for a little chat? He'd be home in time for the picnic.

Well, OK, he said.

He didn't drive, so a detective came out to pick him up. Lapointe wondered if the officers wanted to talk to him, again, about the unsolved rape and murder of his wife's eighty-eight-year-old grandmother, Bernice Martin, more than two years earlier.

Their plan was actually more ambitious. They hoped to make Lapointe confess to the crime. To that end, they'd planned an elaborate ruse. Two rooms in the station were festooned with props—pictures, charts, lists, and diagrams—portraying Lapointe as the killer. A chart said his fingerprints were found on a knife used in the crime. Another linked him to the crime through DNA testing. There was a list of detectives who were on the "Bernice Martin Homicide Task Force."

None of this was true. A suspect who carefully read the "squad assignments" on the task force list might have detected the hokum when he came across the team of "Friday and Gannon," the detectives in the later episodes of TV's *Dragnet*. Regardless, most people in Lapointe's situation would have realized they were in plenty of trouble.

But Lapointe, forty-three, a homely, mentally handicapped man with no history of violence, hadn't a clue. He listened as a sergeant quickly read him his rights, then scribbled his name on a waiver form and went upstairs with a detective. Over the next nine hours, he gave police three statements

From "Reasonable Doubt," *Northeast Magazine, Hartford Courant*, February 21, 1993. Copyright © Hartford Courant. Adapted with permission.

469

admitting guilt in the rape and murder. Then they let him go home, and arrested him the next day.

He was convicted of the crime almost three years later in superior court. Although prosecutors fought to have him executed, he was sentenced to life in prison without chance of parole.

Police, jurors, and prosecutors say they got the right man. But dozens of others—people who know Lapointe, advocates for handicapped persons, lawyers who followed the trial—find the case deeply troubling.

"As far as protection of individual rights, it was the system at its worst. It was a bad case all around," said Hartford defense lawyer William Gerace, who followed the case. That was my reaction as well.

Lapointe didn't get a fair shake. Some believe criminal defendants are coddled and given too many rights and safeguards. Lapointe, who needed them if anybody does, got none. He had no lawyer, his statements weren't taped, and his family wasn't allowed to call or visit during the nine-hour interrogation. Police subjected him to lies, tricks, and intimidation to obtain his confession.

Also, I don't think he did it.

Richard Lapointe was born in Hartford and raised in the city's Charter Oak Terrace housing project. As a child he showed very little promise. He was, and is, short, chubby, weak, and awkward. He wears thick glasses and a hearing aid. He has a head too large for his body, a pointy chin, poor balance, and a slow walk that is several degrees off plumb.

He was slow in school as well. Some kids picked on him and called him "Mister Magoo." The unfairness of this made one gang of kids take Richard under its wing. One of those kids was Jack Jenkins.

"He was the type of kid who, because of his physical stature and appearance, got picked on. He couldn't fight back. He was the classic ninety-pound weakling, so the group I hung out with looked after him," Jenkins said.

In one of life's little ironies, Jenkins had become deputy warden of the Bridgeport jail, where Lapointe was taken after being picked on in the Hartford jail. Jenkins recognized his walk as they brought him in and called out, "Magoo?" Then Jenkins did what he'd done three decades before. He looked out after Mister Magoo.

As a child, Lapointe had remained cheerful despite the ridicule. This was a point of pride; he told a psychologist years later that he felt bigger than the kids who taunted him when he smiled and walked away. He still tries to be accepted as the class clown by telling little jokes, the same jokes over and over, to make people like him.

It wasn't until he was fifteen years old that doctors discovered why Lapointe was an inept student. He had Dandy-Walker Syndrome, a rare hereditary condition now treated at birth, in which a cyst in the lower back of the brain cavity causes parts of the brain to develop abnormally. The cyst often alters the flow of cerebral spinal fluid, causing hydrocephalus, a buildup of fluid that can damage a number of brain functions, such as coordination, speech, memory, and abstract thinking.

Lapointe had the first of five brain operations at fifteen. Doctors put in a shunt, or tube, to draw the fluid out of the cranial cavity.

After his first operation, he tried to return to school. He'd stayed back three times in the first eight grades, then entered Hartford Public High School as a seventeen-year-old freshman. He didn't make it through the year. He said the school board suggested he drop out, because he was only taking up a seat.

After he left school, he settled into life as a dishwasher in a variety of Hartford restaurants. In the mid-1970s he met Karen Martin, a young woman who had a mild case of cerebral palsy and had only partial use of one arm. They married, and in 1979 had a bright and handsome son, Sean. The delivery was difficult for Karen, so Richard had a vasectomy shortly thereafter.

They lived on Richard's dishwashing salary and occasional help from Karen's family. They were so poor at times that when Sean got older Richard would sometimes lower him into Salvation Army bins to grab clothes. Though they were poor, they ate out a good deal because their disabilities made cooking difficult. Waitresses who worked with Richard often gave him the "bomb," the food orders made incorrectly or sent back by customers. Yet the Lapointes struggled to lead a normal life, and somehow got by.

They settled in Manchester in the early 1980s, near some of his wife's relatives. Their favorite was Karen's grandmother, Bernice Martin, whom they called "Nana" or "Mother." Mrs. Martin, a former teacher and Sears saleswoman, was by all accounts an inspirational woman with myriad interests; she organized bingo games and Bible readings for her friends, wrote poems, loved sports, and baked cookies for the volunteer firemen.

She lived in a housing complex for the elderly, Mayfair Gardens, a collection of one-story, wood-and-brick shoeboxes a couple of blocks from the Lapointe home in the north end of town. Richard and Karen settled into a routine that included regular visits to Mrs. Martin's house on Sundays. The Lapointes, devout Catholics, would attend Mass at St. Bridget's Church, have brunch at My Brother's Place, a restaurant on North Main Street, then cross the street to Nana's apartment.

Sean Lapointe had become a Boston Celtics fan, like his dad and great-grandmother, and the Celtics were on TV on Sunday afternoon, March 8, 1987. The family gathered in Mrs. Martin's living room to watch the game and chat. They had coffee and a little something to eat. The Celtics lost a tough one to the Detroit Pistons, 122–119, in overtime. The outcome aside, it was a pleasant visit.

The Lapointes left about 4:00 P.M. and headed home. It was about a ten-minute walk to their house at 75 Union Street, a large two-family that had been turned into a four-unit condominium—Karen's family helped with the purchase—in the comfortable, working-class neighborhood. It was a warm afternoon for early March.

At about 5:45 P.M., Natalie Howard, Mrs. Martin's daughter and Karen's aunt, and her husband, Earle, drove by Mayfair Gardens and saw Mrs. Martin putting the garbage out. "Should we stop?" the husband asked. "No, I'll call her when we go home," Natalie Howard said.

Howard later called her mother twice, but got no answer. So she called the Lapointes at about 8:00 P.M. They were watching TV. Would Richard go over and check on Mother? Sure, Richard said. He walked over and knocked on Mrs. Martin's door. It felt warm, but he didn't think anything of that. He got no answer, so he walked over to the home of a neighbor he knew, Jeannette King. She let him use her phone. He called Karen and Natalie Howard, and said the lights were out and Mrs. Martin must have gone to bed.

She was a night owl. He was told to check again. He walked back to Mrs. Martin's apartment. This time the door was hot, and he could see smoke coming out from under the eaves. He went back to King's home, excited and out of breath, and dialed 911. Firefighters and police found the living room couch on fire, filling the apartment with smoke. Mrs. Martin was on the living room floor, unconscious. A volunteer fireman dragged her out. She was pronounced dead shortly thereafter. The eighty-eight-year-old woman had been bound tightly around the neck and wrists, stabbed, and sexually assaulted. The couch fire was one of three the assailant set in the apartment, apparently to destroy evidence.

Police interviewed dozens of people, including Richard and Karen Lapointe. They said they were at home from about 4:45 until Natalie How-ard called at 8:00 P.M. Although Richard Lapointe remained on the list of twenty-six suspects, investigators thought they knew who the killer was.

They zeroed in on Fred Merrill, a career criminal known as "the peanut butter bandit" because he'd once broken out of jail with a gun slipped to him in a jar of peanut butter. He had been charged in at least two sexual assaults in addition to his record of numerous burglaries, robberies, and four prison escapes. But he was eventually dropped as a suspect by the Manchester police because of his blood type.

There were two bits of forensic evidence found in Bernice Martin's apartment. One was a drop of blood on an envelope that may or may not have belonged to the assailant; the other was a semen stain on the bedspread that probably belonged to the assailant. Tests showed both were left by someone with type A blood. Merrill is type AB negative.

That left the cupboard bare. Murders are relatively rare in Manchester, especially rape-murders of kindly old ladies. The Martin family, which included a state police trooper and other solid citizens, wanted it solved.

About a year after the crime, local officers worked with the FBI's Behavioral Sciences Unit in Quantico, Virginia, to create an "offender's profile." The unit, noted in Thomas Harris's novel *The Silence of the Lambs*, analyzes a crime scene for the characteristics of the criminal. It can, for example, sometimes be determined how experienced the criminal was from how he committed the crime.

Persons close to the case say the profile of Bernice Martin's killer was of a young man, a loner, possibly a member of her family who lived nearby, and knew Mrs. Martin and where she lived, a man who was socially inept and had a weak self-image, a man who had problems with overbearing women.

The group that assembled the profile was headed by New York State Police Lieutenant John Edward Grant, who was spending the year with the FBI. Grant stayed with the case through Lapointe's arrest. The profile, however, didn't produce an instant suspect. After the case had gone unsolved for two years, it was assigned to a new man.

Paul Lombardo, a twelve-year veteran of the force, had been a detective for a little more than two years, and was on his second homicide investigation. He is a tough, dark-haired, no-nonsense, hard-driving cop in the Joe Friday mode.

After reviewing the offender profile and the case file, Lombardo started interviewing the people involved. He interviewed Natalie Howard, and then, on June 8, Richard Lapointe. As he would testify, he found Lapointe's actions "strange" and his denial of committing murder "passive" instead of the "very strong affirmative objection you would expect."

After that, he stopped interviewing suspects. He believed Lapointe was the killer. If correct, it would be a brilliant, 221B Baker Street piece of intuitive police work because, despite all the stuff on the police station walls, there was no evidence linking Lapointe to the crime. Lombardo did learn that Lapointe had type A blood, like that found in the victim's apartment, but so did about 40 percent of the population.

Lombardo contacted Grant, now back at work in New York. Even though some of the profile didn't fit the suspect—Lapointe was neither young nor a loner—Grant said Lapointe would be a "very interesting" possibility.

Working with Grant and the Hartford County State's Attorney's Office, Lombardo set up the sting on the Fourth of July, when he knew Lapointe would have the day off. They'd display the phony evidence props. Lombardo would interrogate Lapointe. Another detective, Michael Morrissey, would go to the Lapointe home and interview Karen.

The interrogation of Richard Lapointe began about 4:00 P.M. in a second-floor office. Lombardo began by telling Lapointe that there was proof that he committed the crime—that his fingerprints had been found on a knife found at the scene. That wasn't true, but police are allowed to lie to suspects or even display phony evidence.

Lapointe denied committing the murder, but eventually asked Lombardo if it were possible for a person to do such a crime and then black out and not remember it.

Lombardo said that was possible.

After an hour or so—neither man could remember exactly—Lapointe gave Lombardo a two-sentence statement: "On March 8 I was responsible for Bernice Martin's death and it was an accident. My mind went blank."

Lapointe then went to the bathroom. Afterward, he recanted that statement, saying he'd given it so he would be allowed to go to the bathroom.

Lapointe asked about using the phone to call his wife or a lawyer. Lombardo said he pushed the phone in front of Lapointe, but didn't leave the room or offer any other assistance. He said Lapointe never picked up the phone. Lapointe said when he asked about calling a lawyer, Lombardo told him: "Later." It's unclear if Lapointe understood why he needed a lawyer. He said he asked because he'd seen it done on a TV show.

Lapointe said Lombardo "played games" to get him to confess. "I'd say, 'You just want me to say I did it,' and he'd say, 'See, you just said you did it.'" Lombardo kept talking. As the evening wore on, Lapointe dictated another statement: "On March 8, 1987, I went to visit Bernice Martin with my wife and son. We left the apartment in the late afternoon and went home. I left my house some time after that to take the dog for a walk. I was at Bernice Martin's apartment with the dog. We were both there together and the time was right. I probably made a pass at her and she said no. So I hit her and I strangled her. If the evidence shows I was there and that I killed her, then I killed her, but I don't remember being there. I made a pass at Bernice because she was a nice person and I thought I could get somewhere with her. She was like a grandmother to me, that I never had."

As Lombardo interviewed Richard, Michael Morrissey arrived at the Lapointe home and began questioning Karen. Morrissey wore a "wire," or hidden microphone, and secretly tape-recorded this conversation with the help of his brother, Officer Joseph Morrissey, who was outside in a patrol car.

From the transcript it was obvious that Morrissey lied to Karen numerous times. He said DNA testing had proved Richard was the killer, that he'd cut his hand and left a drop of blood in the apartment, that neighbors had heard screaming and seen Richard carrying something into the apartment.

Morrissey tried to coax Karen into turning on her husband, threatening her with the loss of her son.

"Richard is going to get arrested, OK? I don't want that to happen to you, because you're going to have to deal with somebody else taking care of your son. Do you know that?" Morrissey said.

Despite this, the fragile woman stuck to her story. "That's not Richard," she said twice, as Morrissey described how Richard supposedly had done the crime. Did Richard ever hit their son? "Never." How did he treat you? "Fine."

Karen added one element she'd forgotten the first time. She said on the night of the killing, Richard went out to walk the dog at about 5:00 P.M., before dinner, but was back "within twenty minutes." She was emphatic about it, saying they had dinner at 5:30 and Richard was there.

Since Bernice Martin was seen alive at 5:45 P.M., this should have been an alibi. But Morrissey didn't see it that way. He returned to headquarters and took over Richard's interrogation. The pitch was that Morrissey had broken the news to the wife, and she wanted him to talk, so now he could tell the whole story.

Curiously, even though Morrissey wore the wire when talking to Karen, there was no tape or transcript of his interrogation of Richard. (Taping was not required by law.) One officer, Wayne Rautenberg, testified that he thought there was a tape of Richard's interview, but none ever surfaced. What did surface, after another four hours of questioning, was a third confession.

It started with the family's visit to Mrs. Martin's apartment, and their walk home at 4:00 P.M.: "After being home awhile I left to walk the dog. I then walked back up to Bernice's apartment and she invited me in. We each had a cup of coffee (I think Bernice had tea) and I sat on the couch. I remember having my matches and my smoking pipe in my jacket pocket. After my coffee I went to the bathroom (which is located off the bedroom). When I came out Bernice was in the bedroom combing her hair. She was wearing a pink house coat type of outer wear with no bra (I could see her breasts when she bent over). I grabbed her with my hand over her waist area. When I did that she pushed me. I threw her on the bed and took off her underwear because I wanted to have intercourse with her. I got my penis inside her for a few strokes and then pulled out and masturbated. I did cum on the bed spread when I was finished. I had already thrown her underwear on the right side of the bed. After the sex she said she was going to tell my wife Karen. I then went to the kitchen and got a steak knife with a hard plastic brown handle and stabbed Bernice in the stomach while she was laying on the couch. The rest of the incident I do not recall although I admit to have strangled her."

Finally, after midnight, Lapointe was confronted by a third interrogator, Captain Joseph Brooks, head of the detective division. Brooks knew Lapointe because both frequented My Brother's Place.

Brooks said he was brought in because Lapointe "continued to vacillate"—that is, he would give a statement, then recant and say he was just parroting what they told him, saying what they wanted to hear so he could go to the bathroom or go home. Police insisted Lapointe was always free to get up and walk out of the station. But Brooks testified that Lapointe told him he didn't know he wasn't under arrest and could leave.

After Morrissey left her home, Karen Lapointe called her mother, Margaret Dana of Farmington. Dana called Karen's brother, Kenneth Martin of Wallingford. They met at Karen's house. At 10:00 P.M., Dana and Kenneth Martin went to the police station. They wanted to find out what was happening with Richard, to see if he needed a lawyer and take him home if possible. Dana testified a police lieutenant told her that he couldn't interrupt the questioning. He also said that Richard had been told about getting a lawyer, but had said he didn't want one.

No one told Lapointe his family members were there. After a half hour, an officer suggested that Dana and Martin go home, assuring them that he would call when Richard could be picked up. Asked why she didn't push for a lawyer, Dana said, "We thought he was just being interviewed. We had no idea what was transpiring that night."

Lapointe told Brooks he was cold, hungry, and tired. Finally, well after 1:00 A.M., they let Lapointe go home—which seemed unusual, to say the least, if he actually had confessed to a sadistic sex murder.

The next morning, July 5, 1989, Lapointe got up and went to work. Meanwhile, Lombardo prepared an application for an arrest warrant. Although Lombardo claimed to have other evidence linking Lapointe to the crime, all he really had were the three confessions he and Morrissey had sweated out of Lapointe over nine hours the night before.

Lapointe was arrested that night.

As his trial approached in superior court in Hartford, Lapointe drew two very good public defenders, Patrick J. Culligan and Christopher M. Cosgrove, and a well-respected judge in David M. Barry. He also drew one of the toughest, most intimidating prosecutors in the system, Rosita M. Creamer.

Culligan and Cosgrove first filed a motion to suppress Richard's confessions. In a seven-week hearing before the judge that began in December 1991, the public defenders tried to show that the confessions had been coerced and were not voluntary, as required by law.

A psychologist and psychiatrist testified that Richard was a mentally damaged man, vulnerable and gullible. He had scored ninety-two on an IQ test, putting him in the thirteenth percentile, and had "no ability to challenge figures of authority"—if told something was true he'd think it was true.

Along with the experts, Culligan and Cosgrove paraded in a host of Manchester residents who knew Richard and described him as a jolly, meek "Mr. Peepers" man who was "slow," "not all there," "very simple," "mildly retarded," and—commonly—"childlike" or "a child in a man's body."

Creamer methodically attacked the expert and character witnesses, as she would later do in front of the jury, emphasizing that, whatever Richard's shortcomings, he was heading a family and holding a job.

Judge Barry denied the motion to suppress the confessions.

Lapointe not only lost his motion, he lost his family and the in-laws who believed "the evidence against him was overwhelming." Possibly succumbing to family pressures, Karen filed for divorce and reclaimed her maiden name.

At Lapointe's eleven-week trial in the spring of 1992, the jury never got to hear Karen. At the hearing to suppress the confession, she weakened her previous statements to the police. She'd said several times earlier that

Richard stayed home after he came back from walking the dog, before 5:30 P.M., on the night of the killing. This time she said that from 6:15 or about 6:30 P.M. to about 7:00 P.M., she was upstairs getting her son ready for bed, so she wasn't sure whether Richard was home then.

When she and Sean came downstairs, she said, Richard was there, watching TV, not sweating or bleeding, looking and acting as he did before.

While she testified, Karen appeared to look away when Richard looked at her. At one point late in the hearing, when the subject of Richard's disabilities came up, Karen blurted, "There's nothing wrong with Richard."

Lapointe's lawyers now felt Karen had turned on her husband, become a potential liability, a loose cannon. They didn't call her to testify again. It was a costly decision because, in retrospect, she might have provided a time frame in which it was almost impossible for Richard to have committed the crime.

With the trial's focus again on his confession, Lapointe took the stand and said several times he didn't kill Bernice Martin. He signed the three confessions, he said, so the officers would let him go home. Creamer shook him with a fierce cross-examination. He seemed uncertain and confused about some events on the evening of Mrs. Martin's death, such as who he called after his first attempt to check on Mrs. Martin. Then she bore in on the confessions. "If your desire was to be thought not guilty, how did you think you would advance that by providing . . . . confessions to the murder?"

"I have no idea," Lapointe replied.

Those who support Lapointe see the cross-examination as another example of his inability to stand up to authority figures and his inclination to tell such people what they want to hear. The jury viewed his testimony differently—as the squirming of a guilty man. Deliberations lasted only one hour.

"The confession was at least 75 percent of it," jury foreman Michael Palin said of the guilty verdict. He and others didn't believe Lapointe would confess so he could go to the bathroom or go home. They also believed the police, as most jurors do.

Even so, when the state sought the death penalty for Lapointe, they decided against capital punishment.

The conviction gave a free pass to Mrs. Martin's murderer. Several likely suspects were not investigated because of the police fixation on Lapointe and the common (and convenient) belief within law enforcement that, short of torture or mental derangement, no one will confess to a crime he did not commit.

Much was made, on the arrest warrant and at the trial, of specific facts that Lapointe provided to police that only the killer would have known. These facts were supposed to be additional proof, beyond the confession, of Lapointe's guilt. They prove nothing. Analyzing them one by one, they are either false or were known to more people than the killer.

The warrant also says that no sperm were found in the semen sample, and that this is consistent with the fact that Lapointe had had a vasectomy. It really proves nothing. Some semen samples don't have sperm in them, because sperm isn't evenly distributed in semen, and heat over 120 degrees destroys sperm, several experts said. Fire officials testified the heat in the apartment fire was between 500 and 600 degrees.

What Lombardo really had was the confession. The confession has so many inconsistencies that it is almost as if Lapointe confessed to the wrong crime.

Let's dismiss the first two confessions as ludicrous and oxymoronic. A rational person cannot admit to having done something he can't remember doing. Let's go to the third confession that Lapointe gave to Detective Morrissey.

In this one, Lapointe leaves to walk the dog, goes over to Mrs. Martin's apartment, has coffee, then goes to the bathroom. When he comes out, Mrs. Martin is sitting in a housecoat with no bra, brushing her hair. Lapointe can see her breasts when she bends over.

He assaults her on the bed. He gets his penis in for a few strokes, then withdraws it and masturbates on the bedspread. She tells him she's going to tell his wife. So he goes and gets a knife and stabs her on the couch, strangles her with his hands, and then doesn't remember anything else.

Family members say Mrs. Martin was a proper woman who wouldn't have appeared as Lapointe said.

Lapointe is supposed to have said, "I had already thrown her underwear on the right side of the bed." Would Richard Lapointe, a man with a weak memory, remember a detail such as that two and a half years later? Or is it something the police fed him, because it happened to correspond with a photo of the scene?

More importantly, the many cuts and bruises in and around the vagina and urethra indicated that the rape was most likely done with a blunt instrument, according to Dr. Arkady Katsnelson, the assistant state medical examiner who performed the autopsy.

Then there is the location of the body. Police believed Mrs. Martin was raped and stabbed, then placed on the living room couch which was then set on fire. So says the warrant. This somewhat corresponds to Lapointe's confession—he says he stabbed Martin on the couch—but not to what experts believe actually happened.

Subsequent testimony by Katsnelson and others showed Mrs. Martin wasn't on the couch. She was found across the room, six or eight feet from the couch. That led to a new theory: that Mrs. Martin was raped and stabbed in the bedroom, and then somehow crawled outside the bedroom door, where she lost consciousness.

Finally, Morrissey was clear that Lapointe admitted strangling Mrs. Martin with both hands. Katsnelson says Mrs. Martin was not strangled with two hands. "This is not a manual strangulation," he said. He said because of the kind of bruises present, it was strangulation by compression, most likely by a blunt object being pushed against the right side of her neck.

Thus, the salient elements of the crime didn't happen the way Lapointe confessed to them. Curiously, his confession did correspond to the police theory of the crime. Is it possible, as Lapointe claims, that police officers "put words in [his] mouth"? Or that he confessed to what he read in the paper? Or some combination of the two. The facts "known only to the killer" also were known to the police.

When I visited Lapointe in prison one day in December 1992, serving his sentence of life without parole plus sixty years, I looked into his big eyes, which don't seem to move together, and asked if he had committed the murder.

"No, I did not," he said quietly, but not what I would call passively. "I got a bad deal." He was cheerful most of the time I was with him. He said the loss of his son was the worst part of it.

The props, the stuff the police hung on the walls, the *Mission Impossible*–style sting the police prepared for Lapointe? It was probably more trouble than it was worth. Lapointe said he only remembered seeing the picture of Mrs. Martin.

Epilogue

On July 5, 1996—seven years and one day after Richard Lapointe succumbed to police trickery and signed multiple confessions to the rape and murder of Bernice Martin—a divided Connecticut Supreme Court affirmed his conviction and life sentence. The pivotal issue on appeal was whether the signed confessions had been voluntary. Five judges in the majority held that, under Connecticut case law, voluntariness need be proved only by a preponderance of the evidence. Under that standard, said the majority, the admission of the confessions at Lapointe's trial had not been "clearly erroneous" and therefore would not be overturned. Two dissenting judges contended that the standard of proof of voluntariness ought not to be a mere preponderance of the evidence but rather beyond a reasonable doubt—as it is in what the dissenters called the "enlightened Northeastern states" of Maine, Massachusetts, New Hampshire, New York, New Jersey, and Rhode Island. By that standard, Lapointe might have been entitled to a new trial. Lapointe's attorneys petitioned the U.S. Supreme Court for certiorari, but it was denied. New attorneys affiliated with Centurion Ministries, the oldest organization in the country devoted to exonerating innocent prisoners, then filed a petition for a state writ of habeas corpus, alleging among other things that the prosecution had withheld exculpatory evidence at Lapointe's trial. Superior Court Judge Stanley T. Fuger denied the petition in 2005. Four years later, the Connecticut Appellate Court reversed Fuger and remanded the case for a hearing, raising Lapointe's hopes of receiving a new trial. As this anthology went to press, however, the Lapointe case remained a striking example of a mentally challenged person's unrequited innocence.

JOHN GEORGE SPIRKO JR.

What he said was plainly false—but it sent him to death row

BOB PAYNTER

ELGIN, OHIO

It was no surprise that John George Spirko Jr. landed in a jail cell in early October 1982, just months after being paroled from a Kentucky prison for murder, just days after getting the snot beat out of him in a bloody bar fight by a gang of bikers, and just hours after waving a sawed-off shotgun in Theresa Fabbro's face in a failed attempt to track down and take revenge on the bikers. Nor was it especially remarkable that, once again behind bars, Spirko cooked up a pair of exotic schemes—contrived in the volatile psyche of a lifelong liar—to wriggle his way out of this new patch of trouble.

That's the way the thirty-six-year-old ex-con had lived his entire life. Thirteen years earlier, while in custody in Flint, Michigan—also after a barroom brawl—he had embarrassed a veteran homicide detective by concocting a detailed, convincing, and altogether phony confession to a series of coed murders then filling the local newspapers. He simply wanted to get out of his jail cell for a few hours of coffee and conversation. Further investigation showed that he had nothing to do with any of the murders.

So it was little wonder that Spirko's imagination sprang to life as he faced a felonious-assault charge for the shotgun-waving incident. The first scheme he came up with was to break out of jail. To that end, he enlisted the help of his girlfriend, Luann Smith. When their plot failed, he came up with scheme number two: in exchange for leniency for himself and his girlfriend-turned-codefendant, he would offer to help solve a high-profile crime then in the headlines—the abduction and murder of Betty Jane Mottinger, the postmaster in Elgin, Ohio, a hamlet of ninety-six souls not far from the Indiana border.

Spirko and the authorities promptly agreed on the terms of his cooperation—a short sentence for himself and probation for Luann Smith, provided

From the series "A Cold-Blooded Liar," *Cleveland Plain Dealer*, January 23–25, 2005. Copyright © Cleveland Plain Dealer. Adapted with permission.

his information proved helpful. He then began spinning a series of ever-changing stories in which he attributed the Mottinger crime to a troupe of dope-shooting, whiskey-guzzling, obscenity-spewing bikers, barflies, and slackers with street names like Rooster, Dino, and Dirty Dan.

Although laced with contradictions, factual errors, and imaginary characters, the tales Spirko proceeded to tell morphed into a prosecution that would send him to death row—for the very crime he'd promised to help solve.

On August 9, 1982, a crystal clear Monday morning in western Ohio, the tiny Elgin post office was robbed of stamps and cash totaling roughly $750 and the forty-eight-year-old postmaster was abducted.

The news was particularly shocking, coming as it did from a burg so quiet and remote that old-timers recalled not a single crime being reported there since World War II. Elgin is in Van Wert County, twenty-two miles due west of Lima, on the way to nowhere. Blink twice along Ohio 81 and you're already through it. The post office is even easier to miss. Housed in a squat, metal-sided hut about sixty yards south of the two-lane highway, the operation was so spare that, in 1982, it had neither a telephone nor running water.

The morning Betty Jane Mottinger disappeared, two Elgin residents—Opal Seibert, who lived across the street from the post office, and Mark Lewis, a truck driver who was heading out of town with a Toledo-bound load of wheat—noticed a stranger standing outside the post office beside a brown, two-tone sedan.

Seibert, a thirty-year resident of Elgin, recognized every face for miles around and knew at once when someone didn't belong. This was one of those times. Sipping coffee in her breezeway, she glanced at the kitchen clock. It was exactly 8:30 A.M. when the lean, clean-shaven stranger stepped slowly from the car and peered around, in all directions, as if to see if anyone was watching. He wore a long-sleeved blue work shirt, and his dark hair was combed straight back. He stood there for several minutes, his upper torso wedged between the car door and the roof, his left arm draped on the door. Seibert's eyes locked onto him. She lost sight of him for a few seconds when her view was blocked by a passing truck. Then the stranger drove off to the south.

As Mark Lewis passed the post office, he noticed the brownish car and the stranger standing in the position Seibert described. Otherwise, however, his description differed from Seibert's. Rather than lean, dark-haired, and clean-shaven, Lewis's stranger was a husky, slightly potbellied man of about 240 pounds, with sandy brown or reddish hair, and, possibly, a light mustache. Also, instead of long-sleeved and blue, Lewis recalled the man's shirt as short-sleeved and green with orange stripes. Neither Seibert nor Lewis saw the man enter or leave the post office, and neither saw Betty Jane Mottinger or anyone else in the car with him.

As the news of the postmaster's disappearance spread, dozens of postal inspectors—agents of the U.S. Postal Inspection Service, which investigates crimes against post-office employees and property—descended on Elgin and surrounding towns and villages, but found few promising leads.

Mottinger's fate remained a mystery until September 19, when the skeletal remains of a woman were found wrapped in a paint-splattered curtain in a soybean field about fifty miles from Elgin near the Blanchard River in Hancock County. The body was so badly decomposed from the summer heat that dental records were needed to identify it. From cuts on her clothing, it appeared that she'd been stabbed thirteen to seventeen times in the chest.

John Spirko's journey to death row began more than a hundred miles and a world away from Elgin in the Toledo suburb of Swanton, where, on October 9, he was arrested and thrown into the Lucas County Jail for harassing Theresa Fabbro with a shotgun. The incident occurred in the parking lot of the Longbranch Saloon, where he'd been beaten by bikers two days earlier.

Facing a felonious assault charge that in all likelihood would send him back to prison, perhaps for life, Spirko set his conniving mind to work. He enlisted Luann Smith in his first connivance, persuading her to smuggle two tungsten steel hacksaw blades in to him at the jail. From one of his cell bars, he cut an eight-inch piece of steel with which, in a daring escape attempt, he smacked a guard. Smith had hidden five hundred dollars and a new shotgun in her car parked around the corner of the jail, but Spirko didn't make it that far.

As a result, a second felonious assault charge was lodged against him, and his girlfriend, who'd never before been in trouble with the law, was charged with aiding and abetting him in the escapade.

The prime suspect in the abduction and slaying of Betty Jane Mottinger at the time of Spirko's arrest and foiled jailbreak was Marion "Sonny" Baumgardner, who was on parole for a post office robbery seven years earlier in Dupont, Ohio, thirty-two miles northeast of Elgin. The postmaster there, also a woman, had been tied up during the crime, but she hadn't been seriously injured.

Baumgardner, who bore some resemblance to the man whom Opal Seibert had seen in front of the Elgin post office, was being sought for questioning about the Mottinger crime, but he hadn't been found. Then, on October 29, three days after Spirko's attempted flight, the *Toledo Blade* reported that Baumgardner had been found, but he had an ironclad alibi—he'd been at work in Pasadena, Texas, on August 9.

The elimination of Baumgardner as a suspect set the investigation back to square one, but to Spirko, sitting in the Lucas County Jail weighing his options, the news evidently was inspirational. Two days after the *Blade* story appeared, he came forward with a proposition: he claimed to have information about the Mottinger crime—information he would reveal in exchange for kid-glove treatment for himself and Luann Smith.

Postal inspectors working on the Mottinger case had never heard of Spirko, but he seemed the sort of person who might know something about, or have been involved in, such a crime.

His rap sheet stretched back to the second grade in Toledo, when he started a fire at school. By age twenty-four he'd been convicted of arson, theft, breaking and entering, forgery, interstate transportation of a stolen car, and murder. At thirty-six, he had spent all but a few years of his adult life behind bars. Thirteen days before the Mottinger kidnapping, he'd been paroled from the Kentucky State Penitentiary at Eddyville, where he'd served twelve years for strangling a seventy-two-year-old woman during a jewelry theft.

An agreement was quickly reached on the conditions of Spirko's cooperation with postal inspectors—Luann Smith would receive probation, avoiding prison time, and he would plead guilty to reduced charges, receive a sentence of no more than five years, to be served in a federal penitentiary, and go into the federal witness protection program.

Spirko soon began a series of at least fifteen interviews with Postal Inspector Paul Hartman, laying out various evolving, but consistently horrifying, accounts of the abduction and murder of Betty Jane Mottinger.

The tales were reminiscent of drive-in slasher flicks, studded with coarse dialogue and detailed descriptions of sickening brutality and a vividly drawn cast, which changed from interview to interview, as did the roles of, among others, Rooster, Dino, and Dirty Dan.

Depending on the rendition—the interviews weren't recorded, so the only record would be Hartman's notes—the abduction followed either a robbery or the botched pickup of a mailed package of heroin. The abductors shoved Mottinger into either the trunk or back seat of a car and whisked her off to a country house, where they held her prisoner, either for several hours or several days, during which she was bound on a living room couch, or confined to an upstairs bedroom, or tied to a pole in the basement. She was beaten, dragged around by the hair, raped, and forced to perform oral sex. When she screamed and flailed and kicked in self-defense, she was stabbed to death, wrapped in a curtain, and her body was dumped in a soybean field.

In his first interview with Hartman on November 29, Spirko claimed merely to have heard about the crime and seen a bag of loot at a Toledo party. In ensuing interviews, as Hartman pressed for details that could be corroborated, Spirko responded with new versions, putting himself closer to the action with each telling. In one version, he witnessed various atrocities. In another, he saw the murder itself. Finally, he even had himself holding Mottinger down trying to keep her quiet, when Rooster suddenly stabbed her to death.

As captivating as the stories may have been, they were shot through with fabrications, contradictions, and what appeared to be wrong guesses about the facts of the case. Spirko told Hartman that Mottinger was wearing a gold watch and a gold necklace when she was killed, but members of her family said she wore neither. Spirko said her hands were bound behind her back with duct tape, but her hands weren't bound with anything when her body was found. He said she'd been stabbed in the back, but she'd been stabbed only in the front. And, perhaps most strikingly, while Hartman apparently never asked Spirko to describe Mottinger, he twice referred to her as a "fat bitch"—although she weighed only 104 pounds and had been described by those who knew her as petite.

The only details that Spirko provided in the interviews that were provably accurate were that Mottinger's body had been left in a soybean field, wrapped in a curtain, and that she had been stabbed many times. But anyone in western Ohio who'd recently read a newspaper or watched television knew those things.

While in prison, Spirko kept a scrapbook, which he left at his sister's home in a Toledo suburb, where Hartman examined it in late 1982.

Among dozens of photos of Spirko's prison buddies, Hartman ran across a snapshot of a slight, calm-looking young man gazing benignly into the camera, gently stroking a kitten. It wasn't the serene photograph but rather the résumé behind it that sparked Hartman's interest, leading him to imagine that the young man—Delaney Gibson Jr.—just might be the dark-haired stranger Opal Seibert had described.

Gibson and Spirko had been cellmates in the late 1970s, when both served time in Kentucky for homicides. Both had been paroled, Spirko in July 1982, Gibson five years earlier. Gibson was everything Spirko was—and more. He had an almost mythical aura about him, a near-legendary capacity to engage in criminal mayhem one day, only to vanish the next. When Hartman happened upon the photo, Gibson, thirty-two, was wanted for two murders in Kentucky and had been on the run for more than a year.

Postal inspectors assembled more photographs of Gibson, taken by authorities in Kentucky years earlier, and showed them to Opal Seibert in January 1983.

"That's the person I saw," Seibert said.

Seibert's identification of Gibson was a new card in Paul Hartman's hand, and he played it with Spirko on January 11, by steering the conversation to the tiny eastern Kentucky mountain of Bear Branch, which Gibson called home.

In a recent interview with the *Cleveland Plain Dealer* from death row, Spirko said that, as he began talking about dopers, Hartman was "lookin' at me and he's smilin' across the table. Then he says, 'You're full of shit. We know who was there. We know who was with you: Delaney Gibson.'" Spirko said he scoffed at that, but Hartman persisted, "'We've got eyewitnesses.'" When told by the *Plain Dealer* what Spirko had said, Hartman responded, "I don't remember that." He denied he'd ever pressured Spirko to say anything.

There's no dispute, however, that Spirko agreed to "sleep on" whatever it was that Hartman said. And sure enough, the next day Spirko told an entirely new story, which was a radical departure from everything he'd said before.

Yes, Spirko now said, Delaney Gibson and two of his cronies had killed Betty Jane Mottinger. After a robbery, they abducted, raped, and stabbed her to death so that she wouldn't be able to identify them. The three had told him all about the crime a few days after it occurred, said Spirko.

That was the last story Spirko told Hartman.

Spirko would later maintain that his rationale for continuing the interviews was just to string Hartman along until Luann Smith received her promised probation—an effort that came to naught. In March 1983, Smith was sentenced to eighteen months in the Ohio Reformatory for Women at Marysville prison.

Delaney Gibson remained on the lam until April 1983, when he was arrested in Canton, North Carolina, where he'd been working as a tomato picker with a crew of migrant farm workers. Upon learning of Gibson's arrest, postal inspectors descended on the Buncombe County Jail in Asheville, where Gibson was held pending extradition to Kentucky.

Gibson denied knowledge of the Mottinger crime and insisted that, in all of 1982, he'd sported a full beard. Also, he said, he'd never been to Elgin, Ohio. Gibson's wife, Margie, and the supervisor of his tomato-picking crew, Juan Flores, both vouched that Spirko indeed had a beard in August 1982. These claims were hardly definitive, of course—Gibson could have grown the beard since August. If—just if—he, his wife, and Flores were telling the truth, Gibson couldn't have been the clean-shaven stranger Seibert saw in front of the Elgin post office. But, apparently, postal inspectors made no effort to verify when Gibson grew the beard.

Gibson was soon extradited to Clay County, Kentucky, where on August 7 he and other inmates overpowered a guard and escaped from jail. Then on September 13, a Van Wert County grand jury indicted him in absentia—along with his talkative former cellmate—for the kidnapping and aggravated murder of the Elgin postmaster, making both men eligible for the death penalty.

Now wanted for three murders, Gibson was on the run until seven days before Christmas, when the FBI caught up with him at a motel just outside Montgomery, Alabama, and charged him with unlawful flight from the Kentucky murder charges. At this point, Hartman pounced on tiny Bear Branch, where Margie Gibson was living. He asked her—for the first time, it seems—about her husband's whereabouts on the morning of August 9, 1982. She said he'd been in North Carolina, where he was working. She added that she, her sister and brother-in-law, Brenda and Michael Bentley, and their children had been on vacation there, with Gibson, from Saturday, August 7, until about 6:30 P.M. Sunday, August 8. If true, that would mean that there were witnesses who could place Gibson more than five hundred miles from Elgin, only fourteen hours before the Mottinger abduction.

Hartman immediately contacted Michael Bentley, who not only said the same thing Margie Gibson said but also had receipts to document their story. Also, he told Hartman, there were photographs—lots of them—taken on the trip showing Gibson with a full beard. Over the next several days, Hartman shuttled between towns in Kentucky and North Carolina doing interviews and verifying the veracity of the receipts Bentley had provided.

On January 11, Margie Gibson gave Hartman eighteen photos showing Delaney, herself, their young son, and the Bentleys driving go-carts at an amusement park and dining at a McDonald's in Candler, North Carolina. Hartman promptly went to Candler and located the restaurant. A few days later, the Bentleys provided forty more photographs purportedly taken on the trip. Hartman confirmed that they had dropped off film for processing at a department store near their home in Ary, Kentucky, on August 10, 1982. In snapshot after snapshot, there was the fugitive Delaney Gibson with a full beard and a thick mop of dark, curly hair.

Given the time and place that the photos appeared to have been taken, it was all but mathematically impossible for Gibson to have been the clean-shaven stranger Opal Seibert had seen on August 9. He would have had to straighten his hair, shave his beard, make a thousand-mile round trip, stop to commit an abduction and murder with Spirko, then grow another full beard without his boss noticing he'd shaved in the meantime.

All this clearly was a problem for the prosecution theory of the Mottinger case. There was, however, an easy solution—simply to hide the photographs. And that's precisely what someone did. Who would remain an open question, but the photos were secreted in a file drawer, apparently separate from other investigative documents pertaining to the case, and not turned over to Spirko's lawyers prior to trial.

Among documents that were turned over to the defense was a memo indicating that a Michael Bentley had claimed that Gibson was in North Carolina the weekend before the Mottinger abduction and that "pictures are purported to have been taken of the weekend in question." Based on that information, defense attorneys twice demanded "all statements of Michael Bentley"—statements that could have alerted them to the existence of the receipts and photographs documenting Gibson's alibi—but these demands went unmet.

John Spirko's trial opened in the Van Wert Court of Common Pleas on July 30, but Delaney Gibson wouldn't be among the witnesses. Three weeks earlier, while awaiting trial for the Kentucky murders, he'd pulled a knife on a deputy sheriff and vanished yet again.

If Gibson had been in the courtroom, he no doubt would have been amazed at Opal Seibert's testimony. When shown an old prison photo of him, clean-shaven, and asked if he was the stranger she'd seen in front of the post office, Seibert told the jury with rock-solid certainty, "That there is his face. He had a different hairdo, but that's him. I don't forget a face." Seibert was one of just two key prosecution witnesses, the other, of course, being Paul Hartman, who testified regarding the "intimate details" of the crime supposedly related to him by Spirko.

Prosecutor Stephen Keister stressed in his summation to the jury both that Spirko told Hartman things that only the killer would know—a dubi-

ous assertion, to say the least—and that Gibson had been positively identified at the scene of the abduction. Keister showed the jurors the old photo
of a bare-chinned Gibson and an artist's rendering of Seibert's clean-shaven
stranger drawn two days after the crime. "I submit to you, it is almost as if the
person who made this drawing back on August 11, 1982, had this picture
from which to make the drawing," said Keister. "You make the comparison.
That identification is there. Delaney Gibson was there that morning."

On August 22, the jury found Spirko guilty and, at the sentencing phase
of his trial two days later, he actually asked the jury to give him the death
penalty—even while insisting he was innocent. "I did not kill Betty Jane
Mottinger," he told the jury. "I did not kidnap Betty Jane Mottinger. But,
I have been convicted for it. From what I have heard, a lady that went to
work, bothered no one, had a family, a husband that loved her, she was
cruelly taken away, brutally murdered. She didn't get no appeal. Nobody
gave her that right. Instead, they just stabbed her to death. They probably
still out there now laughin' about it; laughin' because I got convicted of it.
But she deserved justice, and if that means me, then that's the way it should
be. I'm convicted, I should die. It's simple—simple arithmetic." On April 25,
the jury did as he asked, recommending a death sentence, which the court
imposed four days later.

Four months after Spirko's sentencing, FBI agents found Delaney Gibson hiding in the attic of his father-in-law's home in Bear Branch, but Ohio
authorities didn't move to bring him to trial in the Mottinger case. Gibson proceeded to plead guilty to the two Kentucky murders from the early
1980s and was sentenced to forty years in prison.

In 1995 a major Washington, D.C., law firm* agreed to represent Spirko,
whose appeals had been denied by the Ohio courts. The attorneys assigned
to the case, Thomas C. Hill and Alvin Dunn, filed a petition for a federal
writ of habeas corpus and bored in on the U.S. Postal Service's investigative
files, as Spirko's previous appellate attorneys had done without success.

Postal authorities had steadfastly resisted the release of any files that
hadn't been turned over prior to trial, but in 1996 a court-brokered agreement finally gave Hill and Dunn access to the previously undisclosed files.
There were several references in the files to the photos and other documentation of the Gibson and Bentley families' weekend respite in North
Carolina, but the photos themselves weren't among the materials. Postal

* The firm was Shaw Pittman, which, as a result of a merger, became Pillsbury Winthrop
Shaw Pittman LLP in 2005.

officials said they couldn't find them. Under a federal court order, however, they promised to look in Hartman's personal "desk file." And in the summer of 1997, without saying precisely where the photos had been, they finally were turned over to Spirko's lawyers—as they should have been well in advance of Spirko's trial thirteen years earlier.

Based on the newly discovered information, Hill and Dunn filed an amended habeas petition, alleging that Spirko had been denied due process of law by the prosecution's knowing use of false evidence—that when Stephen Keister put Opal Seibert on the witness stand to identify Delaney Gibson, he knew full well that Gibson had not been in Ohio at the time of the crime.

Gibson was paroled in Kentucky in December 1998 and—because there was no order that he be held to answer for the capital crime for which he was under indictment in Ohio, and for which his purported cohort was on death row—he was a free man.

Six months later, Gibson returned to prison in Kentucky for a parole violation. But in the summer of 2001—in the face of continuing inaction by Ohio authorities—he was released yet again and moved to Louisville.

A U.S. district court judge, meanwhile, had denied Spirko's habeas corpus petition, stating that "the information known to the state, including the information and photos not disclosed to the defense, do not conclusively establish that Gibson was not present in Ohio at 8:30 A.M. on August 9. That information may raise doubts about the likelihood of his being in Elgin, Ohio, that morning, but it does not exclude the possibility that such was the case. The state's assertions about Gibson's involvement were not, therefore, false, much less knowingly so."

The Sixth Circuit affirmed the district court's denial of Spirko's habeas, seeing "no reasonable probability" that the withheld evidence would have made a difference in the outcome of the trial. The decision was released on May 17, 2004, and that very day Van Wert County authorities dismissed all charges against Delaney Gibson.

Stephen Keister, who left the prosecutor's office in 1988 to return to private practice, declined to discuss any aspect of the Spirko case with the *Plain Dealer*, citing the passage of time. "It's been twenty years," he said. "My memory is fading. And a lot of things have been over the dam."

Paul Hartman, who retired from the U.S. Postal Inspection Service in 2000, after nearly three decades in law enforcement, told the *Plain Dealer* he remains certain that Spirko deserves to die for killing Betty Jane Mottinger. "It is my belief that he did it," Hartman said. "If and when they execute him, I will have no qualms. No qualms." Asked about the Gibson photographs, Hartman said he'd put them into the investigative case file "along with everything else" and had "no idea" where they'd been during the thirteen years they'd been missing.

Spirko has never blamed anyone but himself for his predicament.

"I put myself in this position," he told the jury at his sentencing hearing twenty years ago. "I don't actually hold no animosity towards Paul Hartman. . . . I feel one thing. I might be bound for hell, but I know Paul Hartman will be right on my tail-end. And him and I is going to have a go-around in hell. You can believe that."

Epilogue

Thomas Hill and Alvin Dunn, Spirko's lawyers, won seven postponements of Spirko's execution during last-ditch efforts in the courts to overturn his conviction. Failing that, they sought an outright pardon for their client based on what they regarded as overwhelming evidence of his actual innocence. On January 9, 2008, Ohio Governor Ted Strickland commuted Spirko's death sentence to life in prison without parole, citing the absence of physical evidence linking Spirko to the crime and "slim residual doubt" about his guilt.

Hill and Dunn, in an e-mail message to the *Plain Dealer*, lamented, "There can be no joy in the commutation of an innocent man's sentence to life without parole. The positive thing about Governor Strickland's commutation is that the state will now not execute an innocent man and that we can, and will, continue to fight for Mr. Spirko's complete exoneration and release." It appeared, however, that nothing short of finding the real killer would accomplish that.

POLICY RECOMMENDATIONS

The cases profiled in this anthology forcefully demonstrate that the principal reforms of the twentieth century—the supposed abolition of the third degree in the 1930s[1] and the institution of the Miranda warning in 1966[2]—have not adequately addressed the scourge of coerced and false confessions.

Further reform is needed, and needed promptly.

Fortunately, reform concepts have emerged that, we believe, would significantly alleviate the problem of false confessions, while simultaneously enhancing public safety and leading to economies that would free funds to strengthen law enforcement.

The first reform, which should be instituted posthaste by every state and the federal government, is requiring police agencies to electronically record interrogations in their entirety—an idea that already has been implemented in several jurisdictions, and that police and prosecutors in those jurisdictions have come to embrace.

"The best reform that has ever been rammed down my throat," said a top prosecutor in Minnesota,[3] where electronic recording of custodial interrogations has been done under court order since 1994.[4]

Electronic recording creates reliable, objective records of what actually occurs during interrogations. It documents whether threats or promises were made, whether Miranda rights were read and knowingly waived, and whether confessions actually include anomalous facts of the crimes in question or simply echo details provided by the interrogators. Also, of course, electronic records strongly deter coercion of suspects and the fabrication of confessions.

Police have found recording to their liking primarily because it shields them from frivolous allegations of misconduct during interrogations. Similarly, the benefits accrue to prosecutors, judges, public defenders, and, ultimately, society as a whole—as one law journal headline put it, "Everybody Wins."[5]

A common objection to recording is its cost, which is steadily coming down as digital technology advances. But the benefits of recording already appear to greatly outweigh the costs. Motions to suppress confessions based on alleged police misconduct are greatly reduced, saving countless hours not just for police but also for judges, prosecutors, and public defenders. Similarly, untold numbers of costly trials and appeals are avoided because defendants, confronted with an electronic record, are more likely to plead guilty. Also, when bad cases are weeded out, there will be fewer wrongful convictions and, therefore, fewer civil judgments—which often run into seven or eight figures for innocent persons.

Moreover, recording provides another inestimable social dividend—if fewer criminal investigations are derailed by false confessions, the apprehension of actual perpetrators inevitably increases. Leaving the guilty on the street, obviously, poses a serious danger—witness Kenneth M. Tinsley in the Washington case, Terry Wilson Spencer in the Vasquez case, and Brian Dugan in the Hernandez/Cruz case.

There is reason to be hopeful about a future in which electronic recording of interrogations becomes standard police practice. Recording was instituted in only two states during the twentieth century—Minnesota, as noted above, and Alaska.[6] But the glacial pace of the reform has started to pick up. Seven other states—Illinois, Maine, Maryland, New Jersey, New Mexico, Wisconsin, and North Carolina—and the District of Columbia now require custodial recordings in at least some circumstances.[7] Recording has been endorsed or strongly encouraged by the supreme courts of New Hampshire, Iowa, and Massachusetts.[8] And in California, a recording bill has twice passed both houses of the legislature, but was vetoed by Governor Arnold Schwarzenegger.[9]

Perhaps the most promising sign for the future of electronic recording is that it has been implemented voluntarily by hundreds of police departments around the country.[10]

Electronic recording, however, is no panacea.

Additional reforms are urgently needed.

Before getting to those, however, readers may find it helpful to have a little background on the psychological interrogation techniques that led to the false confessions featured in this anthology.

It is no accident that these techniques are widespread—they are taught in police academies across the country and have given rise to an entire industry of consultants. The pioneer and continuing leader in the field is John E. Reid & Associates.[11] "Of necessity," says Reid's 2001 manual, "investigators must deal with criminal suspects on a somewhat lower moral plane than that upon which ethical, law-abiding citizens are expected to conduct their everyday affairs."[12]

Interrogation, obviously, is a guilt-presumptive process. But a problem arises when interrogators, often relying only on hunches, rush to judgment that a suspect is guilty. Once presumed guilty, the suspect is taken into a specially designed room—small, cramped, with barren walls, no telephones or clocks, and no furniture except for chairs.

The interrogation, as taught by Reid, begins with a period of rapport-building. The tone is friendly. The interrogators tell the suspect they only need to hear what, if anything, he or she knows about the crime—a ploy that discourages the invocation of Miranda rights. As the interrogation proceeds, the suspect is abruptly accused of committing the crime, and told, falsely, that the evidence of guilt is overwhelming—fingerprints, blood, hair, witnesses, whatever. Interrogators are trained to cut off any denials—a tactic that destroys the suspect's confidence that all he needs to do is tell the truth.

With the suspect on the brink of hopelessness, the interrogator turns to tactics designed to persuade him that it is in his interest to confess. The inducements range from an appeal to conscience or religious beliefs— "God will forgive you"—to assertions that the criminal justice system treats remorseful defendants more leniently than those who persist in denials. Alternative scenarios of how the crime occurred are suggested—while it might have been premeditated and cold-blooded, it also might have been an accident, self-defense, or a situation that simply got out of hand.

If the suspect claims to have no memory of the crime, the interrogator suggests that it is not uncommon for persons who commit crimes that are totally out of character to erase them from memory and experience a kind of self-protective amnesia. But the interrogator is insistent on one point— the suspect definitely committed the crime.

The ploys build upon one another as the interrogation continues. With each passing hour, the suspect's ability to withstand the pressure withers. Sleep deprivation and hunger exacerbate the sense of hopelessness. Finally, the suspect's resistance collapses and he offers some vague "OK-I-did-it" type of statement. The admission does not end the interrogation, however, because, to win a conviction, the confession must have at least a modicum of specificity—facts that an innocent person would have no way of knowing. But, as several of the cases profiled in this volume show, interrogators often reveal such details—inadvertently or deliberately—through leading questioning, showing crime scene photos, or even taking the suspect to the crime scene.

Electronic recording of the entire interrogation process will document whether corroborative details originated in the mind of the suspect or were suggested during interrogation, but will not prevent innocent suspects from succumbing to the powerful psychological techniques in which the police have been thoroughly schooled.

Some in law enforcement are still in denial about the role standard interrogation techniques play in false confessions. When false confessions come to light, they inevitably blame the suspect. Others in law enforcement readily acknowledge that the techniques do result in some false confessions, but contend that, if the tactics were banned, few guilty persons would ever confess. Whether that is true is an open question, but drawing lines between acceptable and unacceptable tactics is not easy.

Nevertheless, the stories in this volume make it clear that some lines must be drawn—an endeavor to which we now turn our attention.

Duration of interrogation. A recent academic study found that 84 percent of false confessions occurred after interrogations of six hours or longer and that the average duration was more than sixteen hours.[13] Interrogations of such lengths are simply unacceptable. We believe that confessions resulting from interrogations in excess of twelve hours should be categorically inadmissible in court. And confessions following interrogations of more than six hours should be admissible only if the prosecution can establish beyond a reasonable doubt that they were voluntary. To meet the burden, the prosecution would have to show, at a minimum, that steps were taken to alleviate the stress, fatigue, hunger, disorientation, and other environmental factors that are known to have contributed to false confessions.

Polygraphs and voice-stress analyzers. These should be banned—period. Although there is in fact no reliable lie-detection technology, innocent suspects often believe—and are encouraged by their interrogators to believe—that the machines are veritably infallible. Consequently, many suspects are eager to be tested, anticipating that the test will prove they are telling the truth. Then they are devastated when told that they failed. In story after story in this anthology, innocent suspects—Beverly Monroe, Michael Crowe, Peter Reilly, Michael Altenburger, Gerald Martin Anderson, Kevin Fox, and Corey Beale—were told by their interrogators, first, that the so-called lie-detecting devices were infallible and, then, that the tests indicated they were lying. The best remedy for this problem is for the courts to suppress any statement made by suspects after they have been told that polygraphs, or voice-stress analyzers, or any other contraption indicated that they were lying.

Lying by interrogators. Lies by interrogators are commonplace and generally permissible under the 1969 Supreme Court decision *Frazier v. Cupp*.[14] Given that lies are factors in many, if not most, documented cases of false confessions, however, we believe that the Supreme Court should revisit *Frazier*. The interests of justice would be better served by the suppression of all confessions by juveniles, the mentally retarded, and the mentally ill to whom interrogators have lied. Likewise, confessions by normally functioning adults should be suppressed if they were told lies involving family members. It is unconscionable to allow the continuing use of devastatingly hurtful lies such as those inflicted on Kevin Fox (that his wife no longer believed him and his family had stopped loving him) and Donnell Vaughn (that his arrest had caused his grandmother to suffer a heart attack and die).

Implicit promises of leniency. Rarely do interrogators make explicit promises of leniency—for example, that if the suspect confesses, he will be charged only with manslaughter, but, if he refuses to confess, the charge will be murder. Such promises, if proven, would result, under current law, in suppression of any ensuing confessions. Police, however, are taught a process known as pragmatic implication. The idea is to suggest alternative scenarios for crimes—one that it was cold, calculating, and premeditated, the other that it was impulsive, that the result was unintended, or that it was self-defense. The implication is clear—accepting the latter scenario will mitigate, or perhaps eliminate, punishment. To a suspect, even if innocent, it may seem reasonable to cut his losses and confess once he is convinced that continued denials would be futile. Pragmatic implication typically is predicated on a lie—the police almost invariably know the crime was neither accidental nor self-defense. The deception, however, is not why implicit promises should be prohibited during interrogation. Rather, they should be prohibited because the effect of an implicit one is the same as that of an explicit one.

Hypothesizing blackout scenarios. When an innocent suspect is led to believe there is rock-solid evidence that he committed a crime he cannot remember, the only remaining question is why he cannot reconcile the evidence with his memory. At this point, the interrogator offers an explanation—perhaps he committed the crime in a blackout or amnesiac trance. Then the suspect is asked to imagine how he might have committed it, and he compliantly begins to speculate. What he says, naturally, is likely to include information consistent with whatever facts of the crime he learned during his preceding interrogation. Those facts then are misconstrued as knowledge to which only someone involved in the crime would be privy. Because there no doubt are instances when guilty suspects feign memory loss, it would not be reasonable to prohibit police from advancing hypothetical amnesiac scenarios. However, we believe, any statement that follows should be suppressed unless the prosecution can show by clear and convincing evidence that the statement includes a substantial amount of accurate information that was neither imparted during interrogation nor was in the public domain at the time.

Pretrial reliability hearings. Under current law, the only prerequisite for the admission of confessions into evidence at criminal trials is that they be voluntary. At pretrial hearings on motions to suppress, reliability is not an issue—the sole question is voluntariness. This must change. Reliability hearings are hardly a novel concept. They already are common regarding other kinds of evidence—eyewitness identifications, informant testimony, novel forensic evidence, and hearsay. There is no logical reason that confessions proffered by the prosecution should be an exception. There already is a general consensus on what makes an inculpatory statement reliable—substantial corroboration, which is amenable to objective examination before trial. A statement has indisputable veracity if it led the police to physical evidence—a murder weapon, the fruits of a robbery, or bloody clothes—or if it contains facts of the crime that an innocent person either would not know or could not conceivably have guessed. On the other hand, a statement that contradicts the facts of the crime is dubious. Errors in a narrative do not always mean it is false, of course, nor do accurate facts always mean it is true. The question of its reliability, however, is more likely to be fairly and accurately resolved by a judge in pretrial proceedings than by a jury in the emotion-charged atmosphere of trial.

We realize, of course, that reform inevitably faces tremendous resistance—that is the tyranny of the status quo—and that there are legitimate objections to the foregoing proposals. Yet we firmly believe that these concepts deserve serious consideration by police, prosecutors, judges, and legislators, if they want to be part of the solution to the problem of false confessions—rather than part of the problem.

Notes

1. The third degree—that is, the use of physical or mental torture to extract a confession—was abolished following a 1931 report of the National Committee on Law Observation and Enforcement, known popularly as the Wickersham Commission, which documented widespread police brutality during interrogation of suspects, particularly minorities and the poor.

2. *Miranda v. Arizona*, 384 U.S. 436 (1996).

3. See Thomas P. Sullivan, "Electronic Recording of Custodial Interrogations: Everybody Wins," *Journal of Criminal Law and Criminology* 95 (Spring 2005): 1127.

4. *Minnesota v. Scales*, 518 N.W.2d 587 (1994).

5. Sullivan, "Electronic Recording of Custodial Interrogations," 1127.

6. *Stephan v. State*, 711 P.2d 1156 (1985).

7. 750 *Illinois Compiled Statutes*, sec. 405/5–401.5; *Maine Revised Statutes*, tit. 25, sec. 2803B(1)(K); *New Jersey Supreme Court Reports*, 317 (2995); *New Mexico Statutes*, sec. 29-1-16; *Wisconsin Statutes*, sec. 968.073 (2007); *General Statutes of North Carolina*, sec. 15A-211.

8. *State v. Barnett*, 2002 N.H. LEXIS 219; *State v. Hajtic*, 724 N.W. 449 (Iowa 2007); *Commonwealth v. DiGiambattista*, 813 N.E.2d 516 (Mass. 2004).

9. "Governor Vetoes Three Bills on Crime Case Procedures," *Los Angeles Times*, October 16, 2007, B4.

10. Thomas P. Sullivan, Andrew W. Vail, and Howard W. Anderson III, "The Case for Recording Police Interrogation," *Litigation* 34 (Spring 2008): 30–39.

11. The firm's founder and namesake and the late Fred E. Inbau, a professor of law at Northwestern University School of Law, began developing the techniques in the 1950s.

12. Fred E. Inbau, John E. Reid, Joseph P. Buckley, and Brian C. Jayne, *Criminal Interrogation and Confessions*, 4th ed. (Sudbury, Mass.: Jones and Bartlett, 2001).

13. Steven Drizin and Richard Leo, "The Problem of False Confessions in the Post-DNA World," *North Carolina Law Review* 82 (March 2004): 891–1007.

14. *Frazier v. Cupp*, 349 U.S. 731 (1969).

INDEX OF DEFENDANTS AND SUSPECTS

INDEX OF VICTIMS

INDEX OF JURISDICTIONS

NOTES ON CONTRIBUTORS

Editors

Steven A. Drizin is the legal director of the Center on Wrongful Convictions at Northwestern University School of Law in Chicago.

Rob Warden is a former investigative reporter and foreign correspondent for the *Chicago Daily News* and former editor and publisher of *Chicago Lawyer*. Since 1999, he has been the executive director of the Center on Wrongful Convictions.

Contributors

Ken Armstrong—coauthor of the article about Daniel Taylor (page 429)—is a *Seattle Times* investigative reporter who previously worked at the *Chicago Tribune*. He was a Nieman Fellow at Harvard University in 2001.

Alan Berlow—author of the articles about Christopher Ochoa (page 141) and Dick, Tice, Williams, and Wilson (page 415)—is a Maryland freelance journalist and former Southeast Asia correspondent for National Public Radio. He is best known for his acclaimed book *Dead Season: A Story of Murder and Revenge* (1996).

Edwin M. Borchard—author of *Convicting the Innocent*, from which the article about John A. Johnson (page 157) has been adapted—was a professor of law at the Yale University Law School from 1917 until his death in 1951. Prior to his appointment at Yale, he was librarian of Congress.

Tom Condon—author of the article about Richard Lapointe (page 469)—is a columnist and deputy editorial page editor at the *Hartford Courant*.

Donald S. Connery—author of *Guilty Until Proven Innocent*, from which the article on Peter Reilly (page 47) has been adapted—is a freelance journalist based in Connecticut and a member of the Advisory Board of the Center on Wrongful Convictions at Northwestern University School of Law. He is a former foreign correspondent who covered civil wars and revolutions in Asia, Africa, and Europe during the 1950s and 1960s for *Time* and *Life* magazines. In 1962 he covered the Cuban missile crisis from Moscow for NBC as well as *Time*.

John Conroy—author of the article about Madison Hobley (page 297)—is an independent investigative reporter and radio commentator who formerly was a staff writer for the *Chicago Reader*.

Fred J. Cook—coauthor of the article about Melvin Dean Nimer (page 203)—was a prominent investigative reporter in New York from the 1950s until his retirement in the late 1970s. He was perhaps best known for a 1957 report of the Alger Hiss case, to which *The Nation* devoted an entire issue in 1957. He died in 2003 at age ninety-two.

Jim Dwyer—author of the articles about Abdallah Higazy (page 137) and Ozem Goldwire (page 221) and coauthor of *Actual Innocence*, from which the article about Robert Lee Miller Jr. (page 251) has been adapted—is a staff writer at the *New York Times*.

Margaret Edds—author of *An Expendable Man*, from which the article about Earl Washington Jr. (page 235) has been adapted—recently took a buyout from the *Virginian-Pilot*, where she had been an editorial writer for many years.

Paul Eddy—author of the article about Eugene Earl Dykes (page 347)—has been writing about intrigue, corruption, mayhem, and murder for more than twenty-five years, primarily for the *Sunday Times* of London. He was editor of the Insight Team and has coauthored eight nonfiction books covering a spectrum of topics, from war to espionage and terrorism to international drug trafficking. He left the *Sunday Times* in 1985 but has continued writing investigative articles for its Sunday magazine.

William Farr—coauthor of the article about Michael Altenburger (page 71)—was the criminal courts reporter for the *Los Angeles Times* until shortly before his death in 1987, at age fifty-two, after a five-year battle with pancreatic cancer. In his honor, the criminal courts press room was named the Bill Farr Memorial Press Room.

Thomas Frisbie—coauthor of *Victims of Justice Revisited*, from which the article on Alejandro Hernandez and Rolando Cruz (page 317) has been adapted—is an award-winning writer and editor at the *Chicago Sun-Times*, where he has worked since 1976.

Randy Garrett—coauthor of *Victims of Justice Revisited*, the book from which the article on Rolando Cruz and Alejandro Hernandez (page 317) has been adapted—is a mental health technician whose initial writing about the Cruz/Hernandez case appeared in *Chicago Lawyer*.

Gene Gleason—coauthor of the article about Melvin Dean Nimer (page 203)—was a longtime investigative reporter at the *New York World-Telegram and Sun*.

John Grisham—author of the article about Tommy Ward and Karl Fontenot (page 453)—is an Arkansas-born, Mississippi-educated lawyer/politician turned novelist whose books have sold more than 235 million copies worldwide. He has written only one nonfiction book, *The Innocent Man: Murder and Injustice in a Small Town*, from which the article in this anthology has been adapted.

John Kendall—coauthor of the article about Michael Altenburger (page 71)—retired from the *Los Angeles Times* in 1991.

Alex Kotlowitz—author of the article about Romarr Gipson and Elijah Henderson (page 175)—is a Chicago writer best known for his 1992 book *There Are No Children Here*, which the New York Public Library listed as one of the 150 most important books of the twentieth century.

Gerald McFarland—author of *The Counterfeit Man*, from which the article about Jesse and Stephen Boorn (page 163) has been adapted—is a professor of history at the University of Massachusetts, Amherst.

Steve Mills—coauthor of the article about Daniel Taylor (page 429)—is an award-winning *Chicago Tribune* investigative reporter specializing in criminal justice.

Peter Neufeld—coauthor of *Actual Innocence*, from which the article about Robert Lee Miller Jr. (page 251) has been adapted—is an attorney and cofounder of the Innocence Project at the Benjamin N. Cardozo School of Law in New York City.

Bob Paynter—author of the article about John George Spirko Jr. (page 483)—left the *Cleveland Plain Dealer* in 2008, a result of staff cutbacks. He previously worked at the *Akron Beacon Journal*, where he led a team of reporters who won a Pulitzer Prize in 1994 for a yearlong exploration of the impact of race on public life.

James R. Phelan—author of the article about Gerald Martin Anderson (page 81)—was a staff writer for the *Saturday Evening Post* and was best known for his 1976 book *Howard Hughes: The Hidden Years*. He died of lung cancer in 1997 at age eighty-five.

Maurice Possley—a Pulitzer Prize winner and coauthor of the article about Daniel Taylor (page 429)—was a *Chicago Tribune* investigative reporter specializing in criminal justice issues until 2008, when he left as a result of staff cutbacks.

Dana L. Priest—author of the article about David Vasquez (page 269)—covers the intelligence community and national security issues for the *Washington Post* and is an analyst for NBC News. She won the Pulitzer Prize for Beat Reporting in 2006 for her reporting on the CIA's black site prisons. In 2008 the *Post* received the Pulitzer Prize for Public Service based on the work of Priest and two colleagues in exposing mistreatment of wounded veterans at Walter Reed Hospital.

Selwyn Raab—author of *Justice in the Back Room*, from which the article about George Whitmore (page 389) has been adapted—is a former *New York Times* reporter and the author of several nonfiction books about criminal justice and organized crime.

Mark Sauer—coauthor of the *San Diego Union-Tribune* series from which the article about Michael Crowe (page 5) has been adapted—was an investigative reporter at the *Union-Tribune* for thirty years before he left daily journalism in 2007 to pursue a career as a freelance writer/reporter for magazines and television news in San Diego.

Sydney H. Schanberg—author of the article about McCray, Richardson, Salaam, Santana, and Wise (page 193)—is a former *New York Times* foreign correspondent best known for his reporting from Cambodia before the Khmer Rouge took over the country in 1975. His Cambodia coverage won the 1976 Pulitzer Prize for Investigative Reporting.

Barry Scheck—coauthor of *Actual Innocence*, from which the article about Robert Lee Miller Jr. (page 251) has been adapted—is cofounder of the Innocence Project at the Benjamin N. Cardozo School of Law in New York City.

Pete Shellem—author of the series of articles from which the article about Barry Laughman (page 225) has been adapted—reports on wrongful convictions at the *Patriot-News* in Harrisburg, Pennsylvania.

Brendan Smith—author of the article about Donnell Vaughn (page 101)— is the news editor of *Legal Times*.

Bryan Smith—author of the article about Kevin Fox (page 107)—is a senior editor at *Chicago* magazine.

Phil Stanford—author of the article about Laverne Pavlinac (page 367)— left the *Oregonian* in 1994 and currently writes a biweekly column for the *Portland Tribune*.

John Taylor—author of *The Count and the Confession* from which the article about Beverly Monroe (page 19) has been adapted—is a contributing editor at *New York* magazine and a senior writer for *Esquire*.

Don Terry—author of the article about Aaron Patterson (page 383)—is a former reporter for the *Chicago Tribune Magazine*, the *New York Times*, and the *Chicago Defender*.

Alex Tresniowski—author of the article about John Mark Karr (page 361)— is a senior writer at *People* magazine.

Rob Warden—author of the articles about LaVale Burt (page 151) and Steven Paul Linscott (page 279)—is a coeditor of this book.

William S. Warden—author of the article about Thomas M. Bram (page 283)—received a bachelor's degree in political science from the University of Michigan in May 2009. He researched the Bram case in 2006 when he was an intern at the Center on Wrongful Convictions.

John Wilkens—coauthor of the *San Diego Union-Tribune* series from which the article about Michael Crowe (page 5) has been adapted—is an award-winning *Union-Tribune* reporter.

April Witt—author of the articles about Dennis Deonte Green (page 131), Corey Beale (page 377), and Keith Longtin (page 291)—joined the *Washington Post* in 2000 after working nearly a decade at the *Miami Herald*.

Christine Ellen Young—author of the article about Lebrew Jones (page 439)—is an investigative reporter who has worked both for newspapers and television. She has received many awards, including the Alfred I. duPont–Columbia University Silver Baton and a Boston-New England Emmy.

Royalties from this book are being donated
to the Center on Wrongful Convictions

Bluhm Legal Clinic Center on Wrongful Convictions

Mission of the Center

The Center on Wrongful Convictions is dedicated to identifying and rectifying wrongful convictions and other serious miscarriages of justice, raising public awareness of the prevalence, causes, and social costs of wrongful convictions, and reducing the numbers of wrongful convictions by reforming the criminal justice system.

www.law.northwestern.edu/cwc/